tiny dancer

tiny dancer

SIENA CHERSON SIEGEL

art by

MARK SIEGEL

background assistance

ABE ERSKINE

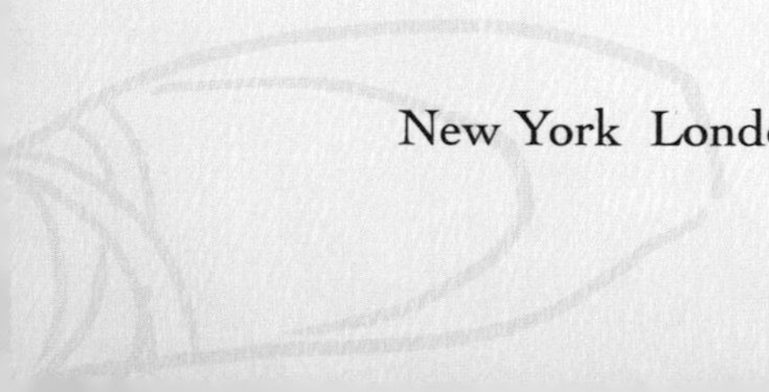

atheneum

New York London Toronto Sydney New Delhi

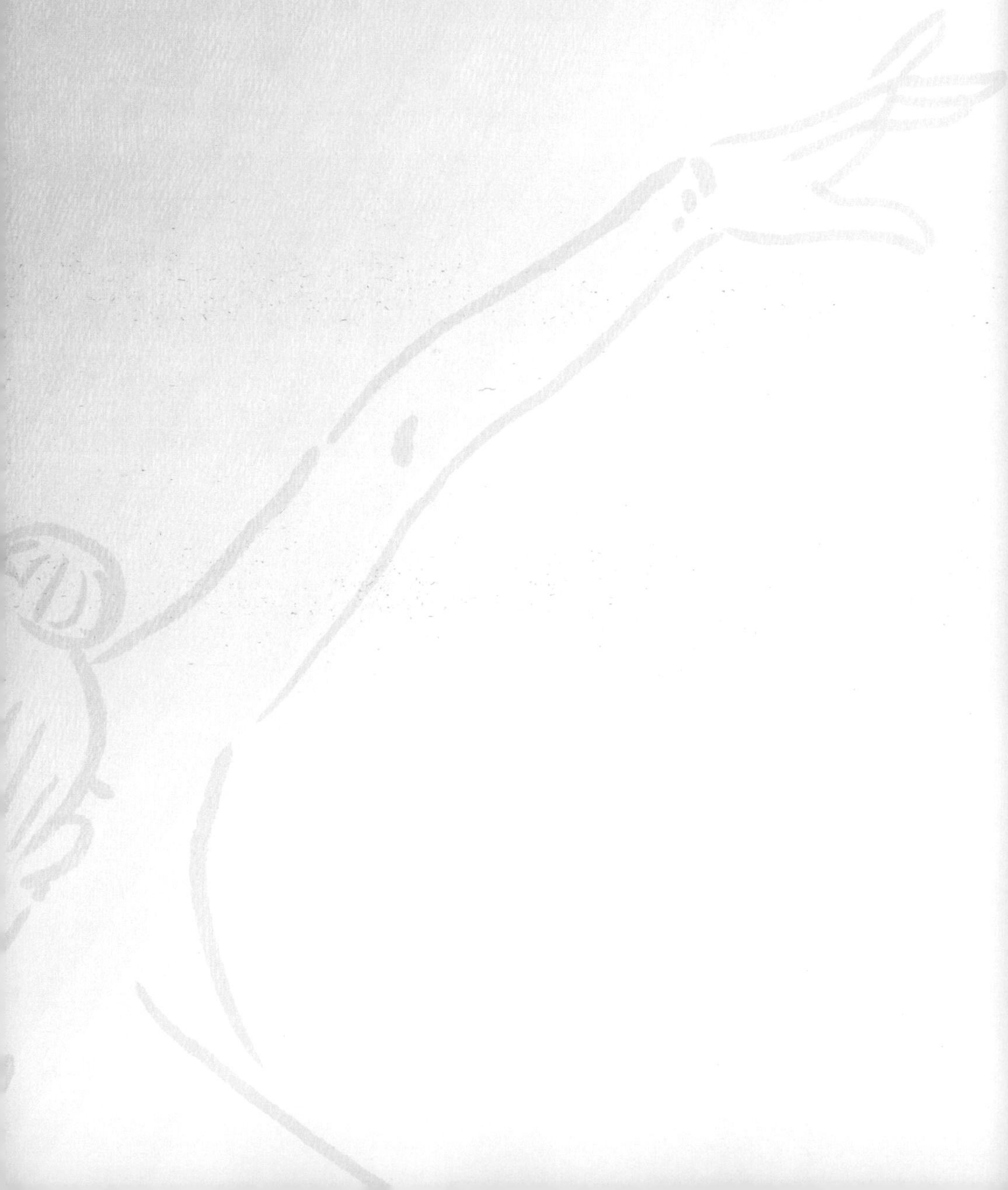

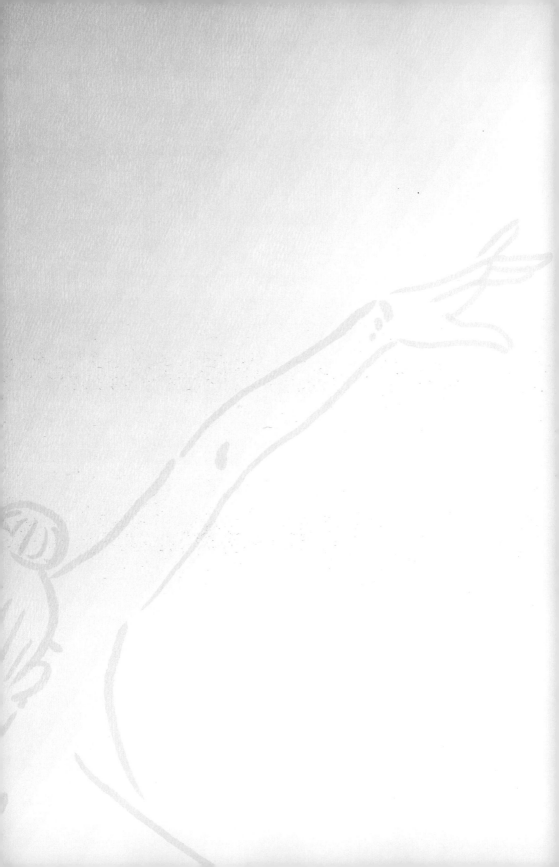

Prelude

Ghost Ballerina

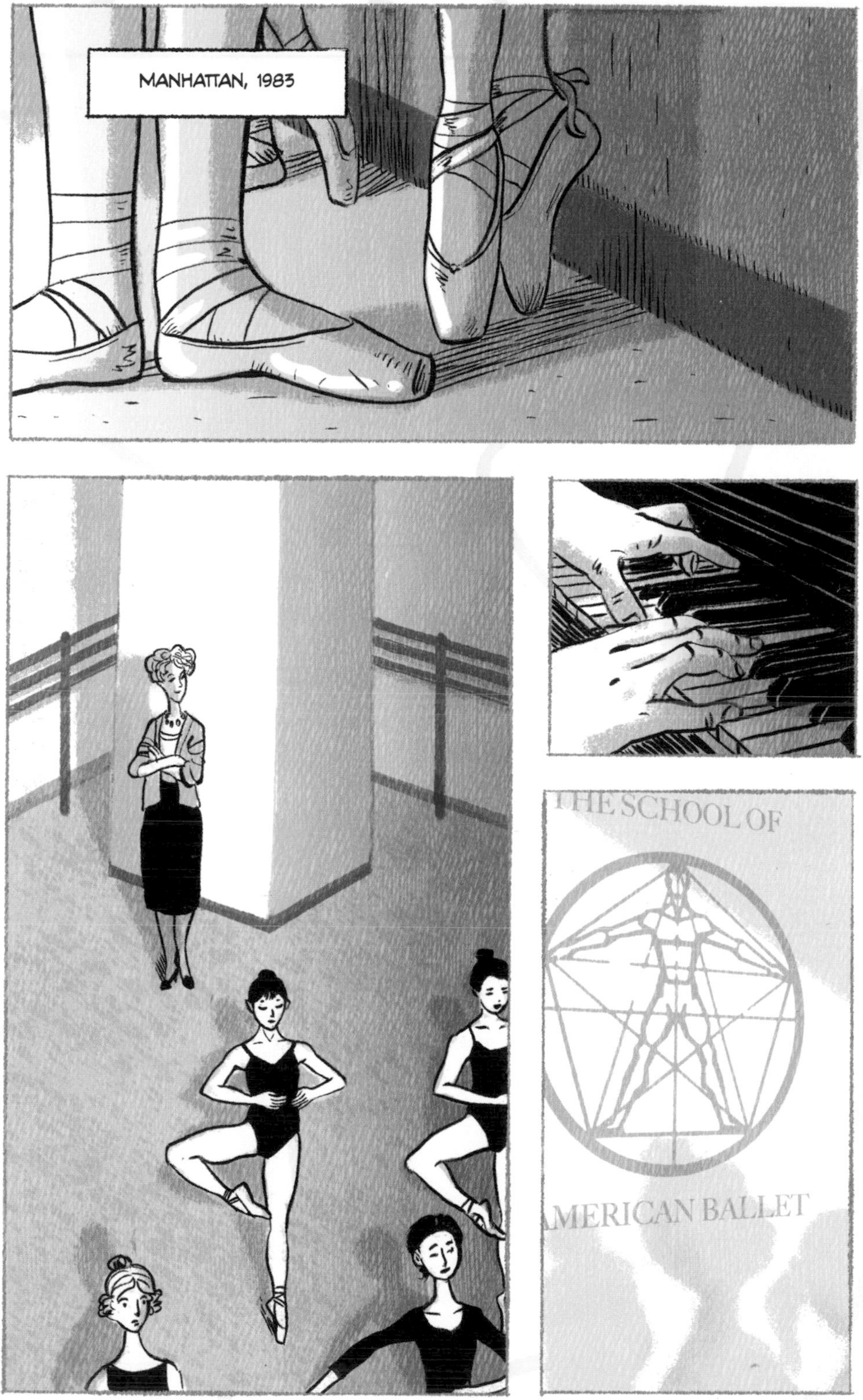
MANHATTAN, 1983
THE SCHOOL OF
AMERICAN BALLET

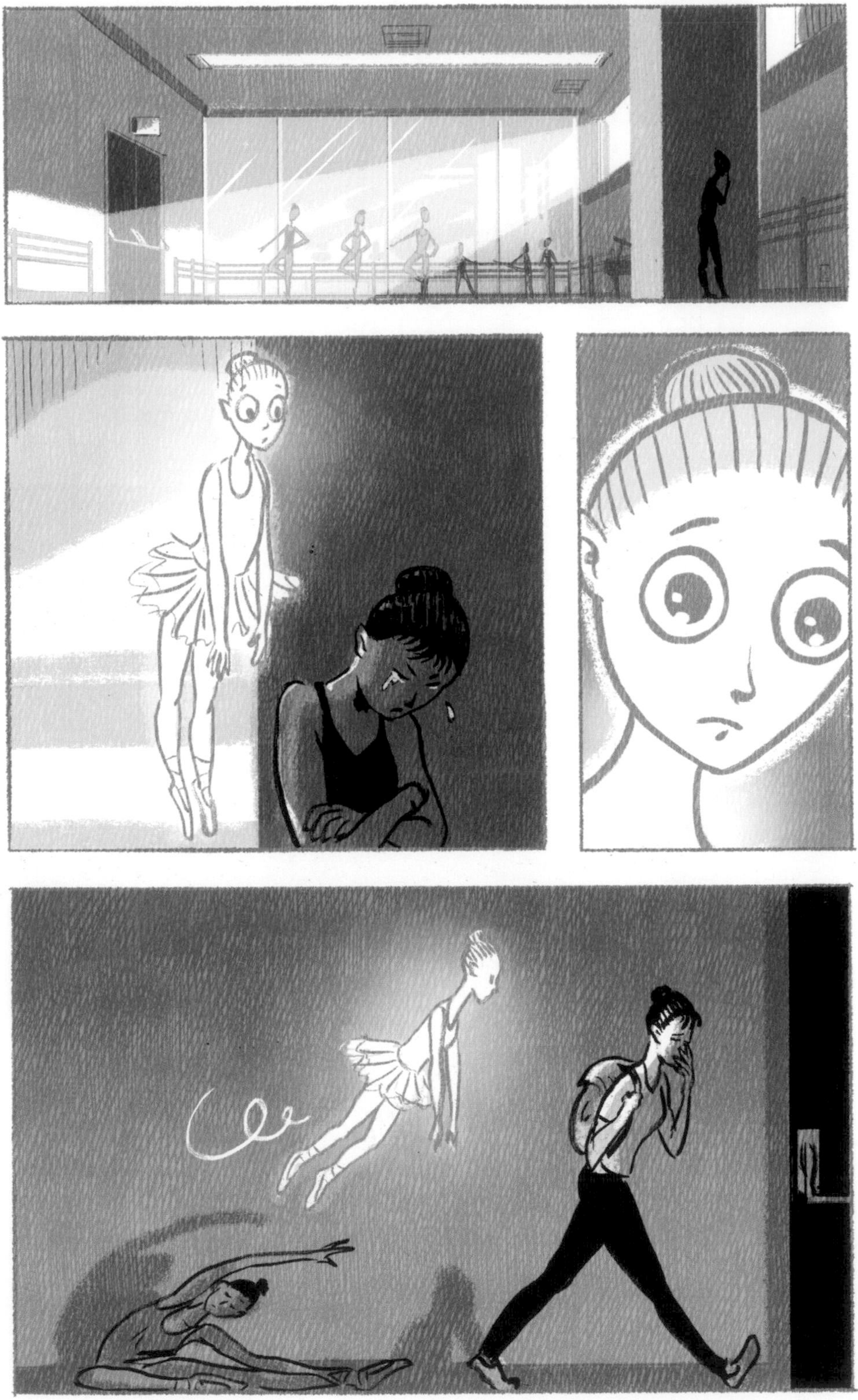

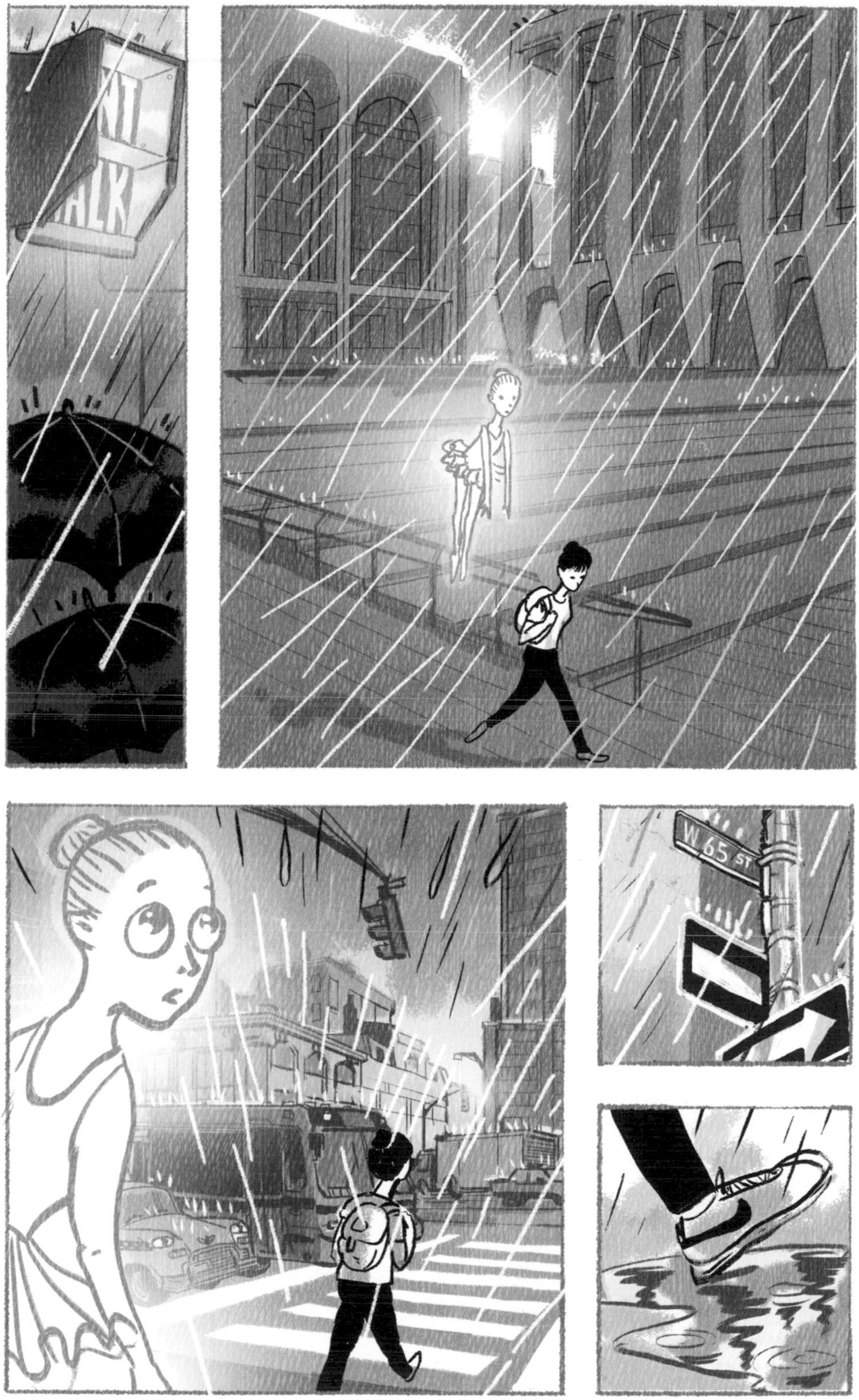
W 65 ST

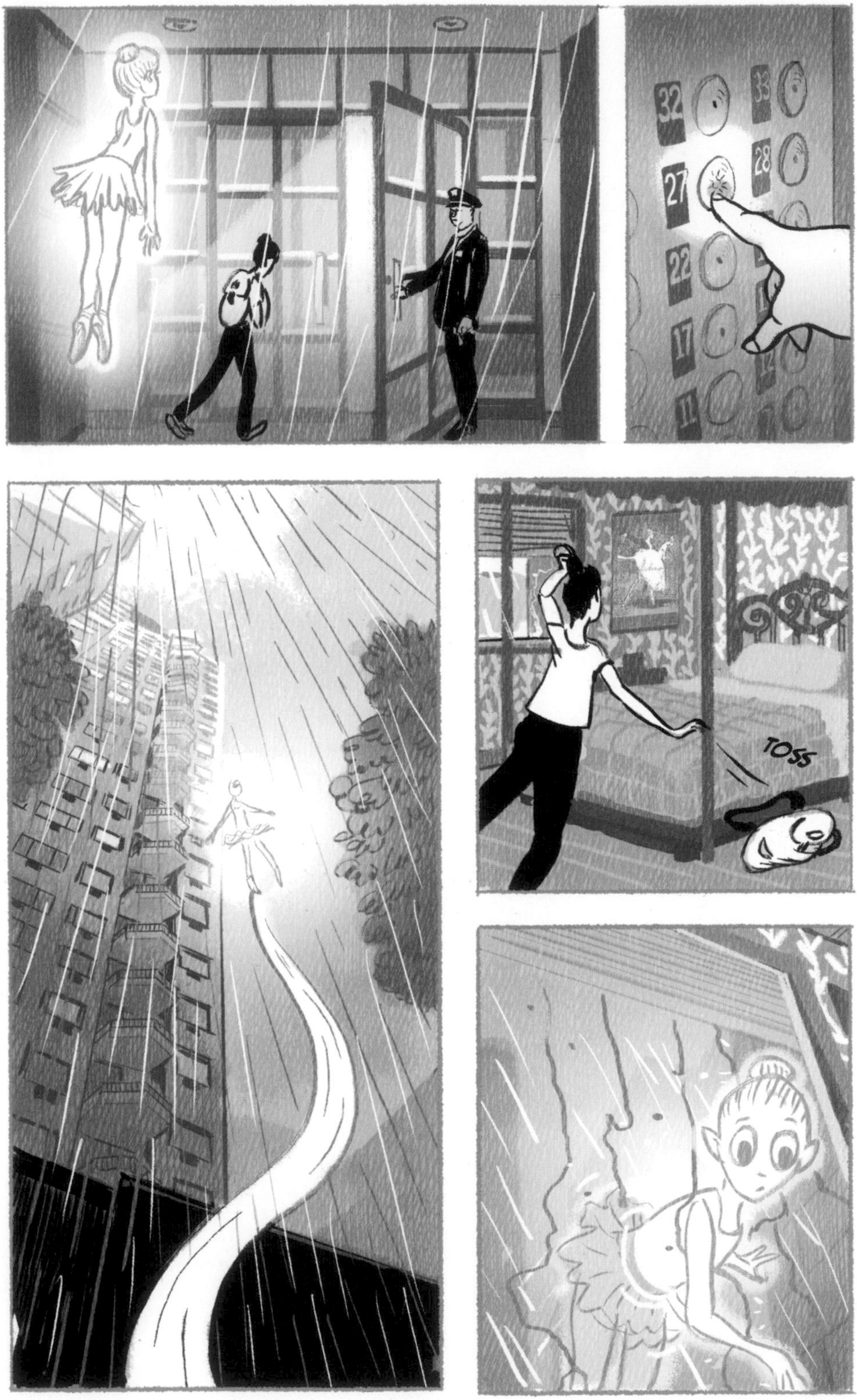
32
33
27
28
22
17
11
TOSS

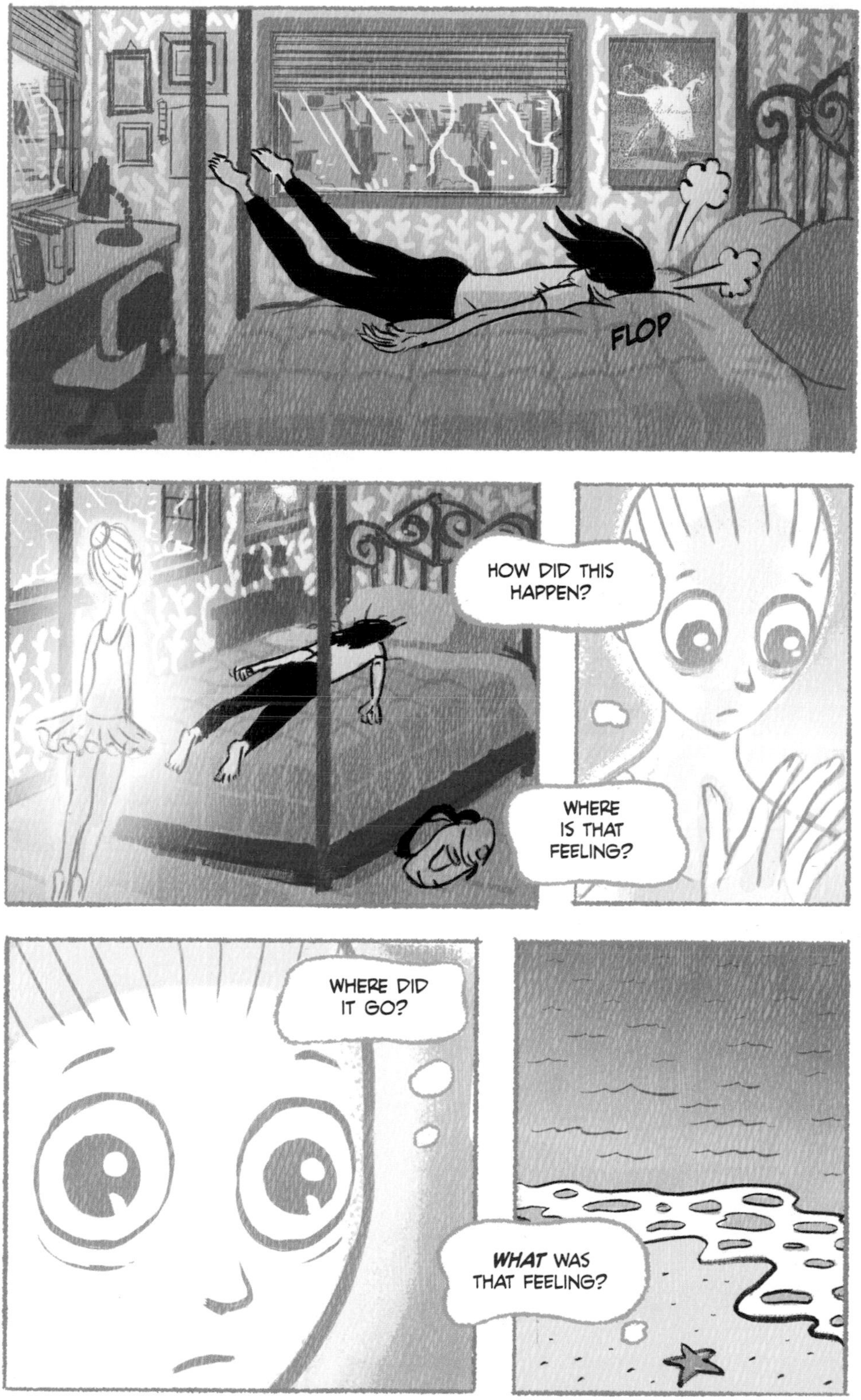
FLOP
HOW DID THIS HAPPEN?
WHERE IS THAT FEELING?
WHERE DID IT GO?
WHAT WAS THAT FEELING?

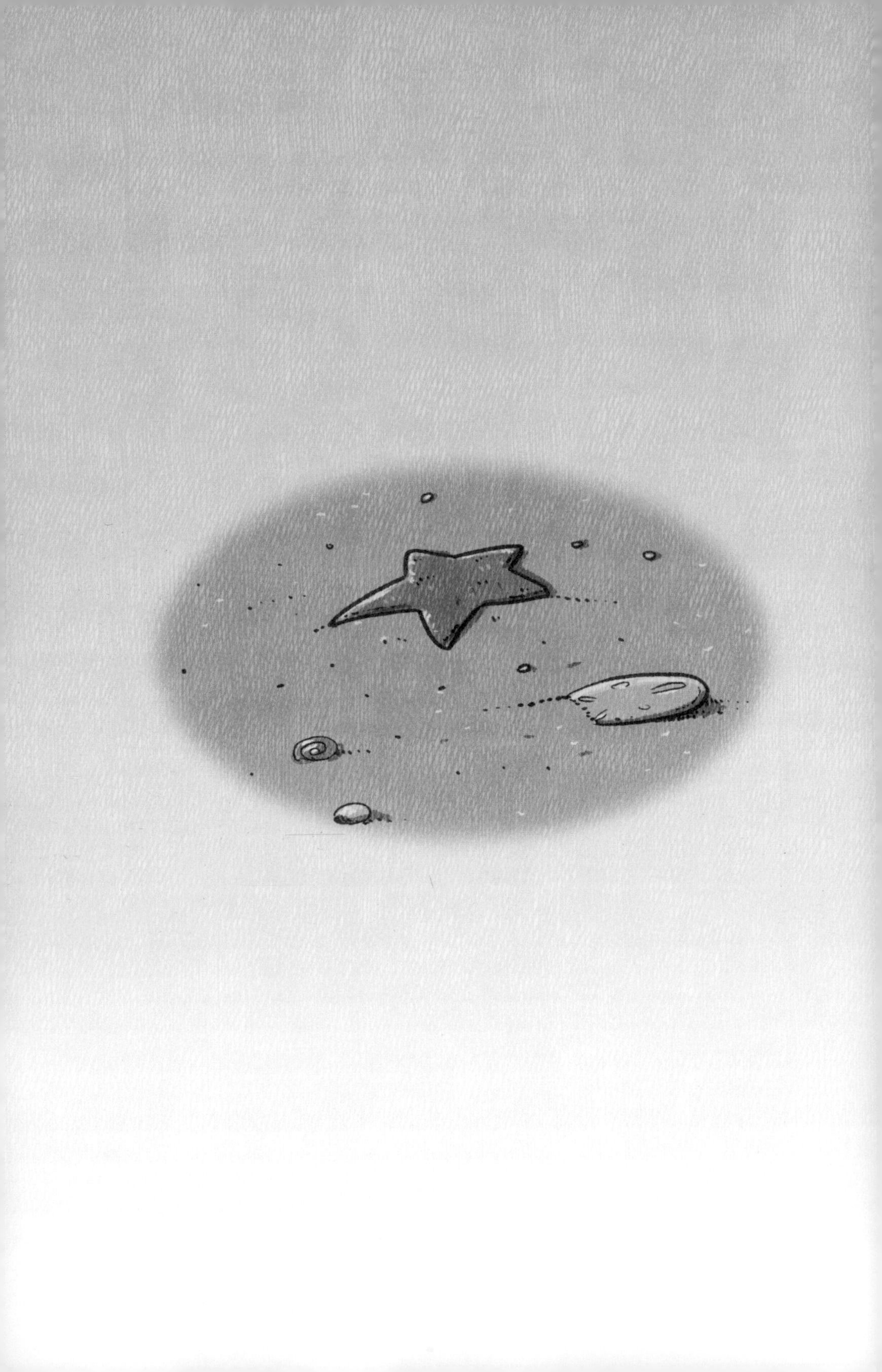

Part 1

A Royal Feeling

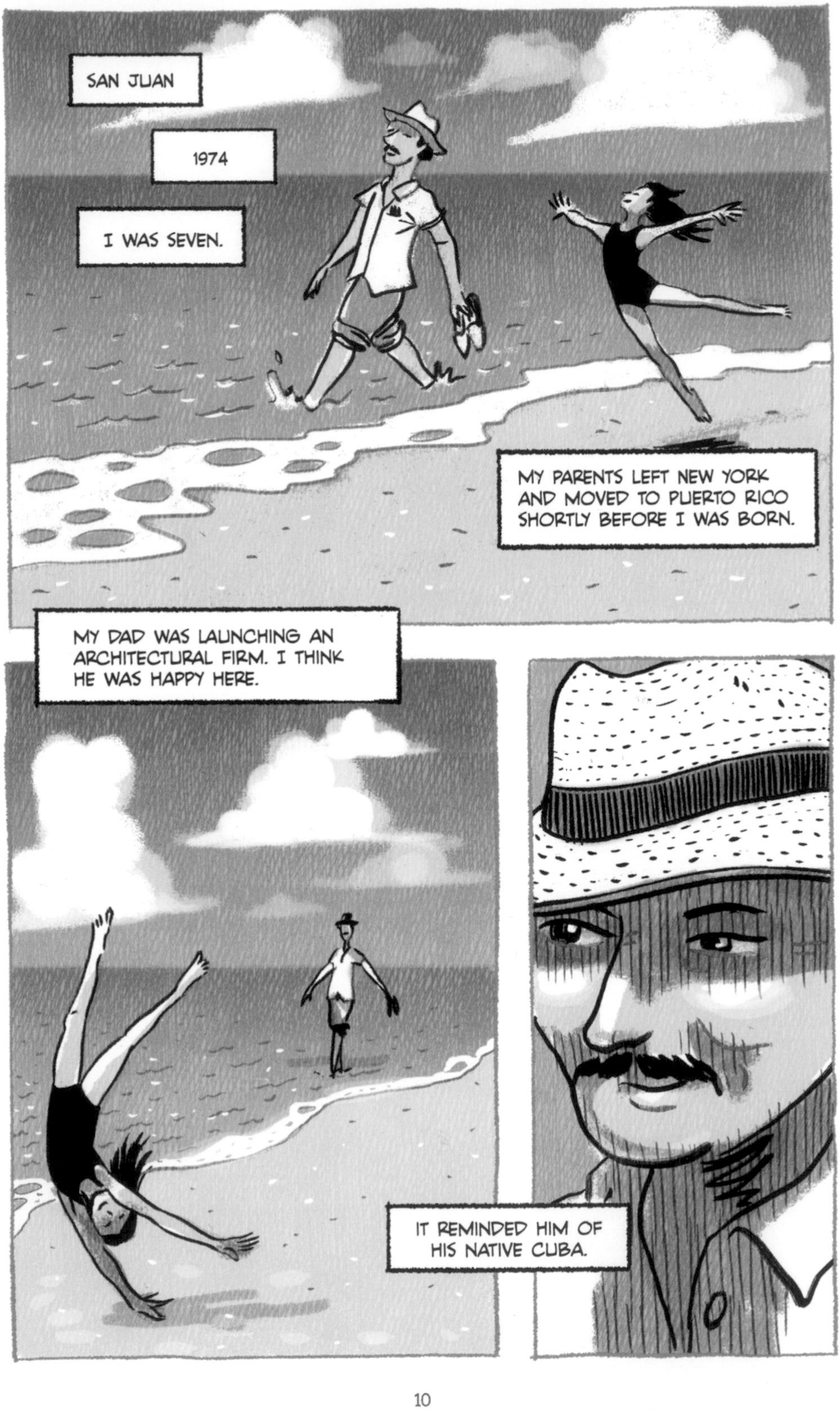
SAN JUAN
1974
I WAS SEVEN.
MY PARENTS LEFT NEW YORK AND MOVED TO PUERTO RICO SHORTLY BEFORE I WAS BORN.
MY DAD WAS LAUNCHING AN ARCHITECTURAL FIRM. I THINK HE WAS HAPPY HERE.
IT REMINDED HIM OF HIS NATIVE CUBA.

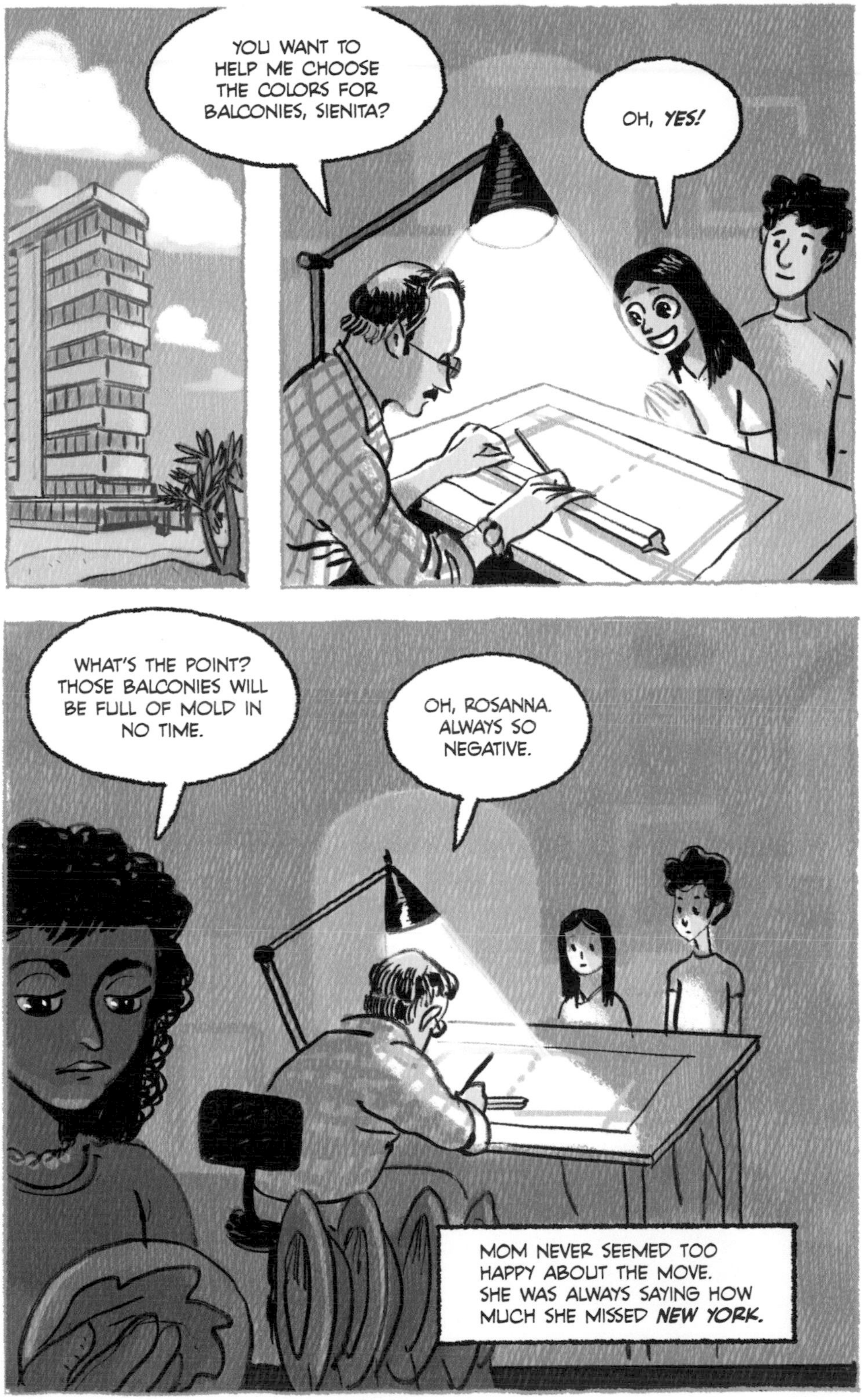

YOU WANT TO HELP ME CHOOSE THE COLORS FOR BALCONIES, SIENITA?
OH, ***YES!***
WHAT'S THE POINT? THOSE BALCONIES WILL BE FULL OF MOLD IN NO TIME.
OH, ROSANNA. ALWAYS SO NEGATIVE.
MOM NEVER SEEMED TOO HAPPY ABOUT THE MOVE. SHE WAS ALWAYS SAYING HOW MUCH SHE MISSED ***NEW YORK.***

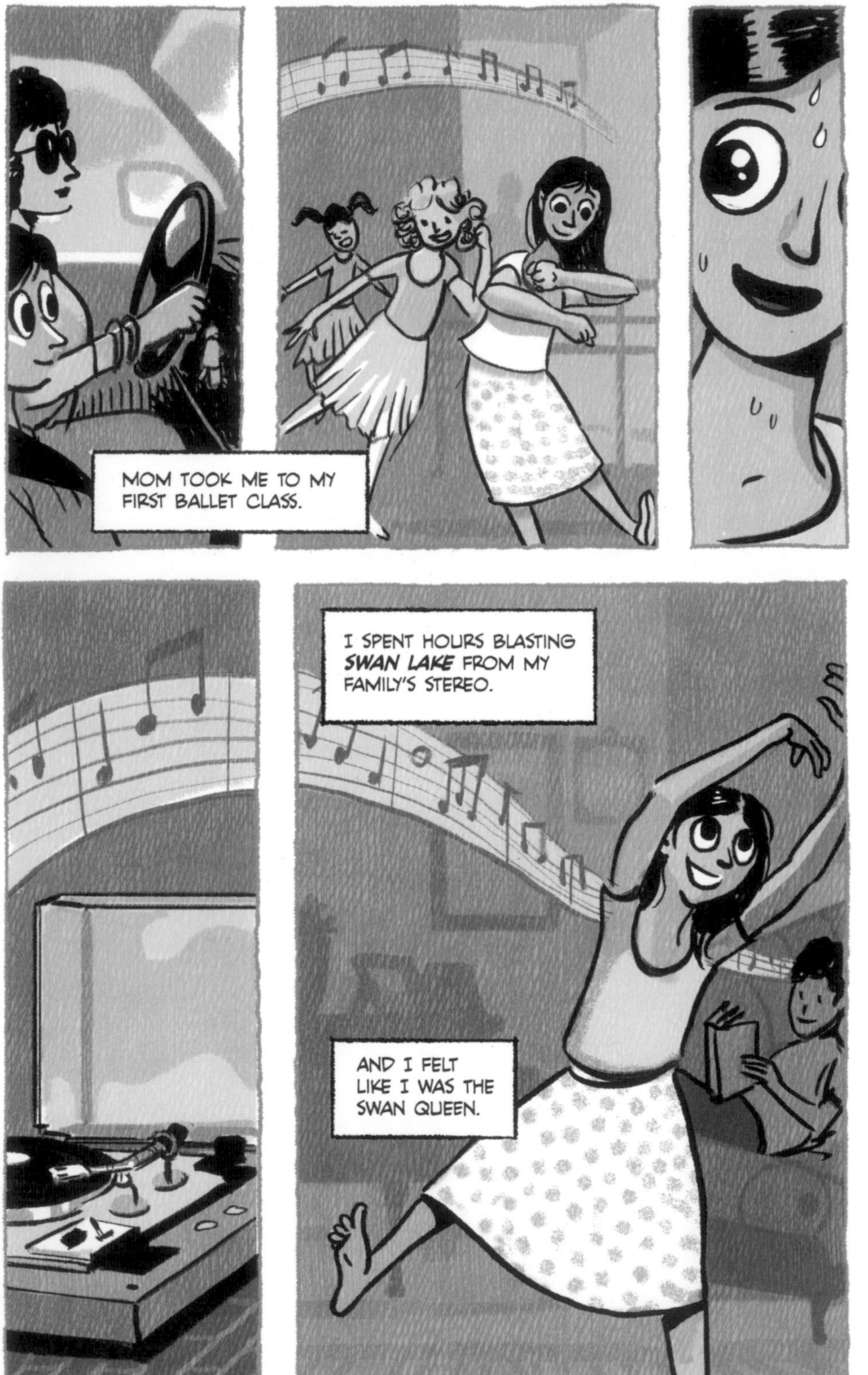
MOM TOOK ME TO MY FIRST BALLET CLASS.
I SPENT HOURS BLASTING *SWAN LAKE* FROM MY FAMILY'S STEREO.
AND I FELT LIKE I WAS THE SWAN QUEEN.

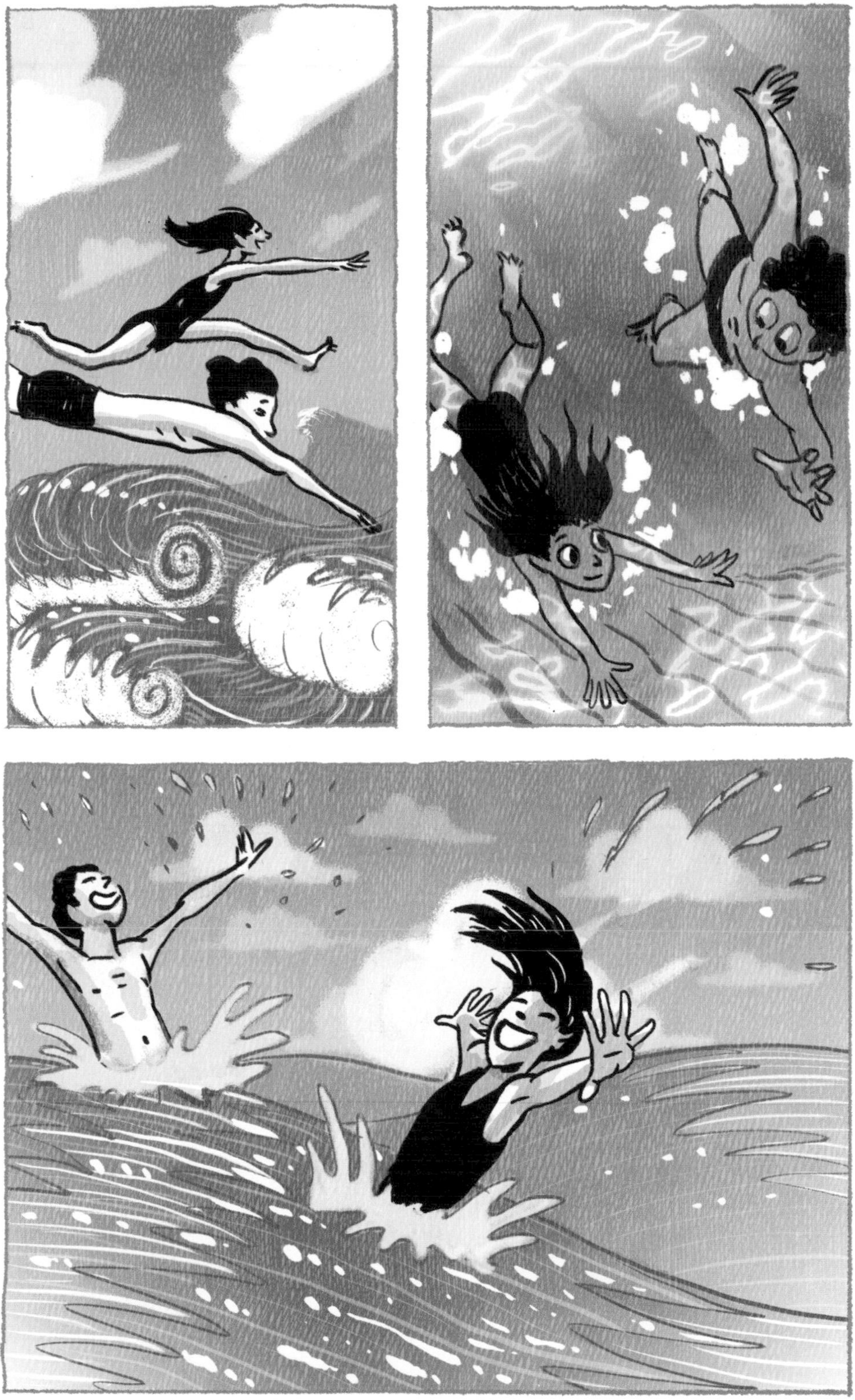

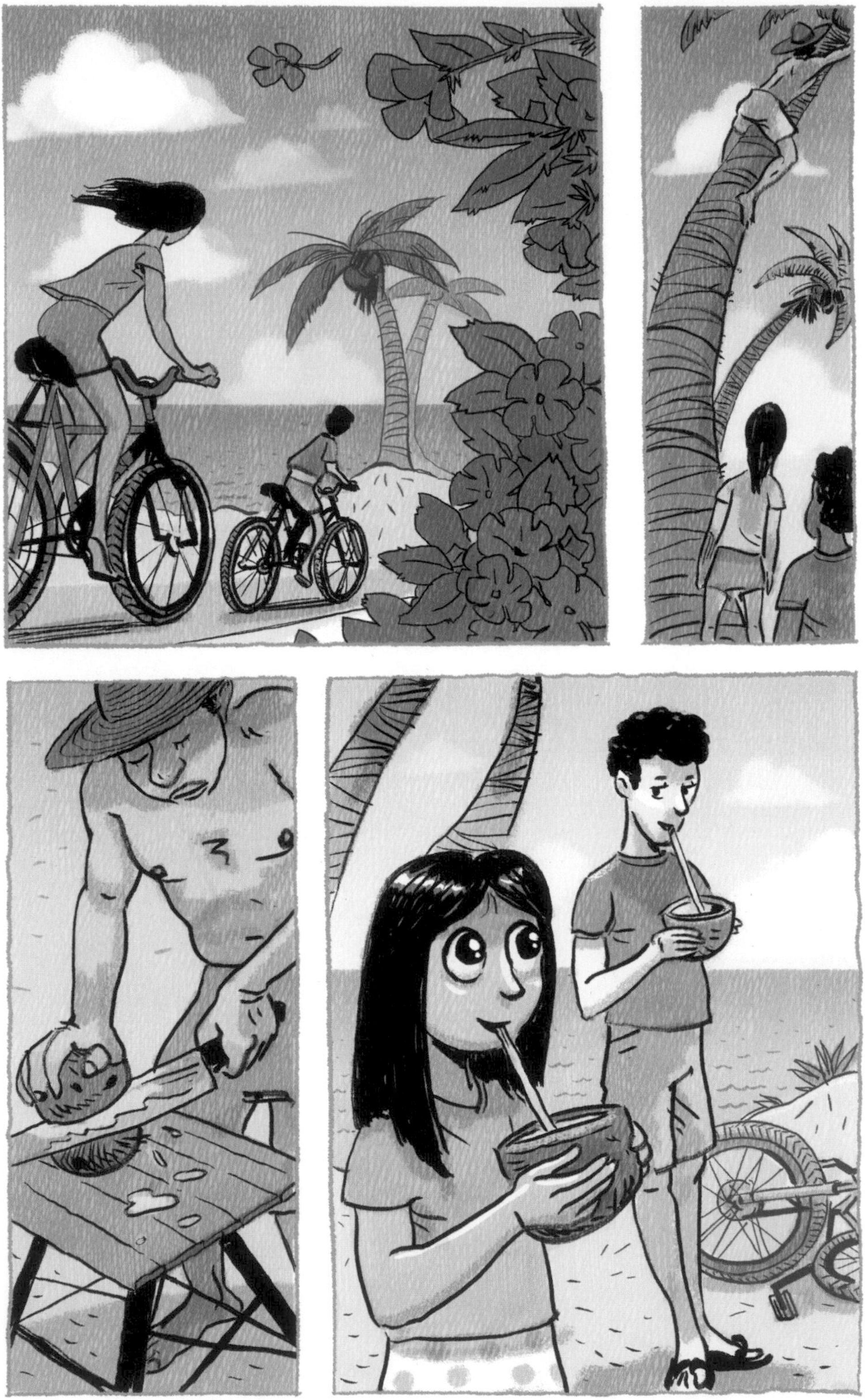

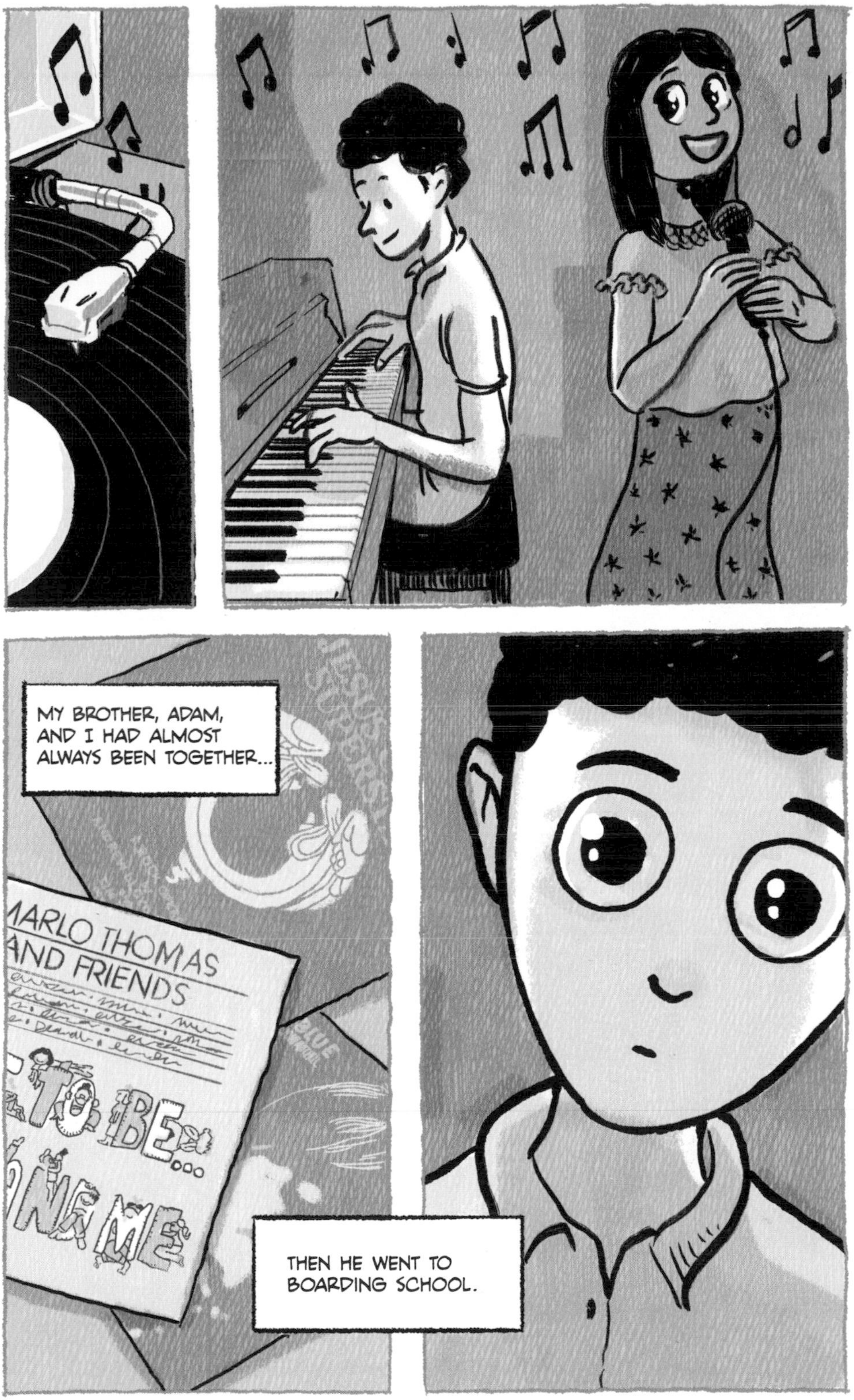
MY BROTHER, ADAM, AND I HAD ALMOST ALWAYS BEEN TOGETHER...
MARLO THOMAS AND FRIENDS
TO BE...
THEN HE WENT TO BOARDING SCHOOL.

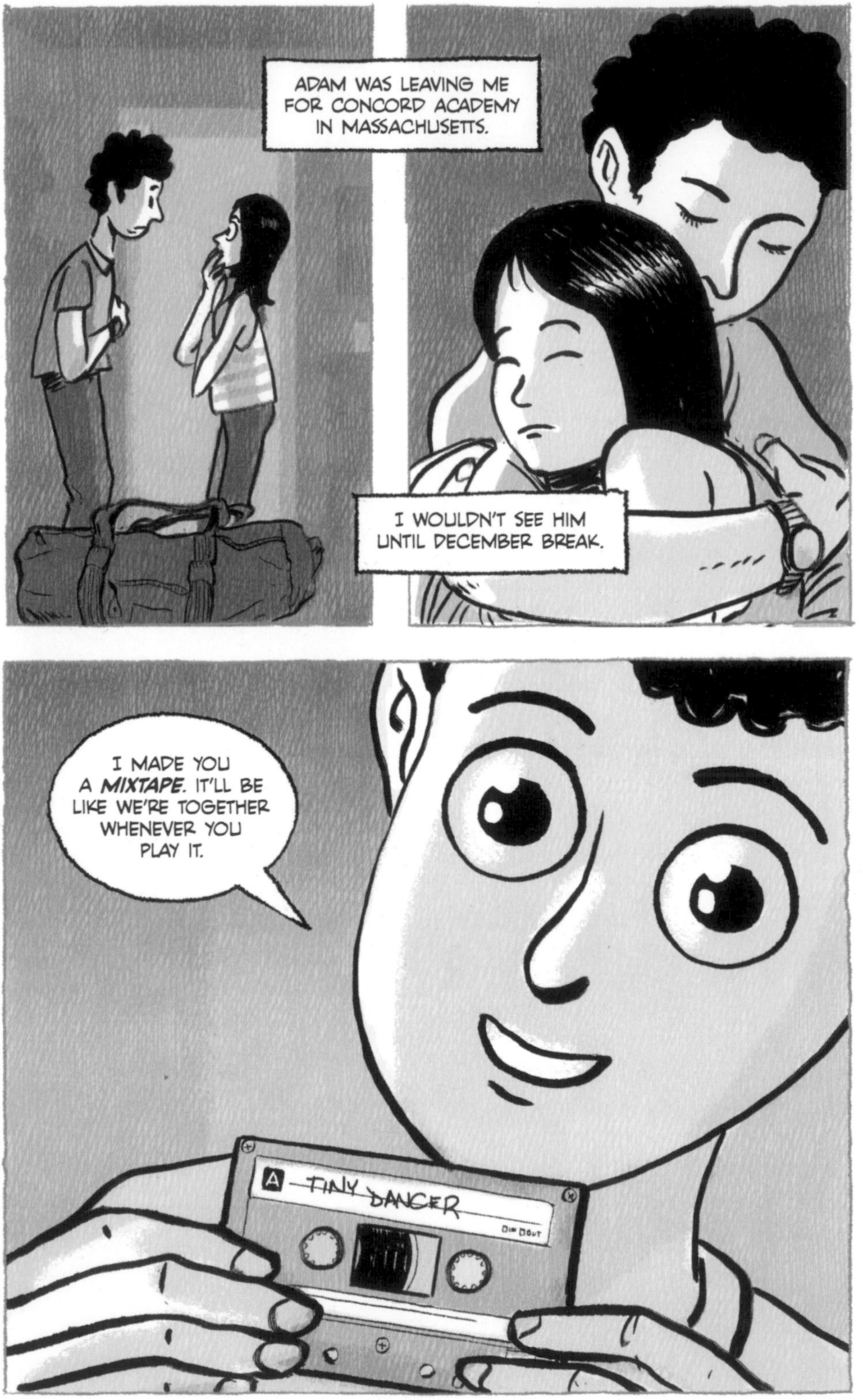
ADAM WAS LEAVING ME FOR CONCORD ACADEMY IN MASSACHUSETTS.
I WOULDN'T SEE HIM UNTIL DECEMBER BREAK.
I MADE YOU A **MIXTAPE**. IT'LL BE LIKE WE'RE TOGETHER WHENEVER YOU PLAY IT.
A
TINY DANCER

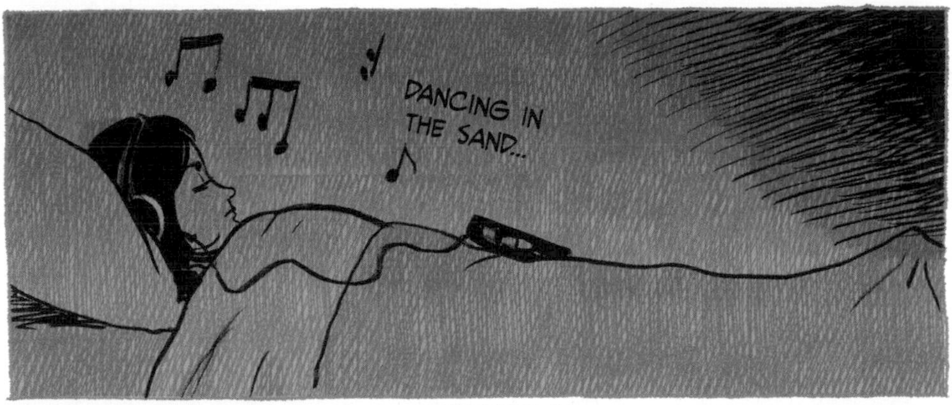
DANCING IN THE SAND...

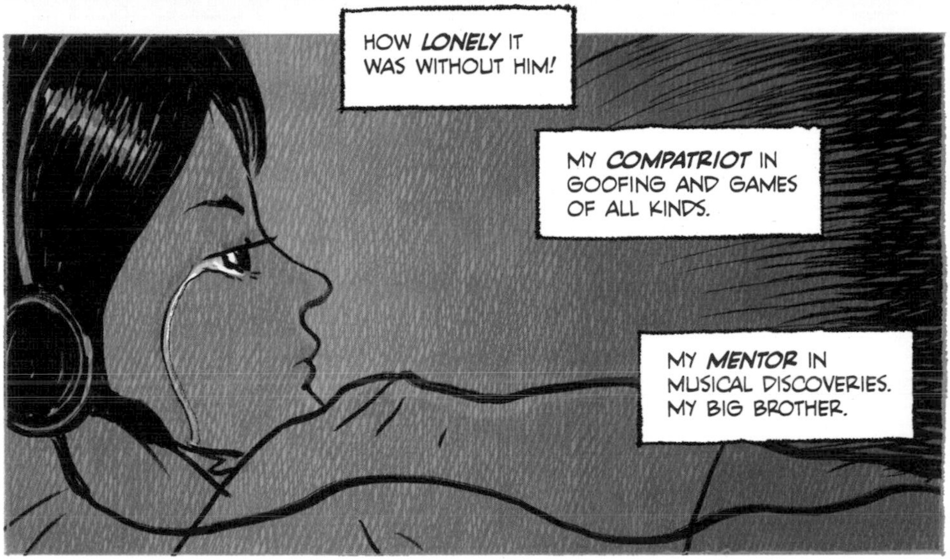
HOW LONELY IT WAS WITHOUT HIM!
MY COMPATRIOT IN GOOFING AND GAMES OF ALL KINDS.
MY MENTOR IN MUSICAL DISCOVERIES. MY BIG BROTHER.

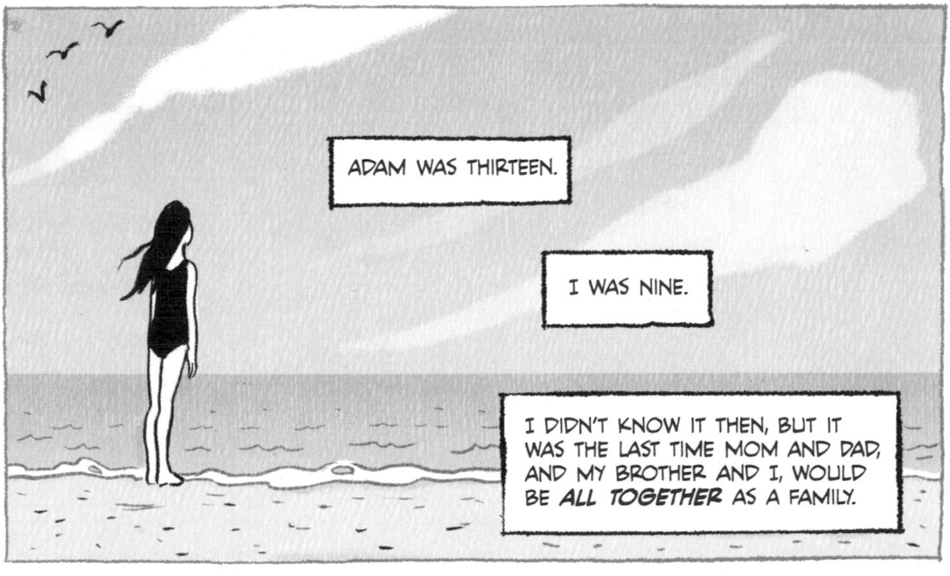
ADAM WAS THIRTEEN.
I WAS NINE.
I DIDN'T KNOW IT THEN, BUT IT WAS THE LAST TIME MOM AND DAD, AND MY BROTHER AND I, WOULD BE ALL TOGETHER AS A FAMILY.

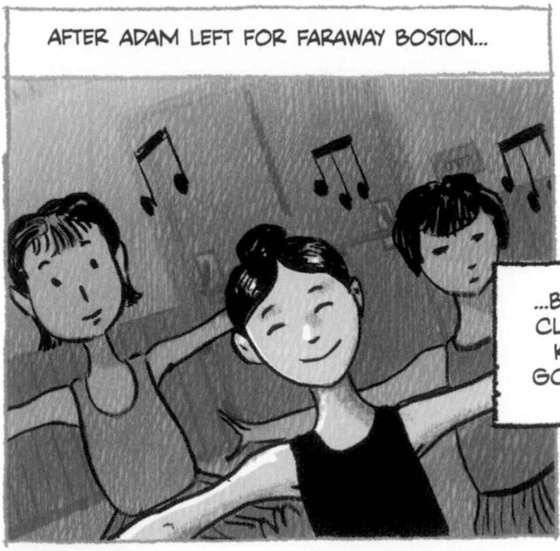
AFTER ADAM LEFT FOR FARAWAY BOSTON...
...BALLET CLASSES KEPT GOING...

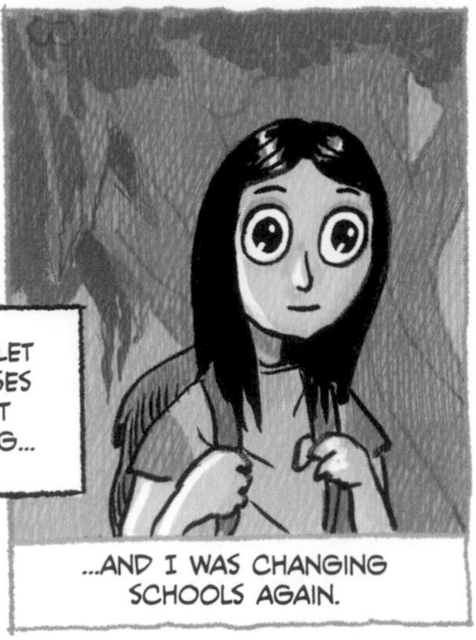
...AND I WAS CHANGING SCHOOLS AGAIN.

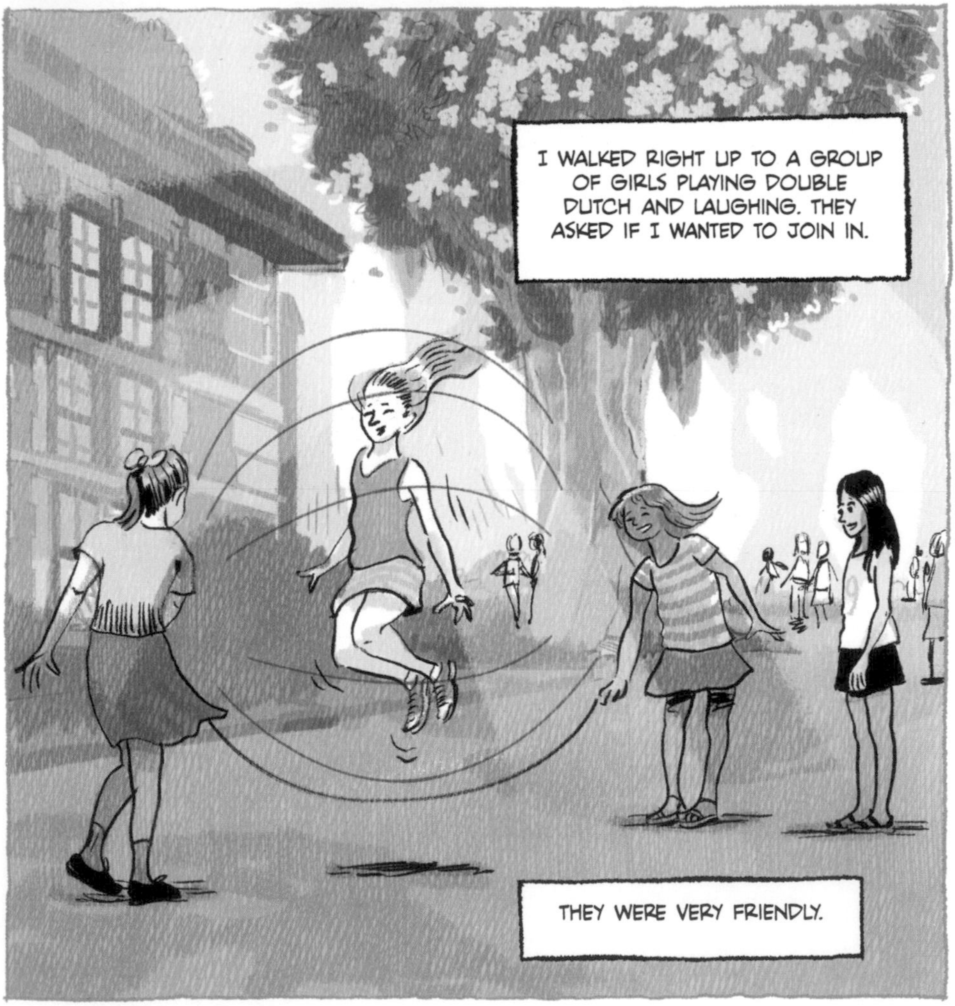
I WALKED RIGHT UP TO A GROUP OF GIRLS PLAYING DOUBLE DUTCH AND LAUGHING. THEY ASKED IF I WANTED TO JOIN IN.
THEY WERE VERY FRIENDLY.

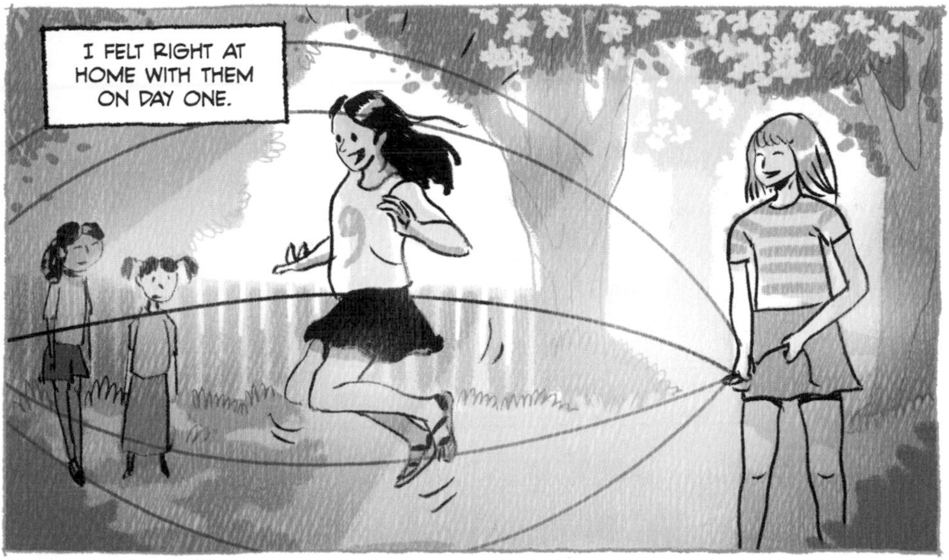
I FELT RIGHT AT HOME WITH THEM ON DAY ONE.

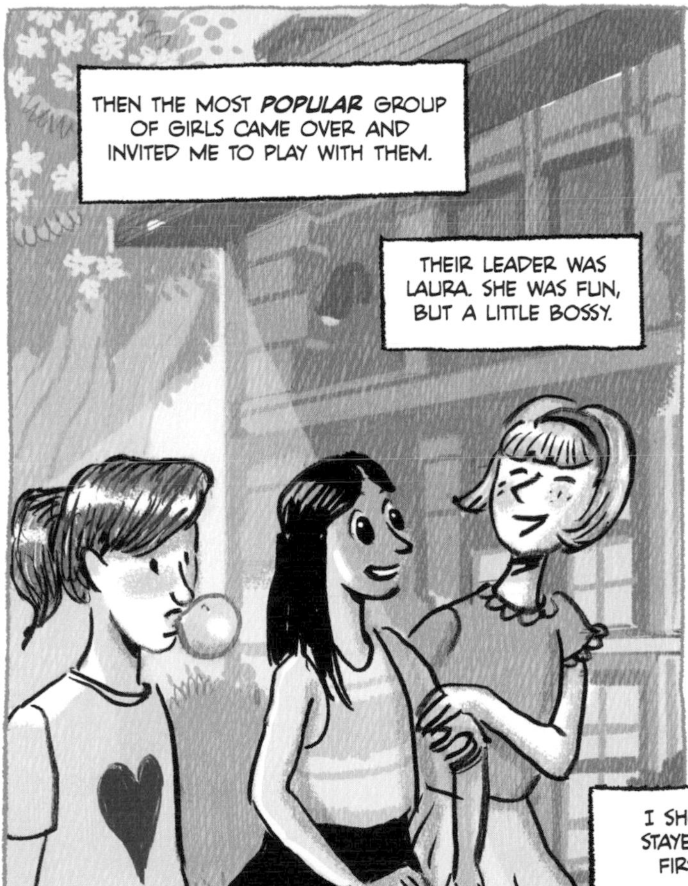
THEN THE MOST ***POPULAR*** GROUP OF GIRLS CAME OVER AND INVITED ME TO PLAY WITH THEM.
THEIR LEADER WAS LAURA. SHE WAS FUN, BUT A LITTLE BOSSY.

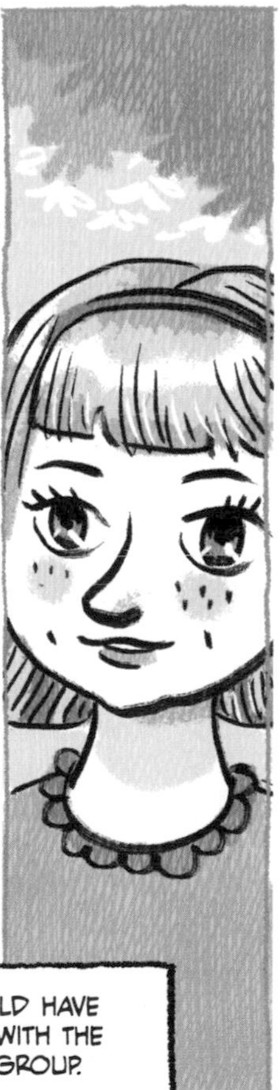
I SHOULD HAVE STAYED WITH THE FIRST GROUP.

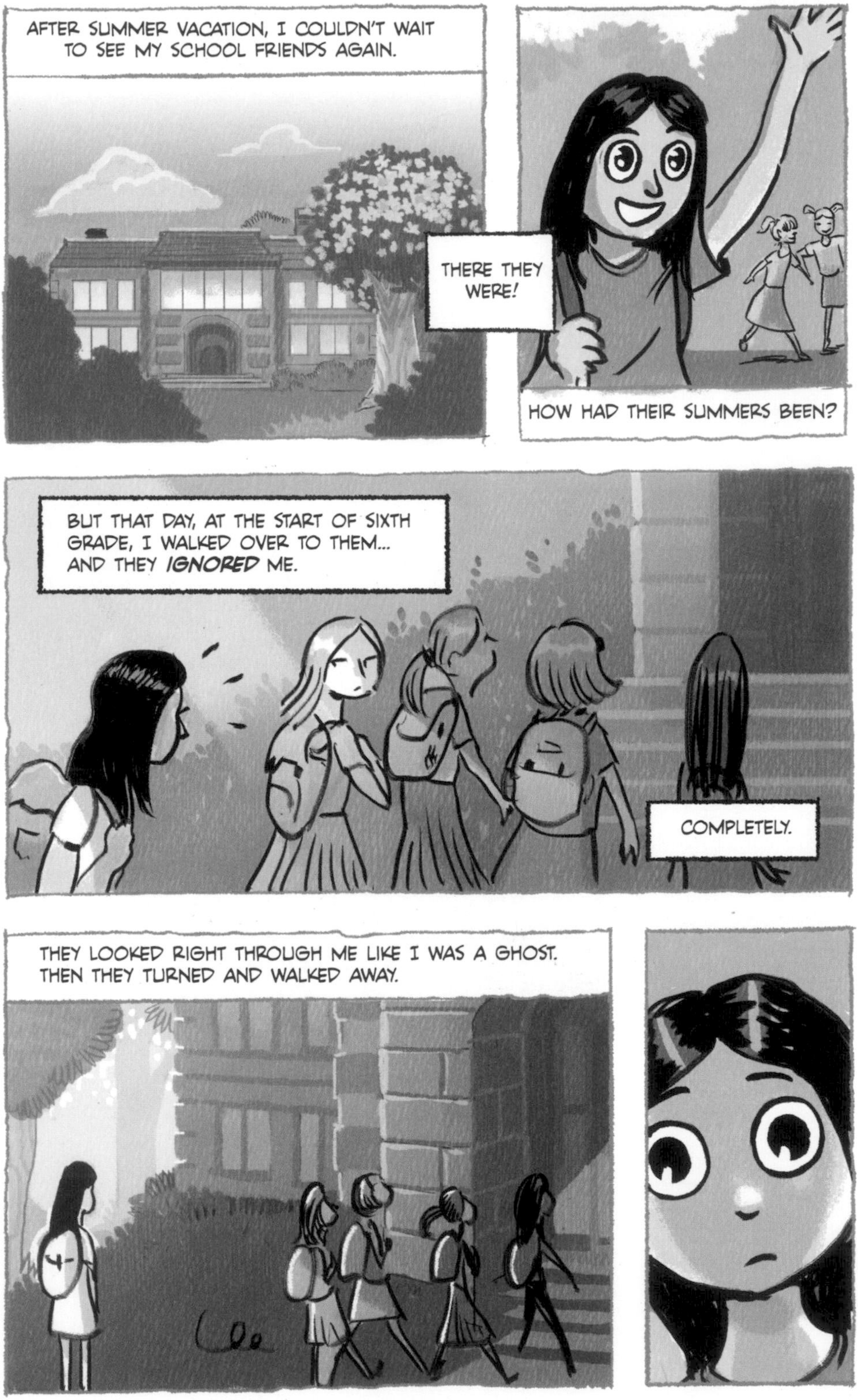
AFTER SUMMER VACATION, I COULDN'T WAIT TO SEE MY SCHOOL FRIENDS AGAIN.
THERE THEY WERE!
HOW HAD THEIR SUMMERS BEEN?
BUT THAT DAY, AT THE START OF SIXTH GRADE, I WALKED OVER TO THEM... AND THEY *IGNORED* ME.
COMPLETELY.
THEY LOOKED RIGHT THROUGH ME LIKE I WAS A GHOST. THEN THEY TURNED AND WALKED AWAY.

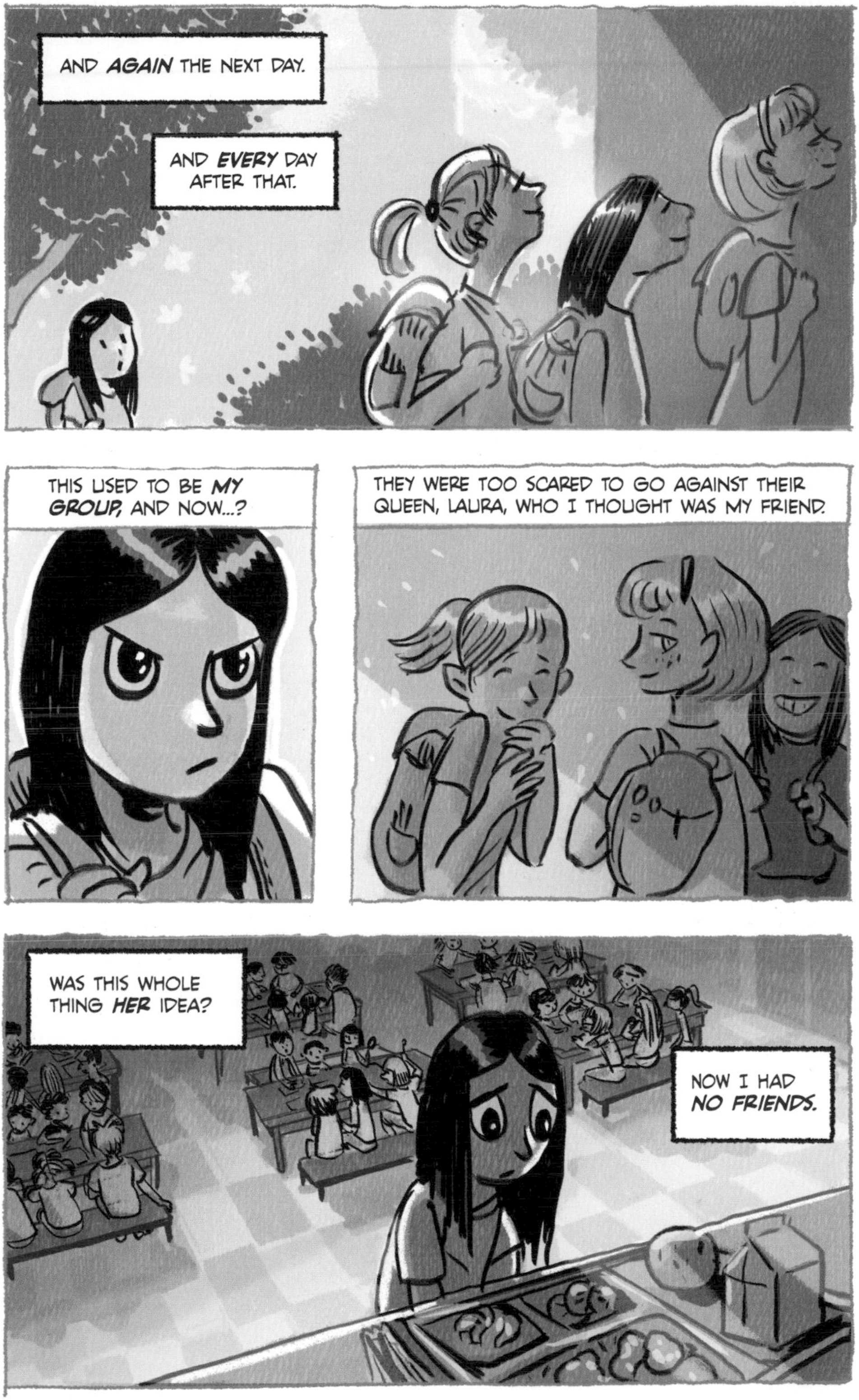
AND AGAIN THE NEXT DAY.
AND EVERY DAY AFTER THAT.
THIS USED TO BE MY GROUP, AND NOW...?
THEY WERE TOO SCARED TO GO AGAINST THEIR QUEEN, LAURA, WHO I THOUGHT WAS MY FRIEND.
WAS THIS WHOLE THING HER IDEA?
NOW I HAD NO FRIENDS.

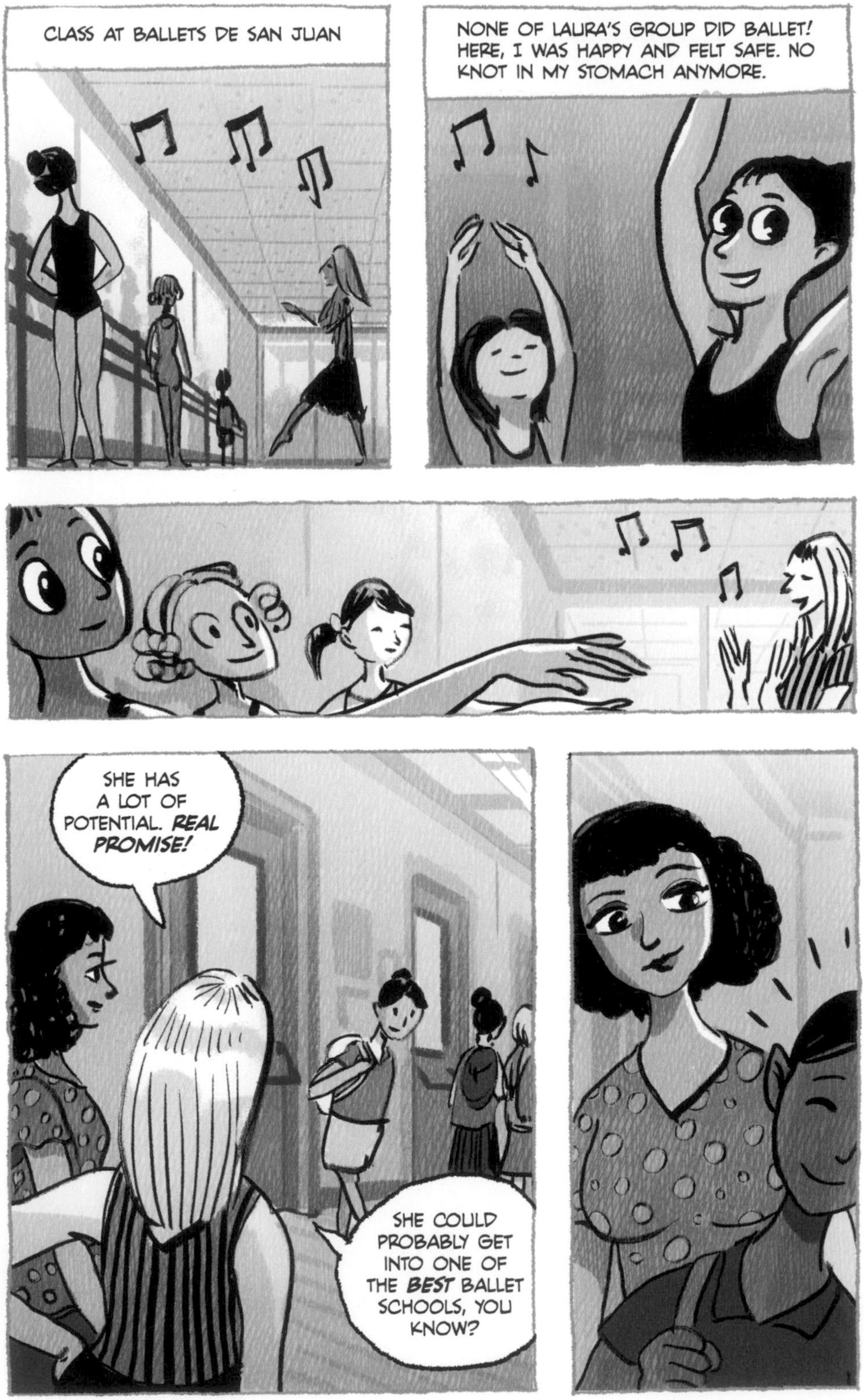
CLASS AT BALLETS DE SAN JUAN
NONE OF LAURA'S GROUP DID BALLET! HERE, I WAS HAPPY AND FELT SAFE. NO KNOT IN MY STOMACH ANYMORE.
SHE HAS A LOT OF POTENTIAL. **REAL PROMISE!**
SHE COULD PROBABLY GET INTO ONE OF THE **BEST** BALLET SCHOOLS, YOU KNOW?

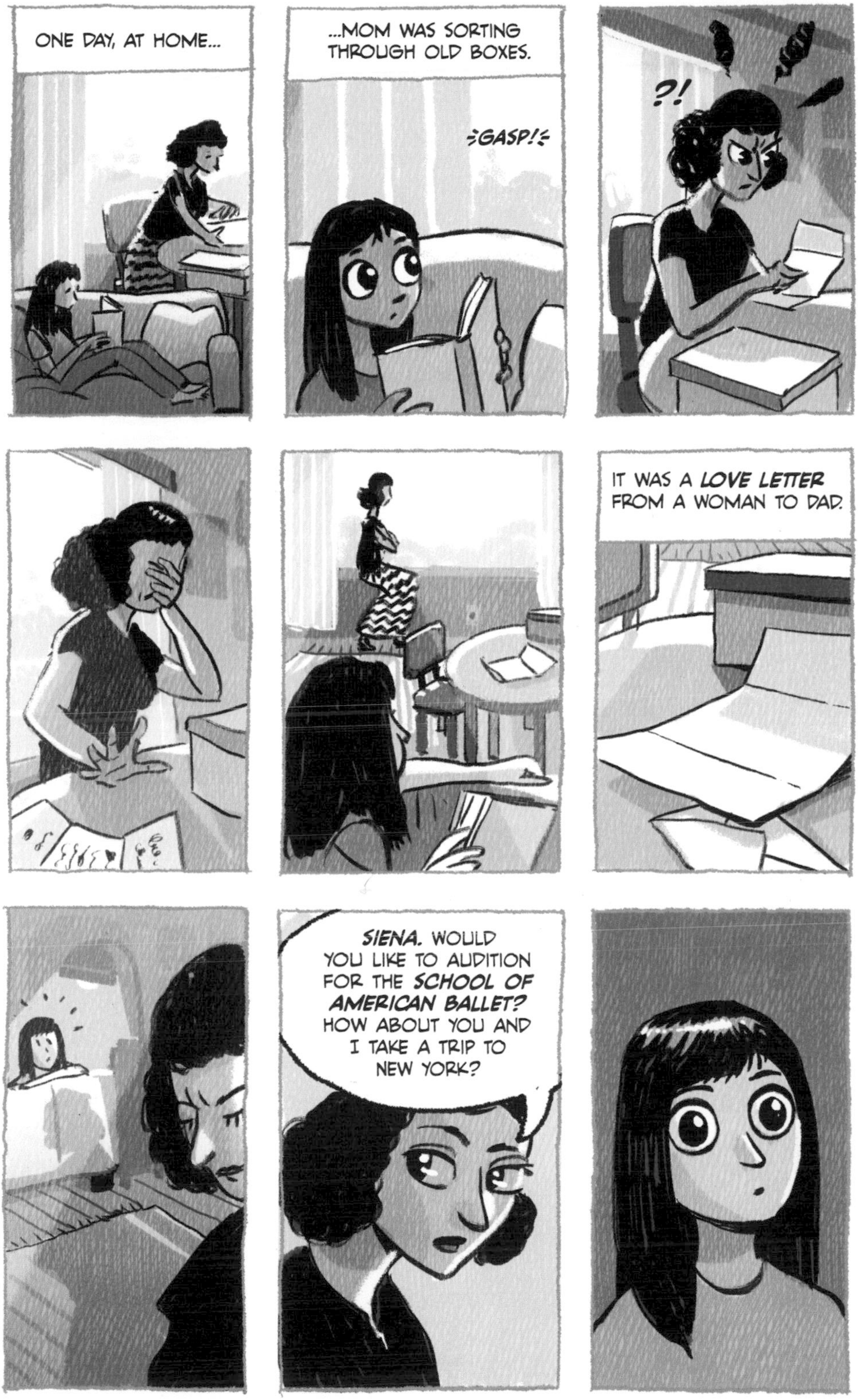
ONE DAY, AT HOME...
...MOM WAS SORTING THROUGH OLD BOXES.
GASP!
?!
IT WAS A LOVE LETTER FROM A WOMAN TO DAD.
SIENA. WOULD YOU LIKE TO AUDITION FOR THE SCHOOL OF AMERICAN BALLET? HOW ABOUT YOU AND I TAKE A TRIP TO NEW YORK?

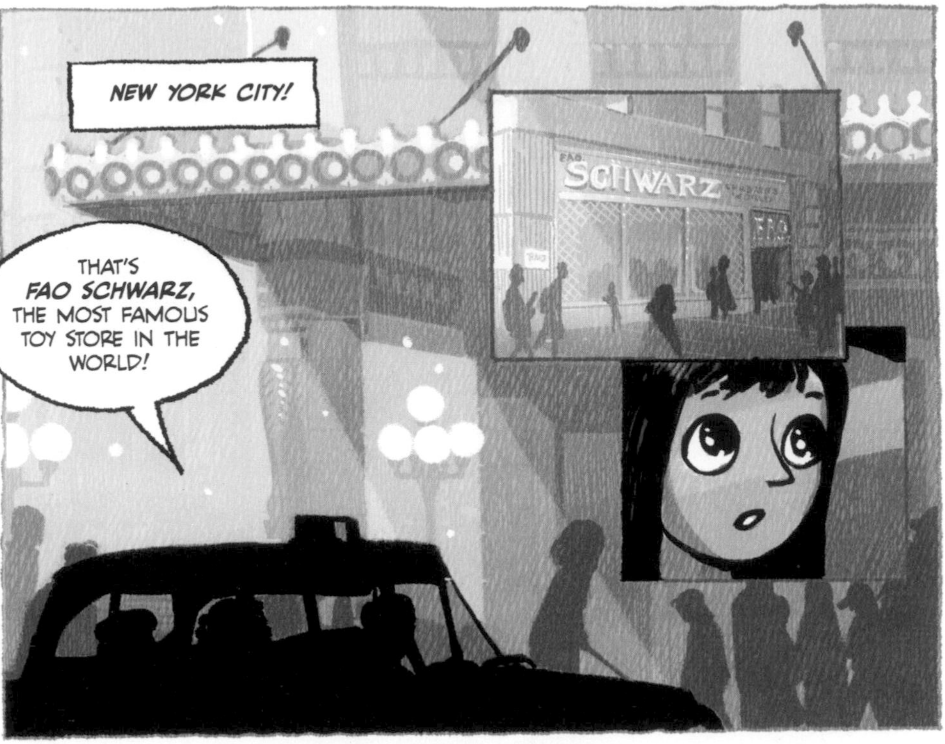
NEW YORK CITY!
THAT'S FAO SCHWARZ, THE MOST FAMOUS TOY STORE IN THE WORLD!
SCHWARZ

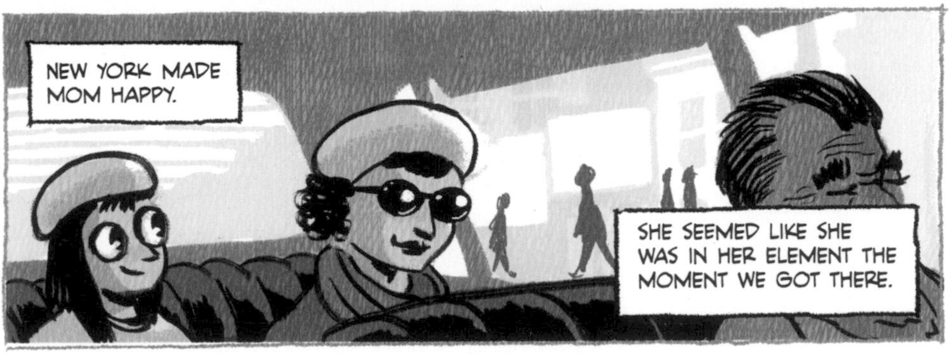
NEW YORK MADE MOM HAPPY.
SHE SEEMED LIKE SHE WAS IN HER ELEMENT THE MOMENT WE GOT THERE.

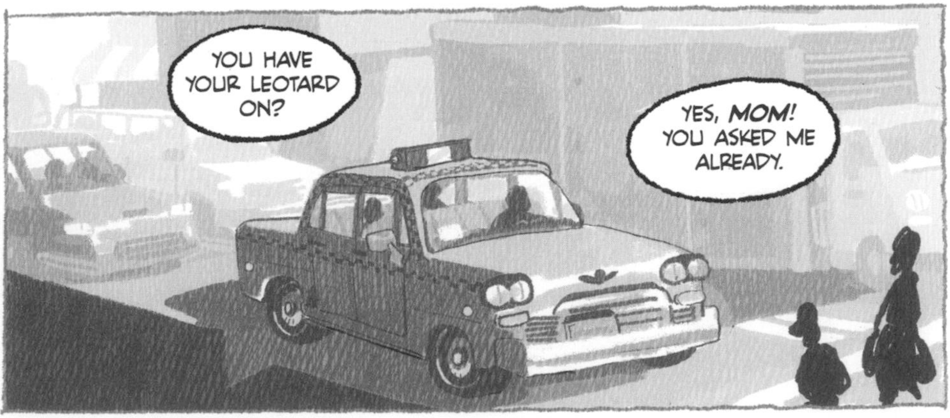
YOU HAVE YOUR LEOTARD ON?
YES, MOM! YOU ASKED ME ALREADY.

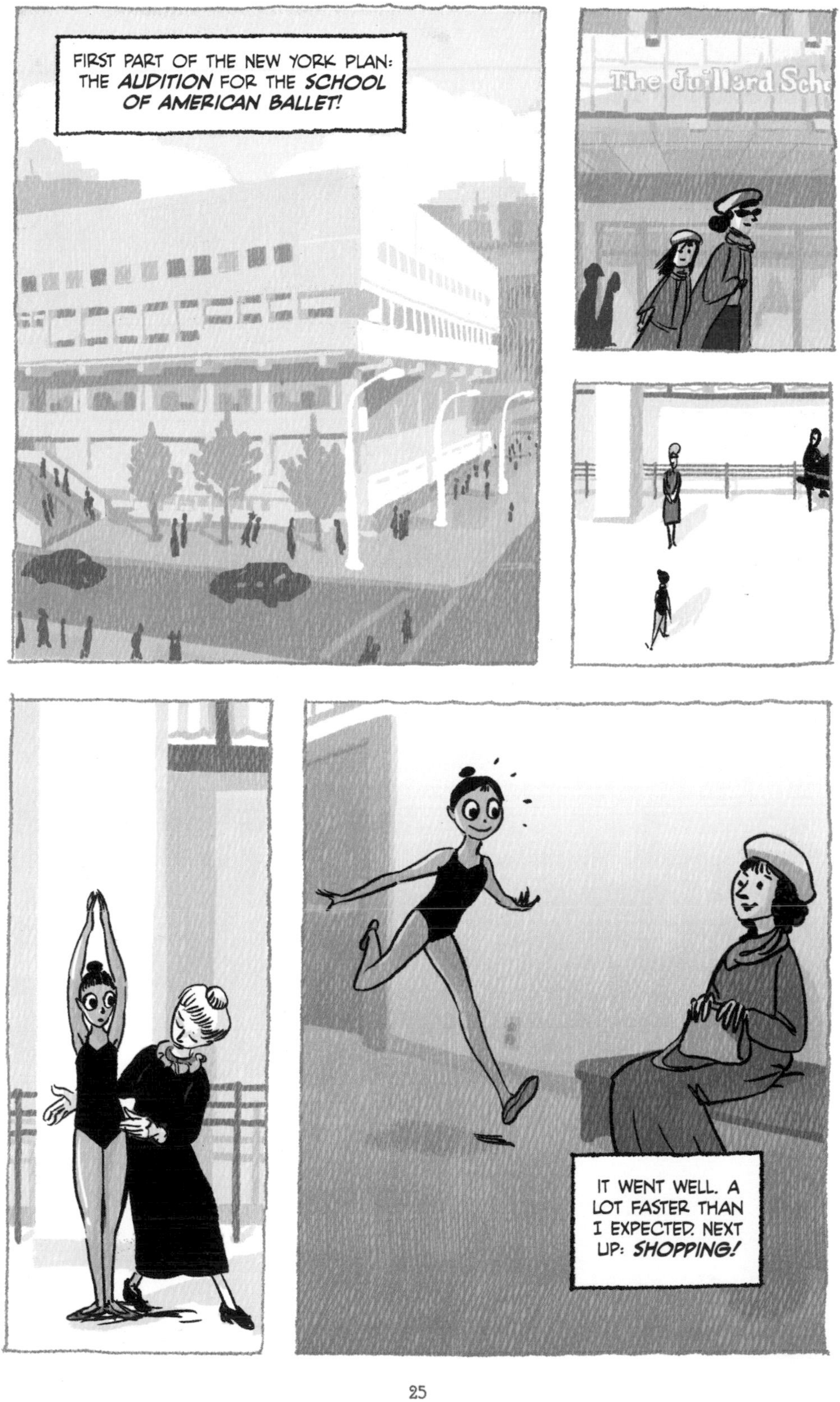
FIRST PART OF THE NEW YORK PLAN: THE AUDITION FOR THE SCHOOL OF AMERICAN BALLET!
The Juillard Scho
IT WENT WELL. A LOT FASTER THAN I EXPECTED. NEXT UP: SHOPPING!

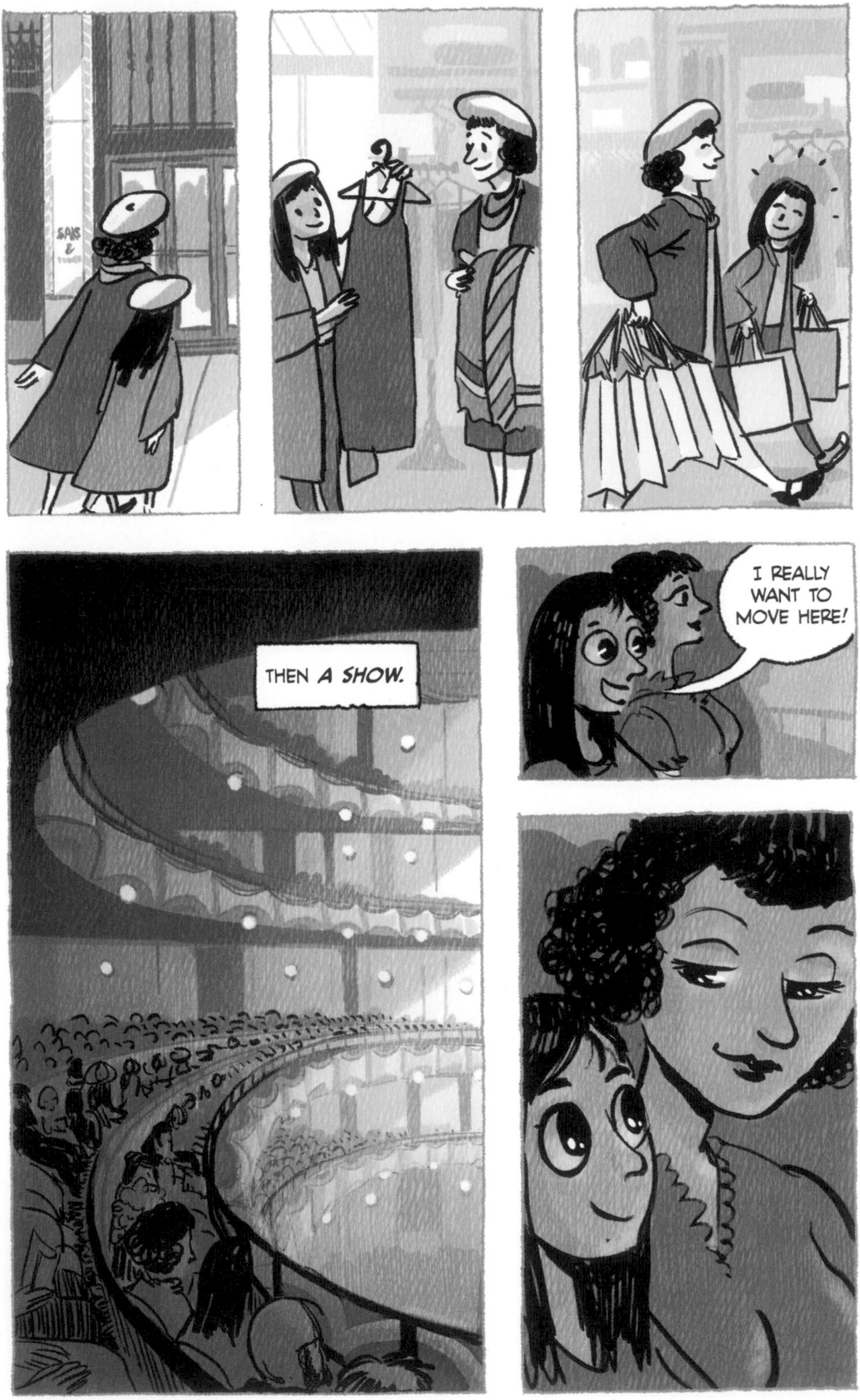
SAKS & [illegible]
THEN A SHOW.
I REALLY WANT TO MOVE HERE!

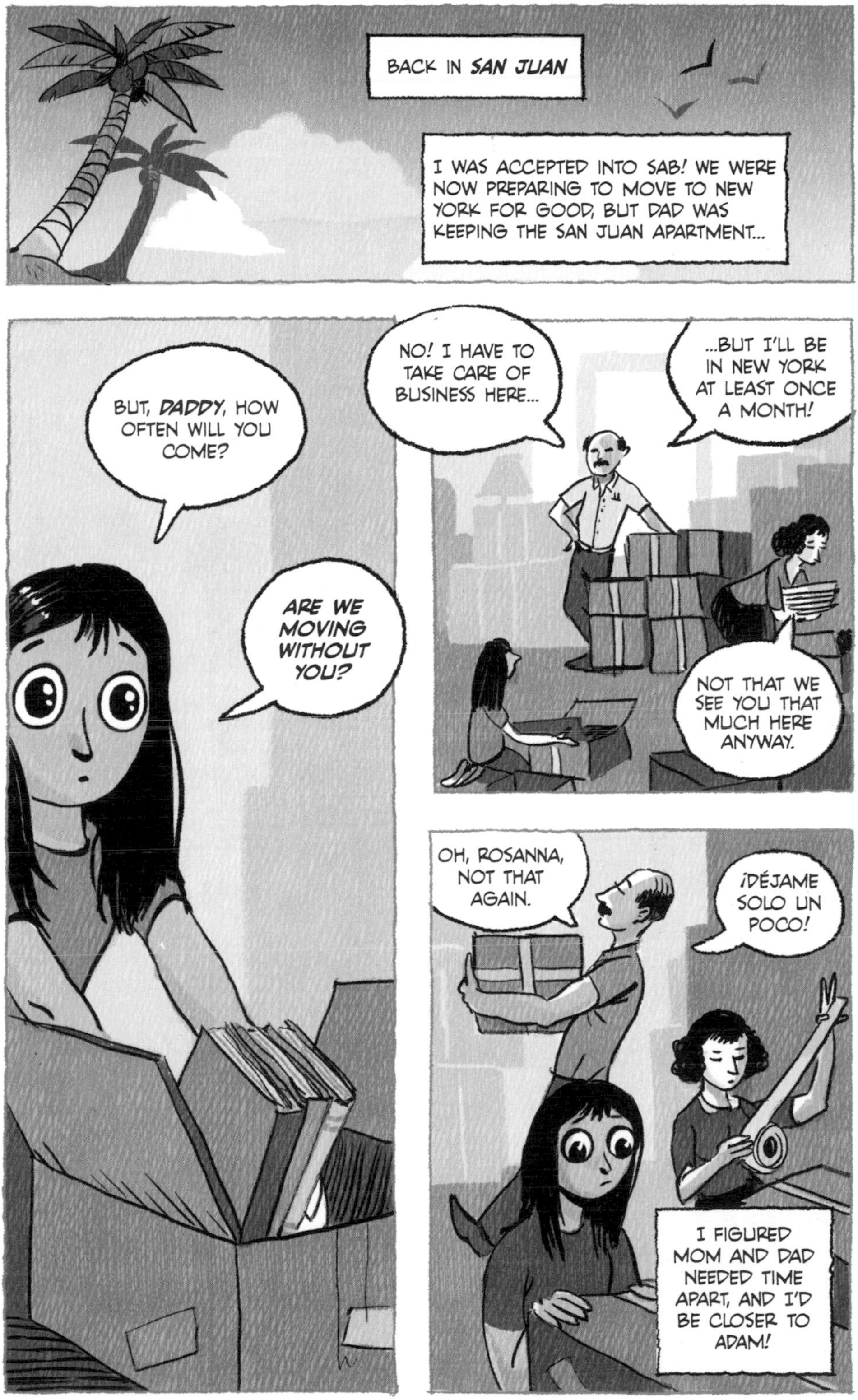
BACK IN SAN JUAN
I WAS ACCEPTED INTO SAB! WE WERE NOW PREPARING TO MOVE TO NEW YORK FOR GOOD, BUT DAD WAS KEEPING THE SAN JUAN APARTMENT...
BUT, DADDY, HOW OFTEN WILL YOU COME?
ARE WE MOVING WITHOUT YOU?
NO! I HAVE TO TAKE CARE OF BUSINESS HERE...
...BUT I'LL BE IN NEW YORK AT LEAST ONCE A MONTH!
NOT THAT WE SEE YOU THAT MUCH HERE ANYWAY.
OH, ROSANNA, NOT THAT AGAIN.
¡DÉJAME SOLO UN POCO!
I FIGURED MOM AND DAD NEEDED TIME APART, AND I'D BE CLOSER TO ADAM!

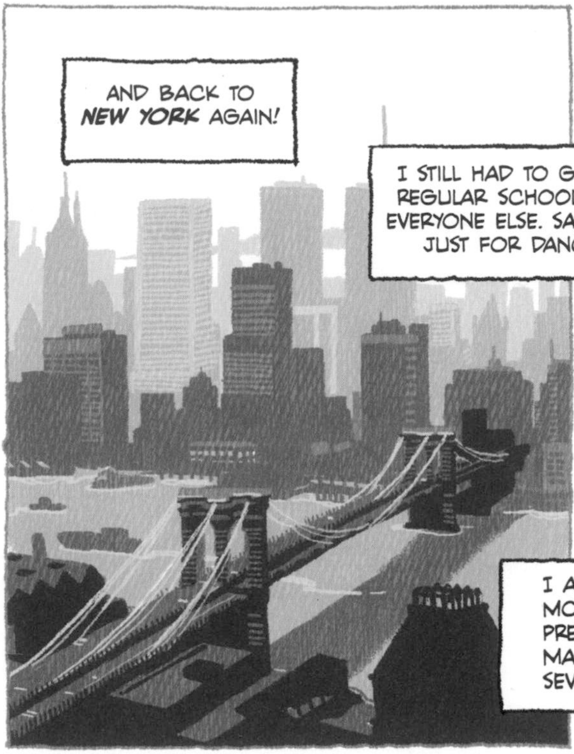
AND BACK TO *NEW YORK* AGAIN!

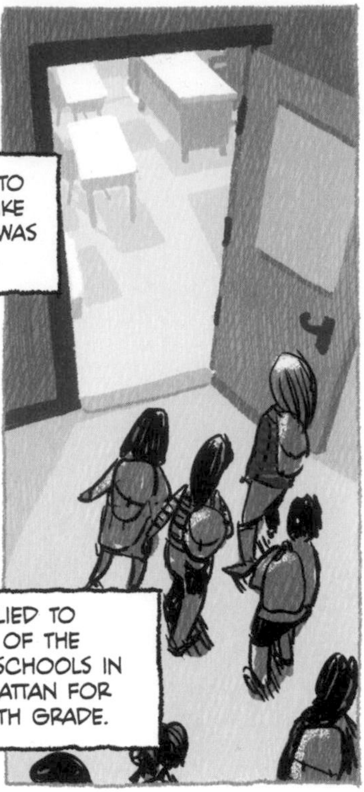
I STILL HAD TO GO TO REGULAR SCHOOL LIKE EVERYONE ELSE. SAB WAS JUST FOR DANCE.
I APPLIED TO MOST OF THE PREP SCHOOLS IN MANHATTAN FOR SEVENTH GRADE.

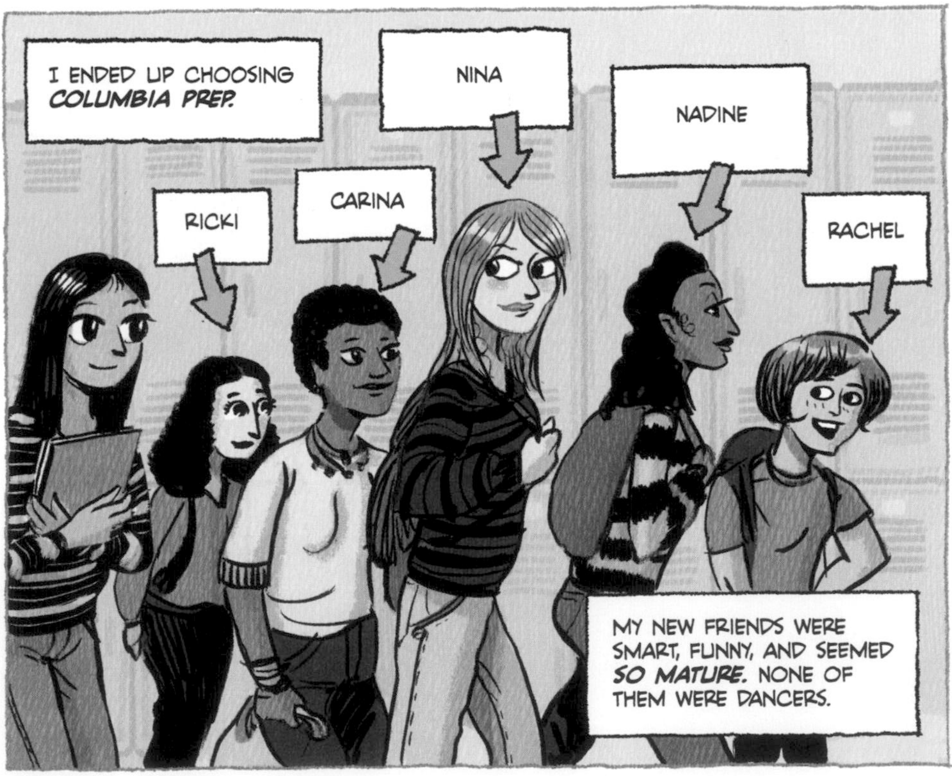
I ENDED UP CHOOSING *COLUMBIA PREP.*
NINA
NADINE
RICKI
CARINA
RACHEL
MY NEW FRIENDS WERE SMART, FUNNY, AND SEEMED *SO MATURE.* NONE OF THEM WERE DANCERS.

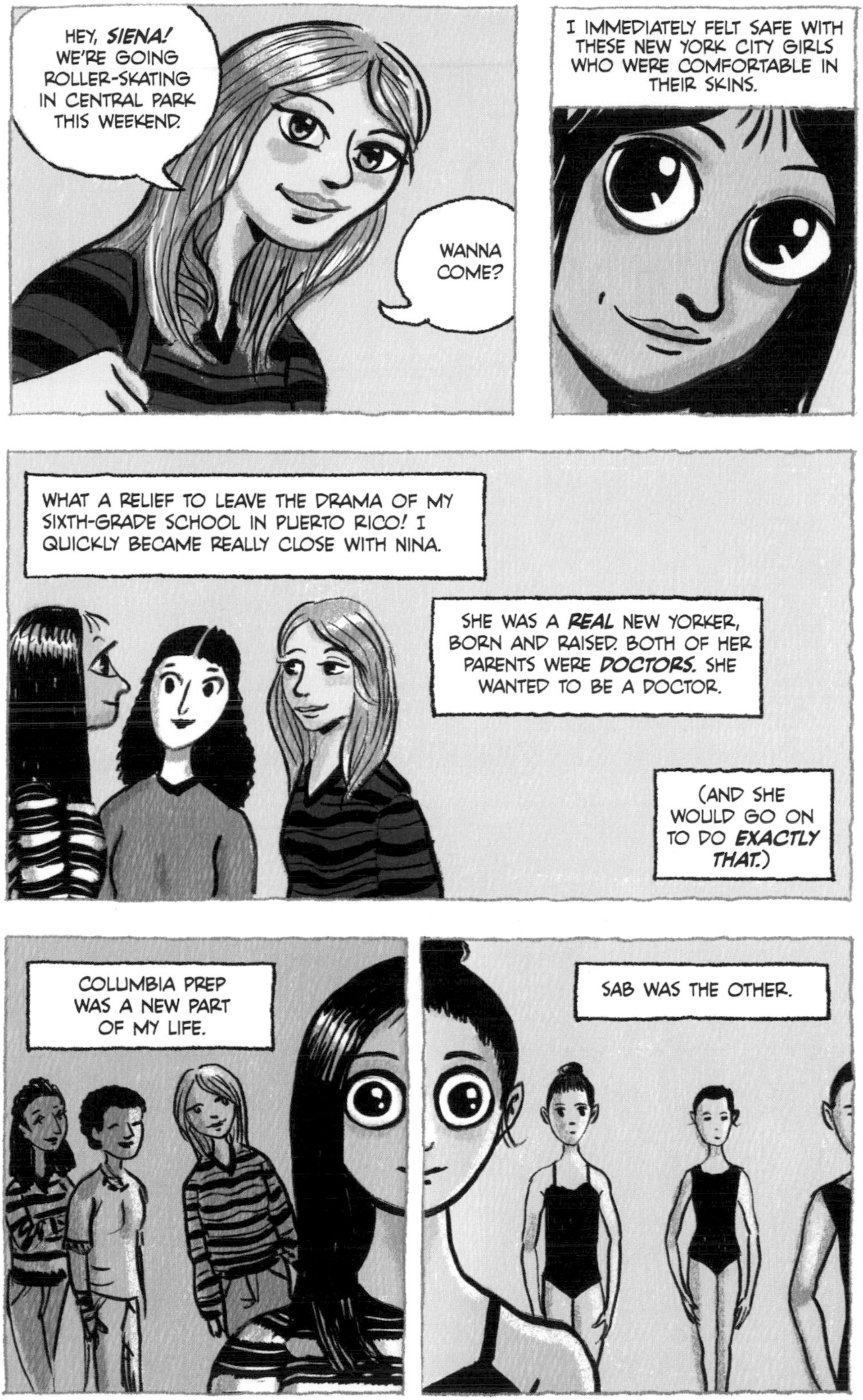
HEY, SIENA! WE'RE GOING ROLLER-SKATING IN CENTRAL PARK THIS WEEKEND.
WANNA COME?
I IMMEDIATELY FELT SAFE WITH THESE NEW YORK CITY GIRLS WHO WERE COMFORTABLE IN THEIR SKINS.
WHAT A RELIEF TO LEAVE THE DRAMA OF MY SIXTH-GRADE SCHOOL IN PUERTO RICO! I QUICKLY BECAME REALLY CLOSE WITH NINA.
SHE WAS A REAL NEW YORKER, BORN AND RAISED. BOTH OF HER PARENTS WERE DOCTORS. SHE WANTED TO BE A DOCTOR.
(AND SHE WOULD GO ON TO DO EXACTLY THAT.)
COLUMBIA PREP WAS A NEW PART OF MY LIFE.
SAB WAS THE OTHER.

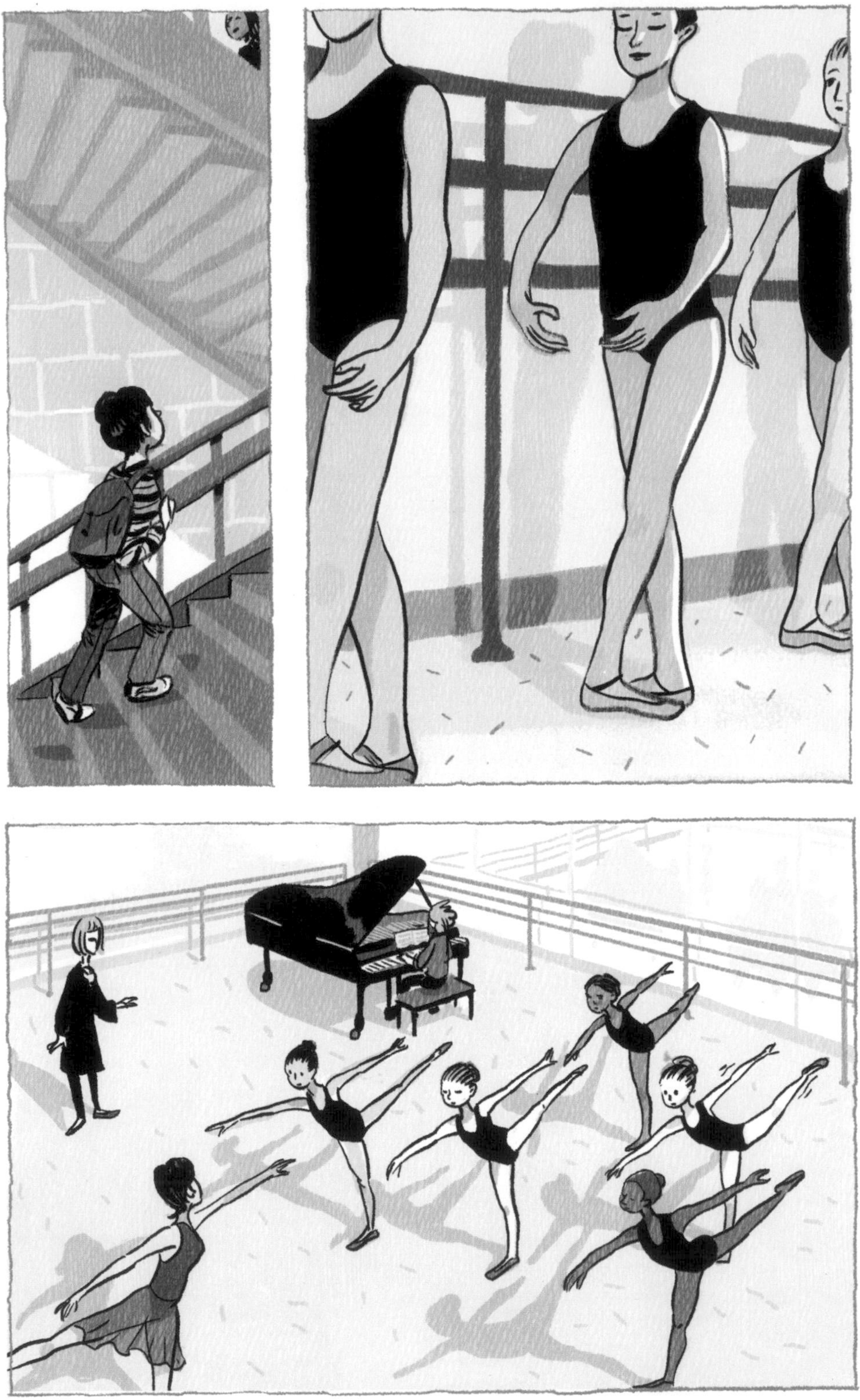

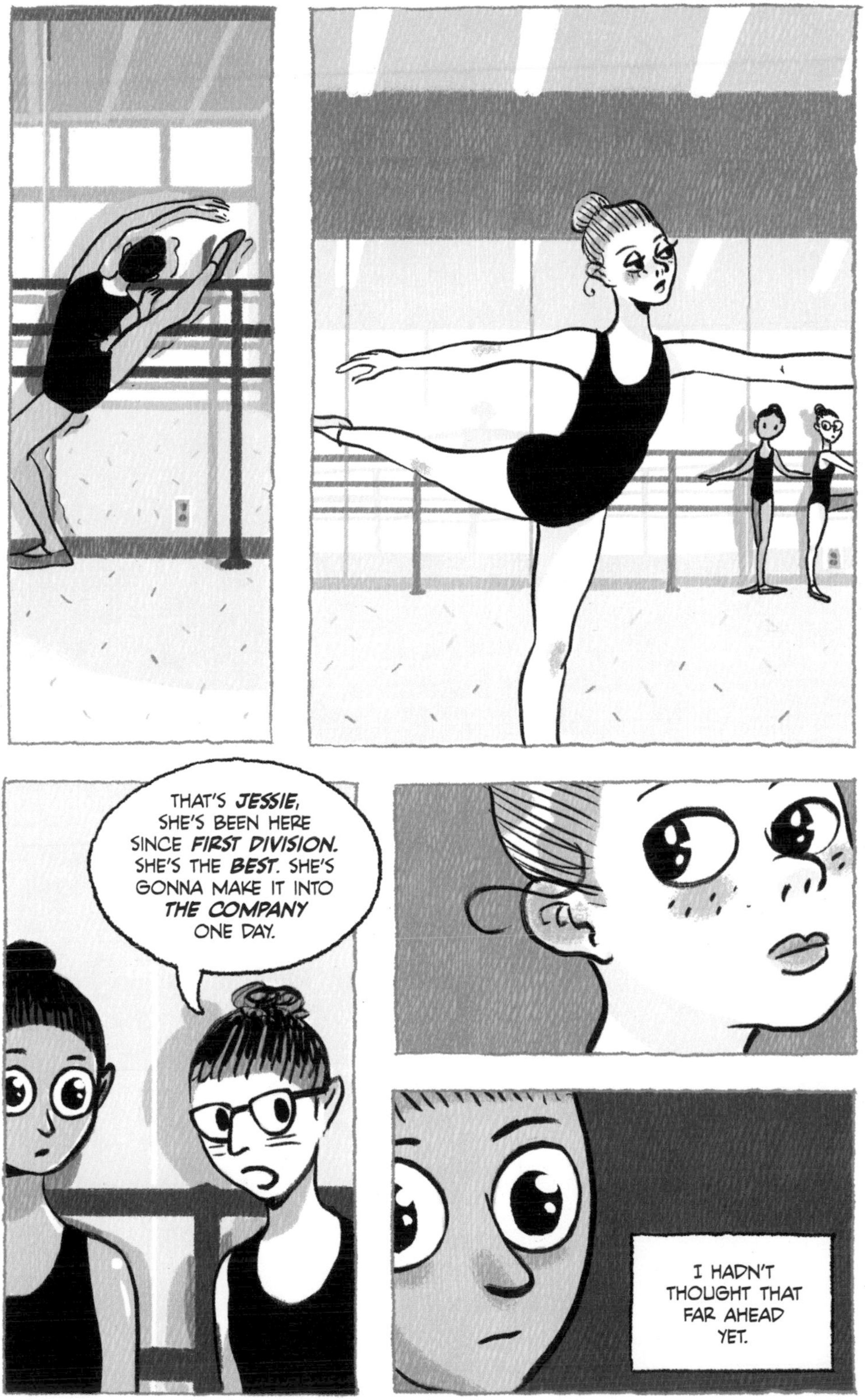
THAT'S JESSIE, SHE'S BEEN HERE SINCE FIRST DIVISION. SHE'S THE BEST. SHE'S GONNA MAKE IT INTO THE COMPANY ONE DAY.
I HADN'T THOUGHT THAT FAR AHEAD YET.

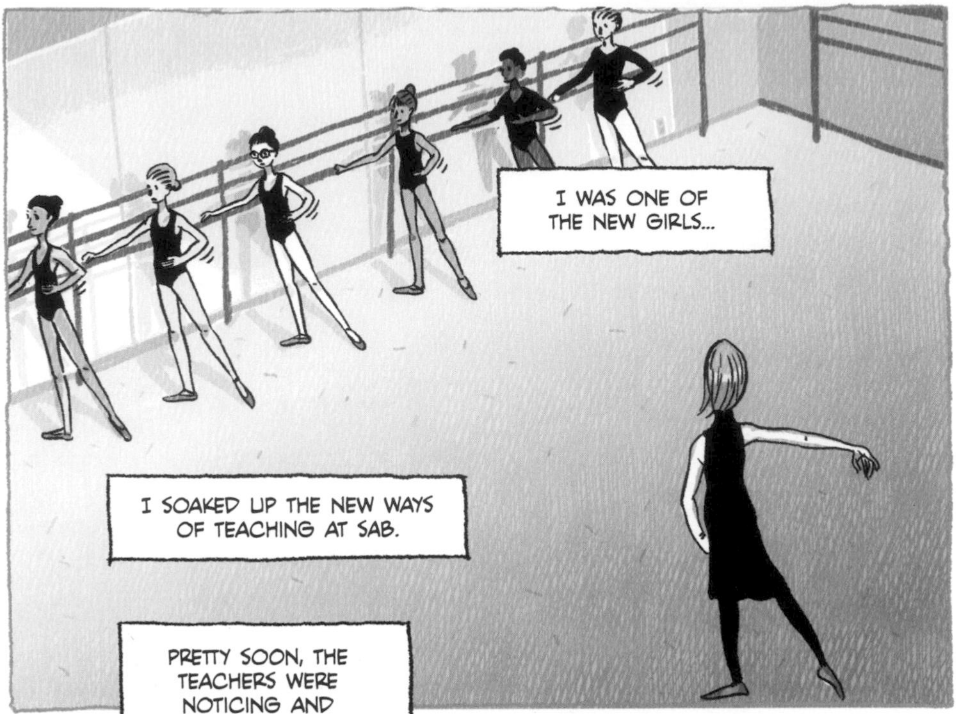
I WAS ONE OF THE NEW GIRLS...
I SOAKED UP THE NEW WAYS OF TEACHING AT SAB.
PRETTY SOON, THE TEACHERS WERE NOTICING AND ENCOURAGING ME.

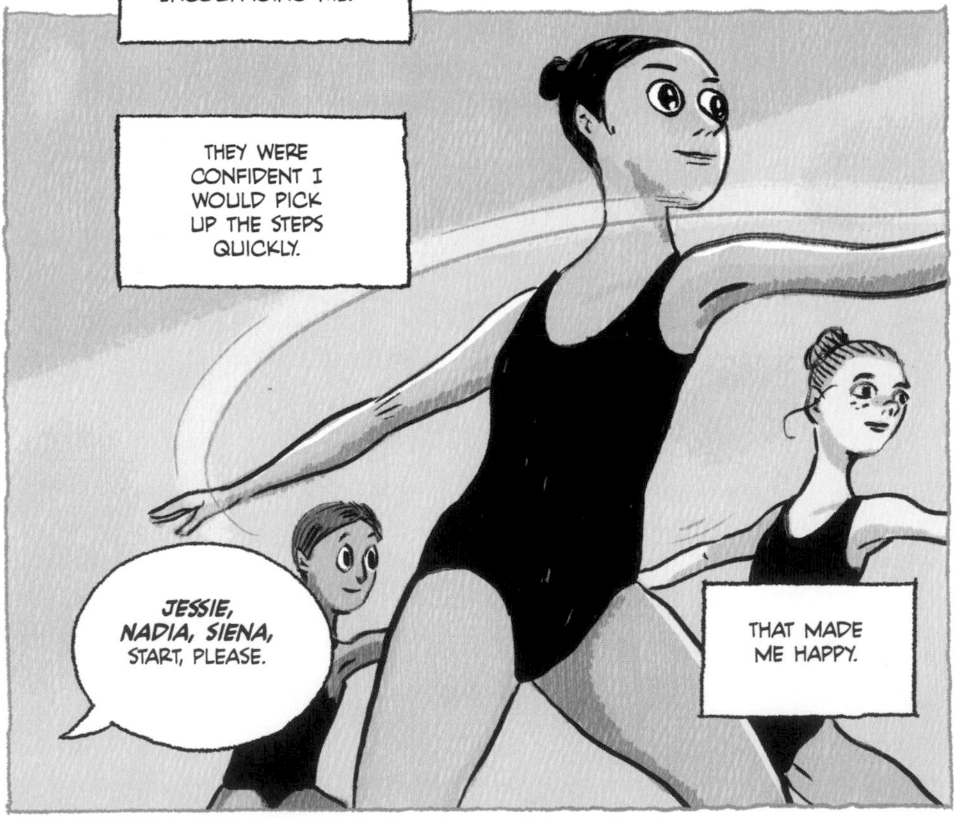
THEY WERE CONFIDENT I WOULD PICK UP THE STEPS QUICKLY.
JESSIE, NADIA, SIENA, START, PLEASE.
THAT MADE ME HAPPY.

THAT FALL, LIFE BECAME BUSY AND VERY EXCITING RIGHT AWAY.

COPPÉLIA Cast

HARLEQUINADE Cast

NUTCRACK Cast

WE STARTED REHEARSING FOR LOTS OF BALLETS.

WE CHILDREN WERE INCLUDED IN MANY OF GEORGE BALANCHINE'S BALLETS, AS LONG AS WE DIDN'T GROW TOO TALL.

JESSIE AND I WERE BOTH CAST IN EVERYTHING, BUT NOT ALWAYS FOR THE SAME PARTS.

PARTS WERE GIVEN ACCORDING TO HEIGHT, AND SHE WAS A LITTLE SHORTER THAN ME.

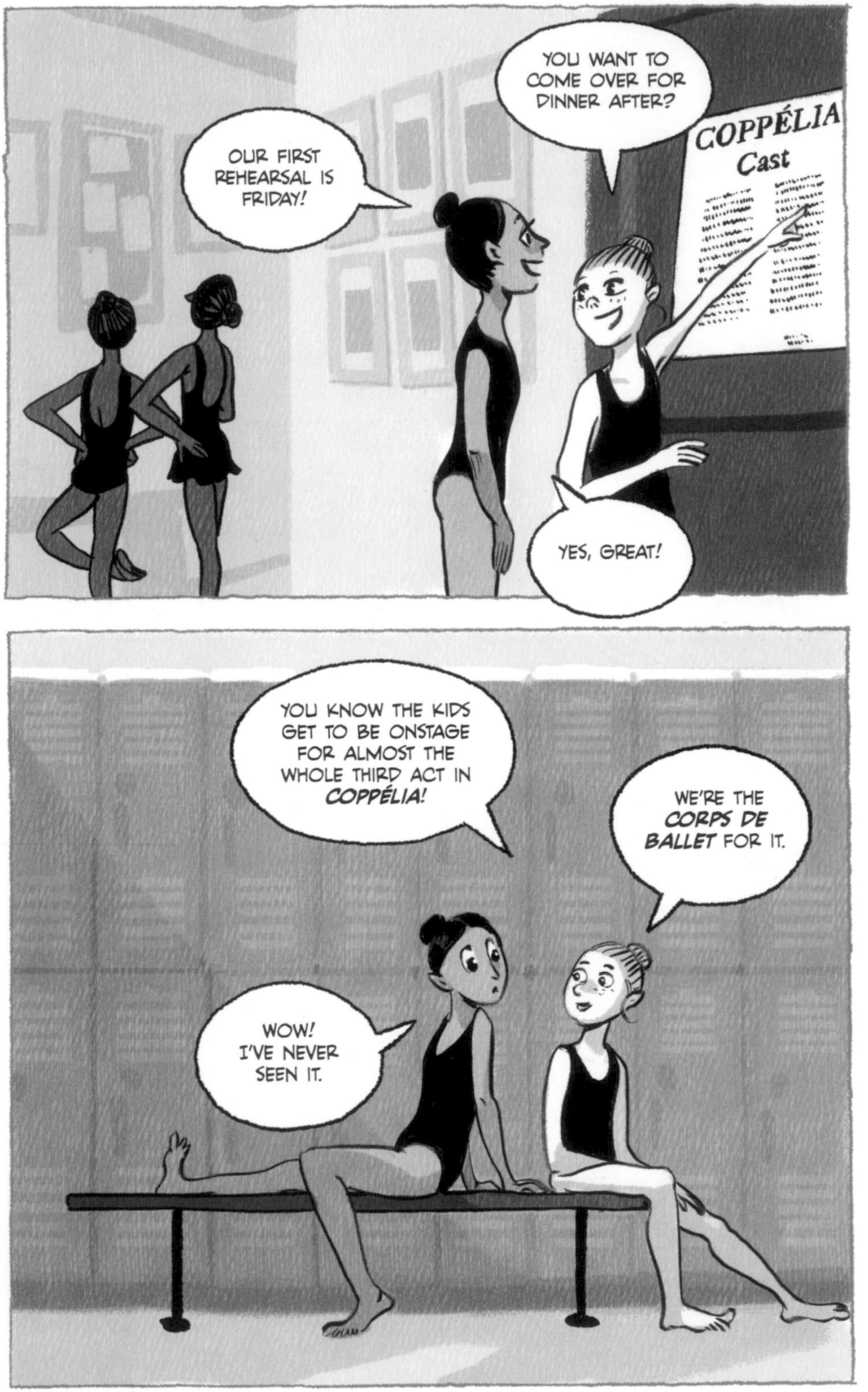
YOU WANT TO COME OVER FOR DINNER AFTER?
COPPÉLIA Cast
OUR FIRST REHEARSAL IS FRIDAY!
YES, GREAT!
YOU KNOW THE KIDS GET TO BE ONSTAGE FOR ALMOST THE WHOLE THIRD ACT IN *COPPÉLIA!*
WE'RE THE *CORPS DE BALLET* FOR IT.
WOW! I'VE NEVER SEEN IT.

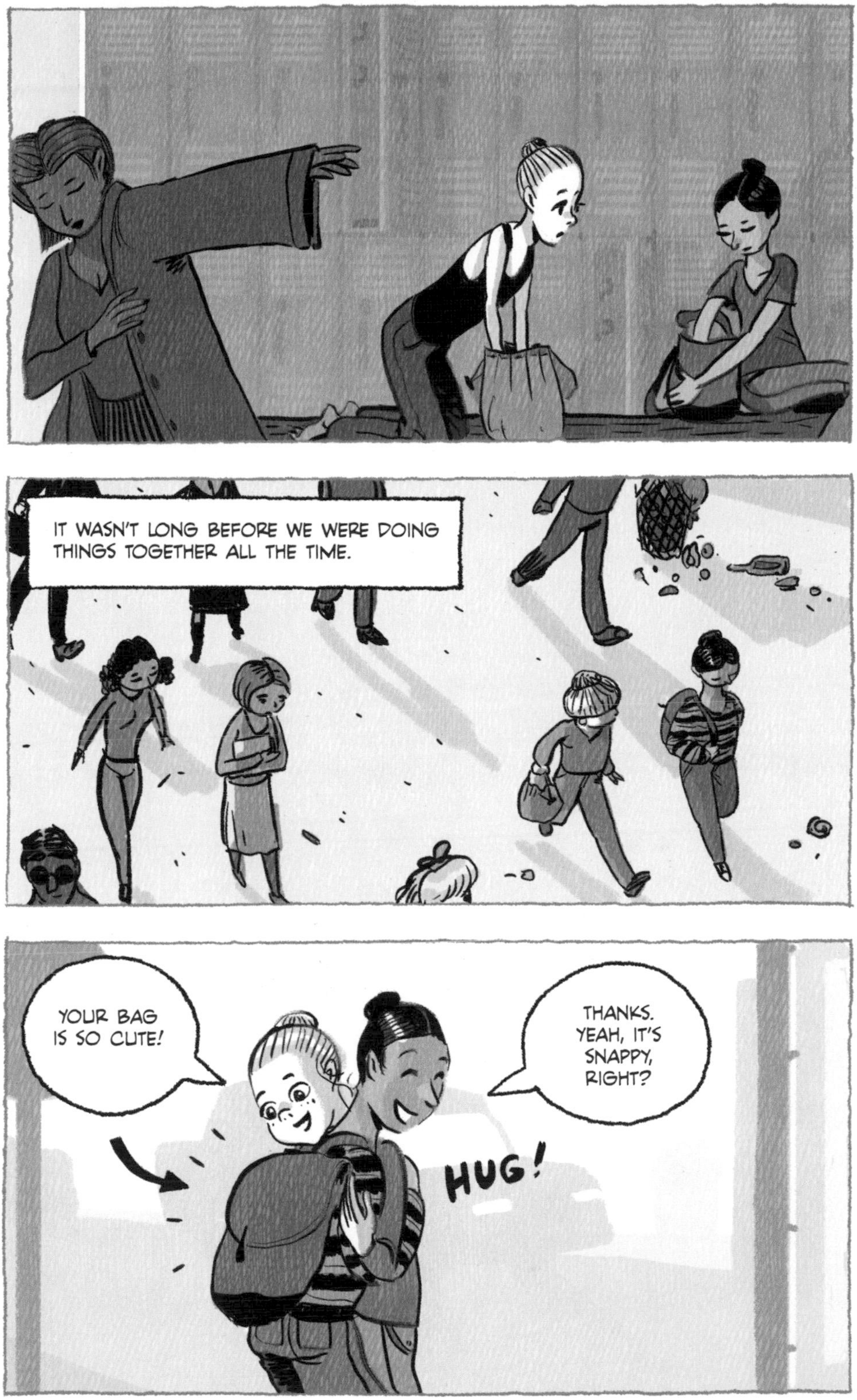
IT WASN'T LONG BEFORE WE WERE DOING THINGS TOGETHER ALL THE TIME.
YOUR BAG IS SO CUTE!
THANKS. YEAH, IT'S SNAPPY, RIGHT?
HUG!

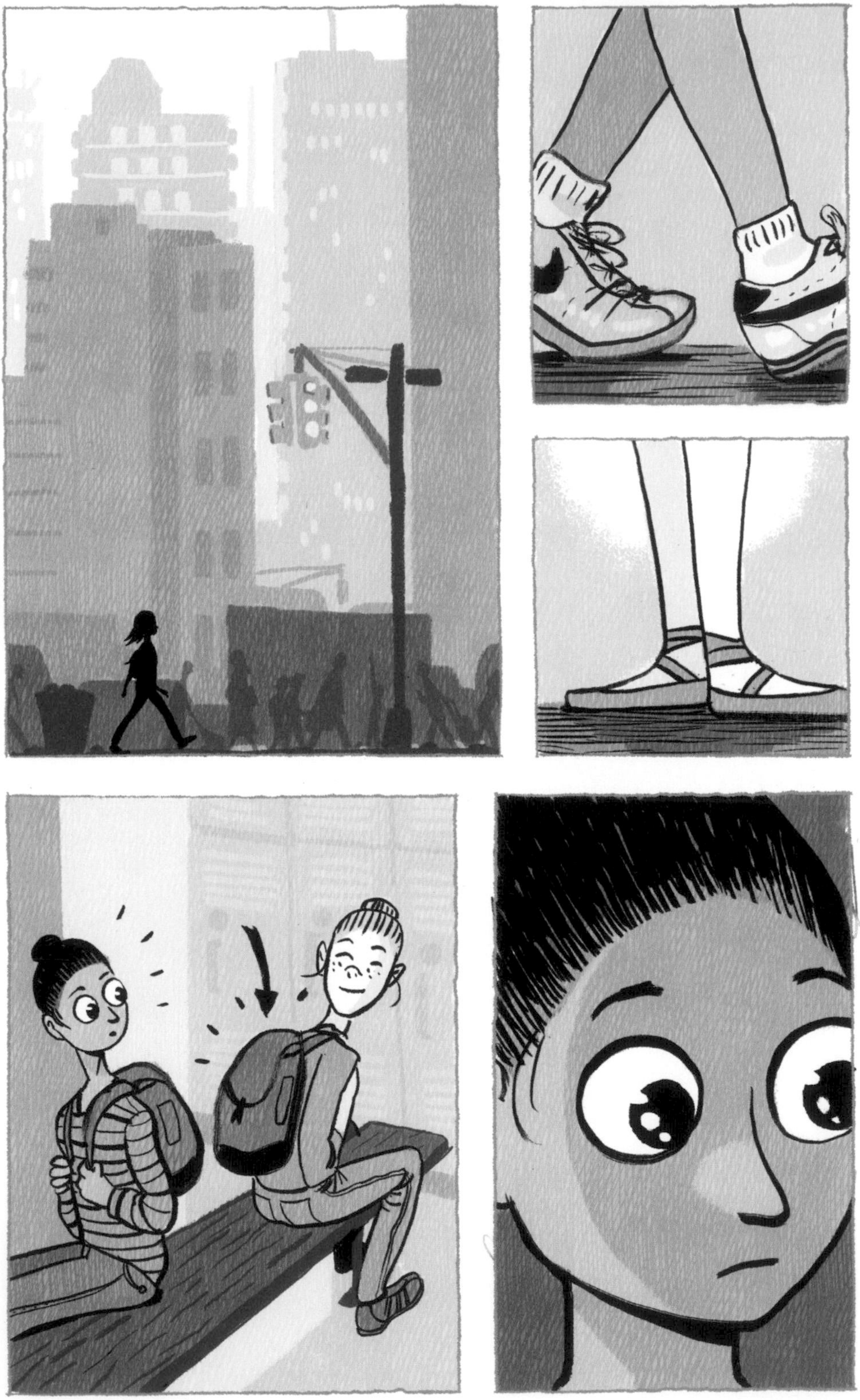

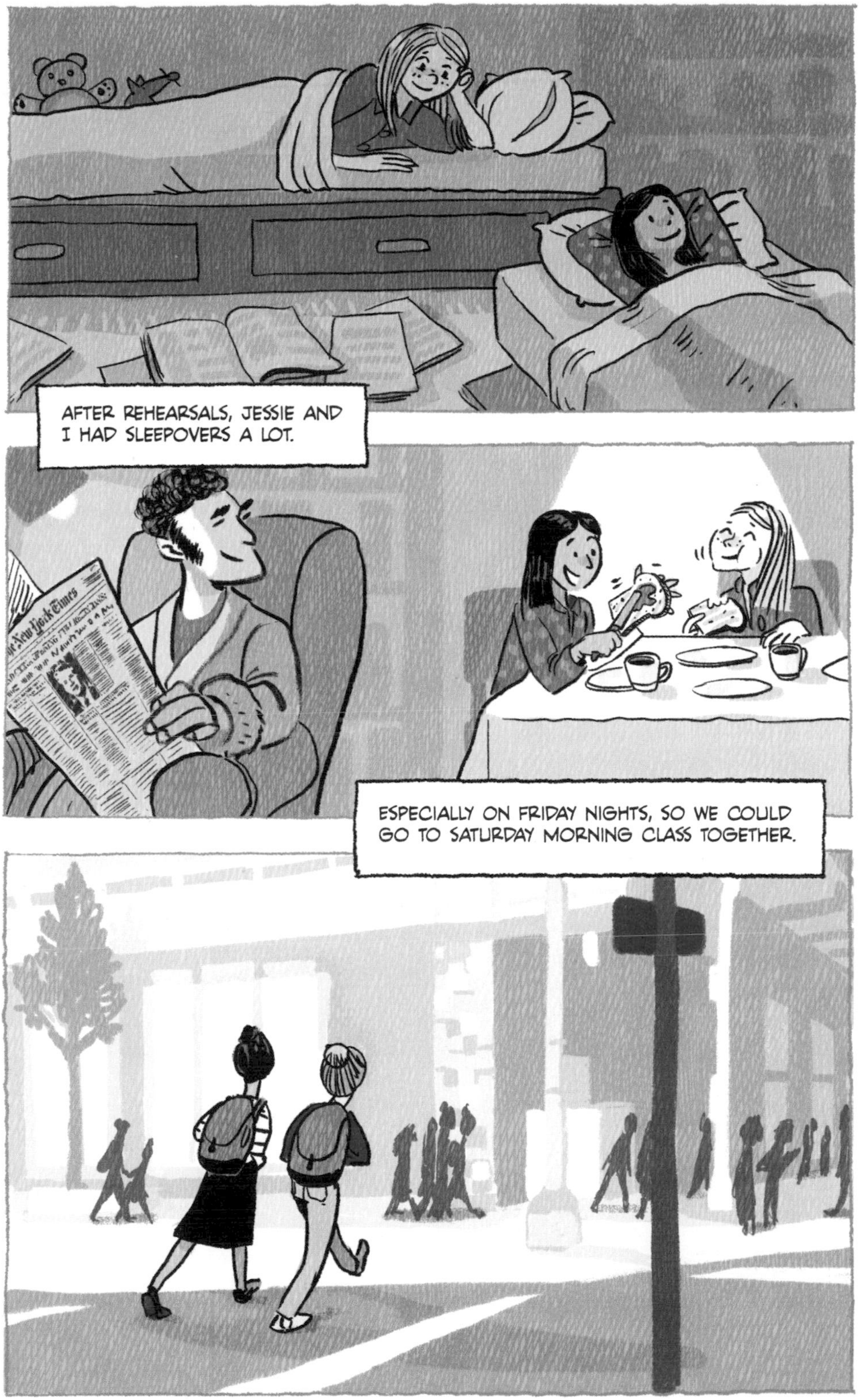
AFTER REHEARSALS, JESSIE AND I HAD SLEEPOVERS A LOT.
ESPECIALLY ON FRIDAY NIGHTS, SO WE COULD GO TO SATURDAY MORNING CLASS TOGETHER.

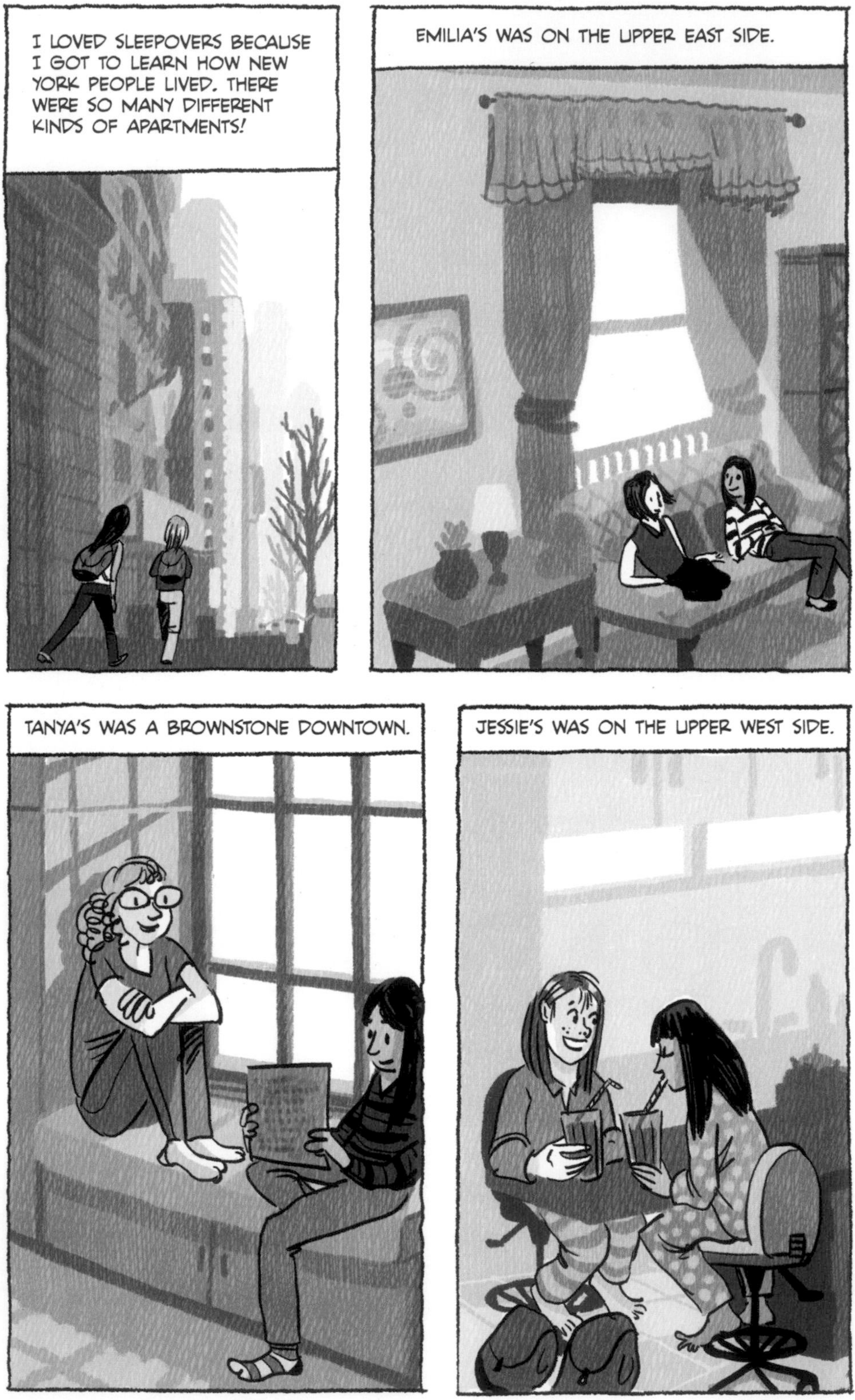
I LOVED SLEEPOVERS BECAUSE I GOT TO LEARN HOW NEW YORK PEOPLE LIVED. THERE WERE SO MANY DIFFERENT KINDS OF APARTMENTS!
EMILIA'S WAS ON THE UPPER EAST SIDE.
TANYA'S WAS A BROWNSTONE DOWNTOWN.
JESSIE'S WAS ON THE UPPER WEST SIDE.

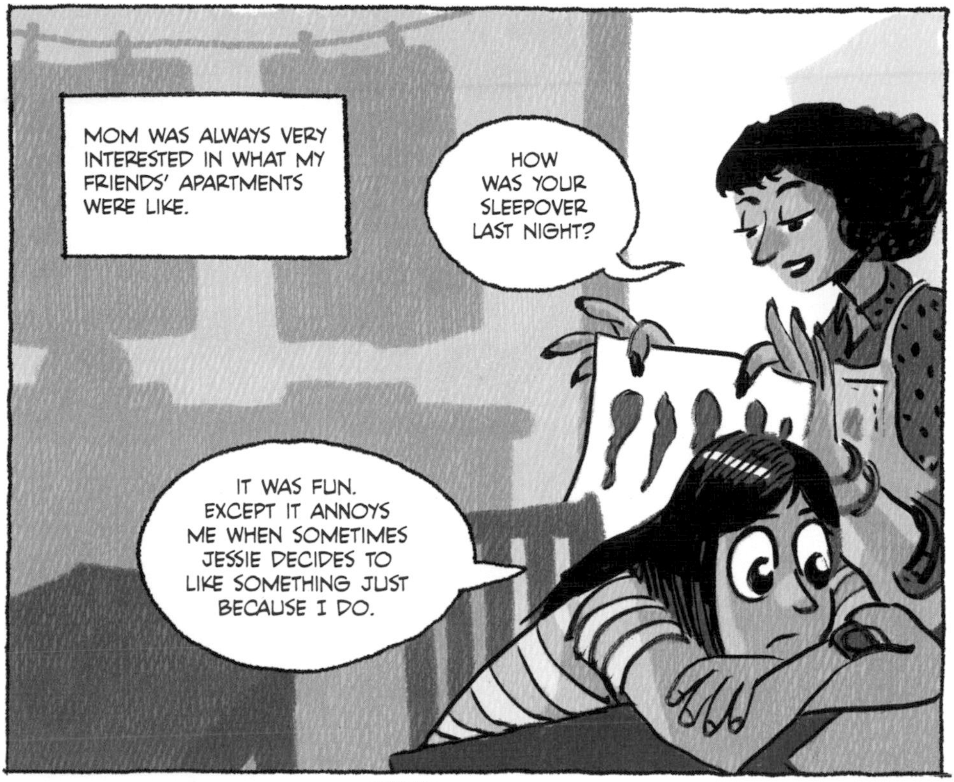
MOM WAS ALWAYS VERY INTERESTED IN WHAT MY FRIENDS' APARTMENTS WERE LIKE.
HOW WAS YOUR SLEEPOVER LAST NIGHT?
IT WAS FUN. EXCEPT IT ANNOYS ME WHEN SOMETIMES JESSIE DECIDES TO LIKE SOMETHING JUST BECAUSE I DO.

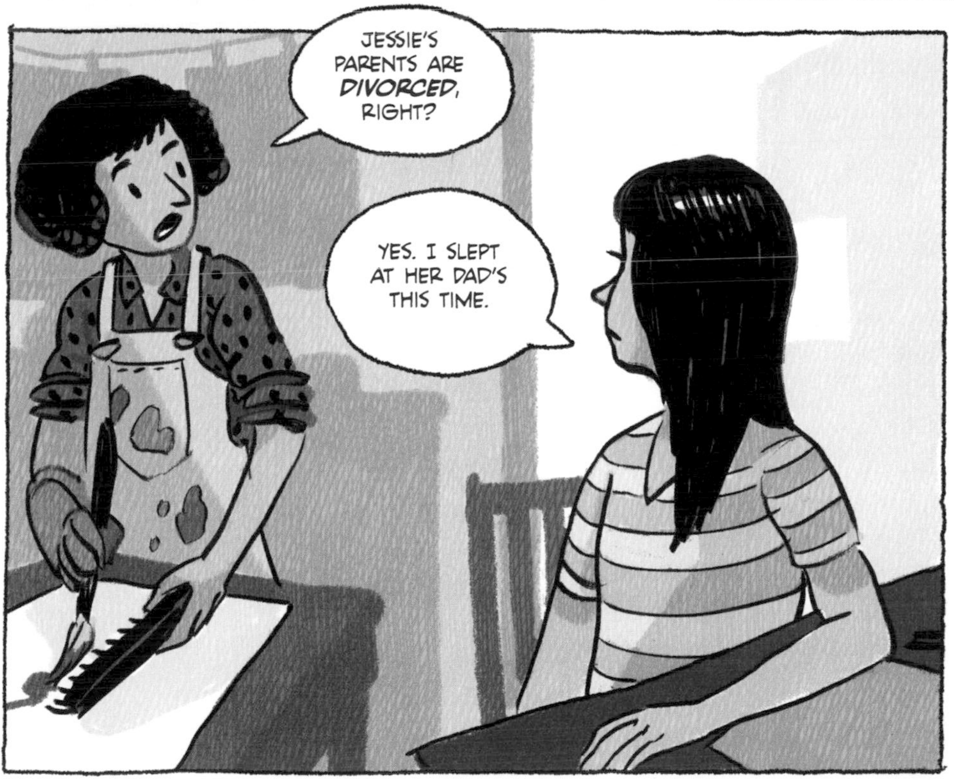
JESSIE'S PARENTS ARE *DIVORCED*, RIGHT?
YES. I SLEPT AT HER DAD'S THIS TIME.

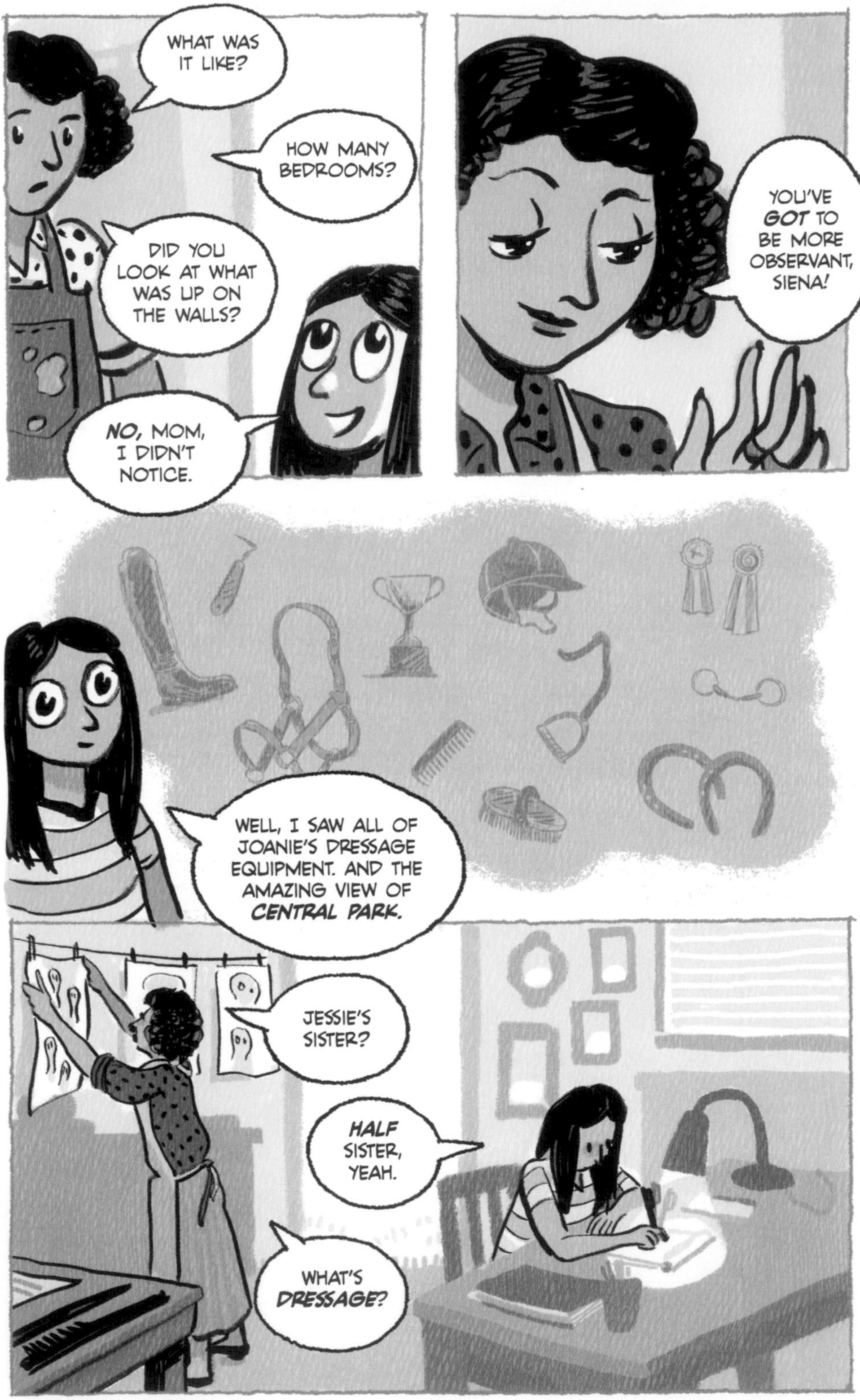
WHAT WAS IT LIKE?
HOW MANY BEDROOMS?
DID YOU LOOK AT WHAT WAS UP ON THE WALLS?
NO, MOM, I DIDN'T NOTICE.
YOU'VE GOT TO BE MORE OBSERVANT, SIENA!
WELL, I SAW ALL OF JOANIE'S DRESSAGE EQUIPMENT. AND THE AMAZING VIEW OF CENTRAL PARK.
JESSIE'S SISTER?
HALF SISTER, YEAH.
WHAT'S DRESSAGE?

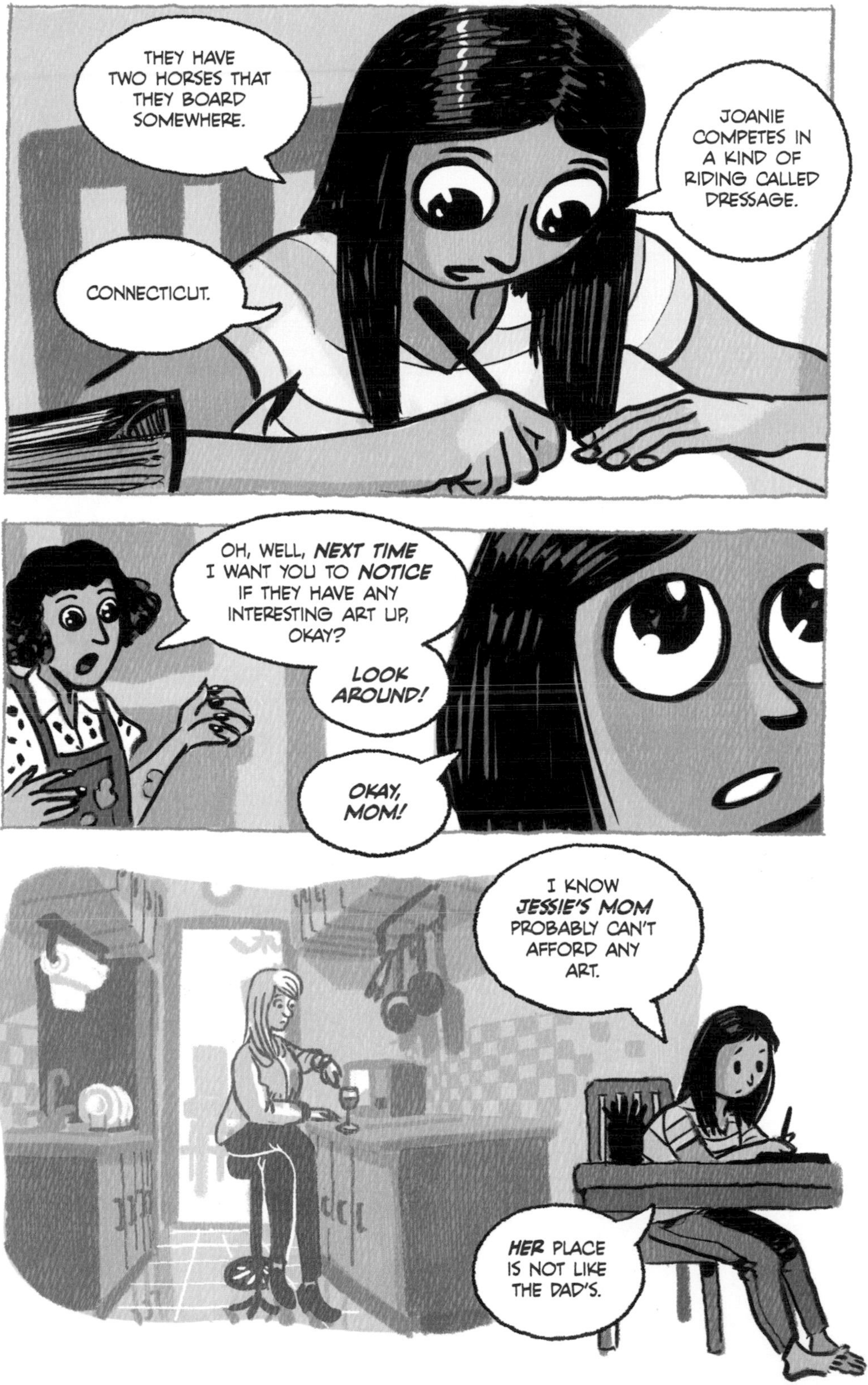
THEY HAVE TWO HORSES THAT THEY BOARD SOMEWHERE.
JOANIE COMPETES IN A KIND OF RIDING CALLED DRESSAGE.
CONNECTICUT.
OH, WELL, *NEXT TIME* I WANT YOU TO *NOTICE* IF THEY HAVE ANY INTERESTING ART UP, OKAY?
LOOK AROUND!
OKAY, MOM!
I KNOW *JESSIE'S MOM* PROBABLY CAN'T AFFORD ANY ART.
HER PLACE IS NOT LIKE THE DAD'S.

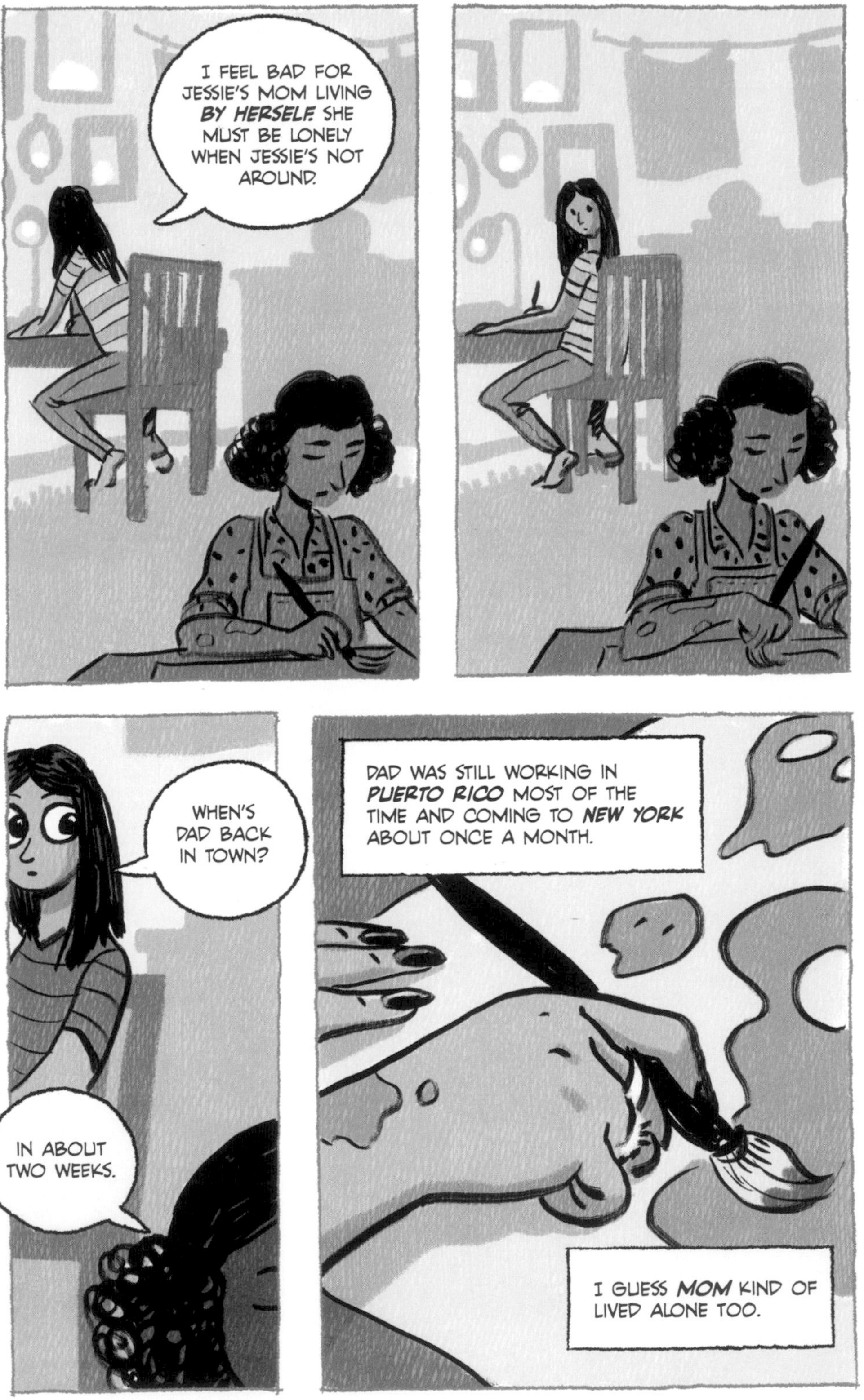
I FEEL BAD FOR JESSIE'S MOM LIVING BY HERSELF. SHE MUST BE LONELY WHEN JESSIE'S NOT AROUND.
WHEN'S DAD BACK IN TOWN?
IN ABOUT TWO WEEKS.
DAD WAS STILL WORKING IN PUERTO RICO MOST OF THE TIME AND COMING TO NEW YORK ABOUT ONCE A MONTH.
I GUESS MOM KIND OF LIVED ALONE TOO.

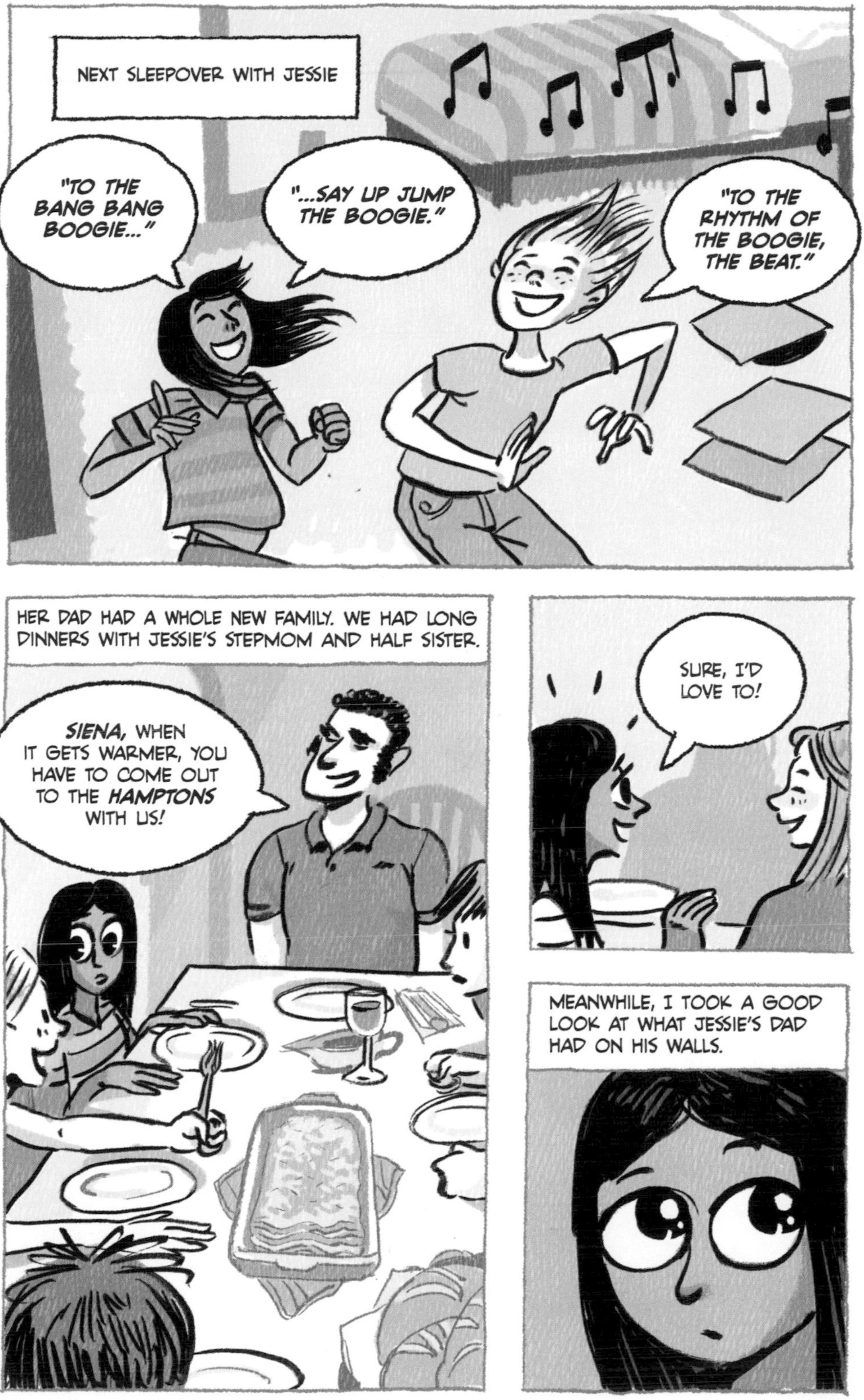
NEXT SLEEPOVER WITH JESSIE
"TO THE BANG BANG BOOGIE..."
"...SAY UP JUMP THE BOOGIE."
"TO THE RHYTHM OF THE BOOGIE, THE BEAT."
HER DAD HAD A WHOLE NEW FAMILY. WE HAD LONG DINNERS WITH JESSIE'S STEPMOM AND HALF SISTER.
SIENA, WHEN IT GETS WARMER, YOU HAVE TO COME OUT TO THE HAMPTONS WITH US!
SURE, I'D LOVE TO!
MEANWHILE, I TOOK A GOOD LOOK AT WHAT JESSIE'S DAD HAD ON HIS WALLS.

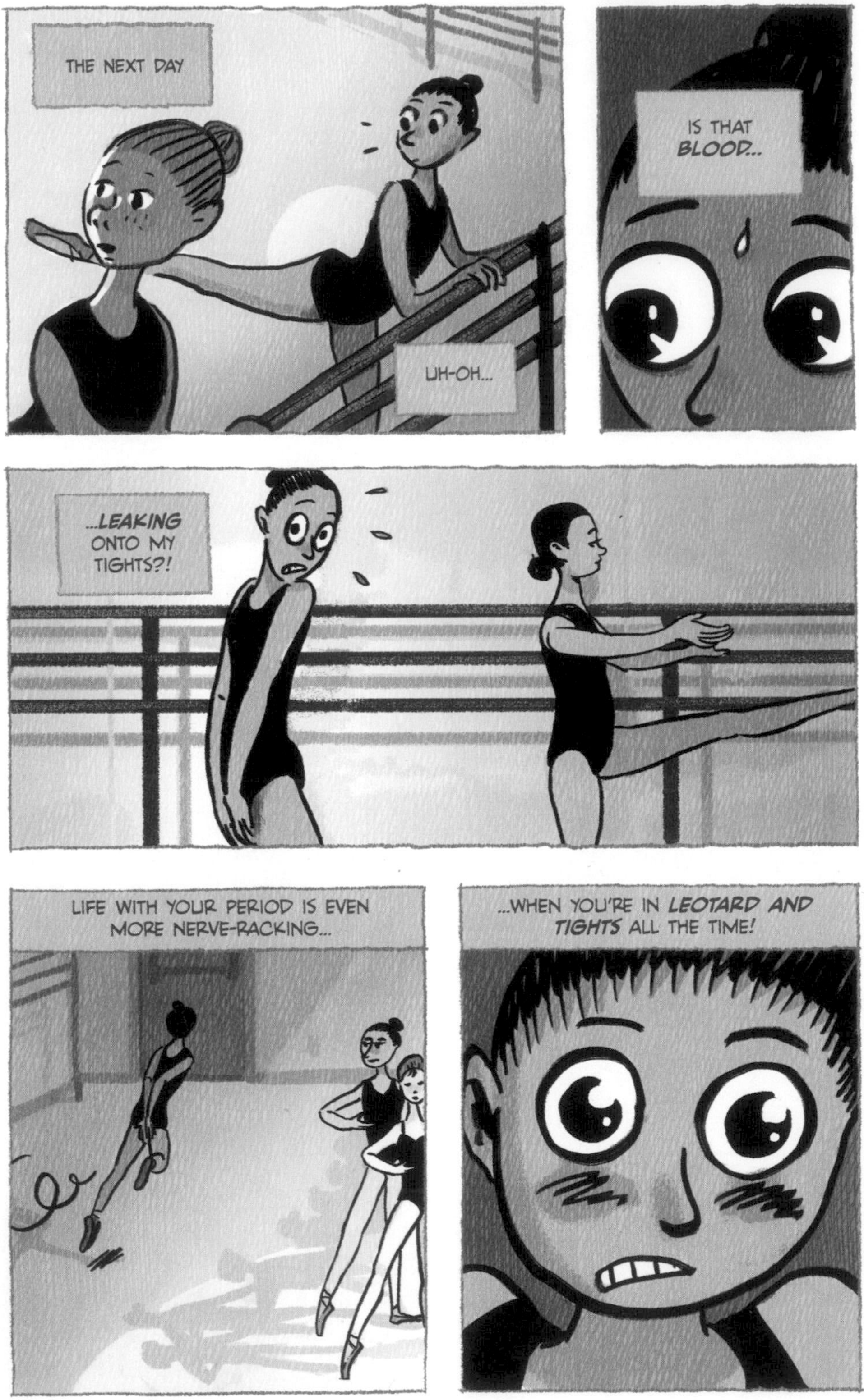
THE NEXT DAY
UH-OH...
IS THAT BLOOD...
...LEAKING ONTO MY TIGHTS?!
LIFE WITH YOUR PERIOD IS EVEN MORE NERVE-RACKING...
...WHEN YOU'RE IN LEOTARD AND TIGHTS ALL THE TIME!

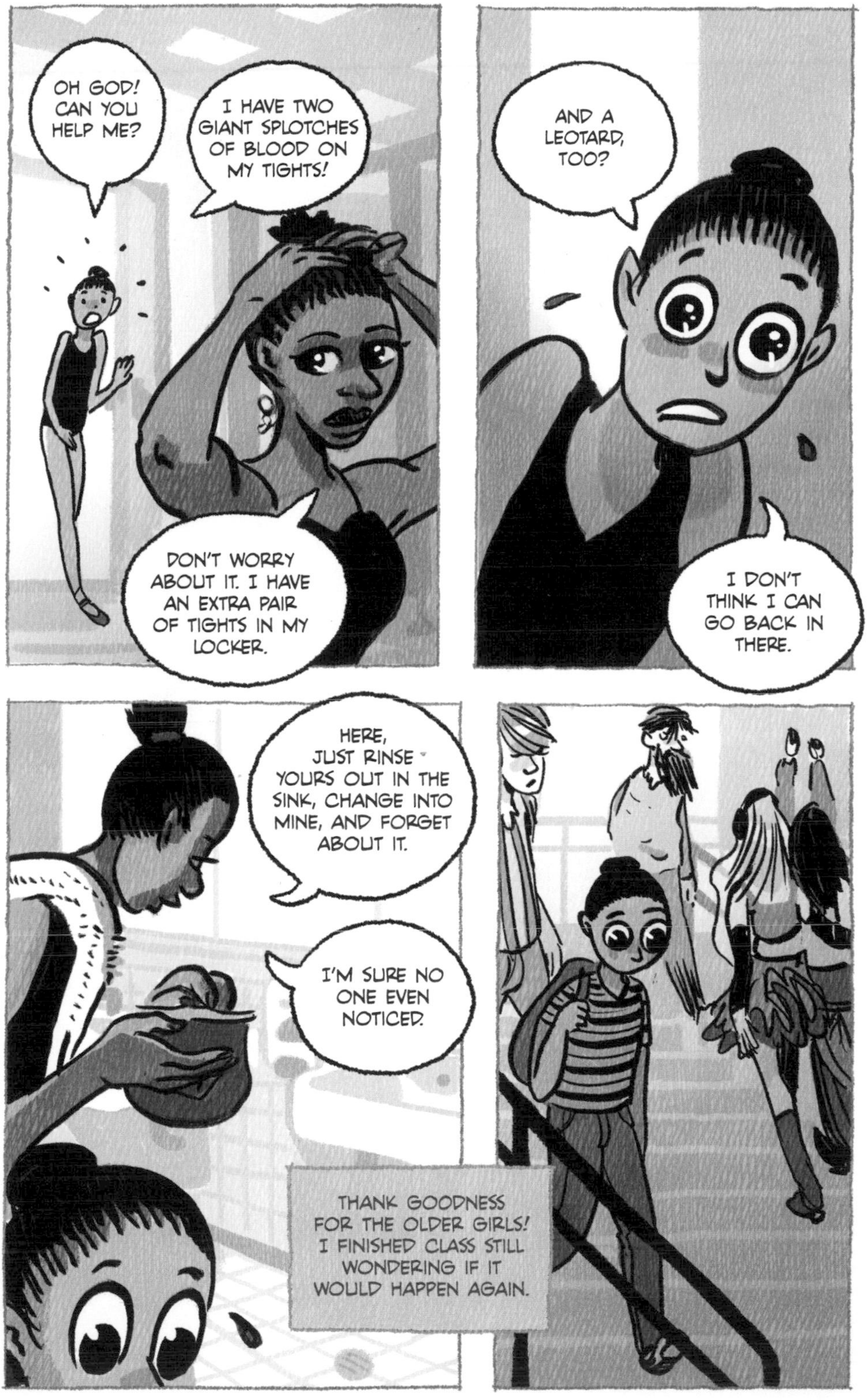
OH GOD! CAN YOU HELP ME?
I HAVE TWO GIANT SPLOTCHES OF BLOOD ON MY TIGHTS!
DON'T WORRY ABOUT IT. I HAVE AN EXTRA PAIR OF TIGHTS IN MY LOCKER.
AND A LEOTARD, TOO?
I DON'T THINK I CAN GO BACK IN THERE.
HERE, JUST RINSE YOURS OUT IN THE SINK, CHANGE INTO MINE, AND FORGET ABOUT IT.
I'M SURE NO ONE EVEN NOTICED.
THANK GOODNESS FOR THE OLDER GIRLS! I FINISHED CLASS STILL WONDERING IF IT WOULD HAPPEN AGAIN.

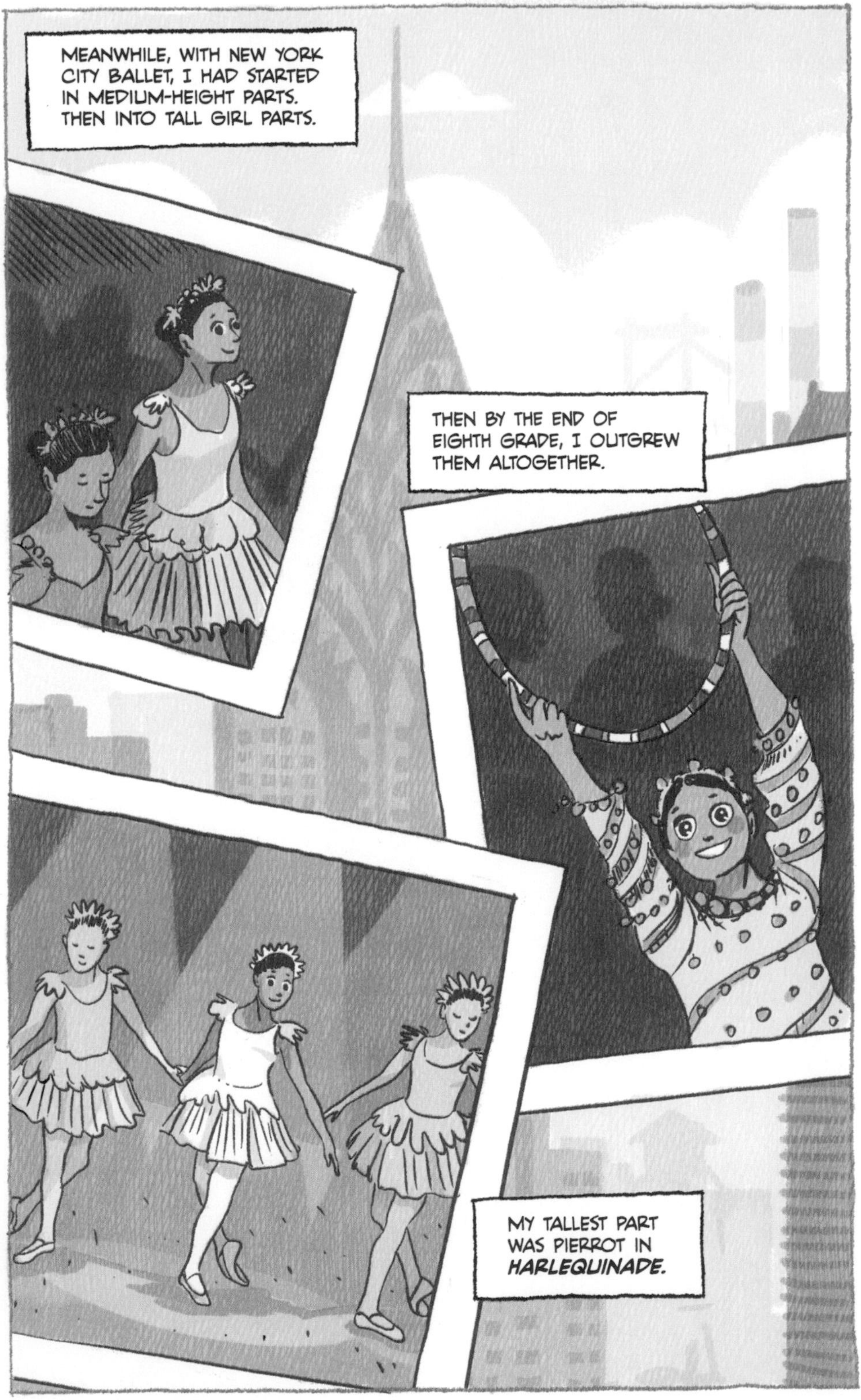
MEANWHILE, WITH NEW YORK CITY BALLET, I HAD STARTED IN MEDIUM-HEIGHT PARTS. THEN INTO TALL GIRL PARTS.
THEN BY THE END OF EIGHTH GRADE, I OUTGREW THEM ALTOGETHER.
MY TALLEST PART WAS PIERROT IN *HARLEQUINADE.*

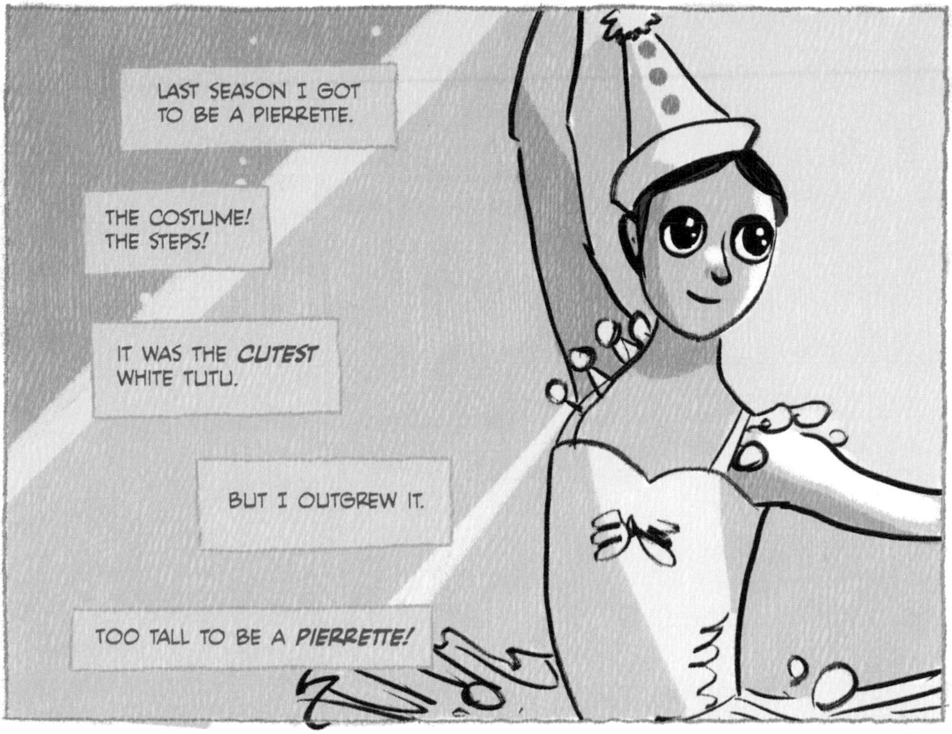
LAST SEASON I GOT TO BE A PIERRETTE.
THE COSTUME! THE STEPS!
IT WAS THE *CUTEST* WHITE TUTU.
BUT I OUTGREW IT.
TOO TALL TO BE A *PIERRETTE!*

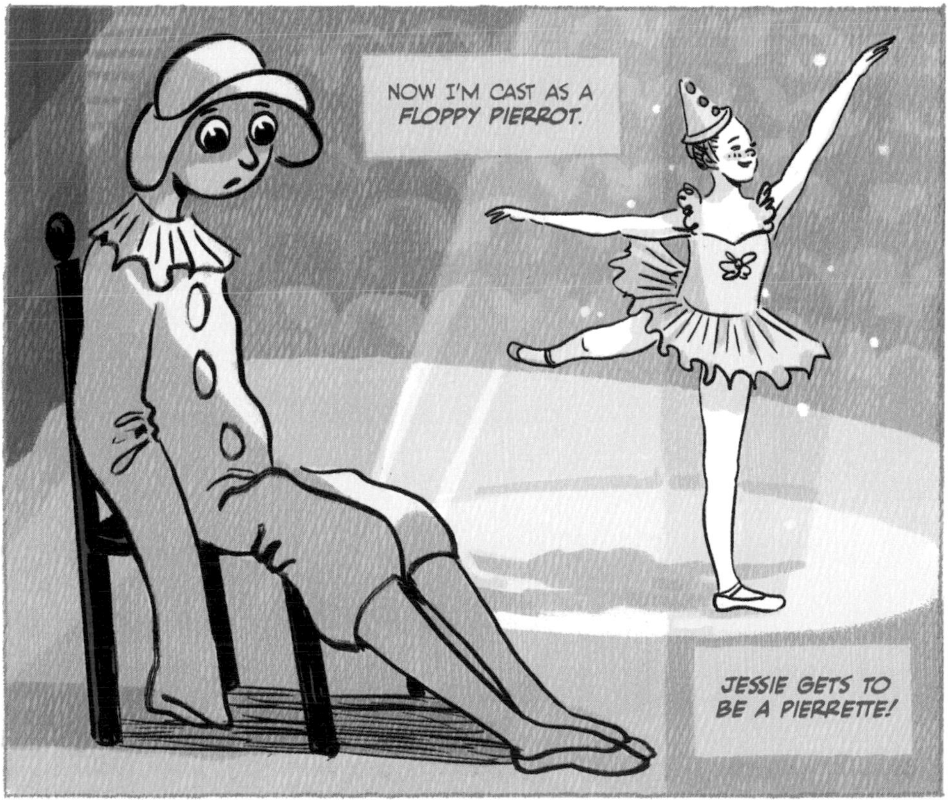
NOW I'M CAST AS A *FLOPPY PIERROT.*
JESSIE GETS TO BE A PIERRETTE!

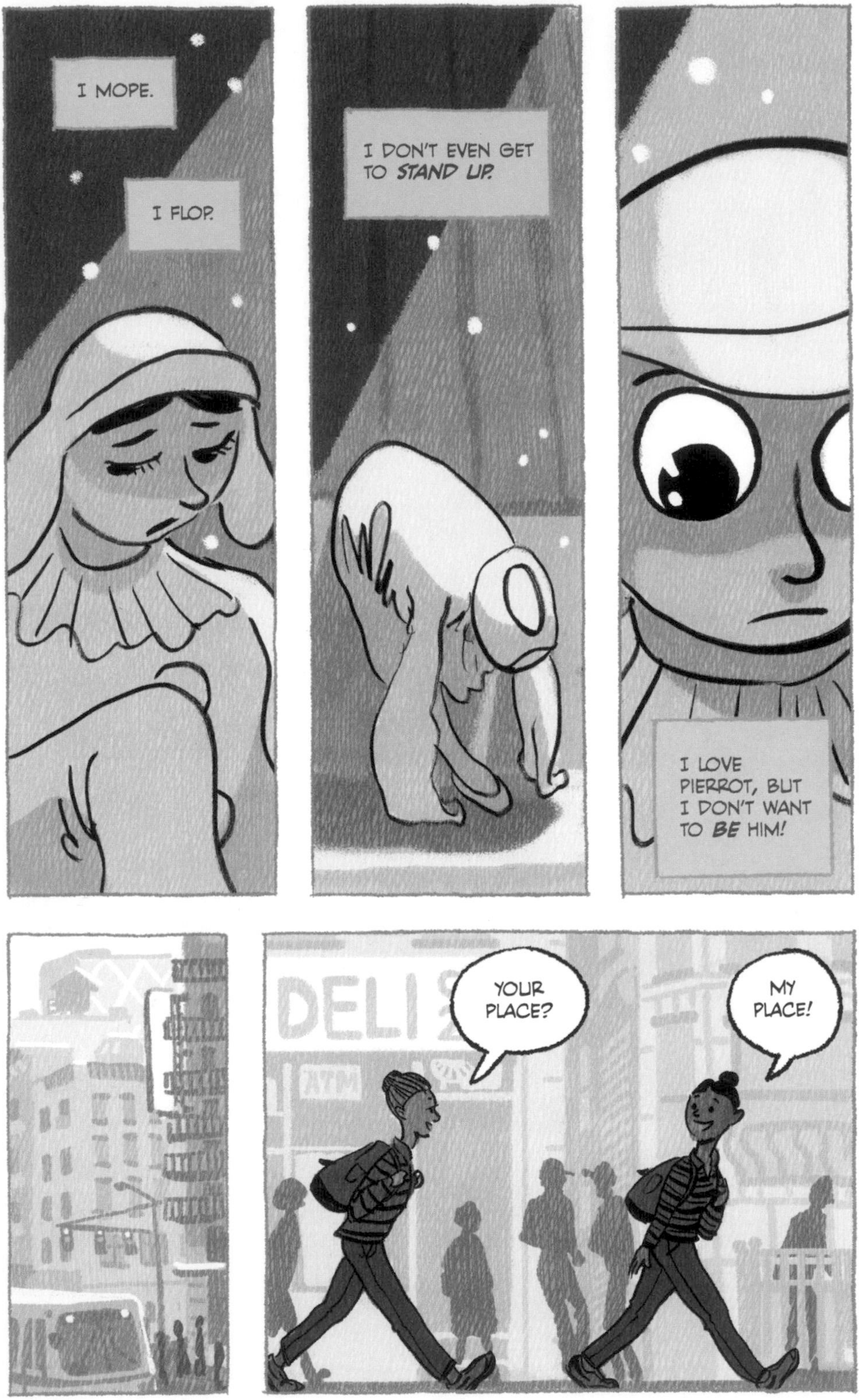

I MOPE.
I FLOP.
I DON'T EVEN GET TO STAND UP.
I LOVE PIERROT, BUT I DON'T WANT TO BE HIM!
DELI
ATM
YOUR PLACE?
MY PLACE!

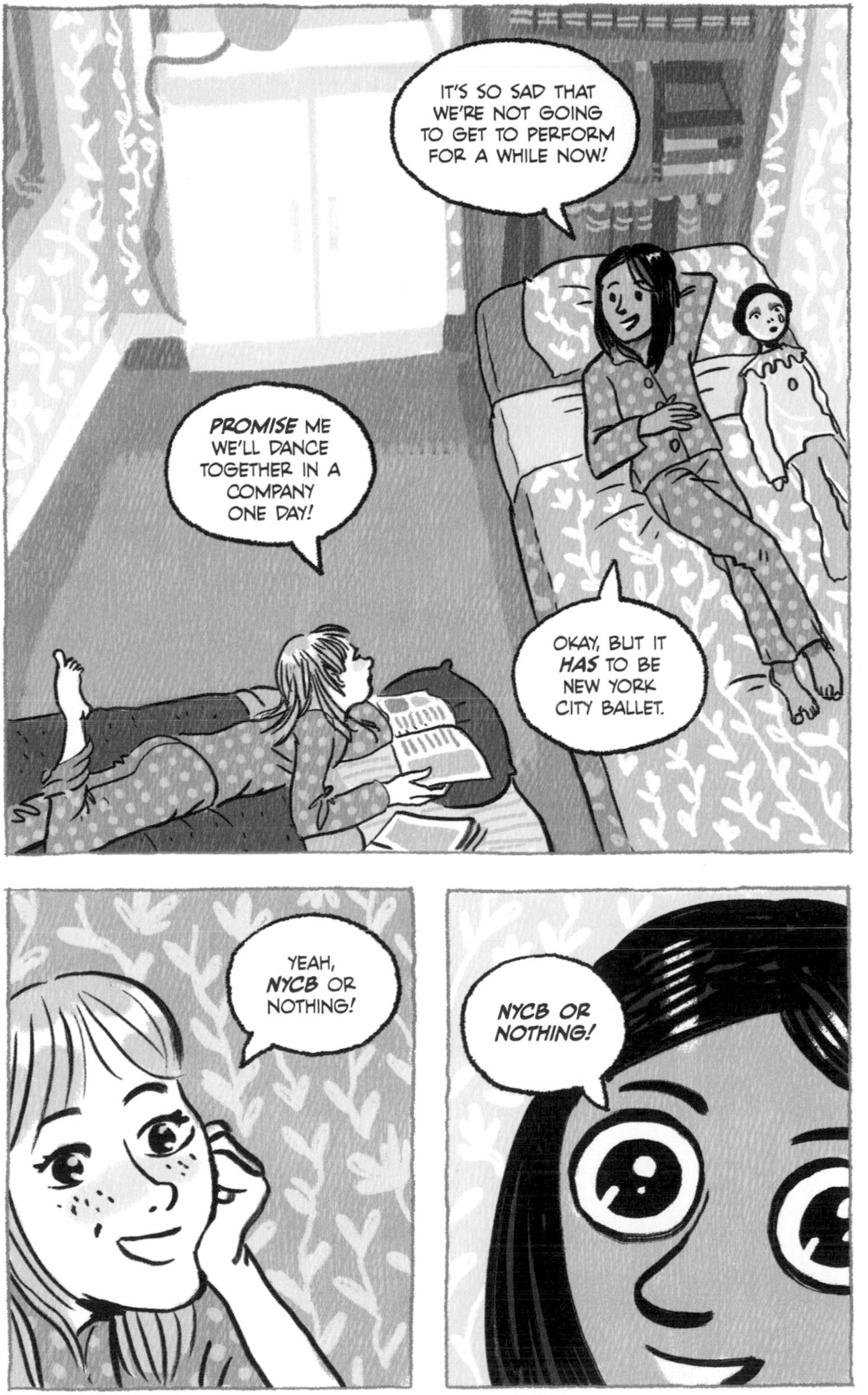
IT'S SO SAD THAT WE'RE NOT GOING TO GET TO PERFORM FOR A WHILE NOW!
PROMISE ME WE'LL DANCE TOGETHER IN A COMPANY ONE DAY!
OKAY, BUT IT HAS TO BE NEW YORK CITY BALLET.
YEAH, NYCB OR NOTHING!
NYCB OR NOTHING!

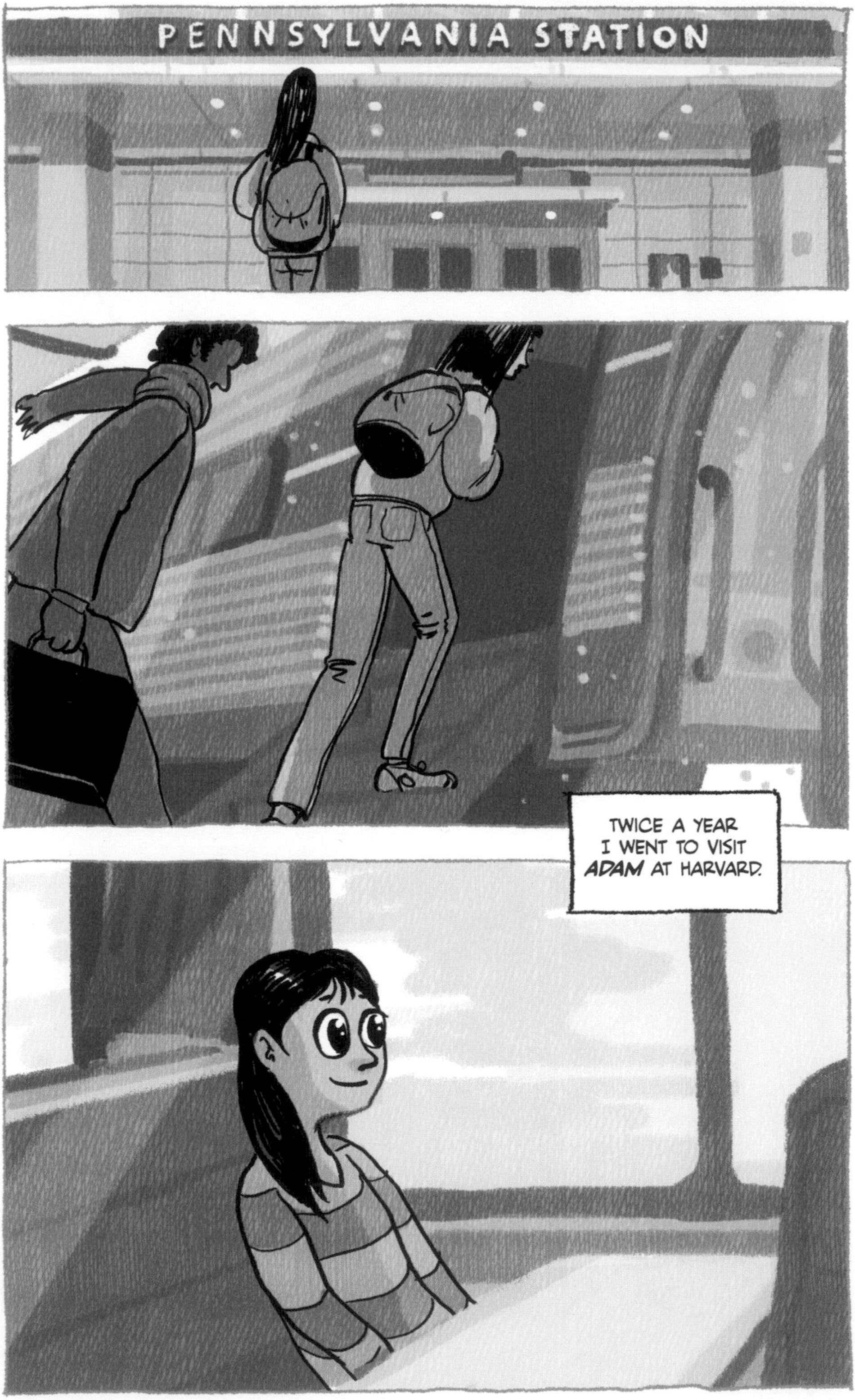
PENNSYLVANIA STATION
TWICE A YEAR I WENT TO VISIT ADAM AT HARVARD.

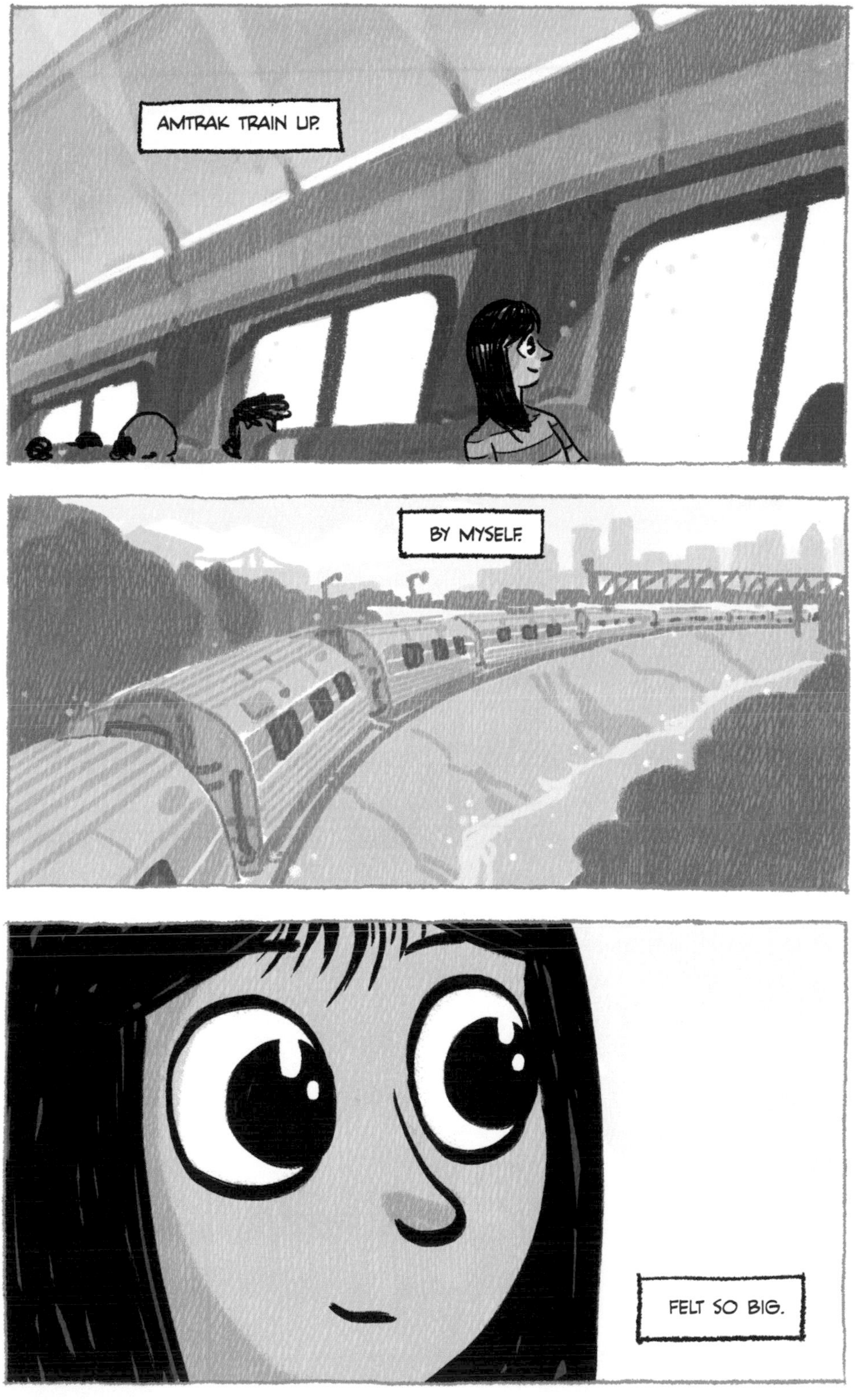
AMTRAK TRAIN UP.
BY MYSELF.
FELT SO BIG.

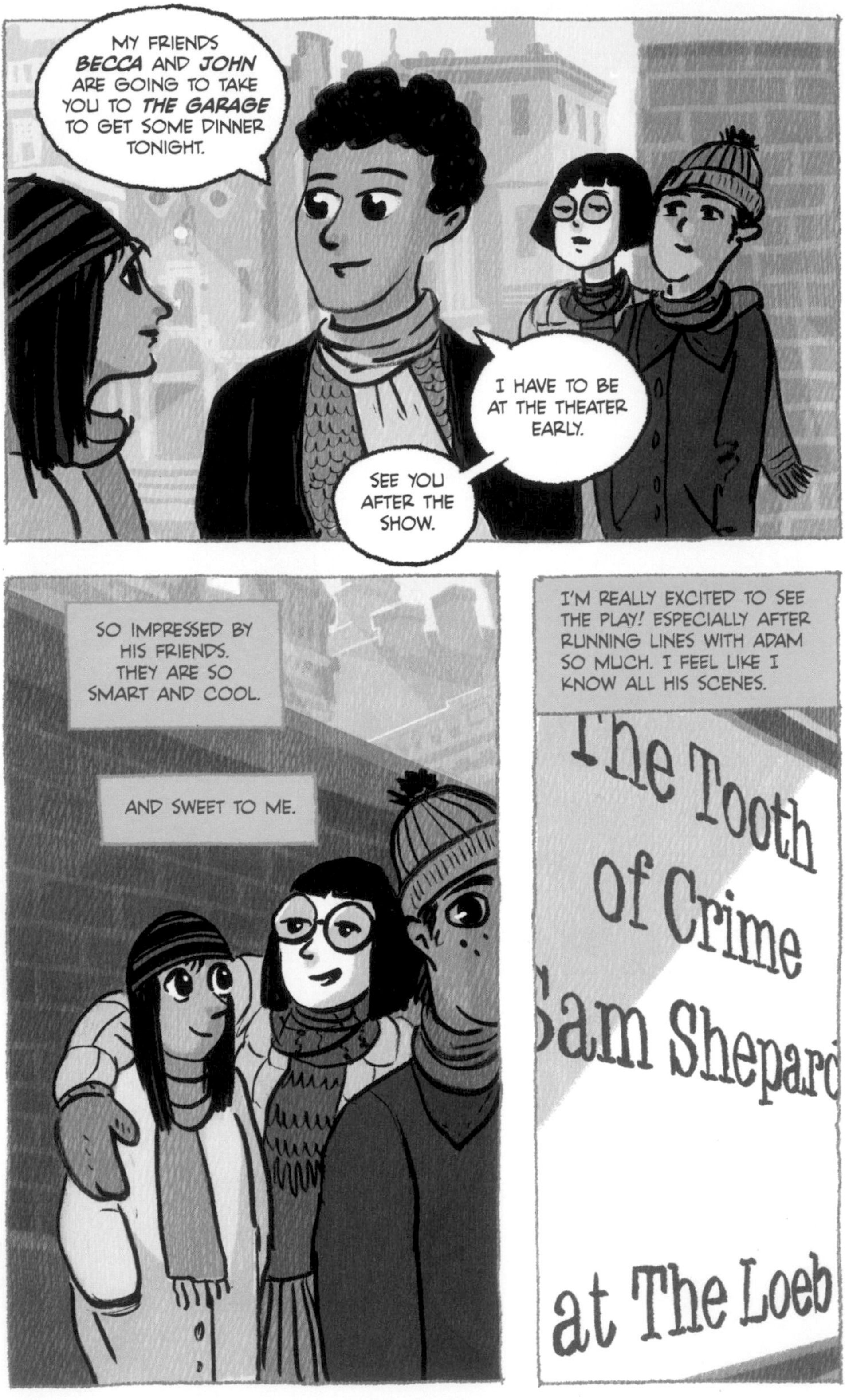
MY FRIENDS *BECCA* AND *JOHN* ARE GOING TO TAKE YOU TO *THE GARAGE* TO GET SOME DINNER TONIGHT.
I HAVE TO BE AT THE THEATER EARLY.
SEE YOU AFTER THE SHOW.
SO IMPRESSED BY HIS FRIENDS. THEY ARE SO SMART AND COOL.
AND SWEET TO ME.
I'M REALLY EXCITED TO SEE THE PLAY! ESPECIALLY AFTER RUNNING LINES WITH ADAM SO MUCH. I FEEL LIKE I KNOW ALL HIS SCENES.
The Tooth
Of Crime
Sam Shepard
at The Loeb

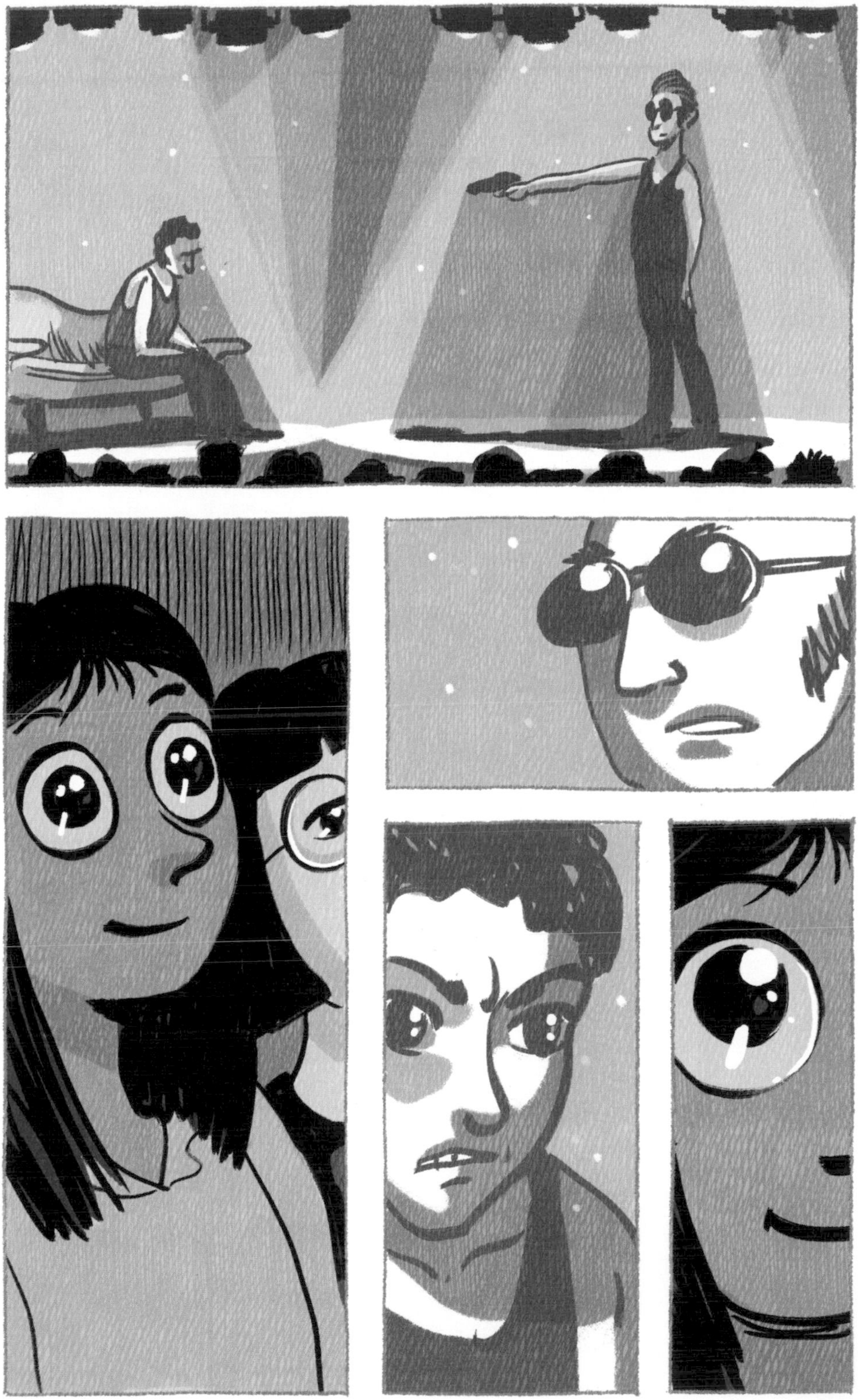

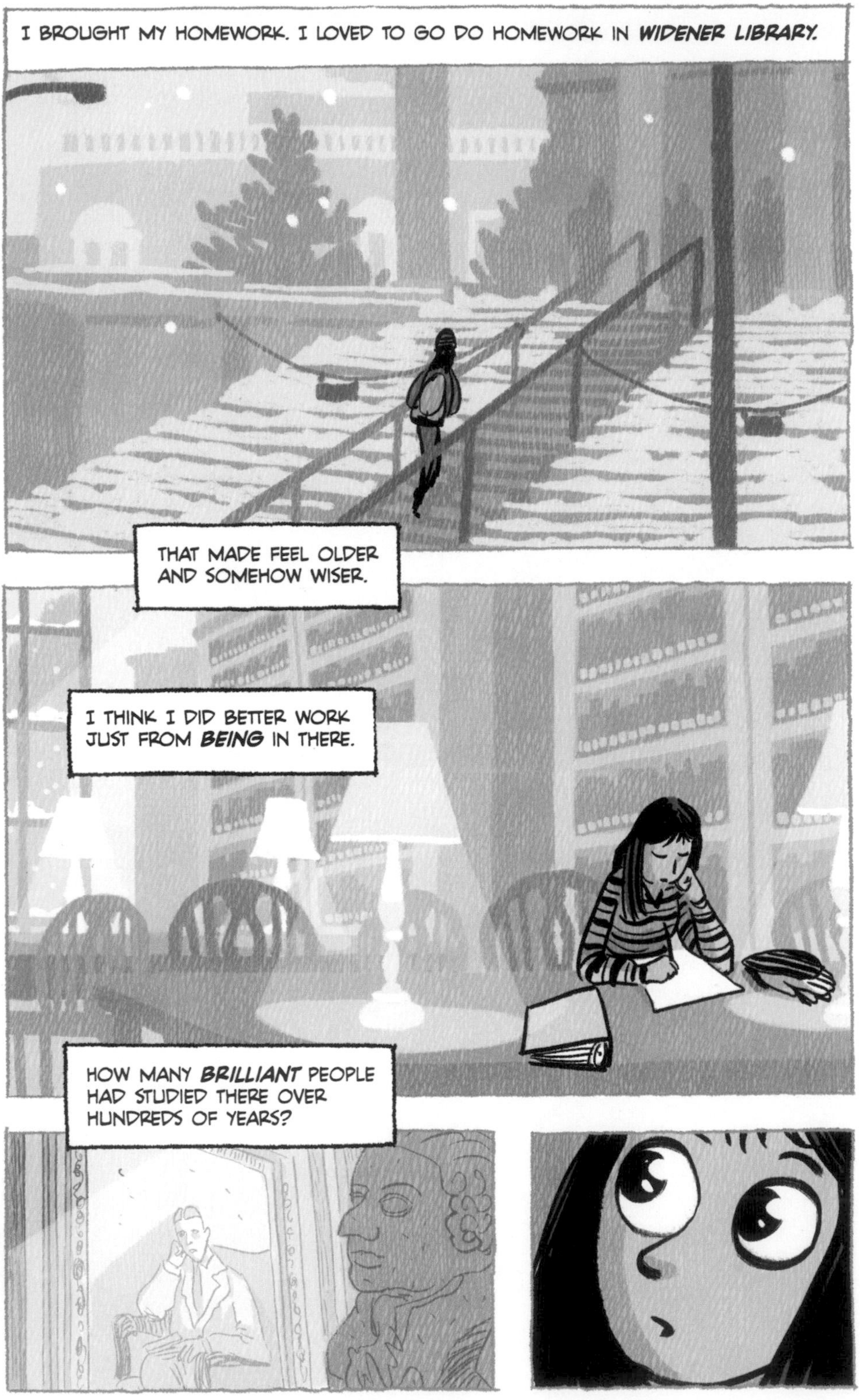
I BROUGHT MY HOMEWORK. I LOVED TO GO DO HOMEWORK IN WIDENER LIBRARY.
THAT MADE FEEL OLDER AND SOMEHOW WISER.
I THINK I DID BETTER WORK JUST FROM BEING IN THERE.
HOW MANY BRILLIANT PEOPLE HAD STUDIED THERE OVER HUNDREDS OF YEARS?

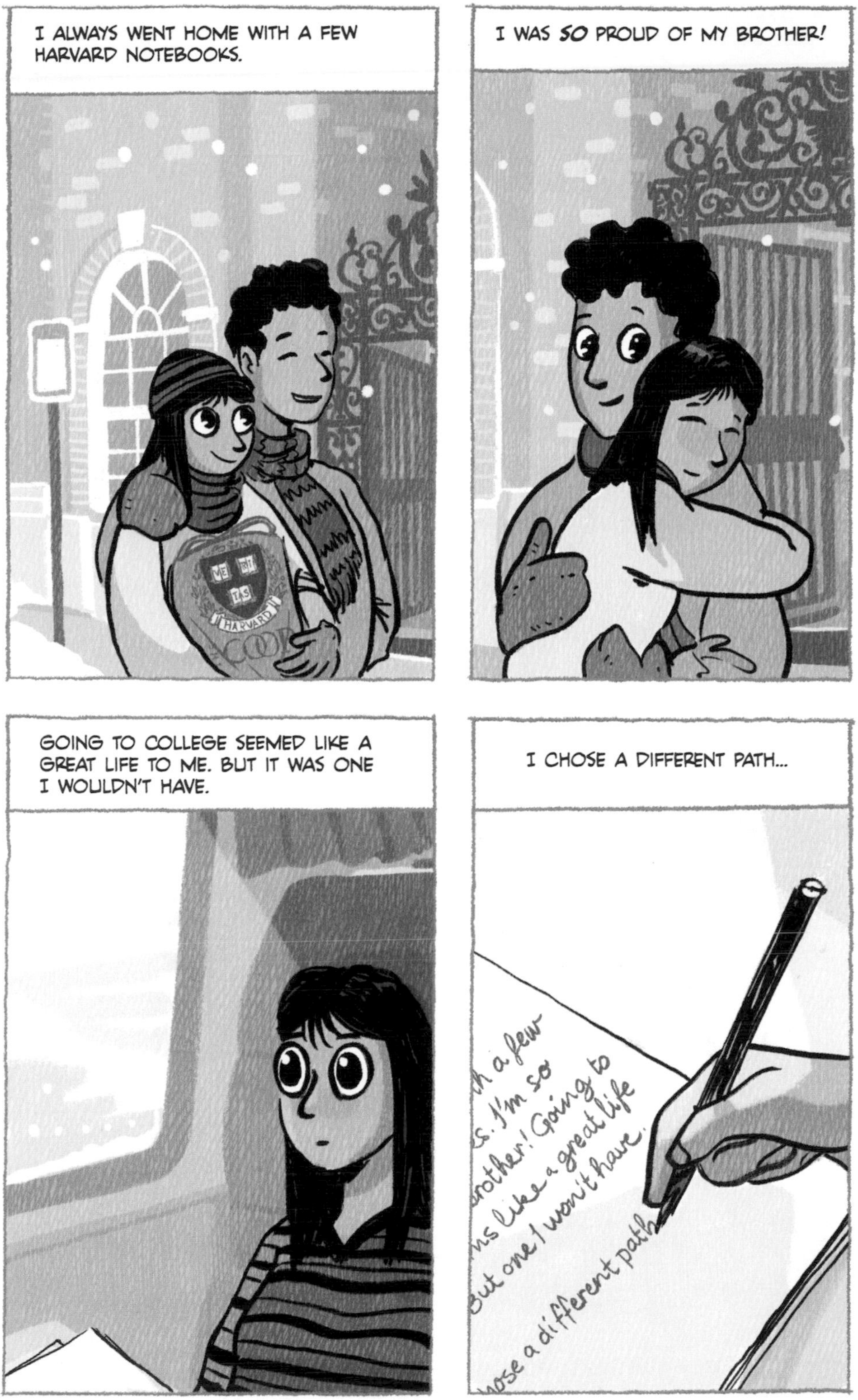
I ALWAYS WENT HOME WITH A FEW HARVARD NOTEBOOKS.
HARVARD
I WAS *SO* PROUD OF MY BROTHER!
GOING TO COLLEGE SEEMED LIKE A GREAT LIFE TO ME. BUT IT WAS ONE I WOULDN'T HAVE.
I CHOSE A DIFFERENT PATH...

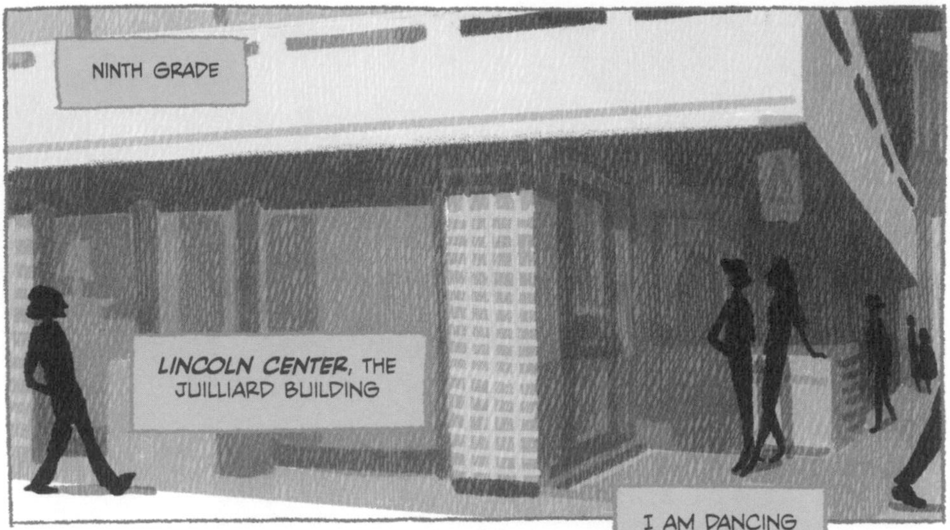
NINTH GRADE
LINCOLN CENTER, THE JUILLIARD BUILDING

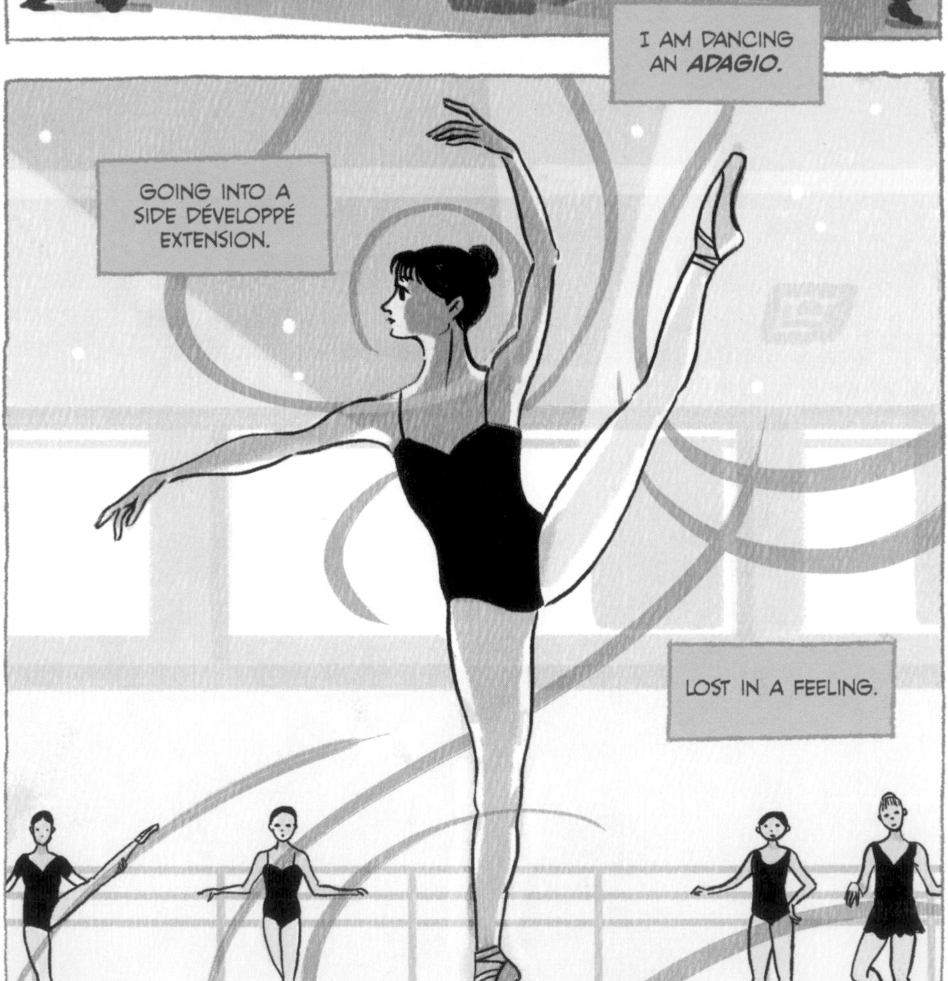
I AM DANCING AN *ADAGIO.*
GOING INTO A SIDE DÉVELOPPÉ EXTENSION.
LOST IN A FEELING.

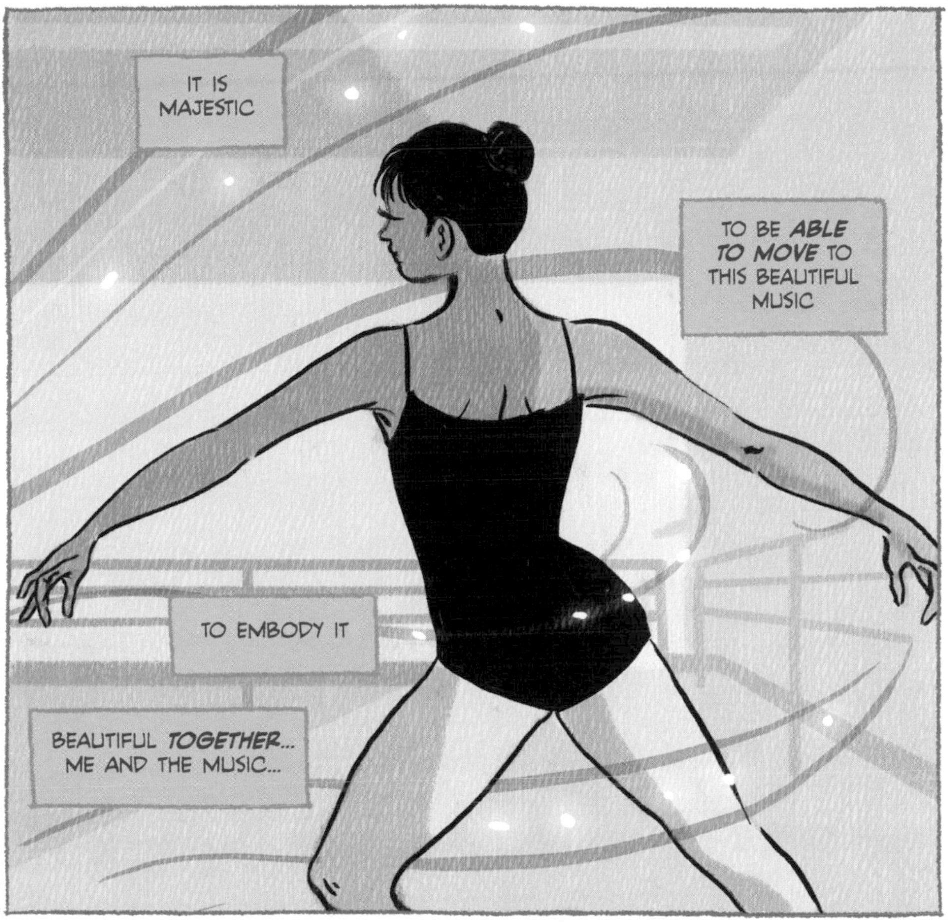
IT IS MAJESTIC
TO BE ABLE TO MOVE TO THIS BEAUTIFUL MUSIC
TO EMBODY IT
BEAUTIFUL TOGETHER... ME AND THE MUSIC...

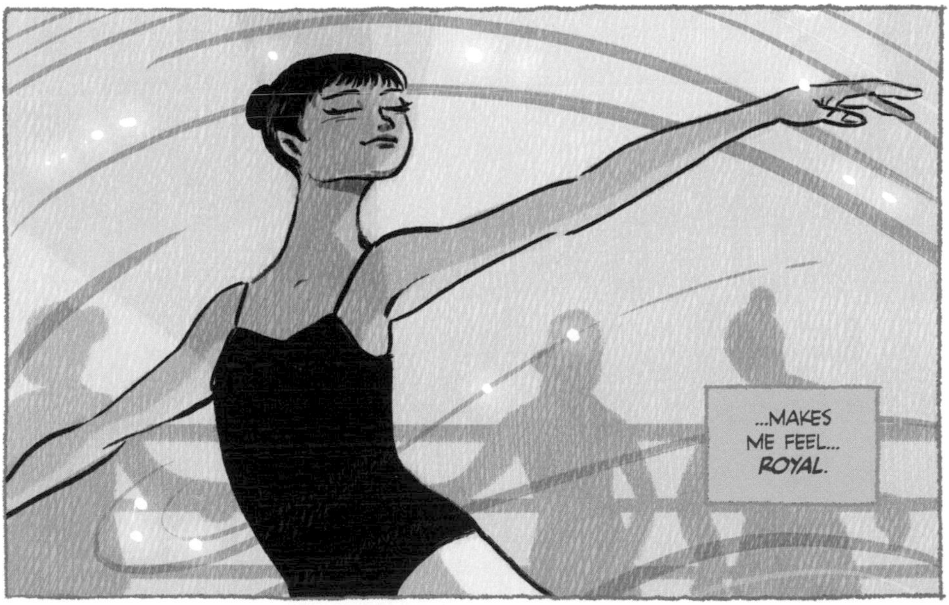
...MAKES ME FEEL... ROYAL.

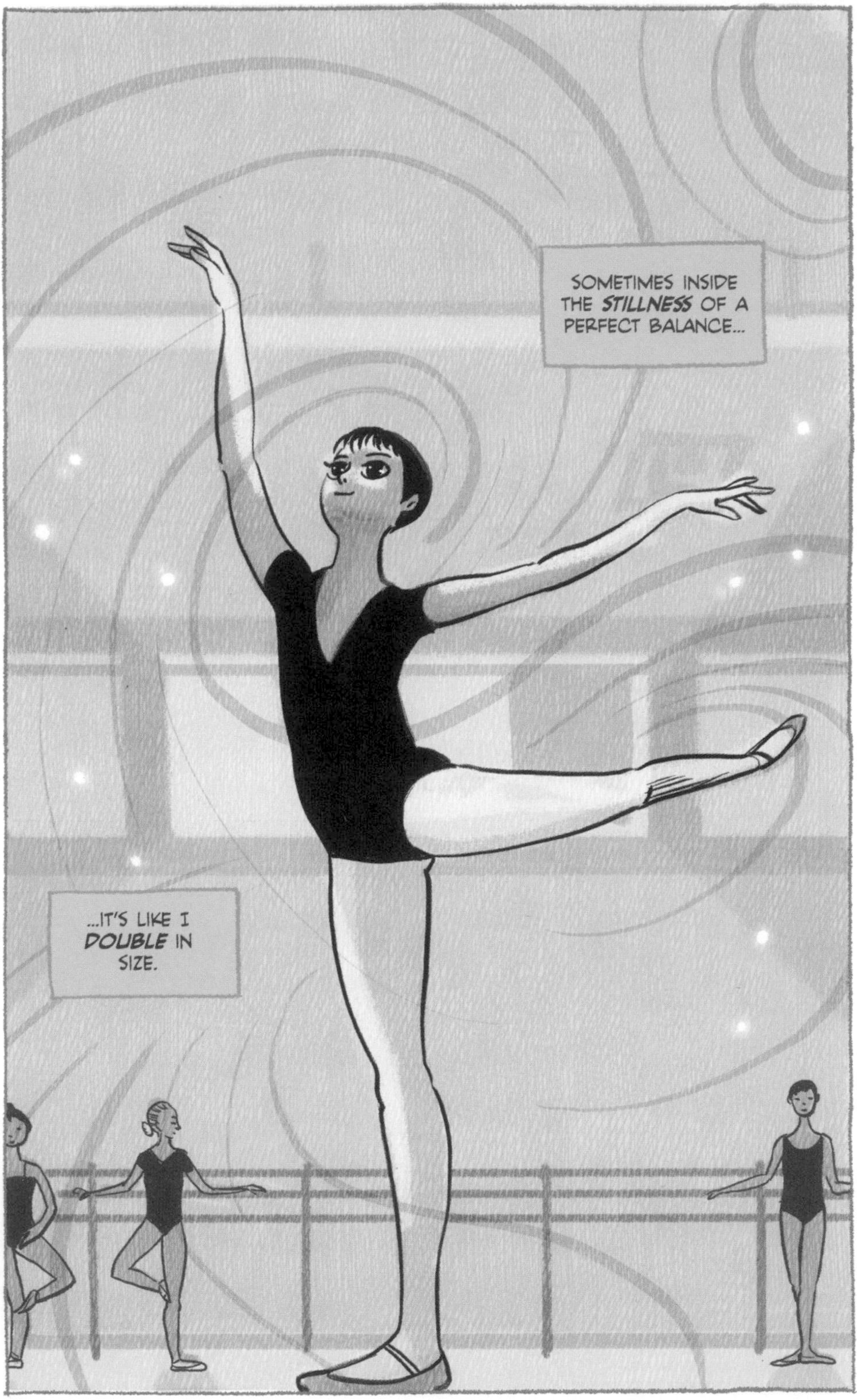
SOMETIMES INSIDE THE STILLNESS OF A PERFECT BALANCE...
...IT'S LIKE I DOUBLE IN SIZE.

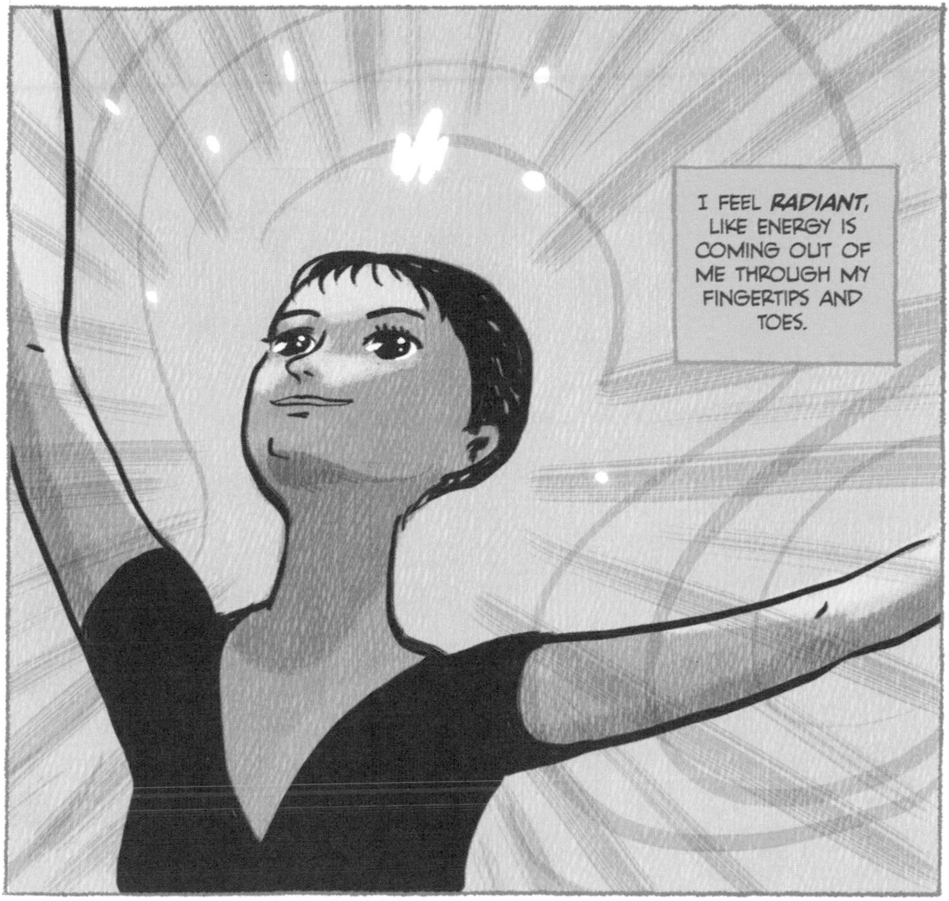
I FEEL ***RADIANT***, LIKE ENERGY IS COMING OUT OF ME THROUGH MY FINGERTIPS AND TOES.

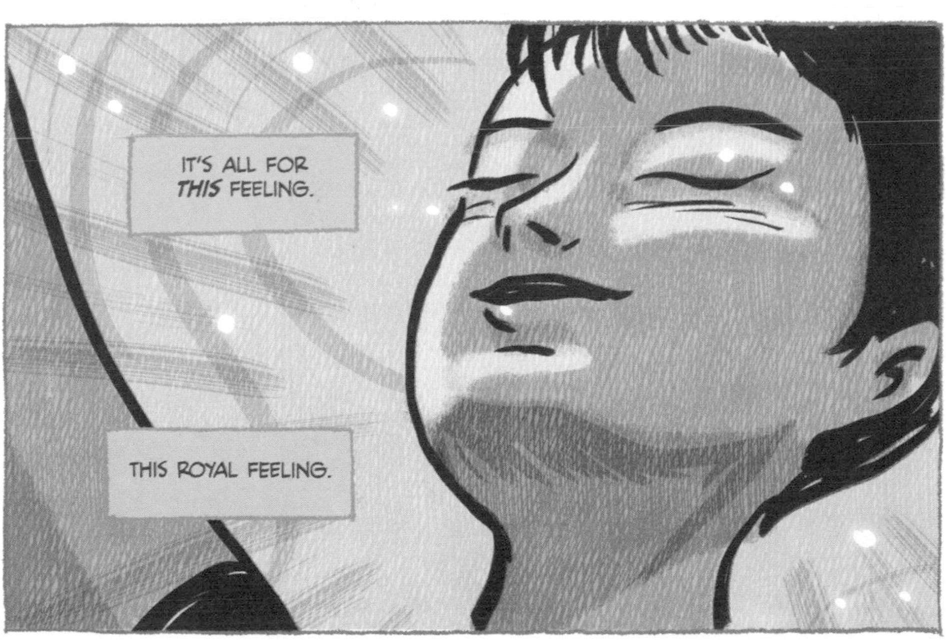
IT'S ALL FOR ***THIS*** FEELING.
THIS ROYAL FEELING.

1982

SPRING WAS *HUMMING.* WHILE EVERYTHING CAME BACK TO LIFE, I HAD A SENSE OF CONFIDENCE AND *HARMONY.*

TULIPS (MY FAVORITE FLOWERS) BURST OUT ON BROADWAY.

I WAS FIFTEEN YEARS OLD AND IN THE BEST BALLET SCHOOL IN THE WORLD.

IN CLASS, I FELT *STRONG AND WELL,* WITH SO MUCH TO LOOK FORWARD TO.

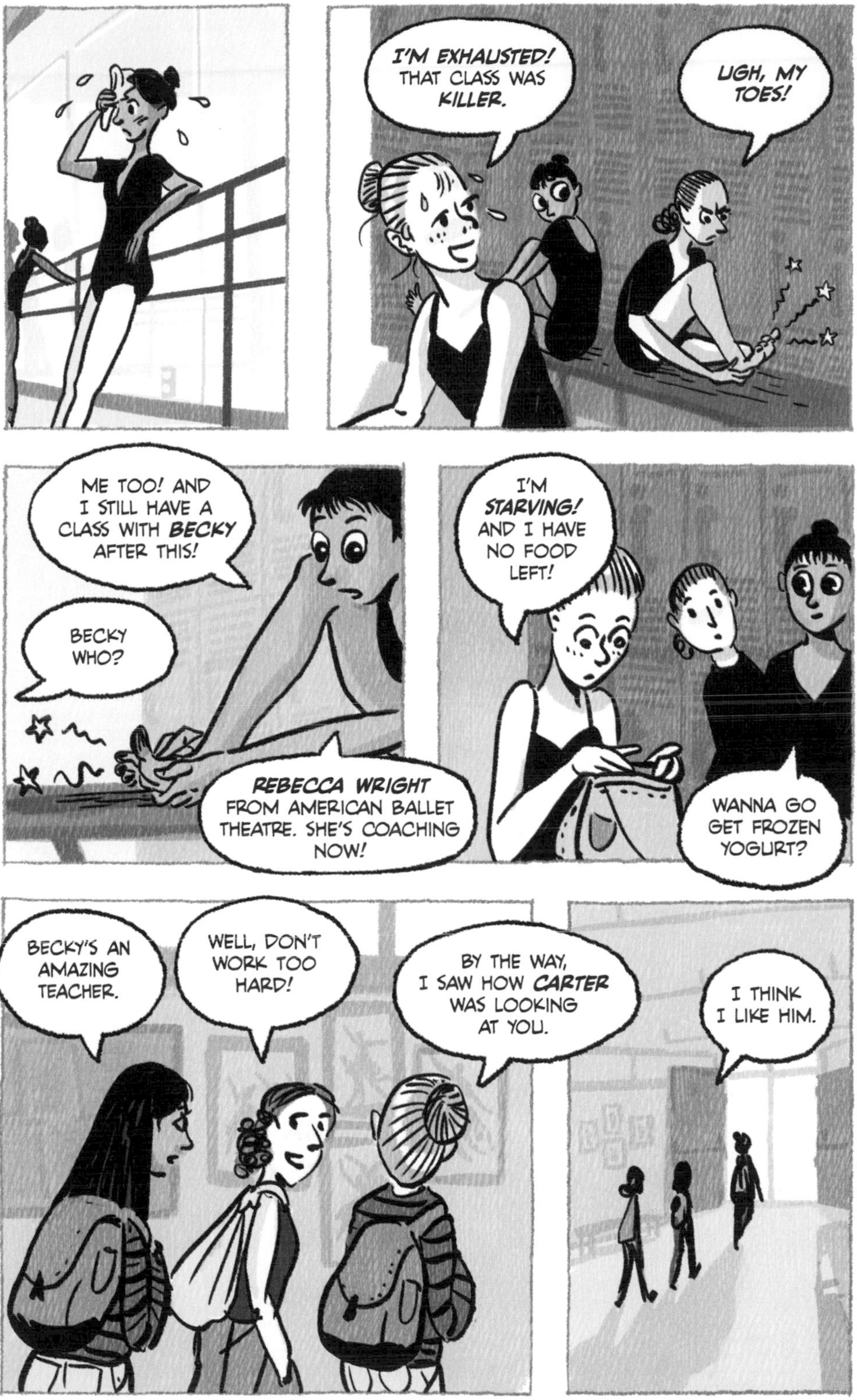
I'M EXHAUSTED! THAT CLASS WAS KILLER.
UGH, MY TOES!
ME TOO! AND I STILL HAVE A CLASS WITH BECKY AFTER THIS!
BECKY WHO?
REBECCA WRIGHT FROM AMERICAN BALLET THEATRE. SHE'S COACHING NOW!
I'M STARVING! AND I HAVE NO FOOD LEFT!
WANNA GO GET FROZEN YOGURT?
BECKY'S AN AMAZING TEACHER.
WELL, DON'T WORK TOO HARD!
BY THE WAY, I SAW HOW CARTER WAS LOOKING AT YOU.
I THINK I LIKE HIM.

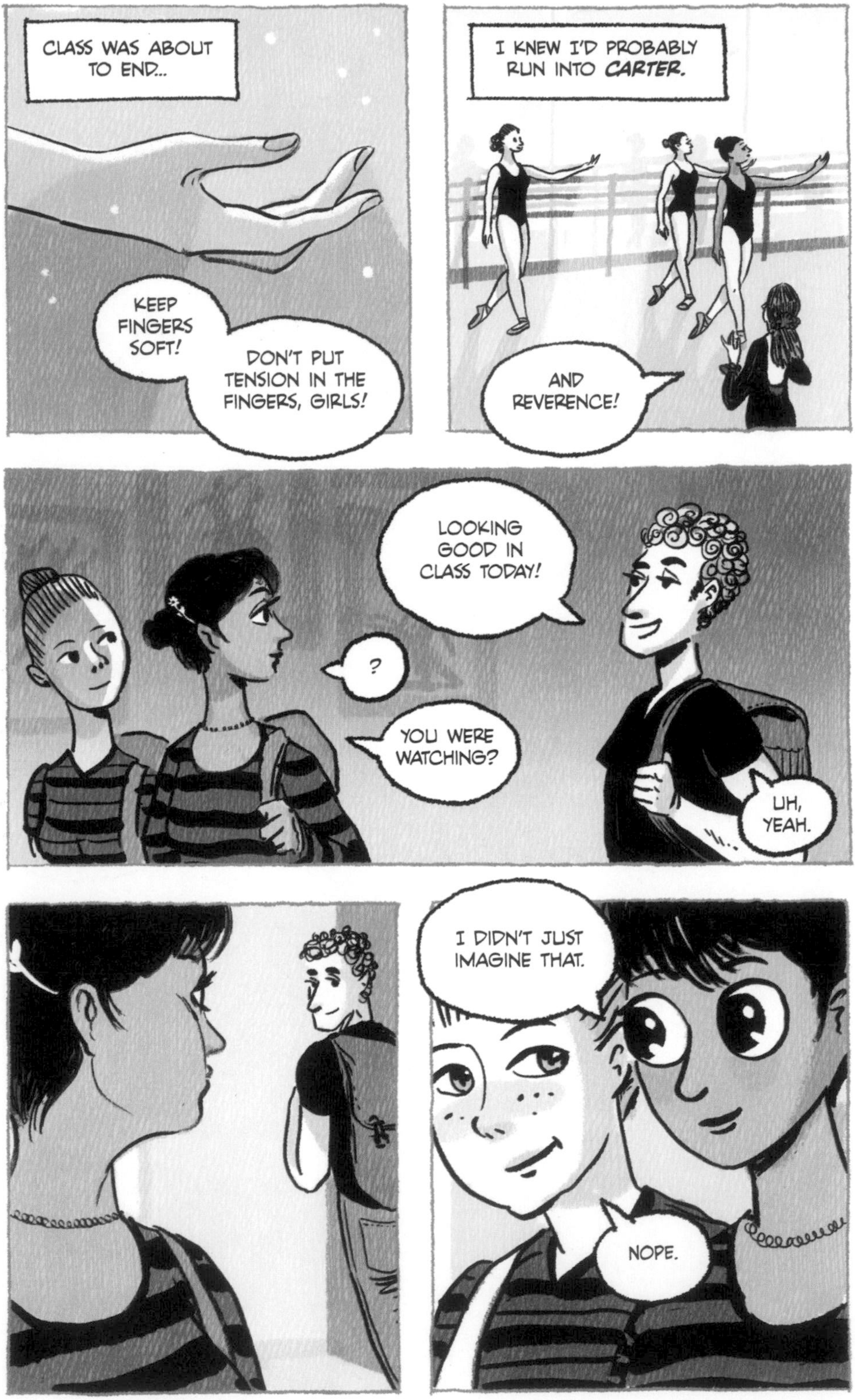
CLASS WAS ABOUT TO END...
KEEP FINGERS SOFT!
DON'T PUT TENSION IN THE FINGERS, GIRLS!
I KNEW I'D PROBABLY RUN INTO CARTER.
AND REVERENCE!
LOOKING GOOD IN CLASS TODAY!
?
YOU WERE WATCHING?
UH, YEAH.
I DIDN'T JUST IMAGINE THAT.
NOPE.

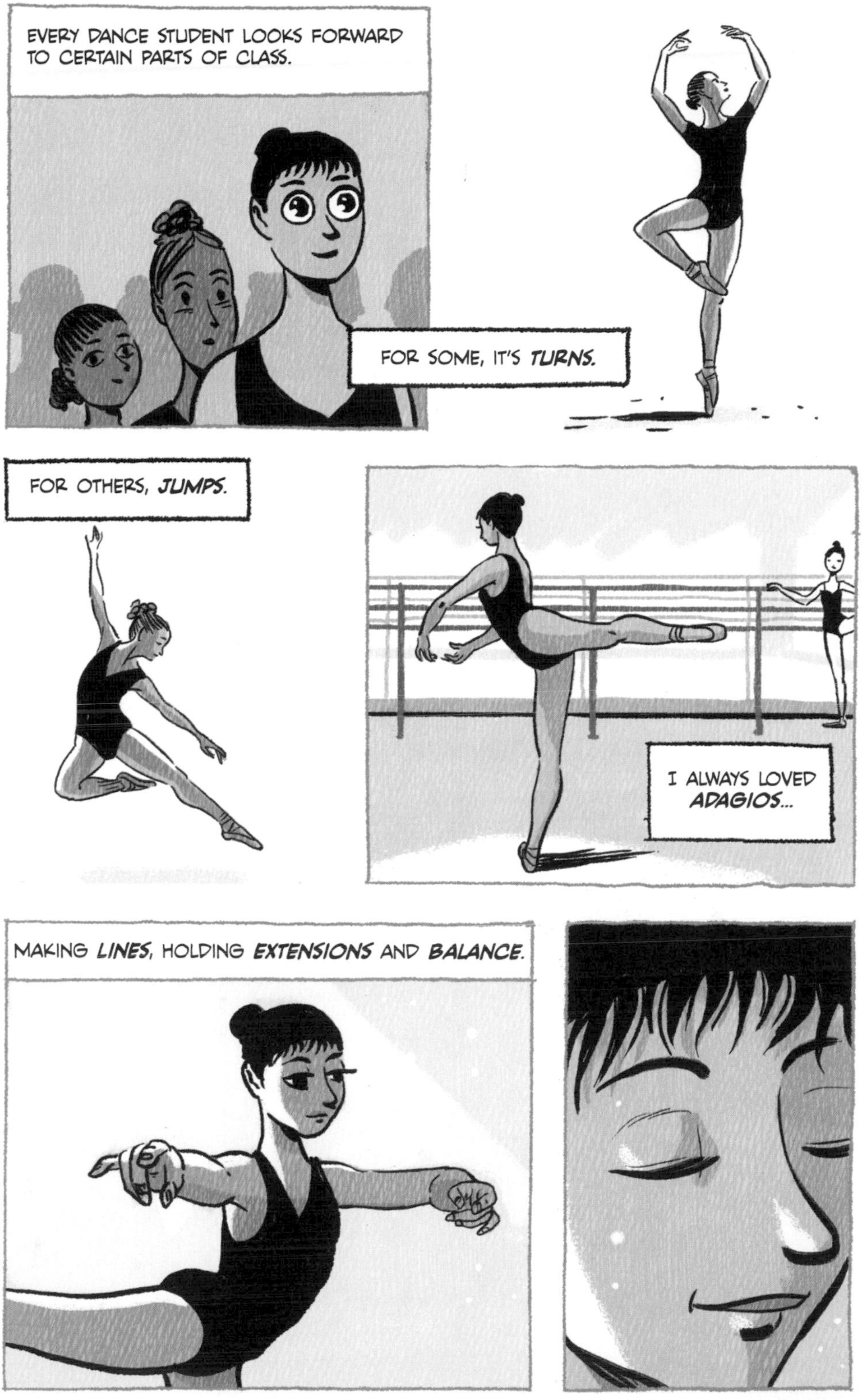
EVERY DANCE STUDENT LOOKS FORWARD TO CERTAIN PARTS OF CLASS.
FOR SOME, IT'S TURNS.
FOR OTHERS, JUMPS.
I ALWAYS LOVED ADAGIOS...
MAKING LINES, HOLDING EXTENSIONS AND BALANCE.

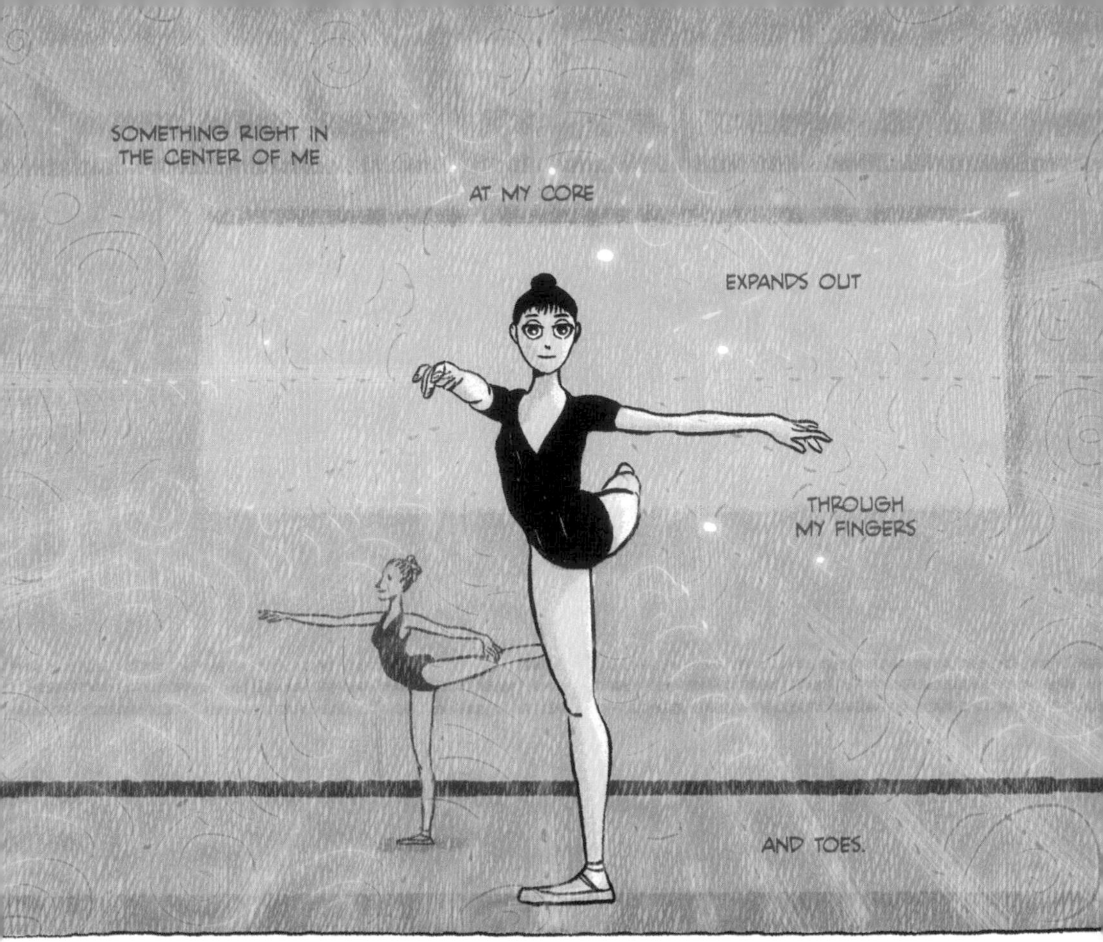
SOMETHING RIGHT IN THE CENTER OF ME
AT MY CORE
EXPANDS OUT
THROUGH MY FINGERS
AND TOES.

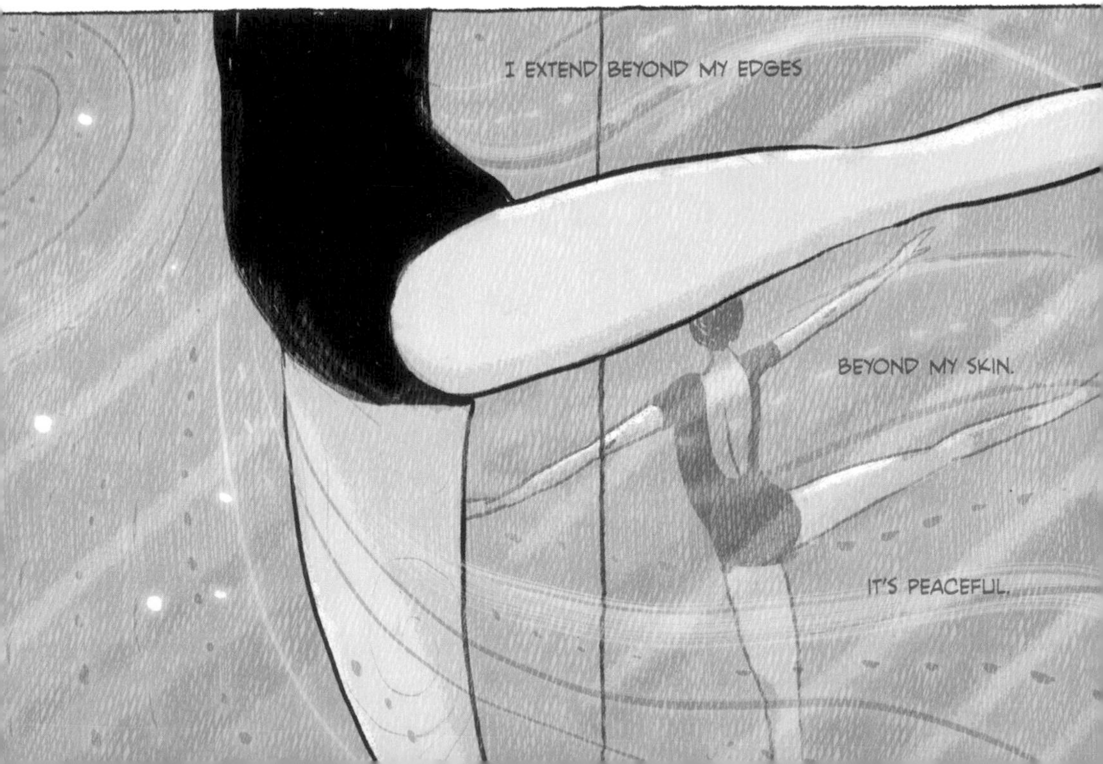
I EXTEND BEYOND MY EDGES
BEYOND MY SKIN.
IT'S PEACEFUL.

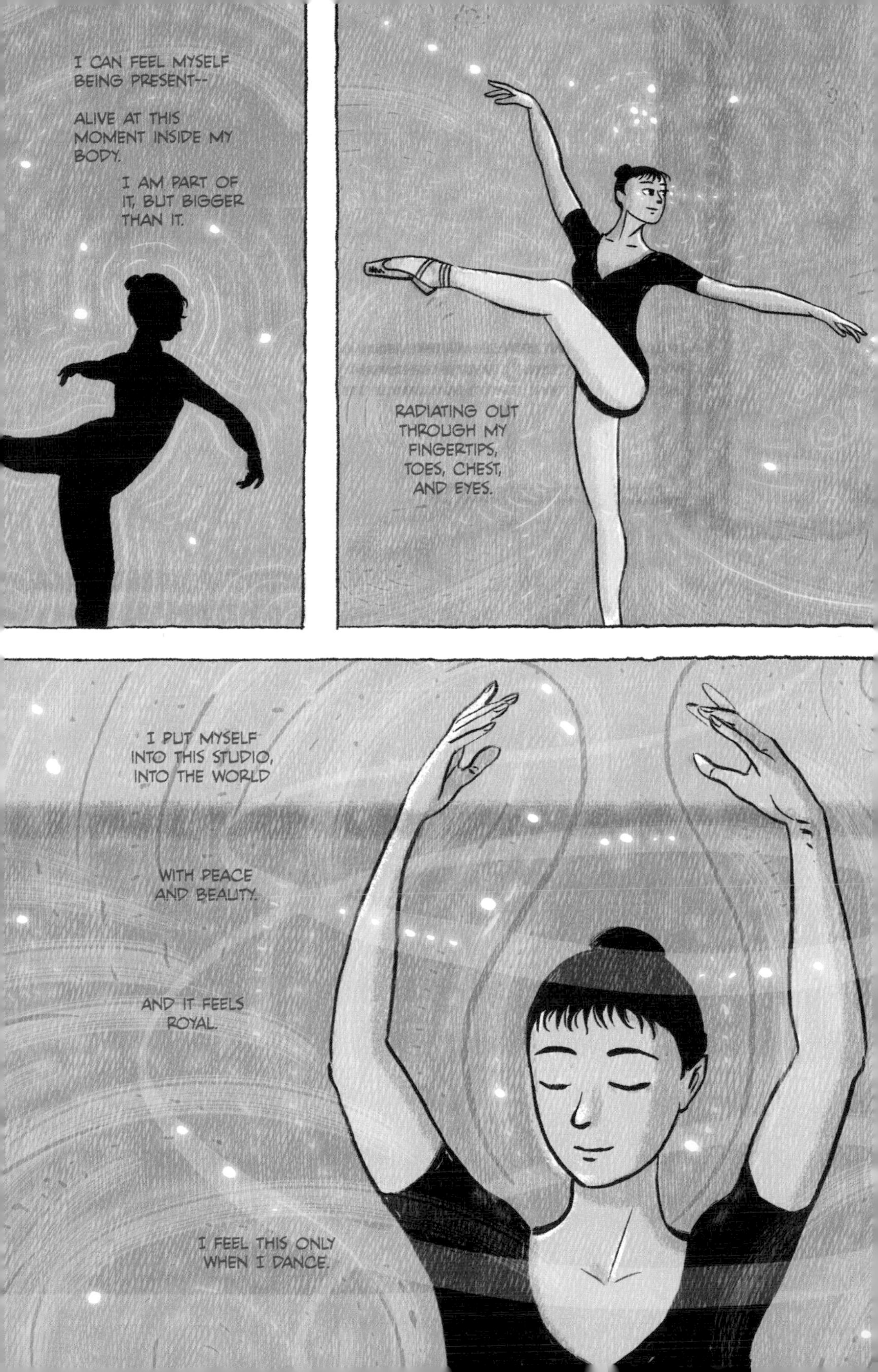
I CAN FEEL MYSELF BEING PRESENT--
ALIVE AT THIS MOMENT INSIDE MY BODY.
I AM PART OF IT, BUT BIGGER THAN IT.
RADIATING OUT THROUGH MY FINGERTIPS, TOES, CHEST, AND EYES.
I PUT MYSELF INTO THIS STUDIO, INTO THE WORLD
WITH PEACE AND BEAUTY.
AND IT FEELS ROYAL.
I FEEL THIS ONLY WHEN I DANCE.

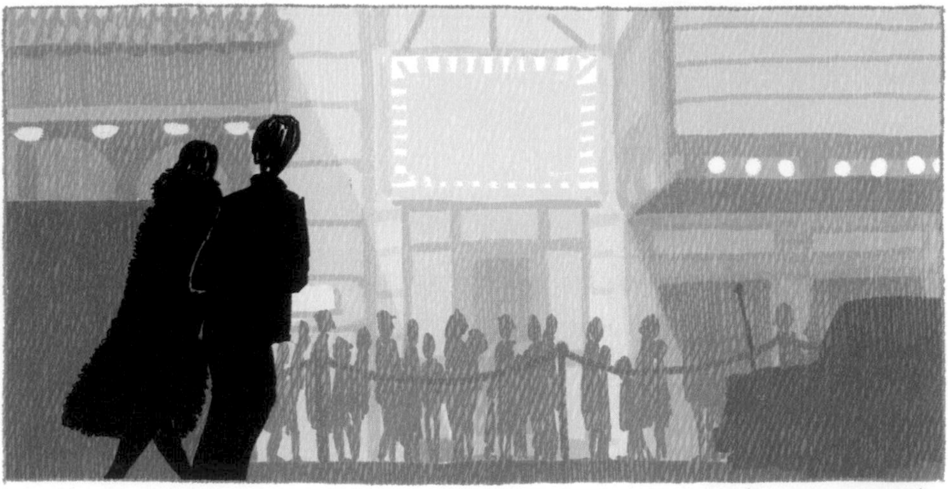

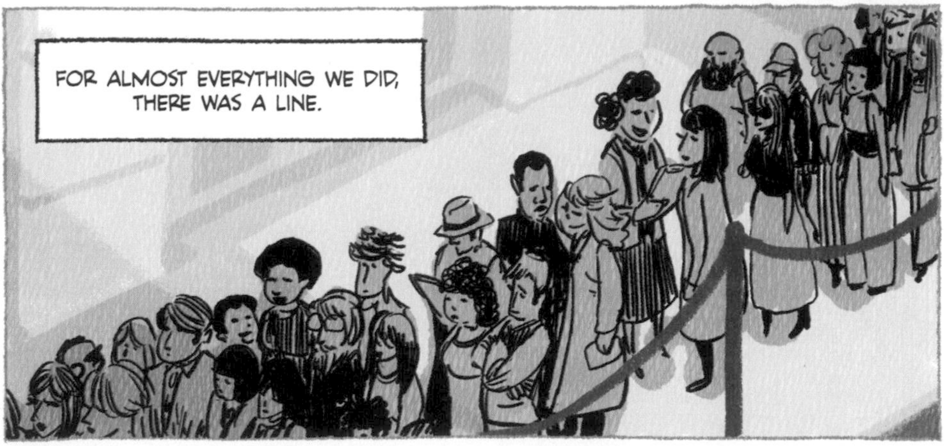
FOR ALMOST EVERYTHING WE DID, THERE WAS A LINE.

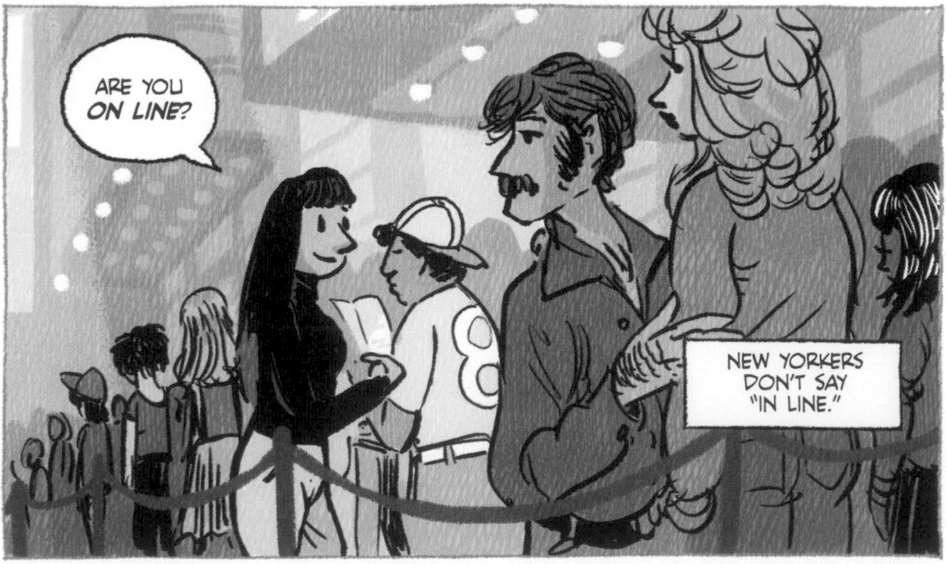
ARE YOU *ON LINE?*
NEW YORKERS DON'T SAY "IN LINE."

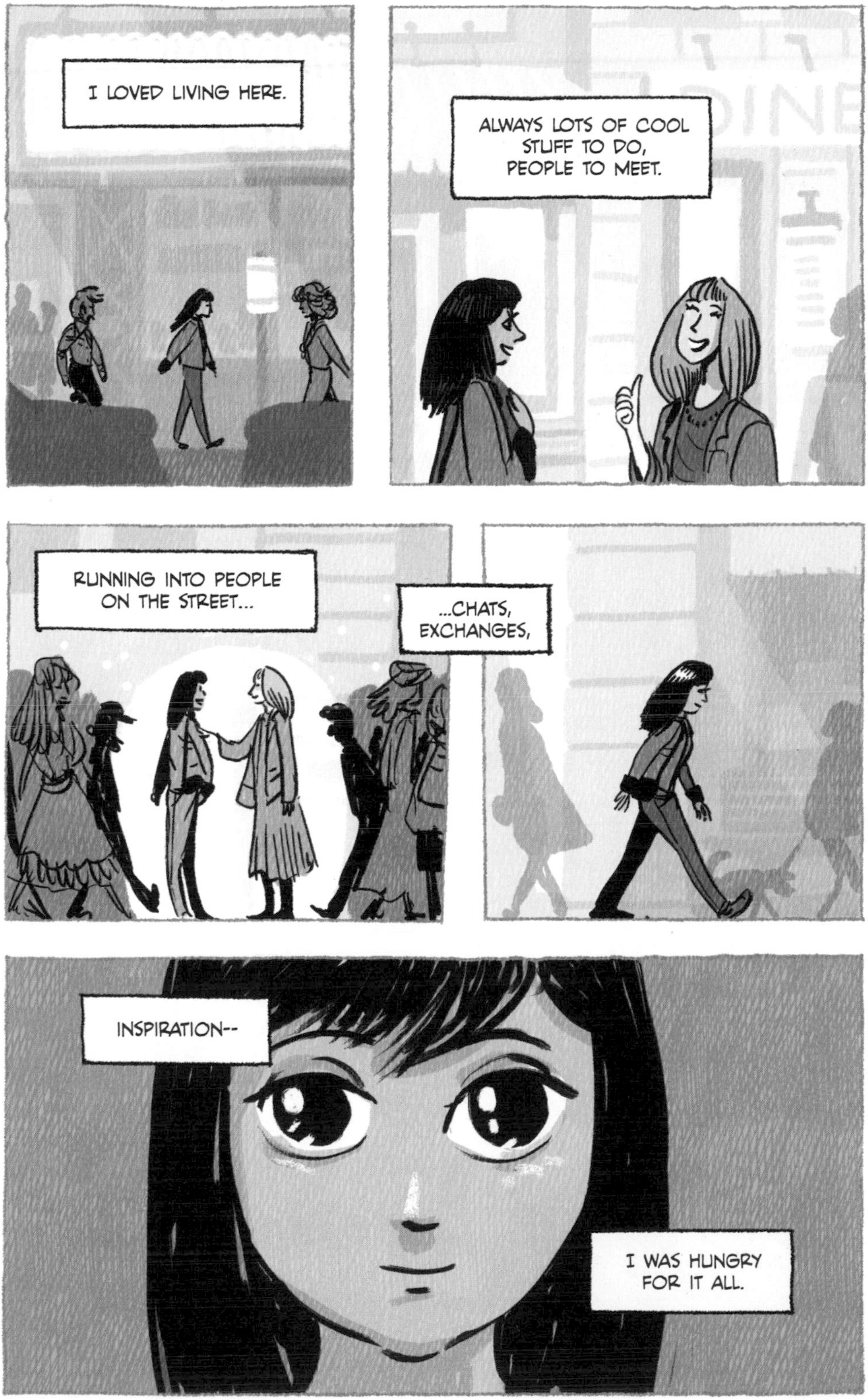
I LOVED LIVING HERE.
ALWAYS LOTS OF COOL STUFF TO DO, PEOPLE TO MEET.
RUNNING INTO PEOPLE ON THE STREET...
...CHATS, EXCHANGES,
INSPIRATION--
I WAS HUNGRY FOR IT ALL.

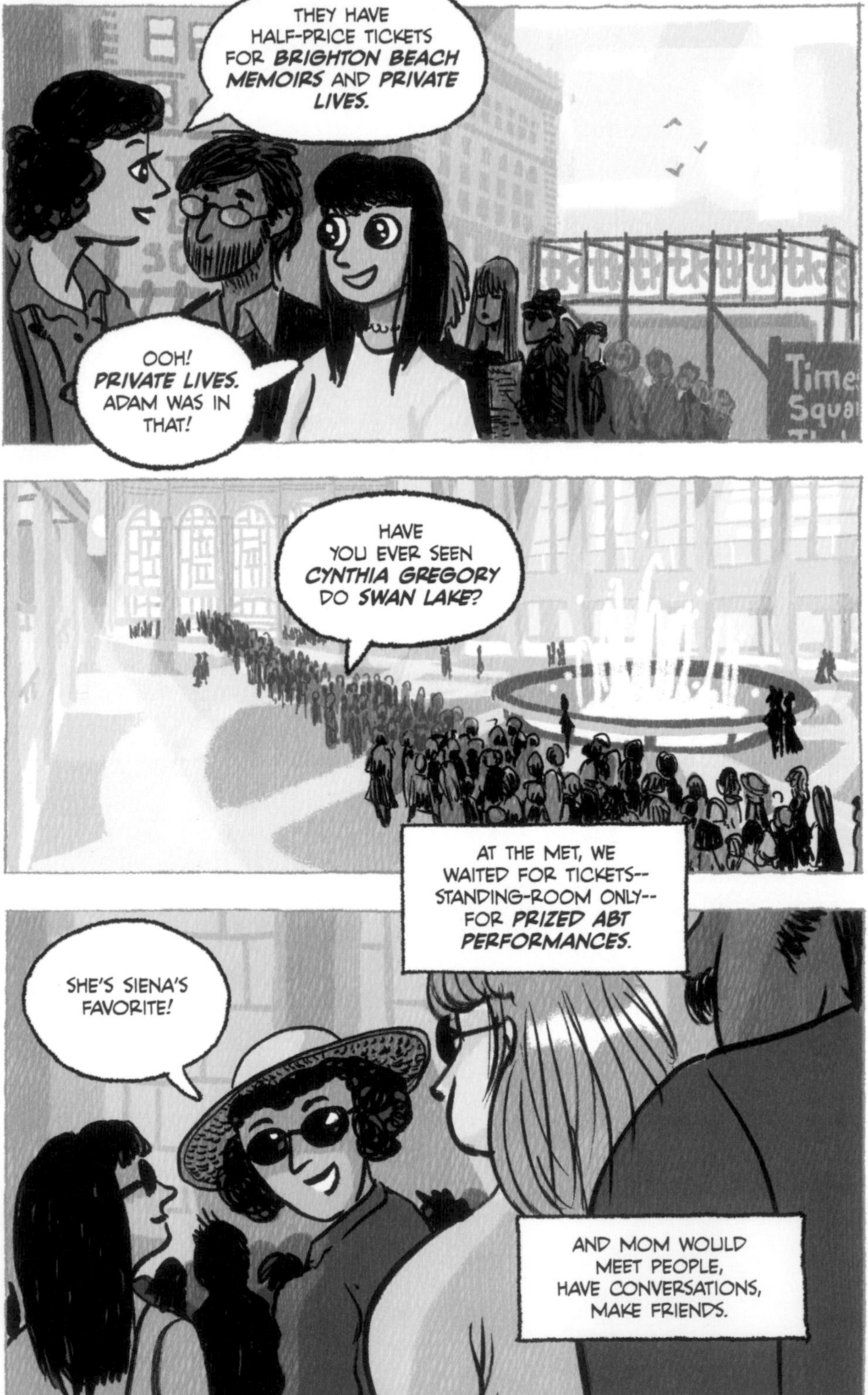
THEY HAVE HALF-PRICE TICKETS FOR **BRIGHTON BEACH MEMOIRS** AND **PRIVATE LIVES.**
OOH! **PRIVATE LIVES.** ADAM WAS IN THAT!
HAVE YOU EVER SEEN **CYNTHIA GREGORY** DO **SWAN LAKE?**
AT THE MET, WE WAITED FOR TICKETS--STANDING-ROOM ONLY--FOR **PRIZED ABT PERFORMANCES.**
SHE'S SIENA'S FAVORITE!
AND MOM WOULD MEET PEOPLE, HAVE CONVERSATIONS, MAKE FRIENDS.

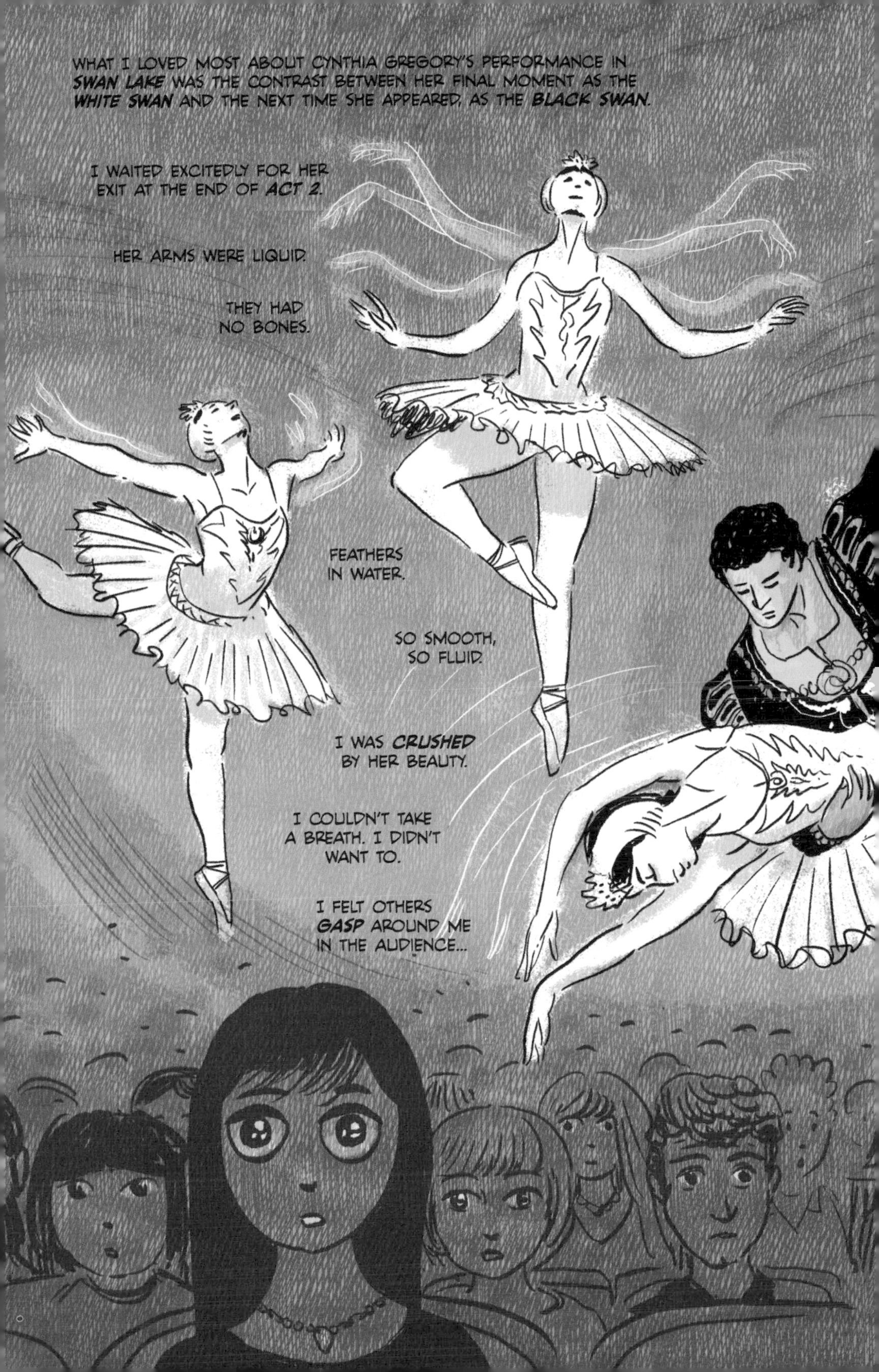
WHAT I LOVED MOST ABOUT CYNTHIA GREGORY'S PERFORMANCE IN SWAN LAKE WAS THE CONTRAST BETWEEN HER FINAL MOMENT AS THE WHITE SWAN AND THE NEXT TIME SHE APPEARED, AS THE BLACK SWAN.
I WAITED EXCITEDLY FOR HER EXIT AT THE END OF ACT 2.
HER ARMS WERE LIQUID.
THEY HAD NO BONES.
FEATHERS IN WATER.
SO SMOOTH, SO FLUID.
I WAS CRUSHED BY HER BEAUTY.
I COULDN'T TAKE A BREATH. I DIDN'T WANT TO.
I FELT OTHERS GASP AROUND ME IN THE AUDIENCE...

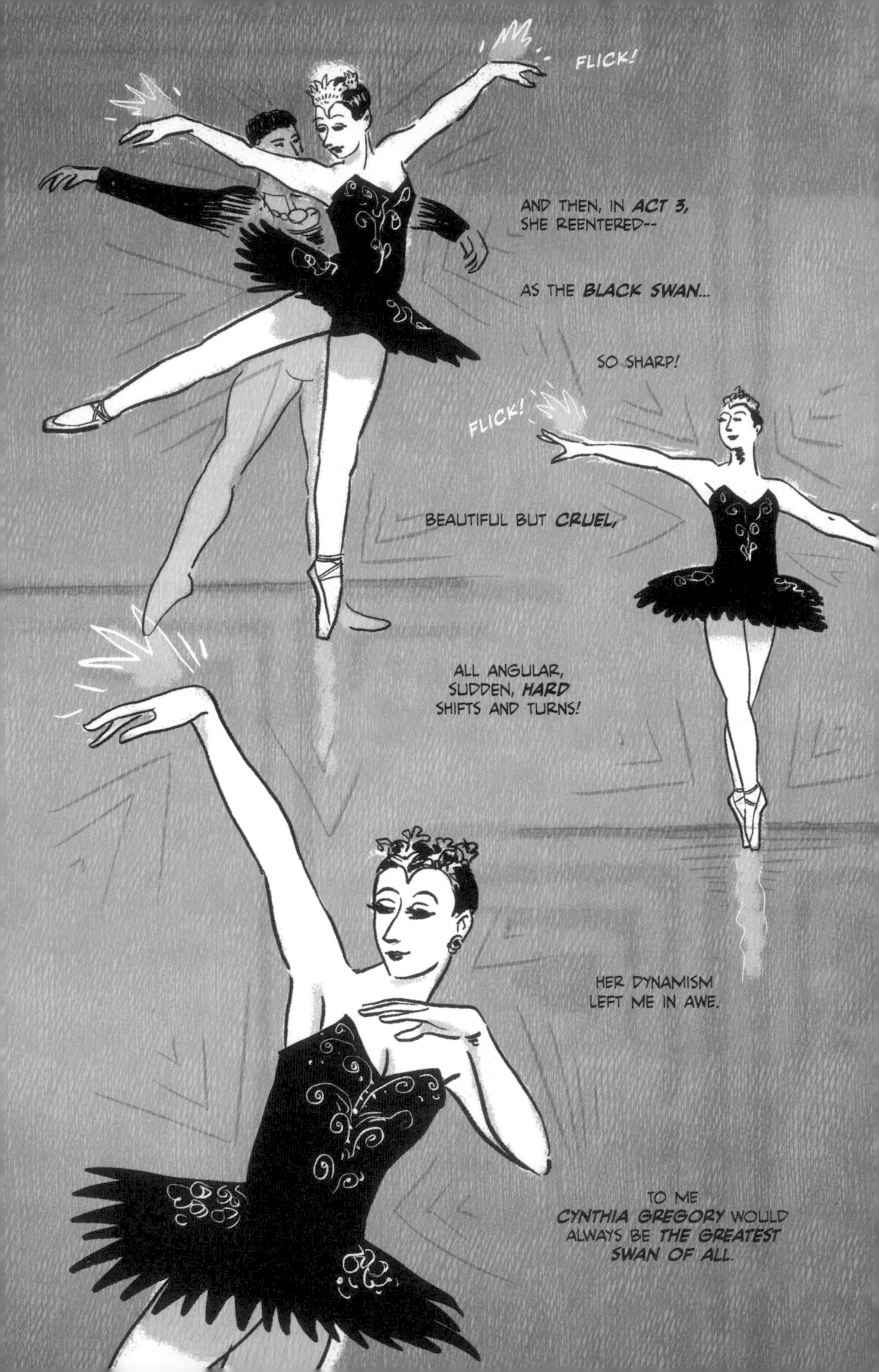
FLICK!
AND THEN, IN ACT 3, SHE REENTERED--
AS THE BLACK SWAN...
SO SHARP!
FLICK!
BEAUTIFUL BUT CRUEL,
ALL ANGULAR, SUDDEN, HARD SHIFTS AND TURNS!
HER DYNAMISM LEFT ME IN AWE.
TO ME CYNTHIA GREGORY WOULD ALWAYS BE THE GREATEST SWAN OF ALL.

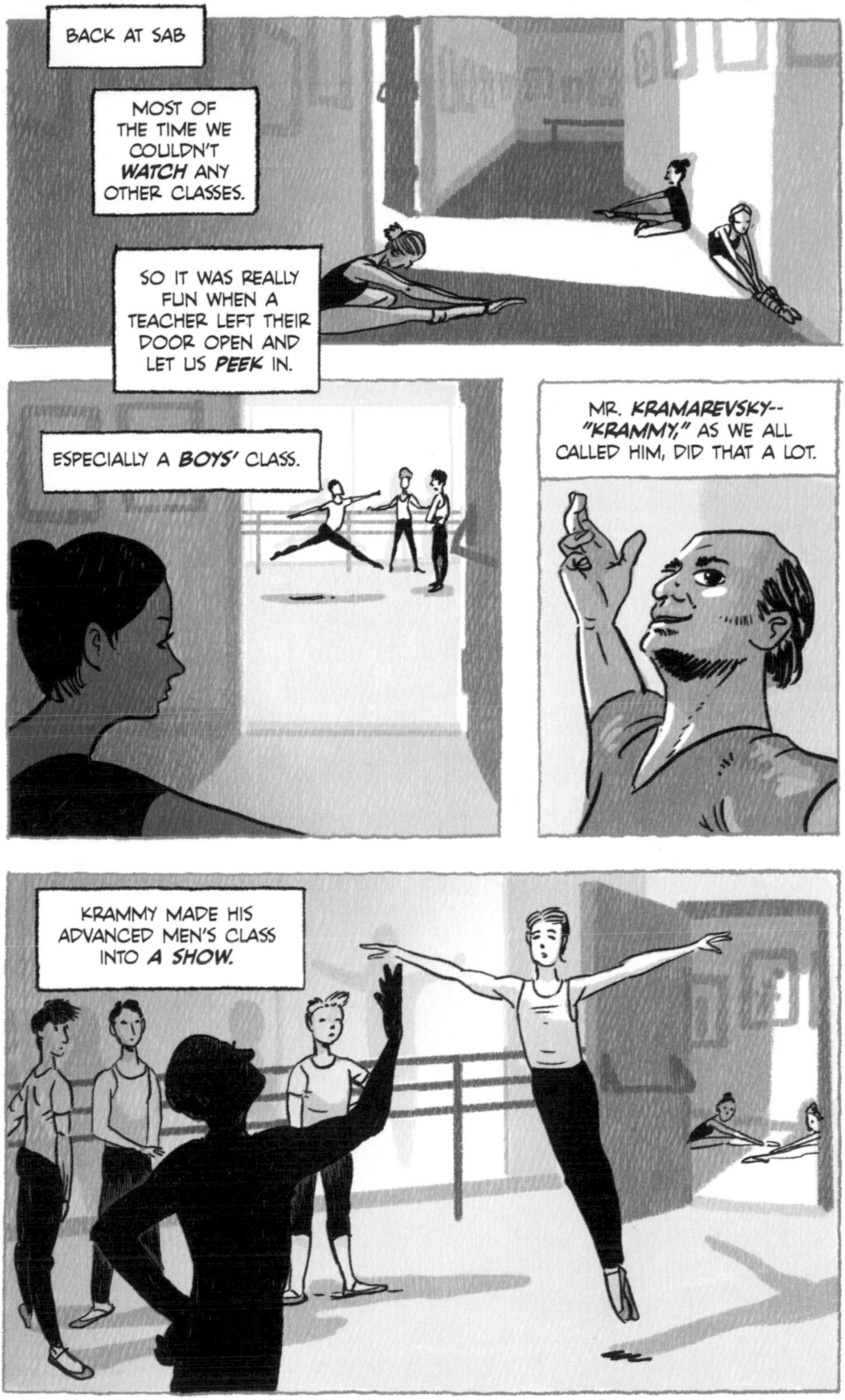
BACK AT SAB
MOST OF THE TIME WE COULDN'T WATCH ANY OTHER CLASSES.
SO IT WAS REALLY FUN WHEN A TEACHER LEFT THEIR DOOR OPEN AND LET US PEEK IN.
ESPECIALLY A BOYS' CLASS.
MR. KRAMAREVSKY-- "KRAMMY," AS WE ALL CALLED HIM, DID THAT A LOT.
KRAMMY MADE HIS ADVANCED MEN'S CLASS INTO A SHOW.

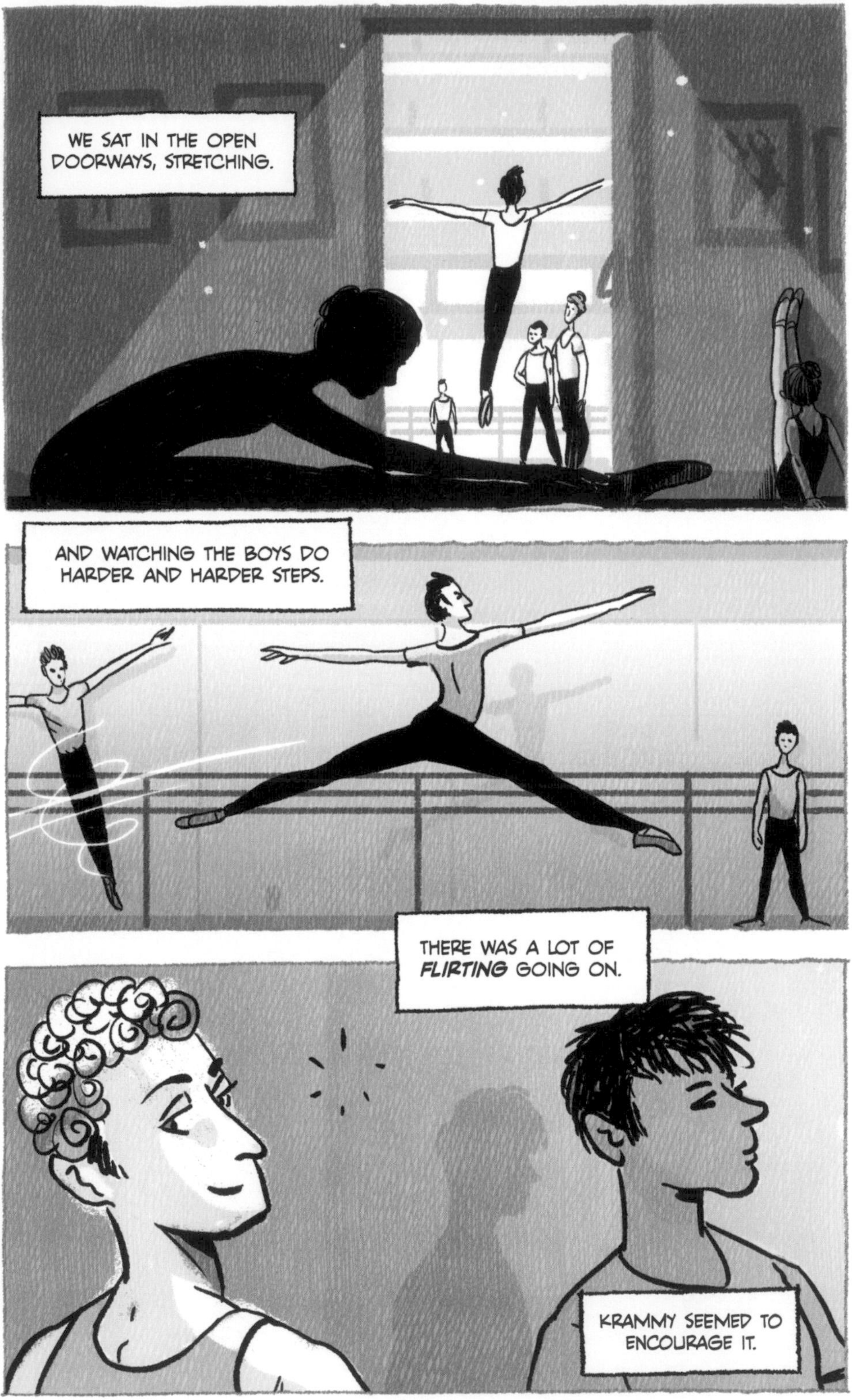
WE SAT IN THE OPEN DOORWAYS, STRETCHING.
AND WATCHING THE BOYS DO HARDER AND HARDER STEPS.
THERE WAS A LOT OF *FLIRTING* GOING ON.
KRAMMY SEEMED TO ENCOURAGE IT.

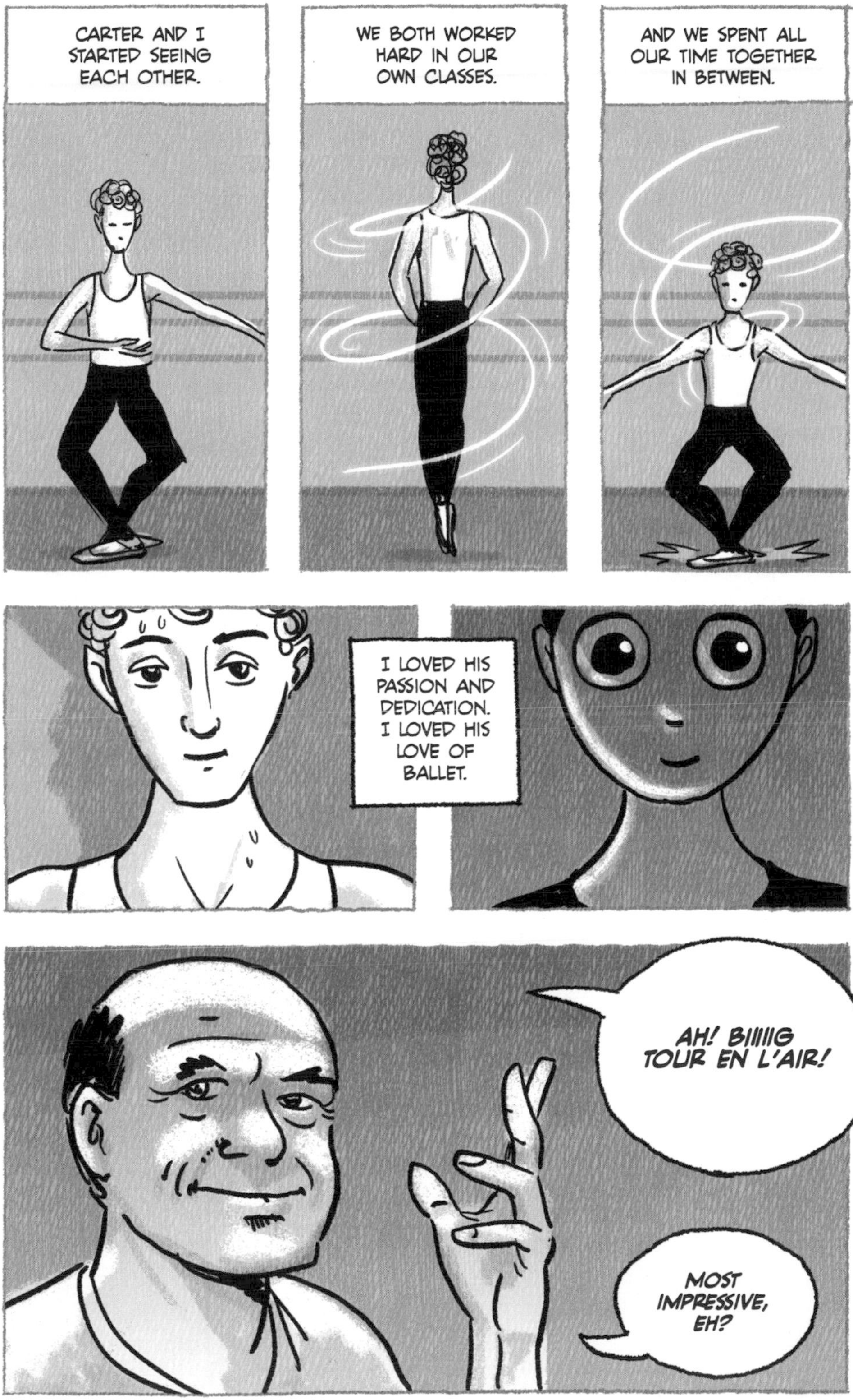
CARTER AND I STARTED SEEING EACH OTHER.
WE BOTH WORKED HARD IN OUR OWN CLASSES.
AND WE SPENT ALL OUR TIME TOGETHER IN BETWEEN.
I LOVED HIS PASSION AND DEDICATION. I LOVED HIS LOVE OF BALLET.
AH! BIIIIIG TOUR EN L'AIR!
MOST IMPRESSIVE, EH?

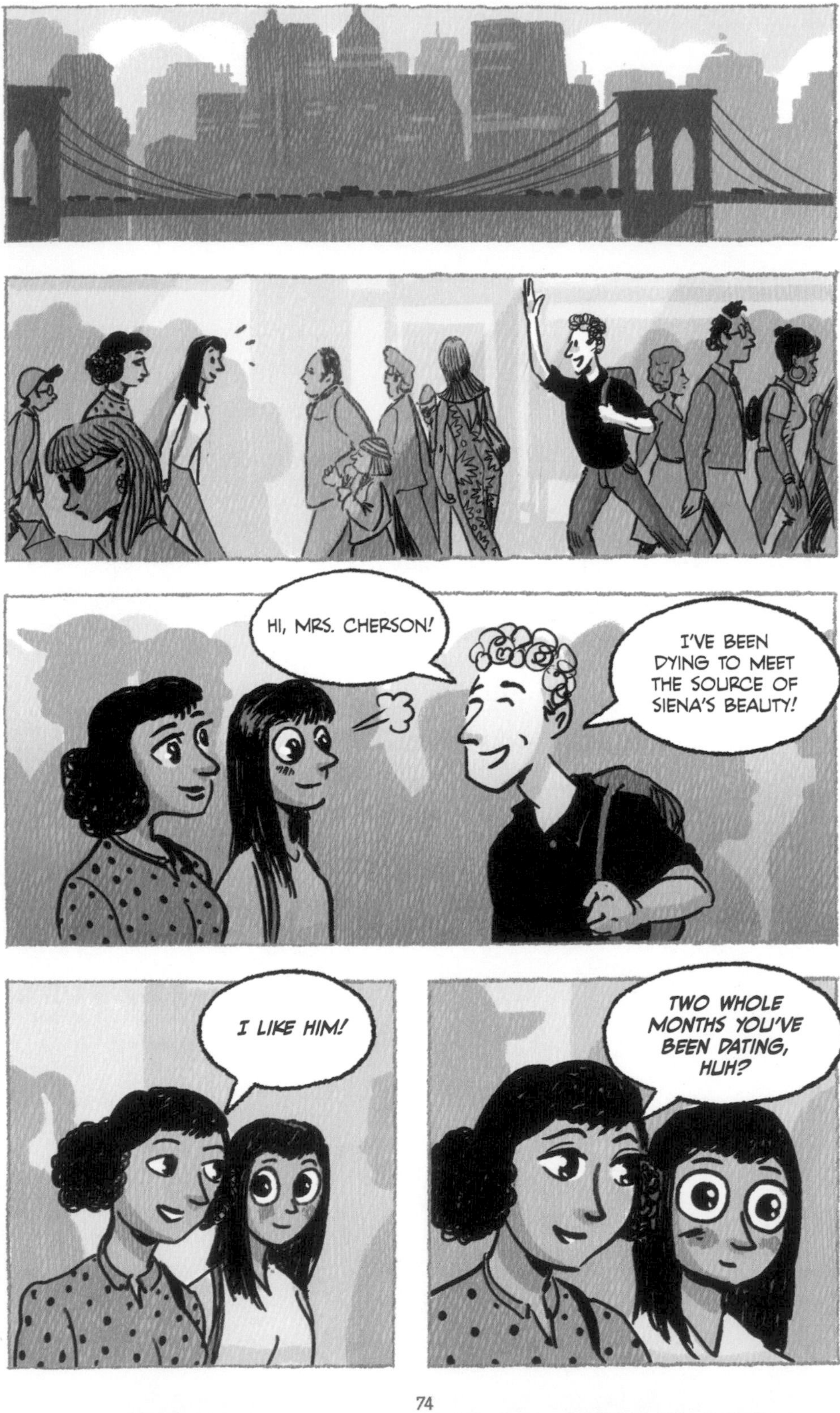
HI, MRS. CHERSON!
I'VE BEEN DYING TO MEET THE SOURCE OF SIENA'S BEAUTY!
I LIKE HIM!
TWO WHOLE MONTHS YOU'VE BEEN DATING, HUH?

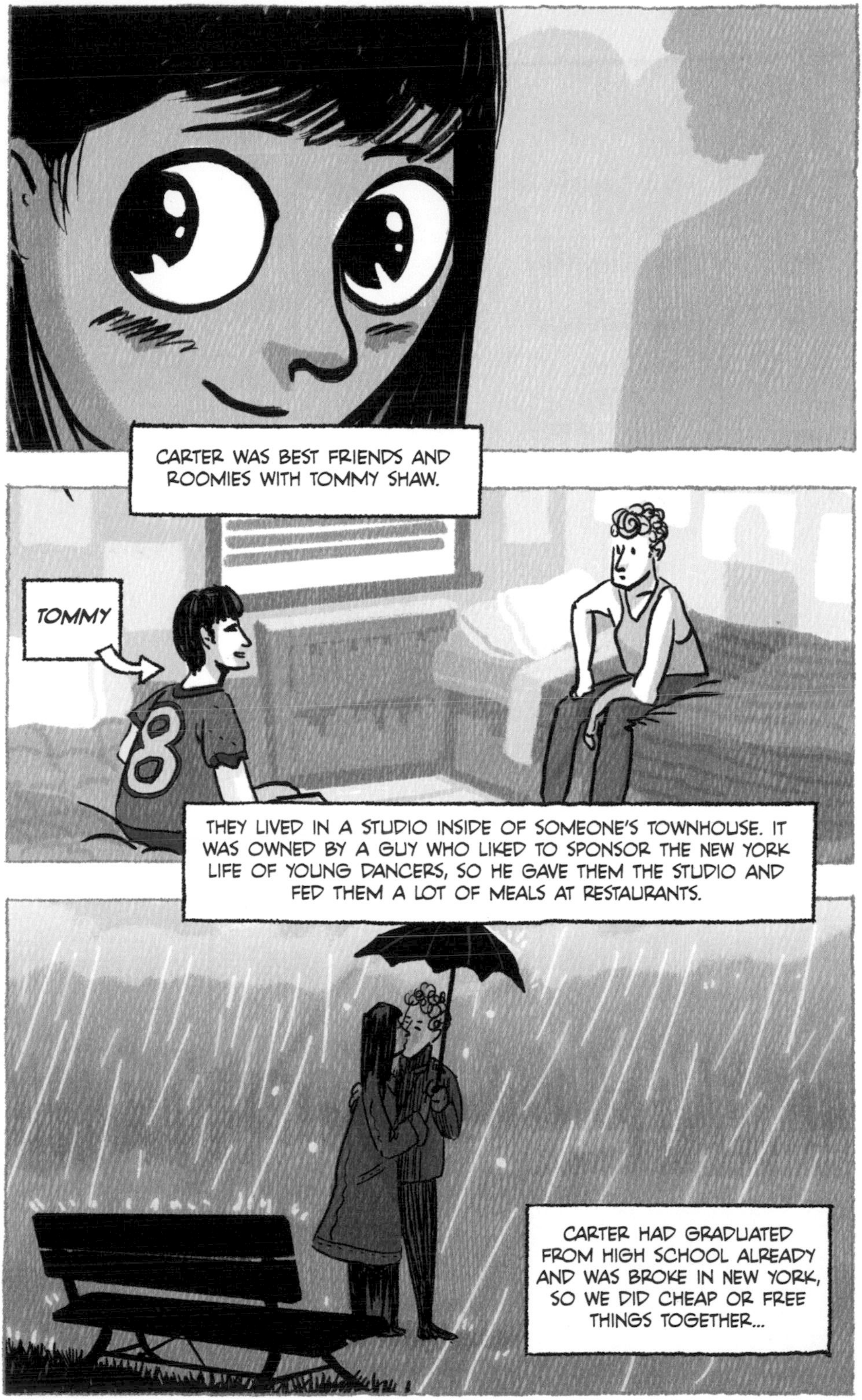
CARTER WAS BEST FRIENDS AND ROOMIES WITH TOMMY SHAW.
TOMMY
THEY LIVED IN A STUDIO INSIDE OF SOMEONE'S TOWNHOUSE. IT WAS OWNED BY A GUY WHO LIKED TO SPONSOR THE NEW YORK LIFE OF YOUNG DANCERS, SO HE GAVE THEM THE STUDIO AND FED THEM A LOT OF MEALS AT RESTAURANTS.
CARTER HAD GRADUATED FROM HIGH SCHOOL ALREADY AND WAS BROKE IN NEW YORK, SO WE DID CHEAP OR FREE THINGS TOGETHER...

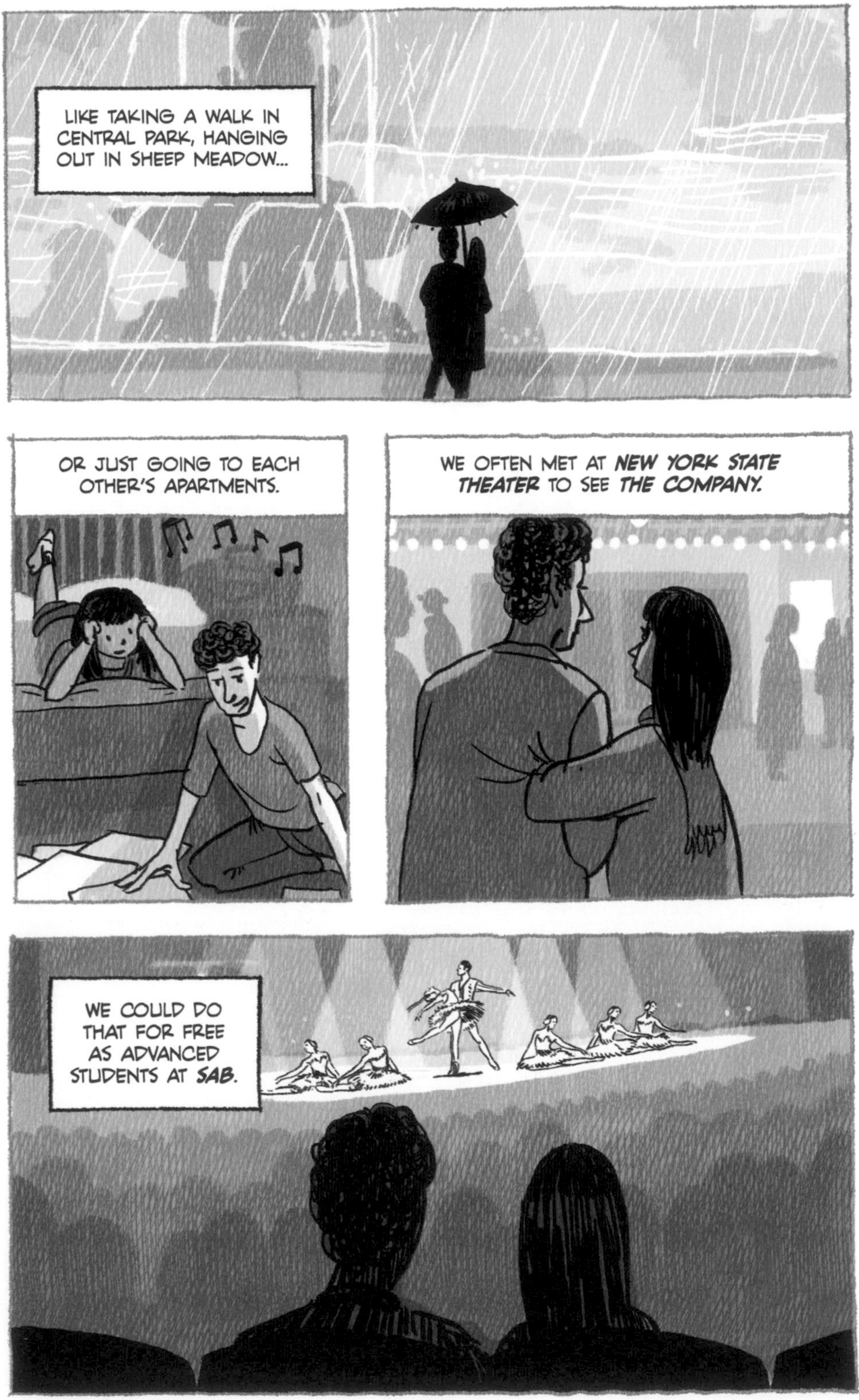
LIKE TAKING A WALK IN CENTRAL PARK, HANGING OUT IN SHEEP MEADOW...
OR JUST GOING TO EACH OTHER'S APARTMENTS.
WE OFTEN MET AT NEW YORK STATE THEATER TO SEE THE COMPANY.
WE COULD DO THAT FOR FREE AS ADVANCED STUDENTS AT SAB.

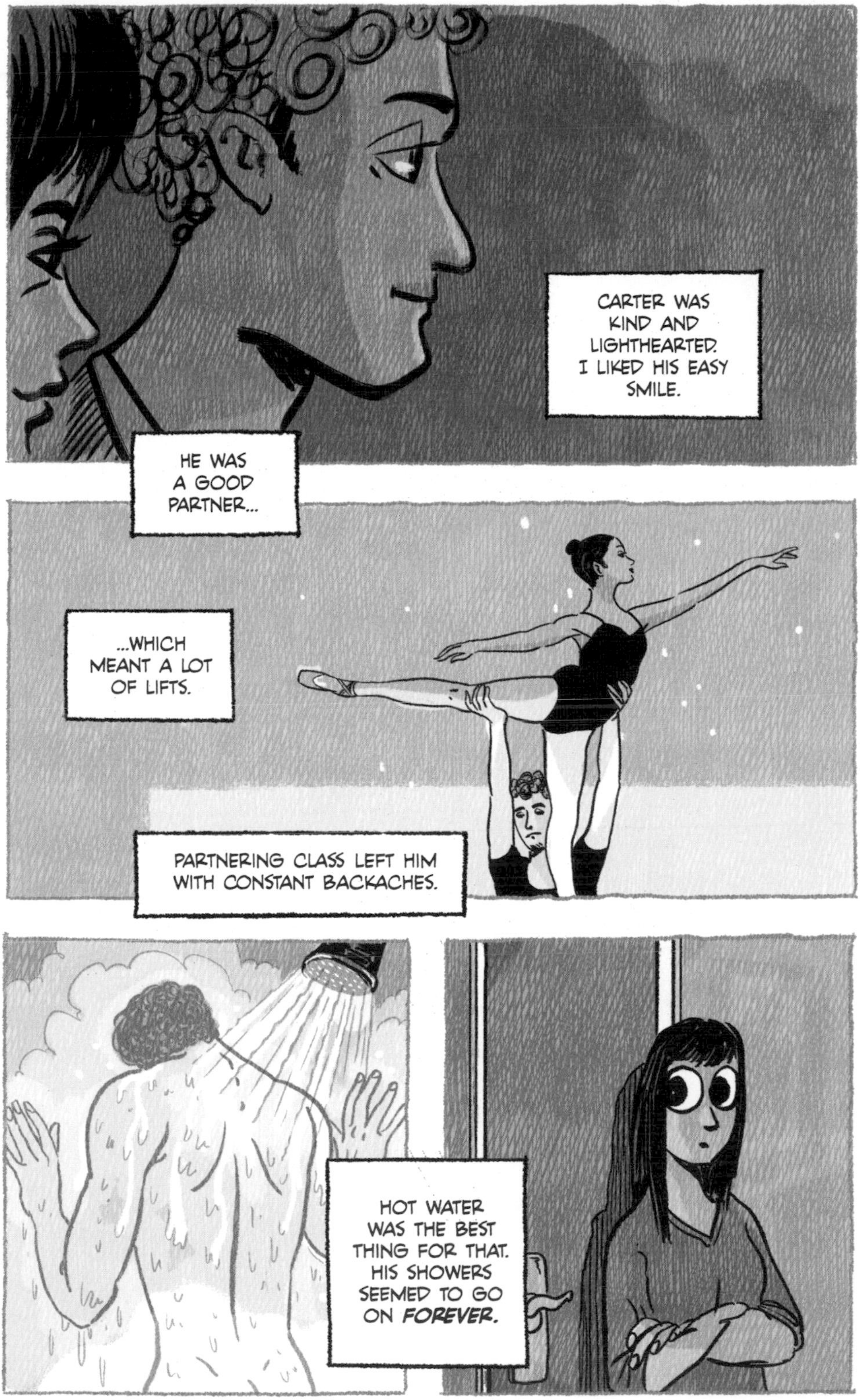
CARTER WAS KIND AND LIGHTHEARTED. I LIKED HIS EASY SMILE.
HE WAS A GOOD PARTNER...
...WHICH MEANT A LOT OF LIFTS.
PARTNERING CLASS LEFT HIM WITH CONSTANT BACKACHES.
HOT WATER WAS THE BEST THING FOR THAT. HIS SHOWERS SEEMED TO GO ON *FOREVER.*

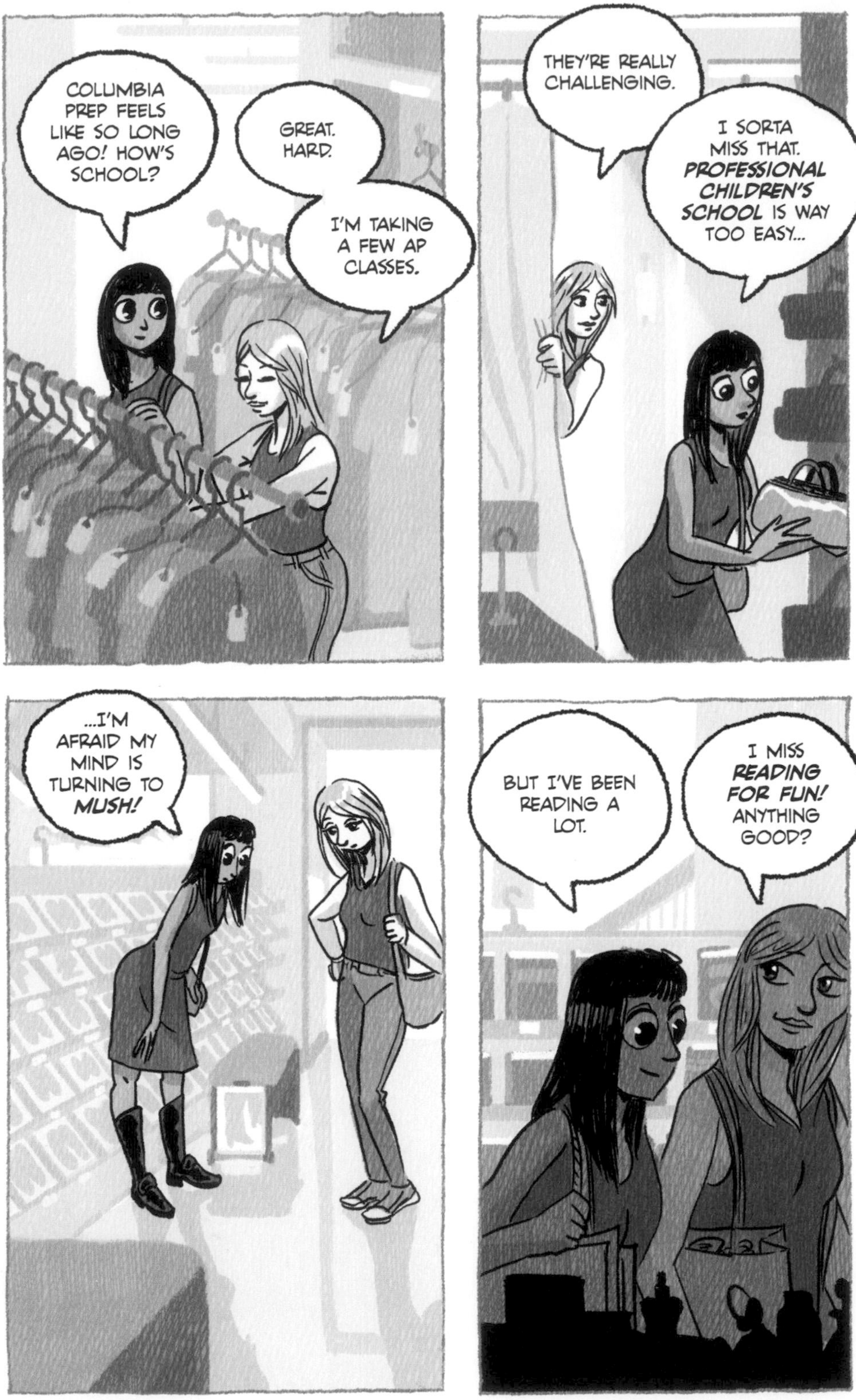
COLUMBIA PREP FEELS LIKE SO LONG AGO! HOW'S SCHOOL?
GREAT. HARD.
I'M TAKING A FEW AP CLASSES.
THEY'RE REALLY CHALLENGING.
I SORTA MISS THAT. PROFESSIONAL CHILDREN'S SCHOOL IS WAY TOO EASY...
...I'M AFRAID MY MIND IS TURNING TO MUSH!
BUT I'VE BEEN READING A LOT.
I MISS READING FOR FUN! ANYTHING GOOD?

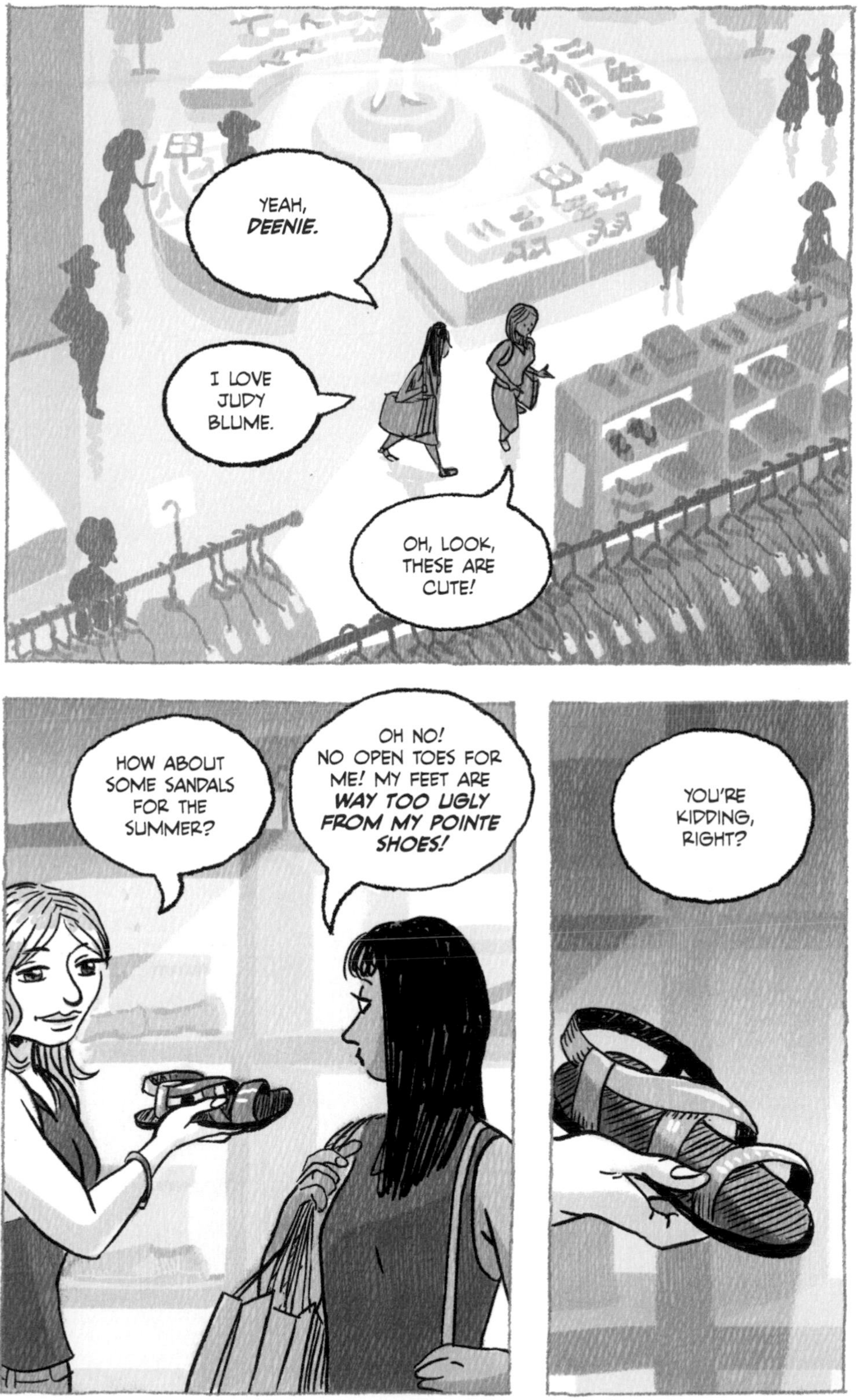
YEAH, ***DEENIE.***
I LOVE JUDY BLUME.
OH, LOOK, THESE ARE CUTE!
HOW ABOUT SOME SANDALS FOR THE SUMMER?
OH NO! NO OPEN TOES FOR ME! MY FEET ARE ***WAY TOO UGLY FROM MY POINTE SHOES!***
YOU'RE KIDDING, RIGHT?

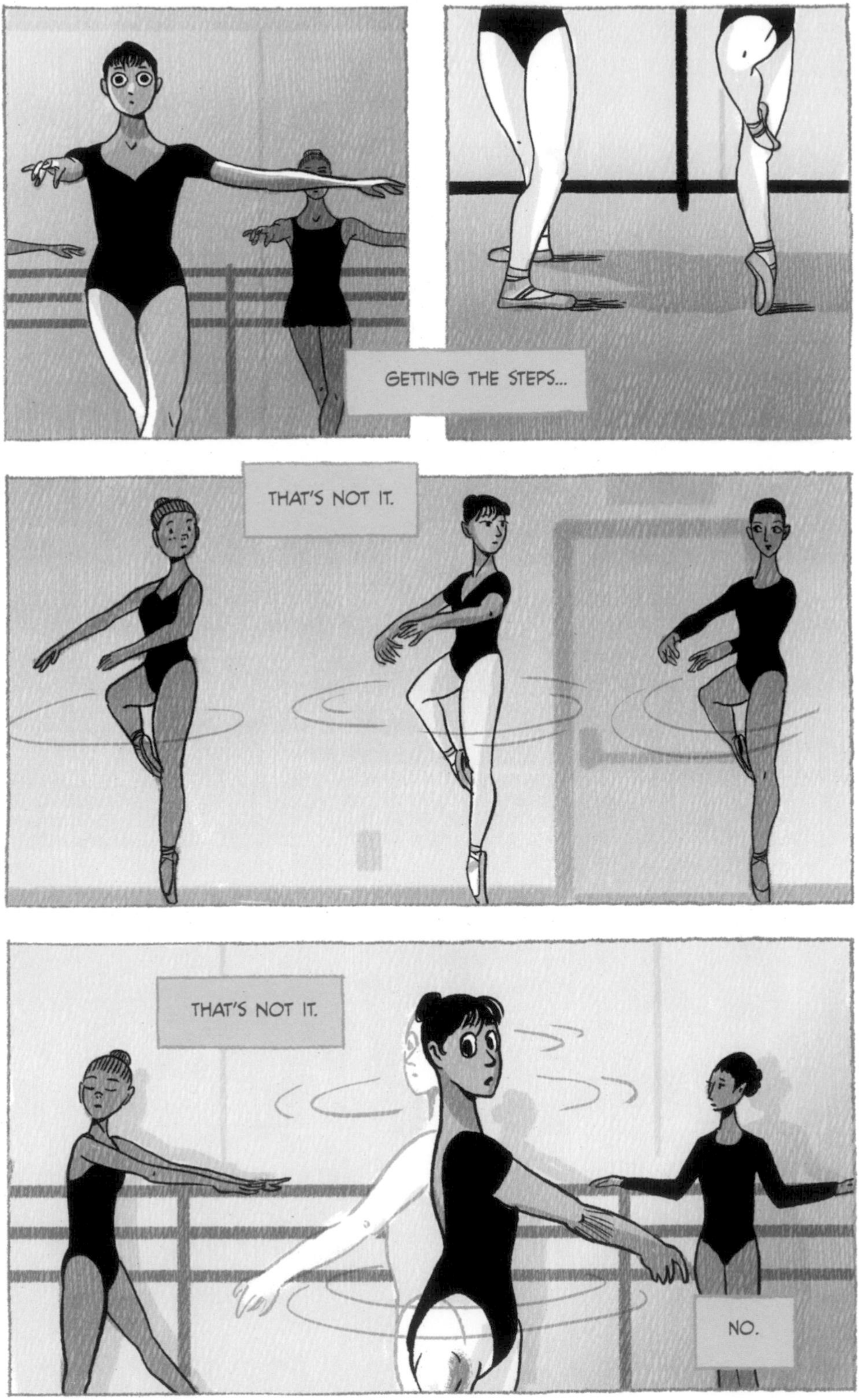
GETTING THE STEPS...
THAT'S NOT IT.
THAT'S NOT IT.
NO.

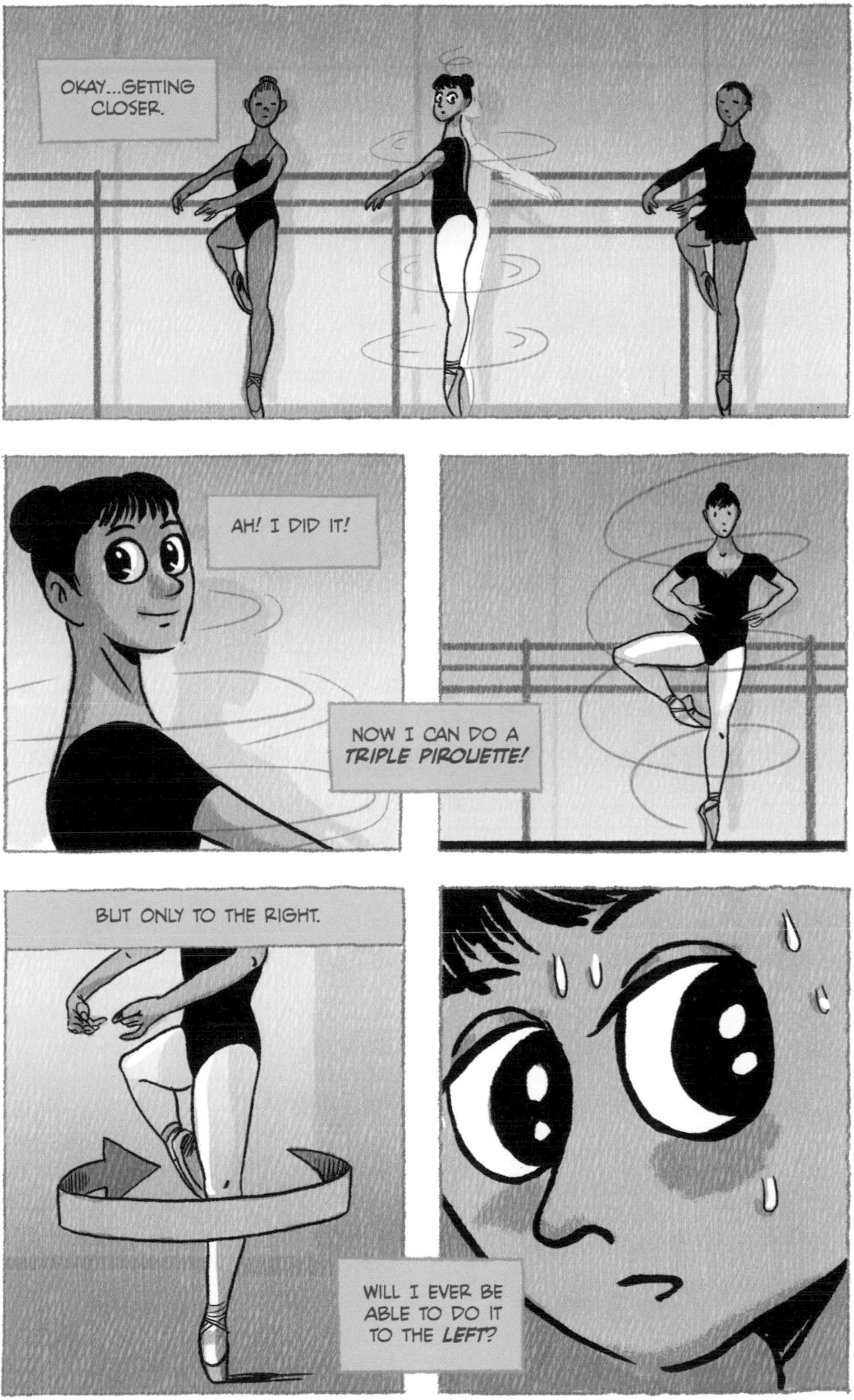
OKAY...GETTING CLOSER.
AH! I DID IT!
NOW I CAN DO A *TRIPLE PIROUETTE!*
BUT ONLY TO THE RIGHT.
WILL I EVER BE ABLE TO DO IT TO THE *LEFT?*

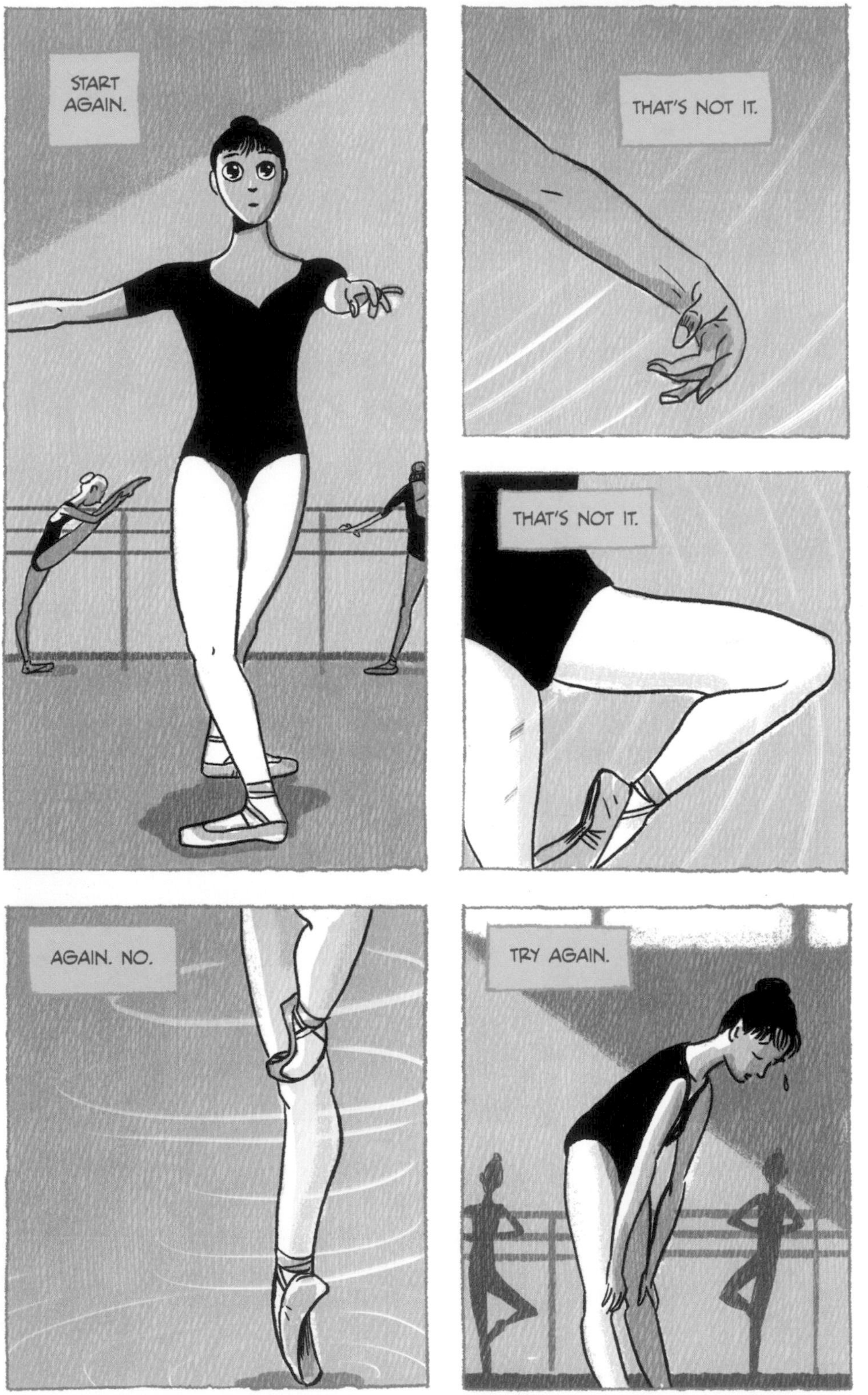
START AGAIN.
THAT'S NOT IT.
THAT'S NOT IT.
AGAIN. NO.
TRY AGAIN.

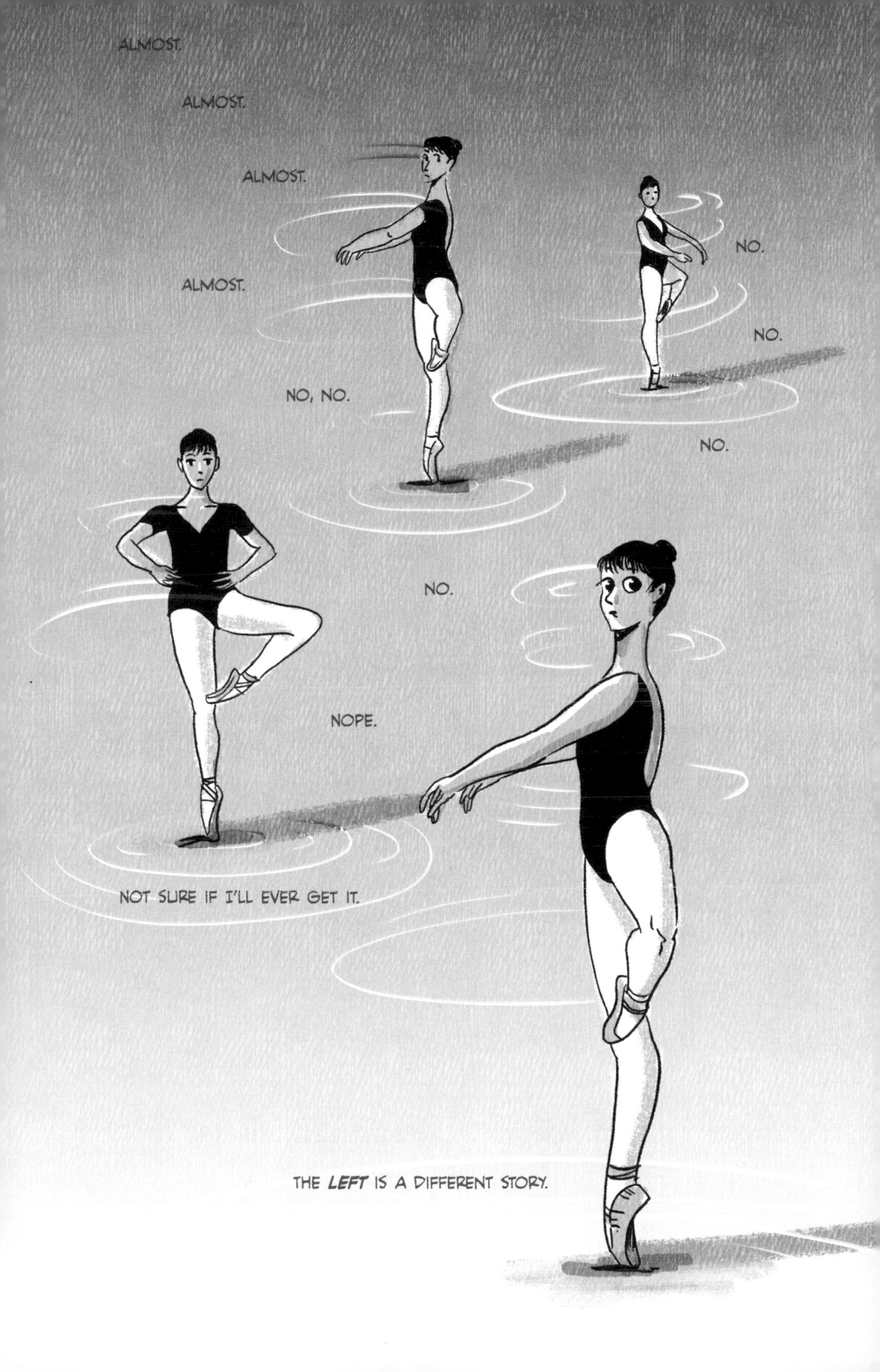

ALMOST.
ALMOST.
ALMOST.
NO.
ALMOST.
NO.
NO, NO.
NO.
NO.
NOPE.
NOT SURE IF I'LL EVER GET IT.
THE *LEFT* IS A DIFFERENT STORY.

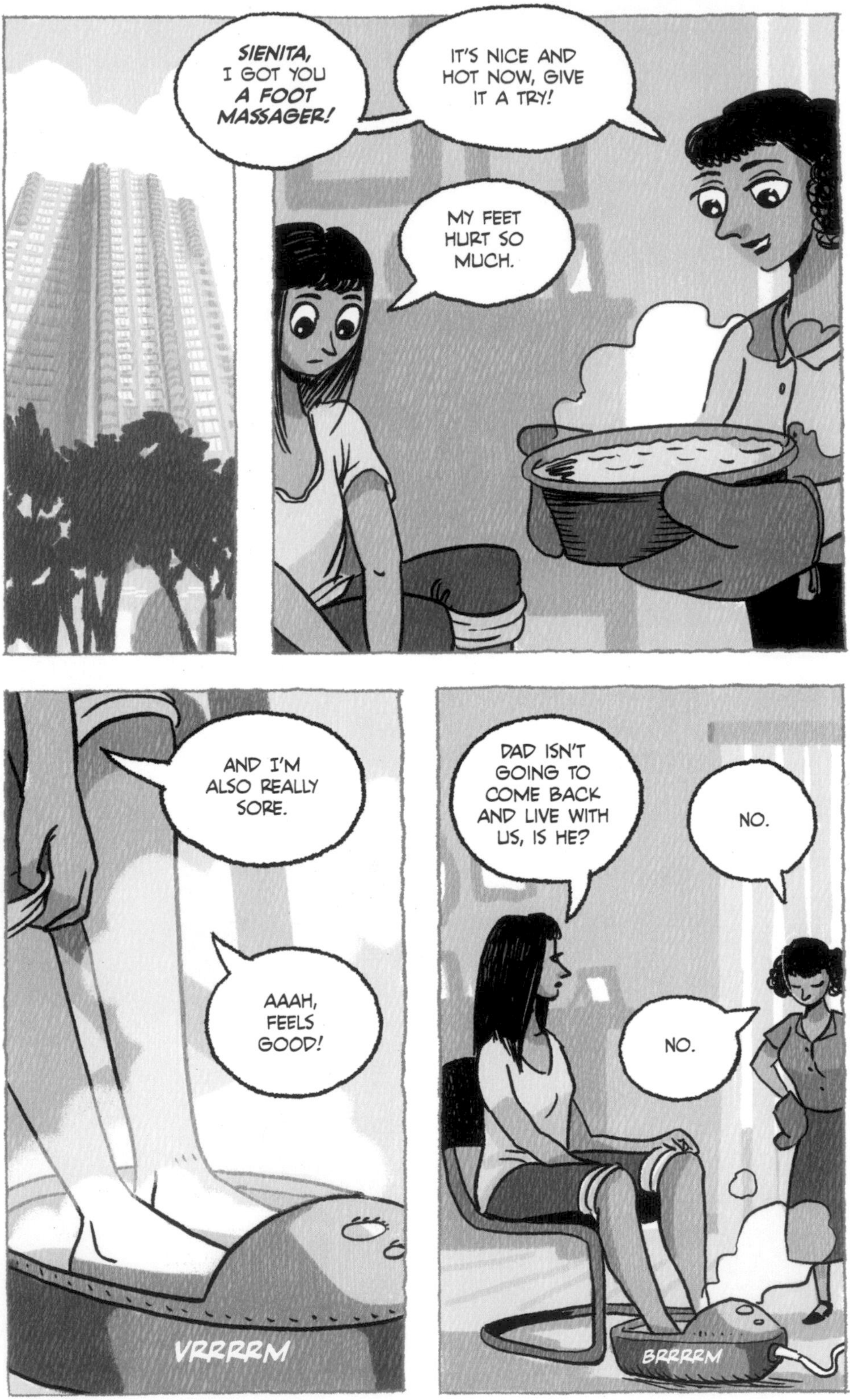
SIENITA, I GOT YOU A FOOT MASSAGER!
IT'S NICE AND HOT NOW, GIVE IT A TRY!
MY FEET HURT SO MUCH.
AND I'M ALSO REALLY SORE.
AAAH, FEELS GOOD!
VRRRRM
DAD ISN'T GOING TO COME BACK AND LIVE WITH US, IS HE?
NO.
NO.
BRRRRM

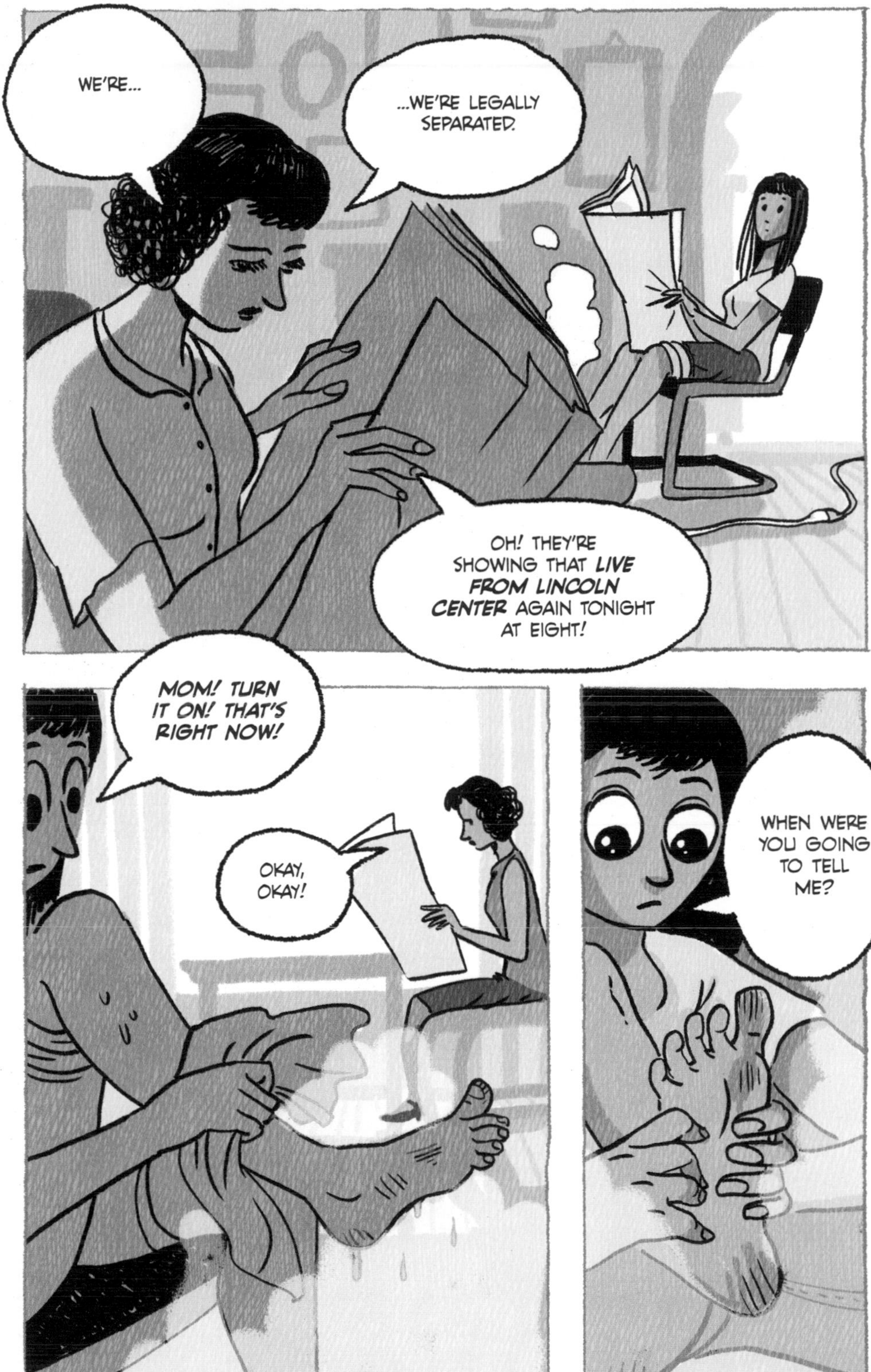
WE'RE...
...WE'RE LEGALLY SEPARATED.
OH! THEY'RE SHOWING THAT *LIVE FROM LINCOLN CENTER* AGAIN TONIGHT AT EIGHT!
MOM! TURN IT ON! THAT'S RIGHT NOW!
OKAY, OKAY!
WHEN WERE YOU GOING TO TELL ME?

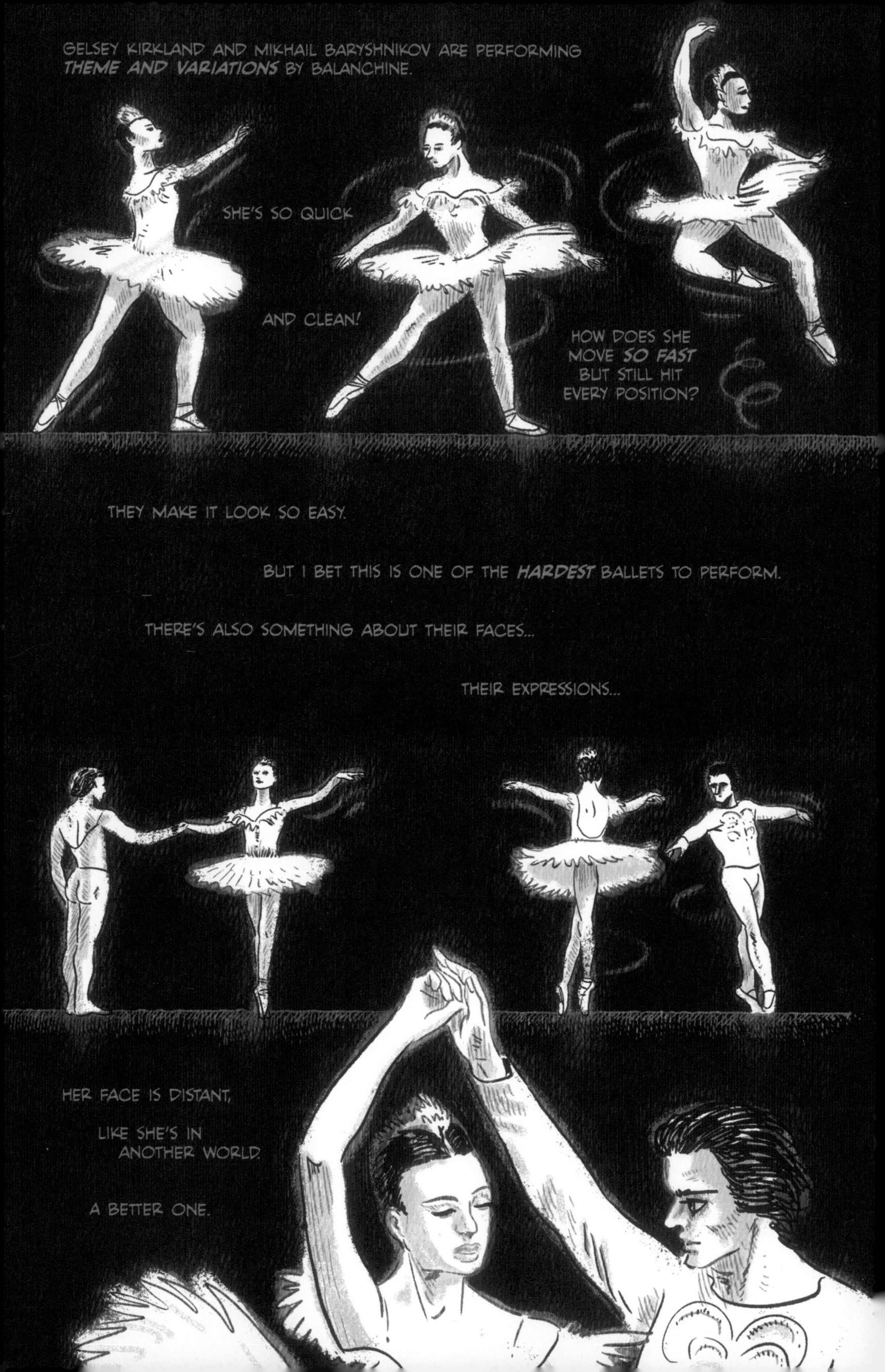
GELSEY KIRKLAND AND MIKHAIL BARYSHNIKOV ARE PERFORMING *THEME AND VARIATIONS* BY BALANCHINE.
SHE'S SO QUICK
AND CLEAN!
HOW DOES SHE MOVE **SO FAST** BUT STILL HIT EVERY POSITION?
THEY MAKE IT LOOK SO EASY.
BUT I BET THIS IS ONE OF THE ***HARDEST*** BALLETS TO PERFORM.
THERE'S ALSO SOMETHING ABOUT THEIR FACES...
THEIR EXPRESSIONS...
HER FACE IS DISTANT,
LIKE SHE'S IN ANOTHER WORLD.
A BETTER ONE.

THE *PAS DE DEUX* IS SO ROMANTIC.

THEY KEEP ATTRACTING AND REPELLING.

IN PERFECT RESPONSE TO THE MUSIC.

THAT MUSIC,
WITH THOSE FACES,
WILL HAUNT ME
FOR YEARS TO COME.

I DREAM OF DANCING SUCH
A PAS DE DEUX WITH MY
BOYFRIEND SOMEDAY.

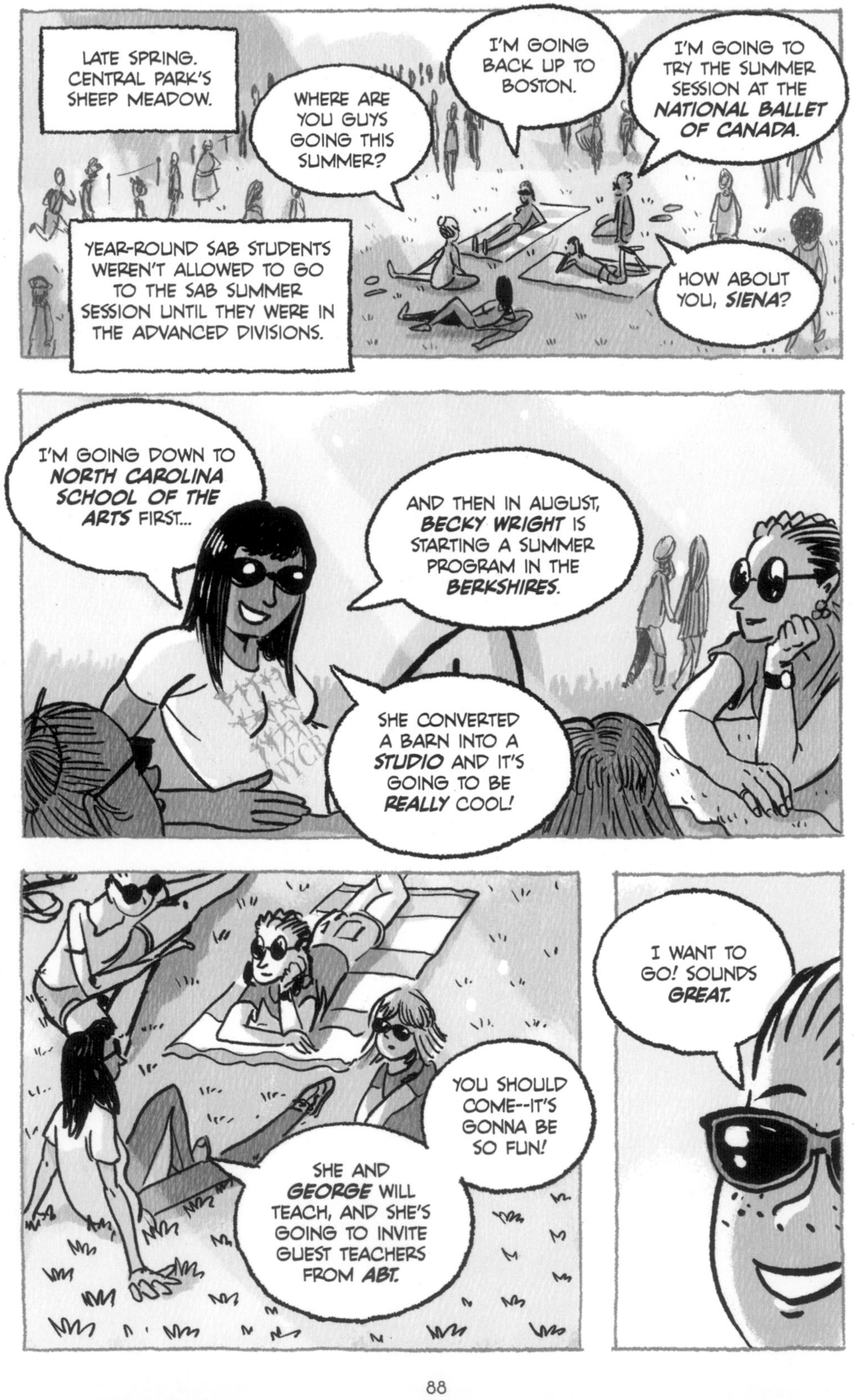
LATE SPRING. CENTRAL PARK'S SHEEP MEADOW.
YEAR-ROUND SAB STUDENTS WEREN'T ALLOWED TO GO TO THE SAB SUMMER SESSION UNTIL THEY WERE IN THE ADVANCED DIVISIONS.
WHERE ARE YOU GUYS GOING THIS SUMMER?
I'M GOING BACK UP TO BOSTON.
I'M GOING TO TRY THE SUMMER SESSION AT THE *NATIONAL BALLET OF CANADA.*
HOW ABOUT YOU, *SIENA?*
I'M GOING DOWN TO *NORTH CAROLINA SCHOOL OF THE ARTS* FIRST...
AND THEN IN AUGUST, *BECKY WRIGHT* IS STARTING A SUMMER PROGRAM IN THE *BERKSHIRES.*
SHE CONVERTED A BARN INTO A *STUDIO* AND IT'S GOING TO BE *REALLY* COOL!
NYCB
YOU SHOULD COME--IT'S GONNA BE SO FUN!
SHE AND *GEORGE* WILL TEACH, AND SHE'S GOING TO INVITE GUEST TEACHERS FROM *ABT.*
I WANT TO GO! SOUNDS *GREAT.*

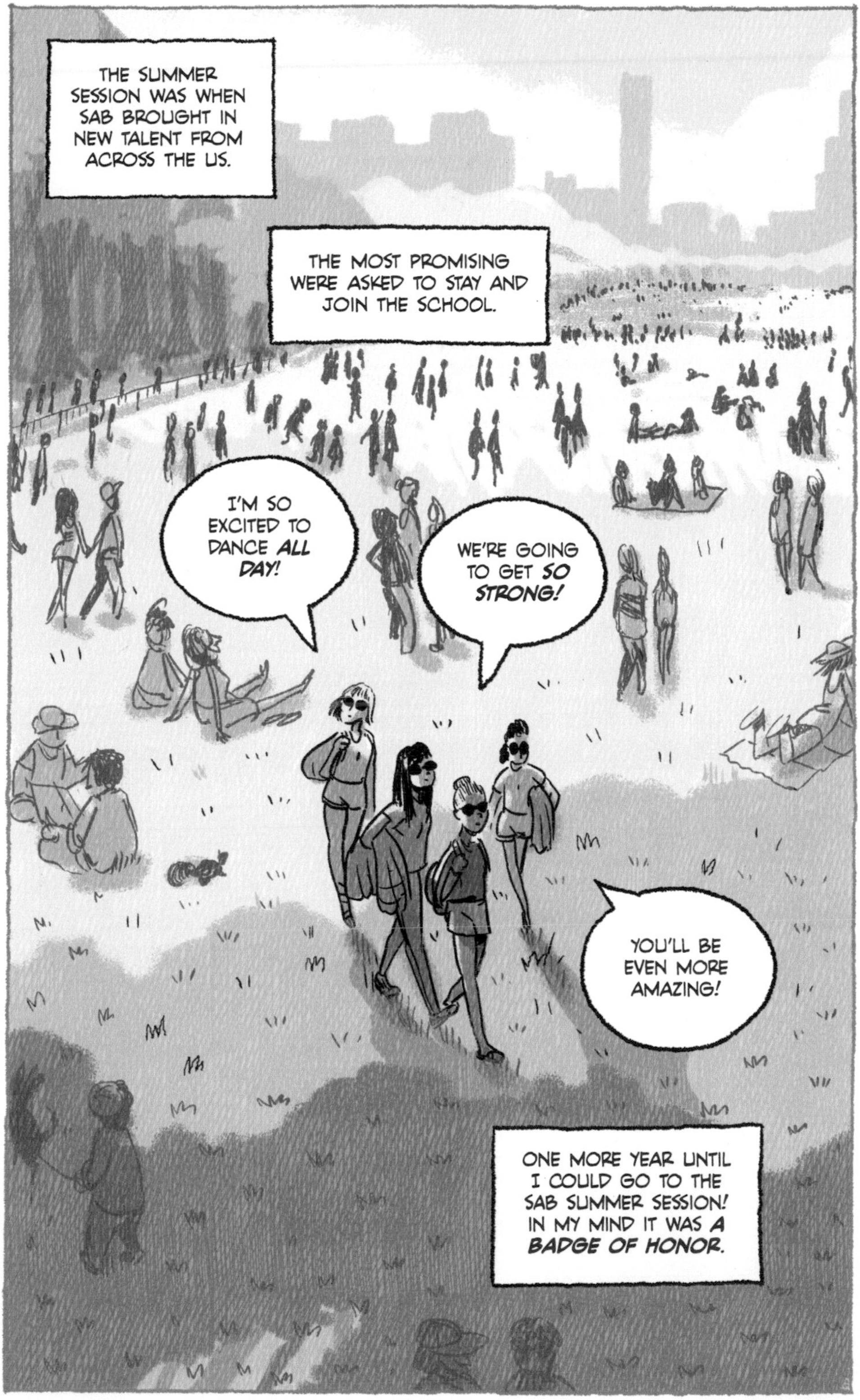
THE SUMMER SESSION WAS WHEN SAB BROUGHT IN NEW TALENT FROM ACROSS THE US.
THE MOST PROMISING WERE ASKED TO STAY AND JOIN THE SCHOOL.
I'M SO EXCITED TO DANCE *ALL DAY!*
WE'RE GOING TO GET *SO STRONG!*
YOU'LL BE EVEN MORE AMAZING!
ONE MORE YEAR UNTIL I COULD GO TO THE SAB SUMMER SESSION! IN MY MIND IT WAS *A BADGE OF HONOR.*

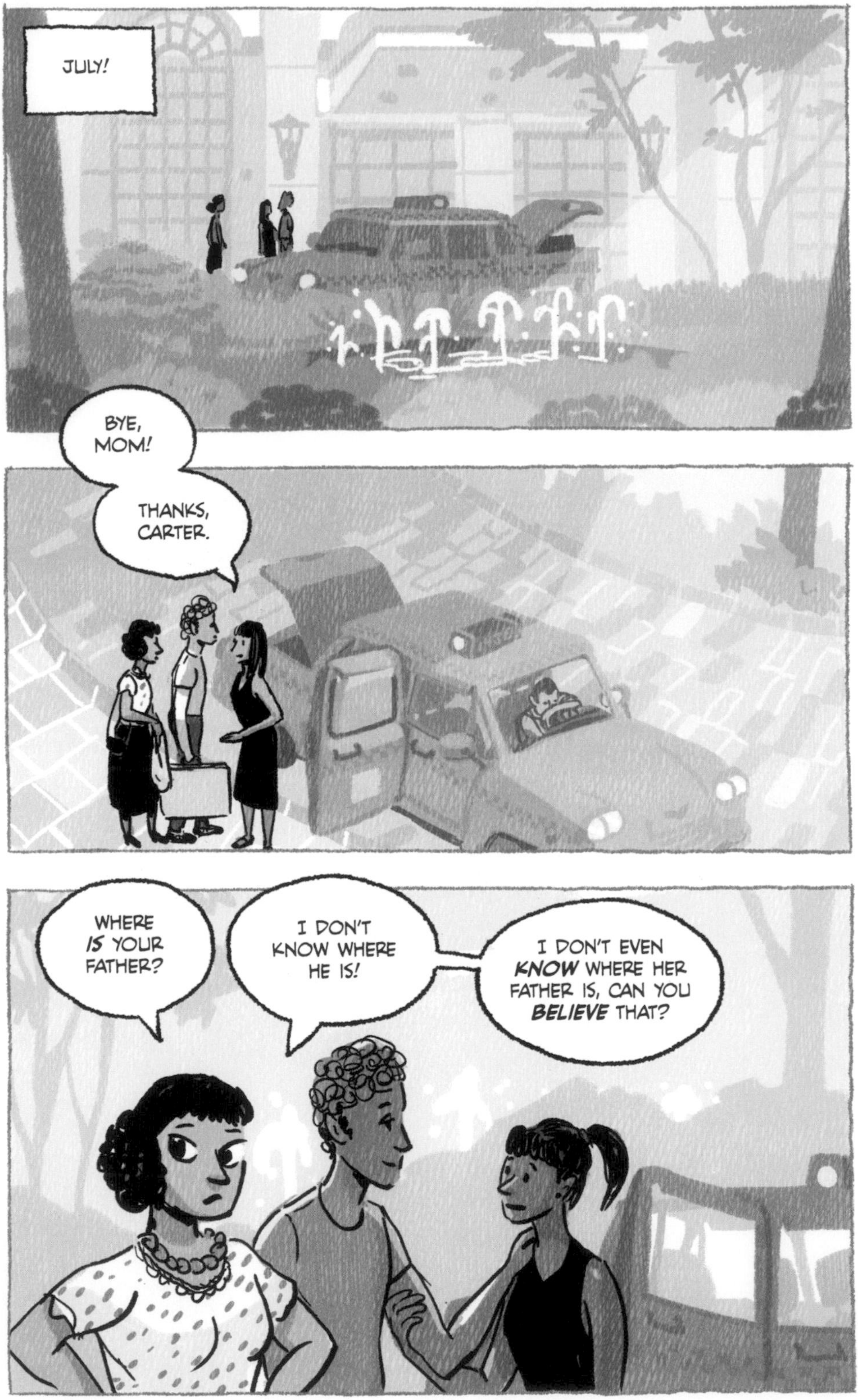
JULY!
BYE, MOM!
THANKS, CARTER.
WHERE *IS* YOUR FATHER?
I DON'T KNOW WHERE HE IS!
I DON'T EVEN *KNOW* WHERE HER FATHER IS, CAN YOU *BELIEVE* THAT?

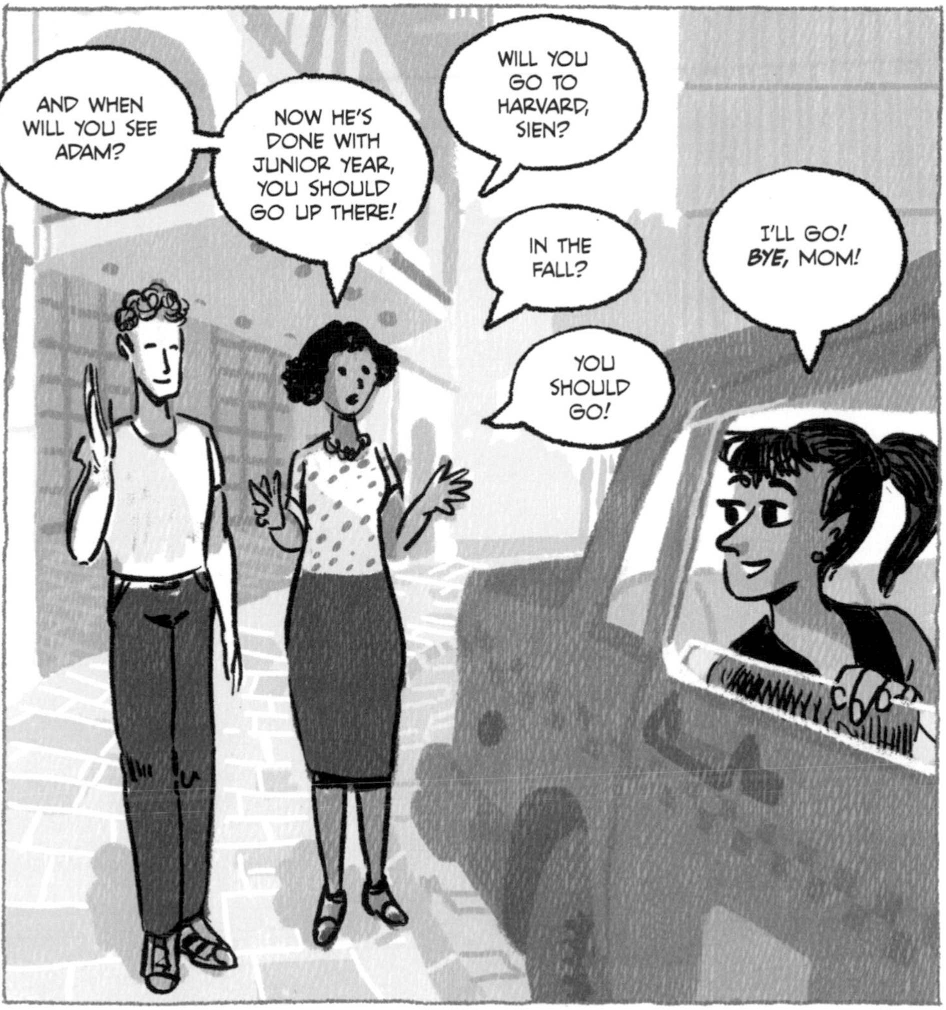
AND WHEN WILL YOU SEE ADAM?
NOW HE'S DONE WITH JUNIOR YEAR, YOU SHOULD GO UP THERE!
WILL YOU GO TO HARVARD, SIEN?
IN THE FALL?
YOU SHOULD GO!
I'LL GO! ***BYE,*** MOM!

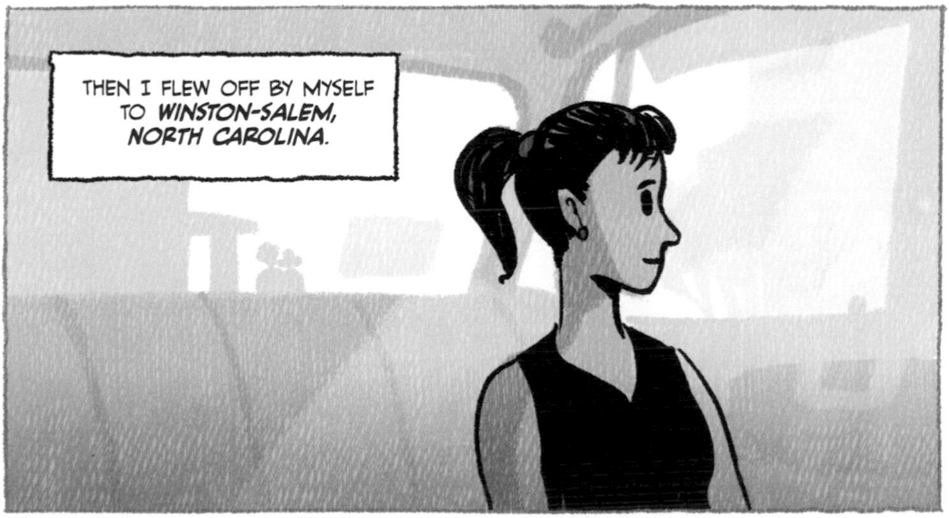
THEN I FLEW OFF BY MYSELF TO ***WINSTON-SALEM, NORTH CAROLINA.***

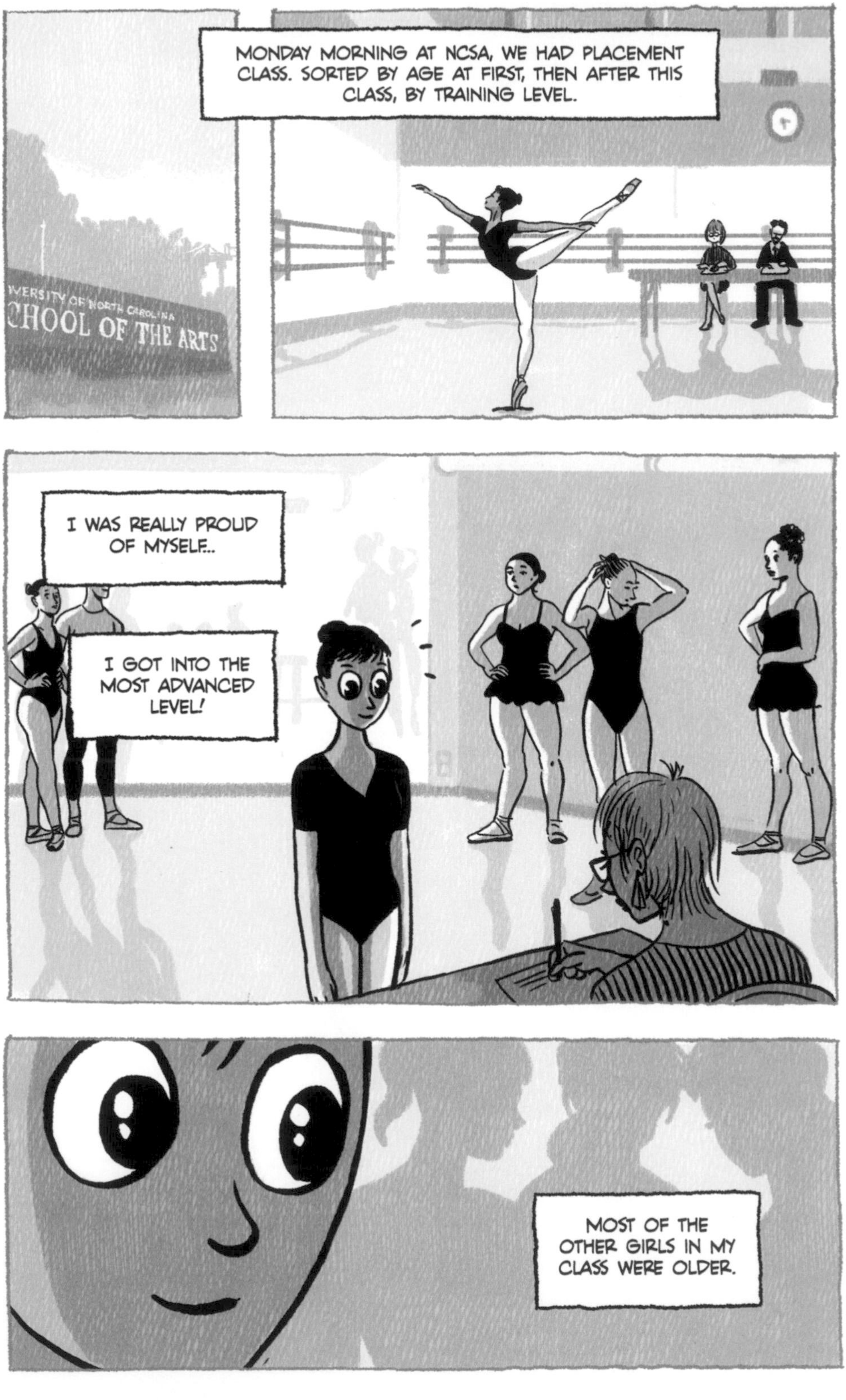
VERSITY OF NORTH CAROLINA
CHOOL OF THE ARTS
MONDAY MORNING AT NCSA, WE HAD PLACEMENT CLASS. SORTED BY AGE AT FIRST, THEN AFTER THIS CLASS, BY TRAINING LEVEL.
I WAS REALLY PROUD OF MYSELF...
I GOT INTO THE MOST ADVANCED LEVEL!
MOST OF THE OTHER GIRLS IN MY CLASS WERE OLDER.

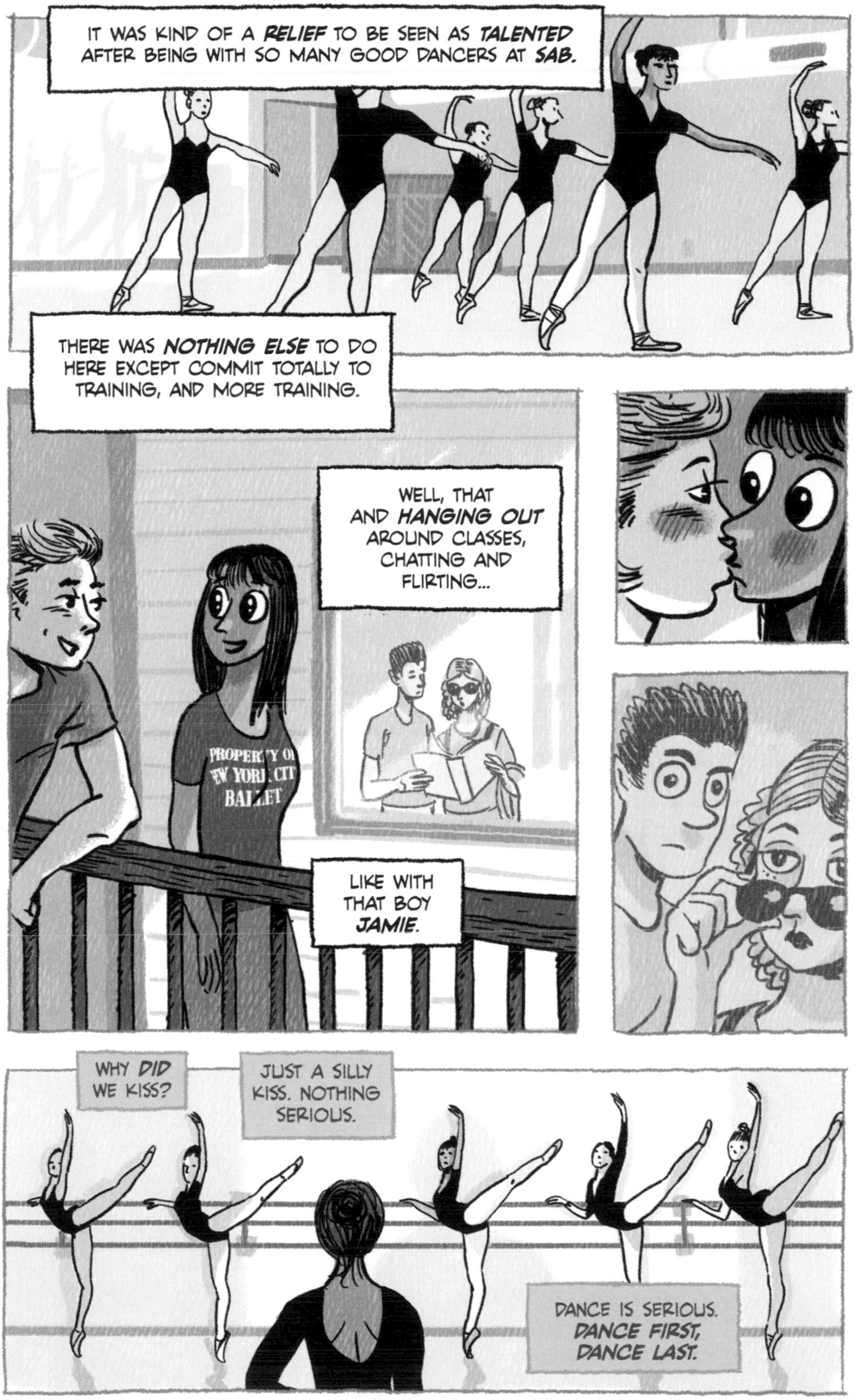
IT WAS KIND OF A RELIEF TO BE SEEN AS TALENTED AFTER BEING WITH SO MANY GOOD DANCERS AT SAB.
THERE WAS NOTHING ELSE TO DO HERE EXCEPT COMMIT TOTALLY TO TRAINING, AND MORE TRAINING.
WELL, THAT AND HANGING OUT AROUND CLASSES, CHATTING AND FLIRTING...
PROPERTY OF NEW YORK CITY BALLET
LIKE WITH THAT BOY JAMIE.
WHY DID WE KISS?
JUST A SILLY KISS. NOTHING SERIOUS.
DANCE IS SERIOUS. DANCE FIRST, DANCE LAST.

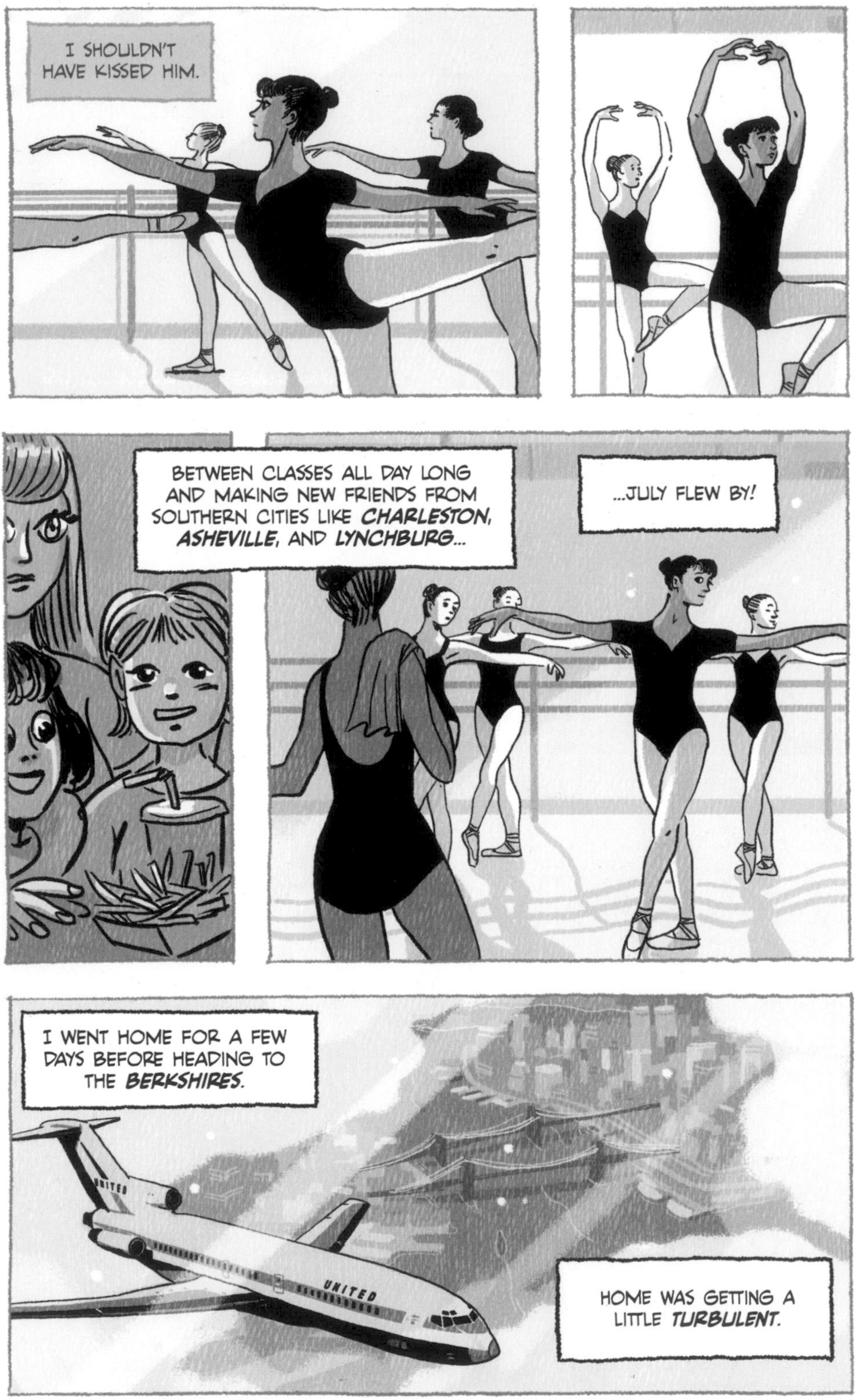
I SHOULDN'T HAVE KISSED HIM.
BETWEEN CLASSES ALL DAY LONG AND MAKING NEW FRIENDS FROM SOUTHERN CITIES LIKE *CHARLESTON, ASHEVILLE*, AND *LYNCHBURG*...
...JULY FLEW BY!
I WENT HOME FOR A FEW DAYS BEFORE HEADING TO THE *BERKSHIRES*.
UNITED
UNITED
HOME WAS GETTING A LITTLE *TURBULENT*.

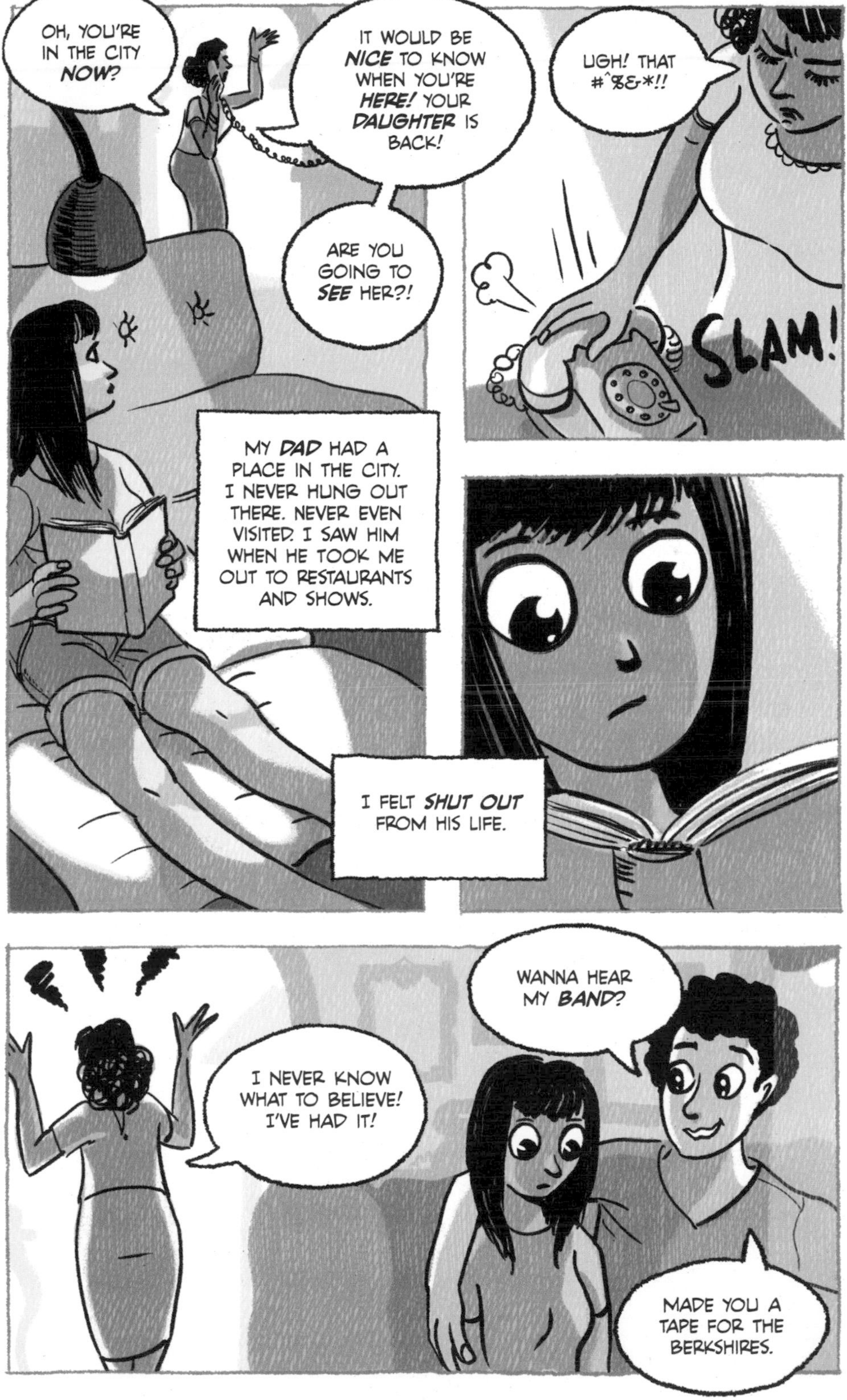

OH, YOU'RE IN THE CITY *NOW?*
IT WOULD BE *NICE* TO KNOW WHEN YOU'RE *HERE!* YOUR *DAUGHTER* IS BACK!
ARE YOU GOING TO *SEE* HER?!
UGH! THAT #^%&*!!
SLAM!
MY *DAD* HAD A PLACE IN THE CITY. I NEVER HUNG OUT THERE. NEVER EVEN VISITED. I SAW HIM WHEN HE TOOK ME OUT TO RESTAURANTS AND SHOWS.
I FELT *SHUT OUT* FROM HIS LIFE.
I NEVER KNOW WHAT TO BELIEVE! I'VE HAD IT!
WANNA HEAR MY *BAND?*
MADE YOU A TAPE FOR THE BERKSHIRES.

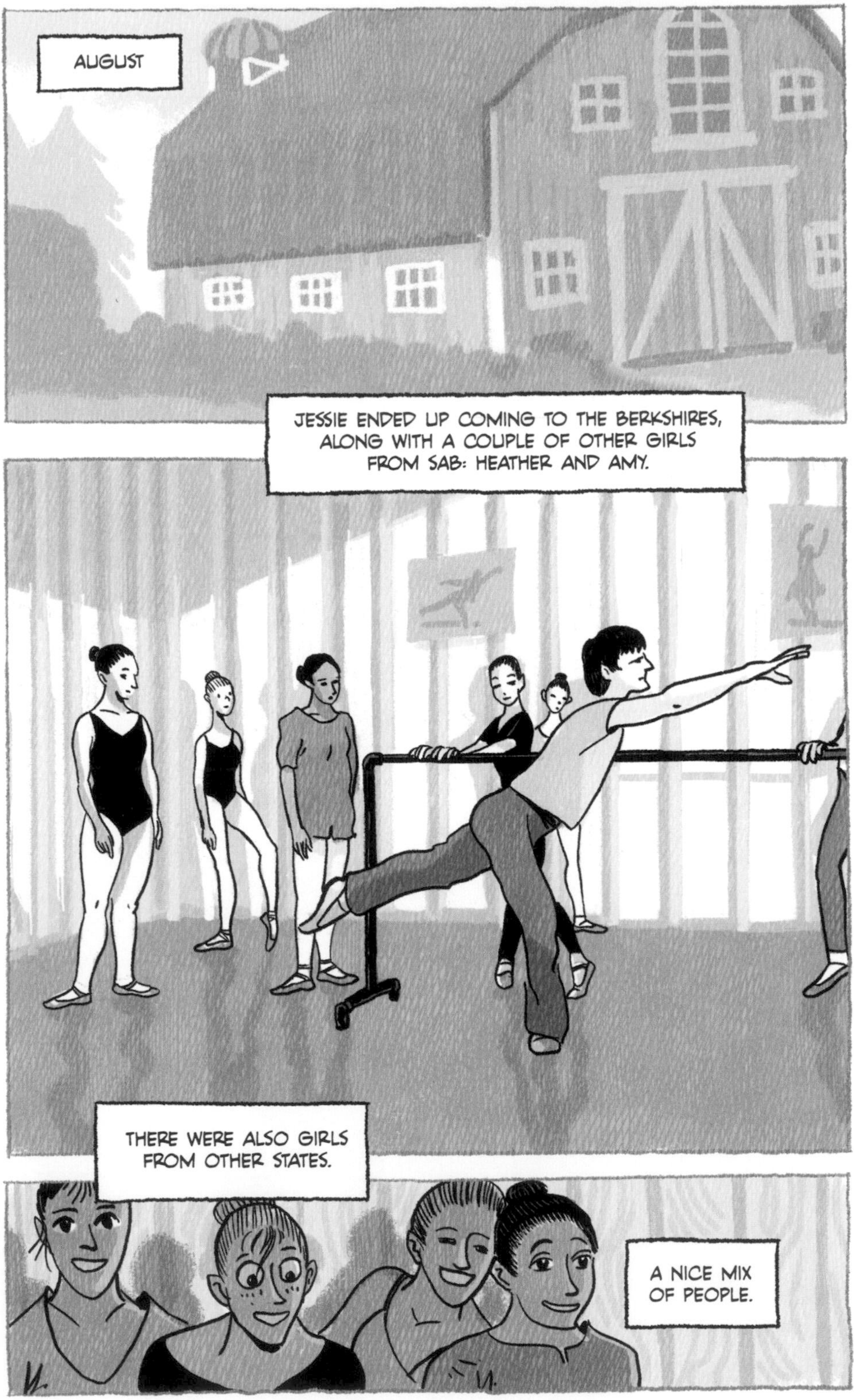
AUGUST
JESSIE ENDED UP COMING TO THE BERKSHIRES, ALONG WITH A COUPLE OF OTHER GIRLS FROM SAB: HEATHER AND AMY.
THERE WERE ALSO GIRLS FROM OTHER STATES.
A NICE MIX OF PEOPLE.

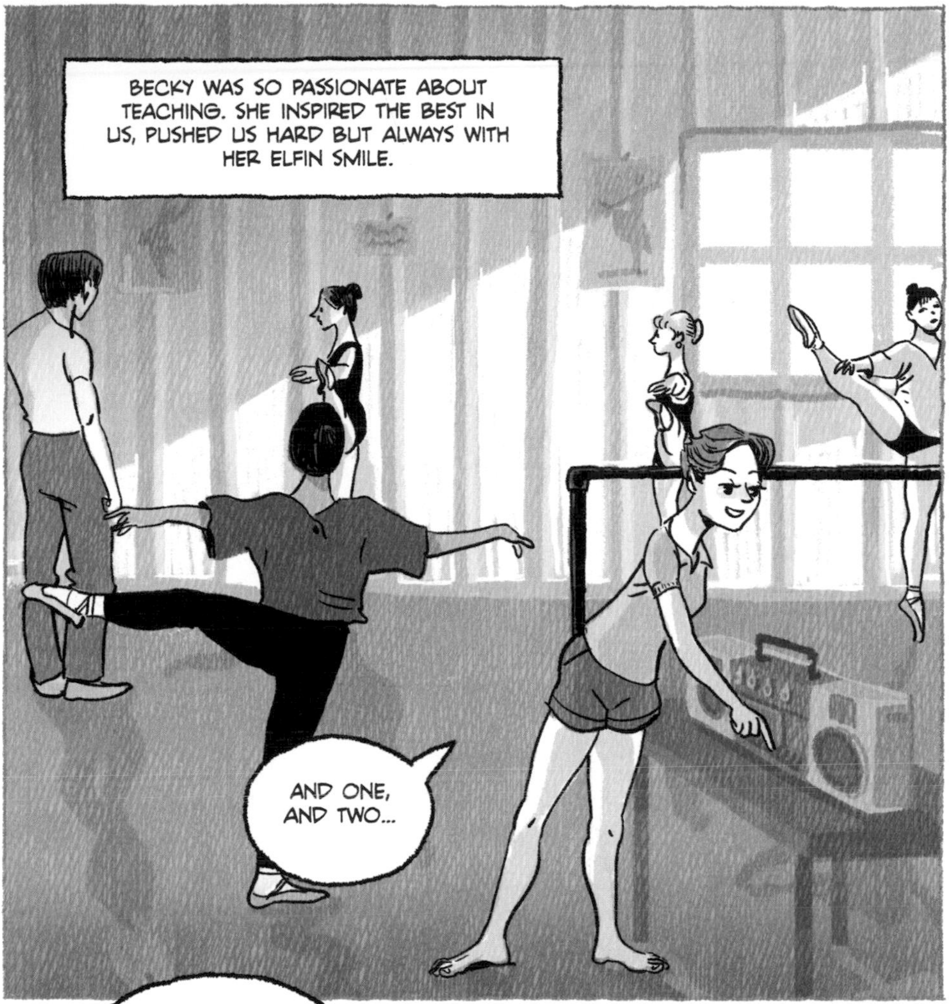
BECKY WAS SO PASSIONATE ABOUT TEACHING. SHE INSPIRED THE BEST IN US, PUSHED US HARD BUT ALWAYS WITH HER ELFIN SMILE.
AND ONE, AND TWO...

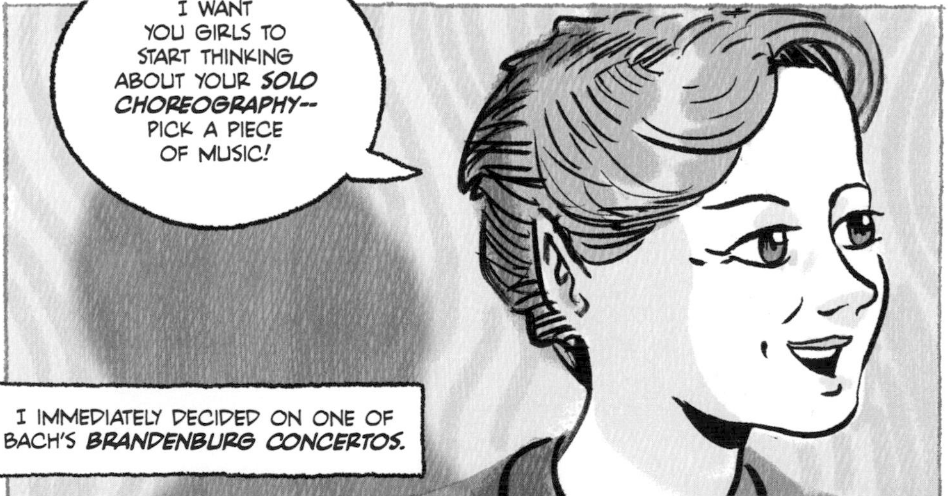
I WANT YOU GIRLS TO START THINKING ABOUT YOUR *SOLO CHOREOGRAPHY*-- PICK A PIECE OF MUSIC!
I IMMEDIATELY DECIDED ON ONE OF BACH'S *BRANDENBURG CONCERTOS.*

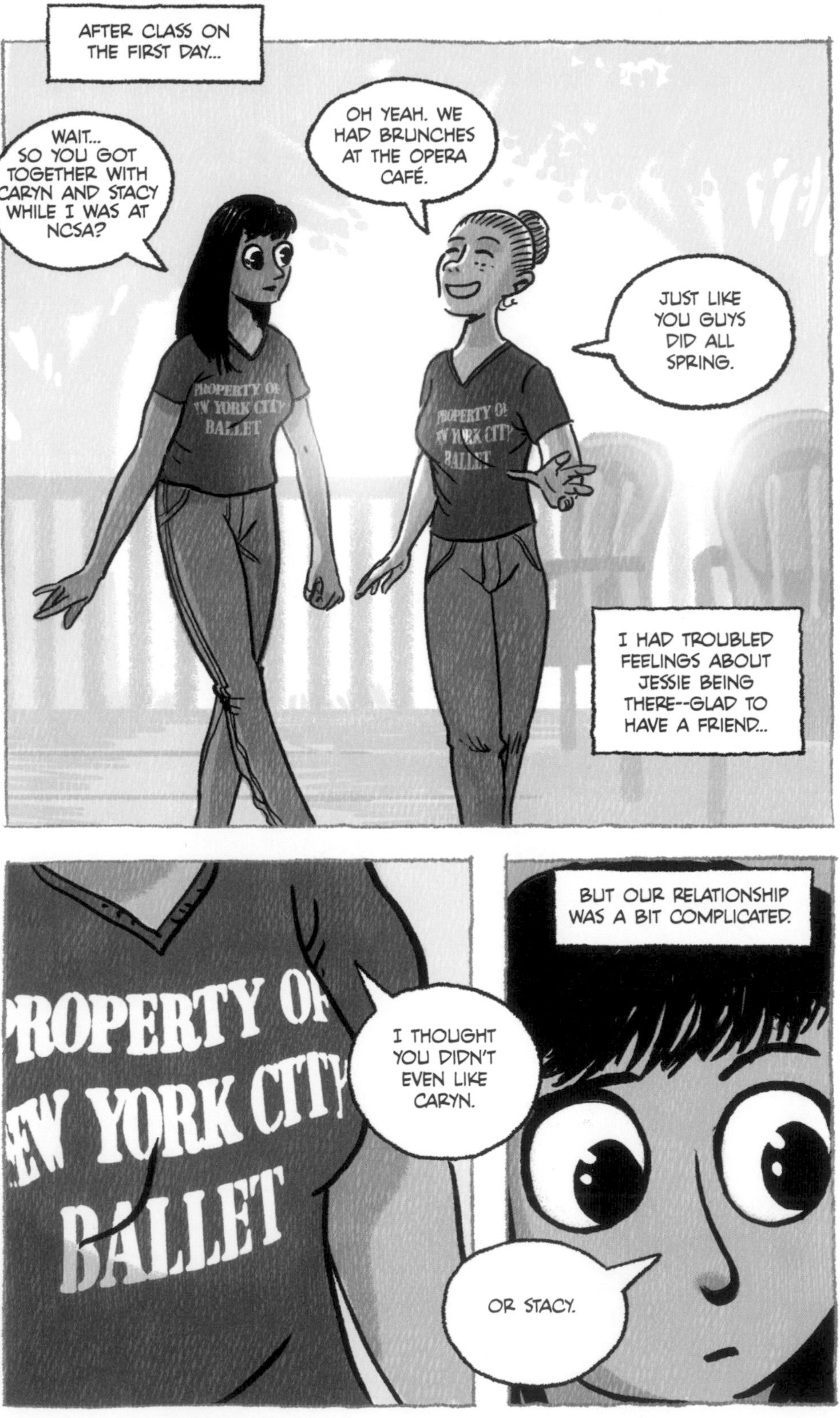

AFTER CLASS ON THE FIRST DAY...
WAIT... SO YOU GOT TOGETHER WITH CARYN AND STACY WHILE I WAS AT NCSA?
OH YEAH. WE HAD BRUNCHES AT THE OPERA CAFÉ.
JUST LIKE YOU GUYS DID ALL SPRING.
PROPERTY OF NEW YORK CITY BALLET
I HAD TROUBLED FEELINGS ABOUT JESSIE BEING THERE--GLAD TO HAVE A FRIEND...
BUT OUR RELATIONSHIP WAS A BIT COMPLICATED.
I THOUGHT YOU DIDN'T EVEN LIKE CARYN.
OR STACY.

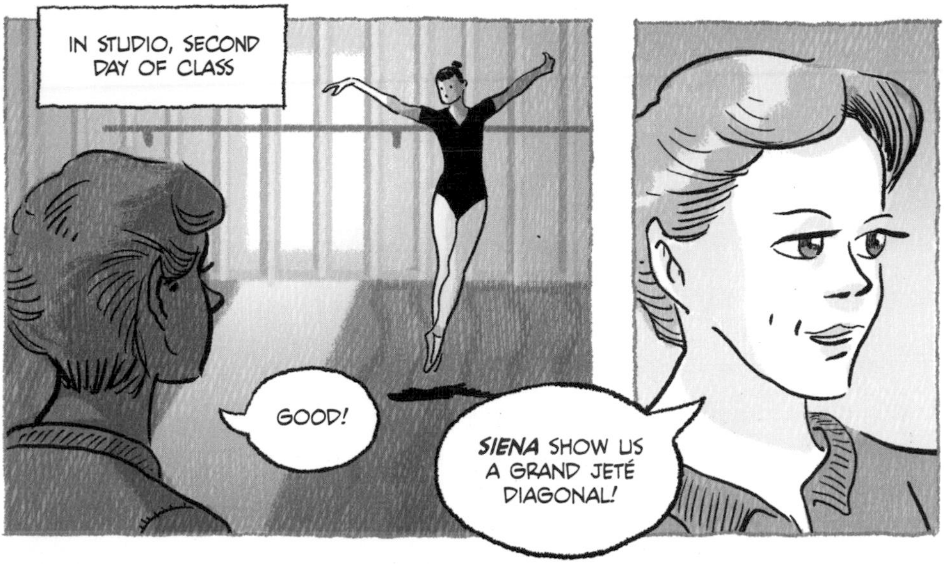
IN STUDIO, SECOND DAY OF CLASS
GOOD!
SIENA SHOW US A GRAND JETÉ DIAGONAL!

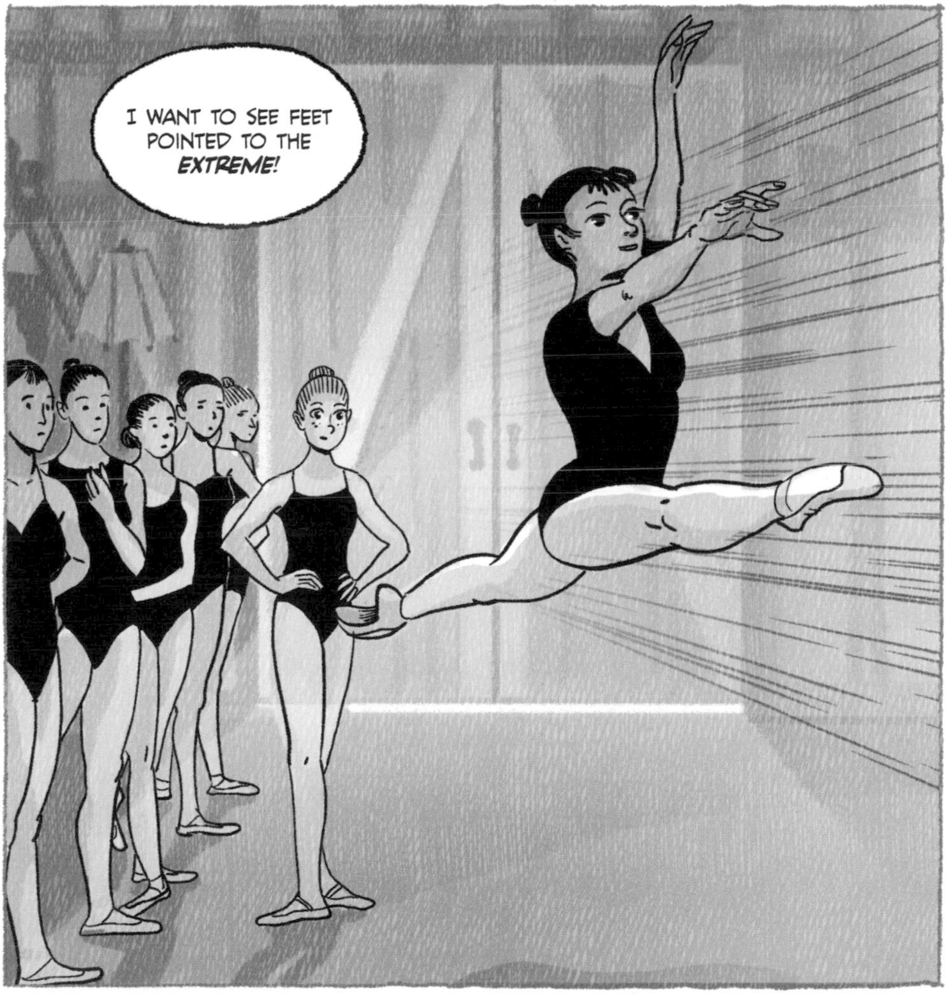
I WANT TO SEE FEET POINTED TO THE EXTREME!

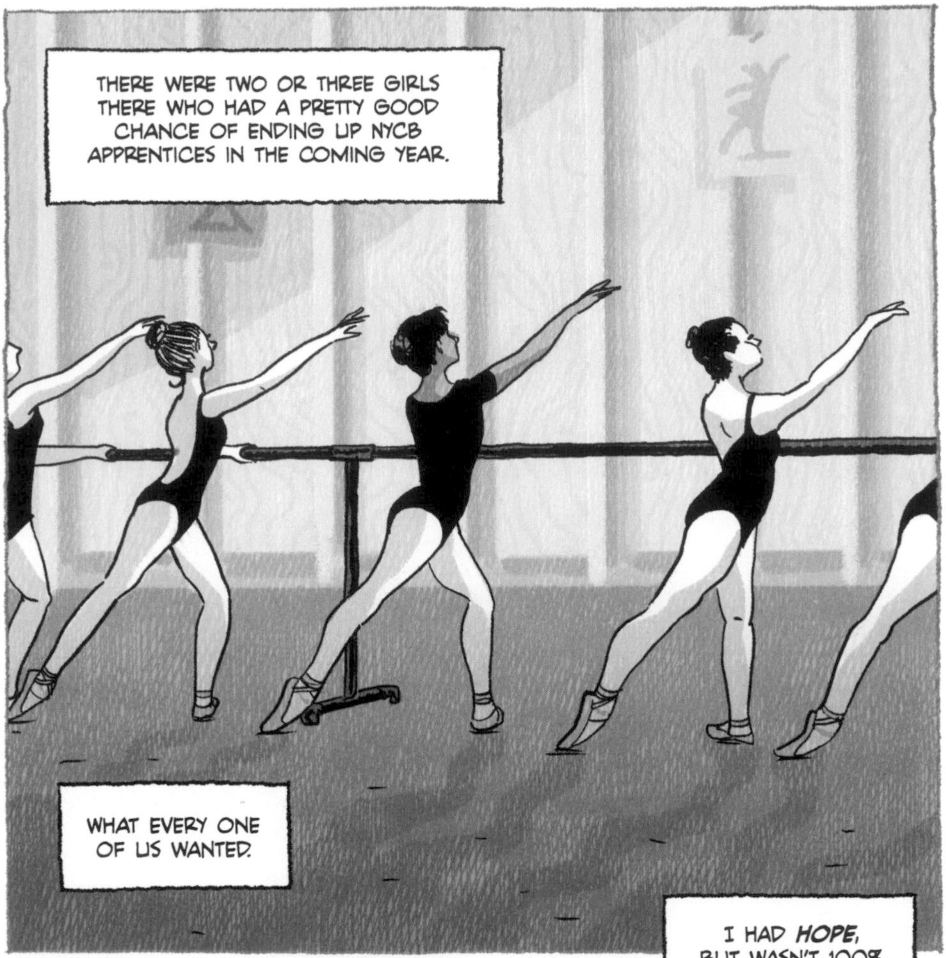
THERE WERE TWO OR THREE GIRLS THERE WHO HAD A PRETTY GOOD CHANCE OF ENDING UP NYCB APPRENTICES IN THE COMING YEAR.
WHAT EVERY ONE OF US WANTED.

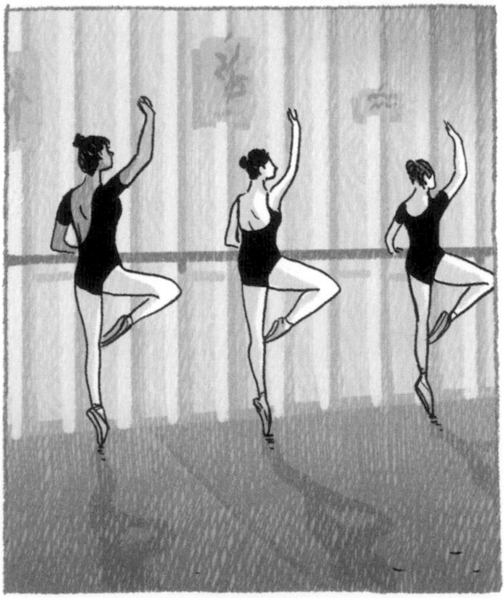

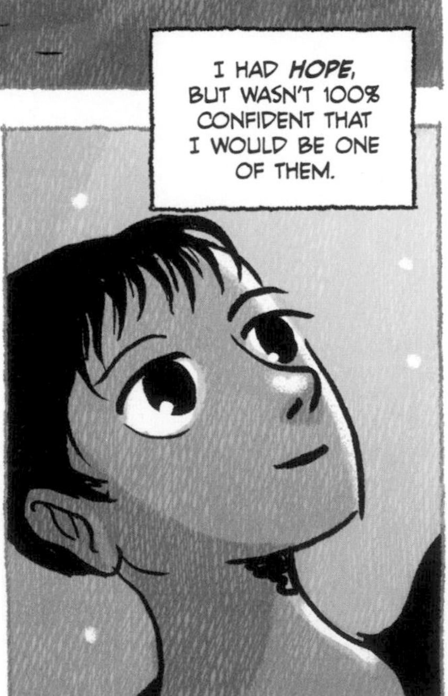
I HAD ***HOPE***, BUT WASN'T 100% CONFIDENT THAT I WOULD BE ONE OF THEM.

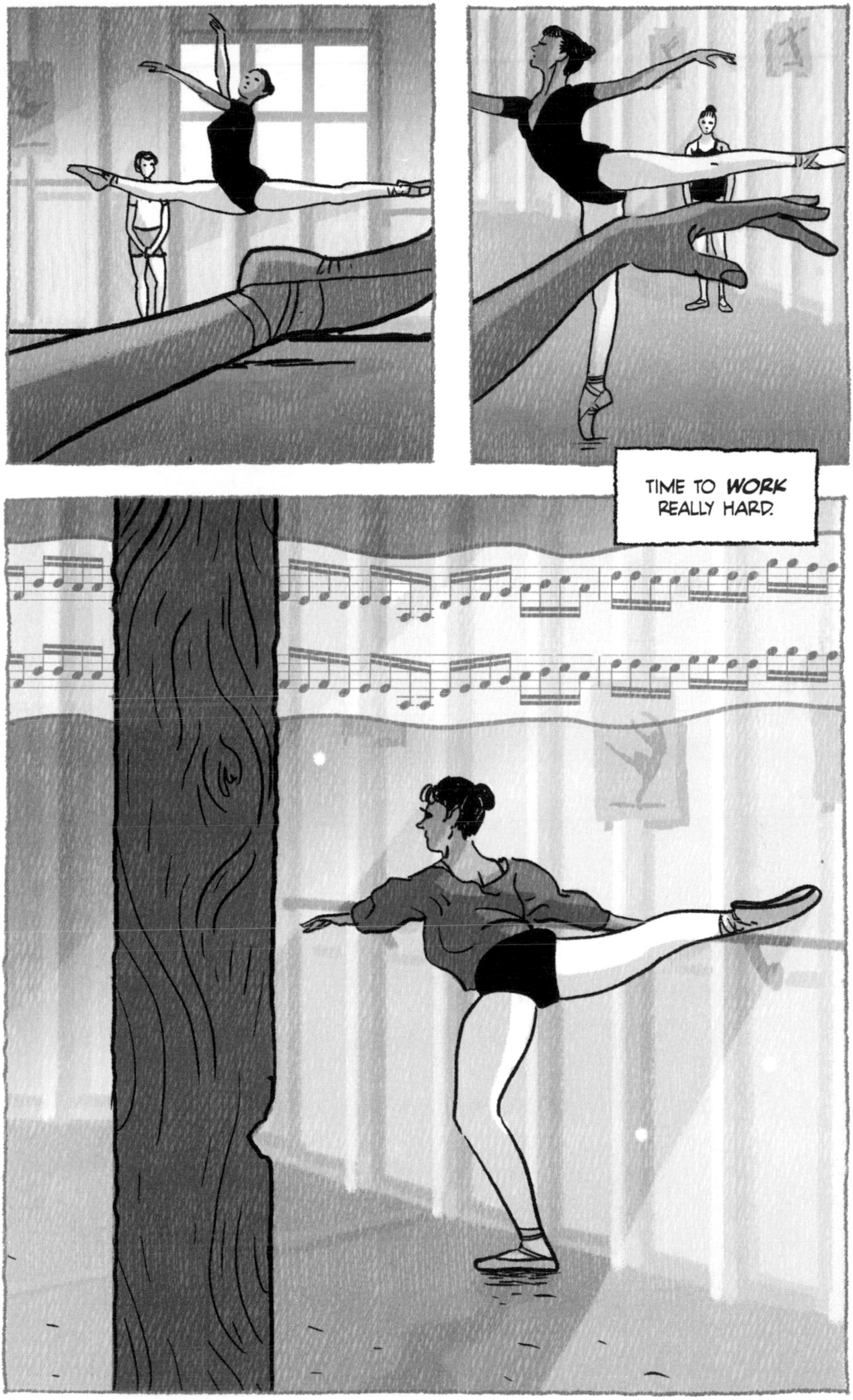
TIME TO WORK REALLY HARD.

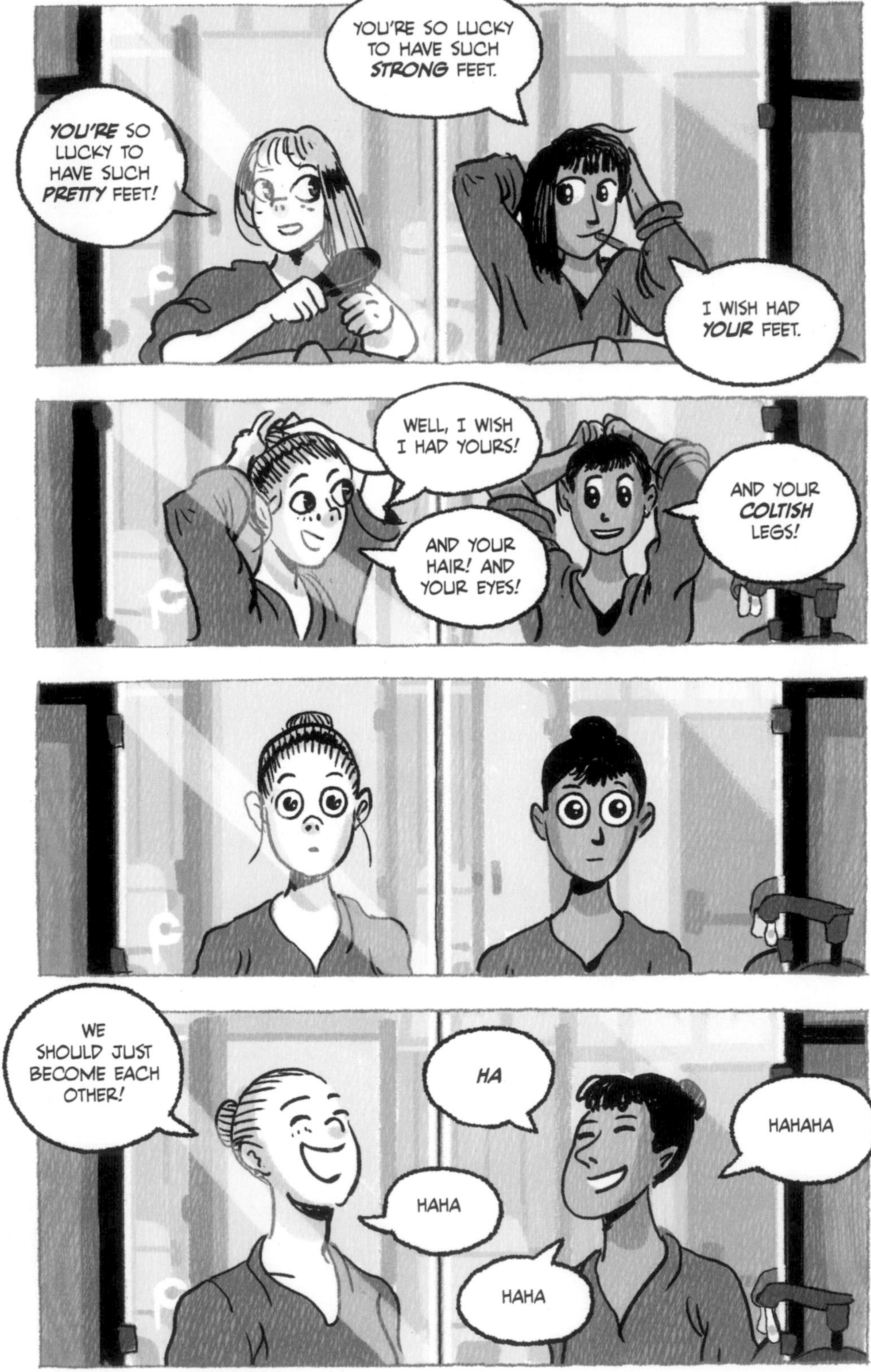
YOU'RE SO LUCKY TO HAVE SUCH PRETTY FEET!
YOU'RE SO LUCKY TO HAVE SUCH STRONG FEET.
I WISH HAD YOUR FEET.
WELL, I WISH I HAD YOURS!
AND YOUR HAIR! AND YOUR EYES!
AND YOUR COLTISH LEGS!
WE SHOULD JUST BECOME EACH OTHER!
HA
HAHA
HAHA
HAHAHA

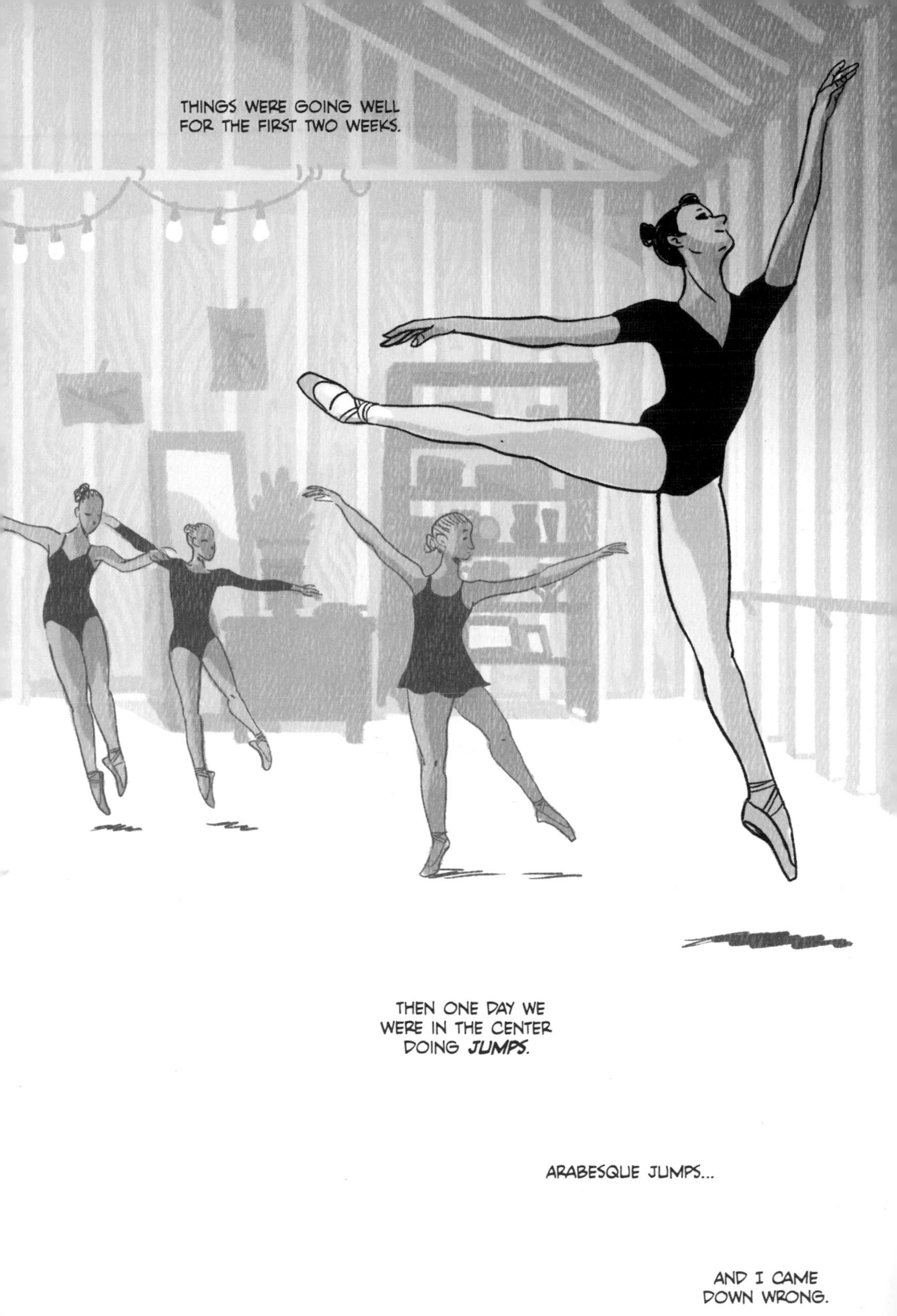
THINGS WERE GOING WELL FOR THE FIRST TWO WEEKS.
THEN ONE DAY WE WERE IN THE CENTER DOING *JUMPS*.
ARABESQUE JUMPS...
AND I CAME DOWN WRONG.

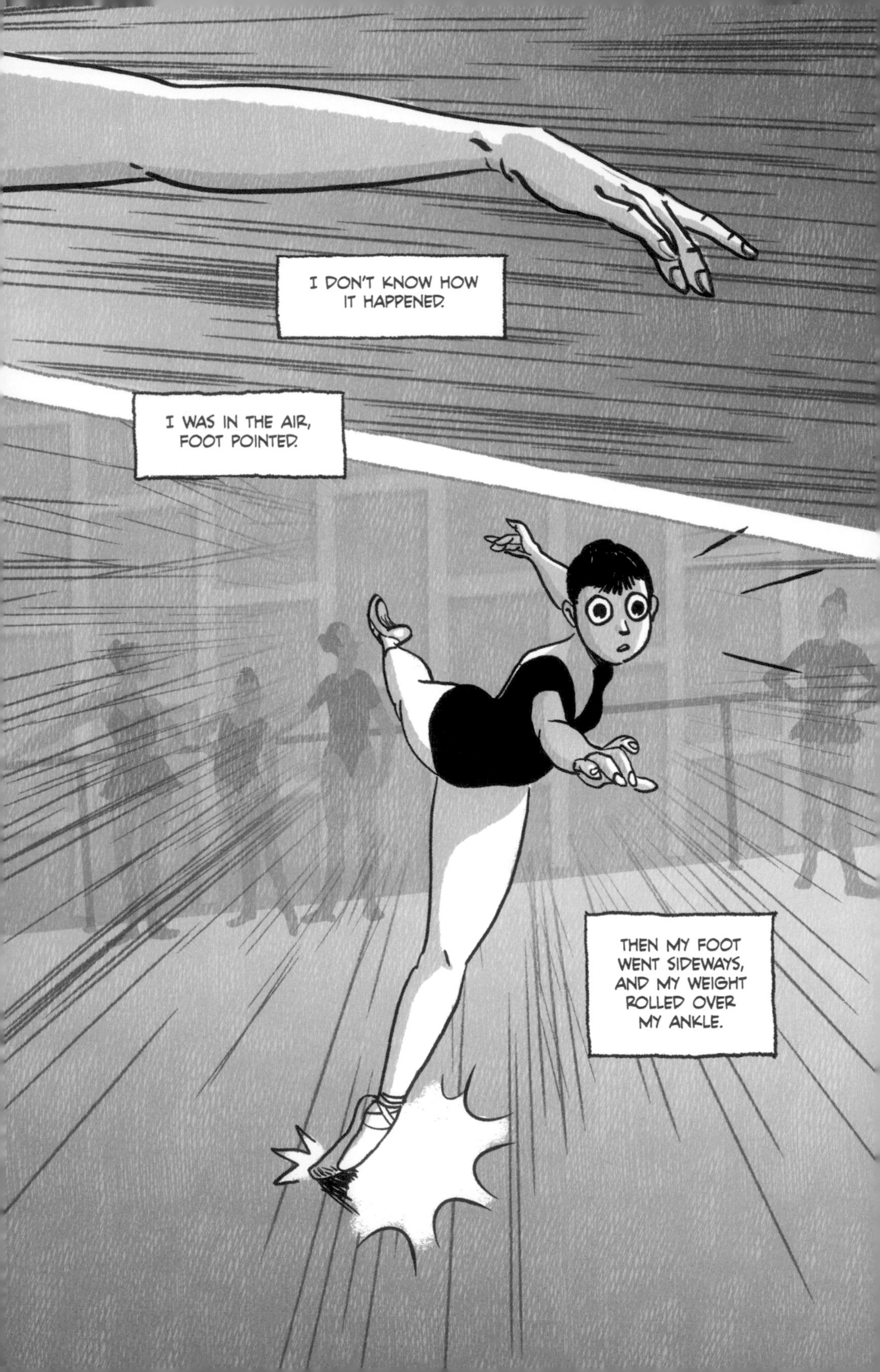
I DON'T KNOW HOW IT HAPPENED.
I WAS IN THE AIR, FOOT POINTED.
THEN MY FOOT WENT SIDEWAYS, AND MY WEIGHT ROLLED OVER MY ANKLE.

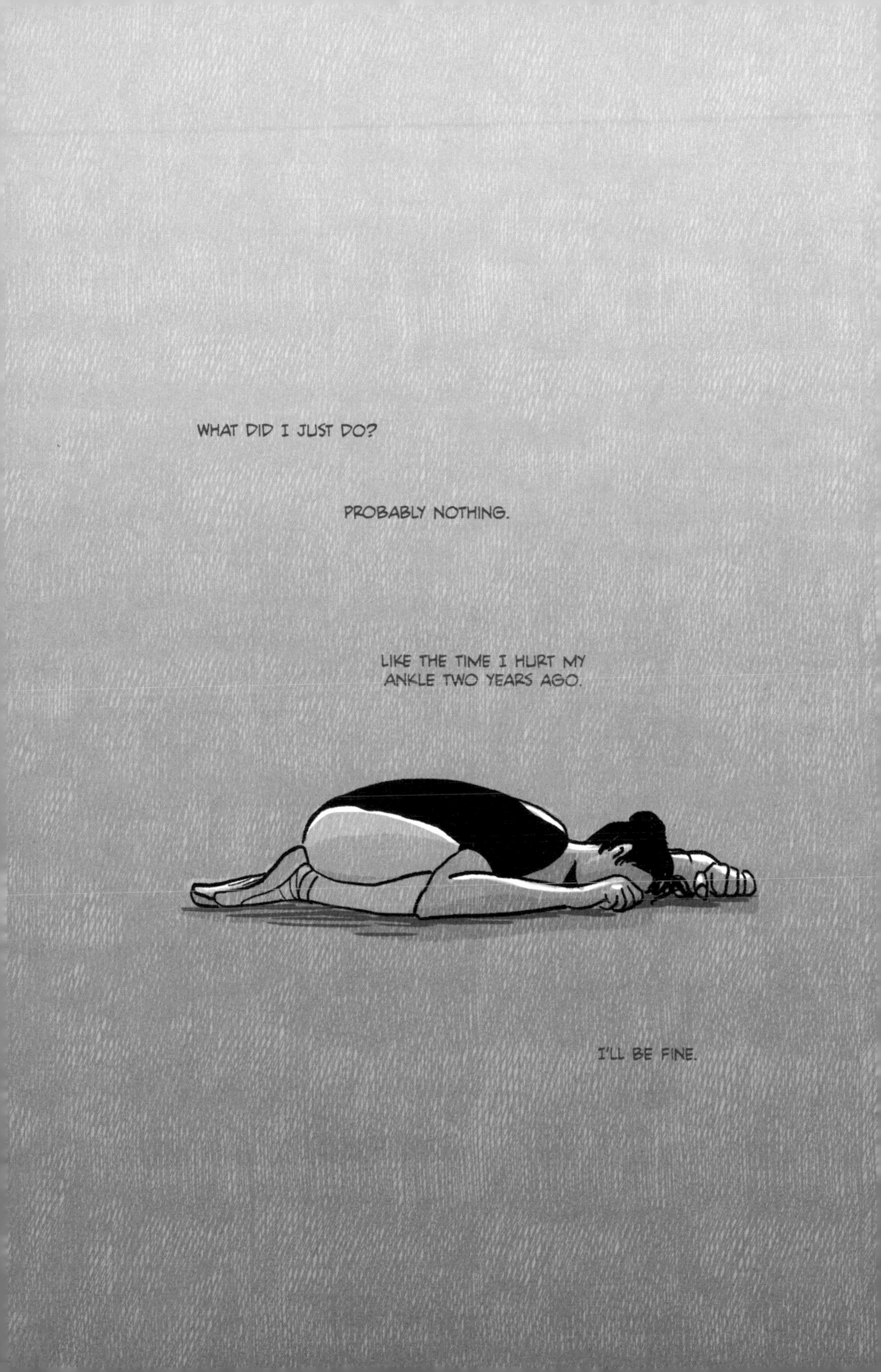

WHAT DID I JUST DO?

PROBABLY NOTHING.

LIKE THE TIME I HURT MY
ANKLE TWO YEARS AGO.

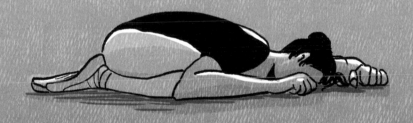

I'LL BE FINE.

IT'S SWELLING UP.

I'M SCARED IT
MIGHT BE BAD.

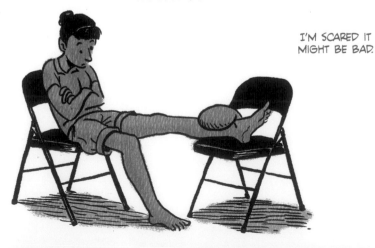

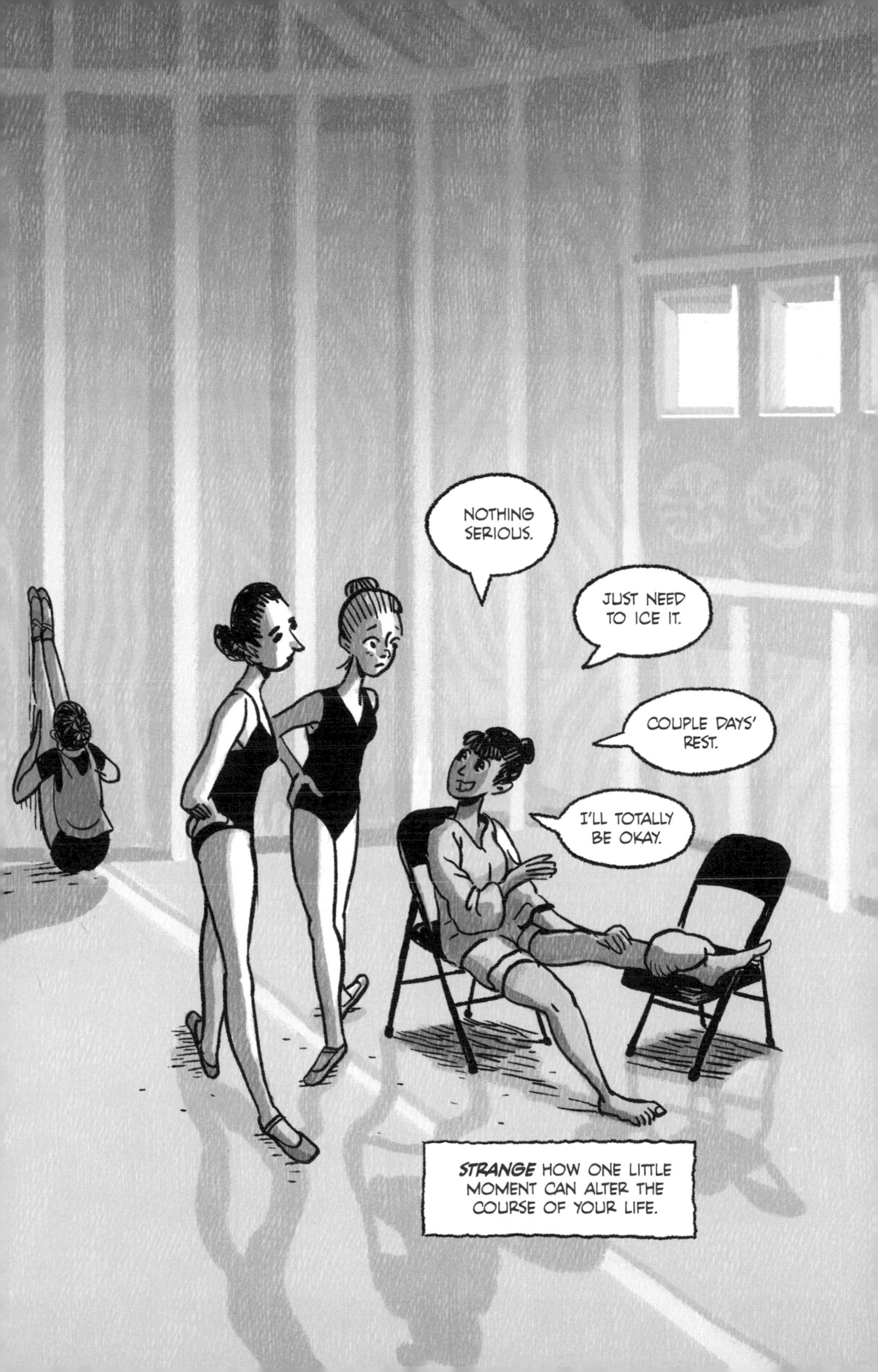
NOTHING SERIOUS.
JUST NEED TO ICE IT.
COUPLE DAYS' REST.
I'LL TOTALLY BE OKAY.
STRANGE HOW ONE LITTLE MOMENT CAN ALTER THE COURSE OF YOUR LIFE.

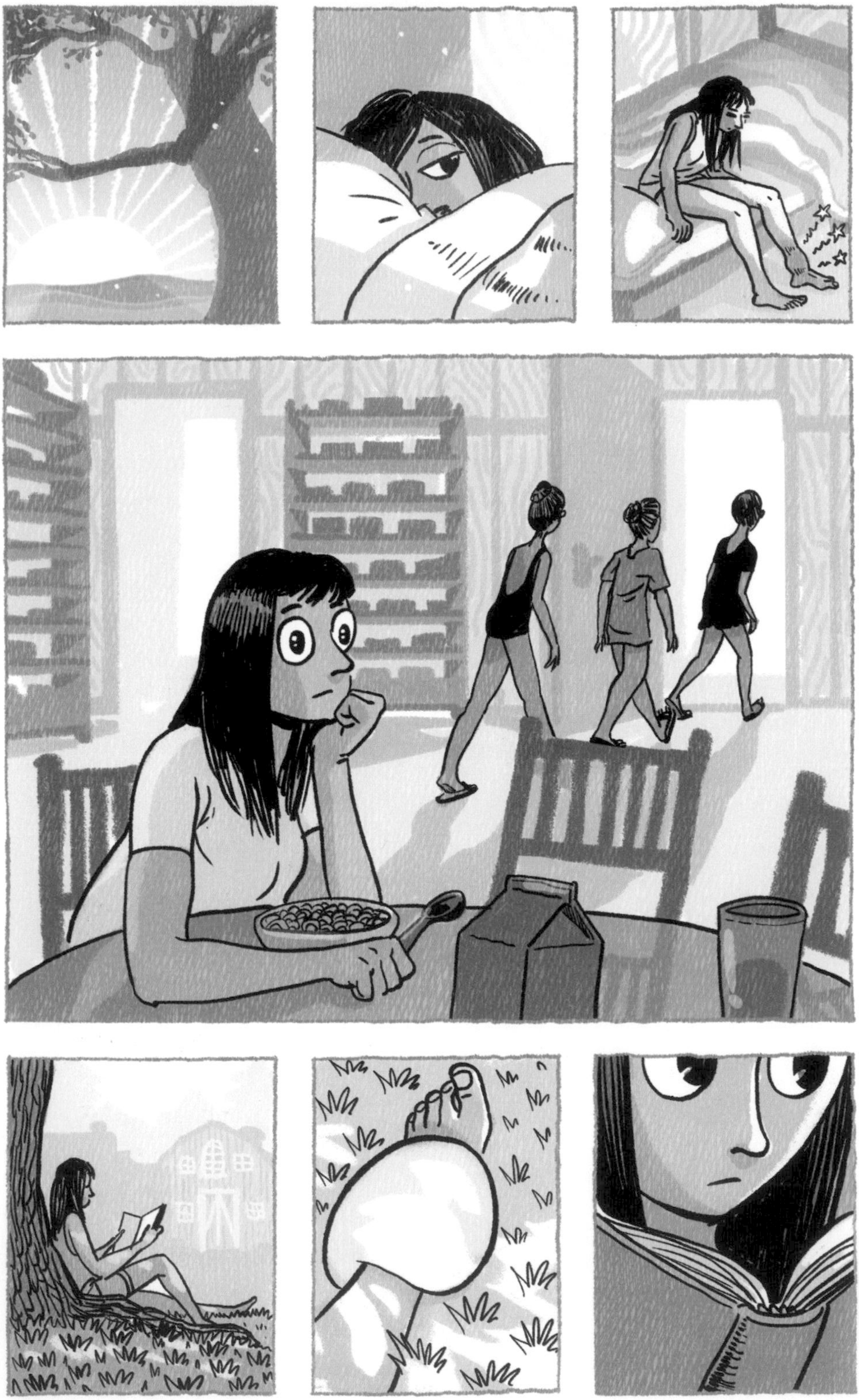

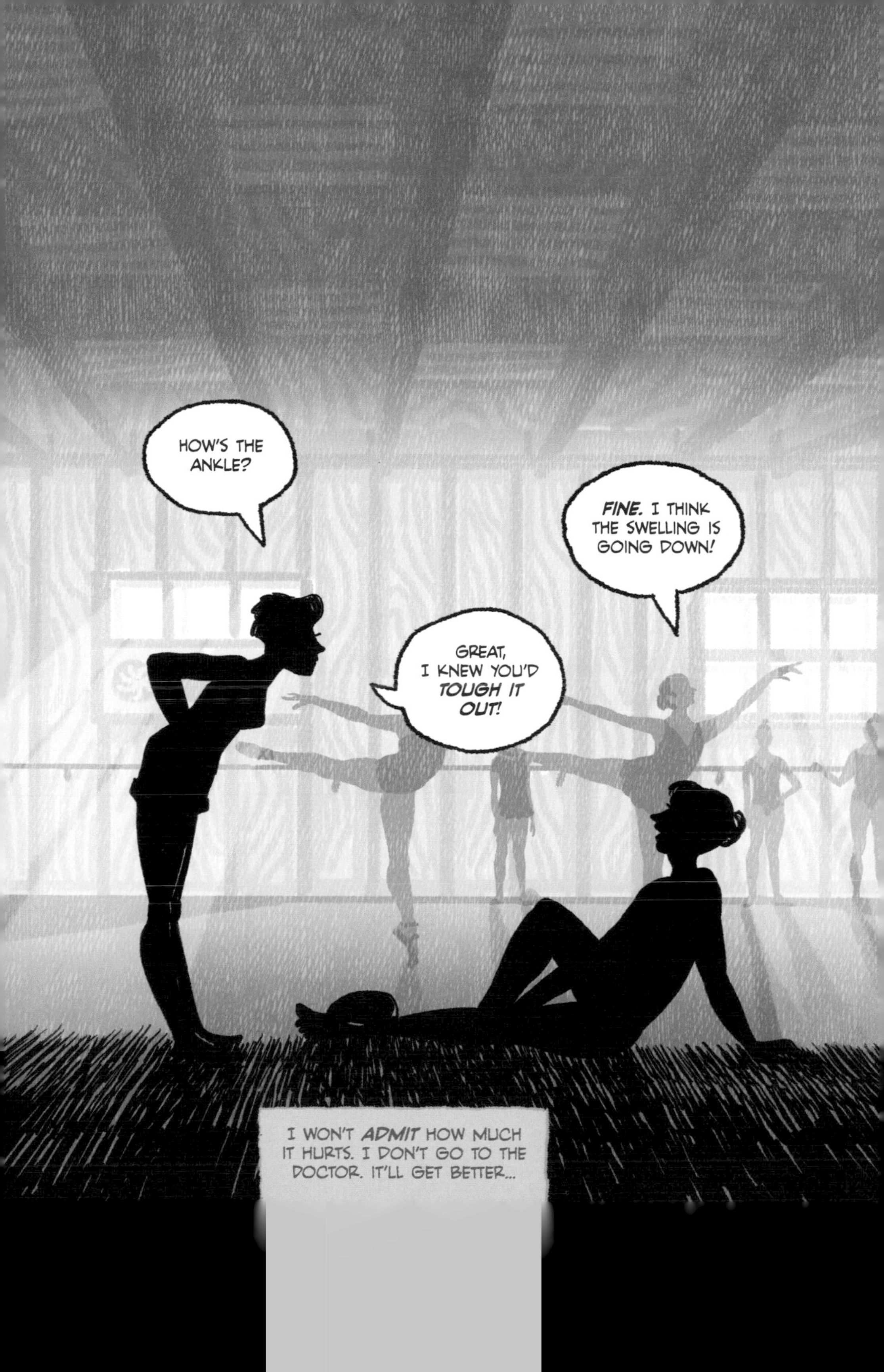
HOW'S THE ANKLE?
FINE. I THINK THE SWELLING IS GOING DOWN!
GREAT, I KNEW YOU'D TOUGH IT OUT!
I WON'T ADMIT HOW MUCH IT HURTS. I DON'T GO TO THE DOCTOR. IT'LL GET BETTER...

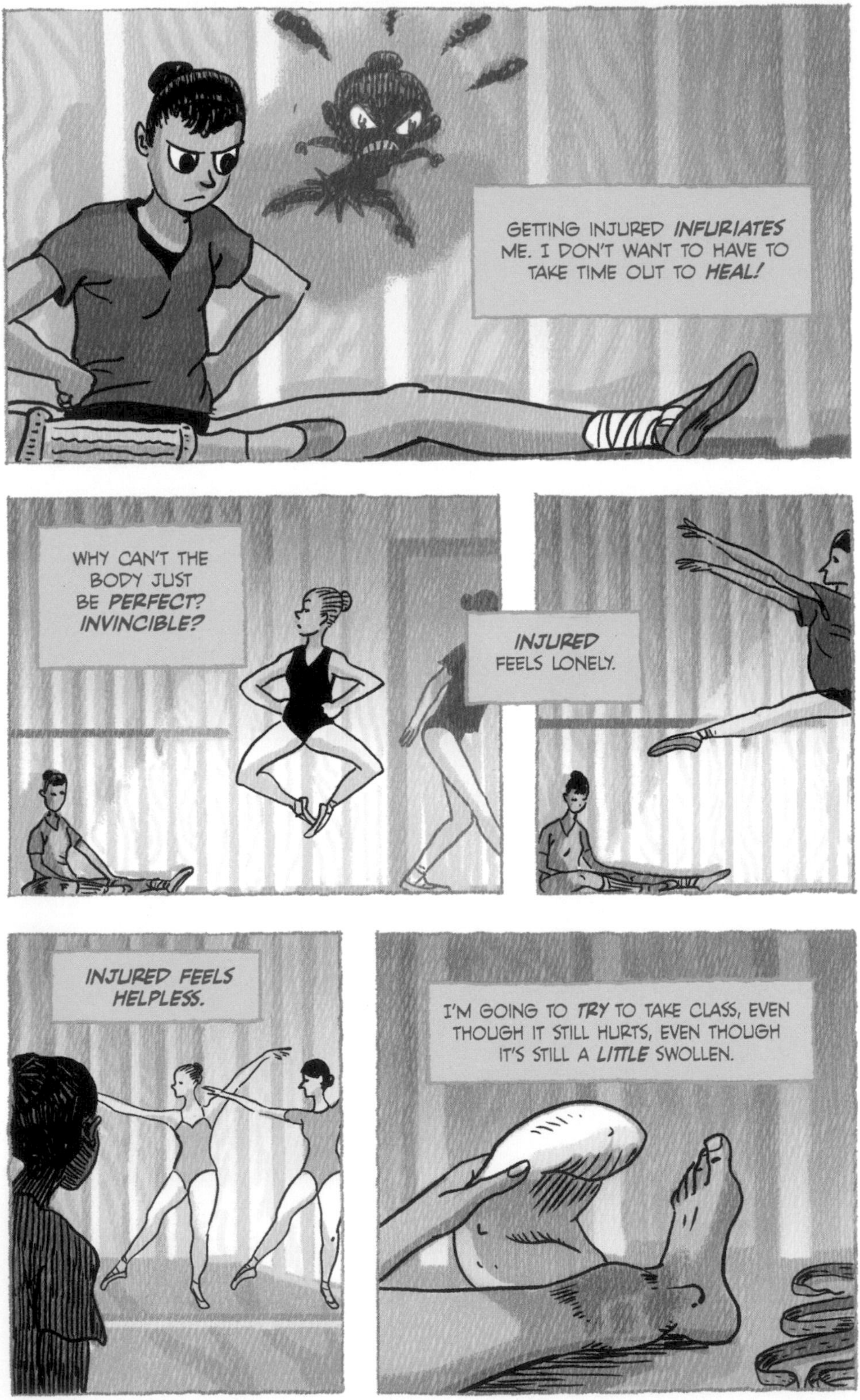
GETTING INJURED *INFURIATES* ME. I DON'T WANT TO HAVE TO TAKE TIME OUT TO *HEAL!*
WHY CAN'T THE BODY JUST BE *PERFECT? INVINCIBLE?*
INJURED FEELS LONELY.
INJURED FEELS HELPLESS.
I'M GOING TO *TRY* TO TAKE CLASS, EVEN THOUGH IT STILL HURTS, EVEN THOUGH IT'S STILL A *LITTLE* SWOLLEN.

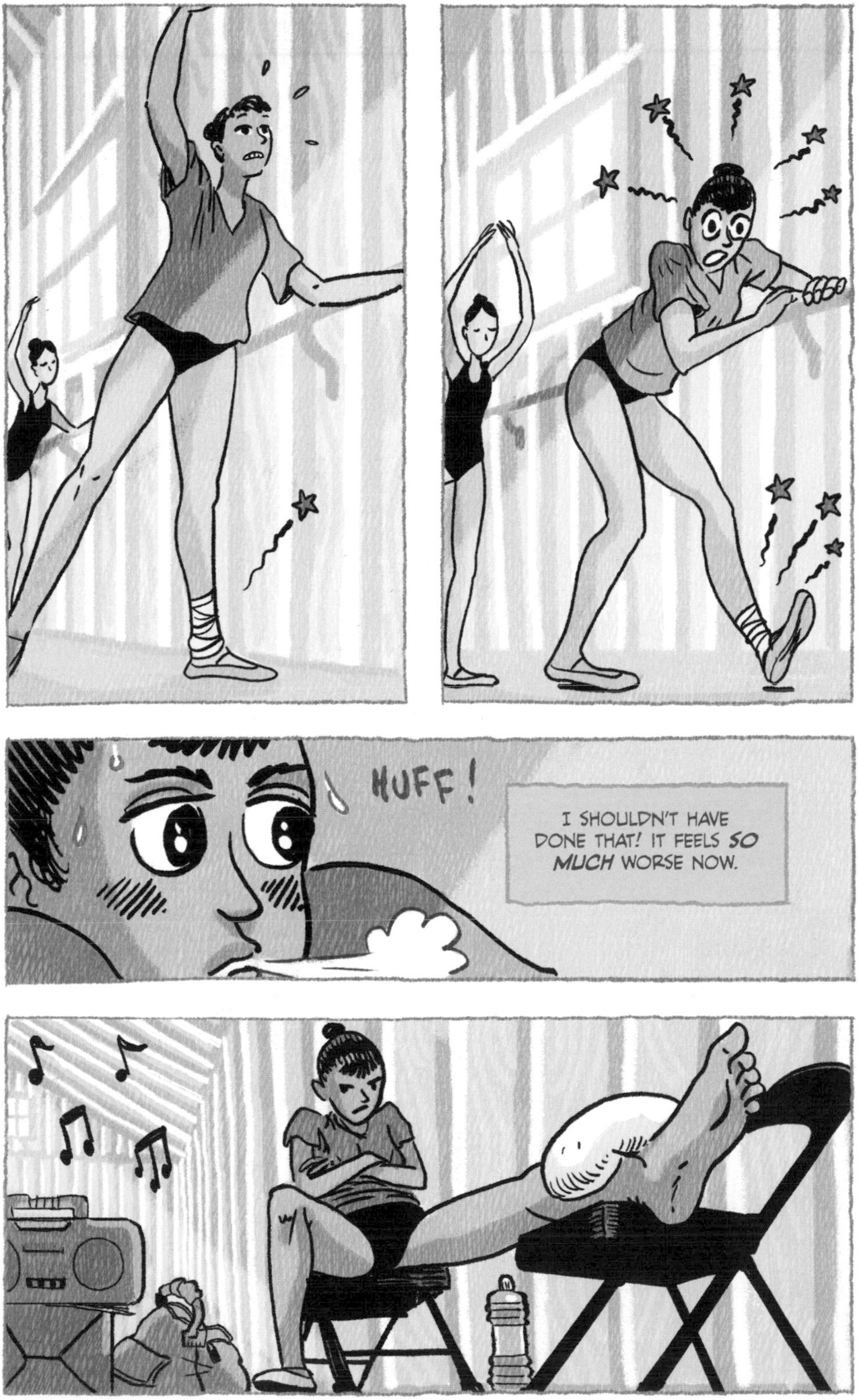
HUFF!
I SHOULDN'T HAVE DONE THAT! IT FEELS SO MUCH WORSE NOW.

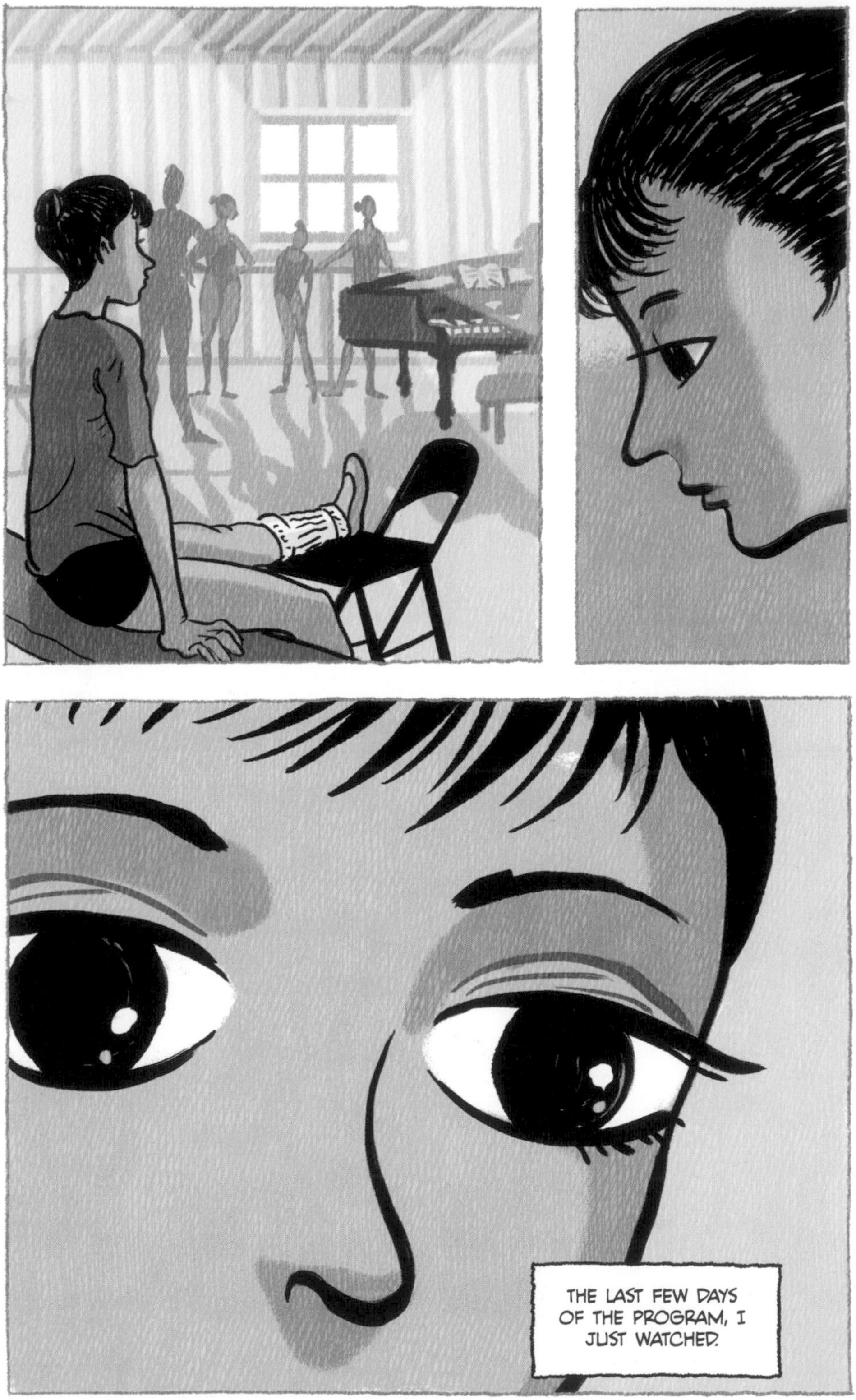
THE LAST FEW DAYS OF THE PROGRAM, I JUST WATCHED.

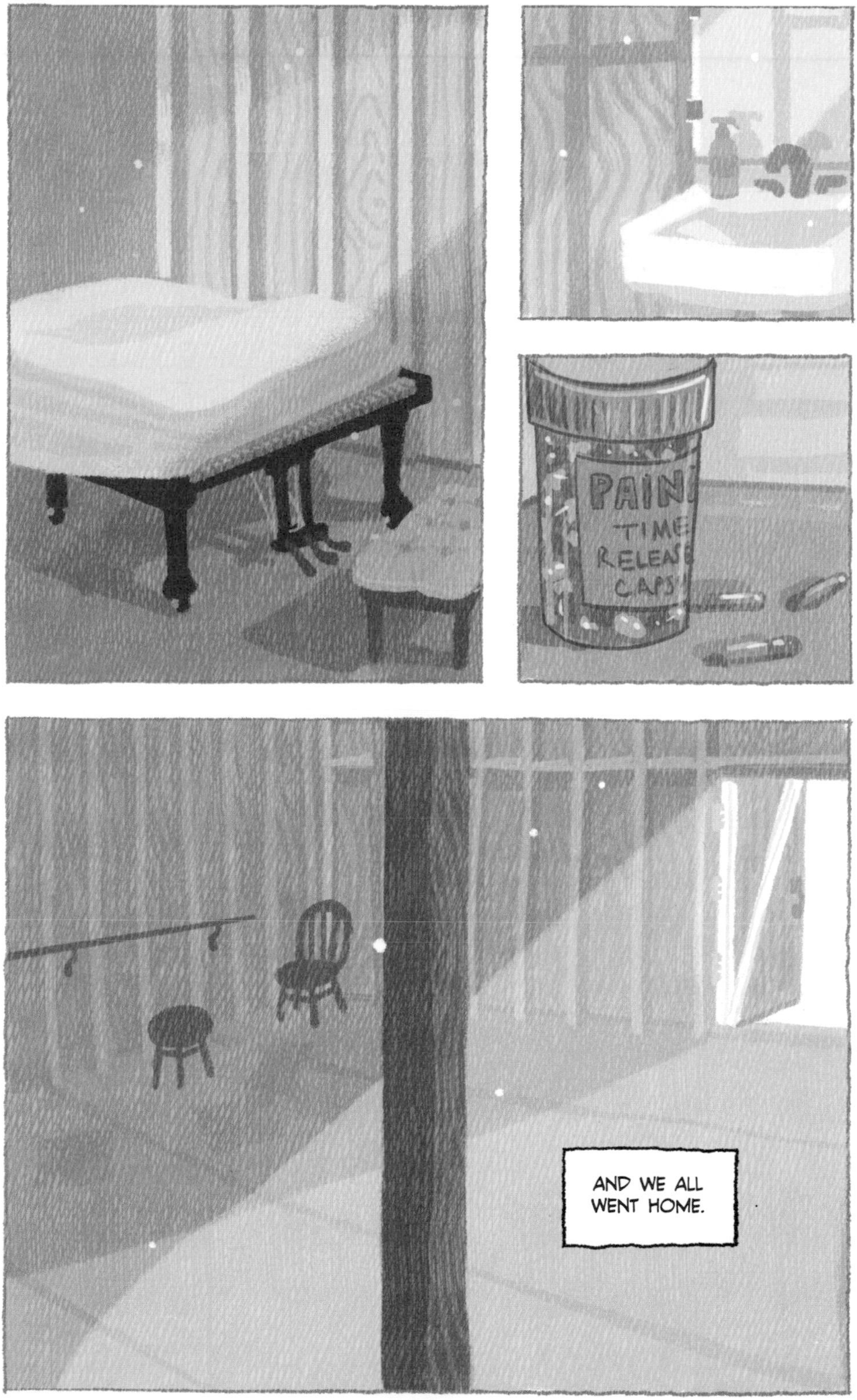
PAIN
TIME
RELEAS
CAPS
AND WE ALL WENT HOME.

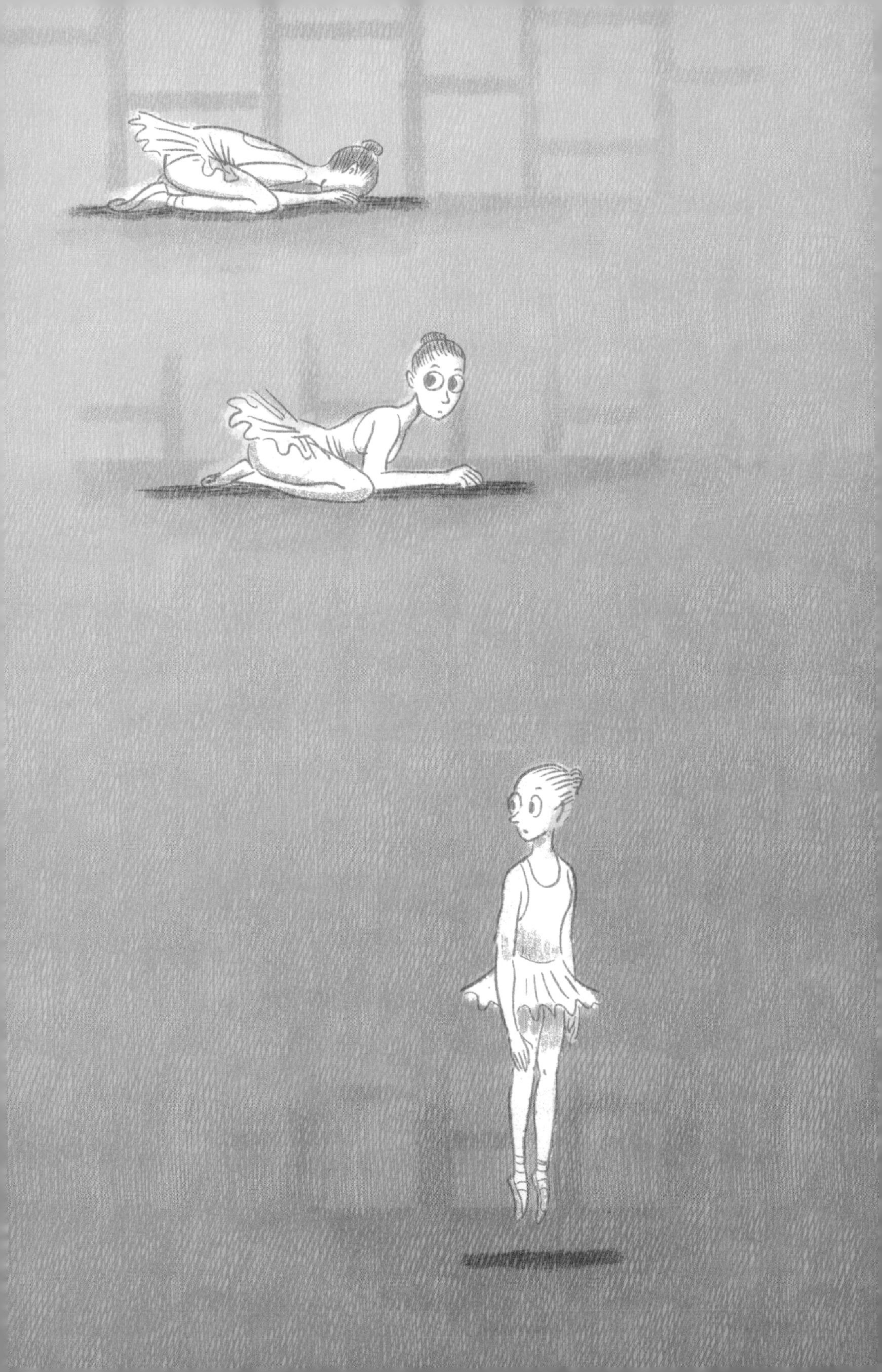

Part 2

The Narrowing Road

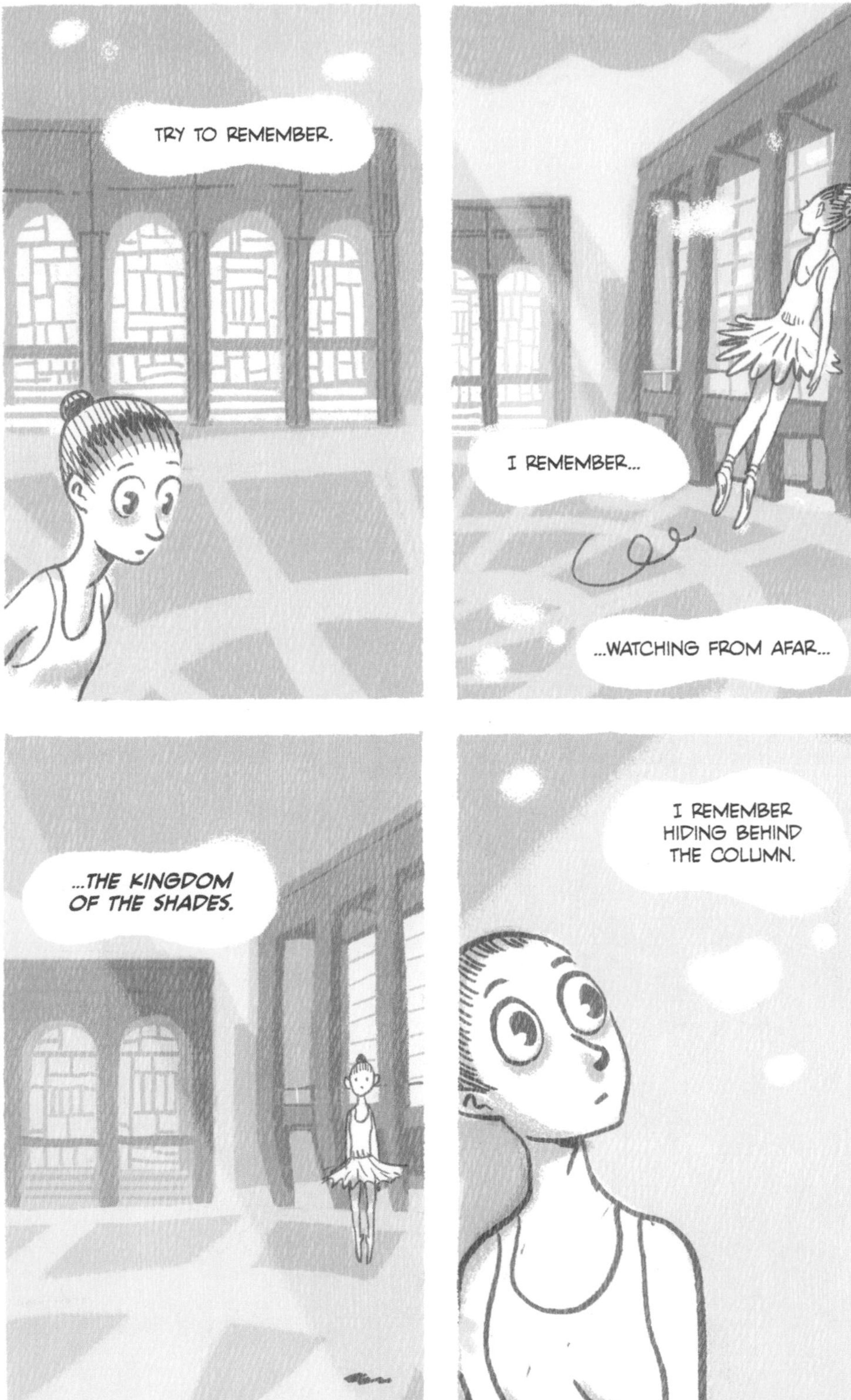
TRY TO REMEMBER.
I REMEMBER...
...WATCHING FROM AFAR...
...THE KINGDOM OF THE SHADES.
I REMEMBER HIDING BEHIND THE COLUMN.

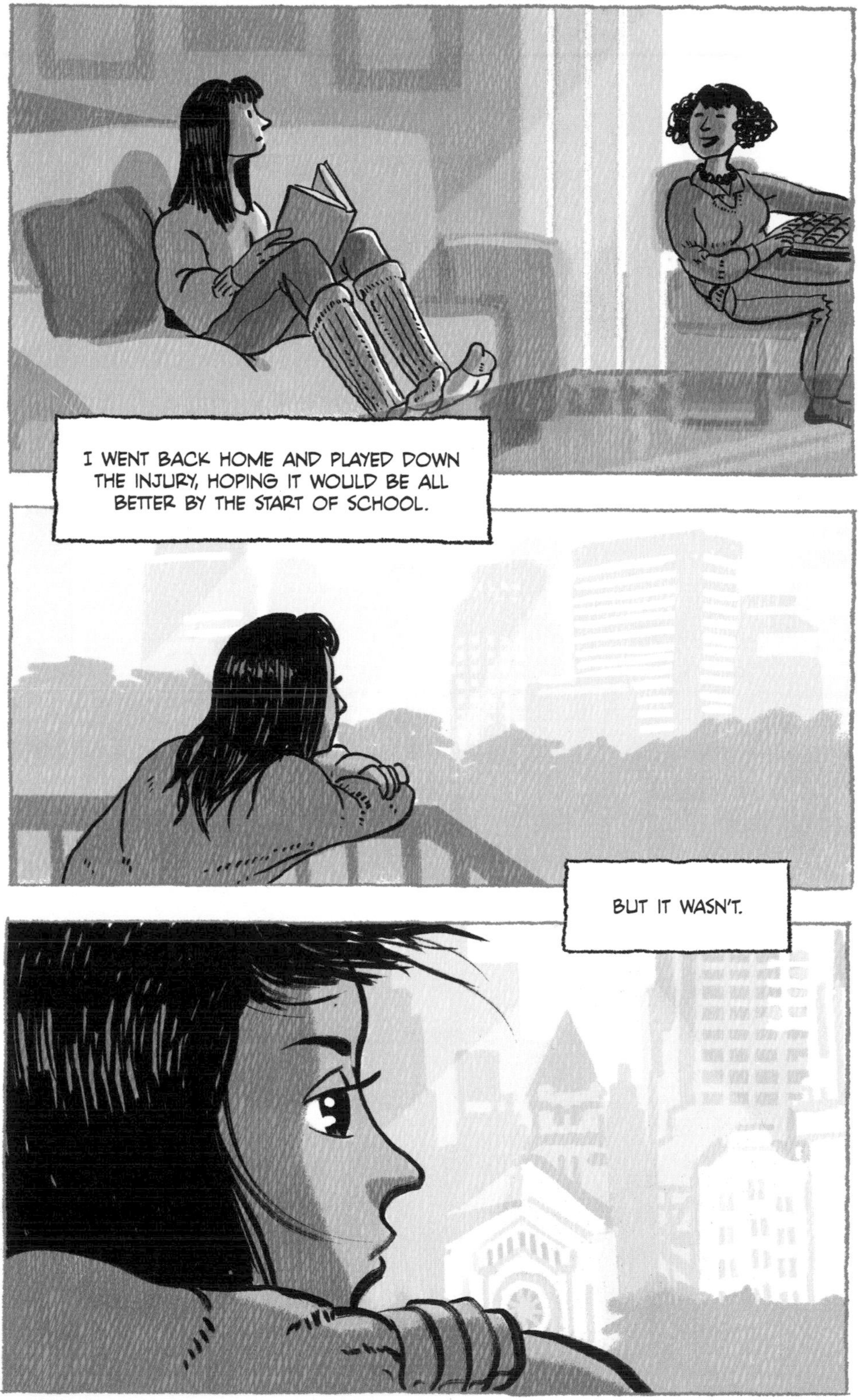
I WENT BACK HOME AND PLAYED DOWN THE INJURY, HOPING IT WOULD BE ALL BETTER BY THE START OF SCHOOL.
BUT IT WASN'T.

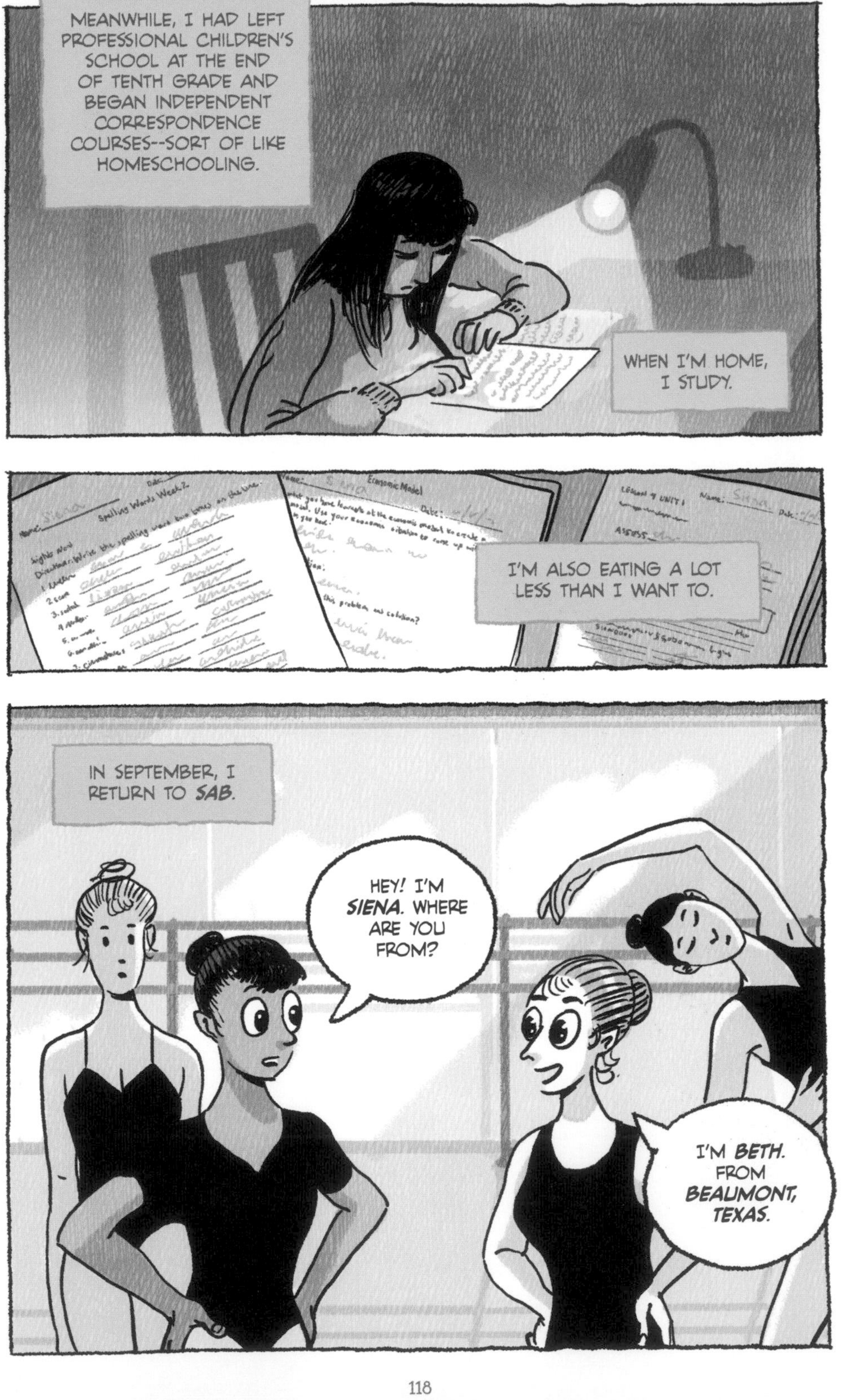
MEANWHILE, I HAD LEFT PROFESSIONAL CHILDREN'S SCHOOL AT THE END OF TENTH GRADE AND BEGAN INDEPENDENT CORRESPONDENCE COURSES--SORT OF LIKE HOMESCHOOLING.
WHEN I'M HOME, I STUDY.
I'M ALSO EATING A LOT LESS THAN I WANT TO.
IN SEPTEMBER, I RETURN TO *SAB*.
HEY! I'M *SIENA*. WHERE ARE YOU FROM?
I'M *BETH*. FROM *BEAUMONT, TEXAS*.

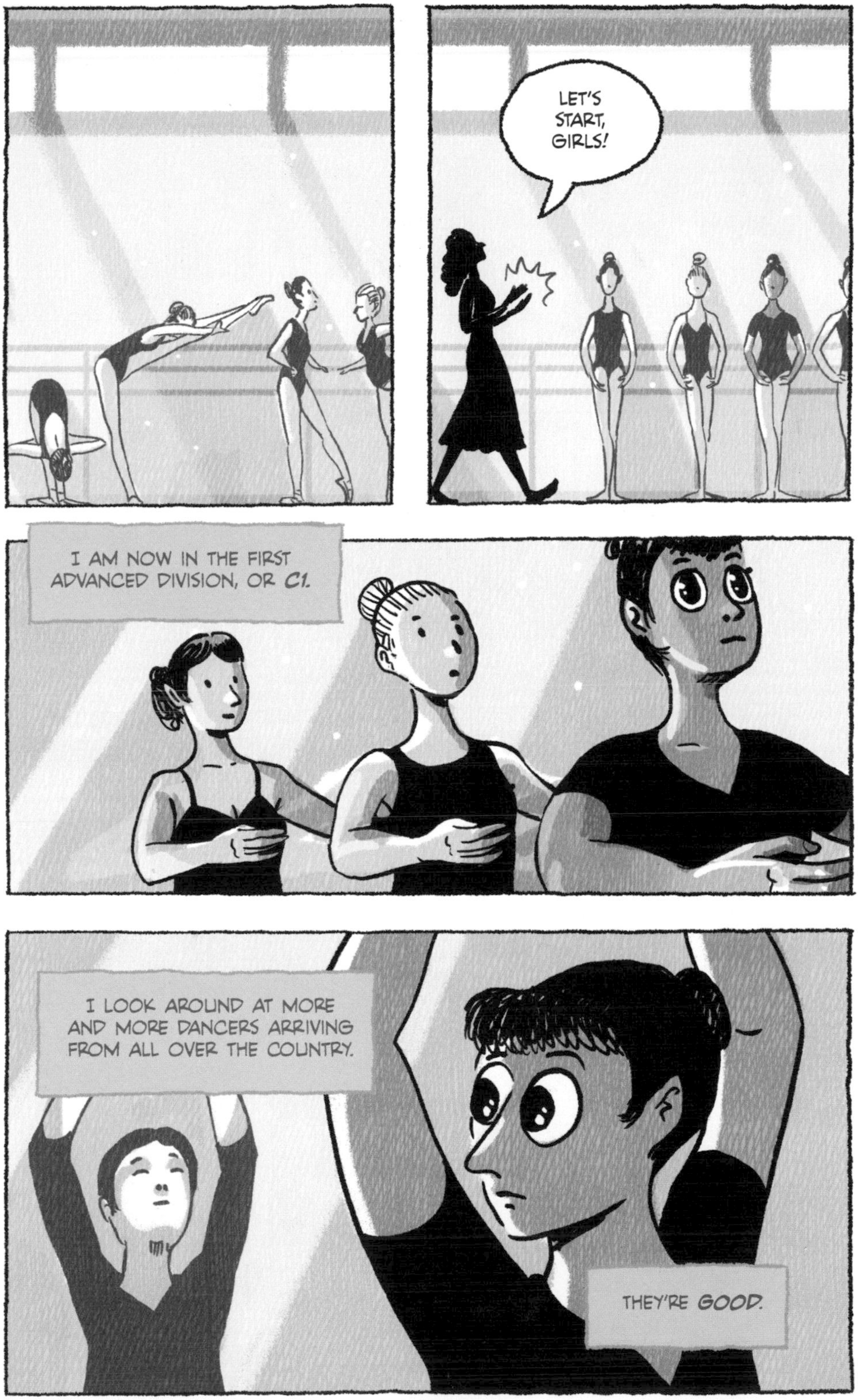
LET'S START, GIRLS!
I AM NOW IN THE FIRST ADVANCED DIVISION, OR C1.
I LOOK AROUND AT MORE AND MORE DANCERS ARRIVING FROM ALL OVER THE COUNTRY.
THEY'RE GOOD.

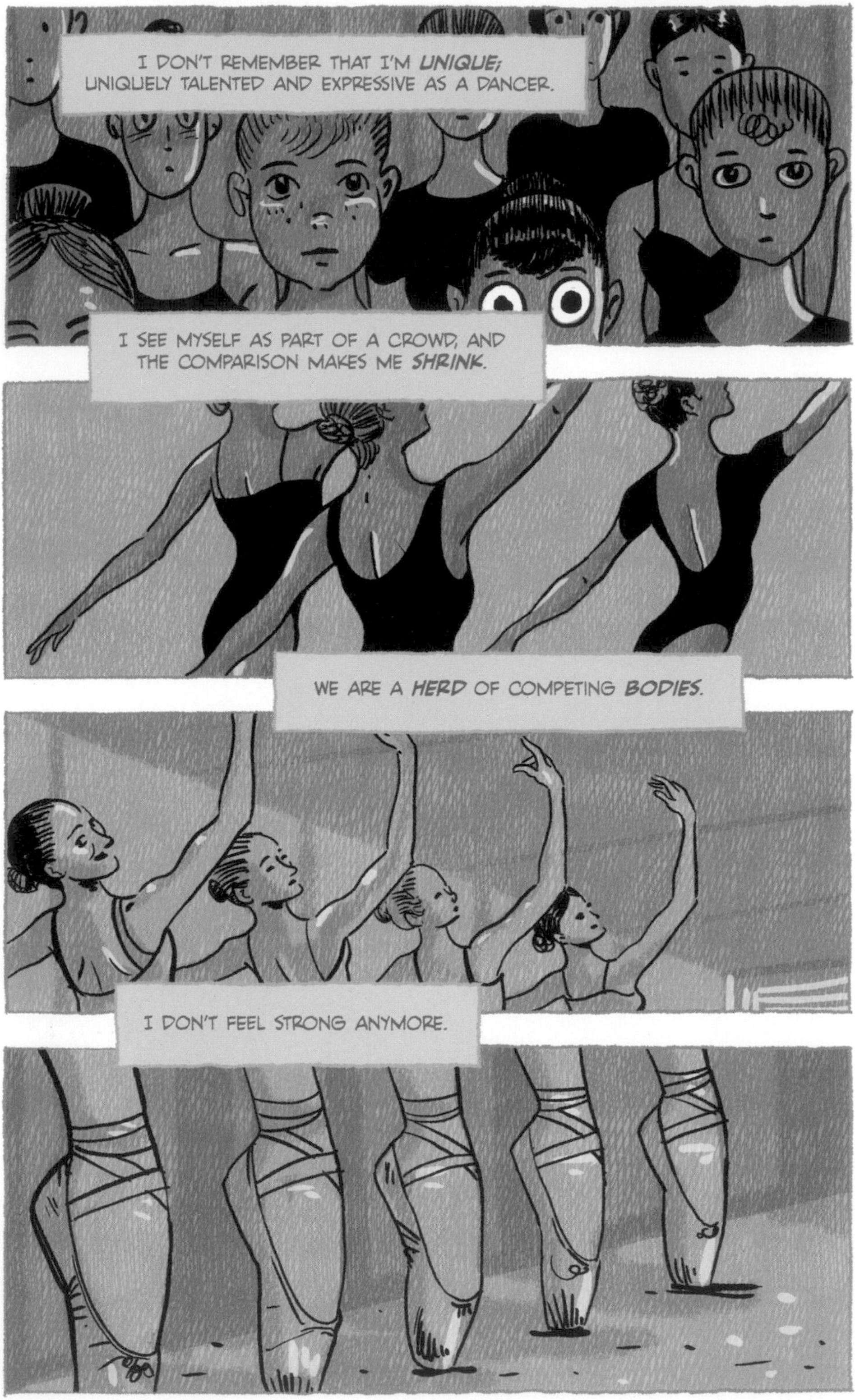
I DON'T REMEMBER THAT I'M UNIQUE; UNIQUELY TALENTED AND EXPRESSIVE AS A DANCER.
I SEE MYSELF AS PART OF A CROWD, AND THE COMPARISON MAKES ME SHRINK.
WE ARE A HERD OF COMPETING BODIES.
I DON'T FEEL STRONG ANYMORE.

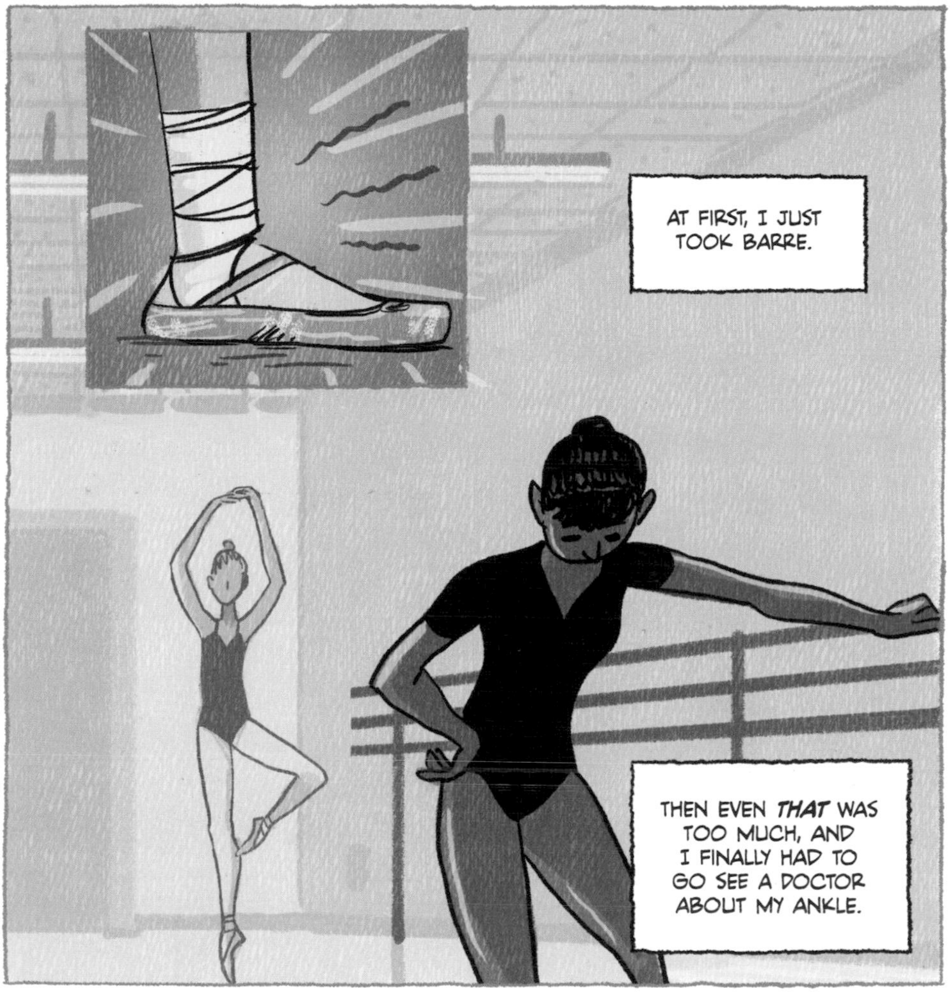
AT FIRST, I JUST TOOK BARRE.
THEN EVEN *THAT* WAS TOO MUCH, AND I FINALLY HAD TO GO SEE A DOCTOR ABOUT MY ANKLE.

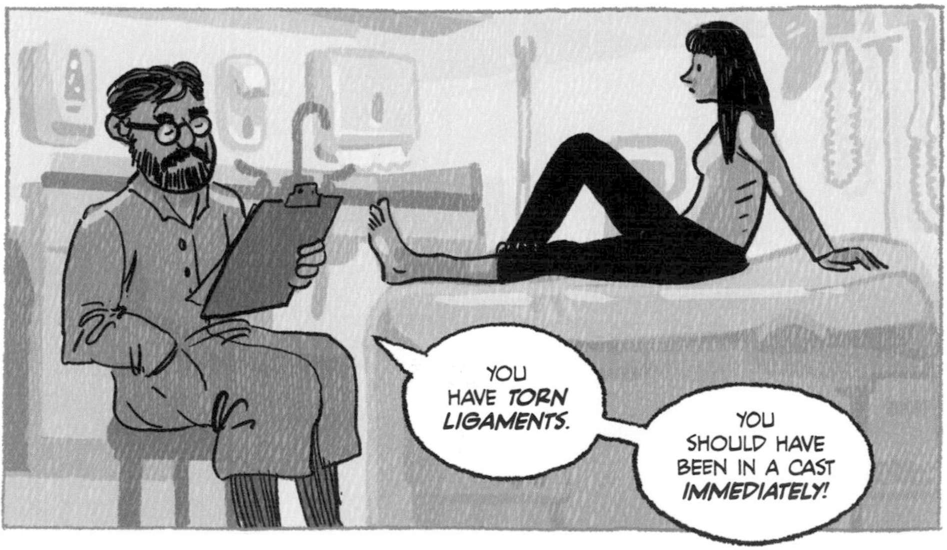
YOU HAVE *TORN LIGAMENTS*.
YOU SHOULD HAVE BEEN IN A CAST *IMMEDIATELY!*

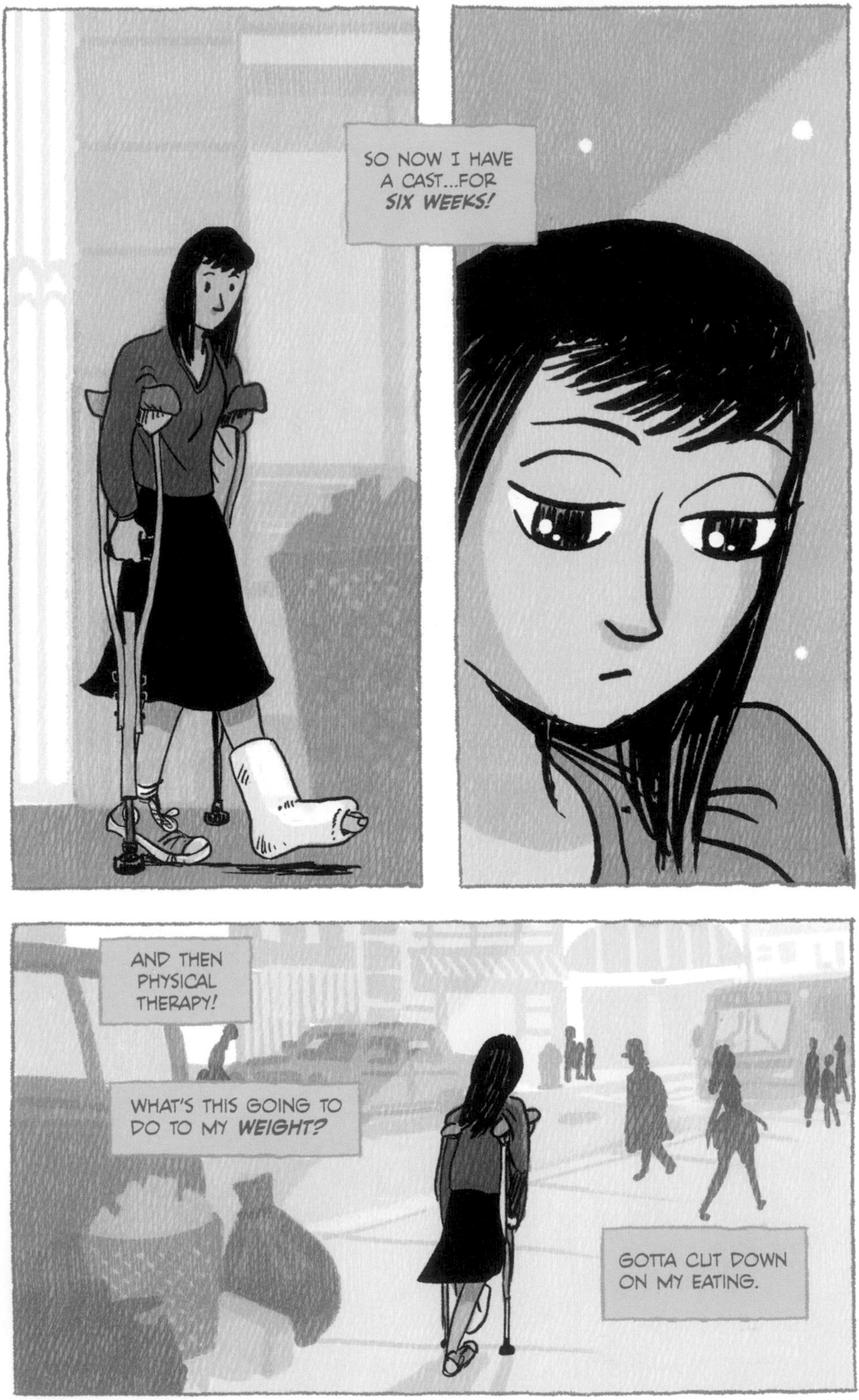
SO NOW I HAVE A CAST...FOR SIX WEEKS!
AND THEN PHYSICAL THERAPY!
WHAT'S THIS GOING TO DO TO MY WEIGHT?
GOTTA CUT DOWN ON MY EATING.

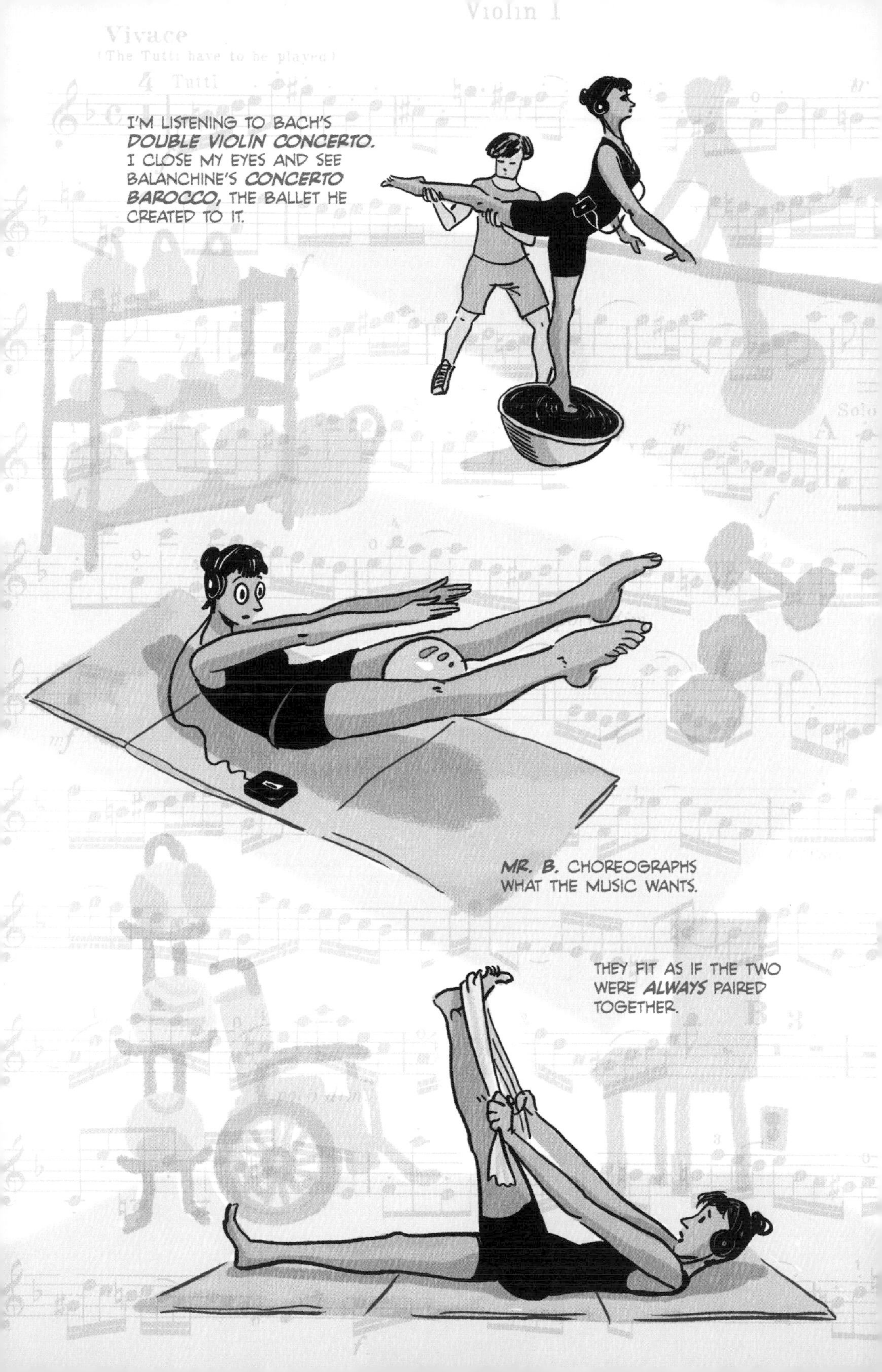
Violin I
Vivace
(The Tutti have to be played)
4 Tutti
I'M LISTENING TO BACH'S *DOUBLE VIOLIN CONCERTO.* I CLOSE MY EYES AND SEE BALANCHINE'S *CONCERTO BAROCCO,* THE BALLET HE CREATED TO IT.
Solo
A
MR. B. CHOREOGRAPHS WHAT THE MUSIC WANTS.
THEY FIT AS IF THE TWO WERE *ALWAYS* PAIRED TOGETHER.
B

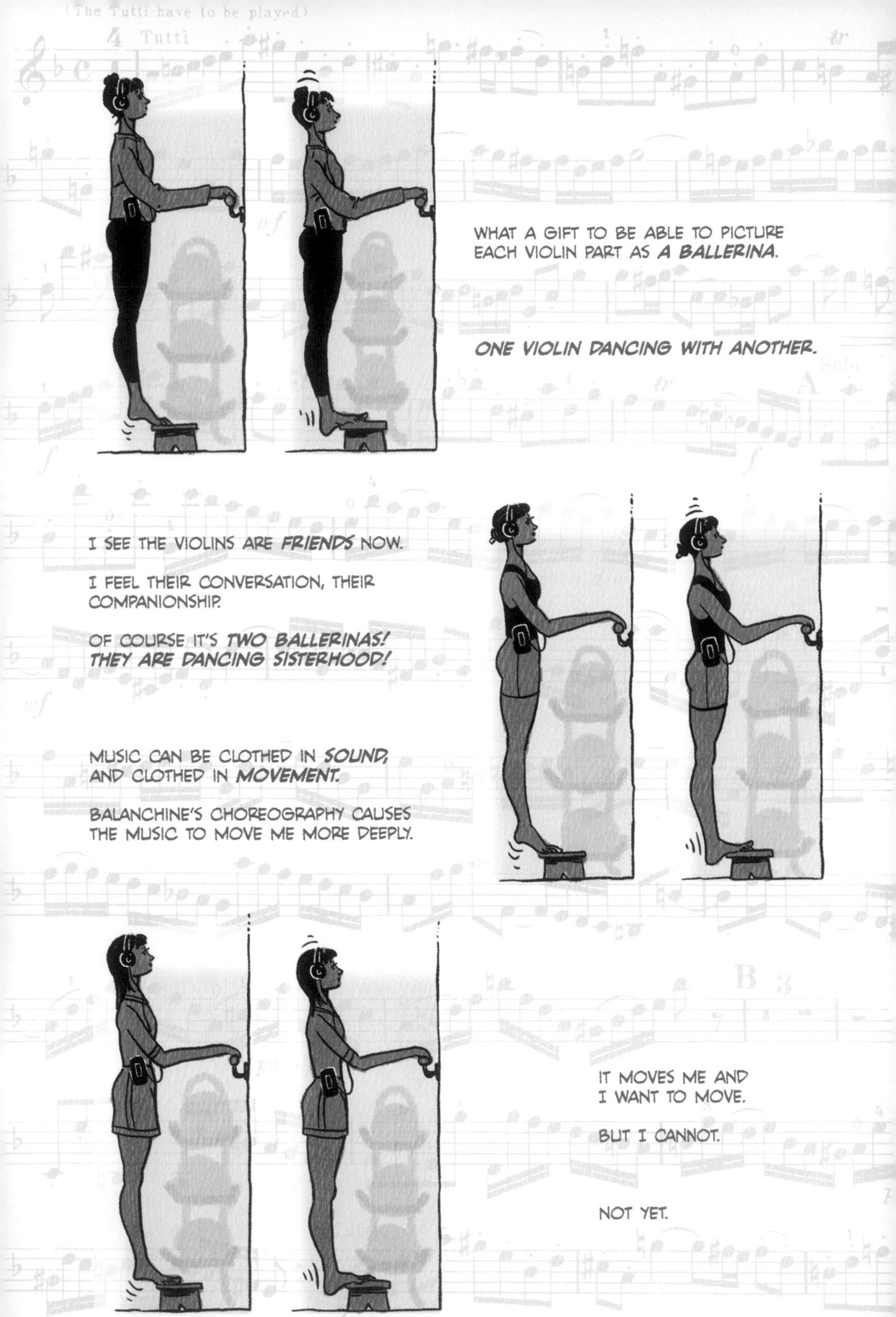
(The Tutti have to be played)
Tutti
WHAT A GIFT TO BE ABLE TO PICTURE EACH VIOLIN PART AS *A BALLERINA.*
ONE VIOLIN DANCING WITH ANOTHER.
Solo
I SEE THE VIOLINS ARE *FRIENDS* NOW.
I FEEL THEIR CONVERSATION, THEIR COMPANIONSHIP.
OF COURSE IT'S *TWO BALLERINAS! THEY ARE DANCING SISTERHOOD!*
MUSIC CAN BE CLOTHED IN *SOUND,* AND CLOTHED IN *MOVEMENT.*
BALANCHINE'S CHOREOGRAPHY CAUSES THE MUSIC TO MOVE ME MORE DEEPLY.
IT MOVES ME AND I WANT TO MOVE.
BUT I CANNOT.
NOT YET.

NEW YORK STATE THEATER, TWO MONTHS LATER

STANDING IN THE BACK OF *THE FIRST RING.* WATCHING *NYCB* WITH CARTER.

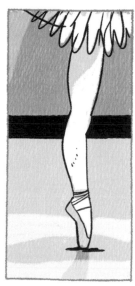

WOW! THOSE HOPS EN POINTE WERE INCREDIBLE!

I DID SOME HOPS TODAY. AND IT WAS ROUGH! I THOUGHT MY ANKLE WAS GONNA *CRACK.*

IT'LL BE OKAY. YOU CAN'T *HOLD BACK!*

JUST START *GOING FOR IT.*

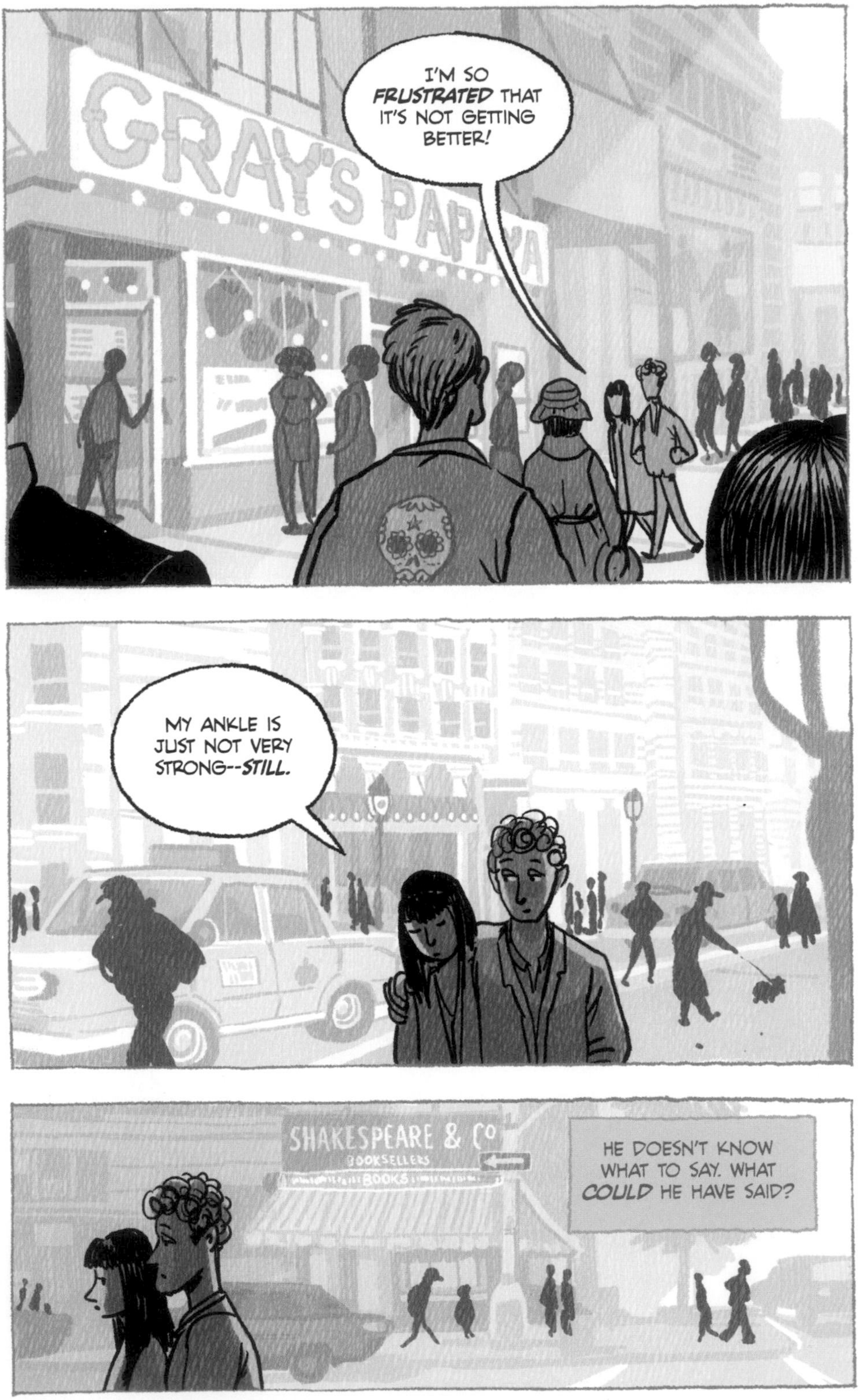
GRAY'S PAPAYA
I'M SO FRUSTRATED THAT IT'S NOT GETTING BETTER!
MY ANKLE IS JUST NOT VERY STRONG--STILL.
SHAKESPEARE & Co
BOOKSELLERS
BOOKS
HE DOESN'T KNOW WHAT TO SAY. WHAT COULD HE HAVE SAID?

ANOTHER DAY

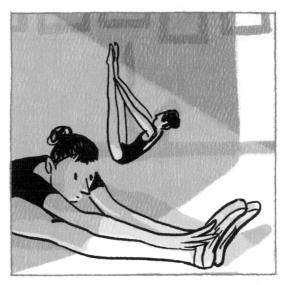

ADVANCED MEN'S CLASS

CARTER IS SHOWING OFF FOR ME.

BUT TODAY IT DOESN'T *CHEER ME UP.*

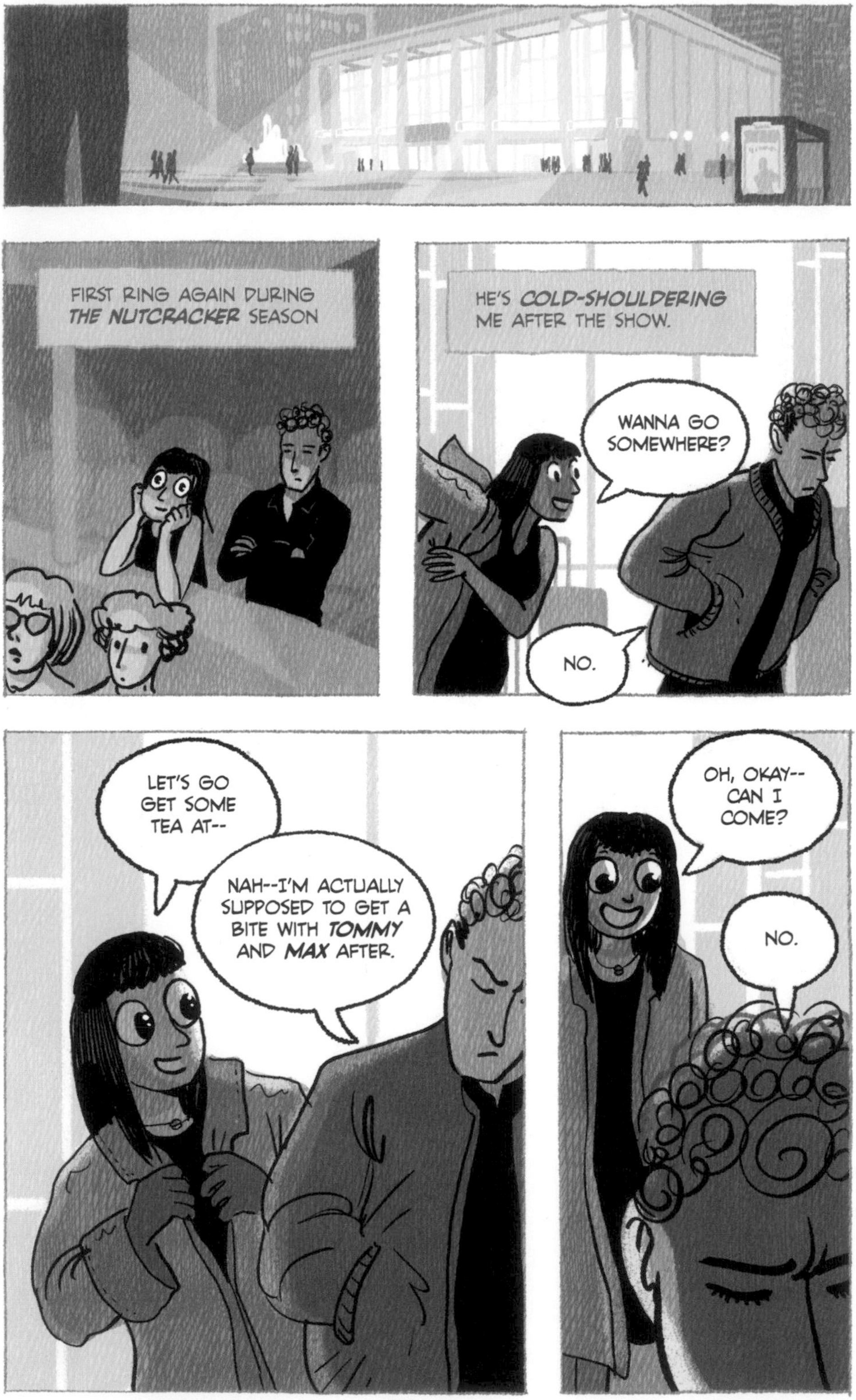
FIRST RING AGAIN DURING *THE NUTCRACKER* SEASON
HE'S *COLD-SHOULDERING* ME AFTER THE SHOW.
WANNA GO SOMEWHERE?
NO.
LET'S GO GET SOME TEA AT--
NAH--I'M ACTUALLY SUPPOSED TO GET A BITE WITH *TOMMY* AND *MAX* AFTER.
OH, OKAY-- CAN I COME?
NO.

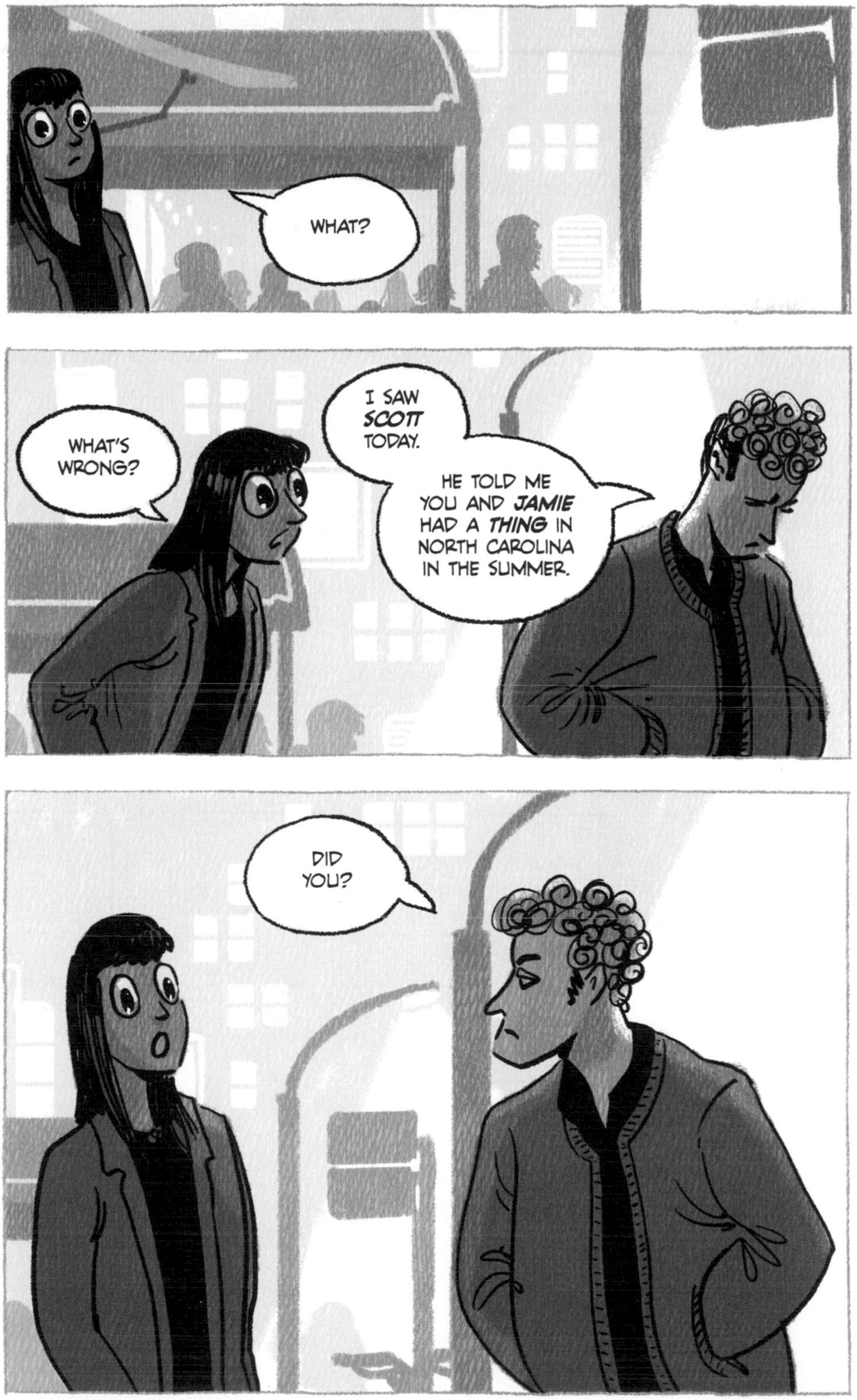
WHAT?
WHAT'S WRONG?
I SAW SCOTT TODAY.
HE TOLD ME YOU AND JAMIE HAD A THING IN NORTH CAROLINA IN THE SUMMER.
DID YOU?

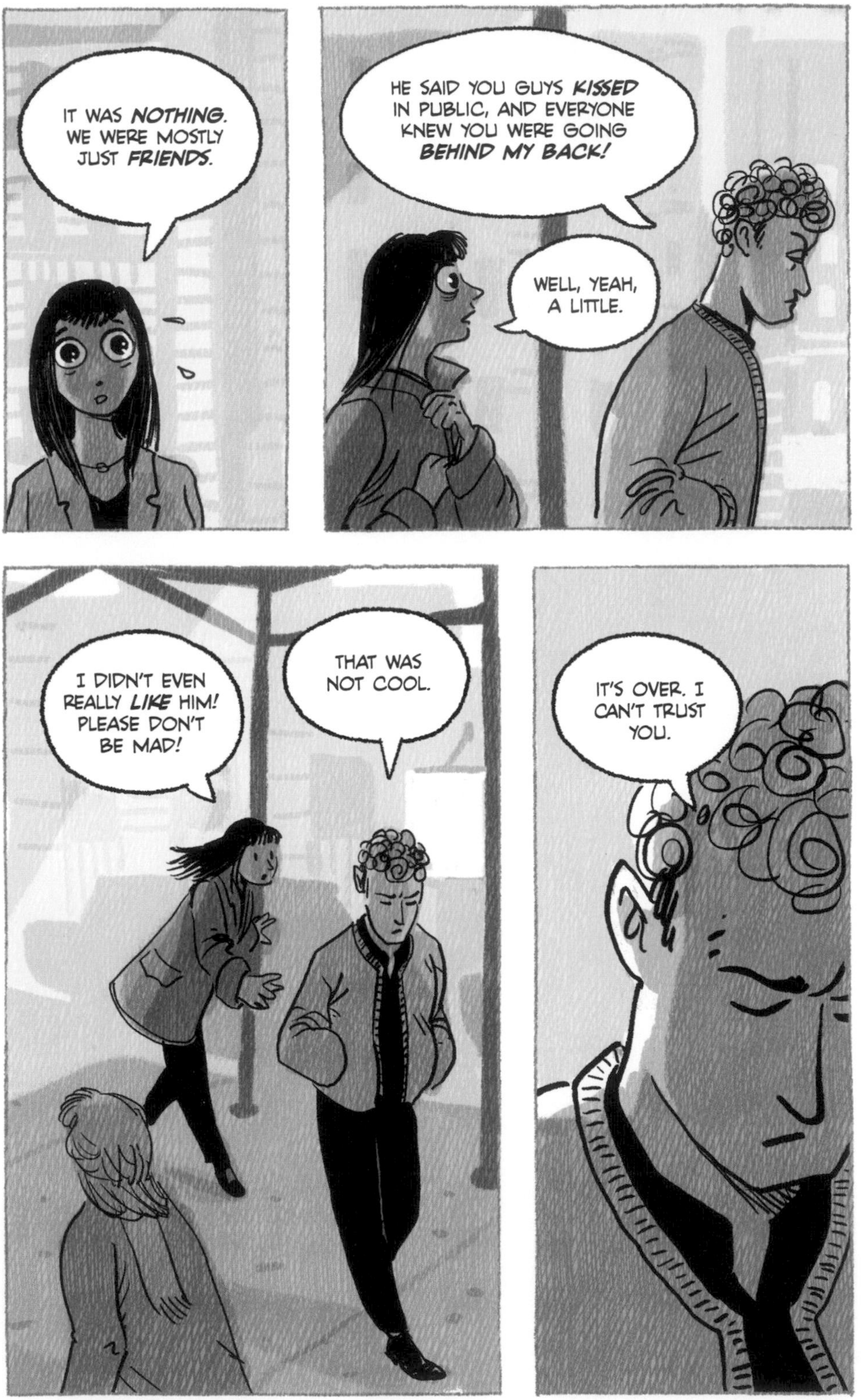
IT WAS **NOTHING**. WE WERE MOSTLY JUST **FRIENDS**.
HE SAID YOU GUYS **KISSED** IN PUBLIC, AND EVERYONE KNEW YOU WERE GOING **BEHIND MY BACK!**
WELL, YEAH, A LITTLE.
I DIDN'T EVEN REALLY **LIKE** HIM! PLEASE DON'T BE MAD!
THAT WAS NOT COOL.
IT'S OVER. I CAN'T TRUST YOU.

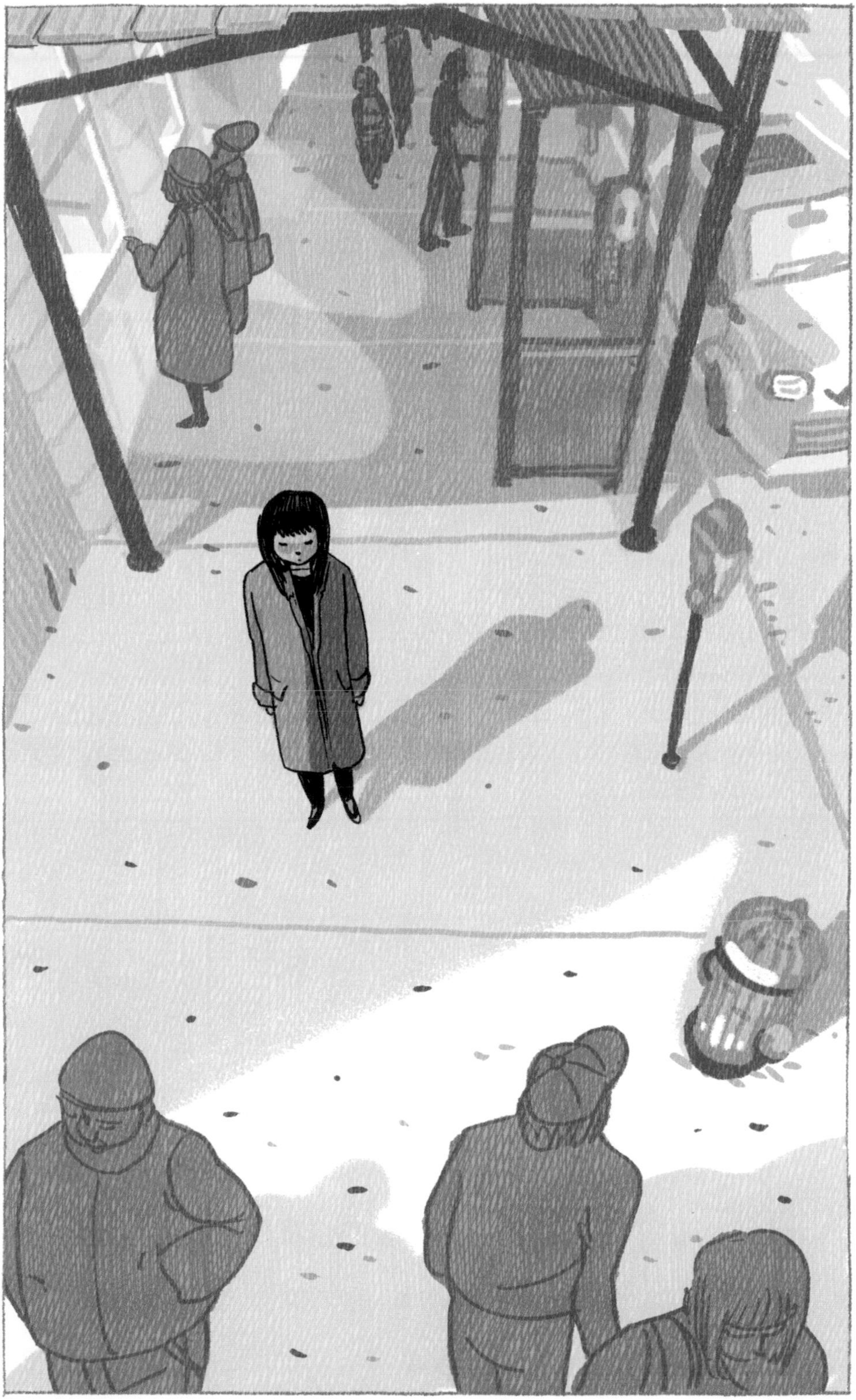

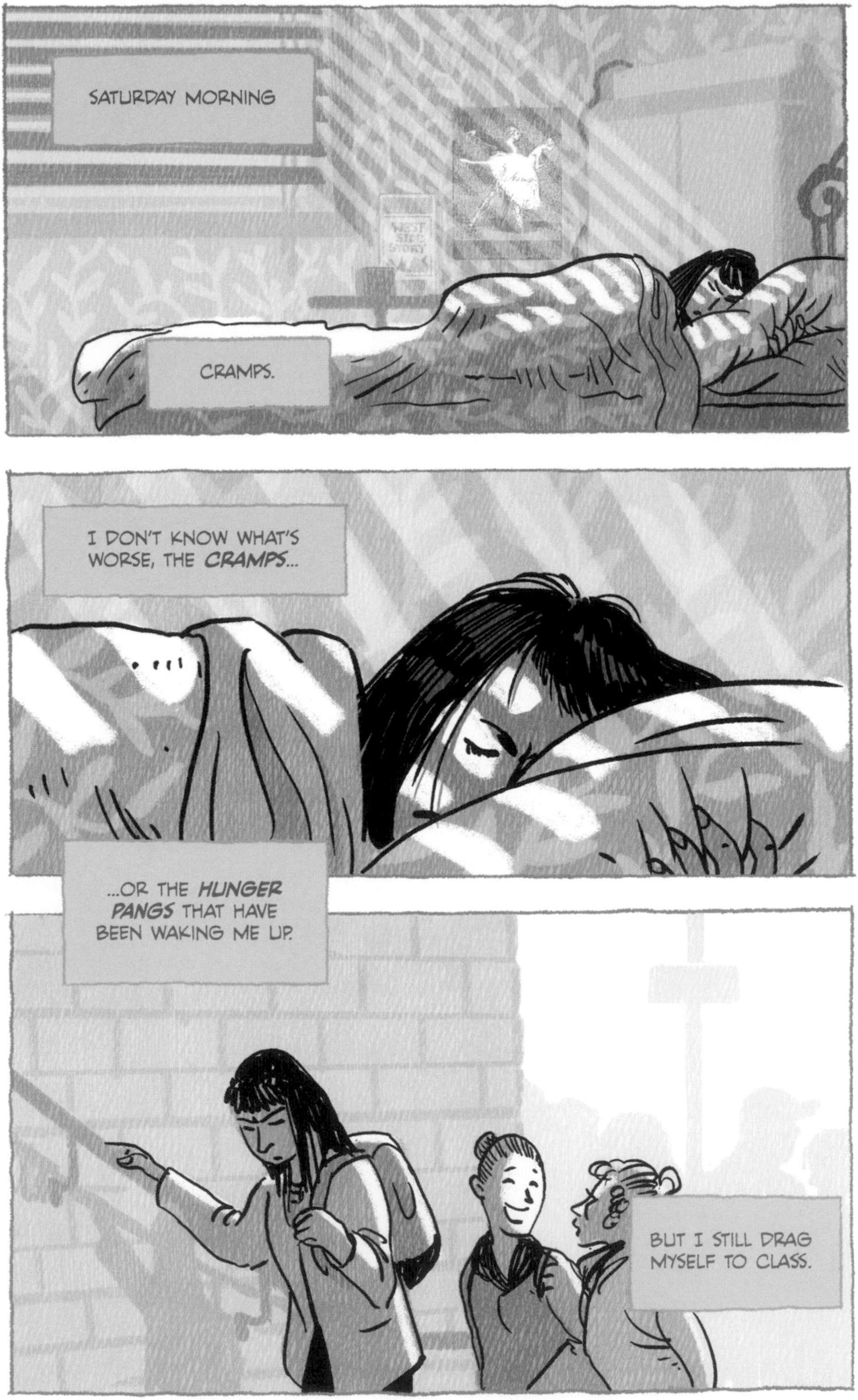
SATURDAY MORNING
WEST SIDE STORY
CRAMPS.
I DON'T KNOW WHAT'S WORSE, THE *CRAMPS*...
...OR THE ***HUNGER PANGS*** THAT HAVE BEEN WAKING ME UP.
BUT I STILL DRAG MYSELF TO CLASS.

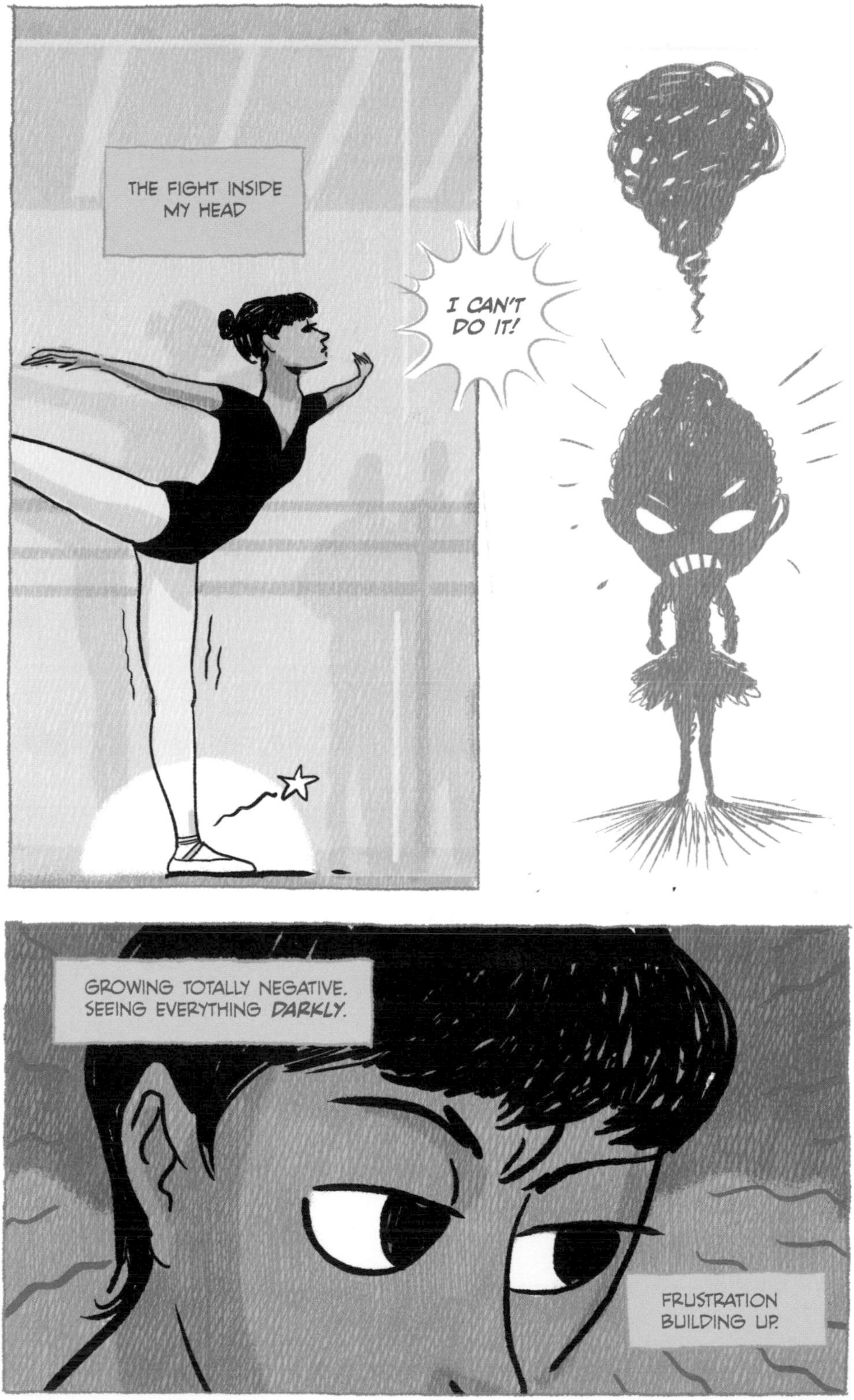
THE FIGHT INSIDE MY HEAD
I CAN'T DO IT!
GROWING TOTALLY NEGATIVE. SEEING EVERYTHING DARKLY.
FRUSTRATION BUILDING UP.

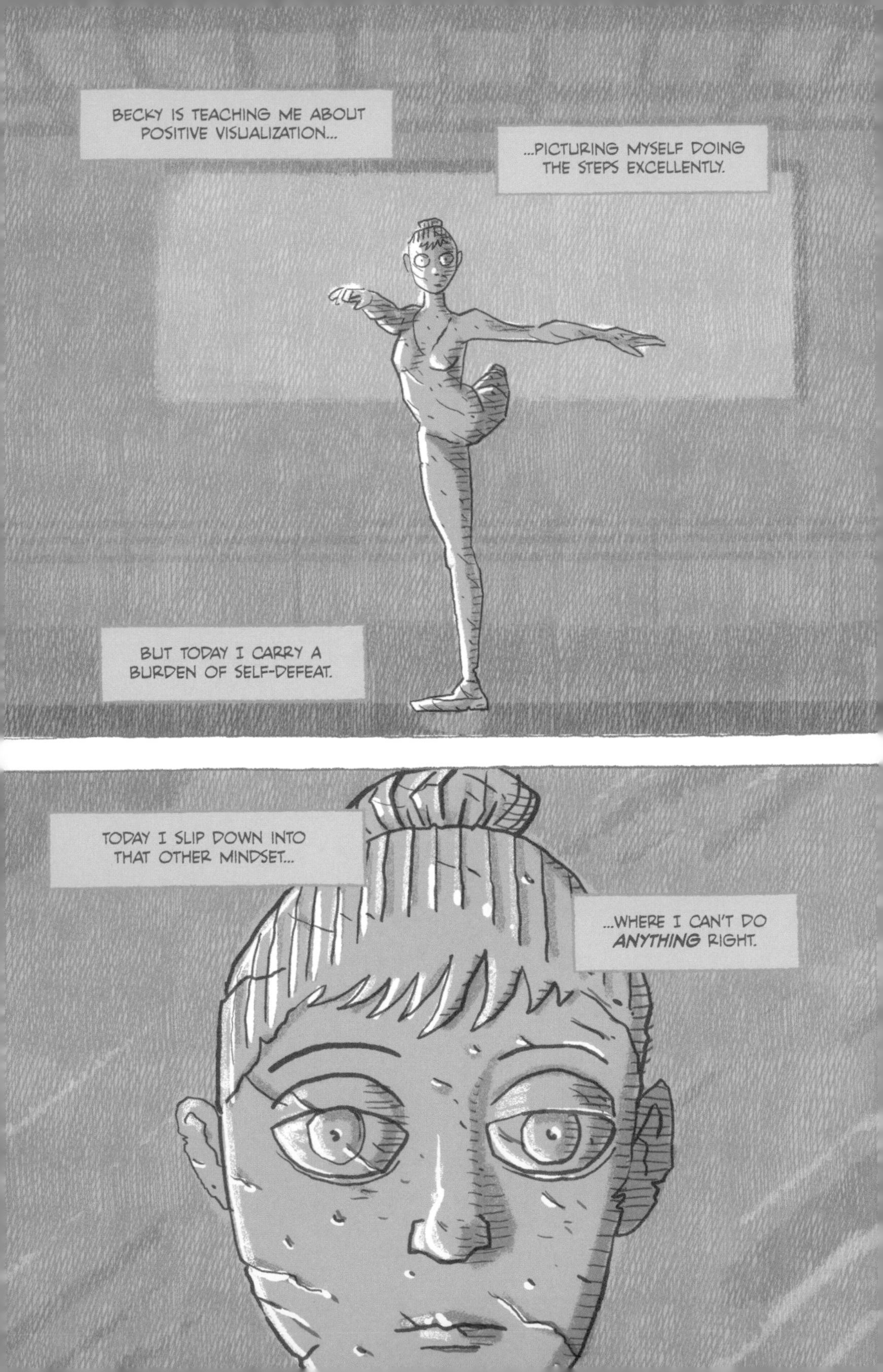
BECKY IS TEACHING ME ABOUT POSITIVE VISUALIZATION...
...PICTURING MYSELF DOING THE STEPS EXCELLENTLY.
BUT TODAY I CARRY A BURDEN OF SELF-DEFEAT.
TODAY I SLIP DOWN INTO THAT OTHER MINDSET...
...WHERE I CAN'T DO *ANYTHING* RIGHT.

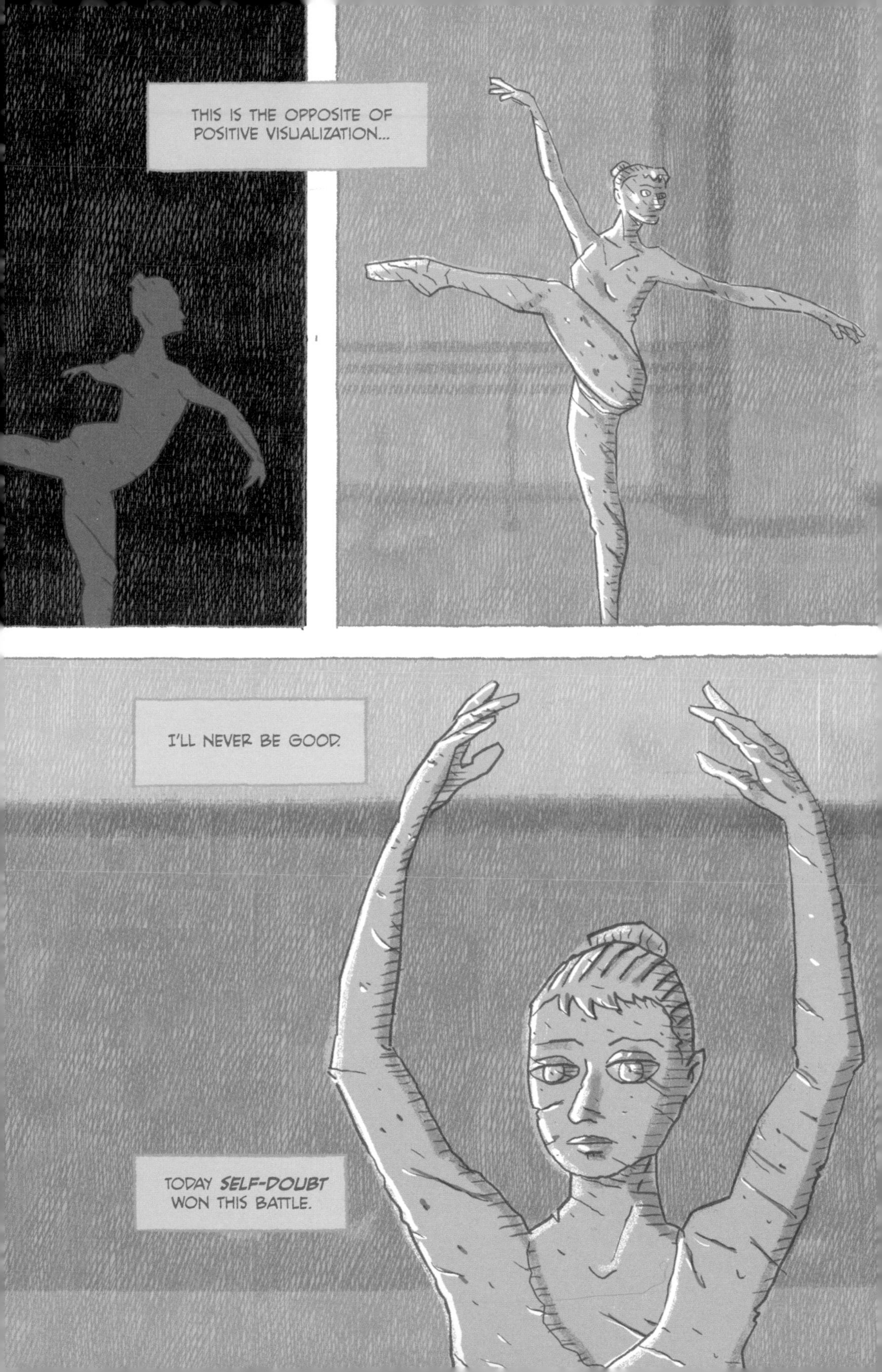
THIS IS THE OPPOSITE OF POSITIVE VISUALIZATION...
I'LL NEVER BE GOOD.
TODAY *SELF-DOUBT* WON THIS BATTLE.

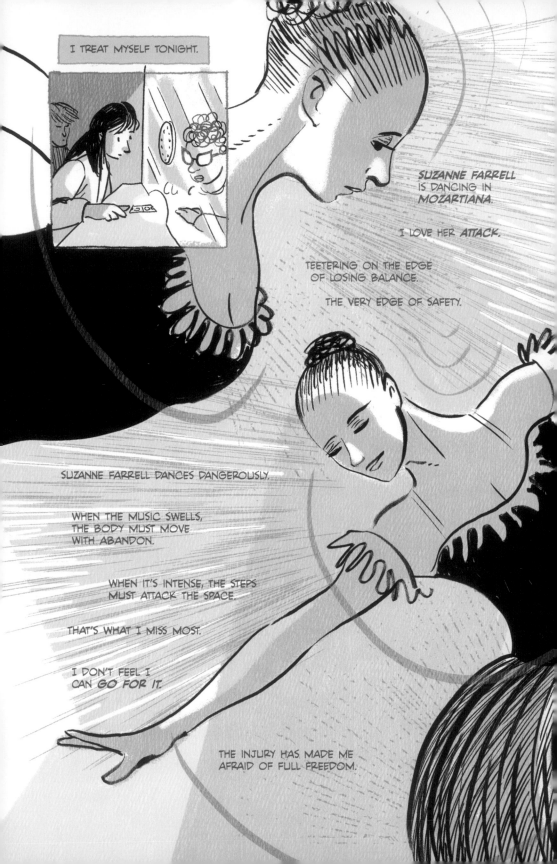

I TREAT MYSELF TONIGHT.

SUZANNE FARRELL IS DANCING IN *MOZARTIANA*.

I LOVE HER *ATTACK*.

TEETERING ON THE EDGE OF LOSING BALANCE.

THE VERY EDGE OF SAFETY.

SUZANNE FARRELL DANCES DANGEROUSLY.

WHEN THE MUSIC SWELLS, THE BODY MUST MOVE WITH ABANDON.

WHEN IT'S INTENSE, THE STEPS MUST ATTACK THE SPACE.

THAT'S WHAT I MISS MOST.

I DON'T FEEL I CAN *GO FOR IT*.

THE INJURY HAS MADE ME AFRAID OF FULL FREEDOM.

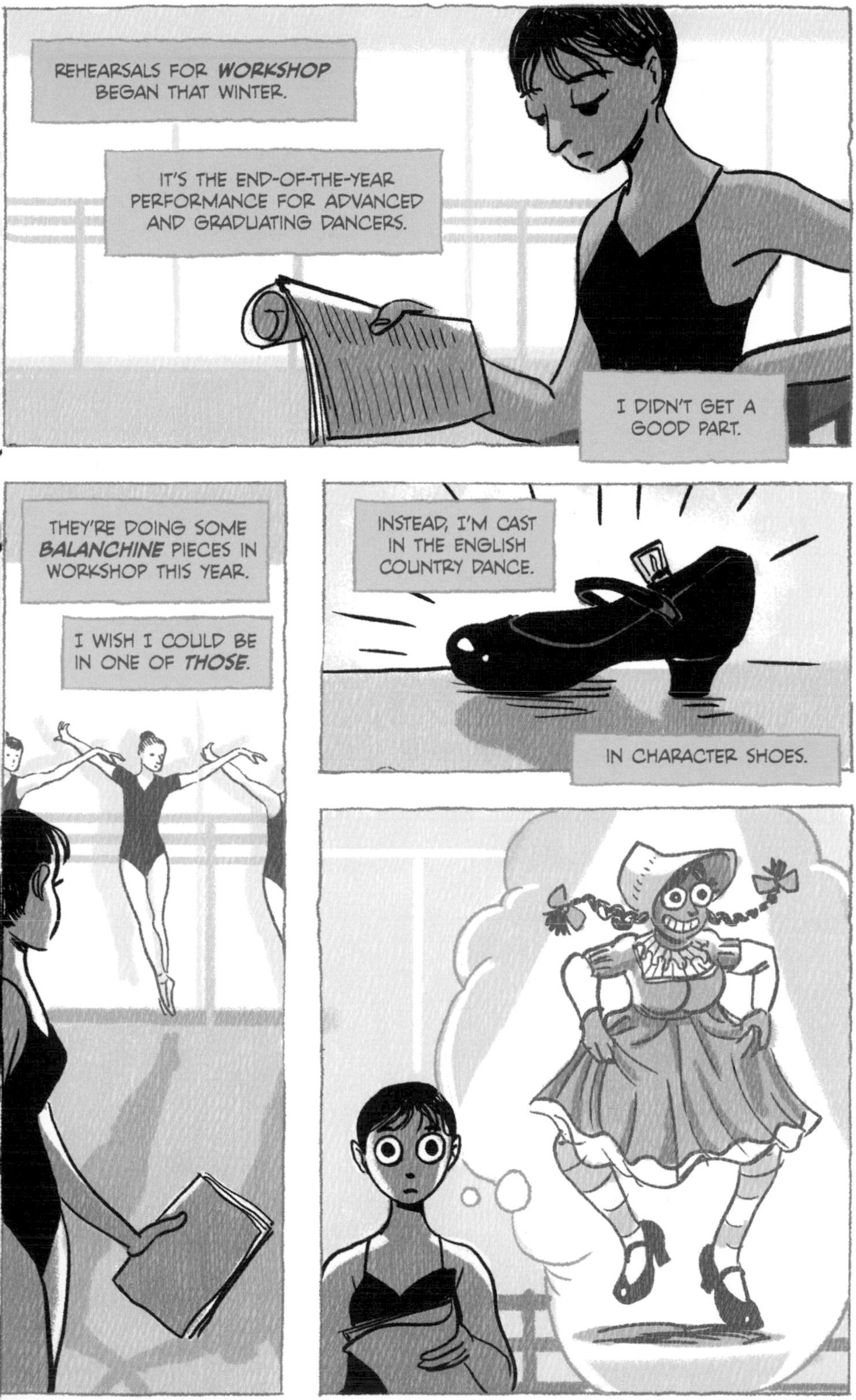
REHEARSALS FOR WORKSHOP BEGAN THAT WINTER.
IT'S THE END-OF-THE-YEAR PERFORMANCE FOR ADVANCED AND GRADUATING DANCERS.
I DIDN'T GET A GOOD PART.
THEY'RE DOING SOME BALANCHINE PIECES IN WORKSHOP THIS YEAR.
I WISH I COULD BE IN ONE OF THOSE.
INSTEAD, I'M CAST IN THE ENGLISH COUNTRY DANCE.
IN CHARACTER SHOES.

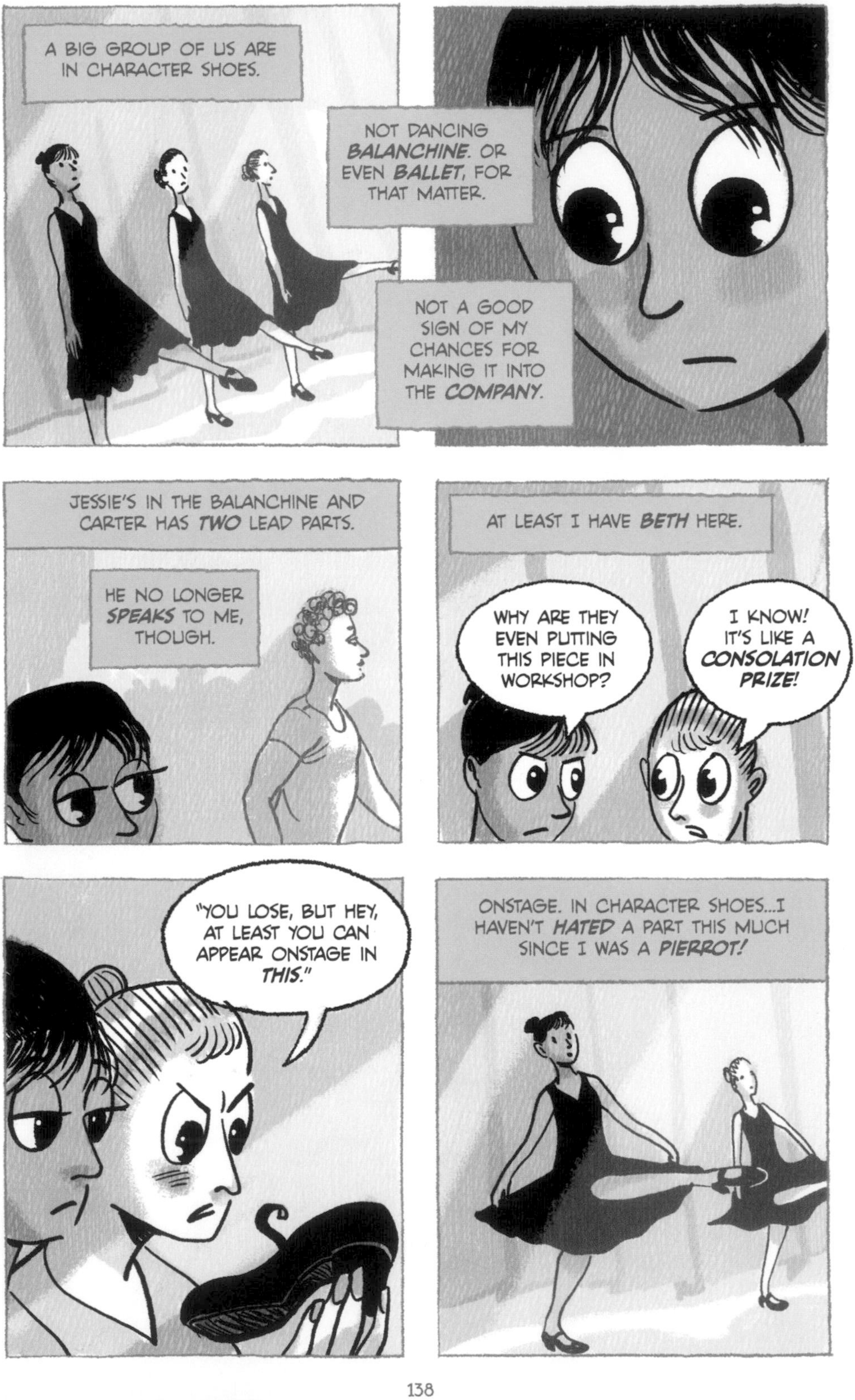
A BIG GROUP OF US ARE IN CHARACTER SHOES.
NOT DANCING *BALANCHINE*. OR EVEN *BALLET*, FOR THAT MATTER.
NOT A GOOD SIGN OF MY CHANCES FOR MAKING IT INTO THE *COMPANY*.
JESSIE'S IN THE BALANCHINE AND CARTER HAS *TWO* LEAD PARTS.
HE NO LONGER *SPEAKS* TO ME, THOUGH.
AT LEAST I HAVE *BETH* HERE.
WHY ARE THEY EVEN PUTTING THIS PIECE IN WORKSHOP?
I KNOW! IT'S LIKE A *CONSOLATION PRIZE!*
"YOU LOSE, BUT HEY, AT LEAST YOU CAN APPEAR ONSTAGE IN *THIS*."
ONSTAGE. IN CHARACTER SHOES...I HAVEN'T *HATED* A PART THIS MUCH SINCE I WAS A *PIERROT!*

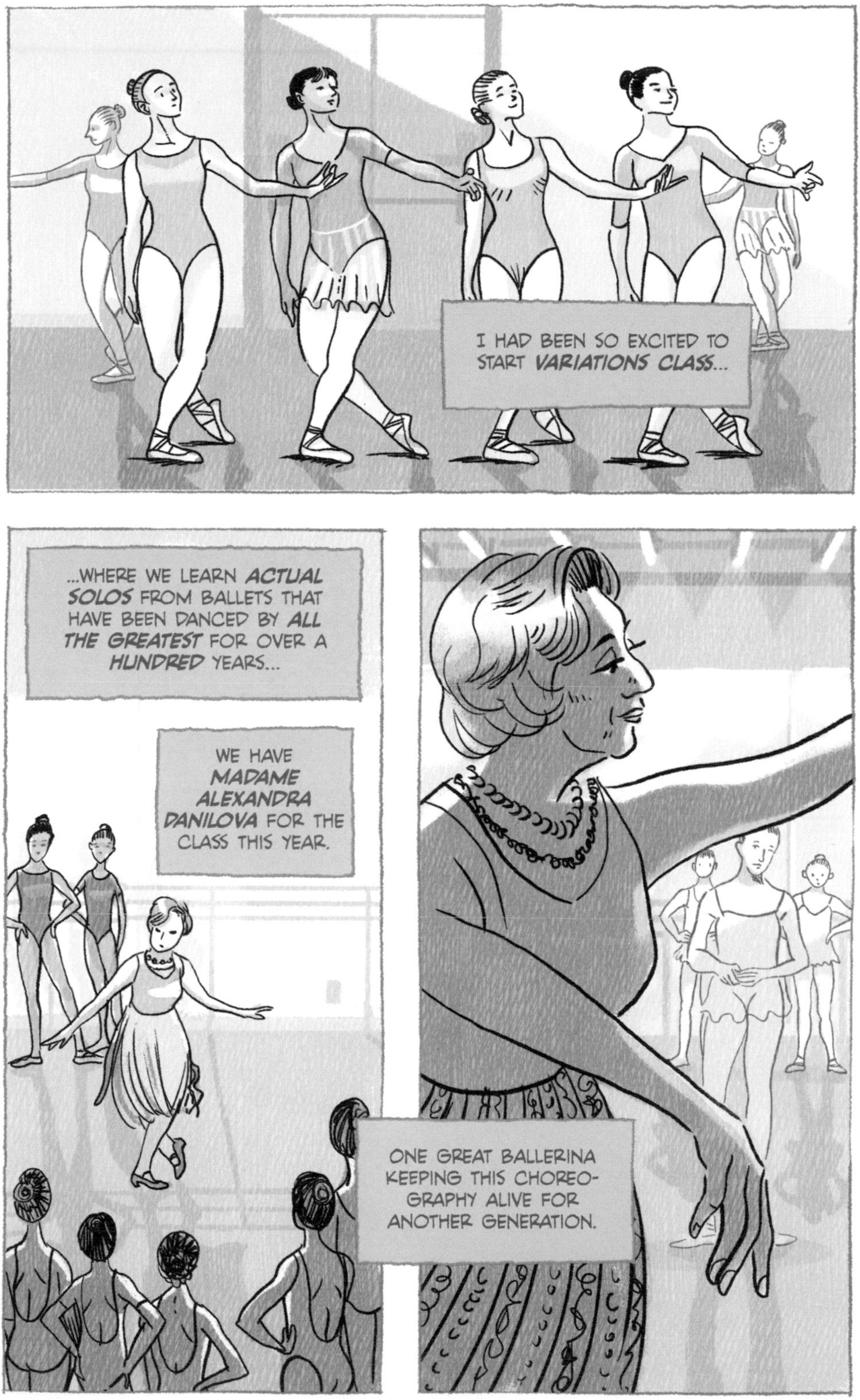
I HAD BEEN SO EXCITED TO START VARIATIONS CLASS...
...WHERE WE LEARN ACTUAL SOLOS FROM BALLETS THAT HAVE BEEN DANCED BY ALL THE GREATEST FOR OVER A HUNDRED YEARS...
WE HAVE MADAME ALEXANDRA DANILOVA FOR THE CLASS THIS YEAR.
ONE GREAT BALLERINA KEEPING THIS CHOREOGRAPHY ALIVE FOR ANOTHER GENERATION.

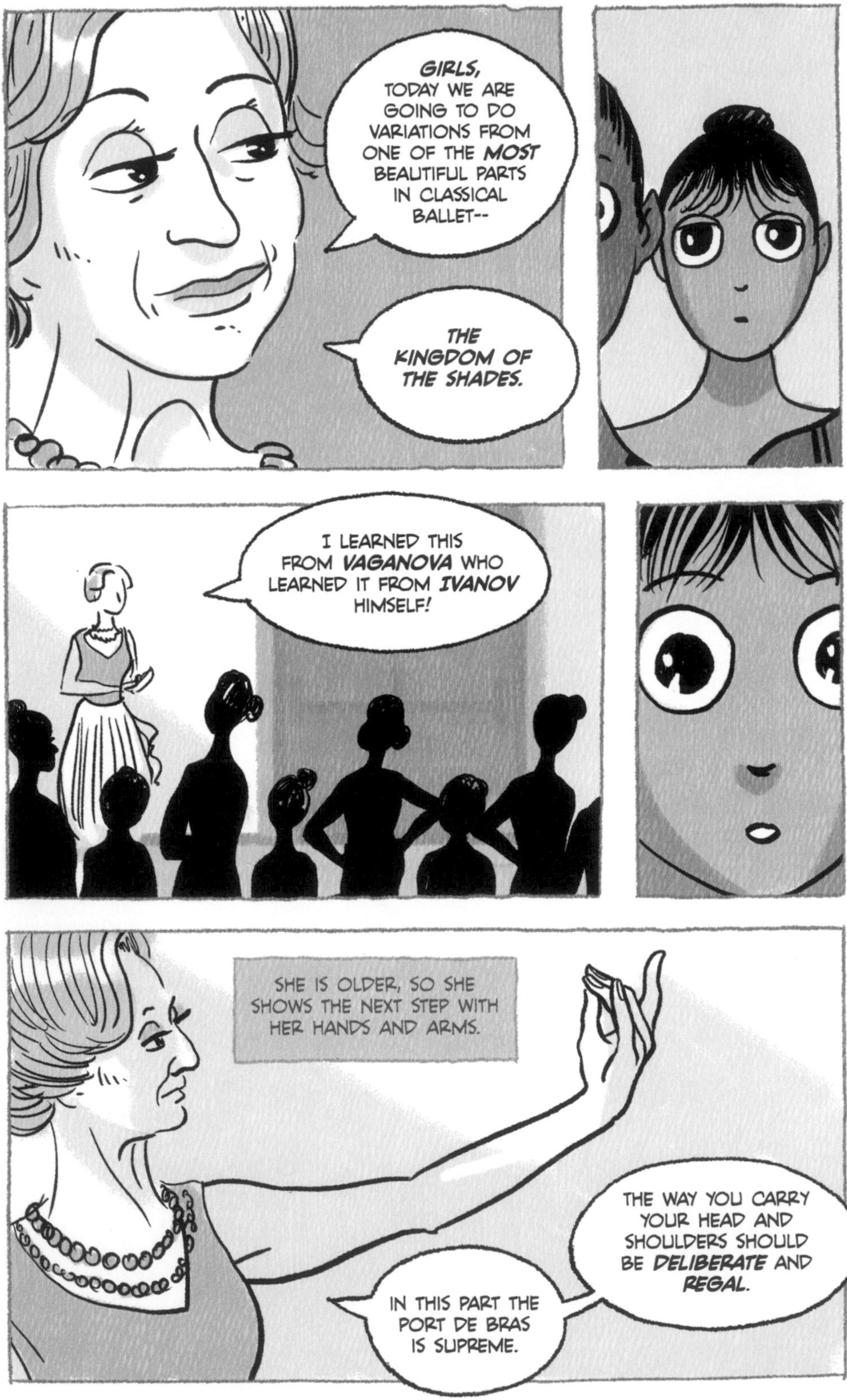
GIRLS, TODAY WE ARE GOING TO DO VARIATIONS FROM ONE OF THE MOST BEAUTIFUL PARTS IN CLASSICAL BALLET--
THE KINGDOM OF THE SHADES.
I LEARNED THIS FROM VAGANOVA WHO LEARNED IT FROM IVANOV HIMSELF!
SHE IS OLDER, SO SHE SHOWS THE NEXT STEP WITH HER HANDS AND ARMS.
THE WAY YOU CARRY YOUR HEAD AND SHOULDERS SHOULD BE DELIBERATE AND REGAL.
IN THIS PART THE PORT DE BRAS IS SUPREME.

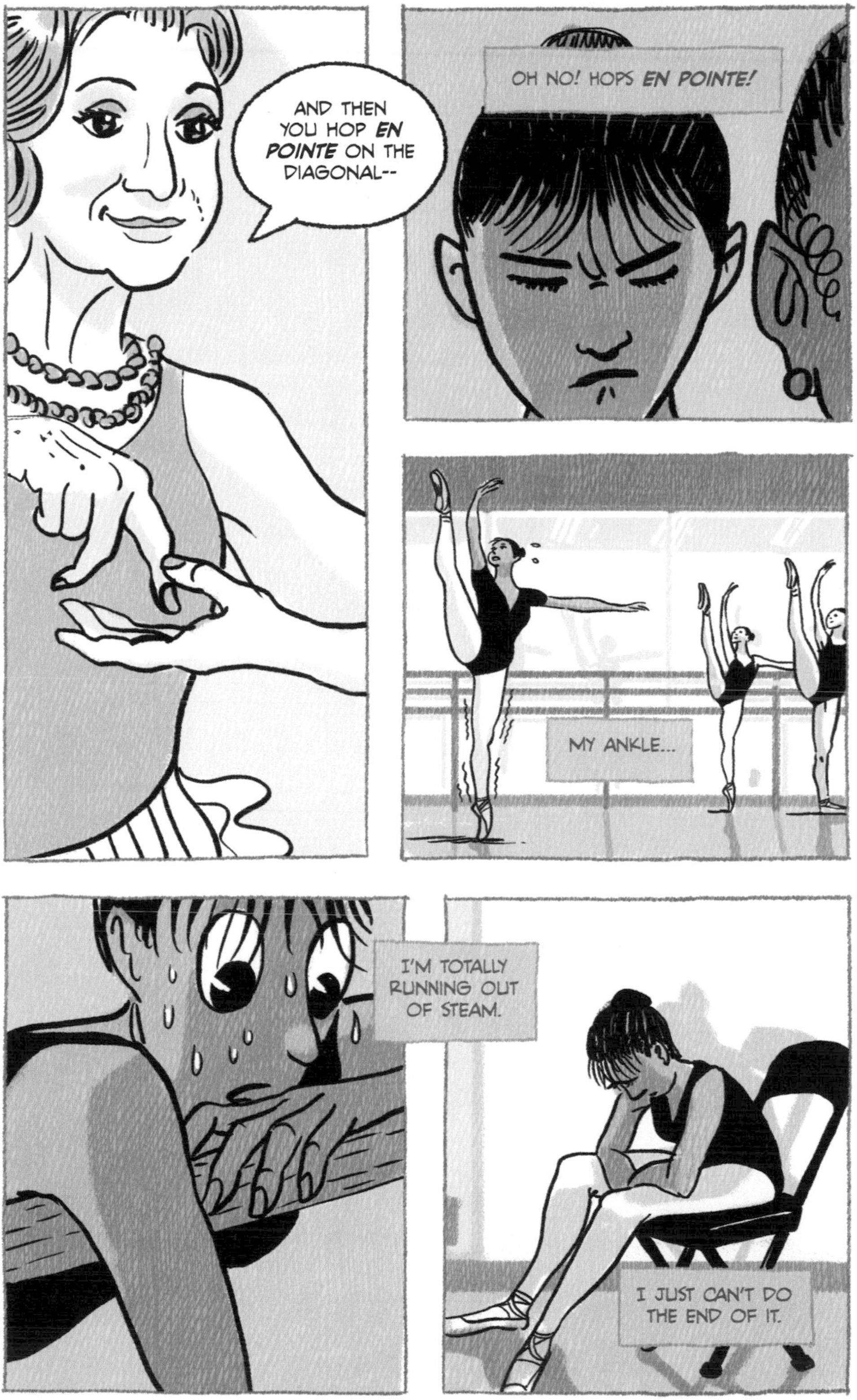
AND THEN YOU HOP *EN POINTE* ON THE DIAGONAL--
OH NO! HOPS *EN POINTE!*
MY ANKLE...
I'M TOTALLY RUNNING OUT OF STEAM.
I JUST CAN'T DO THE END OF IT.

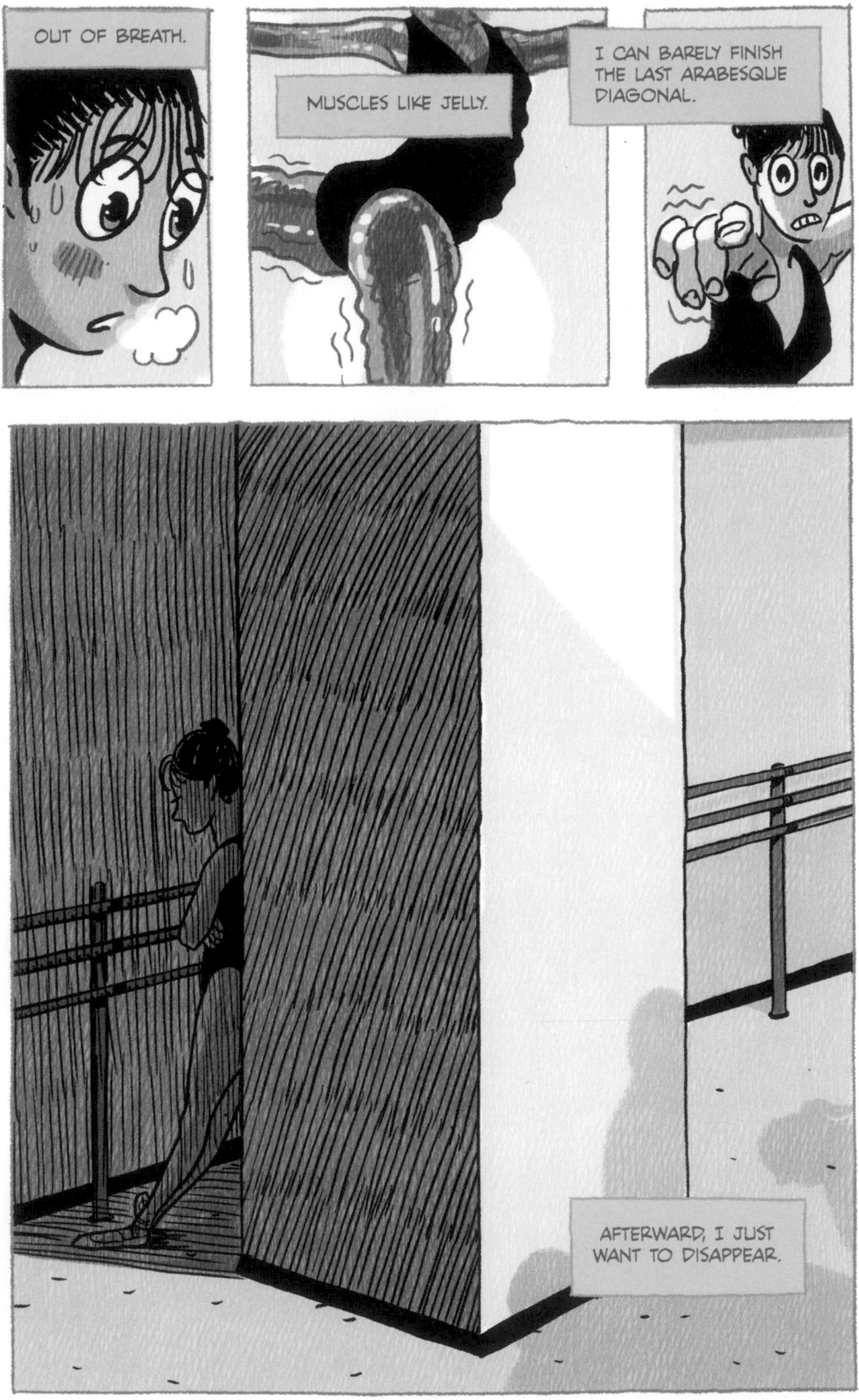
OUT OF BREATH.
MUSCLES LIKE JELLY.
I CAN BARELY FINISH THE LAST ARABESQUE DIAGONAL.
AFTERWARD, I JUST WANT TO DISAPPEAR.

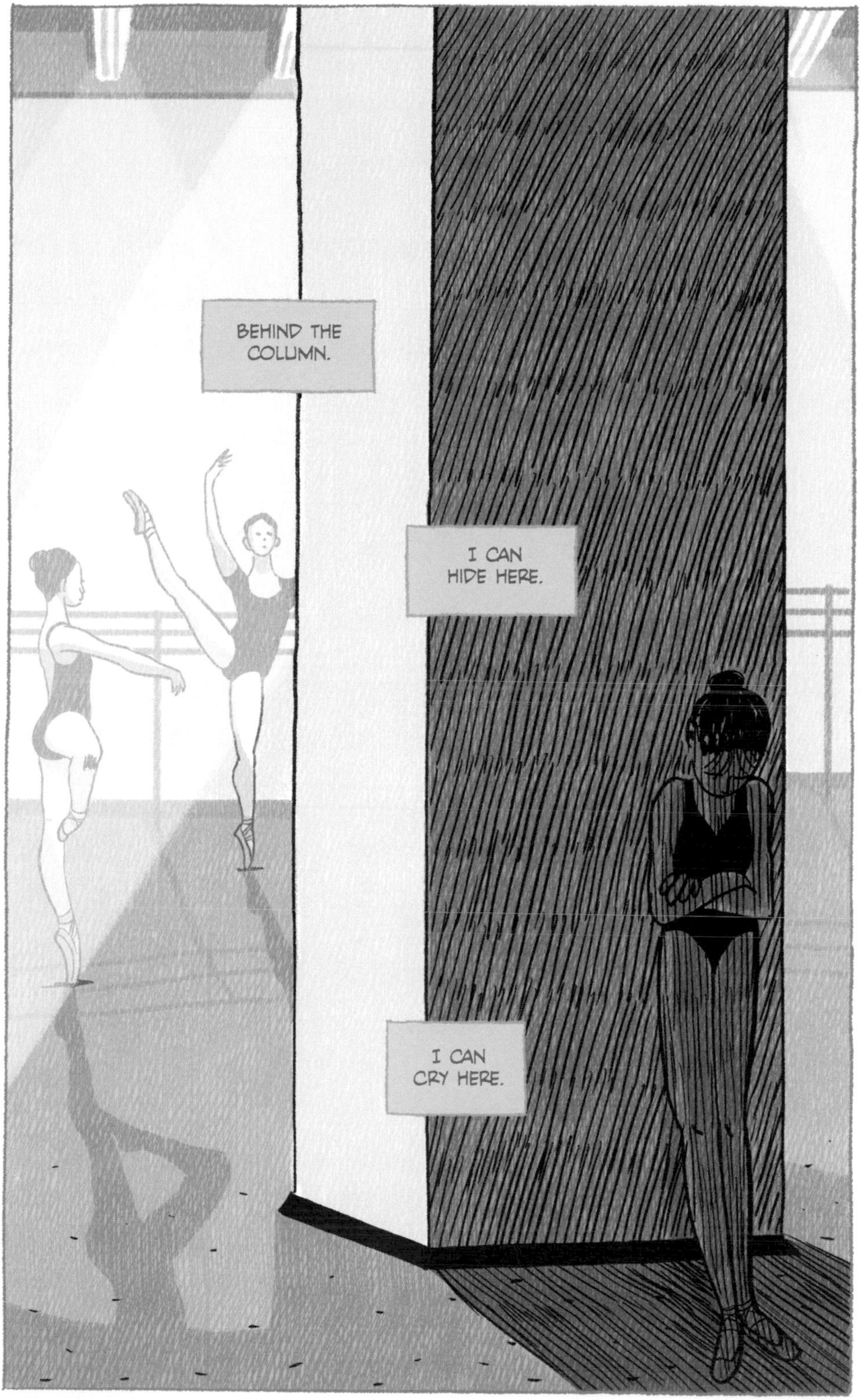
BEHIND THE COLUMN.
I CAN HIDE HERE.
I CAN CRY HERE.

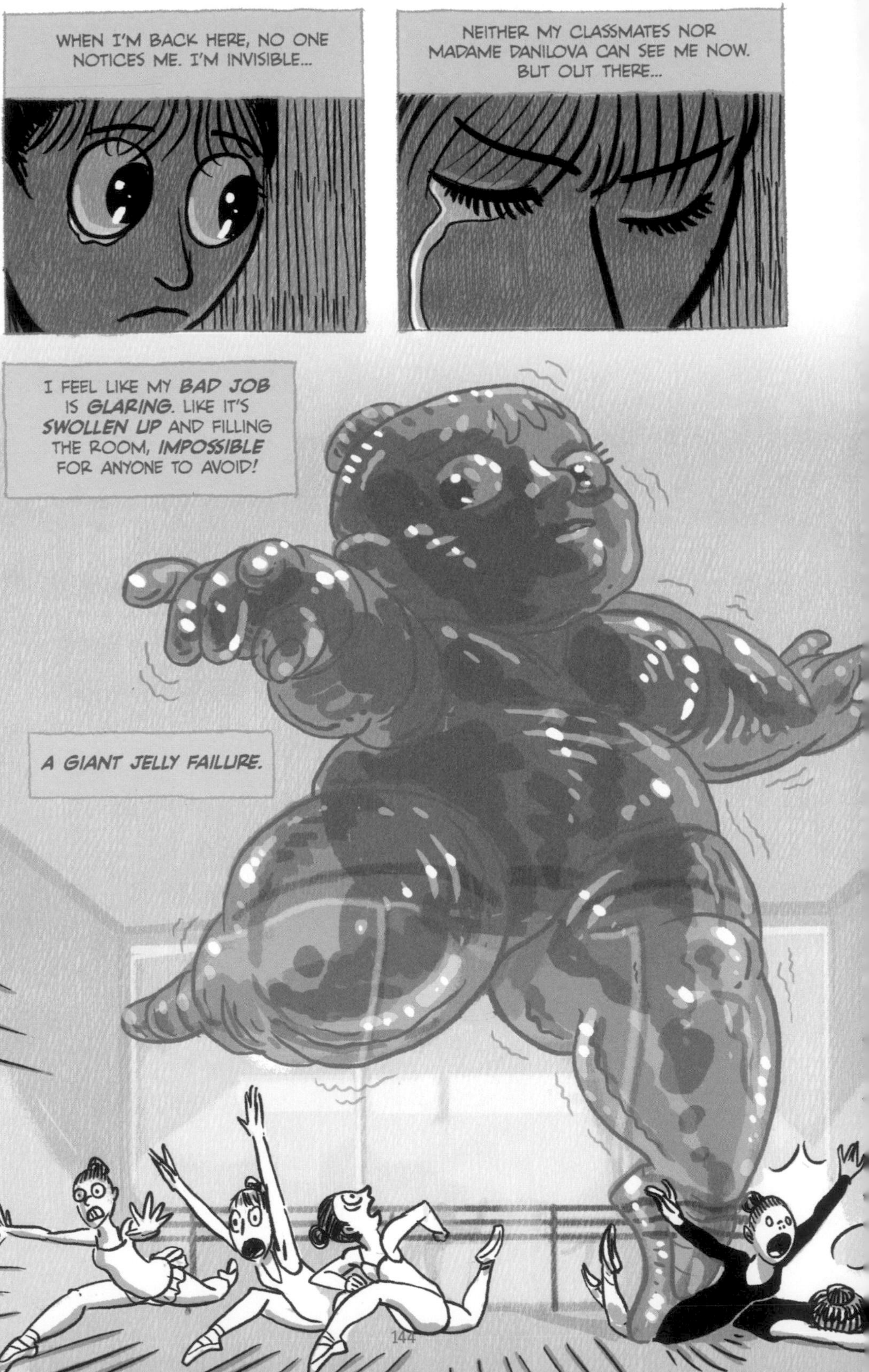
WHEN I'M BACK HERE, NO ONE NOTICES ME. I'M INVISIBLE...
NEITHER MY CLASSMATES NOR MADAME DANILOVA CAN SEE ME NOW. BUT OUT THERE...
I FEEL LIKE MY BAD JOB IS GLARING. LIKE IT'S SWOLLEN UP AND FILLING THE ROOM, IMPOSSIBLE FOR ANYONE TO AVOID!
A GIANT JELLY FAILURE.

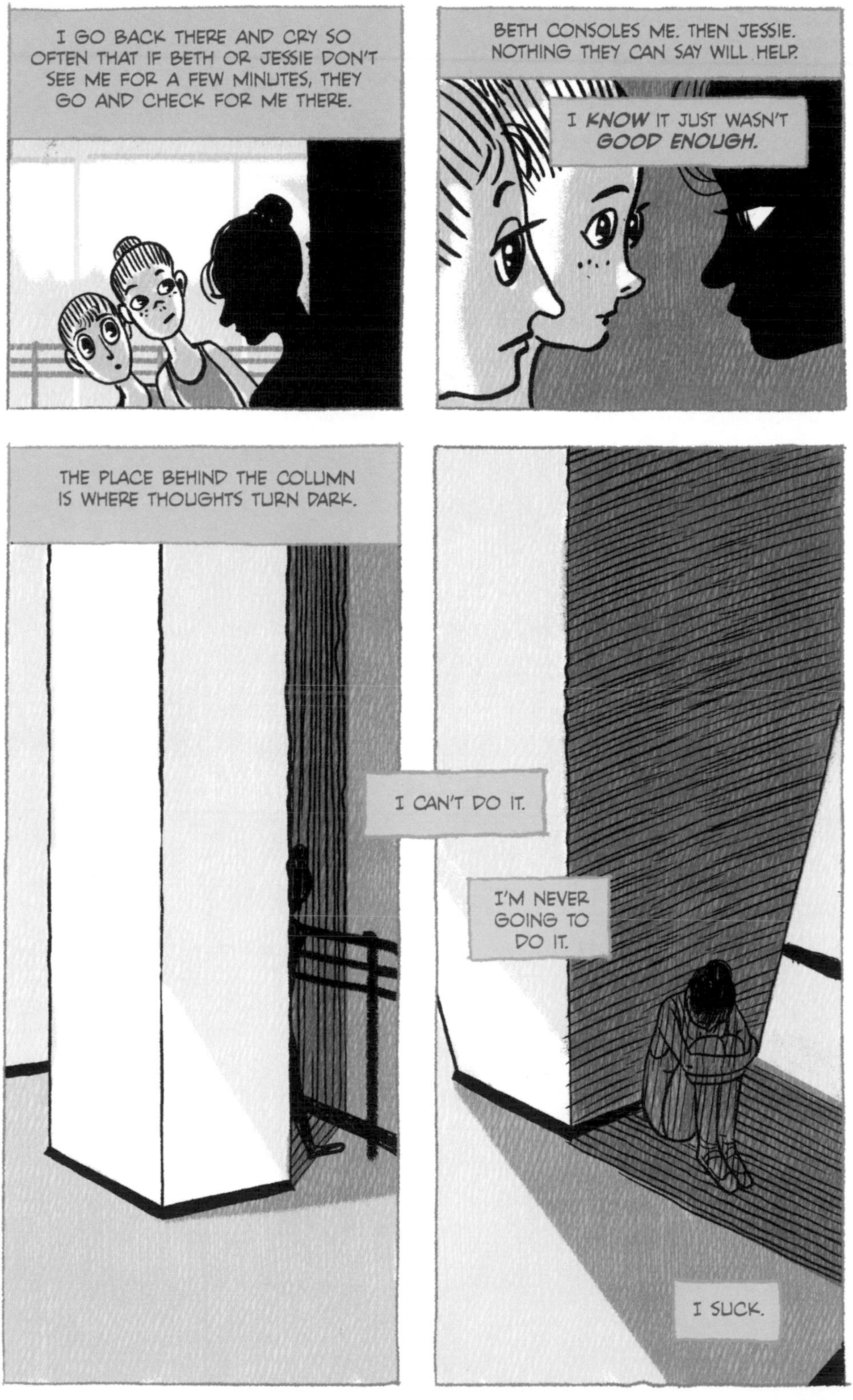
I GO BACK THERE AND CRY SO OFTEN THAT IF BETH OR JESSIE DON'T SEE ME FOR A FEW MINUTES, THEY GO AND CHECK FOR ME THERE.
BETH CONSOLES ME. THEN JESSIE. NOTHING THEY CAN SAY WILL HELP.
I KNOW IT JUST WASN'T GOOD ENOUGH.
THE PLACE BEHIND THE COLUMN IS WHERE THOUGHTS TURN DARK.
I CAN'T DO IT.
I'M NEVER GOING TO DO IT.
I SUCK.

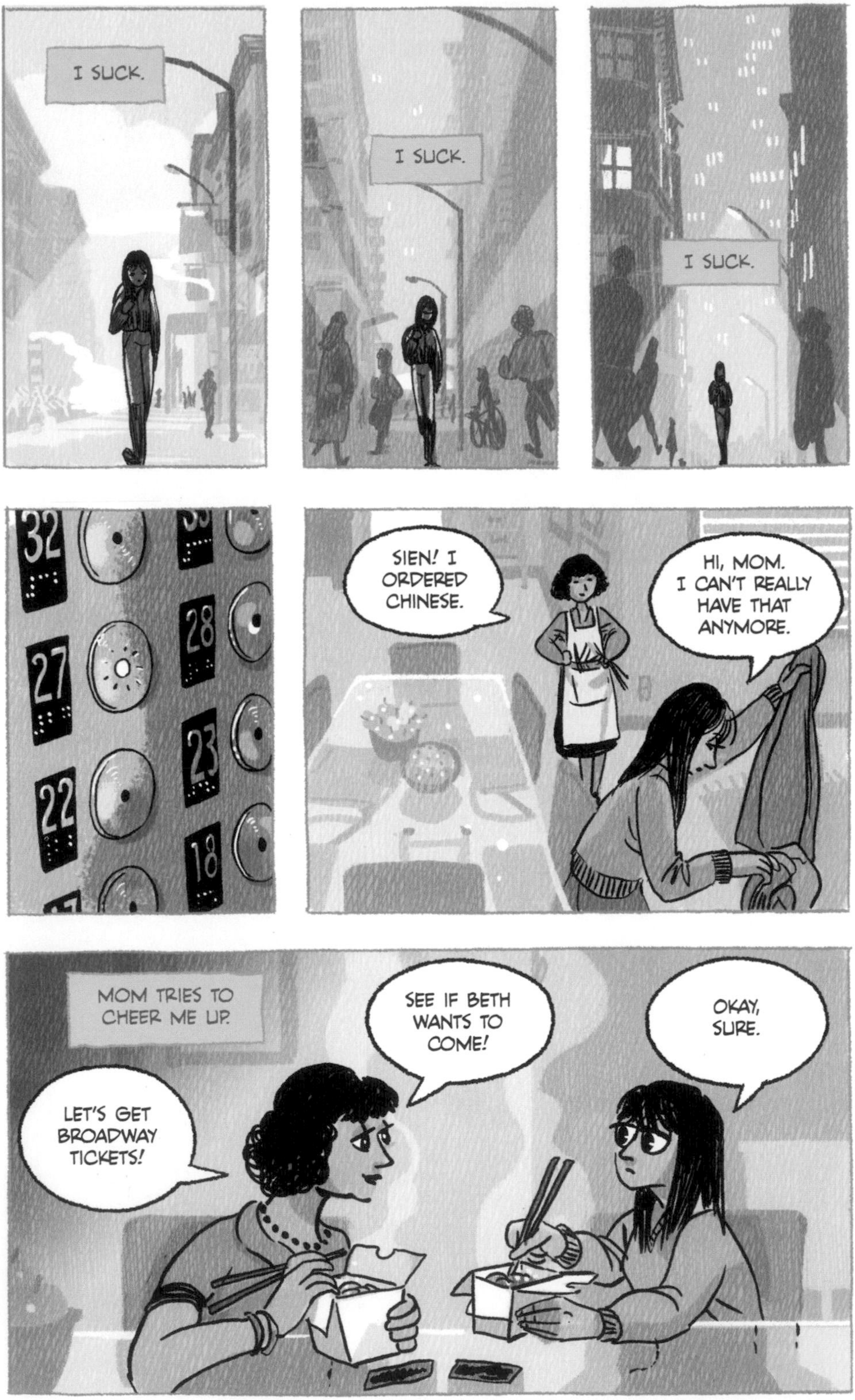
I SUCK.
I SUCK.
I SUCK.
SIEN! I ORDERED CHINESE.
HI, MOM. I CAN'T REALLY HAVE THAT ANYMORE.
MOM TRIES TO CHEER ME UP.
LET'S GET BROADWAY TICKETS!
SEE IF BETH WANTS TO COME!
OKAY, SURE.

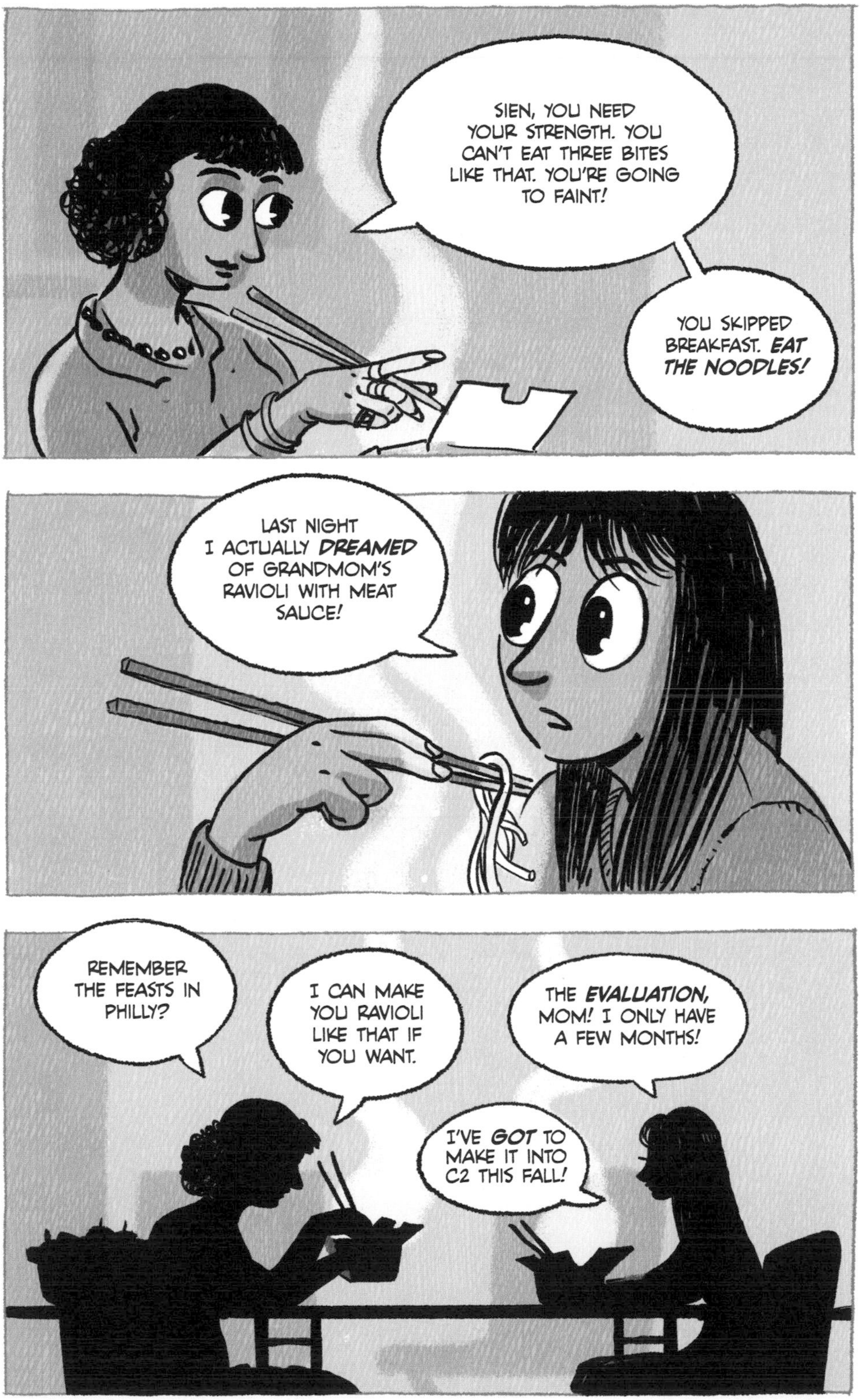
SIEN, YOU NEED YOUR STRENGTH. YOU CAN'T EAT THREE BITES LIKE THAT. YOU'RE GOING TO FAINT!
YOU SKIPPED BREAKFAST. ***EAT THE NOODLES!***
LAST NIGHT I ACTUALLY ***DREAMED*** OF GRANDMOM'S RAVIOLI WITH MEAT SAUCE!
REMEMBER THE FEASTS IN PHILLY?
I CAN MAKE YOU RAVIOLI LIKE THAT IF YOU WANT.
THE ***EVALUATION,*** MOM! I ONLY HAVE A FEW MONTHS!
I'VE ***GOT*** TO MAKE IT INTO C2 THIS FALL!

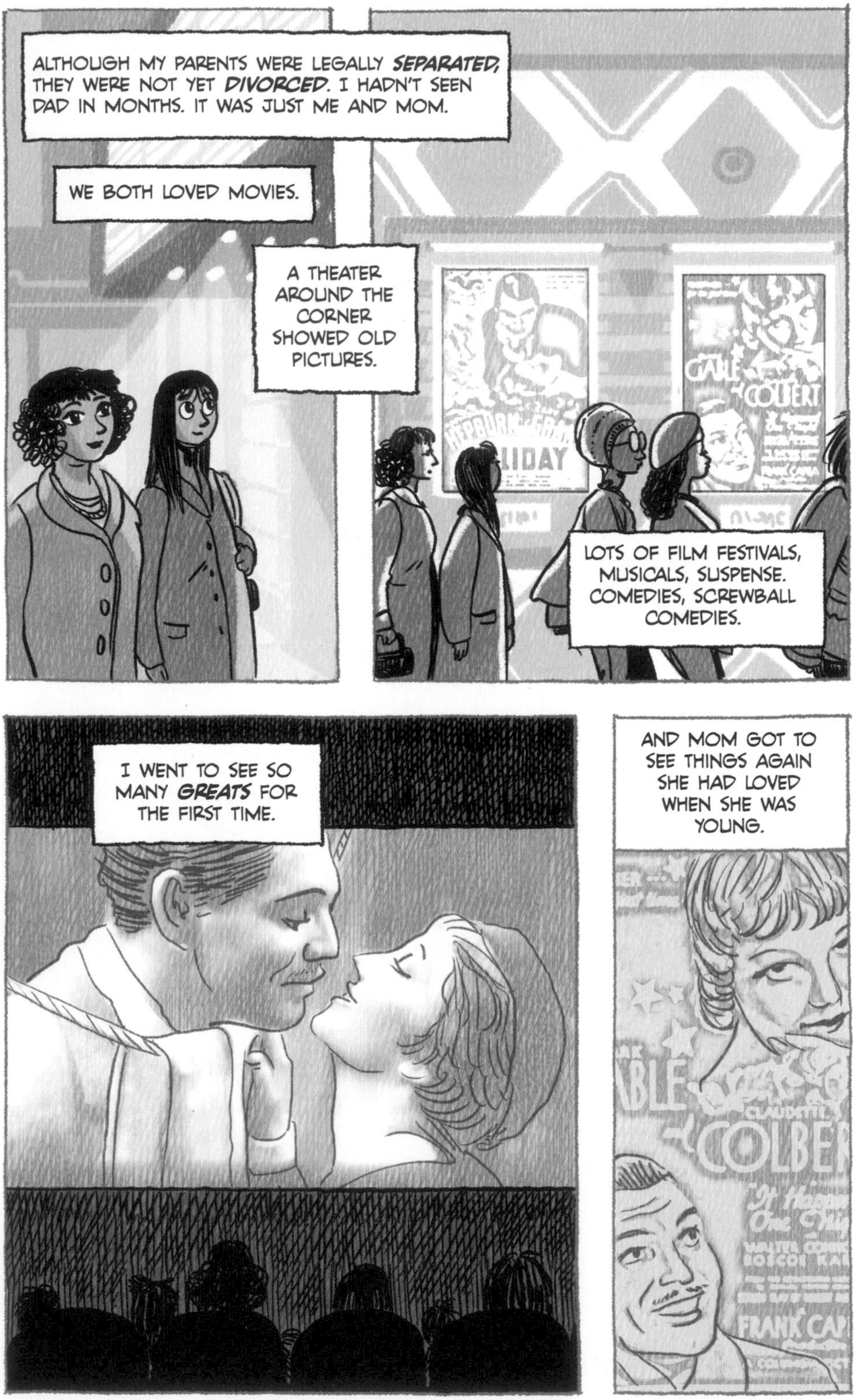
ALTHOUGH MY PARENTS WERE LEGALLY SEPARATED, THEY WERE NOT YET DIVORCED. I HADN'T SEEN DAD IN MONTHS. IT WAS JUST ME AND MOM.
WE BOTH LOVED MOVIES.
A THEATER AROUND THE CORNER SHOWED OLD PICTURES.
GABLE
COLBERT
LOTS OF FILM FESTIVALS, MUSICALS, SUSPENSE. COMEDIES, SCREWBALL COMEDIES.
I WENT TO SEE SO MANY GREATS FOR THE FIRST TIME.
AND MOM GOT TO SEE THINGS AGAIN SHE HAD LOVED WHEN SHE WAS YOUNG.

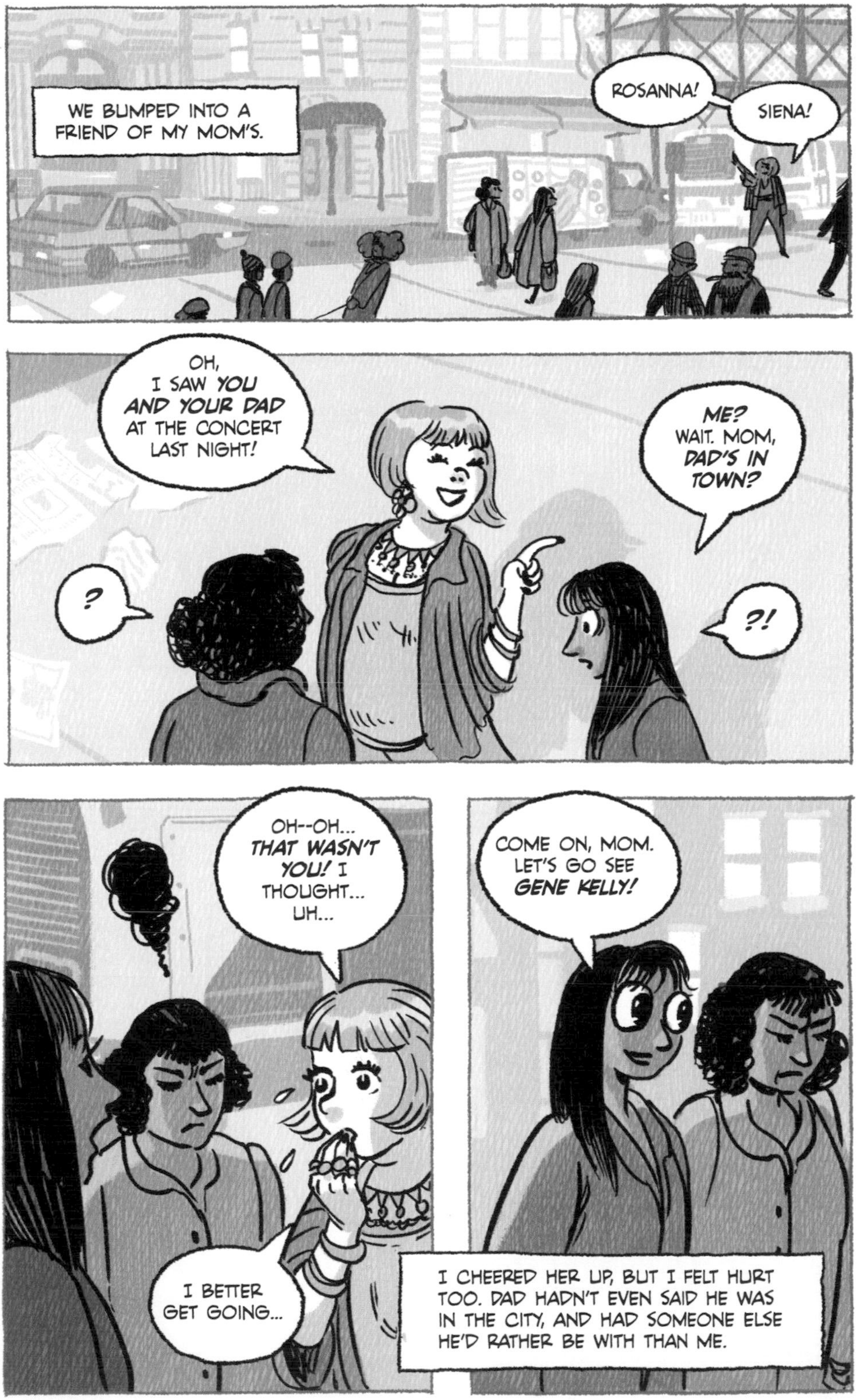
WE BUMPED INTO A FRIEND OF MY MOM'S.
ROSANNA!
SIENA!
OH, I SAW YOU AND YOUR DAD AT THE CONCERT LAST NIGHT!
ME? WAIT. MOM, DAD'S IN TOWN?
?
?!
OH--OH... THAT WASN'T YOU! I THOUGHT... UH...
I BETTER GET GOING...
COME ON, MOM. LET'S GO SEE GENE KELLY!
I CHEERED HER UP, BUT I FELT HURT TOO. DAD HADN'T EVEN SAID HE WAS IN THE CITY, AND HAD SOMEONE ELSE HE'D RATHER BE WITH THAN ME.

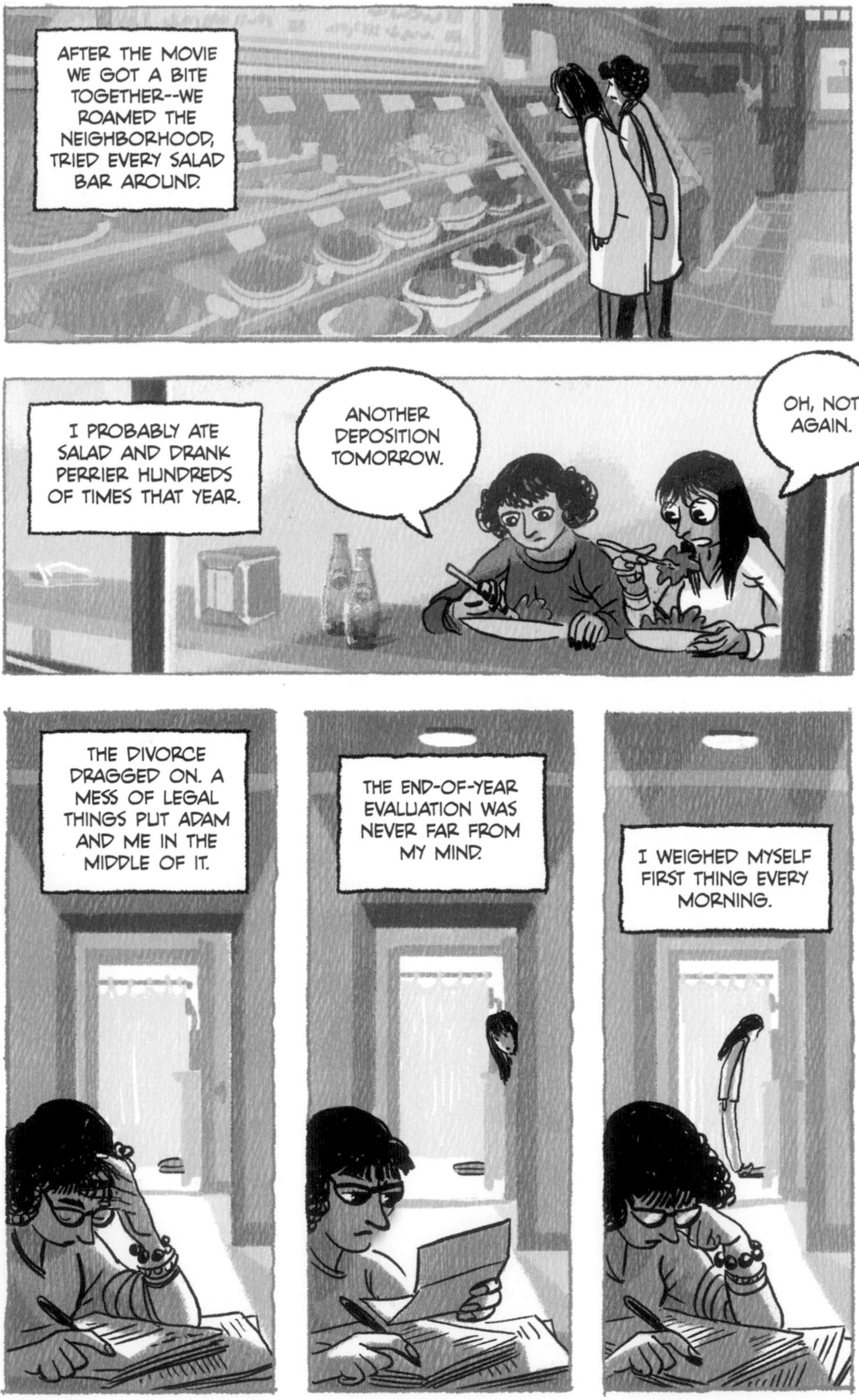
AFTER THE MOVIE WE GOT A BITE TOGETHER--WE ROAMED THE NEIGHBORHOOD, TRIED EVERY SALAD BAR AROUND.
I PROBABLY ATE SALAD AND DRANK PERRIER HUNDREDS OF TIMES THAT YEAR.
ANOTHER DEPOSITION TOMORROW.
OH, NOT AGAIN.
THE DIVORCE DRAGGED ON. A MESS OF LEGAL THINGS PUT ADAM AND ME IN THE MIDDLE OF IT.
THE END-OF-YEAR EVALUATION WAS NEVER FAR FROM MY MIND.
I WEIGHED MYSELF FIRST THING EVERY MORNING.

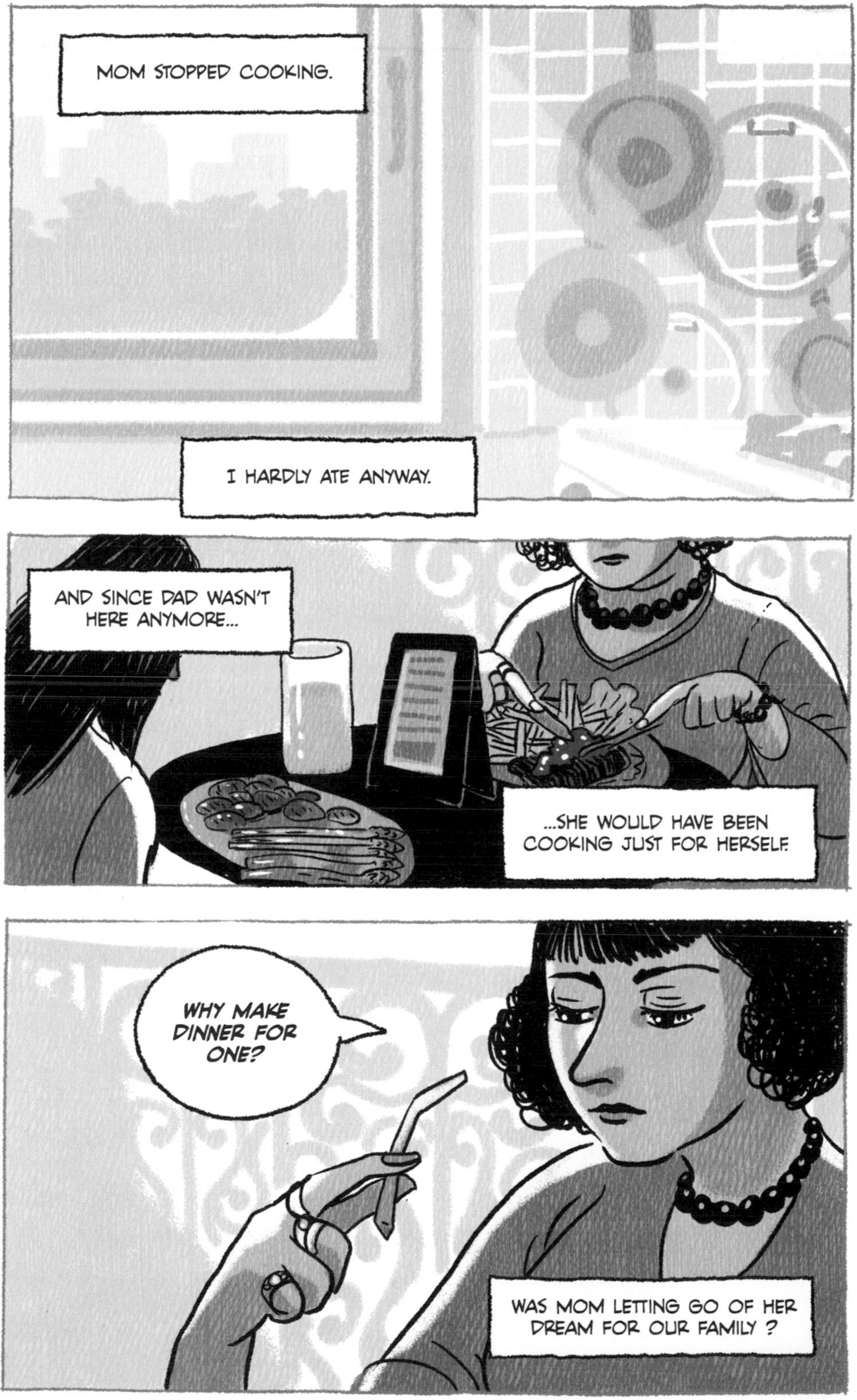
MOM STOPPED COOKING.
I HARDLY ATE ANYWAY.
AND SINCE DAD WASN'T HERE ANYMORE...
...SHE WOULD HAVE BEEN COOKING JUST FOR HERSELF.
WHY MAKE DINNER FOR ONE?
WAS MOM LETTING GO OF HER DREAM FOR OUR FAMILY ?

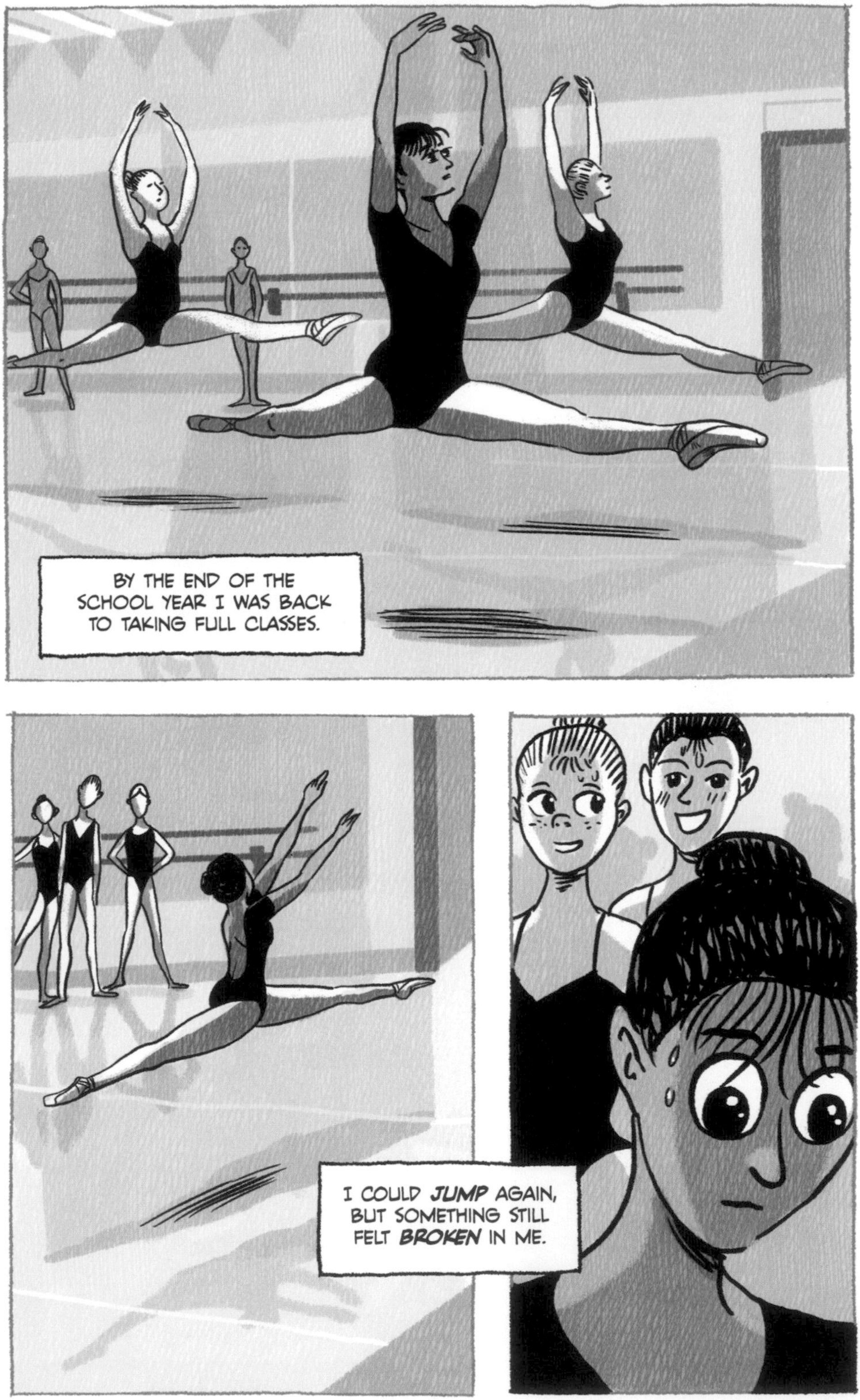
BY THE END OF THE SCHOOL YEAR I WAS BACK TO TAKING FULL CLASSES.
I COULD *JUMP* AGAIN, BUT SOMETHING STILL FELT *BROKEN* IN ME.

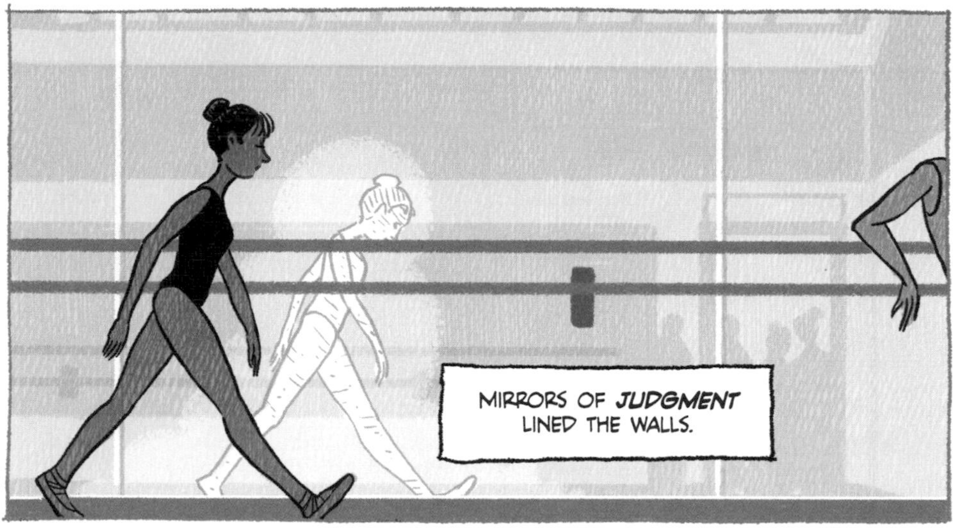
MIRRORS OF ***JUDGMENT*** LINED THE WALLS.

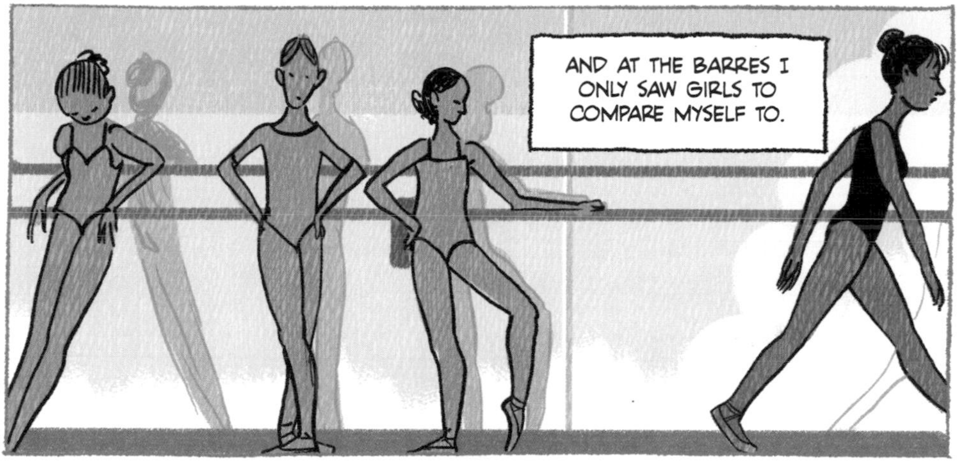
AND AT THE BARRES I ONLY SAW GIRLS TO COMPARE MYSELF TO.

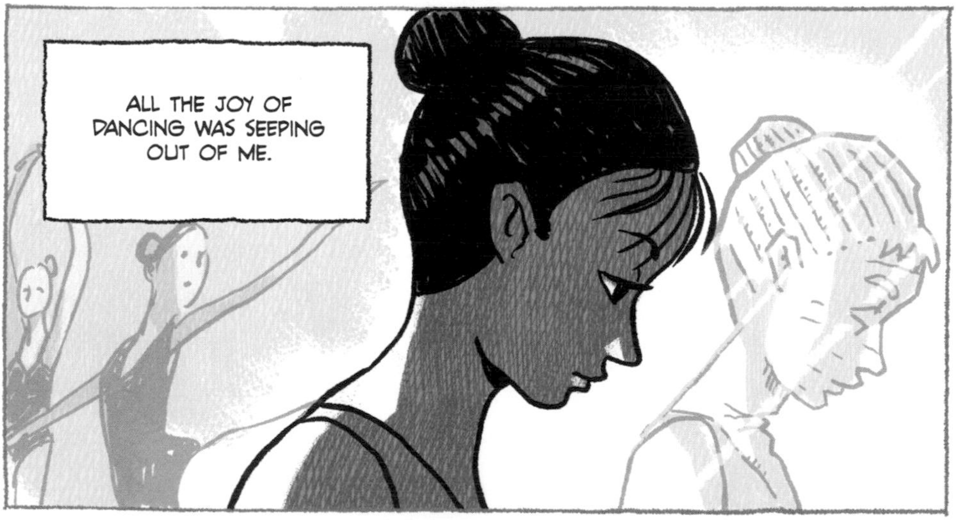
ALL THE JOY OF DANCING WAS SEEPING OUT OF ME.

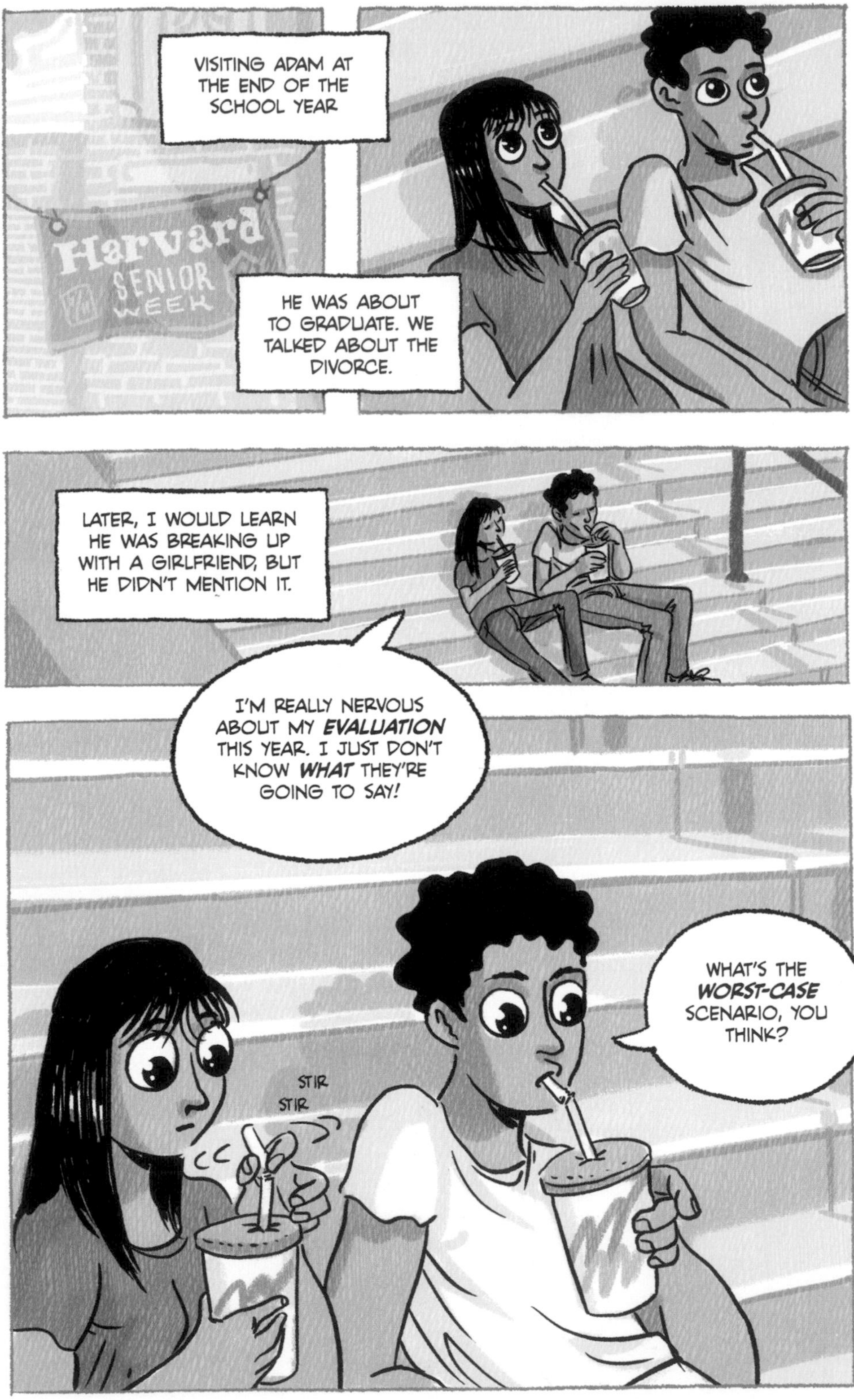
VISITING ADAM AT THE END OF THE SCHOOL YEAR
Harvard SENIOR WEEK
HE WAS ABOUT TO GRADUATE. WE TALKED ABOUT THE DIVORCE.
LATER, I WOULD LEARN HE WAS BREAKING UP WITH A GIRLFRIEND, BUT HE DIDN'T MENTION IT.
I'M REALLY NERVOUS ABOUT MY ***EVALUATION*** THIS YEAR. I JUST DON'T KNOW ***WHAT*** THEY'RE GOING TO SAY!
WHAT'S THE ***WORST-CASE*** SCENARIO, YOU THINK?
STIR
STIR

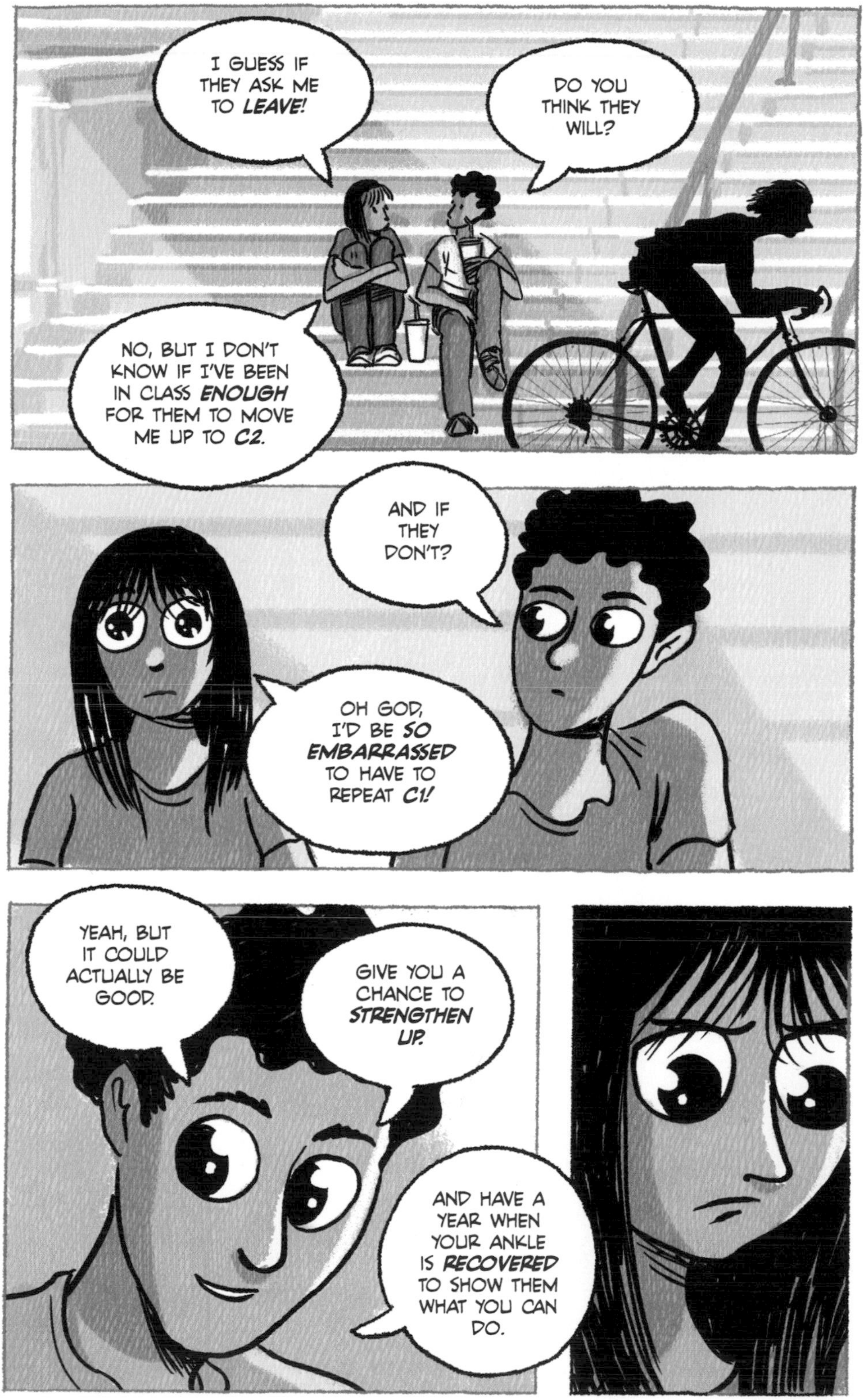
I GUESS IF THEY ASK ME TO LEAVE!
DO YOU THINK THEY WILL?
NO, BUT I DON'T KNOW IF I'VE BEEN IN CLASS ENOUGH FOR THEM TO MOVE ME UP TO C2.
AND IF THEY DON'T?
OH GOD, I'D BE SO EMBARRASSED TO HAVE TO REPEAT C1!
YEAH, BUT IT COULD ACTUALLY BE GOOD.
GIVE YOU A CHANCE TO STRENGTHEN UP.
AND HAVE A YEAR WHEN YOUR ANKLE IS RECOVERED TO SHOW THEM WHAT YOU CAN DO.

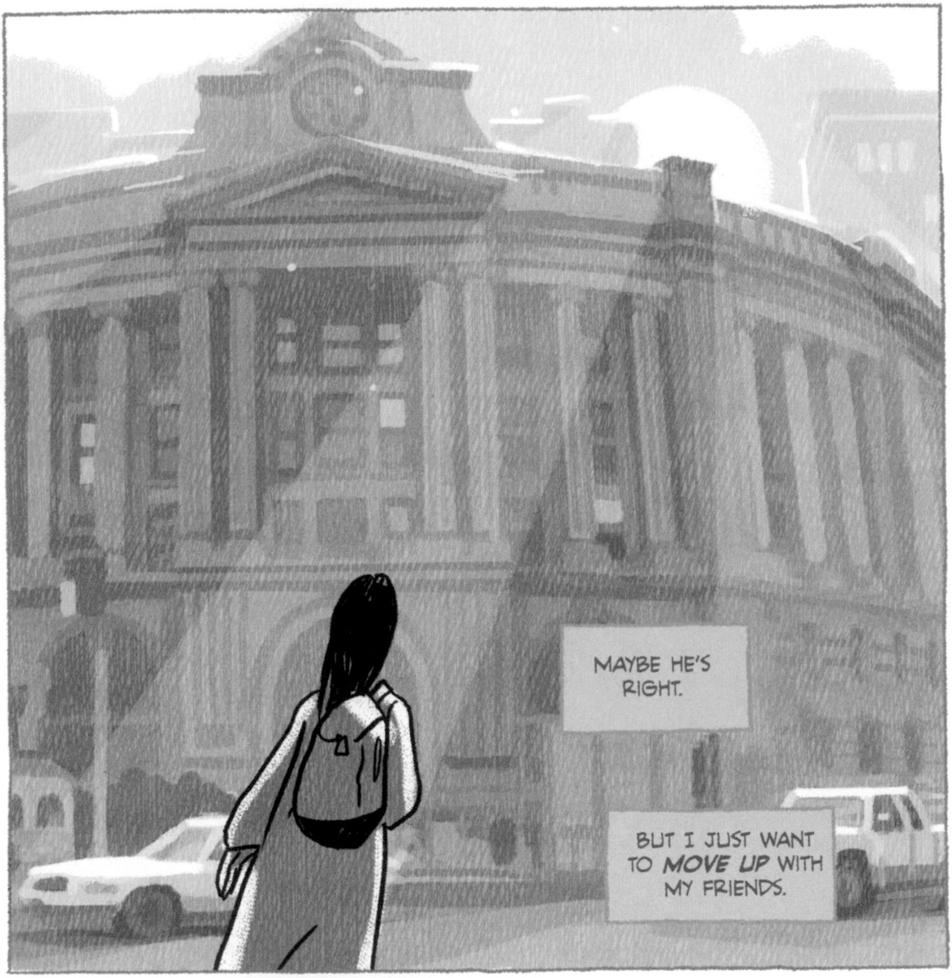
MAYBE HE'S RIGHT.
BUT I JUST WANT TO MOVE UP WITH MY FRIENDS.

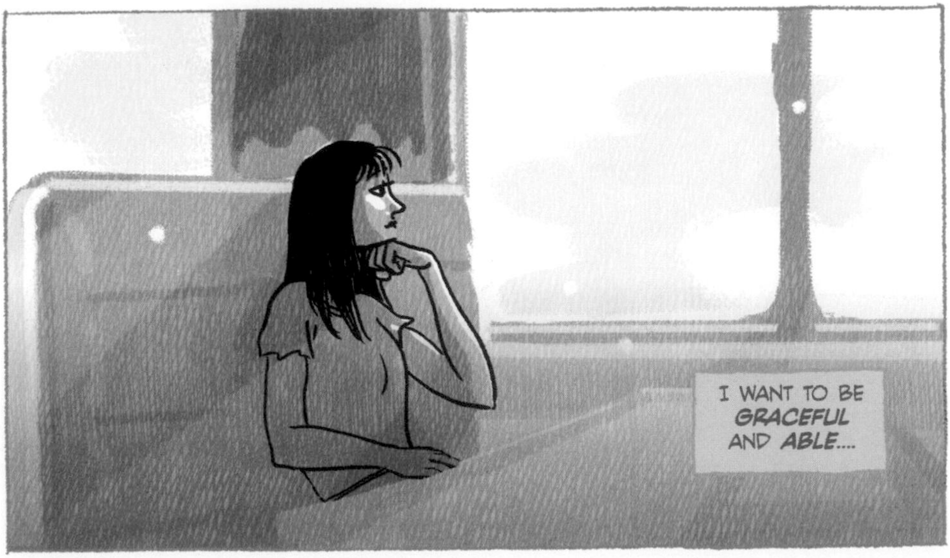
I WANT TO BE GRACEFUL AND ABLE....

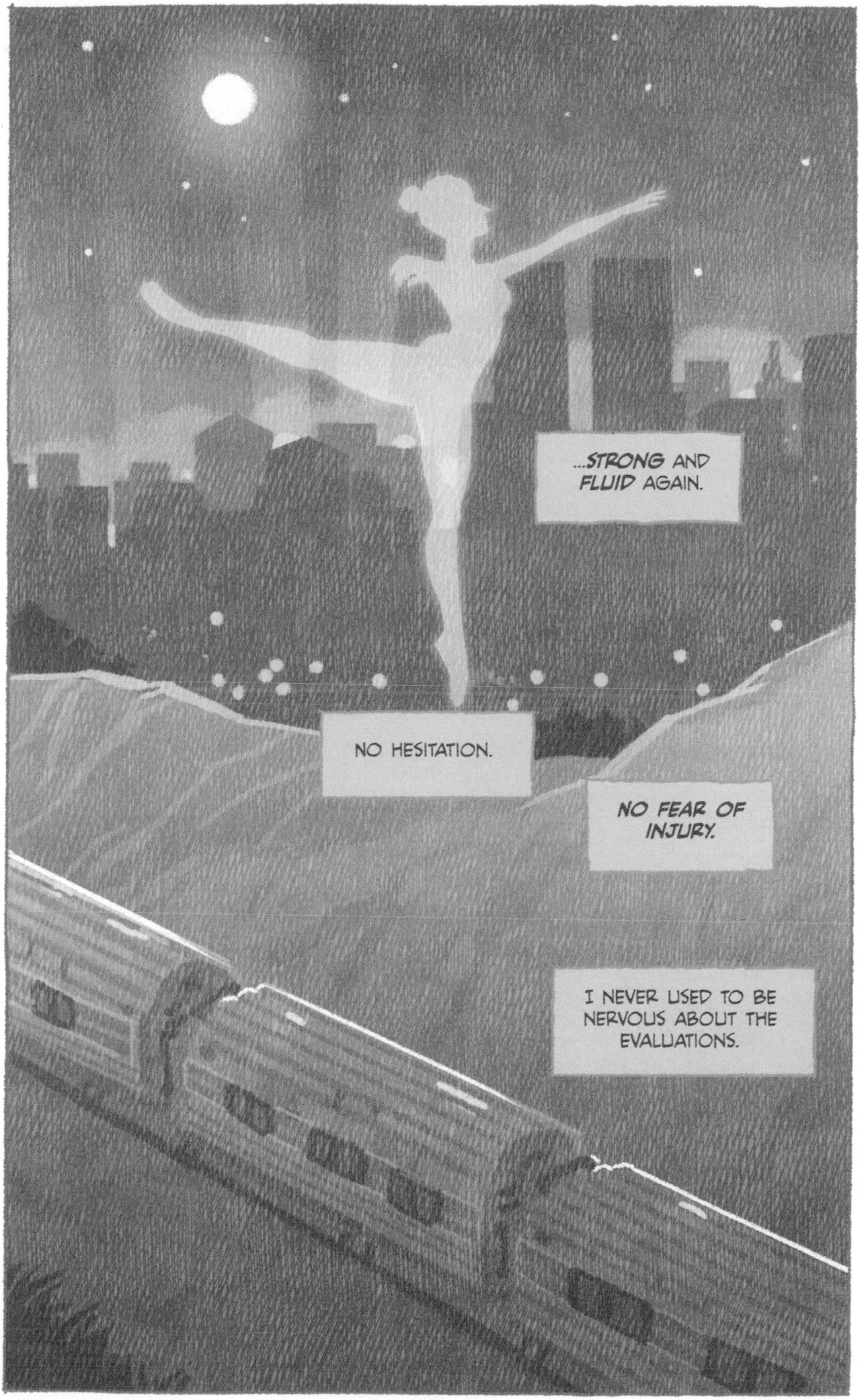
...STRONG AND FLUID AGAIN.
NO HESITATION.
NO FEAR OF INJURY.
I NEVER USED TO BE NERVOUS ABOUT THE EVALUATIONS.

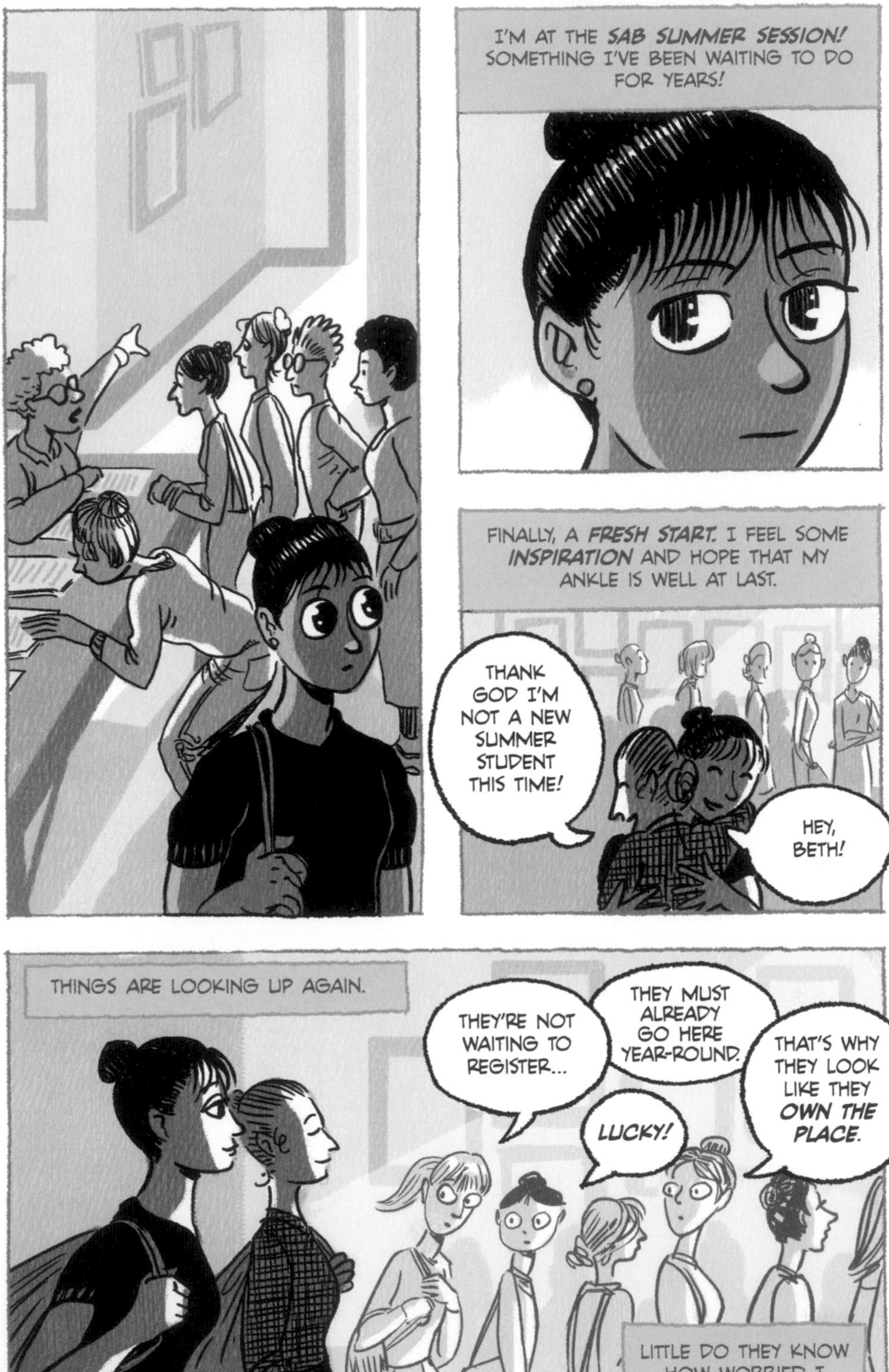
I'M AT THE ***SAB SUMMER SESSION!*** SOMETHING I'VE BEEN WAITING TO DO FOR YEARS!
FINALLY, A ***FRESH START.*** I FEEL SOME ***INSPIRATION*** AND HOPE THAT MY ANKLE IS WELL AT LAST.
THANK GOD I'M NOT A NEW SUMMER STUDENT THIS TIME!
HEY, BETH!
THINGS ARE LOOKING UP AGAIN.
THEY'RE NOT WAITING TO REGISTER...
THEY MUST ALREADY GO HERE YEAR-ROUND.
LUCKY!
THAT'S WHY THEY LOOK LIKE THEY ***OWN THE PLACE.***
LITTLE DO THEY KNOW HOW WORRIED I REALLY AM.

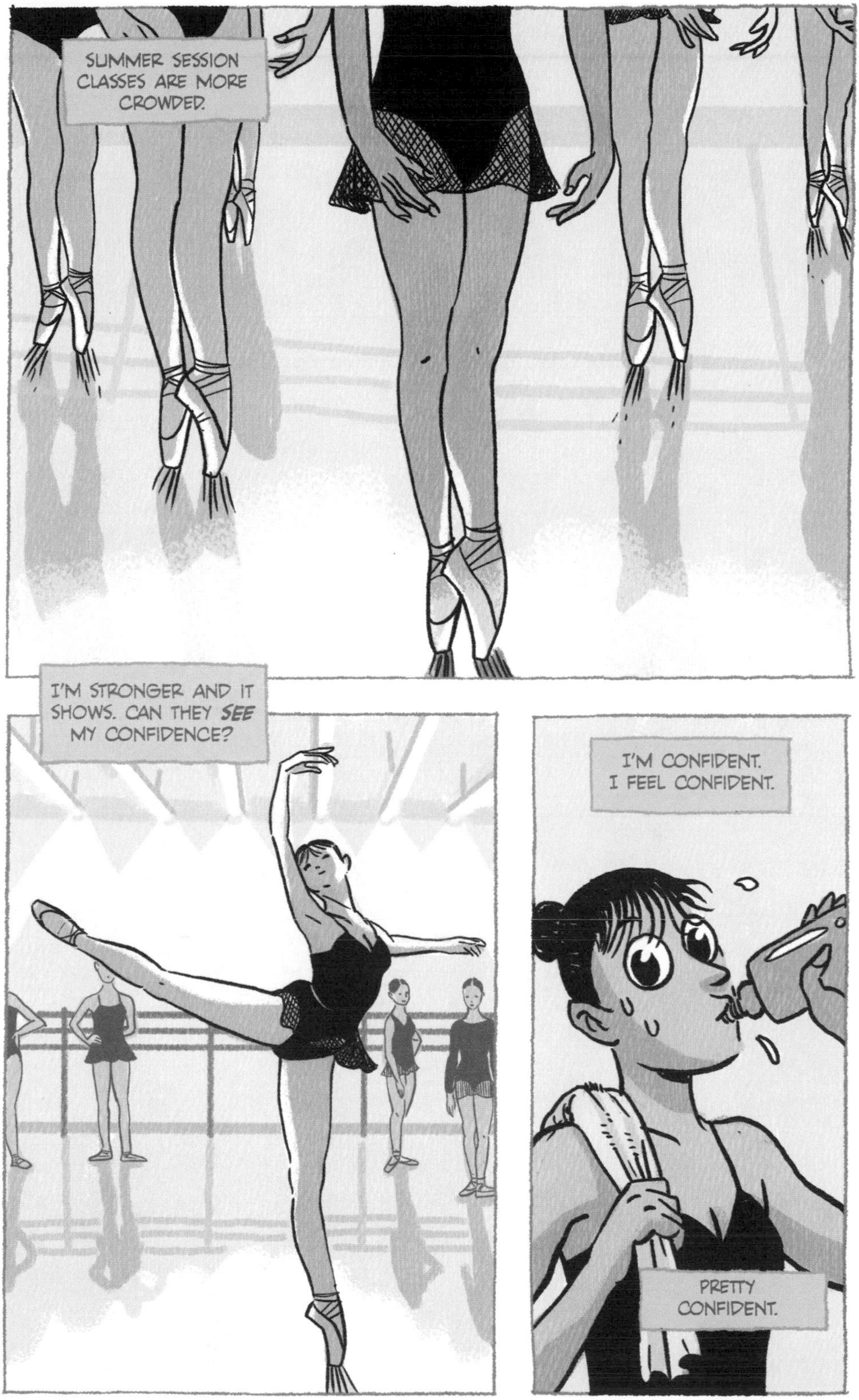
SUMMER SESSION CLASSES ARE MORE CROWDED.
I'M STRONGER AND IT SHOWS. CAN THEY *SEE* MY CONFIDENCE?
I'M CONFIDENT. I FEEL CONFIDENT.
PRETTY CONFIDENT.

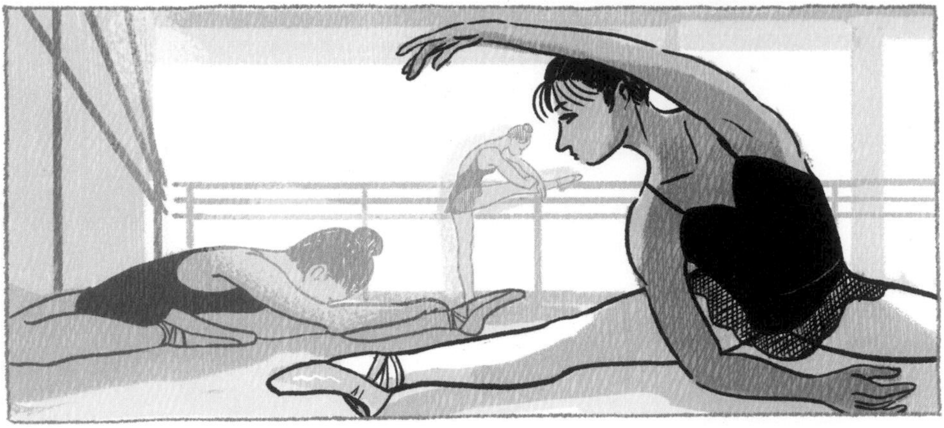

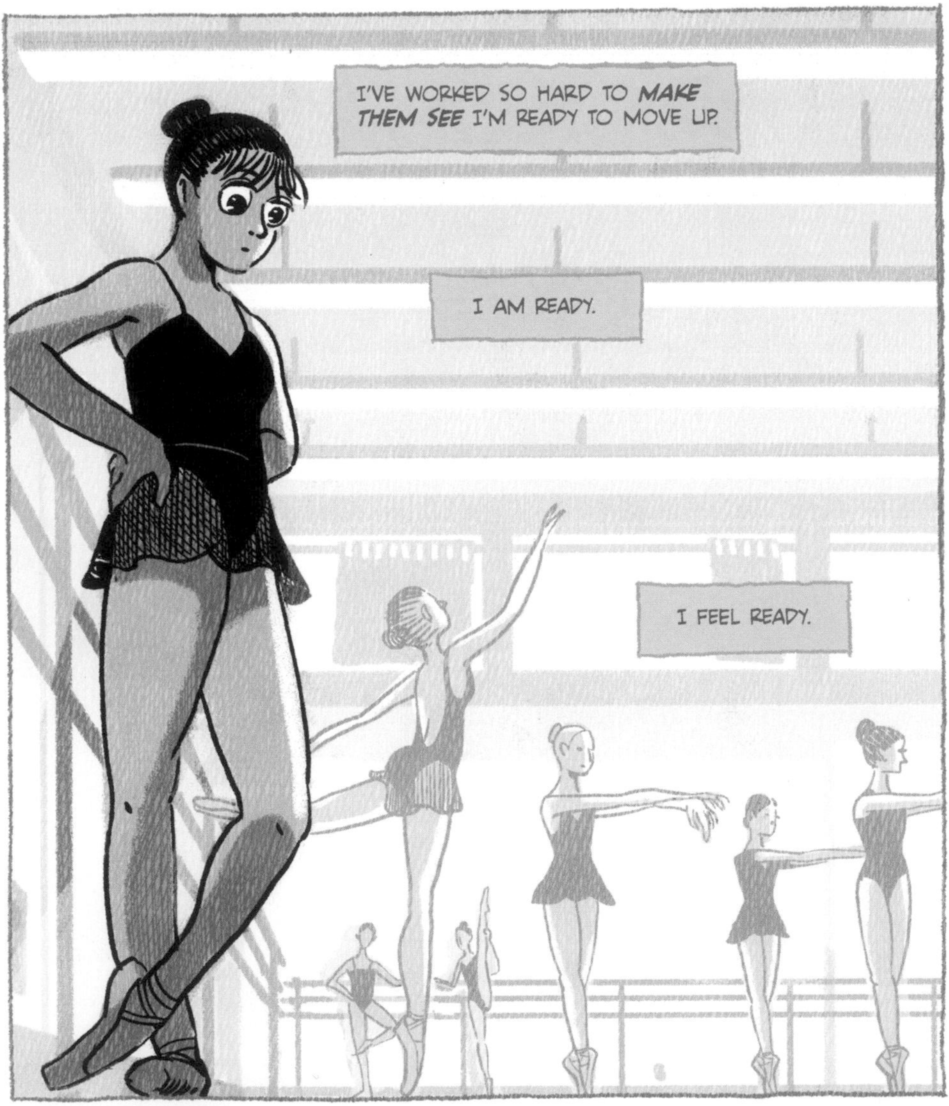
I'VE WORKED SO HARD TO MAKE THEM SEE I'M READY TO MOVE UP.
I AM READY.
I FEEL READY.

IT'S THE END OF SUMMER.

THE EVALUATION CALL.

I'M LISTENING ON THE
OTHER LINE.

WE'RE CONCERNED
ABOUT SIENA'S
PROGRESS THIS
YEAR.

SIENA WILL
HAVE TO
REPEAT C1.

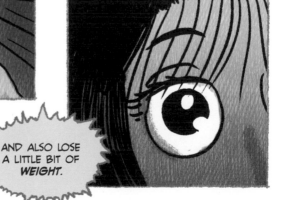

AND ALSO LOSE
A LITTLE BIT OF
WEIGHT.

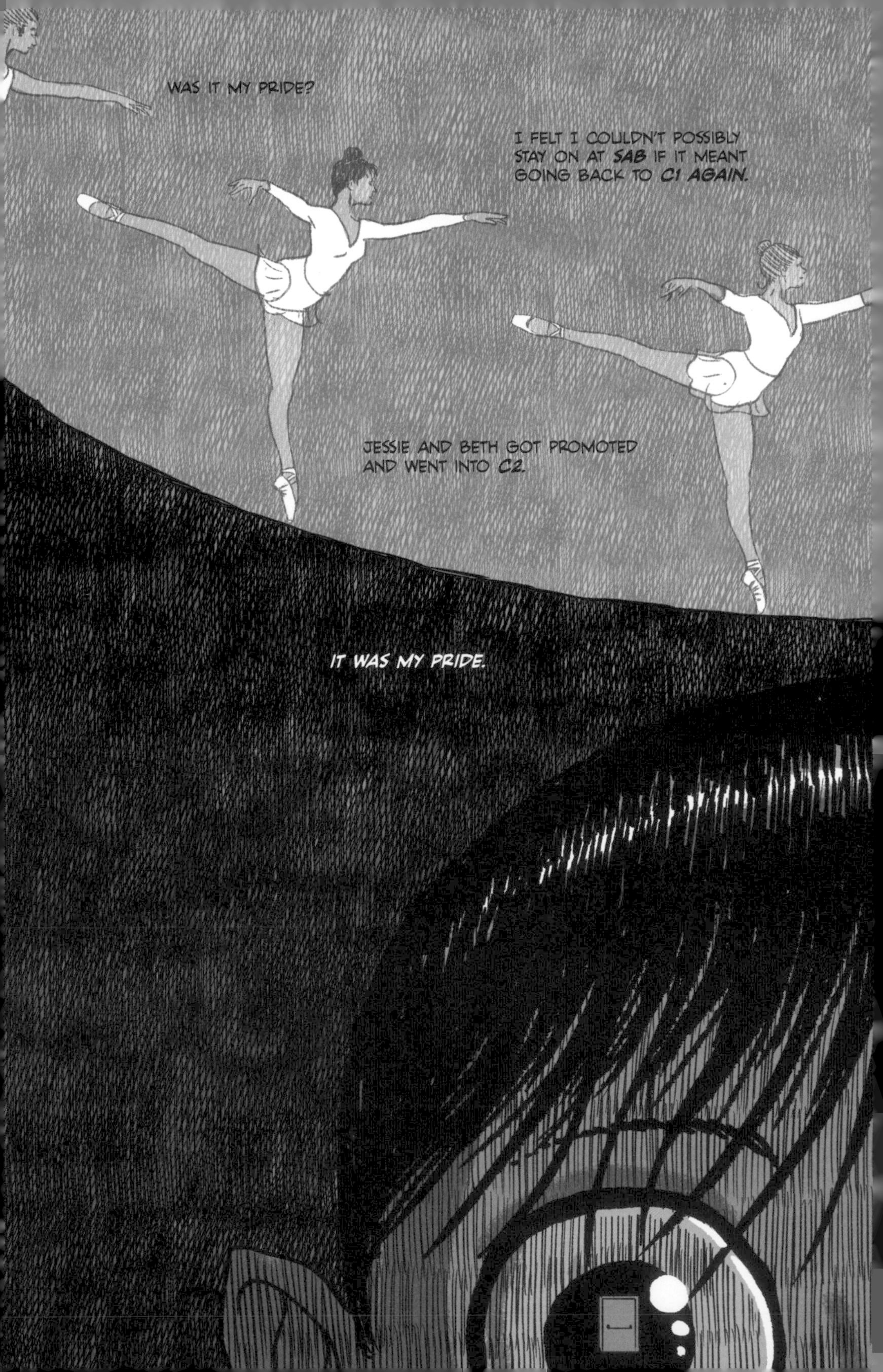
WAS IT MY PRIDE?
I FELT I COULDN'T POSSIBLY STAY ON AT SAB IF IT MEANT GOING BACK TO C1 AGAIN.
JESSIE AND BETH GOT PROMOTED AND WENT INTO C2.
IT WAS MY PRIDE.

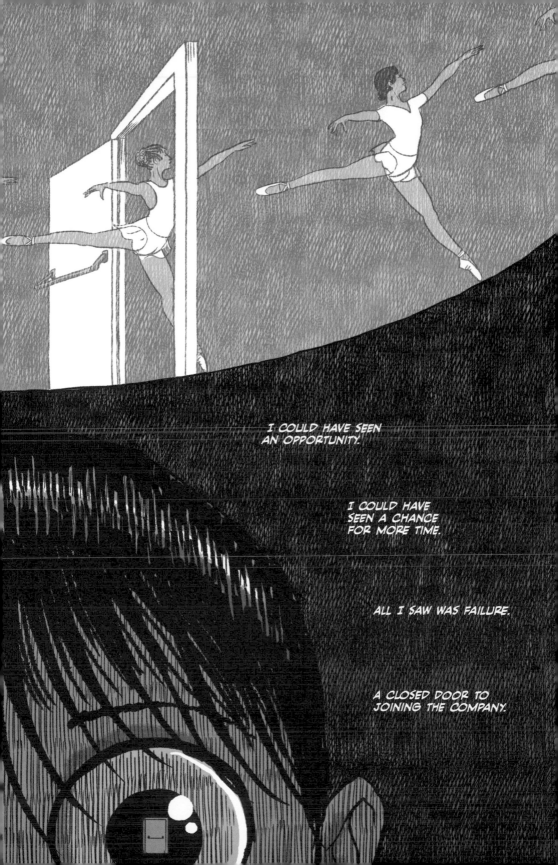

I COULD HAVE SEEN
AN OPPORTUNITY.

I COULD HAVE
SEEN A CHANCE
FOR MORE TIME.

ALL I SAW WAS FAILURE.

A CLOSED DOOR TO
JOINING THE COMPANY.

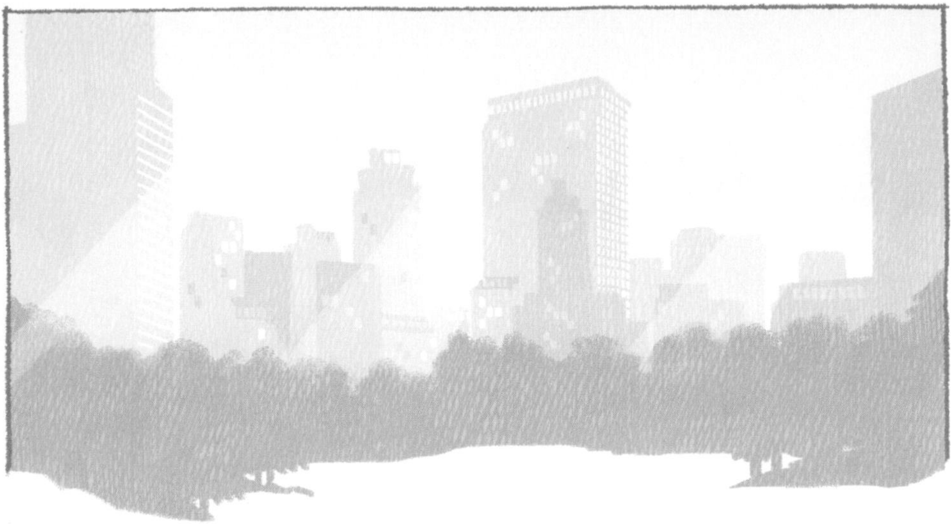

I DECIDED TO LEAVE
THE SCHOOL.

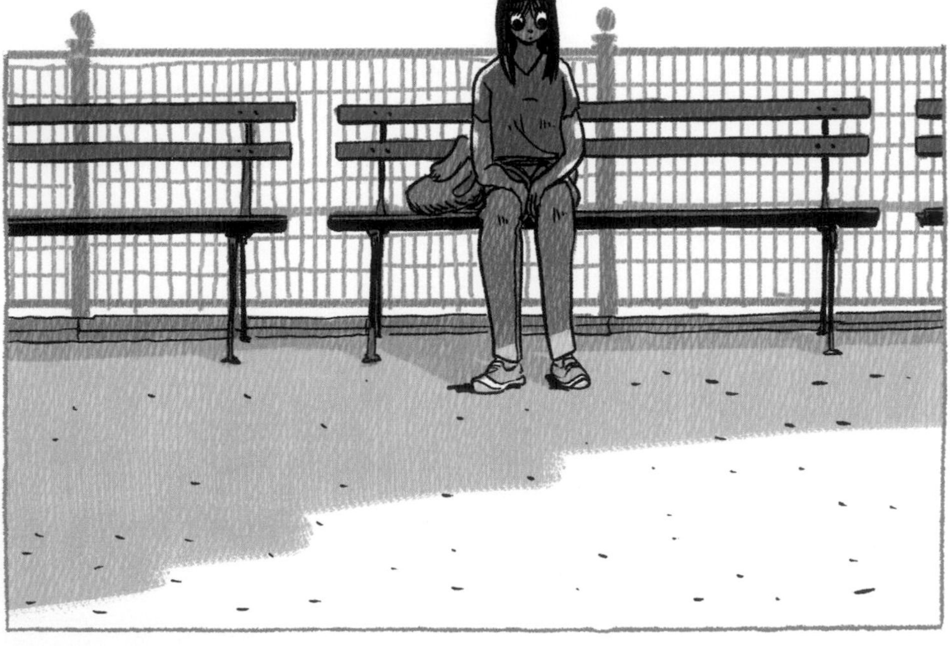

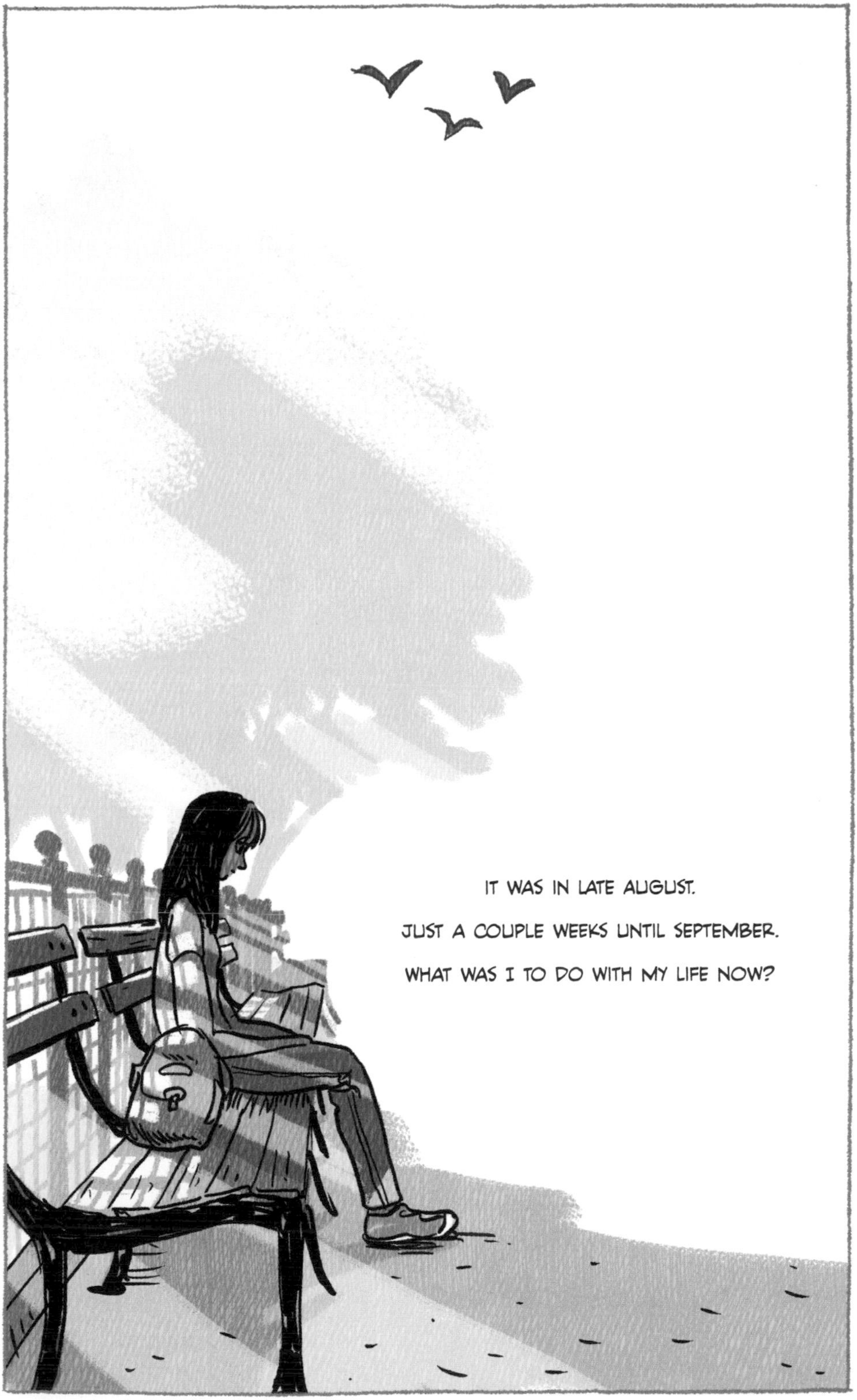
IT WAS IN LATE AUGUST.
JUST A COUPLE WEEKS UNTIL SEPTEMBER.
WHAT WAS I TO DO WITH MY LIFE NOW?

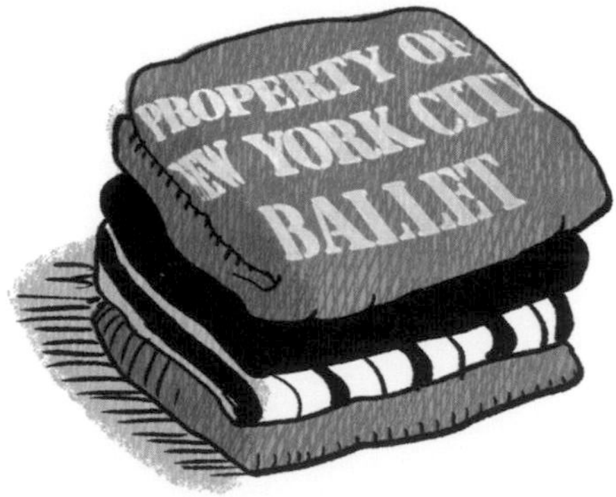
PROPERTY OF
NEW YORK CITY
BALLET

Part 3

The Kingdom of the Shades

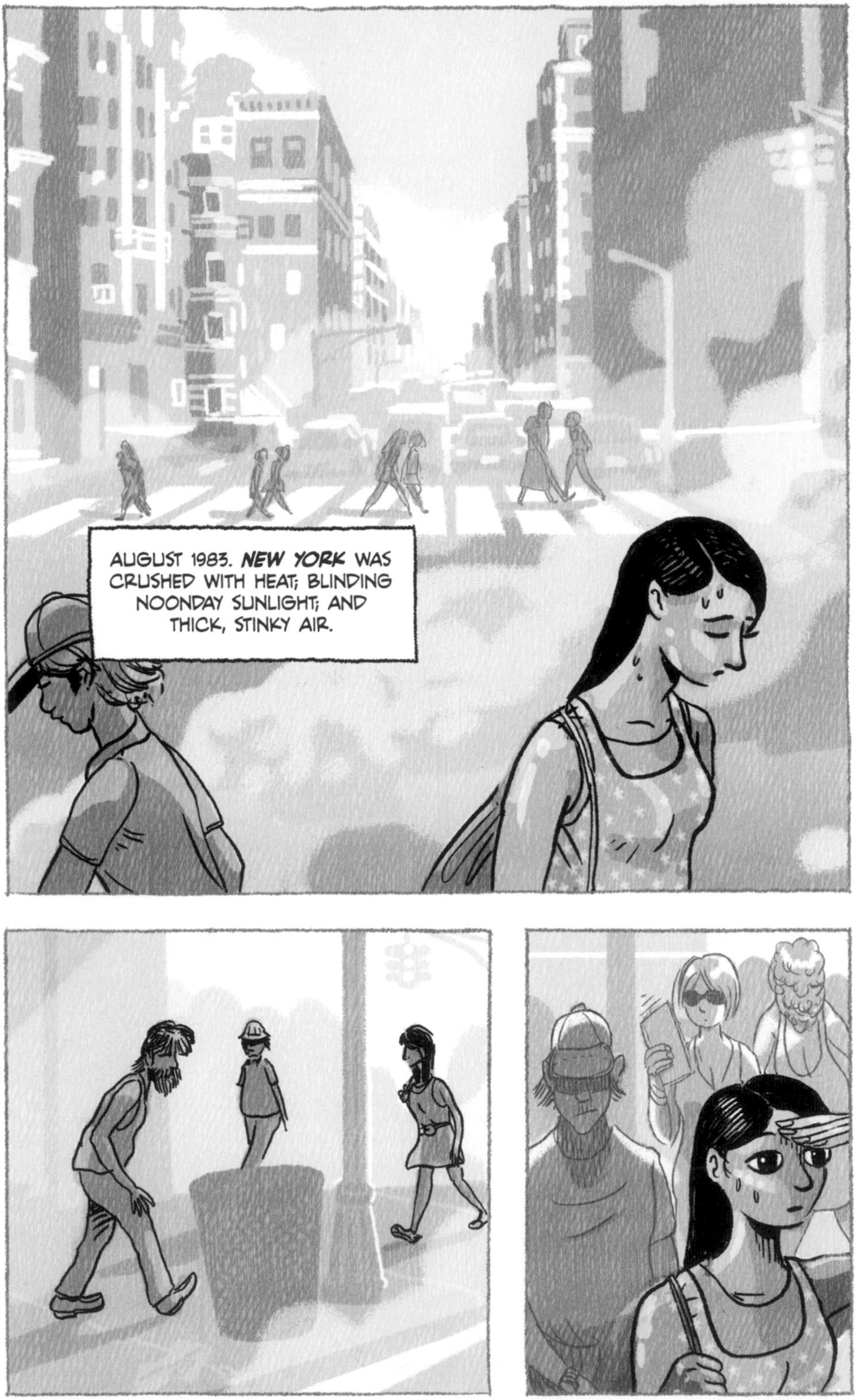
AUGUST 1983. NEW YORK WAS CRUSHED WITH HEAT; BLINDING NOONDAY SUNLIGHT; AND THICK, STINKY AIR.

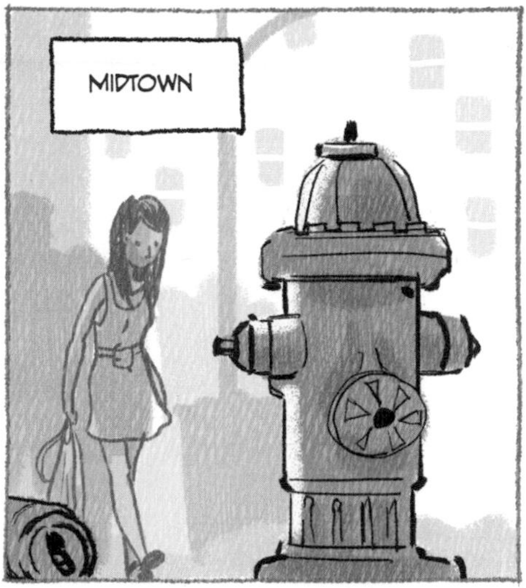
MIDTOWN

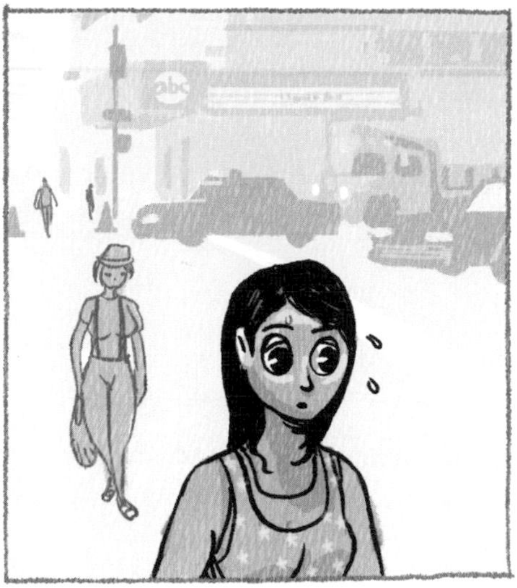

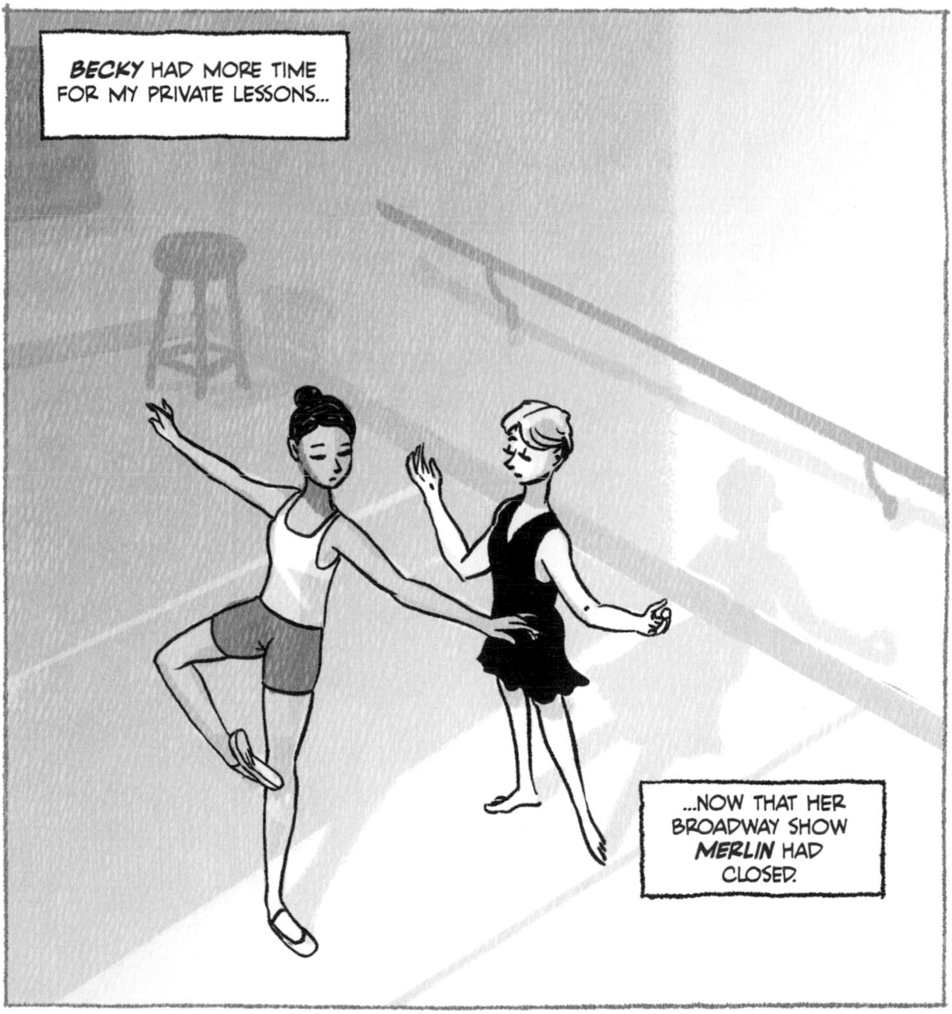
BECKY HAD MORE TIME FOR MY PRIVATE LESSONS...
...NOW THAT HER BROADWAY SHOW *MERLIN* HAD CLOSED.

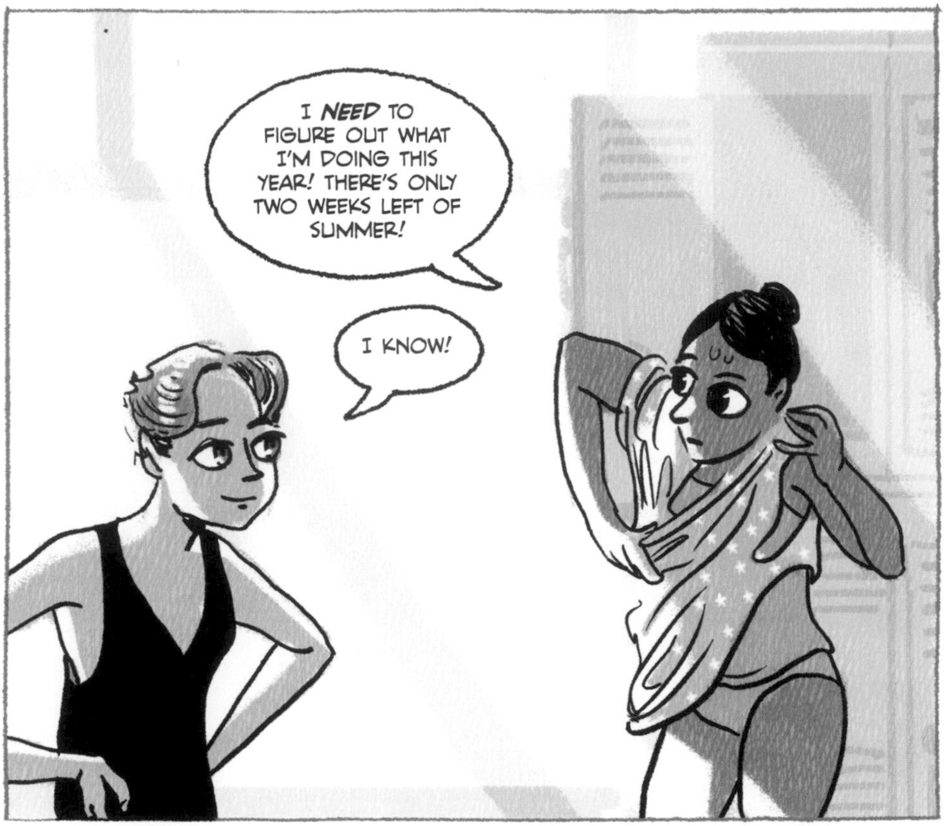
I NEED TO FIGURE OUT WHAT I'M DOING THIS YEAR! THERE'S ONLY TWO WEEKS LEFT OF SUMMER!
I KNOW!

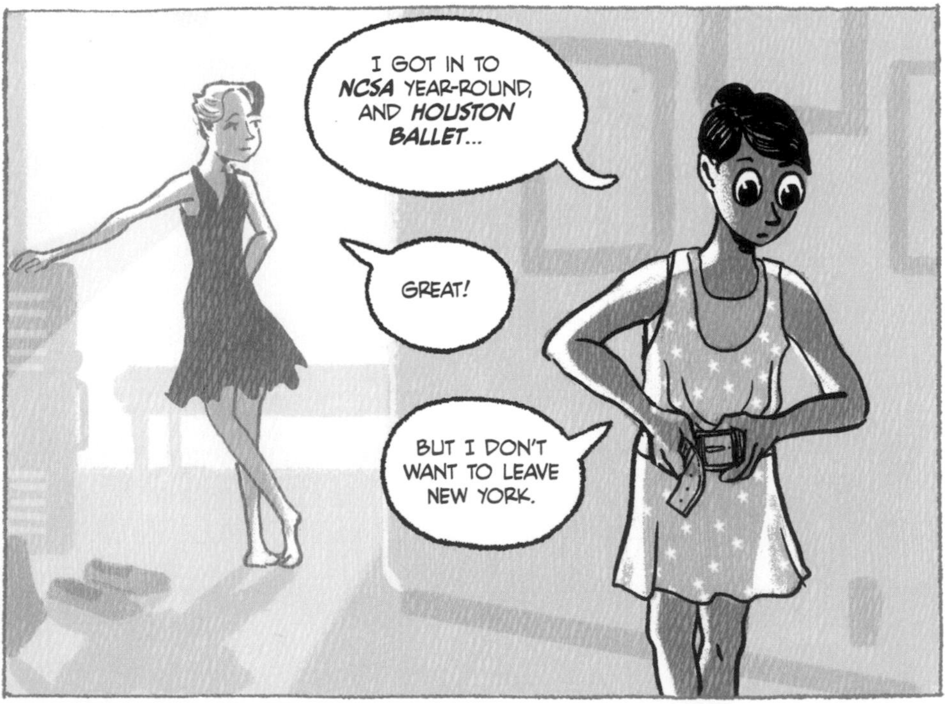
I GOT IN TO NCSA YEAR-ROUND, AND HOUSTON BALLET...
GREAT!
BUT I DON'T WANT TO LEAVE NEW YORK.

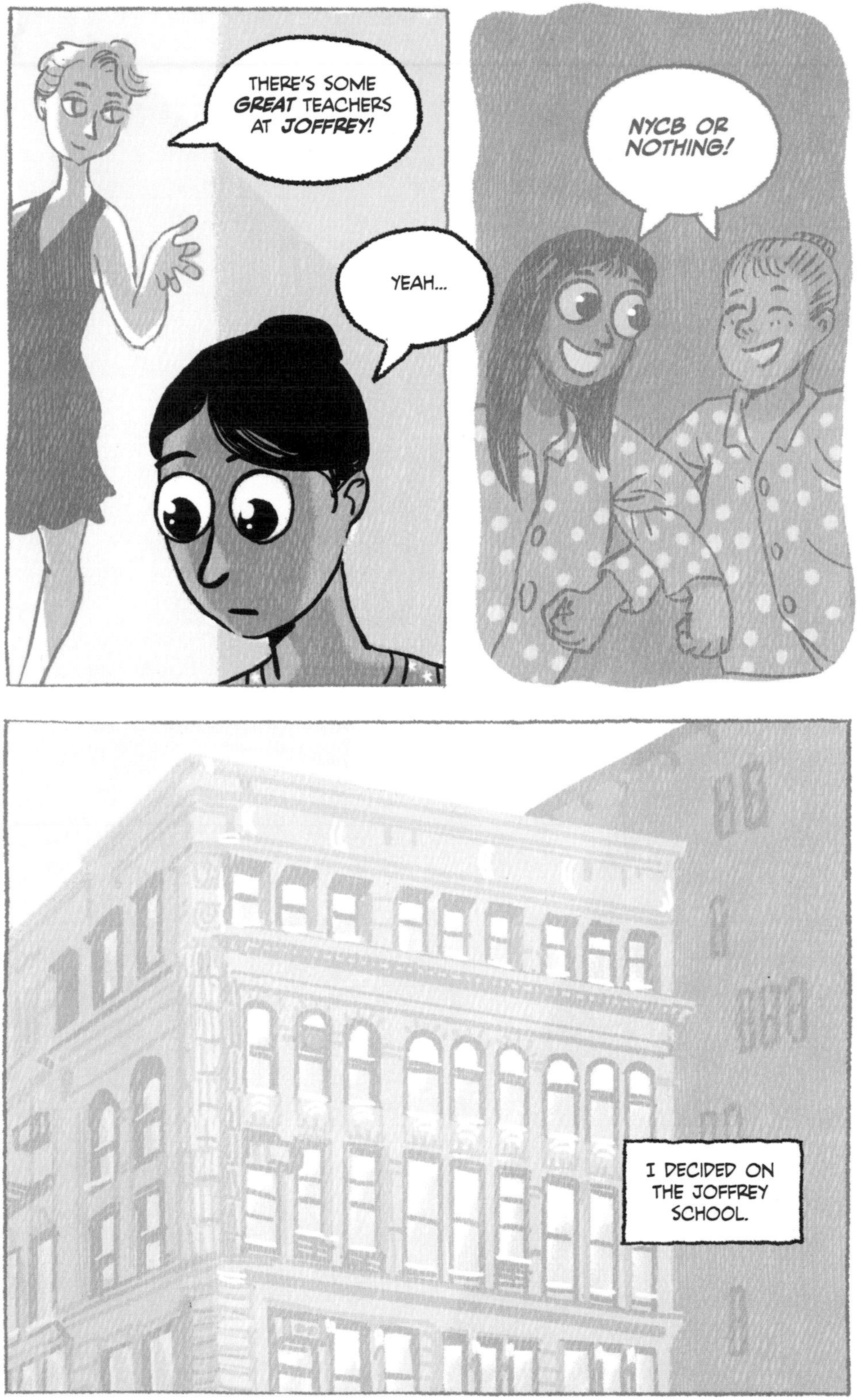
THERE'S SOME GREAT TEACHERS AT JOFFREY!
YEAH...
NYCB OR NOTHING!
I DECIDED ON THE JOFFREY SCHOOL.

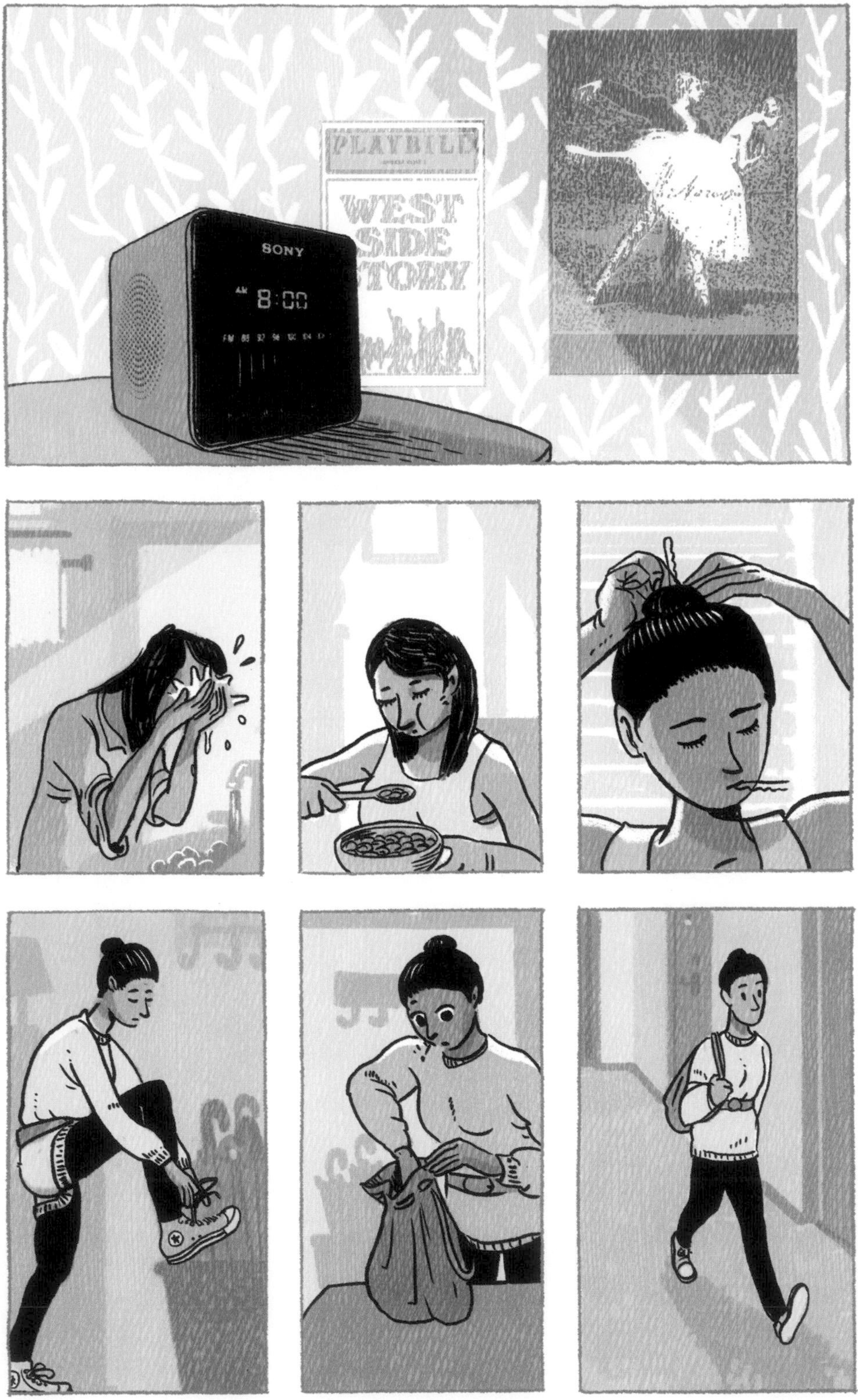
SONY
8:00
PLAYBILL
WEST SIDE STORY

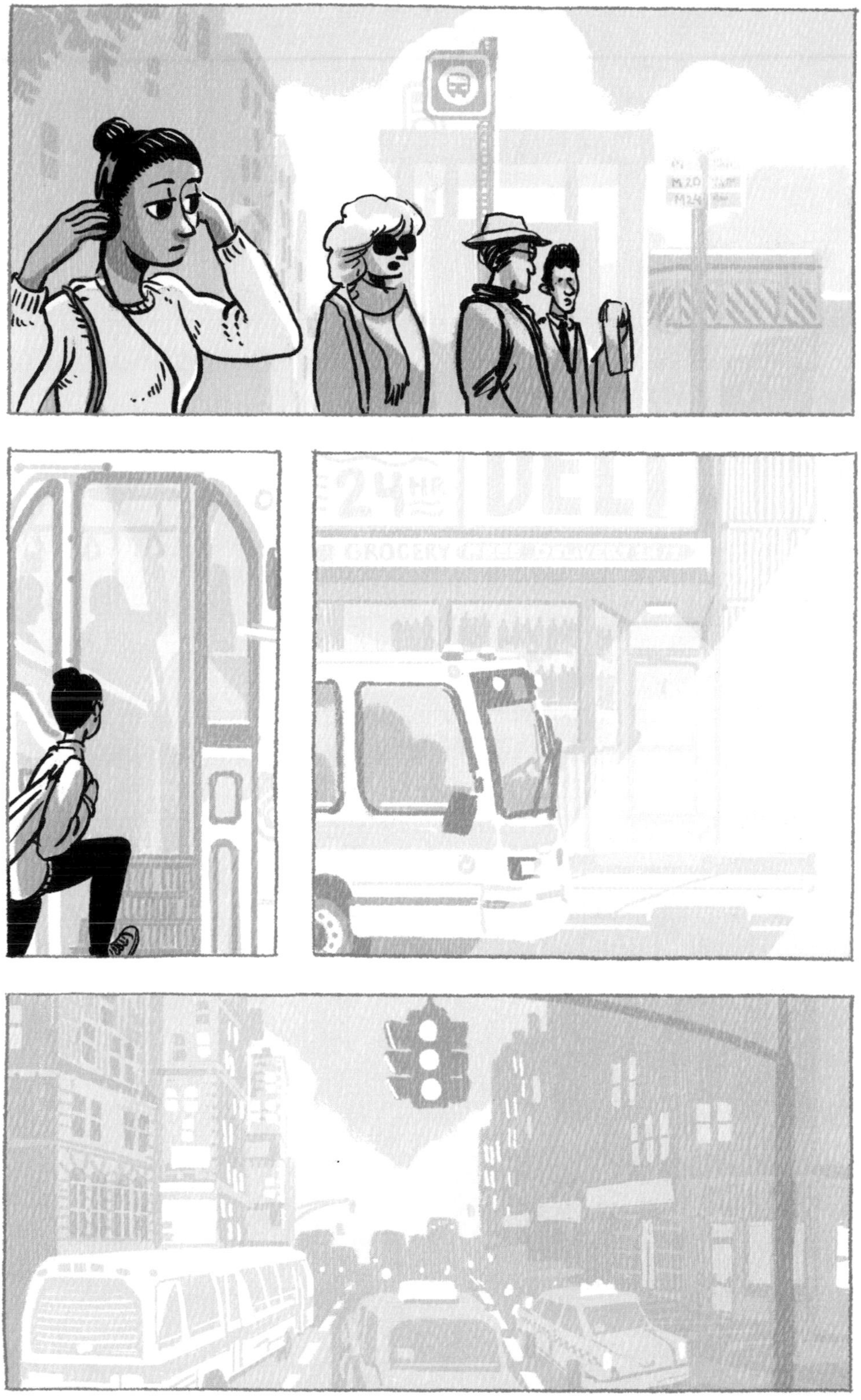
M20
M24
24HR
GROCERY

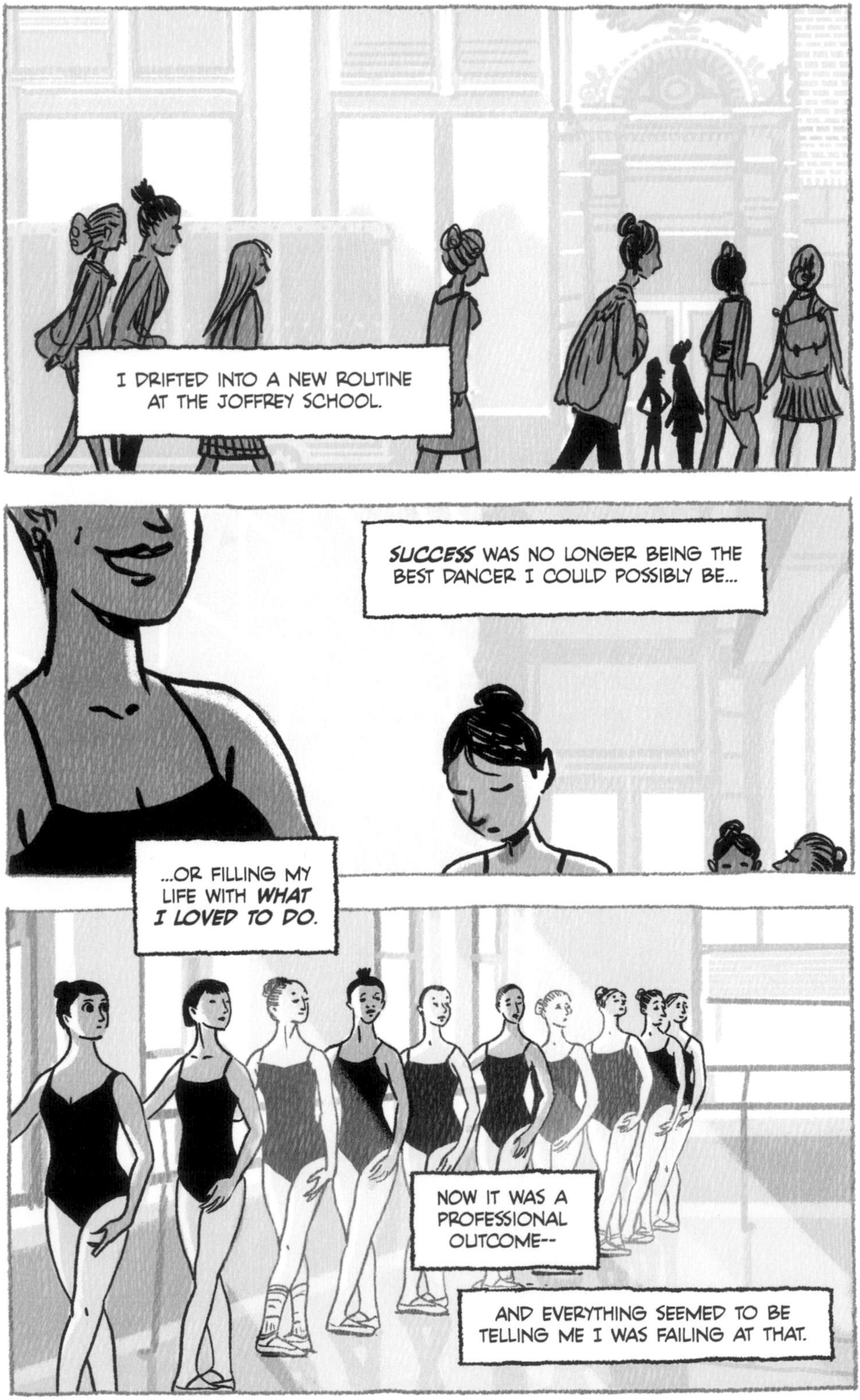
I DRIFTED INTO A NEW ROUTINE AT THE JOFFREY SCHOOL.
SUCCESS WAS NO LONGER BEING THE BEST DANCER I COULD POSSIBLY BE...
...OR FILLING MY LIFE WITH WHAT I LOVED TO DO.
NOW IT WAS A PROFESSIONAL OUTCOME--
AND EVERYTHING SEEMED TO BE TELLING ME I WAS FAILING AT THAT.

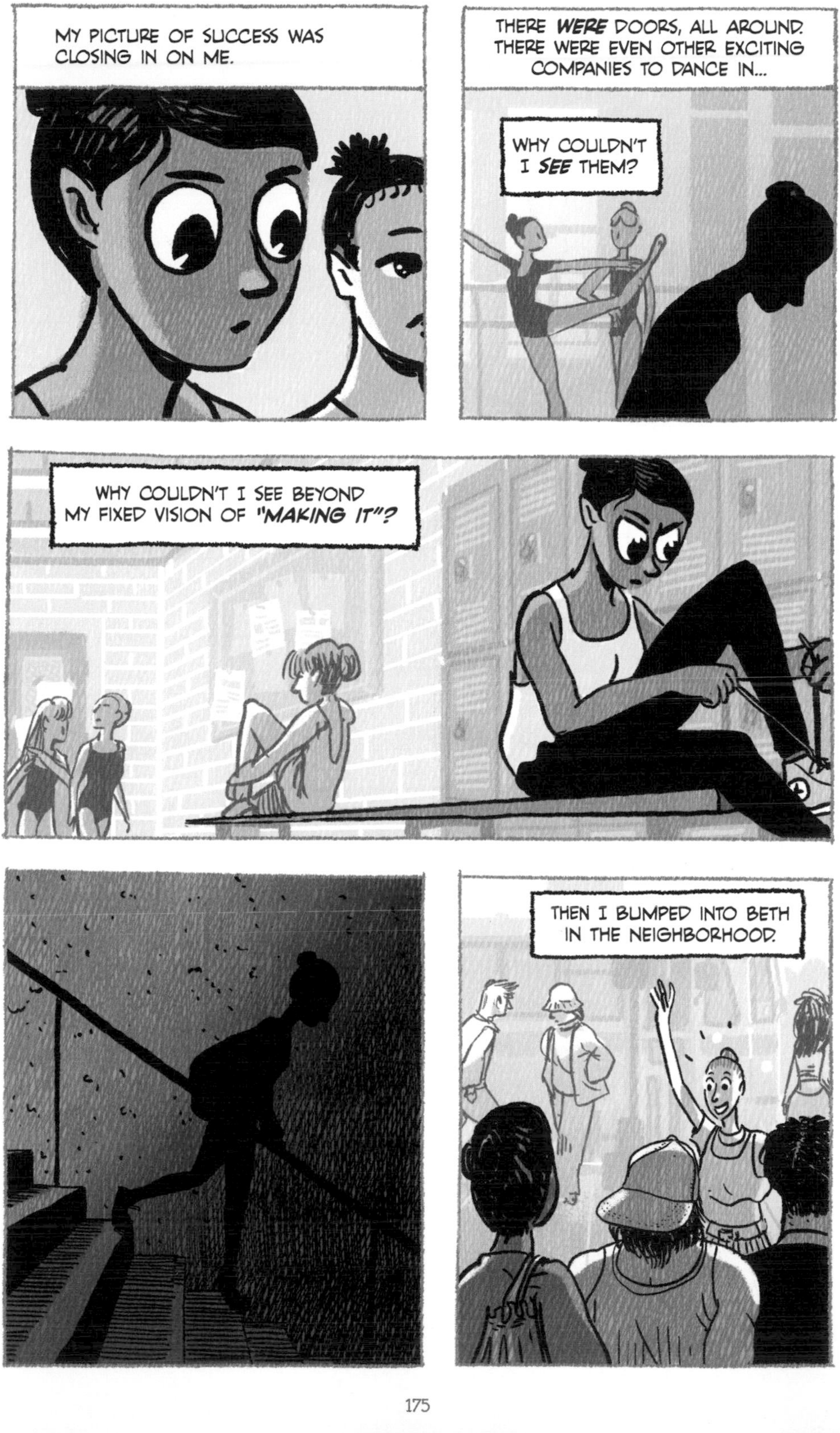

MY PICTURE OF SUCCESS WAS CLOSING IN ON ME.
THERE WERE DOORS, ALL AROUND. THERE WERE EVEN OTHER EXCITING COMPANIES TO DANCE IN...
WHY COULDN'T I SEE THEM?
WHY COULDN'T I SEE BEYOND MY FIXED VISION OF "MAKING IT"?
THEN I BUMPED INTO BETH IN THE NEIGHBORHOOD.

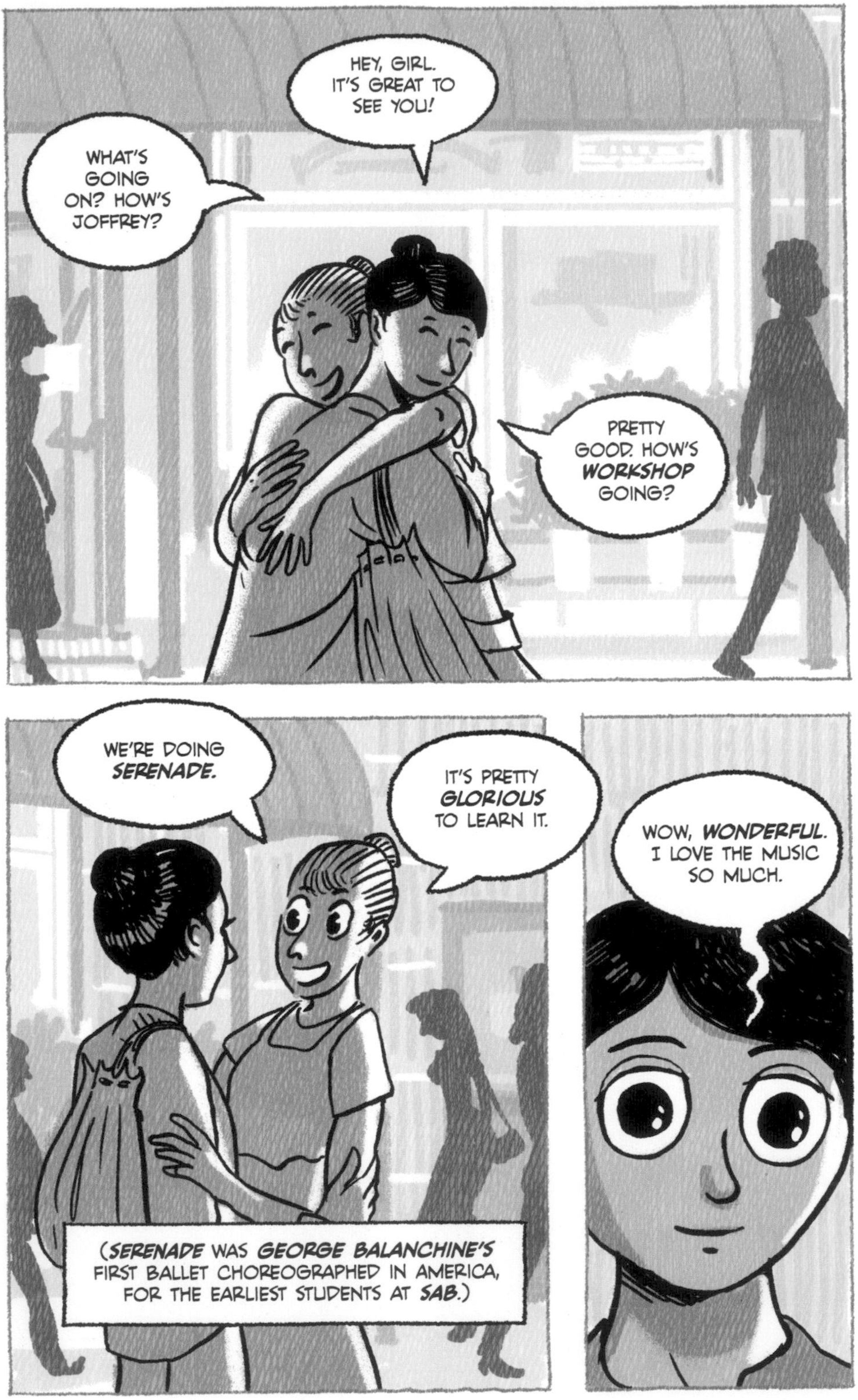
WHAT'S GOING ON? HOW'S JOFFREY?
HEY, GIRL. IT'S GREAT TO SEE YOU!
PRETTY GOOD. HOW'S **WORKSHOP** GOING?
WE'RE DOING ***SERENADE.***
IT'S PRETTY ***GLORIOUS*** TO LEARN IT.
(***SERENADE*** WAS ***GEORGE BALANCHINE'S*** FIRST BALLET CHOREOGRAPHED IN AMERICA, FOR THE EARLIEST STUDENTS AT ***SAB***.)
WOW, ***WONDERFUL.*** I LOVE THE MUSIC SO MUCH.

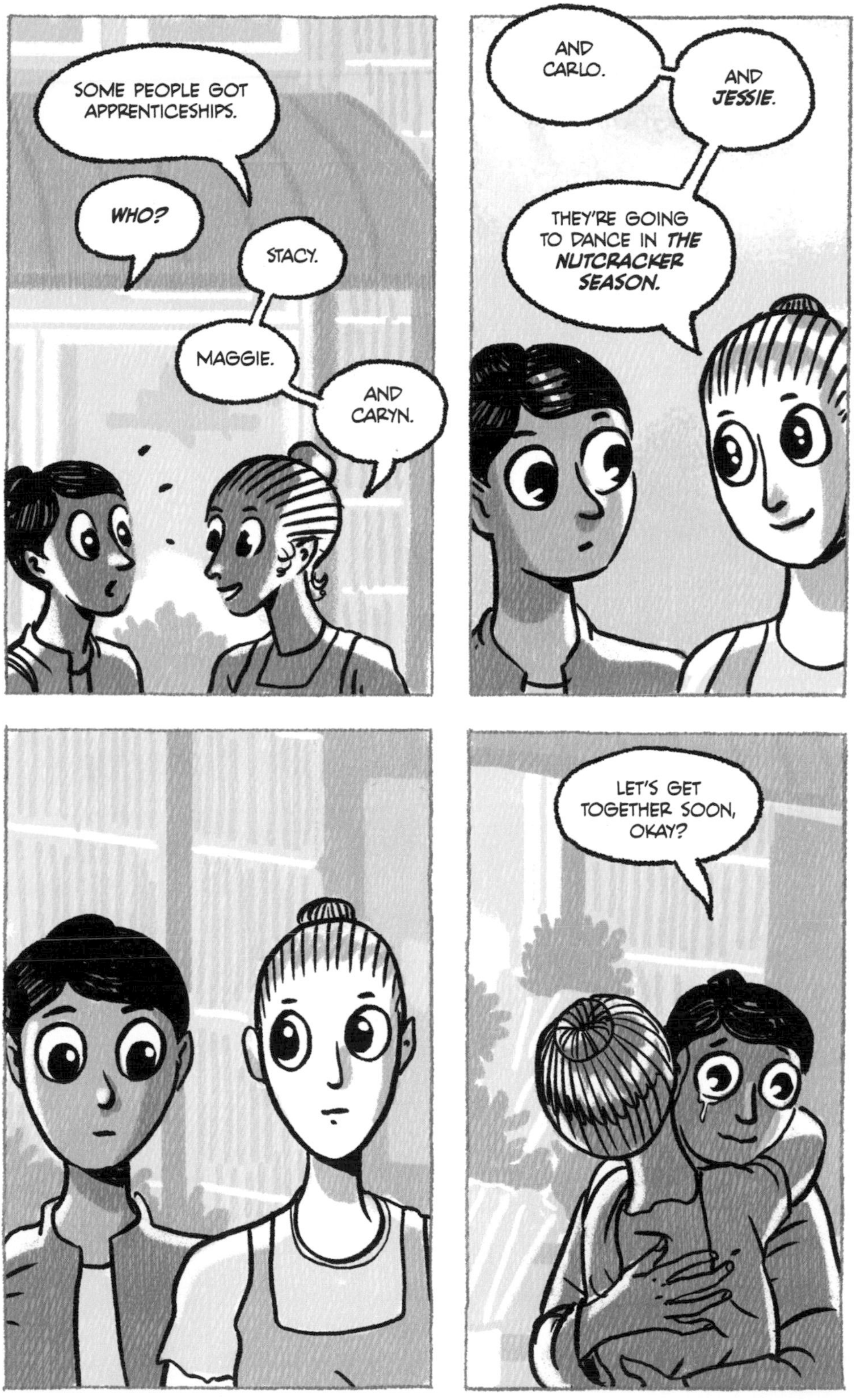
SOME PEOPLE GOT APPRENTICESHIPS.
WHO?
STACY.
MAGGIE.
AND CARYN.
AND CARLO.
AND JESSIE.
THEY'RE GOING TO DANCE IN THE NUTCRACKER SEASON.
LET'S GET TOGETHER SOON, OKAY?

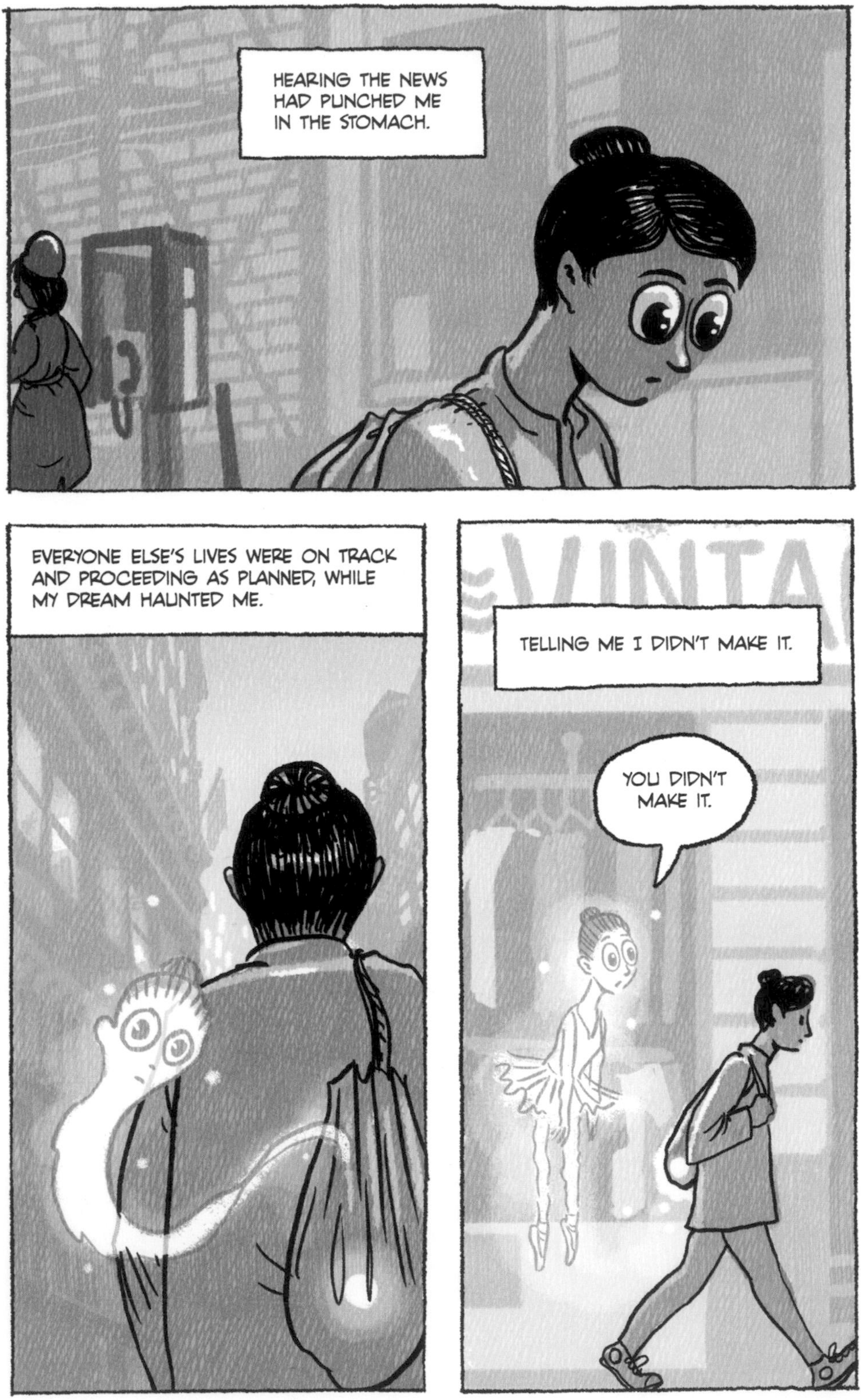
HEARING THE NEWS HAD PUNCHED ME IN THE STOMACH.
EVERYONE ELSE'S LIVES WERE ON TRACK AND PROCEEDING AS PLANNED, WHILE MY DREAM HAUNTED ME.
TELLING ME I DIDN'T MAKE IT.
YOU DIDN'T MAKE IT.

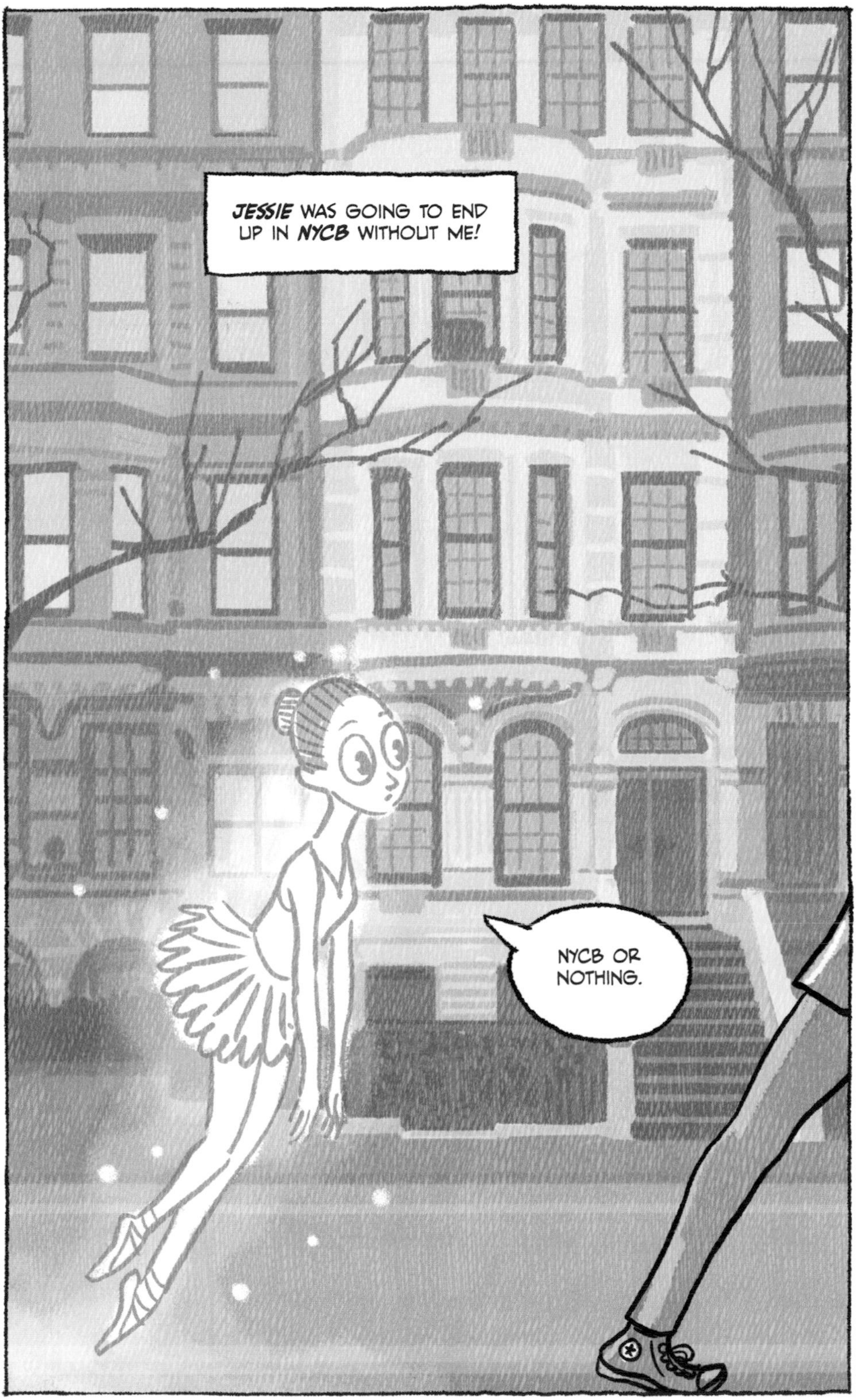
JESSIE WAS GOING TO END UP IN NYCB WITHOUT ME!
NYCB OR NOTHING.

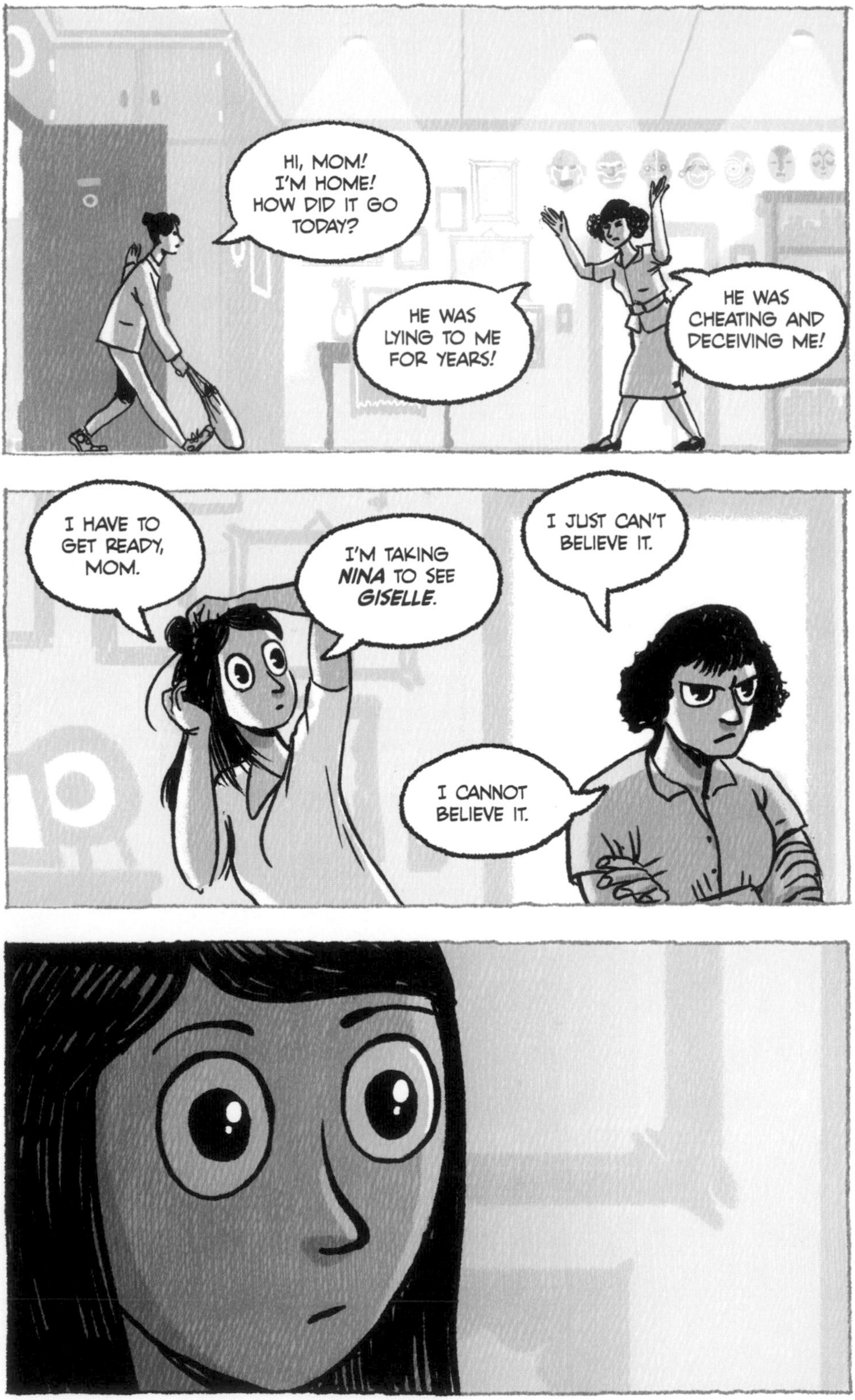
HI, MOM! I'M HOME! HOW DID IT GO TODAY?
HE WAS LYING TO ME FOR YEARS!
HE WAS CHEATING AND DECEIVING ME!
I HAVE TO GET READY, MOM.
I'M TAKING *NINA* TO SEE *GISELLE*.
I JUST CAN'T BELIEVE IT.
I CANNOT BELIEVE IT.

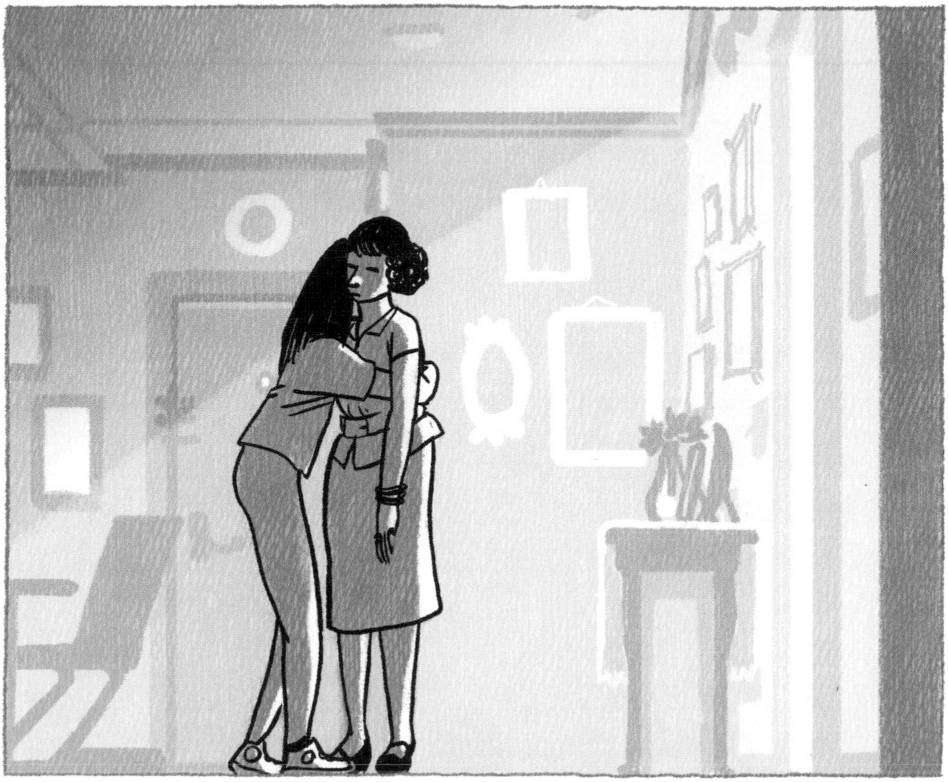

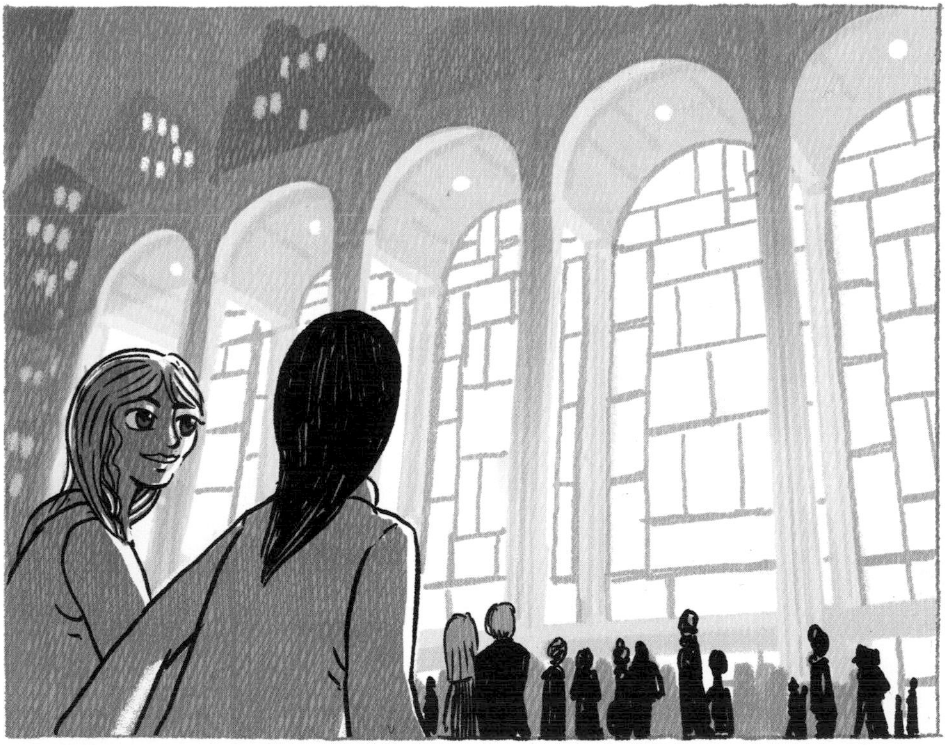

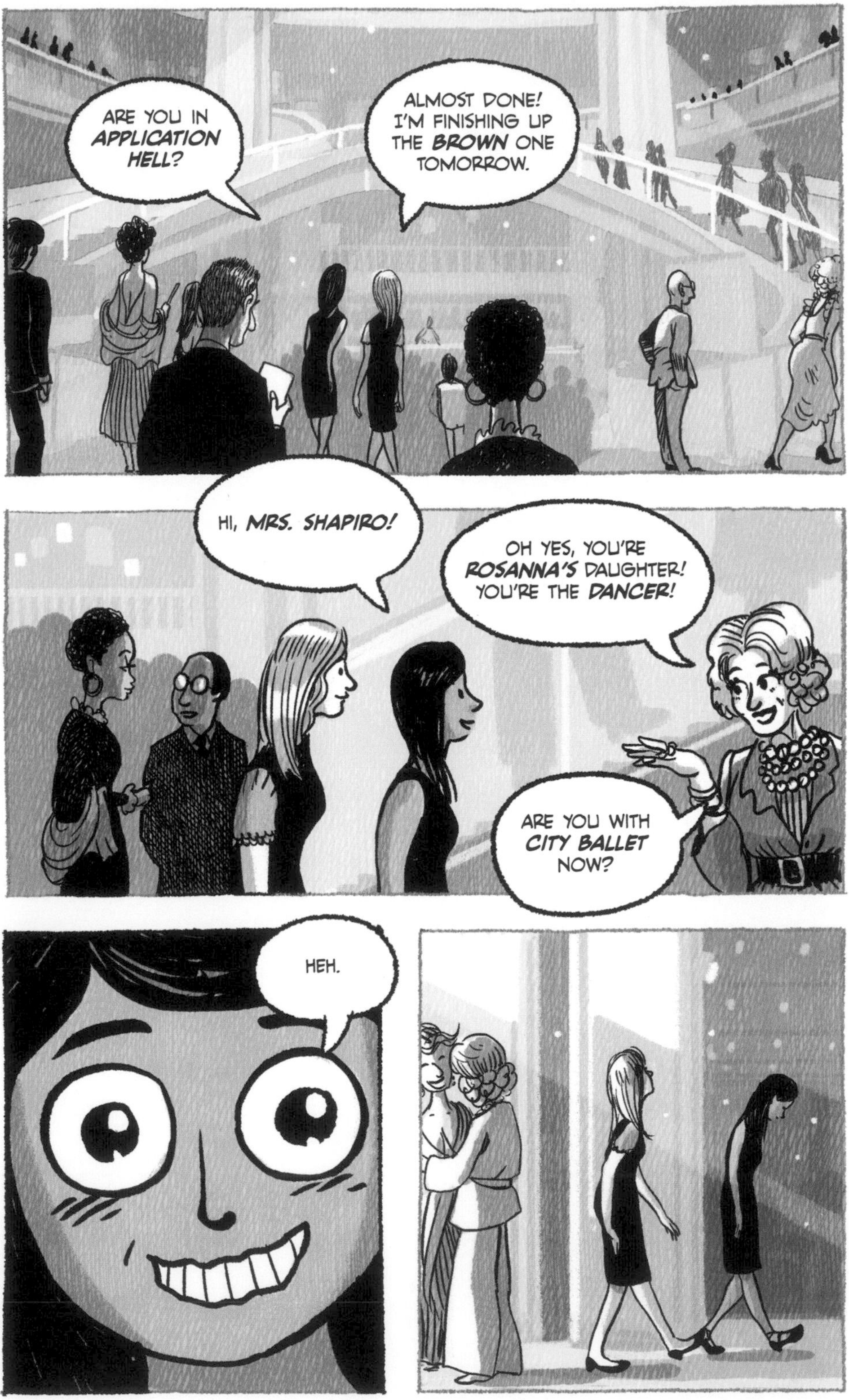
ARE YOU IN APPLICATION HELL?
ALMOST DONE! I'M FINISHING UP THE BROWN ONE TOMORROW.
HI, MRS. SHAPIRO!
OH YES, YOU'RE ROSANNA'S DAUGHTER! YOU'RE THE DANCER!
ARE YOU WITH CITY BALLET NOW?
HEH.

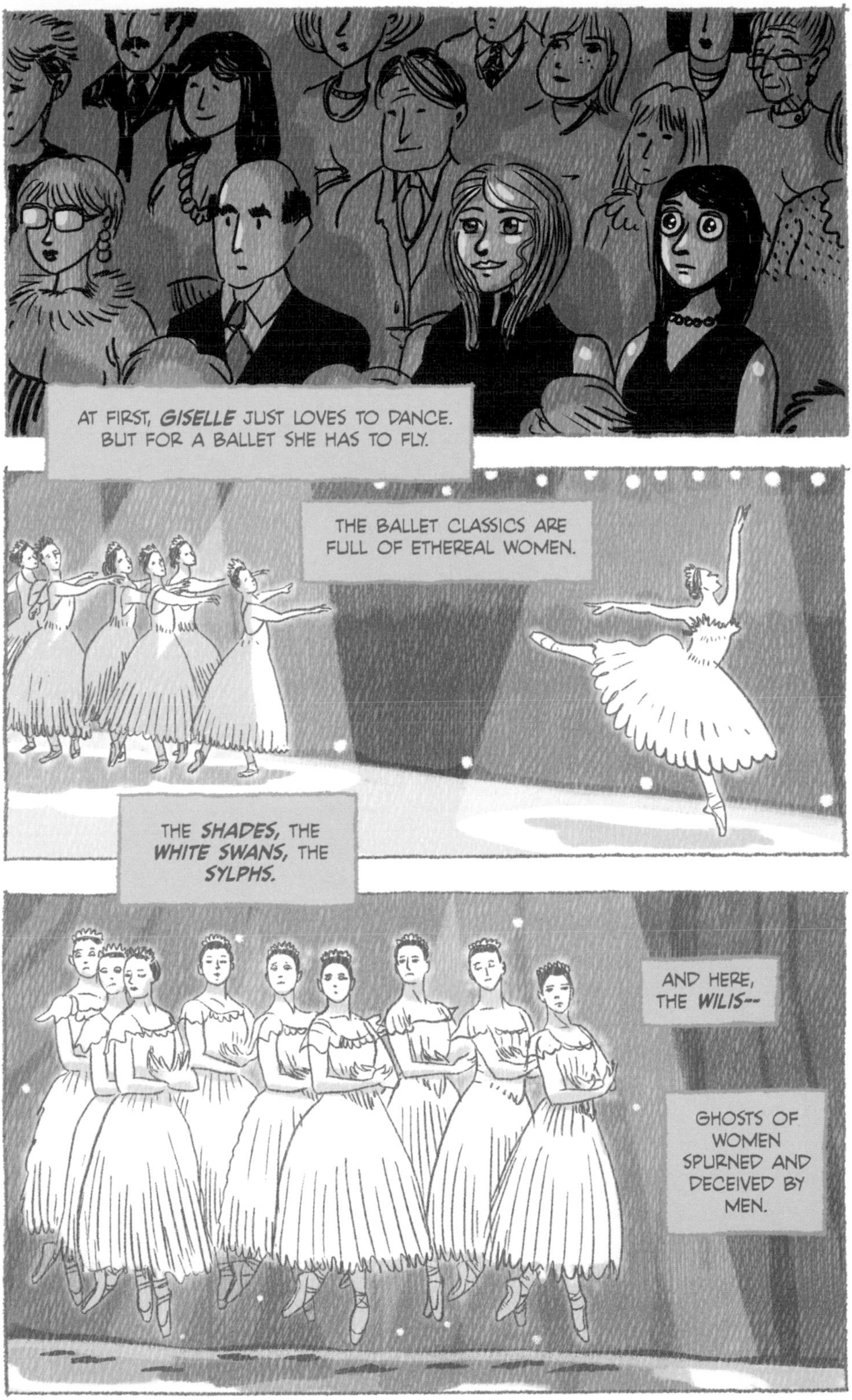
AT FIRST, GISELLE JUST LOVES TO DANCE. BUT FOR A BALLET SHE HAS TO FLY.
THE BALLET CLASSICS ARE FULL OF ETHEREAL WOMEN.
THE SHADES, THE WHITE SWANS, THE SYLPHS.
AND HERE, THE WILIS--
GHOSTS OF WOMEN SPURNED AND DECEIVED BY MEN.

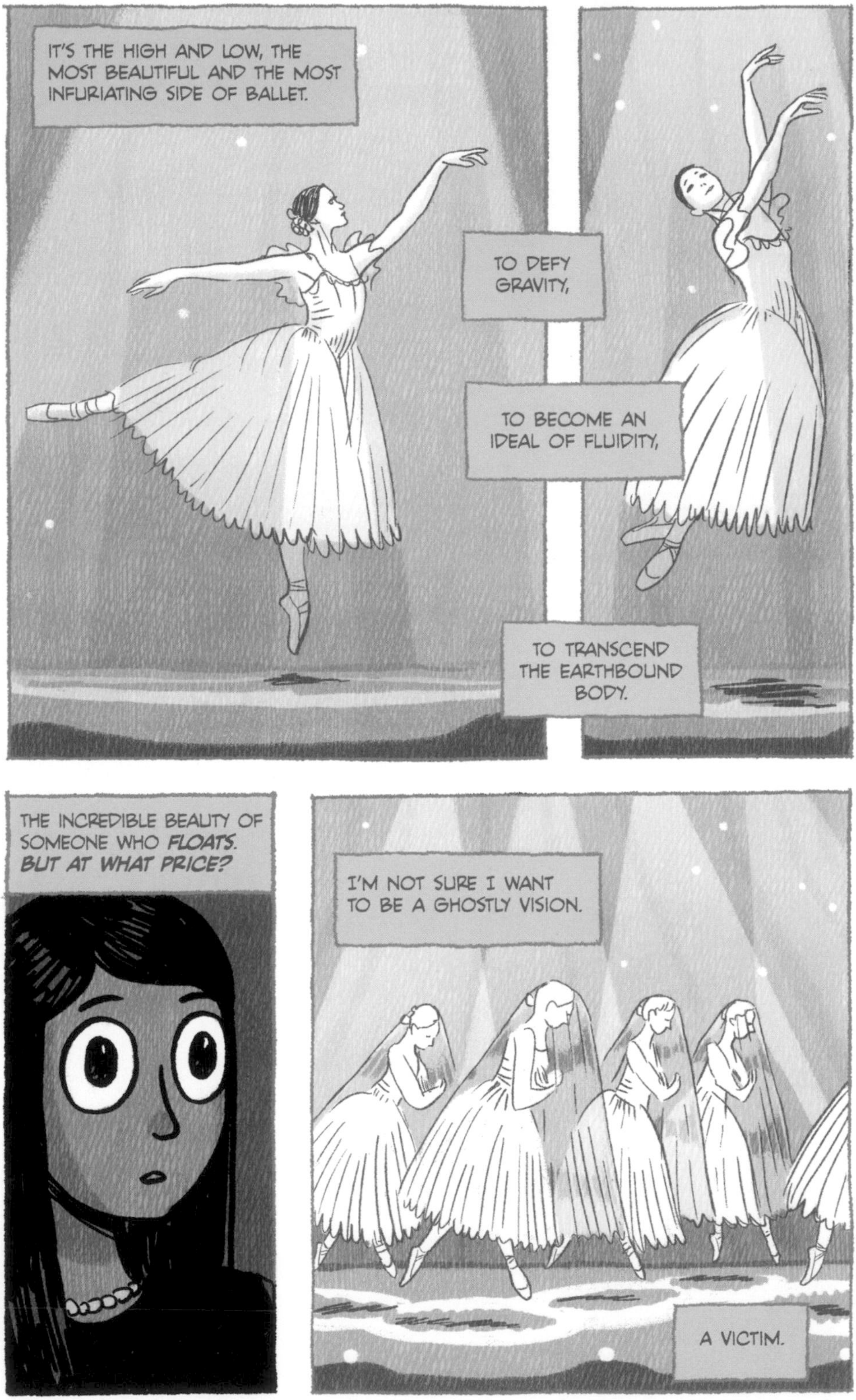
IT'S THE HIGH AND LOW, THE MOST BEAUTIFUL AND THE MOST INFURIATING SIDE OF BALLET.
TO DEFY GRAVITY,
TO BECOME AN IDEAL OF FLUIDITY,
TO TRANSCEND THE EARTHBOUND BODY.
THE INCREDIBLE BEAUTY OF SOMEONE WHO *FLOATS.* *BUT AT WHAT PRICE?*
I'M NOT SURE I WANT TO BE A GHOSTLY VISION.
A VICTIM.

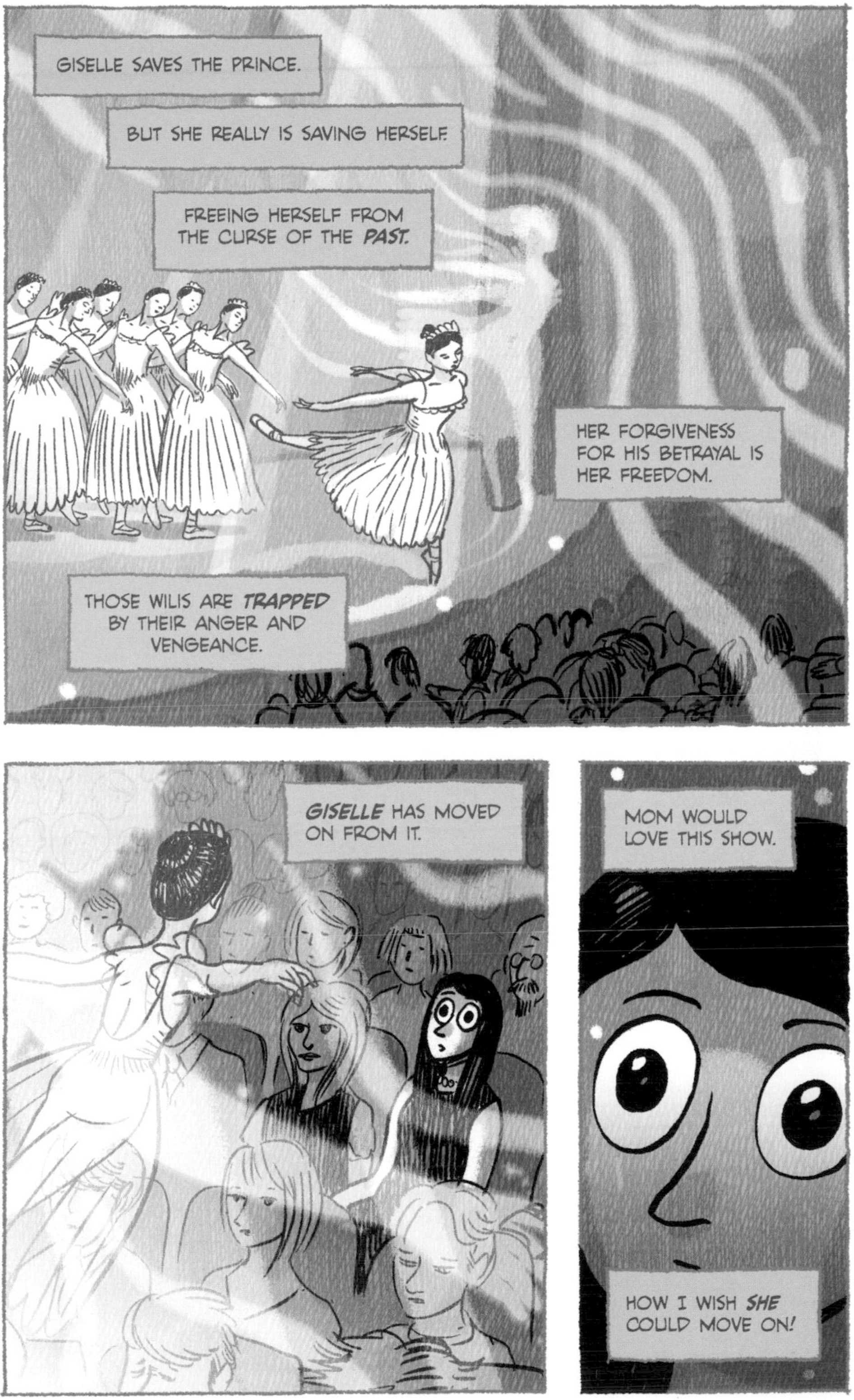
GISELLE SAVES THE PRINCE.
BUT SHE REALLY IS SAVING HERSELF.
FREEING HERSELF FROM THE CURSE OF THE *PAST.*
HER FORGIVENESS FOR HIS BETRAYAL IS HER FREEDOM.
THOSE WILIS ARE *TRAPPED* BY THEIR ANGER AND VENGEANCE.
GISELLE HAS MOVED ON FROM IT.
MOM WOULD LOVE THIS SHOW.
HOW I WISH *SHE* COULD MOVE ON!

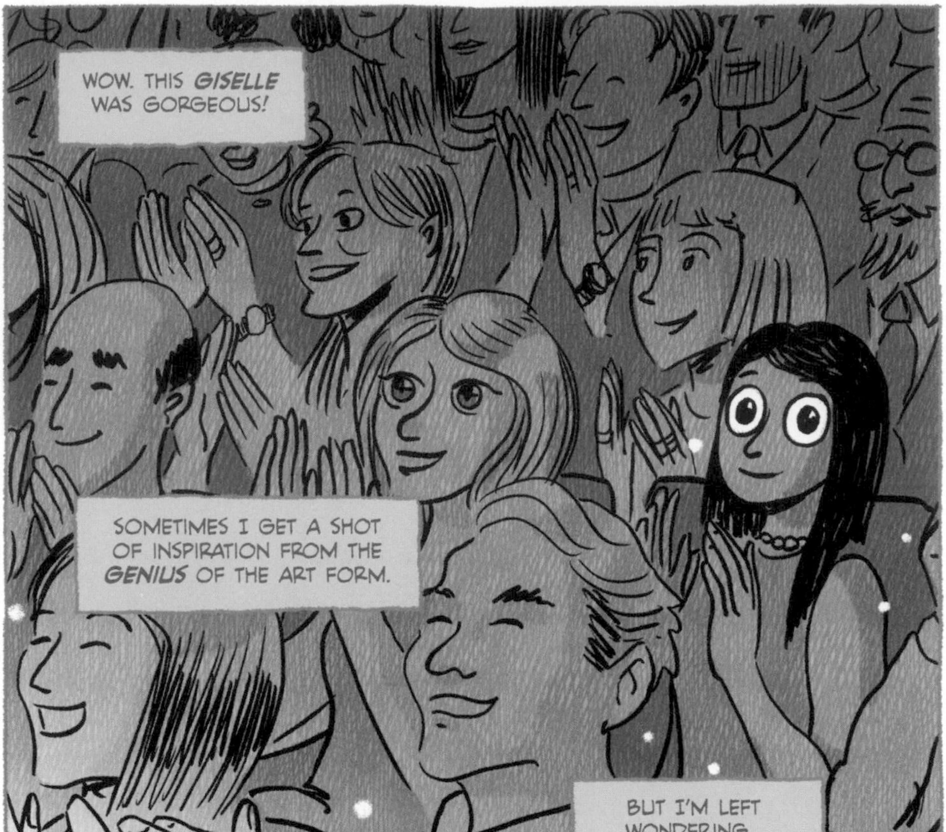
WOW. THIS *GISELLE* WAS GORGEOUS!
SOMETIMES I GET A SHOT OF INSPIRATION FROM THE *GENIUS* OF THE ART FORM.
BUT I'M LEFT WONDERING...

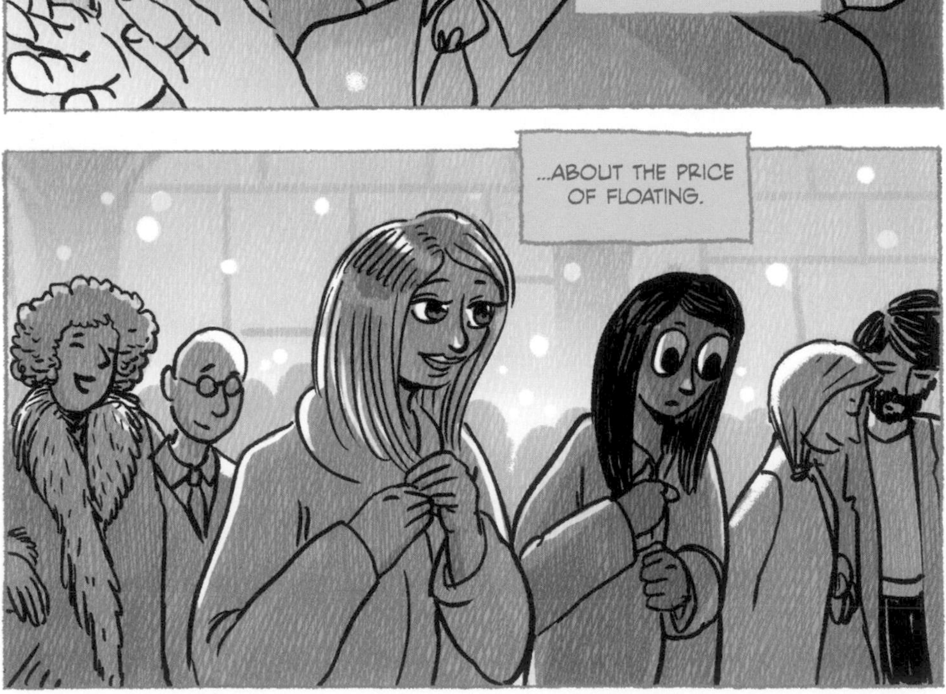
...ABOUT THE PRICE OF FLOATING.

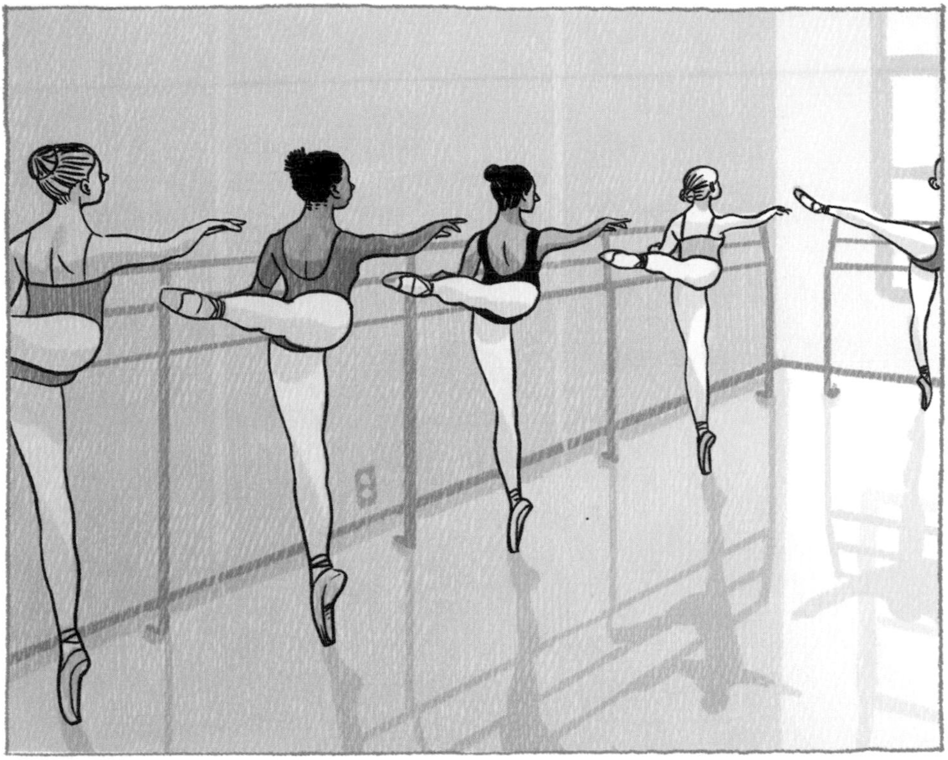

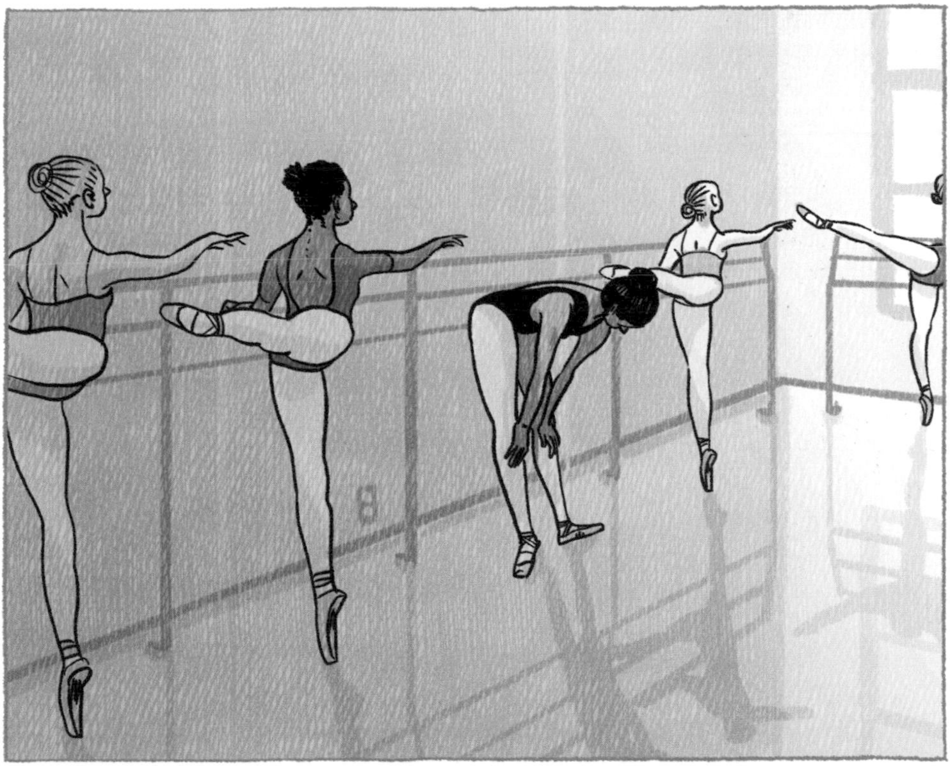

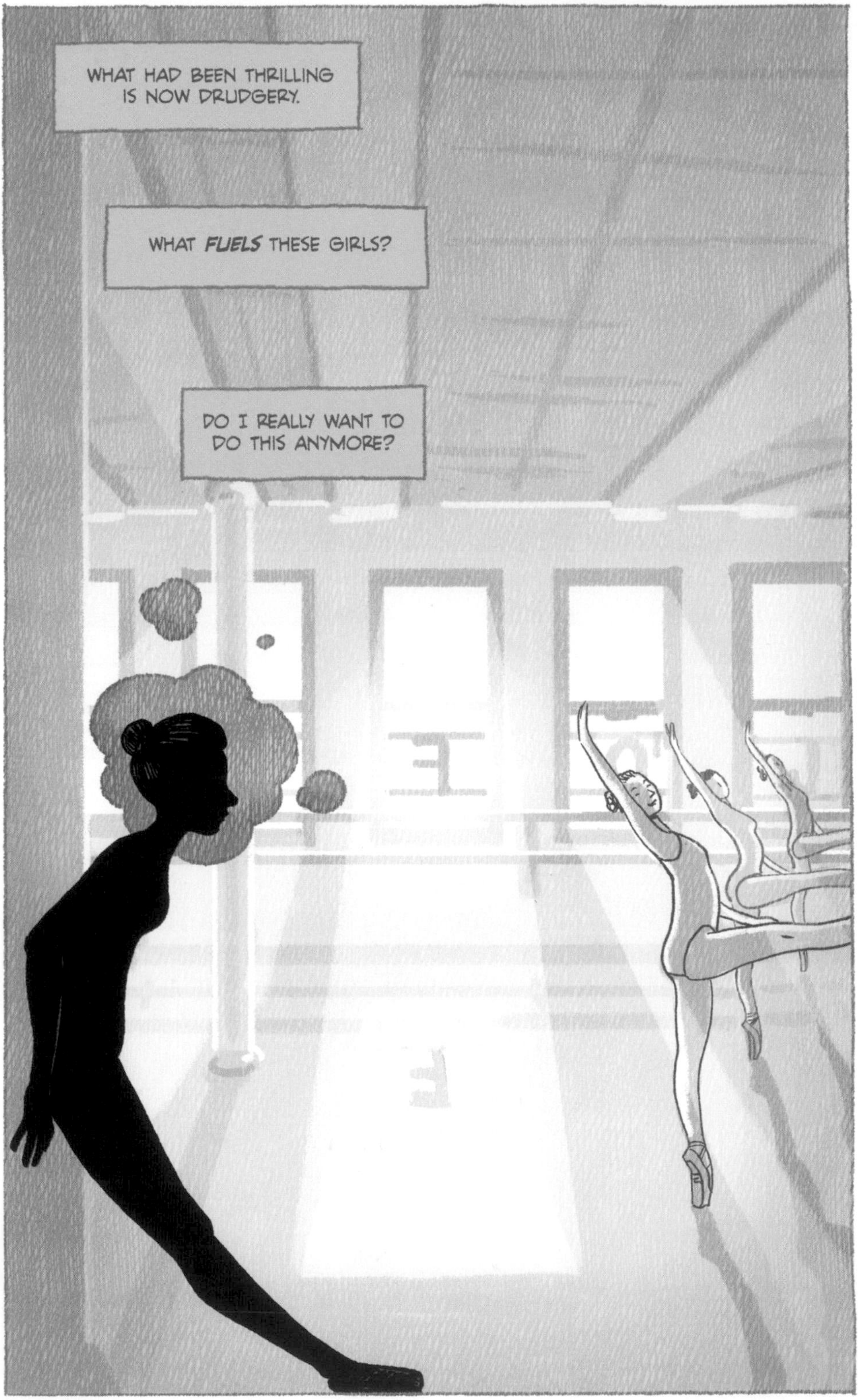
WHAT HAD BEEN THRILLING IS NOW DRUDGERY.
WHAT *FUELS* THESE GIRLS?
DO I REALLY WANT TO DO THIS ANYMORE?

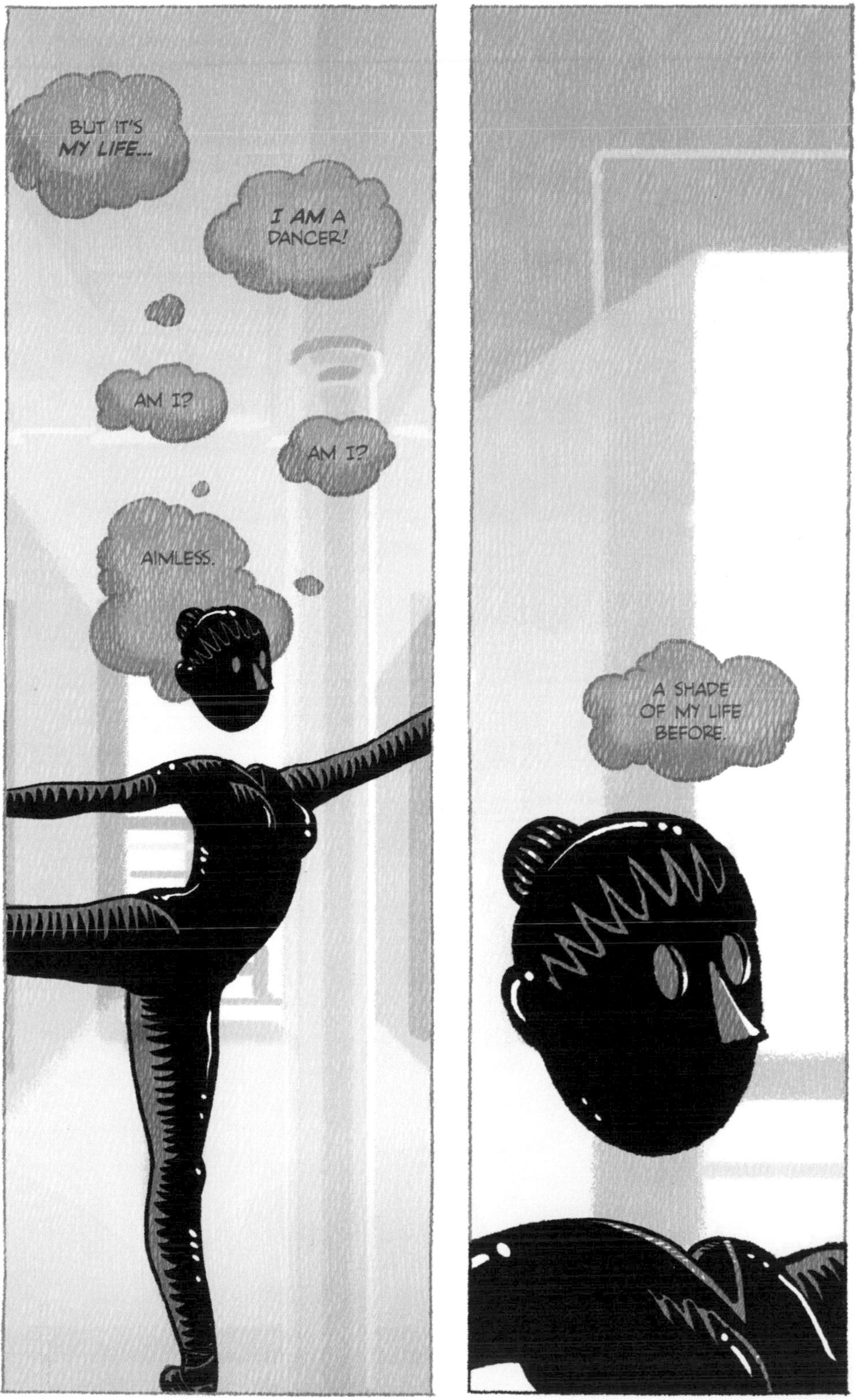
BUT IT'S MY LIFE...
I AM A DANCER!
AM I?
AM I?
AIMLESS.
A SHADE OF MY LIFE BEFORE.

A FEW MONTHS
PASSED LIKE THIS.

IT WAS GETTING
HARDER AND HARDER
TO WORK HARD.

DISCOURAGEMENT
SEEMED TO BE A
CONSTANT PARTNER.

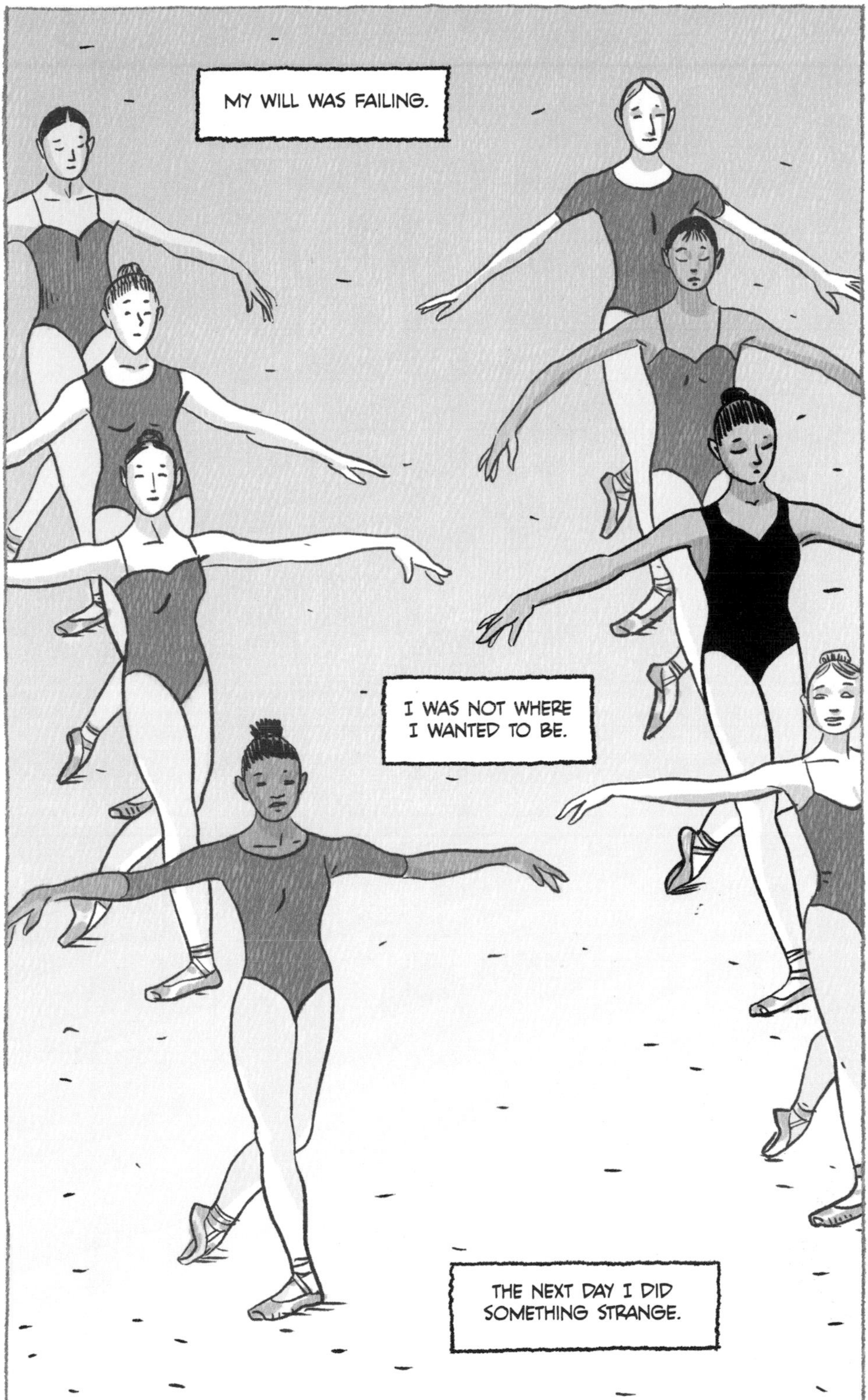
MY WILL WAS FAILING.
I WAS NOT WHERE I WANTED TO BE.
THE NEXT DAY I DID SOMETHING STRANGE.

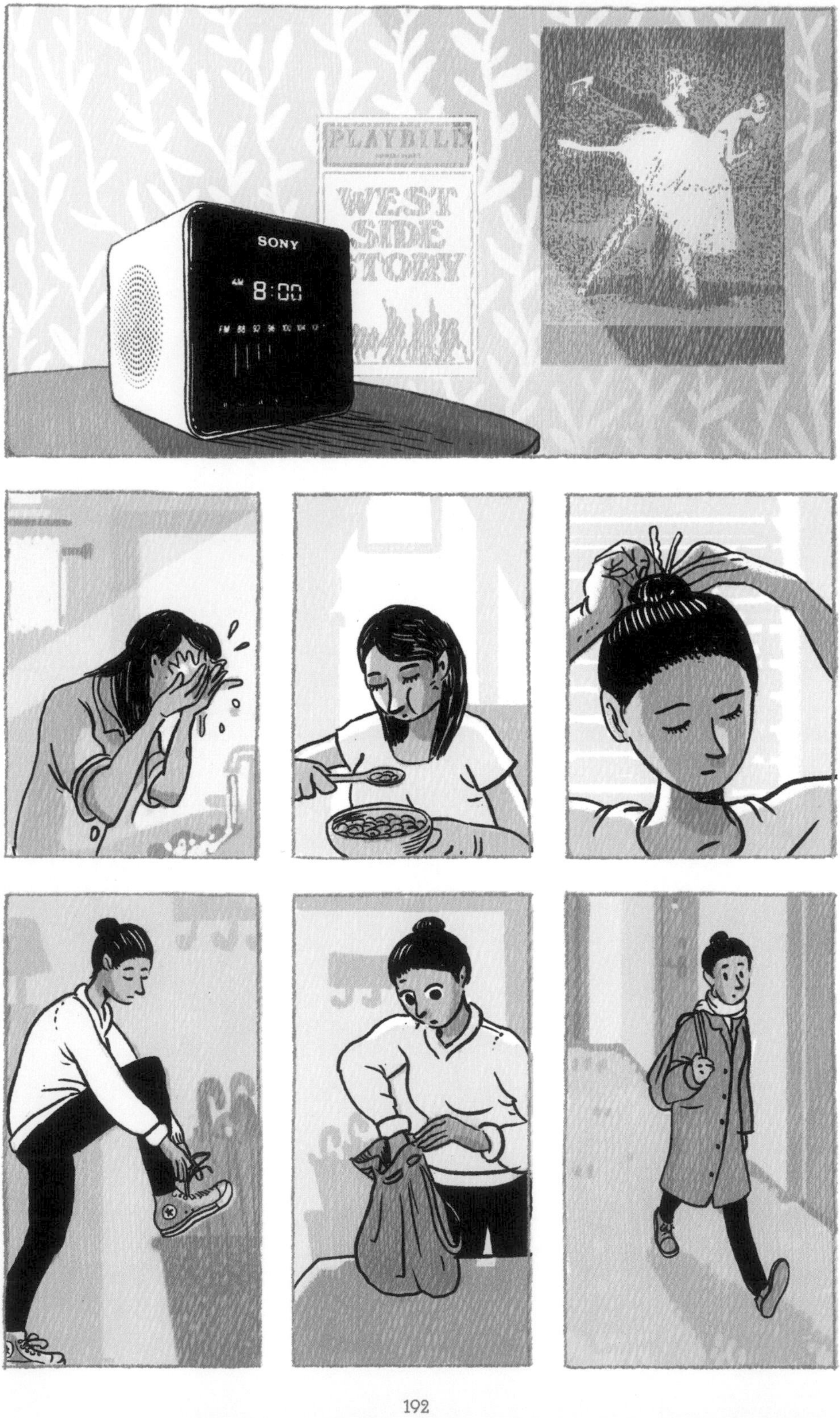
SONY
8:00
PLAYBILL
WEST SIDE STORY

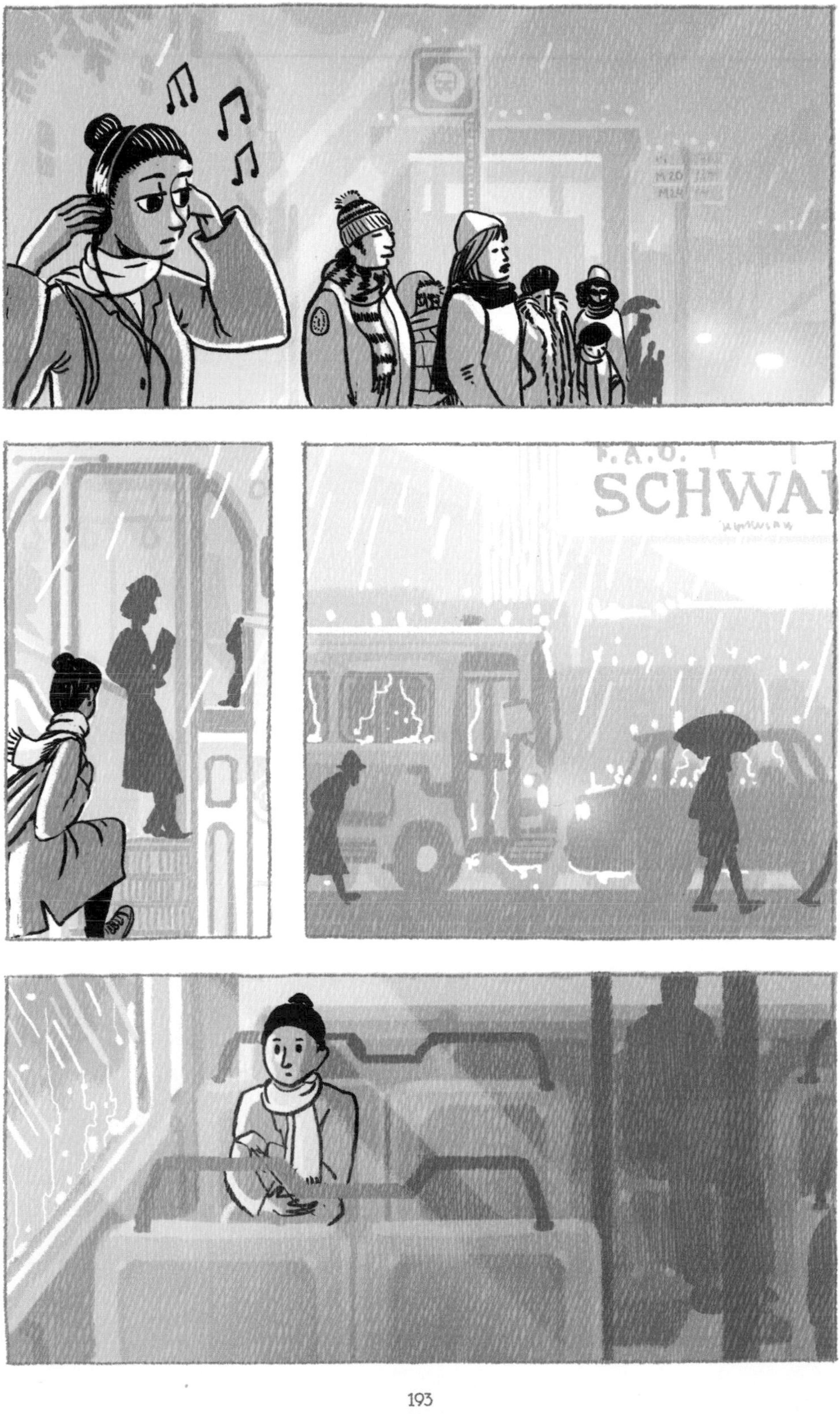
F.A.O.
SCHWA

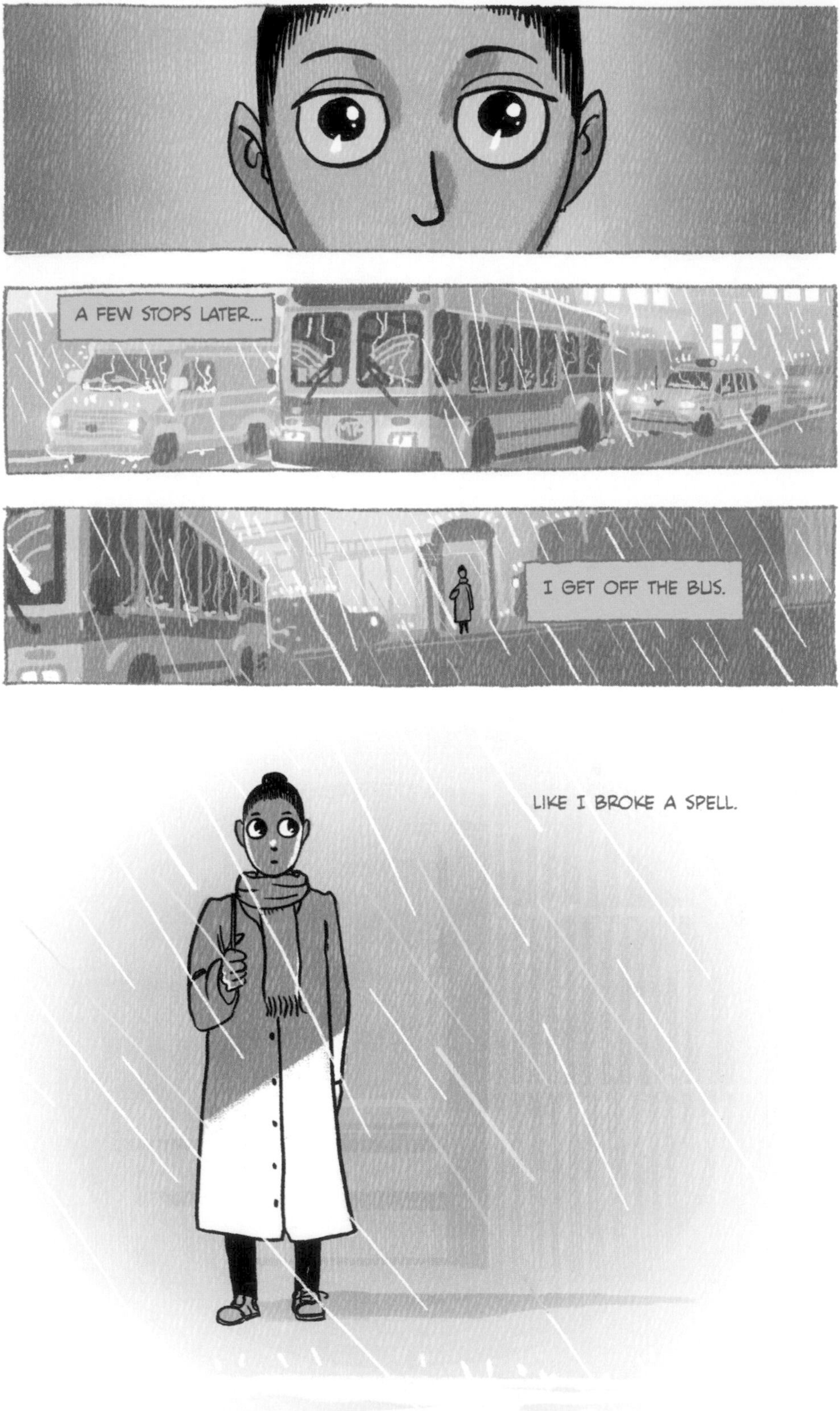
A FEW STOPS LATER...
I GET OFF THE BUS.
LIKE I BROKE A SPELL.

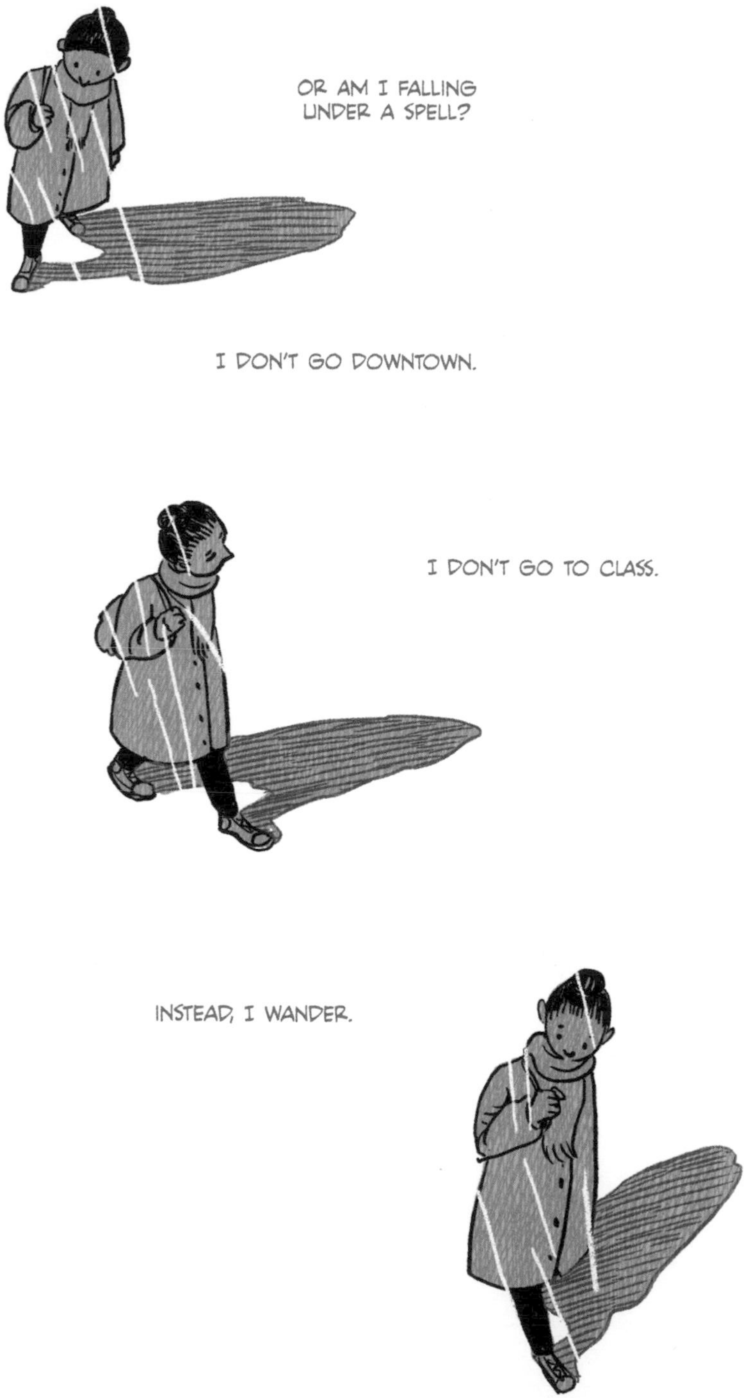
OR AM I FALLING UNDER A SPELL?
I DON'T GO DOWNTOWN.
I DON'T GO TO CLASS.
INSTEAD, I WANDER.

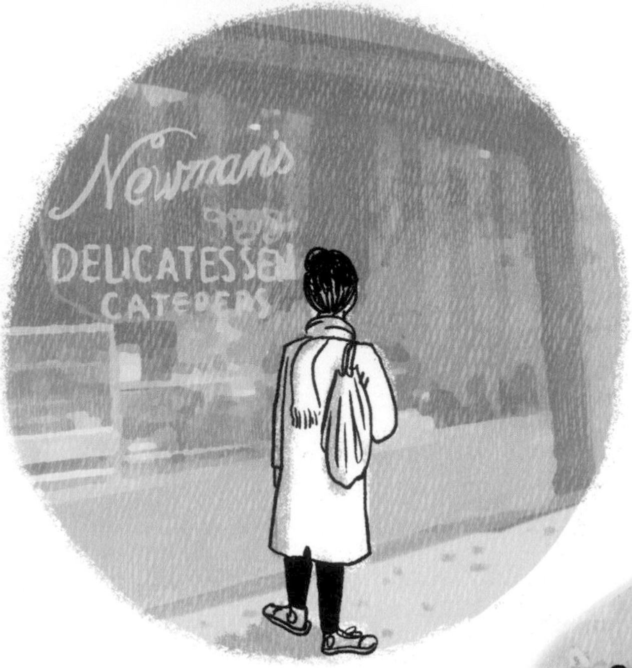
Newman's
DELICATESSEN

I HOVER AROUND
A COUPLE DELIS.

I DRIFT INTO
BLOOMINGDALE'S...

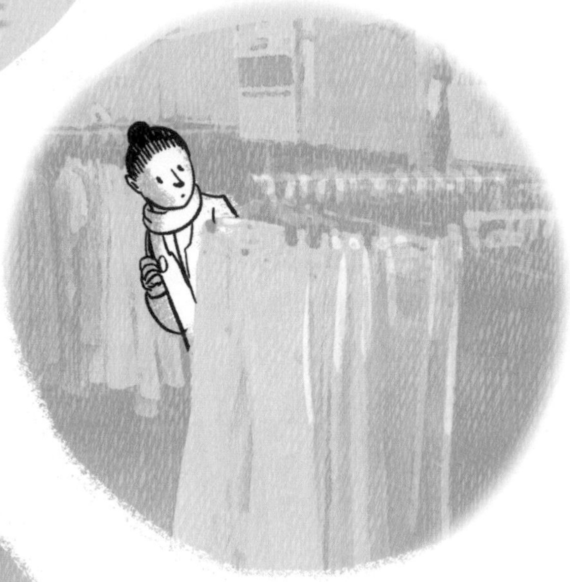

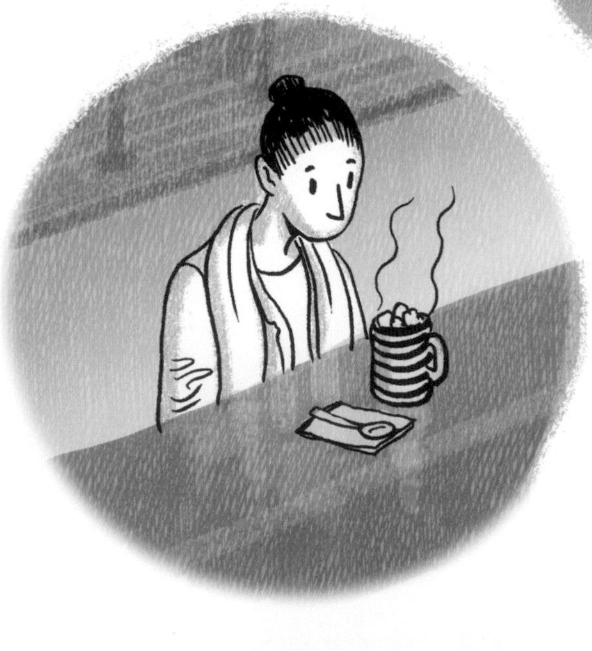

...WHERE I SIT AT THE
COFFEE SHOP FOR A
HOT CHOCOLATE.

LATER, I WALK INTO A DINER IN MIDTOWN.

EAT TORTELLINI.

FOR SO LONG I'VE AVOIDED FOOD LIKE THIS.

BUT IT ISN'T THE TREAT I HAD HOPED.

IT DOESN'T HAVE MUCH TASTE AT ALL.

THE NEXT DAY--
I DO IT AGAIN.

AND AGAIN.

AND THE DAY AFTER THAT.

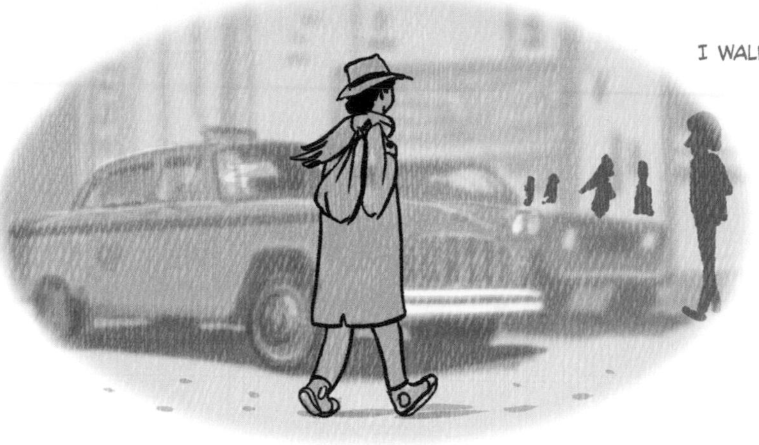

I WALK THE STREETS.

LIKE IN A DREAM.

I HAUNT THE
UPPER EAST SIDE.

WHERE I WON'T
BE LIKELY TO
BUMP INTO MOM.

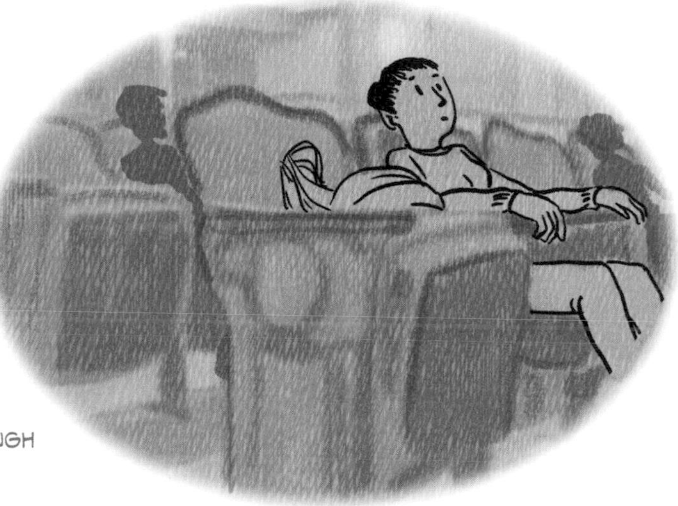

I SIT THROUGH
MOVIES.

EAT ALONE.

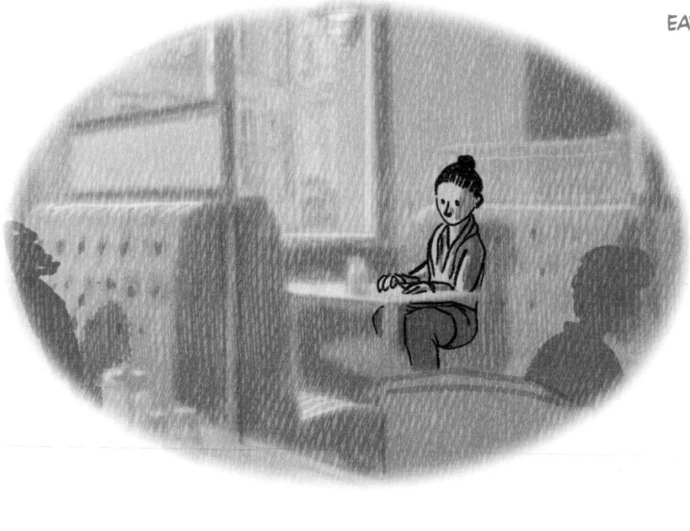

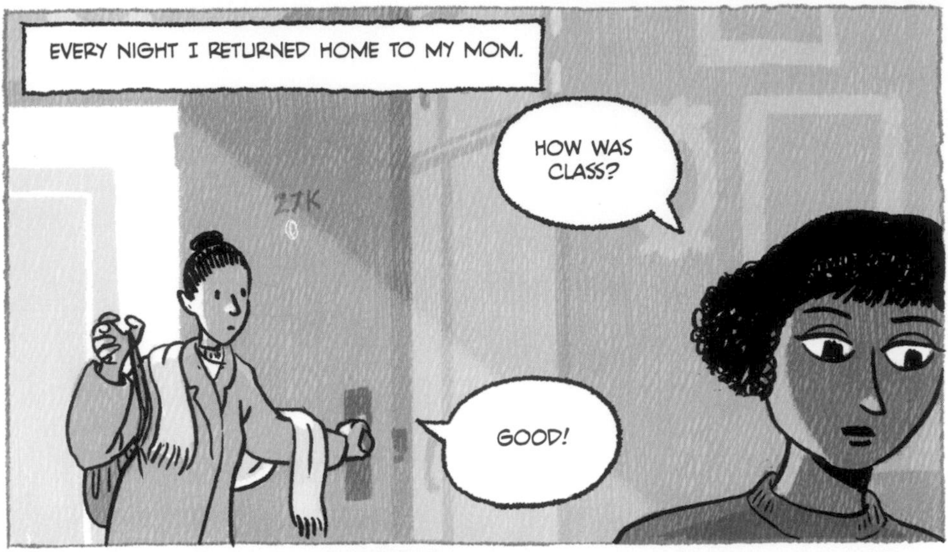
EVERY NIGHT I RETURNED HOME TO MY MOM.
HOW WAS CLASS?
GOOD!

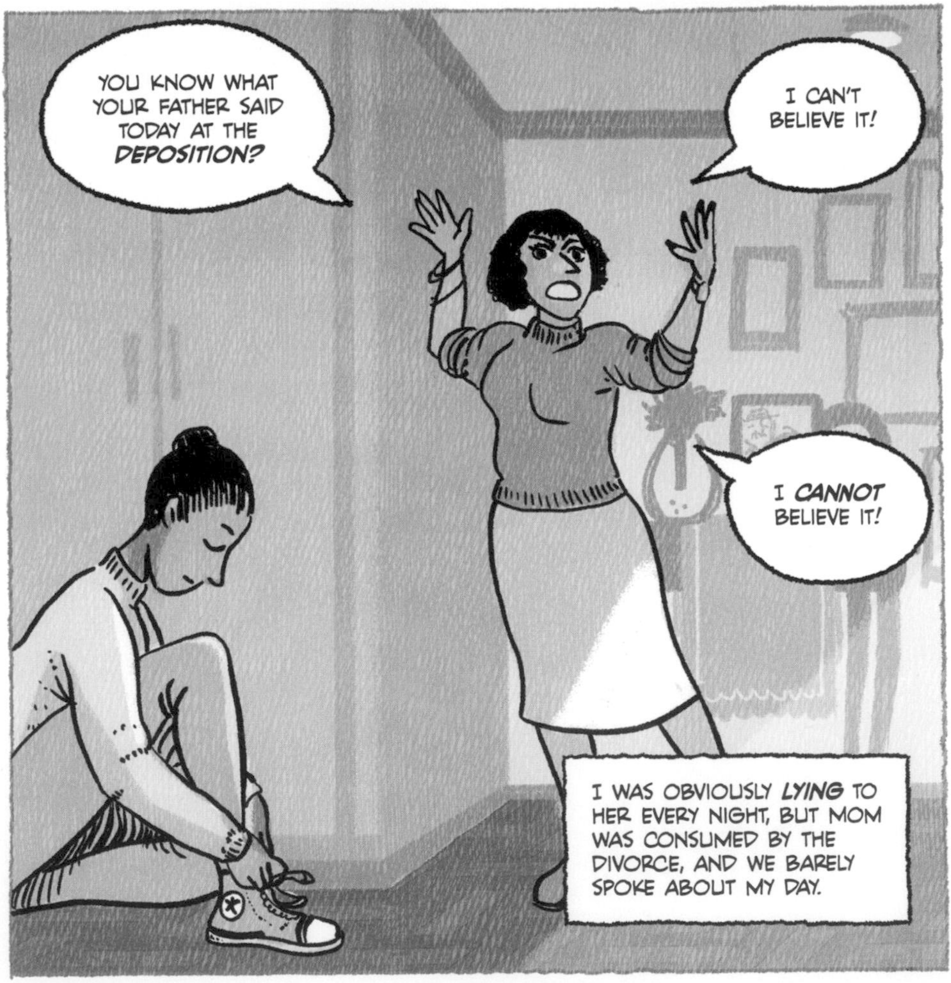
YOU KNOW WHAT YOUR FATHER SAID TODAY AT THE *DEPOSITION?*
I CAN'T BELIEVE IT!
I *CANNOT* BELIEVE IT!
I WAS OBVIOUSLY *LYING* TO HER EVERY NIGHT, BUT MOM WAS CONSUMED BY THE DIVORCE, AND WE BARELY SPOKE ABOUT MY DAY.

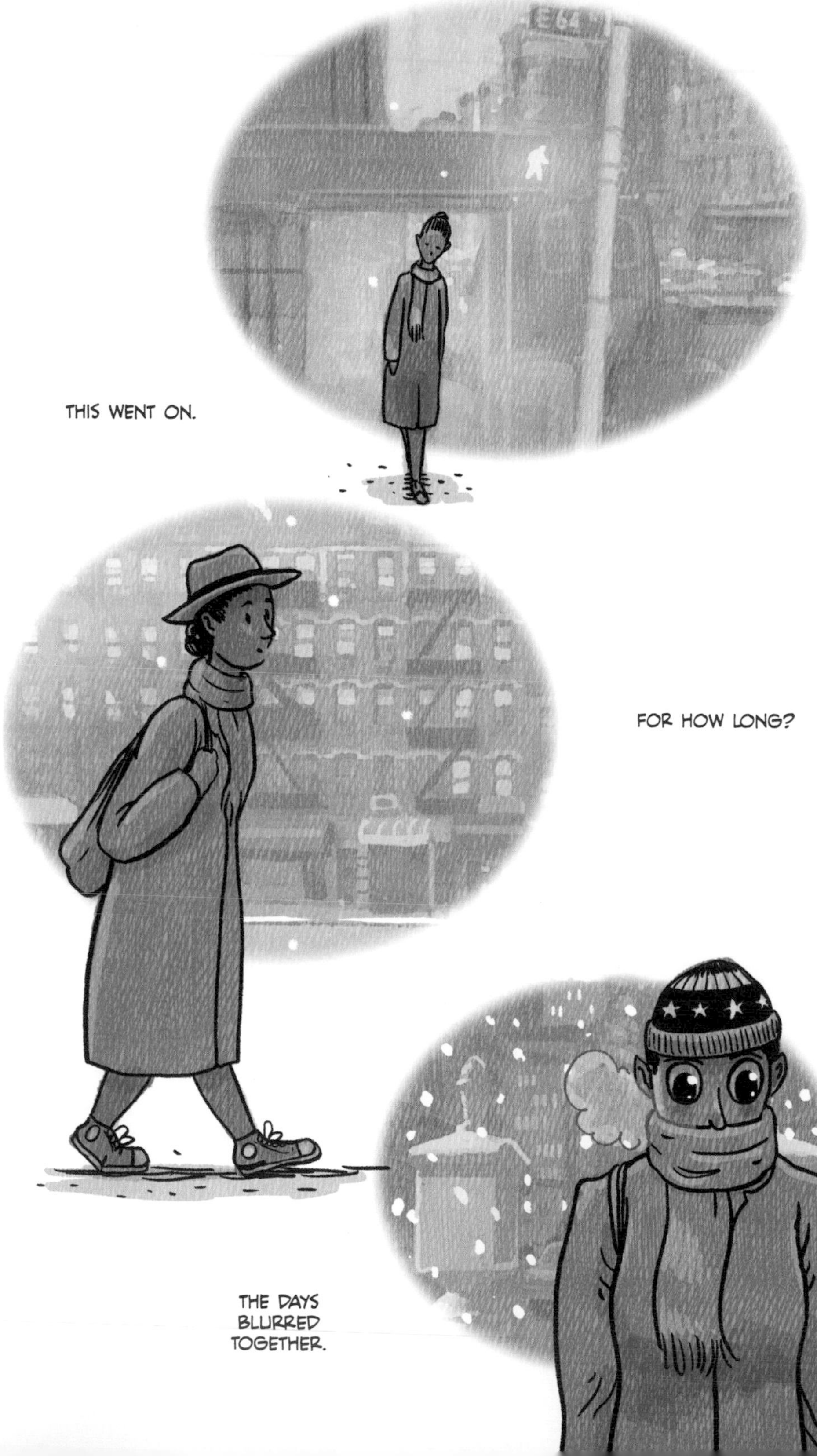
E 64
THIS WENT ON.
FOR HOW LONG?
THE DAYS
BLURRED
TOGETHER.

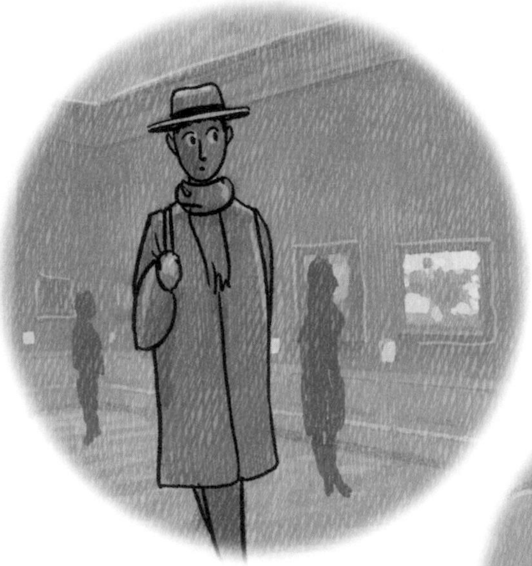

THIS IS GREAT.

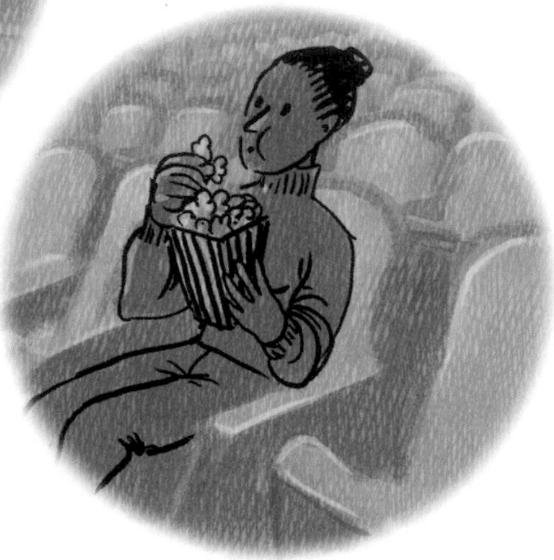

I'M FREE TO DO
WHATEVER I WANT!

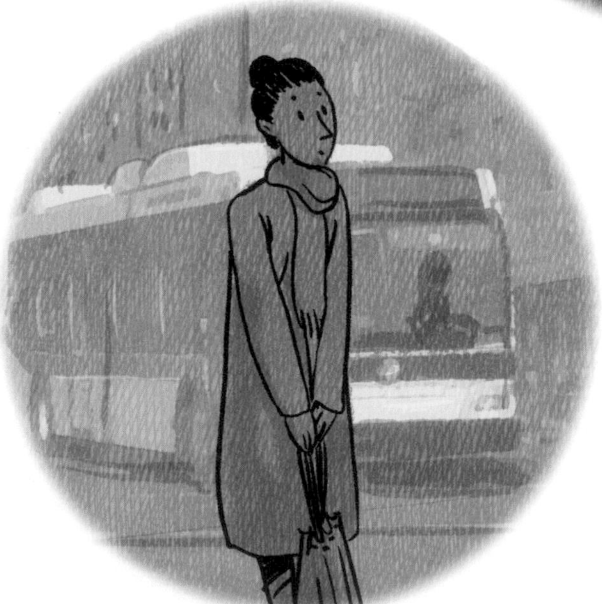

WHAT SHOULD I DO TODAY?

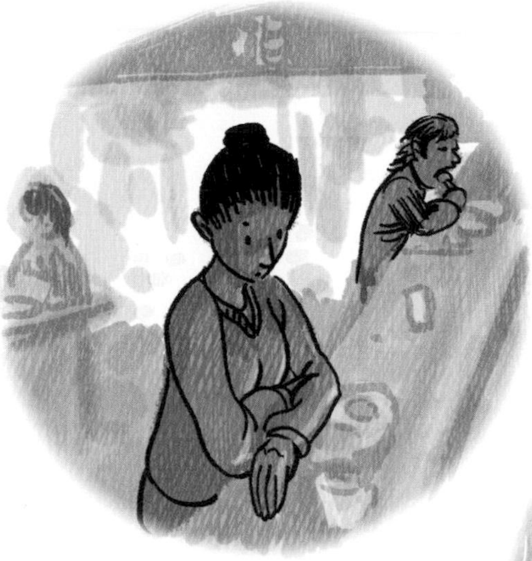

BUT I'M RUNNING
OUT OF IDEAS...

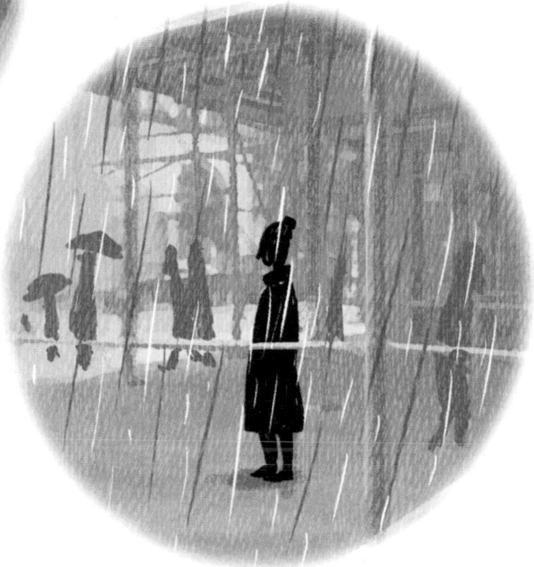

NO ONE TO BE WITH.

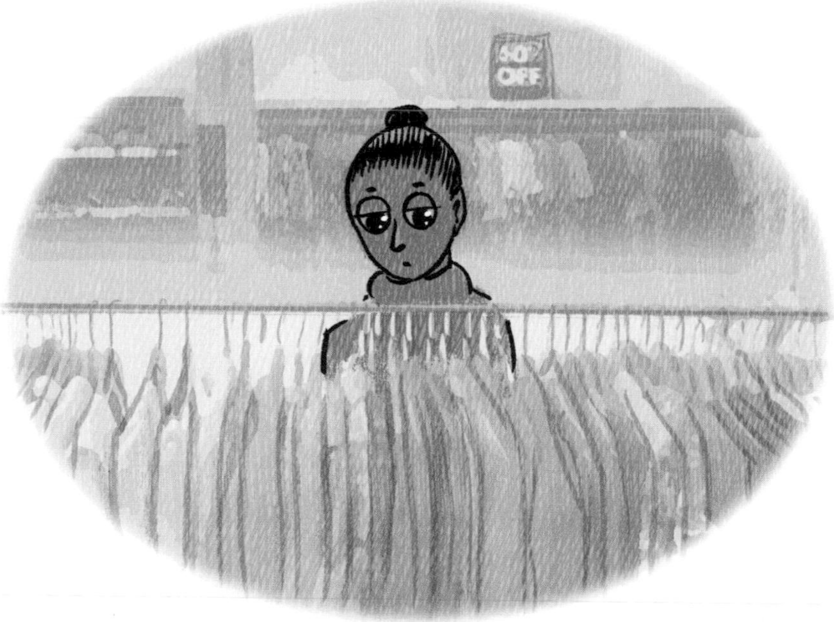
60% OFF

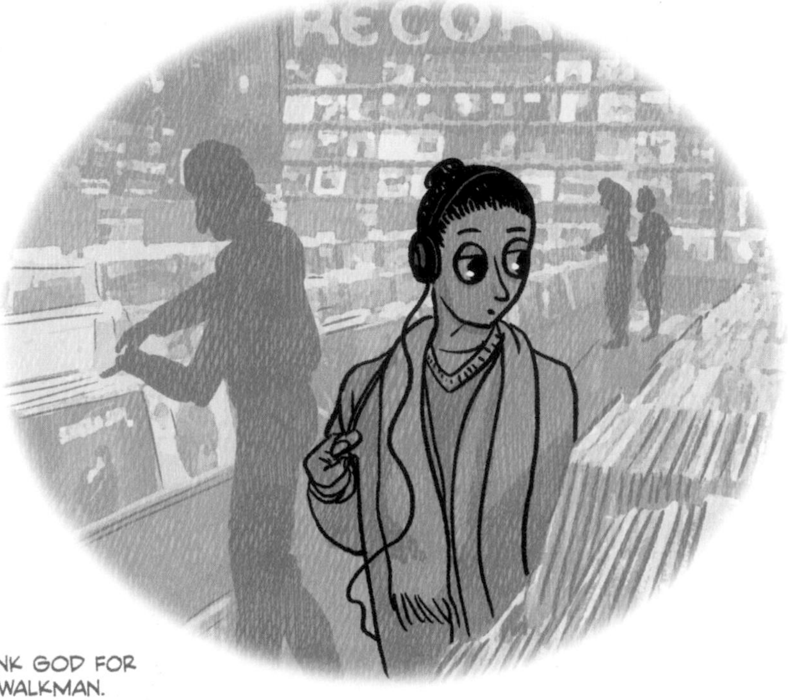

THANK GOD FOR
MY WALKMAN.

U2 KEEPS ME
COMPANY.

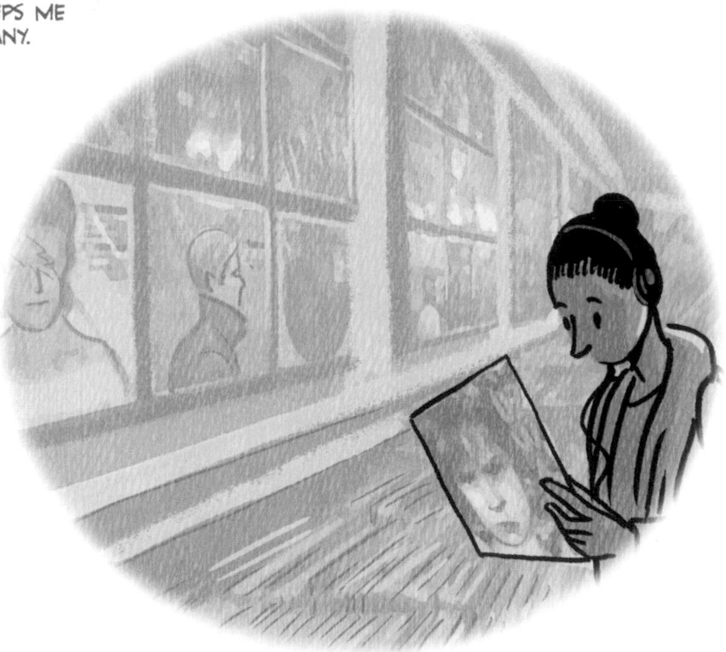

THEIR ANGER STIRS SOMETHING IN ME.

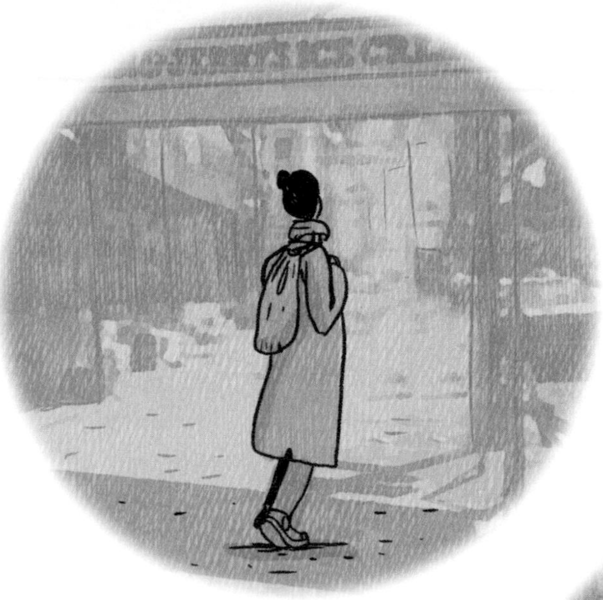

I'M ANGRY TOO.

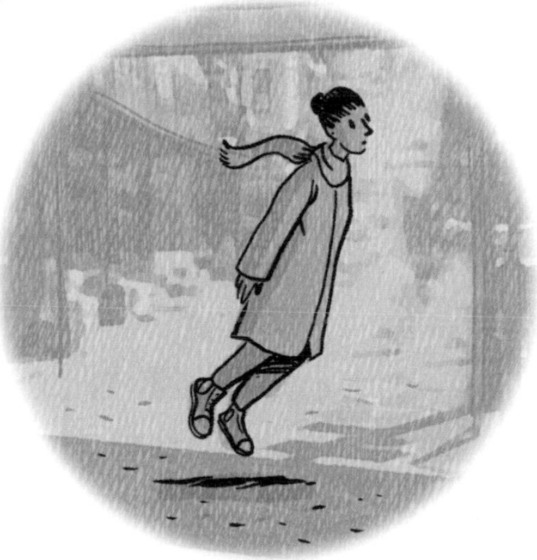

BUT I DON'T EVEN KNOW
WHAT ABOUT, REALLY.

THEN ONE EVENING,
AS I DRIFT BACK HOME...

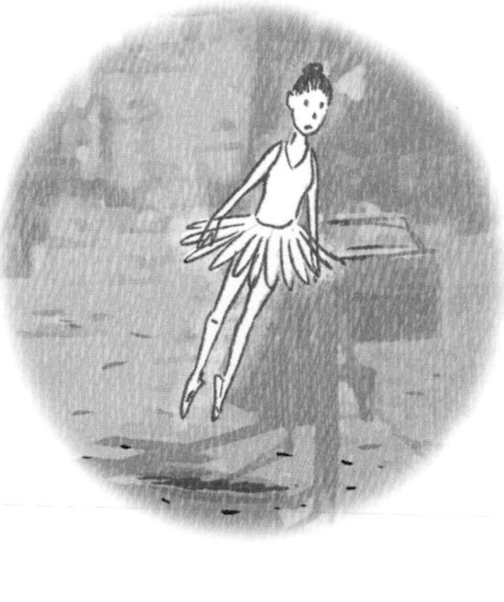

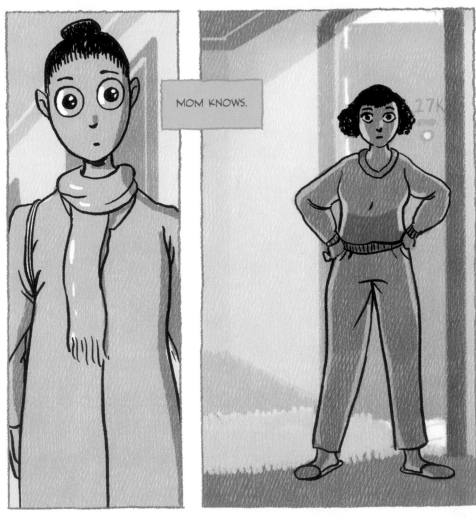

MOM KNOWS.

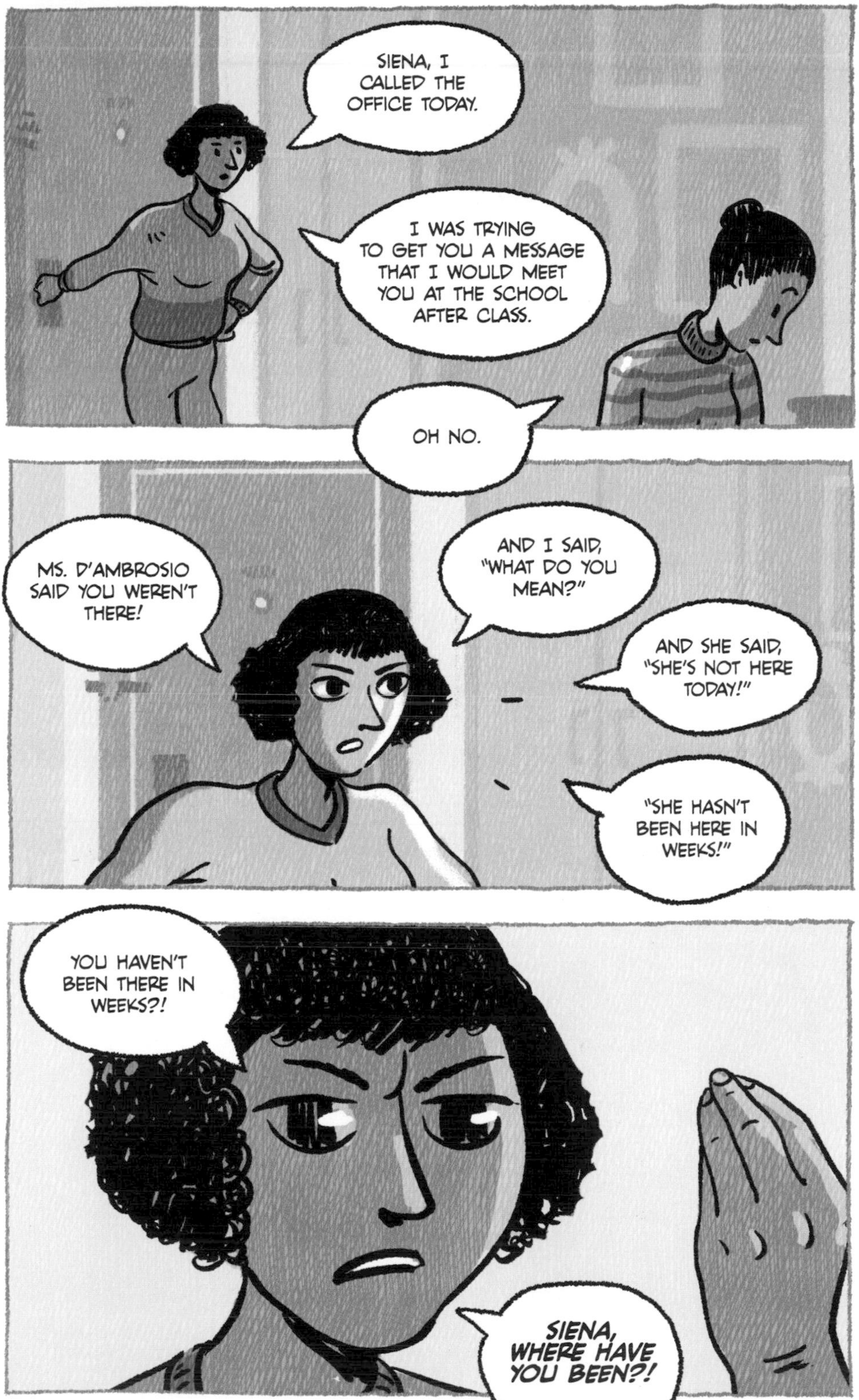
SIENA, I CALLED THE OFFICE TODAY.
I WAS TRYING TO GET YOU A MESSAGE THAT I WOULD MEET YOU AT THE SCHOOL AFTER CLASS.
OH NO.
MS. D'AMBROSIO SAID YOU WEREN'T THERE!
AND I SAID, "WHAT DO YOU MEAN?"
AND SHE SAID, "SHE'S NOT HERE TODAY!"
"SHE HASN'T BEEN HERE IN WEEKS!"
YOU HAVEN'T BEEN THERE IN WEEKS?!
SIENA, WHERE HAVE YOU BEEN?!

MOM...

I HAVEN'T BEEN ABLE TO GET MYSELF TO CLASS. I JUST CAN'T DO IT ANYMORE.

YOU DON'T LIKE THE SCHOOL? IS IT THE TEACHERS?

NO, MOM.

I FELT LIKE I *COULDN'T* TELL YOU. I DIDN'T WANT TO LET YOU AND DADDY DOWN AFTER ALL YOU'VE DONE TO SUPPORT MY BALLET LIFE.

I WAS SO SCARED TO TELL YOU.

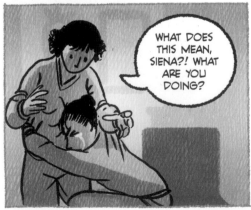

WHAT DOES THIS MEAN, SIENA?! WHAT ARE YOU DOING?

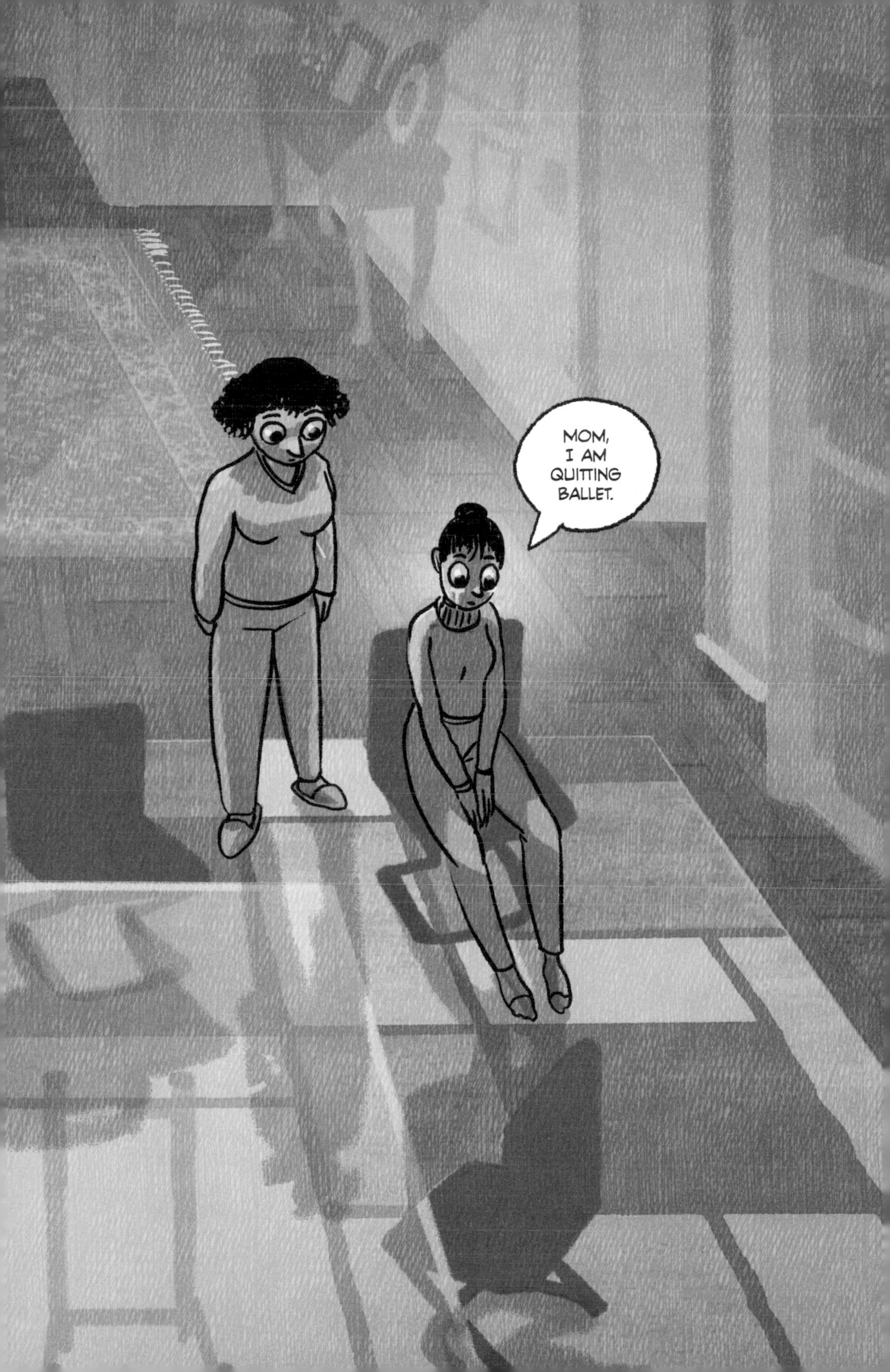
MOM, I AM QUITTING BALLET.

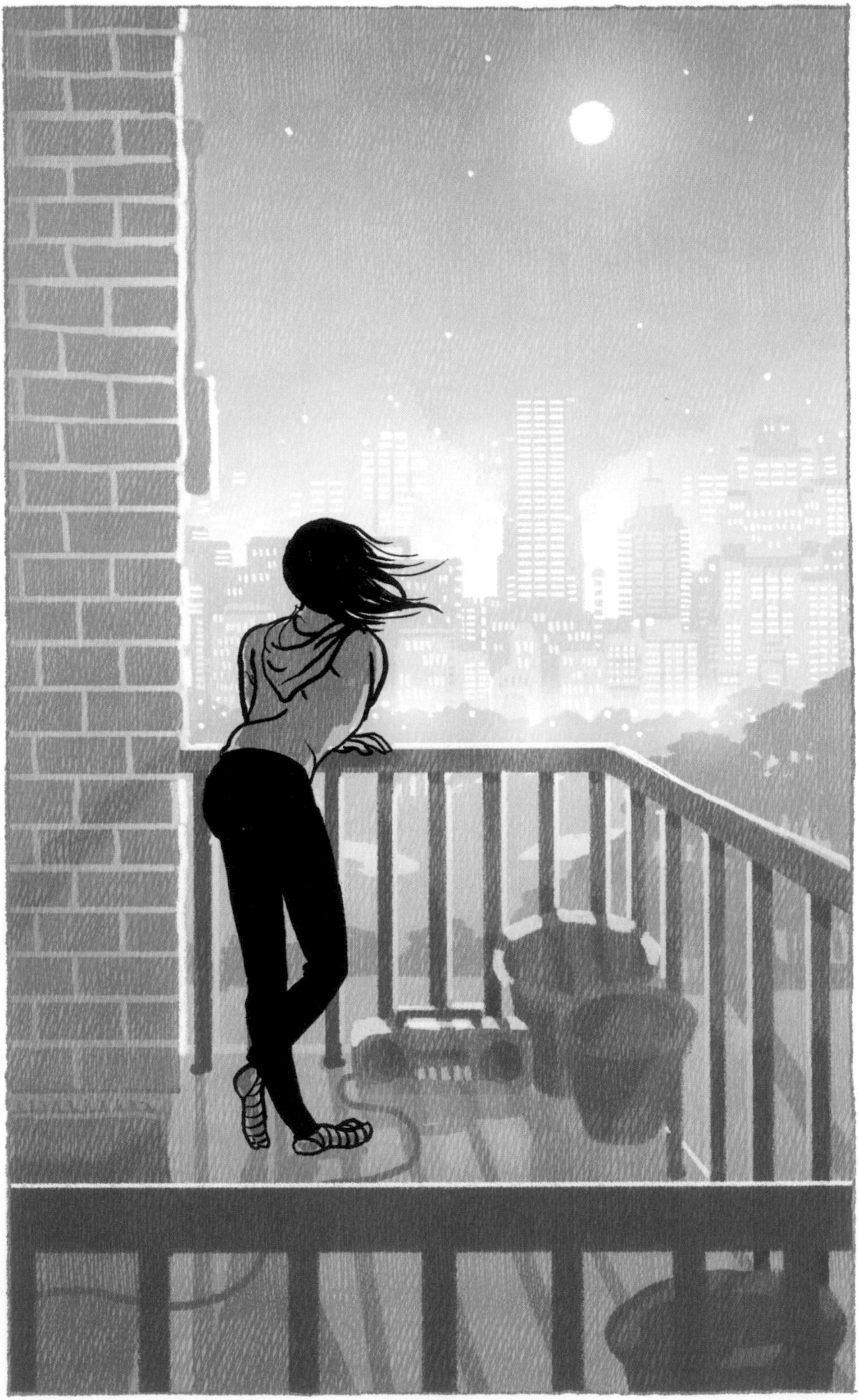

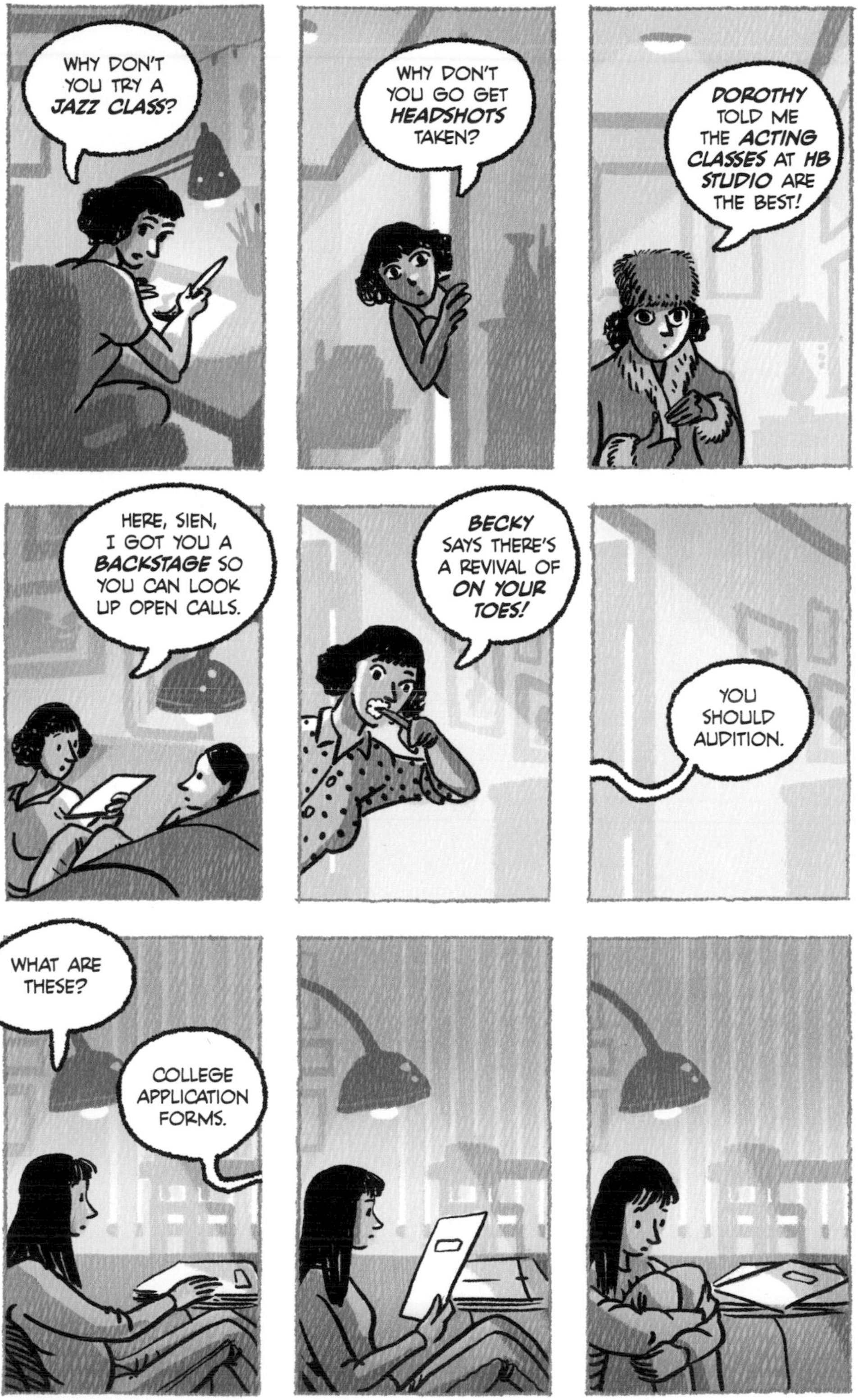
WHY DON'T YOU TRY A JAZZ CLASS?
WHY DON'T YOU GO GET HEADSHOTS TAKEN?
DOROTHY TOLD ME THE ACTING CLASSES AT HB STUDIO ARE THE BEST!
HERE, SIEN, I GOT YOU A BACKSTAGE SO YOU CAN LOOK UP OPEN CALLS.
BECKY SAYS THERE'S A REVIVAL OF ON YOUR TOES!
YOU SHOULD AUDITION.
WHAT ARE THESE?
COLLEGE APPLICATION FORMS.

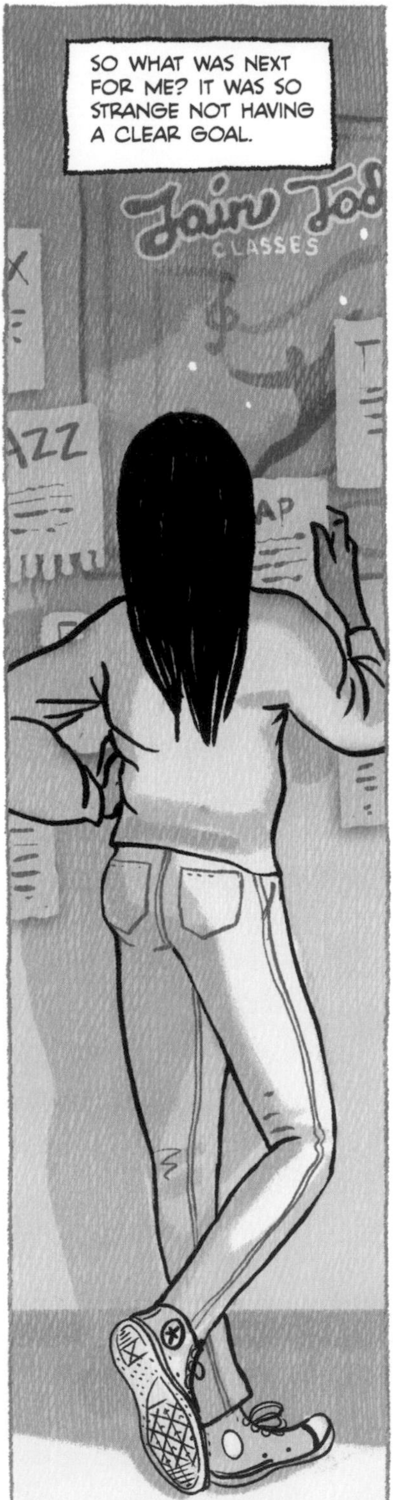
SO WHAT WAS NEXT FOR ME? IT WAS SO STRANGE NOT HAVING A CLEAR GOAL.
CLASSES

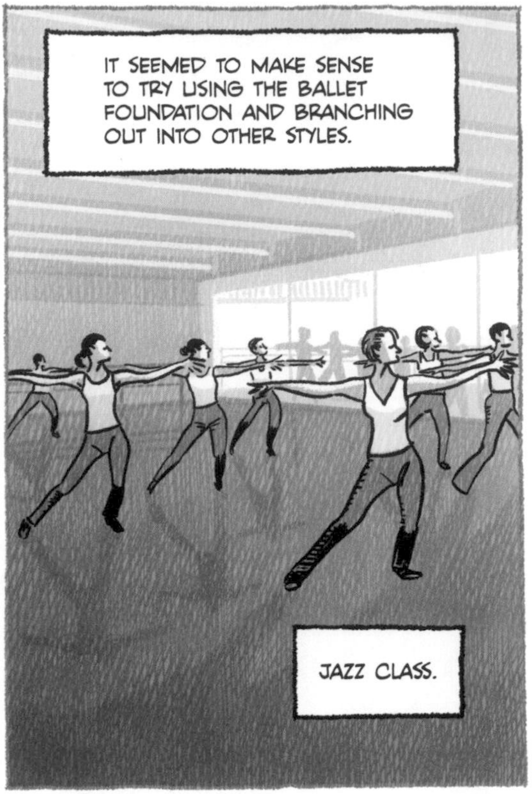
IT SEEMED TO MAKE SENSE TO TRY USING THE BALLET FOUNDATION AND BRANCHING OUT INTO OTHER STYLES.
JAZZ CLASS.

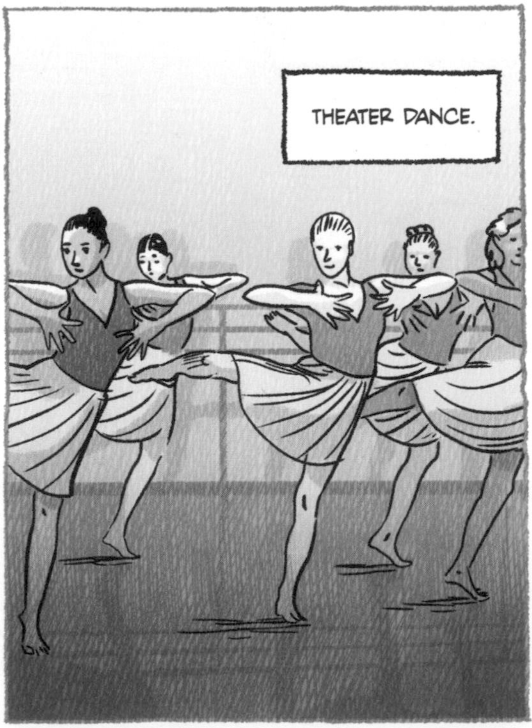
THEATER DANCE.

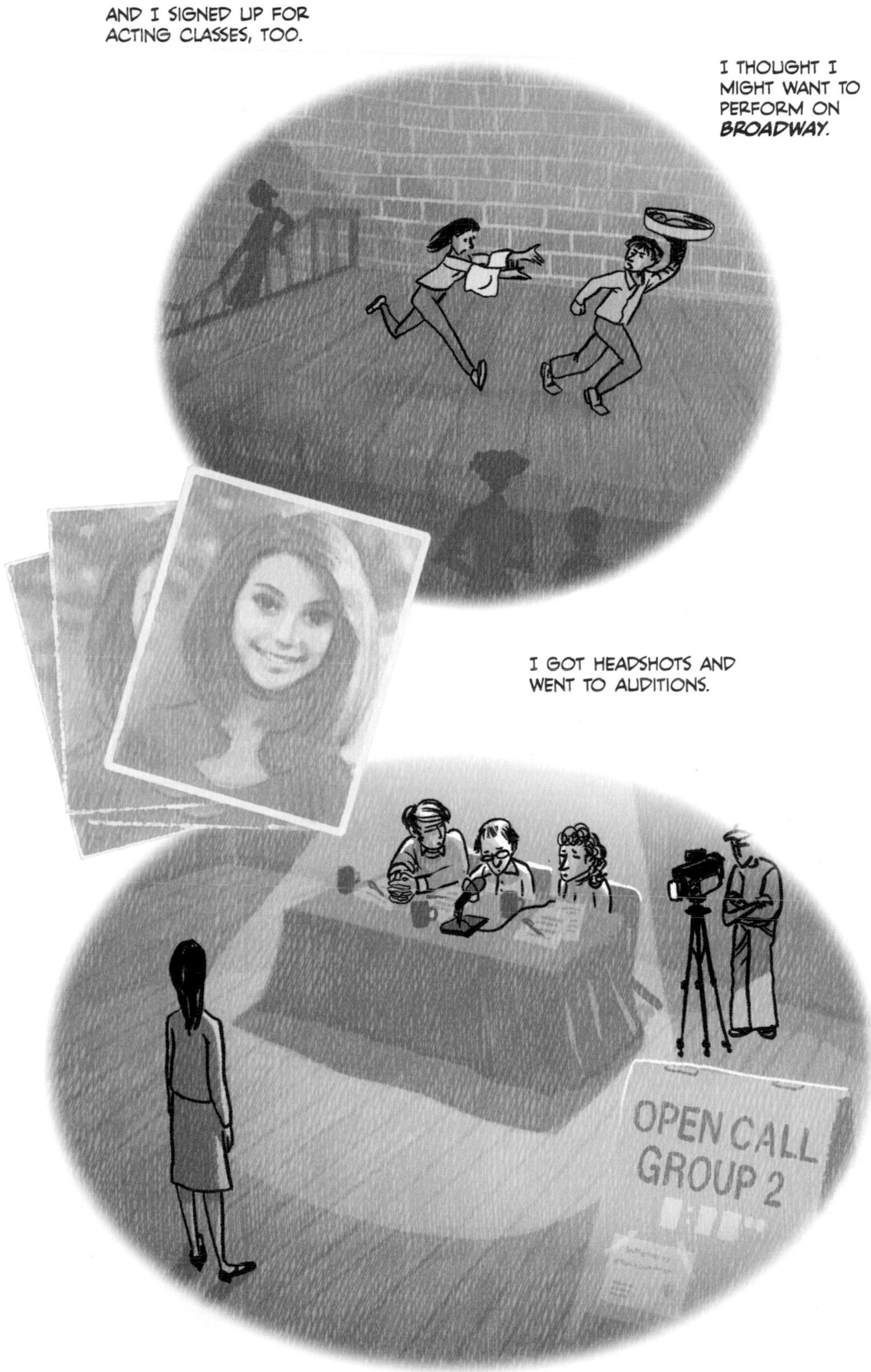
AND I SIGNED UP FOR ACTING CLASSES, TOO.
I THOUGHT I MIGHT WANT TO PERFORM ON BROADWAY.
I GOT HEADSHOTS AND WENT TO AUDITIONS.
OPEN CALL GROUP 2

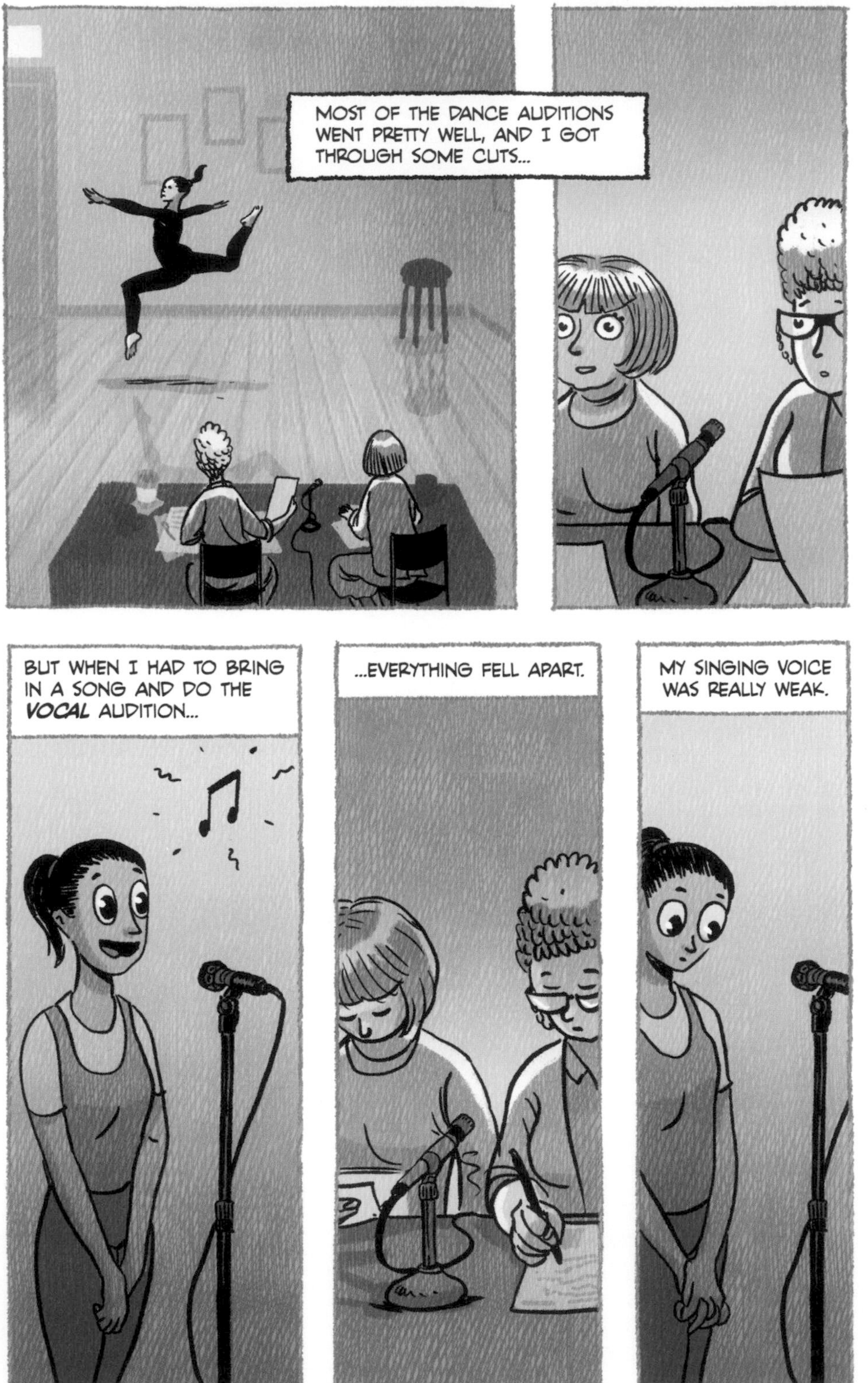
MOST OF THE DANCE AUDITIONS WENT PRETTY WELL, AND I GOT THROUGH SOME CUTS...
BUT WHEN I HAD TO BRING IN A SONG AND DO THE *VOCAL* AUDITION...
...EVERYTHING FELL APART.
MY SINGING VOICE WAS REALLY WEAK.

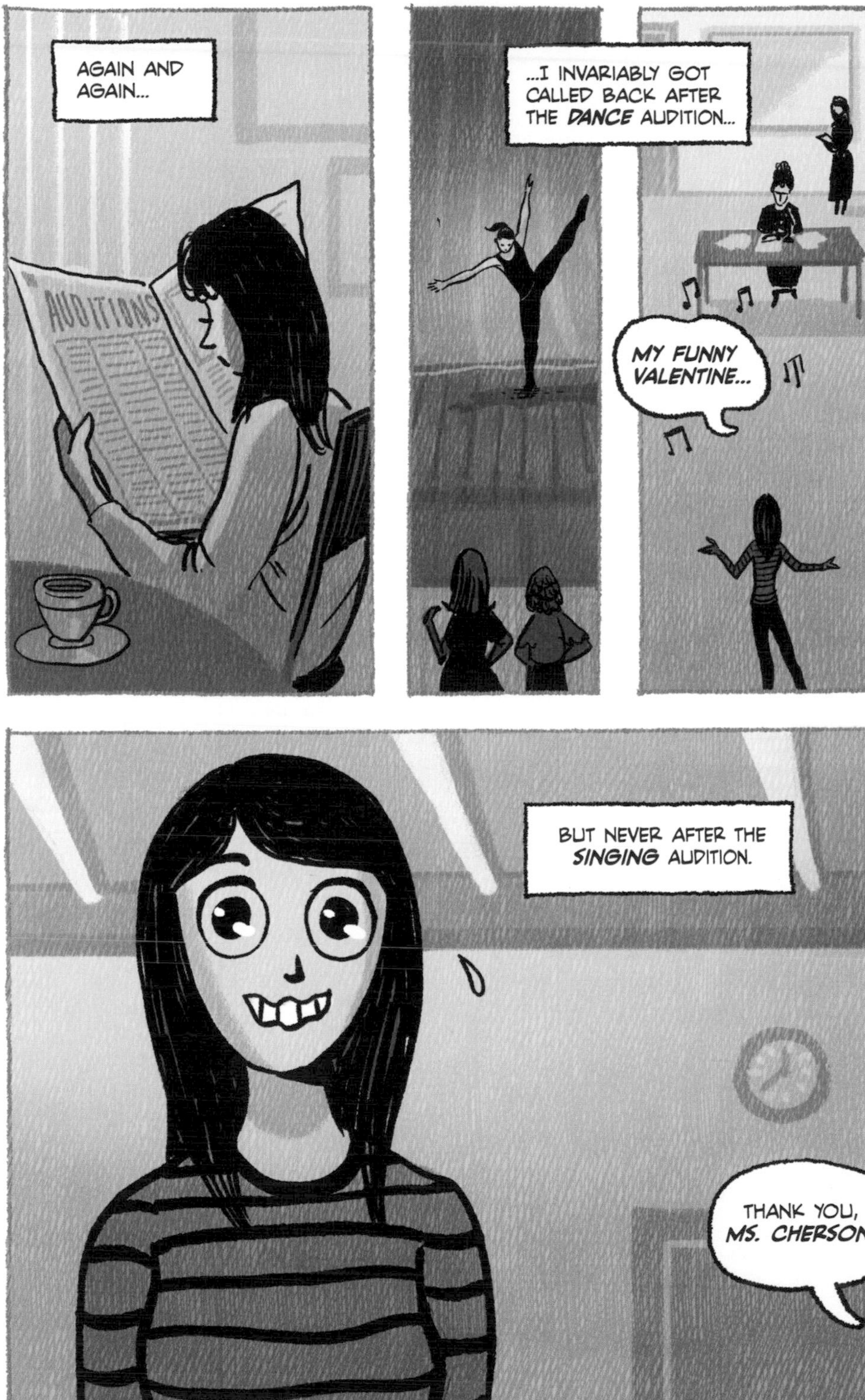
AGAIN AND AGAIN...
AUDITIONS
...I INVARIABLY GOT CALLED BACK AFTER THE DANCE AUDITION...
MY FUNNY VALENTINE...
BUT NEVER AFTER THE SINGING AUDITION.
THANK YOU, MS. CHERSON.

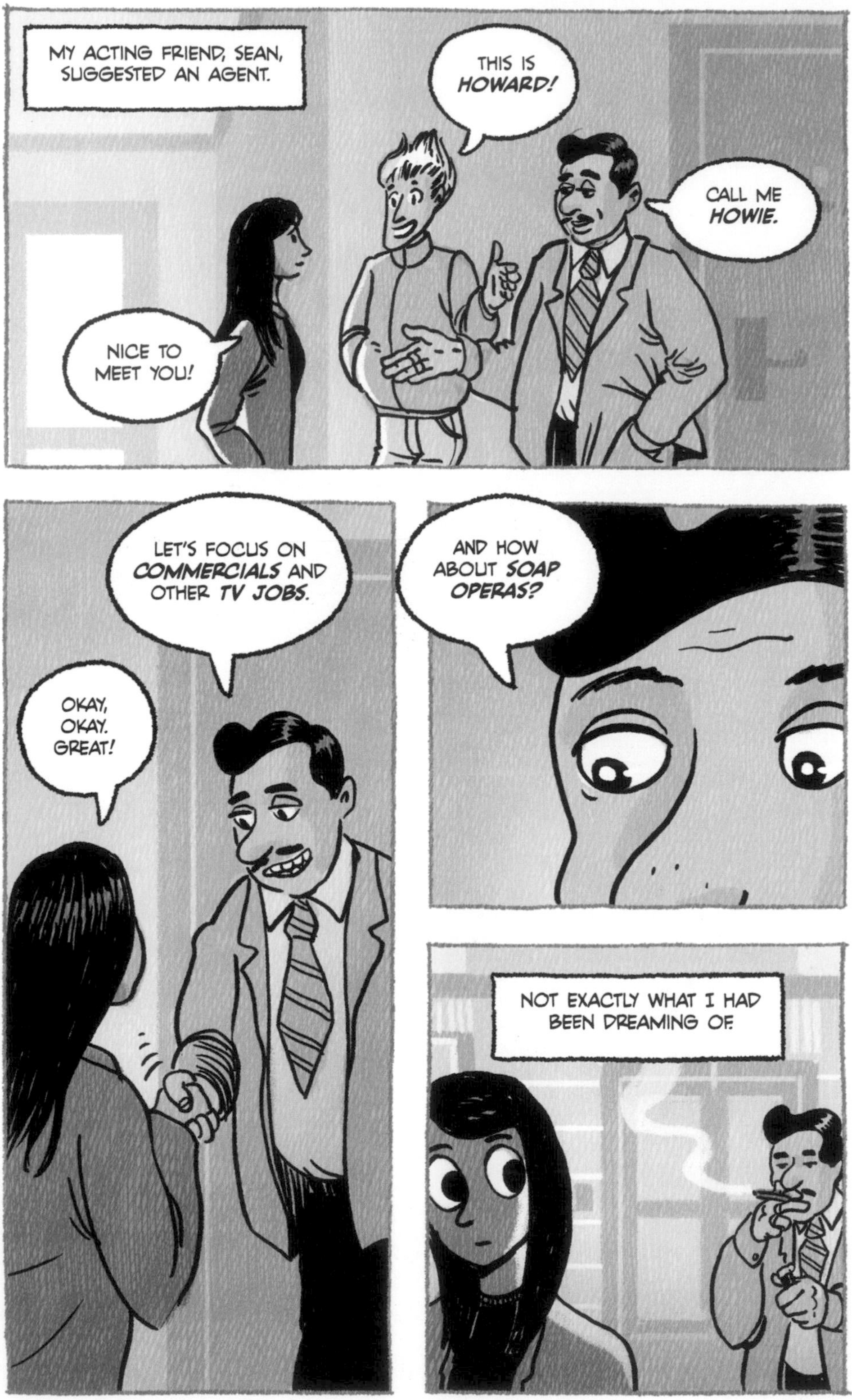
MY ACTING FRIEND, SEAN, SUGGESTED AN AGENT.
THIS IS *HOWARD!*
CALL ME *HOWIE.*
NICE TO MEET YOU!
LET'S FOCUS ON *COMMERCIALS* AND OTHER *TV JOBS.*
OKAY, OKAY. GREAT!
AND HOW ABOUT *SOAP OPERAS?*
NOT EXACTLY WHAT I HAD BEEN DREAMING OF.

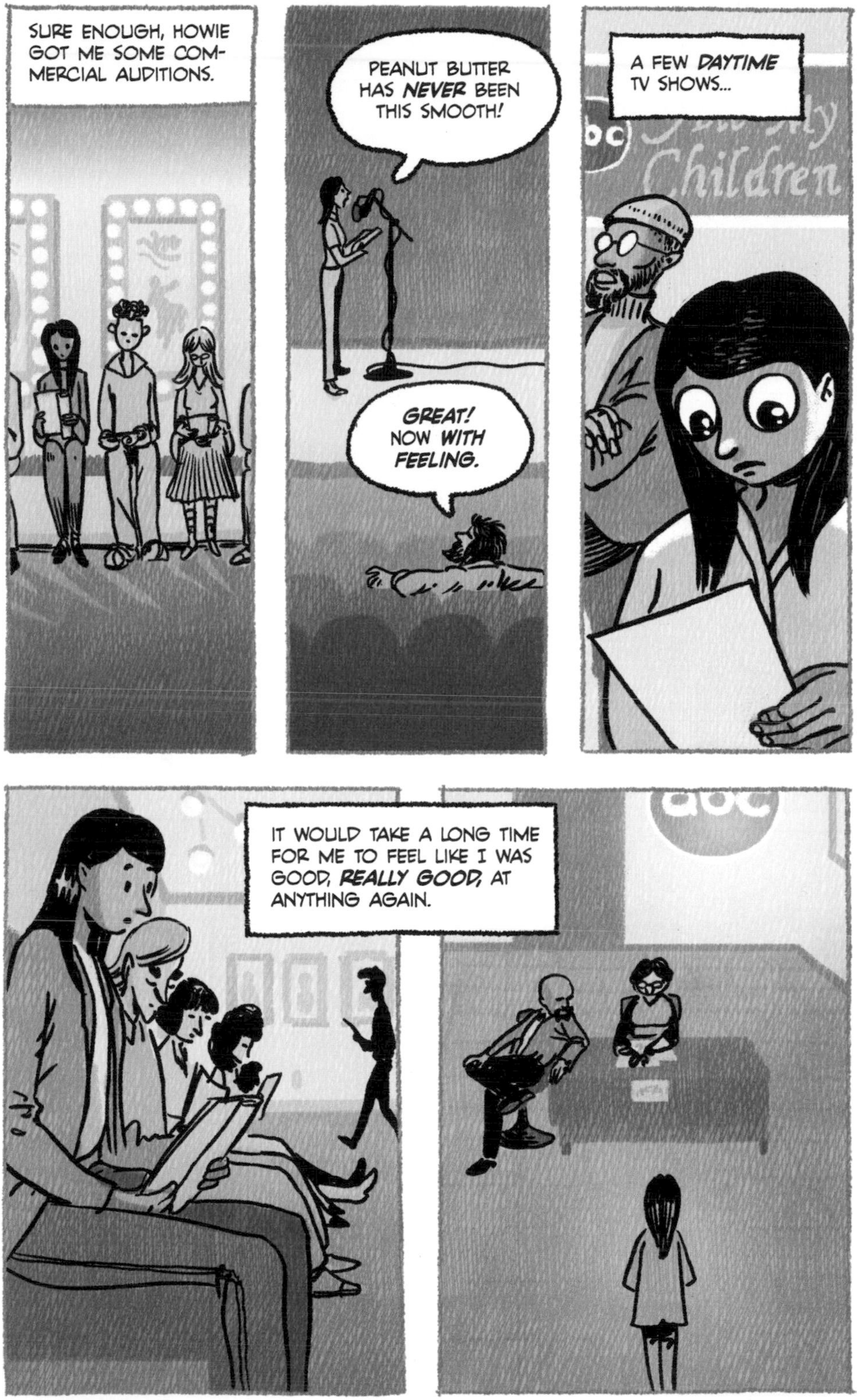
SURE ENOUGH, HOWIE GOT ME SOME COMMERCIAL AUDITIONS.
PEANUT BUTTER HAS ***NEVER*** BEEN THIS SMOOTH!
GREAT! NOW ***WITH FEELING.***
A FEW ***DAYTIME*** TV SHOWS...
IT WOULD TAKE A LONG TIME FOR ME TO FEEL LIKE I WAS GOOD, ***REALLY GOOD,*** AT ANYTHING AGAIN.

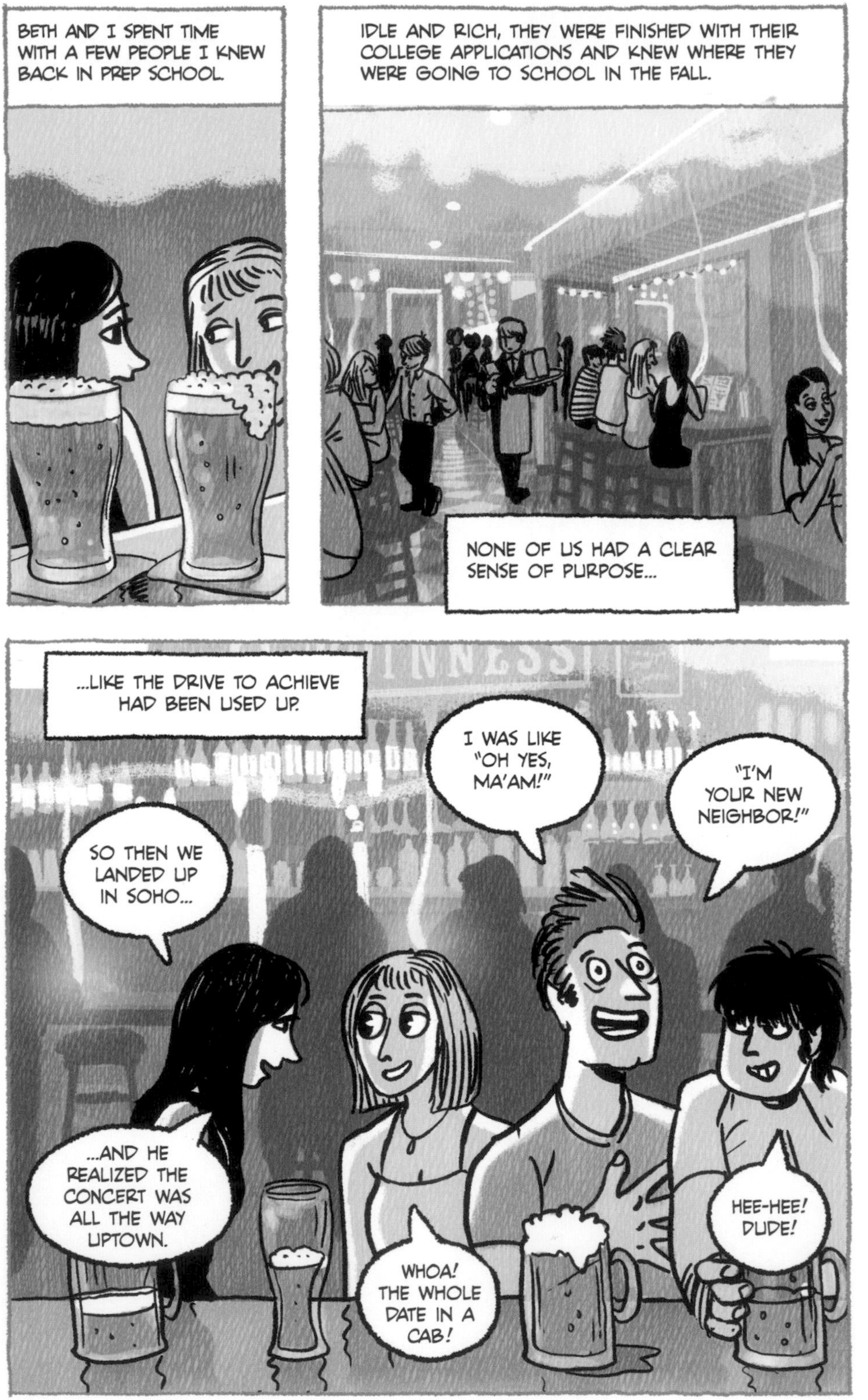
BETH AND I SPENT TIME WITH A FEW PEOPLE I KNEW BACK IN PREP SCHOOL.
IDLE AND RICH, THEY WERE FINISHED WITH THEIR COLLEGE APPLICATIONS AND KNEW WHERE THEY WERE GOING TO SCHOOL IN THE FALL.
NONE OF US HAD A CLEAR SENSE OF PURPOSE...
...LIKE THE DRIVE TO ACHIEVE HAD BEEN USED UP.
SO THEN WE LANDED UP IN SOHO...
I WAS LIKE "OH YES, MA'AM!"
"I'M YOUR NEW NEIGHBOR!"
...AND HE REALIZED THE CONCERT WAS ALL THE WAY UPTOWN.
WHOA! THE WHOLE DATE IN A CAB!
HEE-HEE! DUDE!

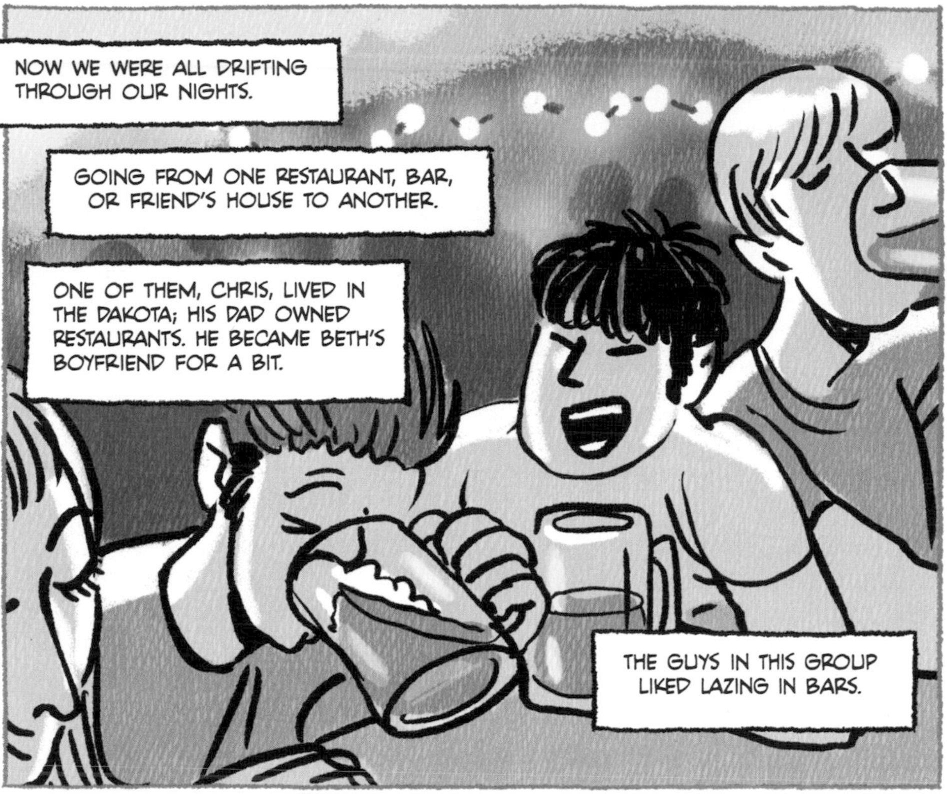
NOW WE WERE ALL DRIFTING THROUGH OUR NIGHTS.
GOING FROM ONE RESTAURANT, BAR, OR FRIEND'S HOUSE TO ANOTHER.
ONE OF THEM, CHRIS, LIVED IN THE DAKOTA; HIS DAD OWNED RESTAURANTS. HE BECAME BETH'S BOYFRIEND FOR A BIT.
THE GUYS IN THIS GROUP LIKED LAZING IN BARS.

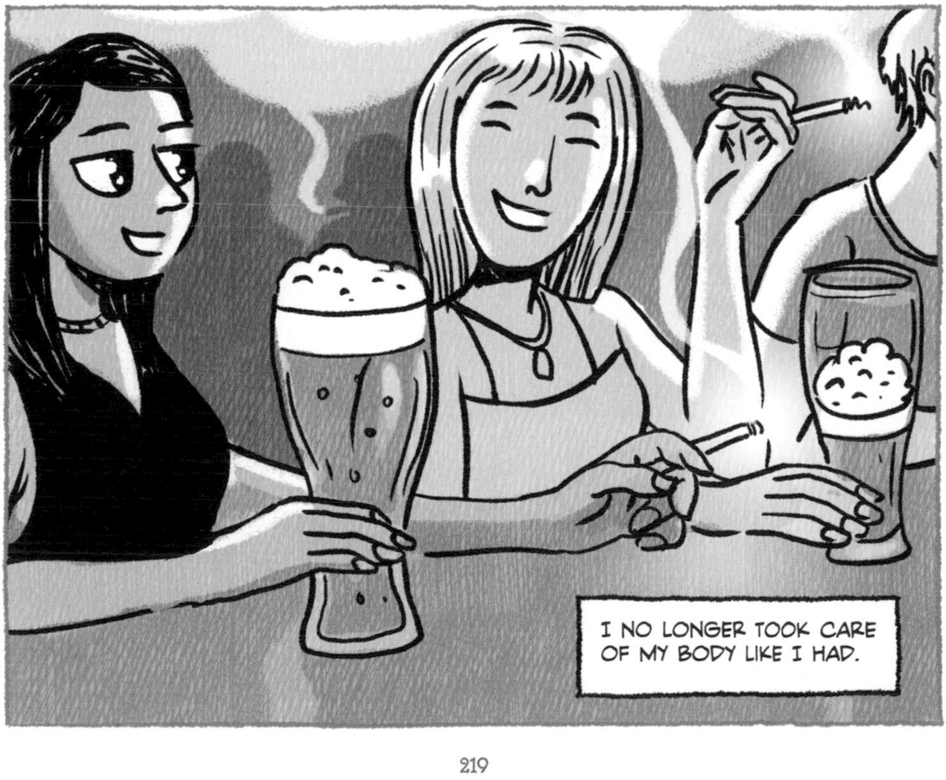
I NO LONGER TOOK CARE OF MY BODY LIKE I HAD.

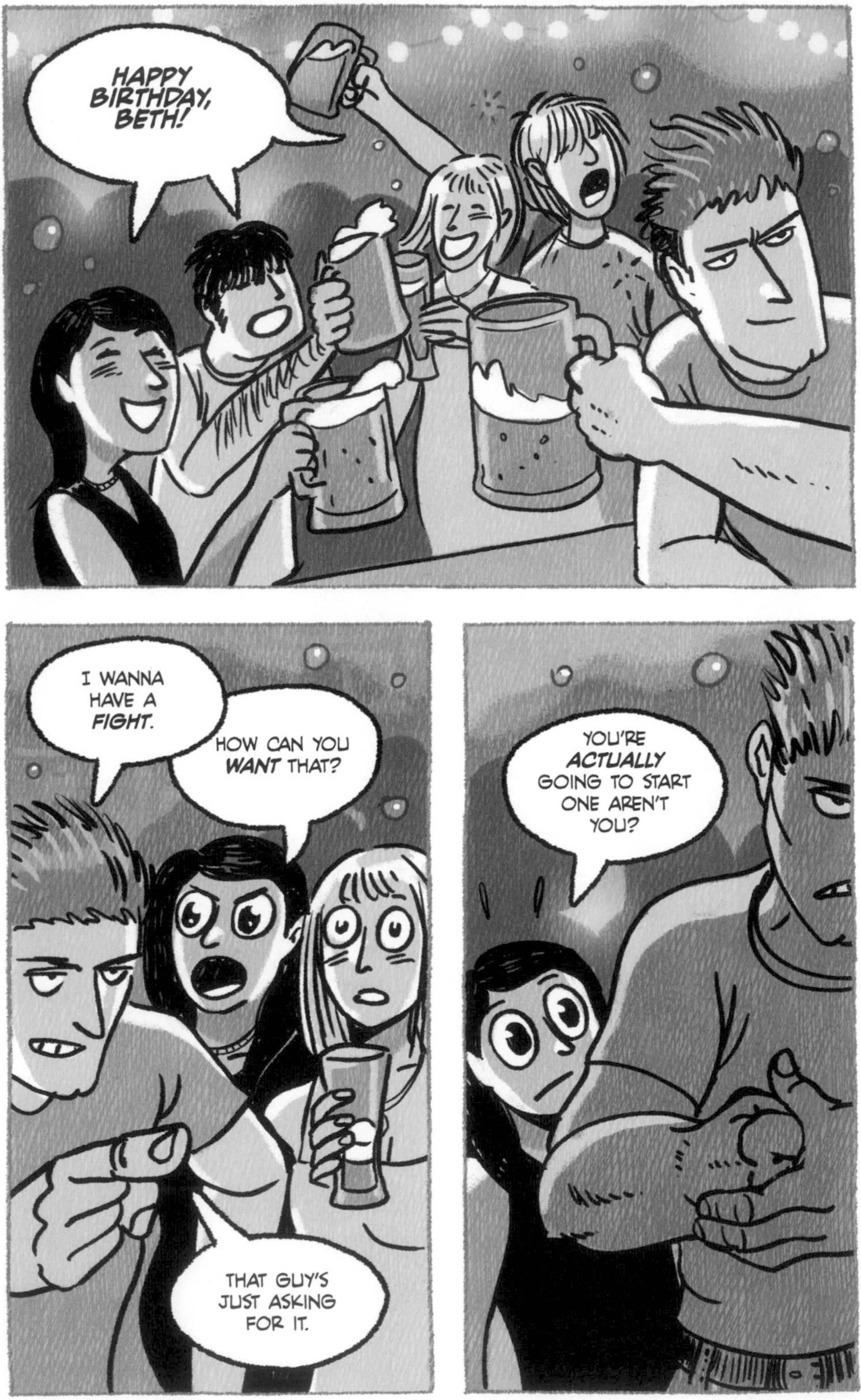
HAPPY BIRTHDAY, BETH!
I WANNA HAVE A FIGHT.
HOW CAN YOU WANT THAT?
THAT GUY'S JUST ASKING FOR IT.
YOU'RE ACTUALLY GOING TO START ONE AREN'T YOU?

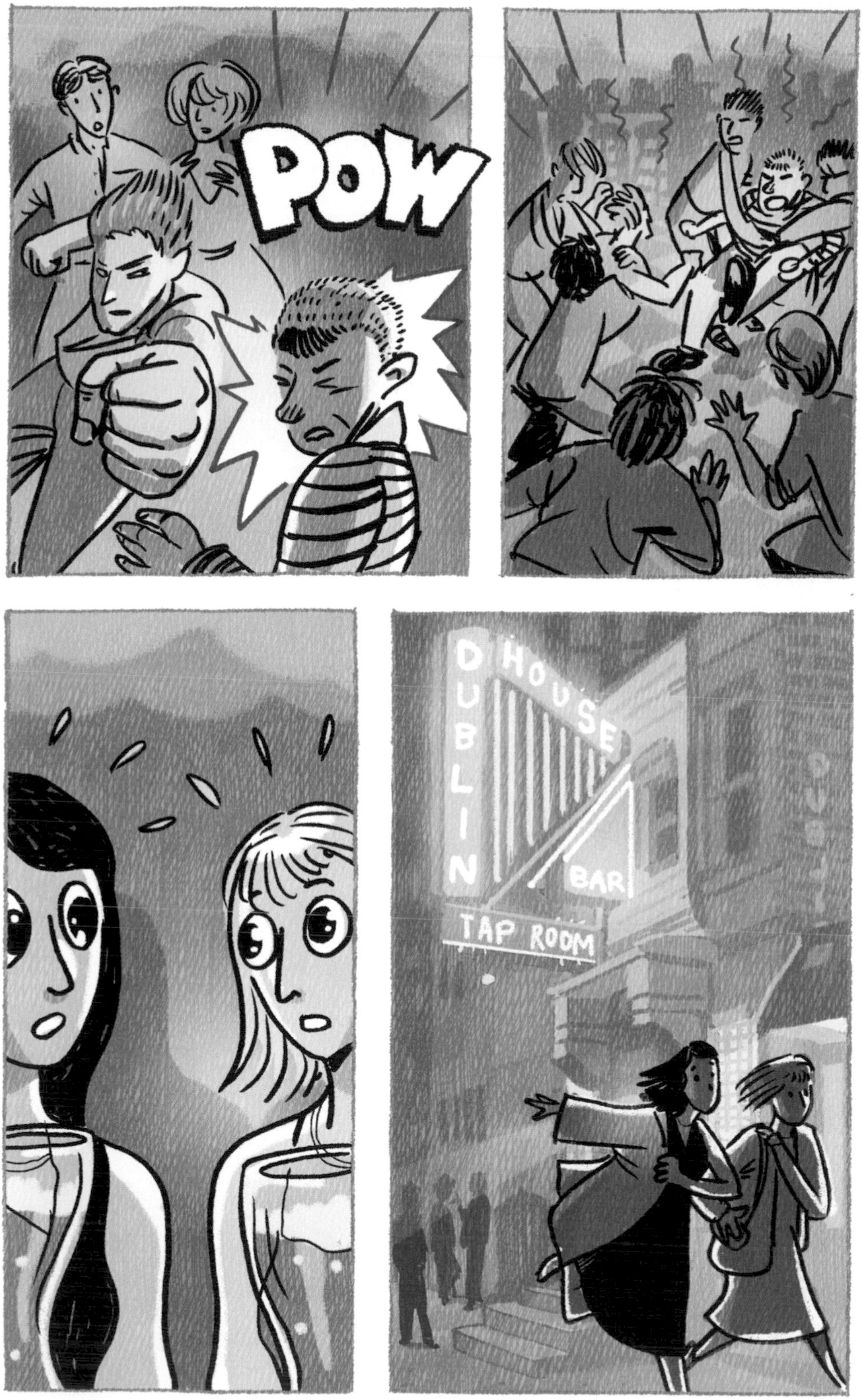
POW
DUBLIN HOUSE
BAR
TAP ROOM

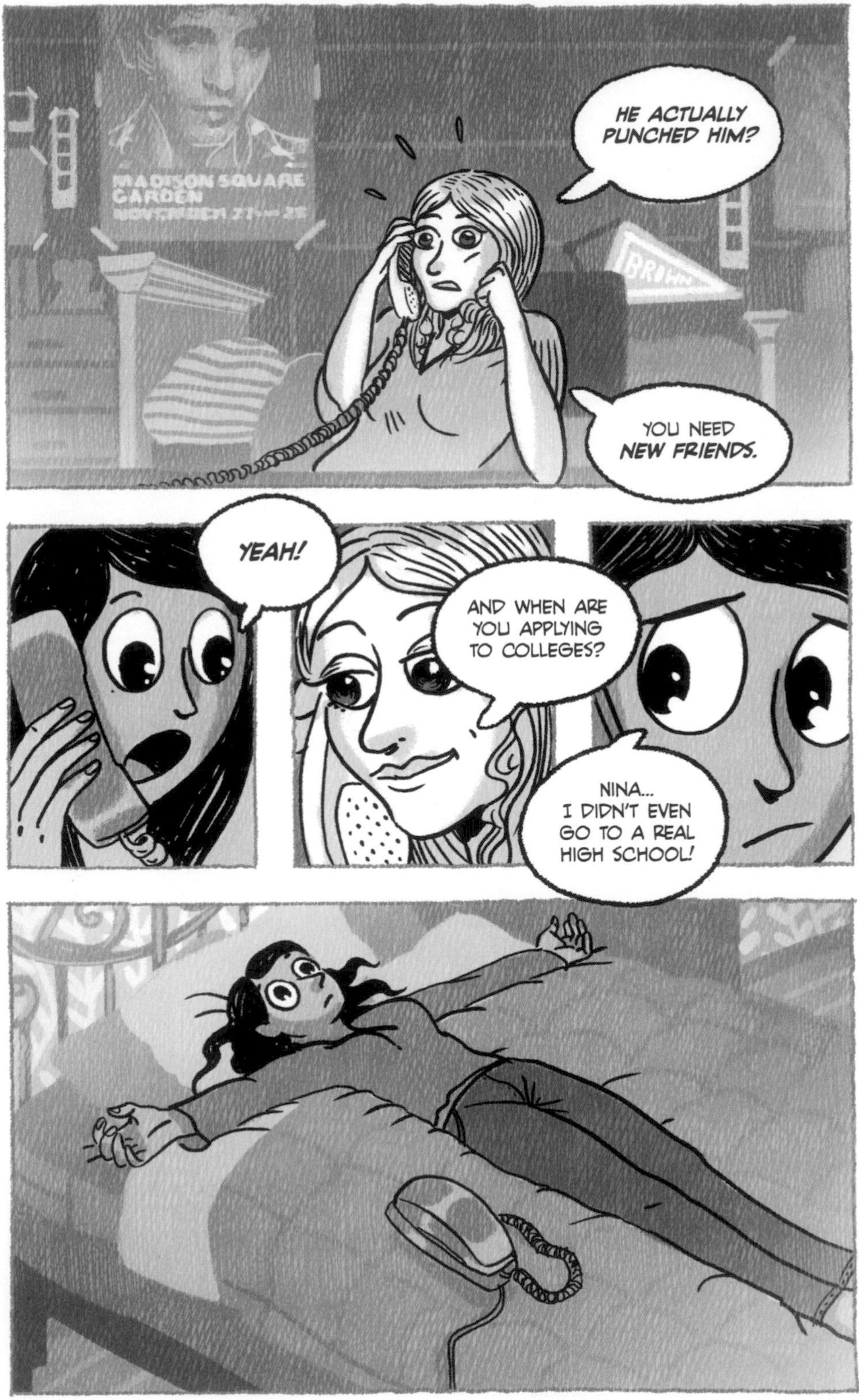
MADISON SQUARE GARDEN
HE ACTUALLY PUNCHED HIM?
YOU NEED NEW FRIENDS.
YEAH!
AND WHEN ARE YOU APPLYING TO COLLEGES?
NINA... I DIDN'T EVEN GO TO A REAL HIGH SCHOOL!

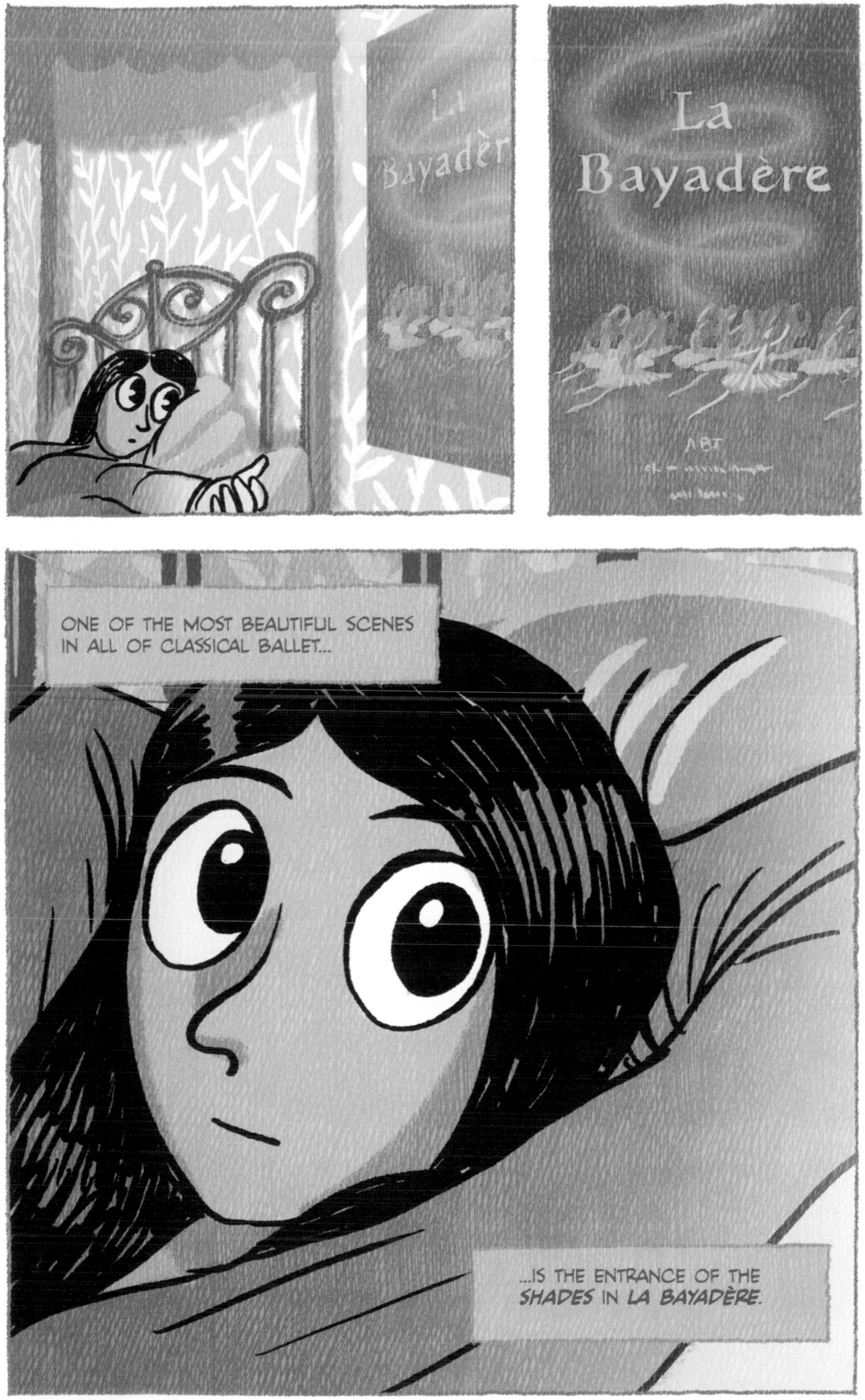
La Bayadère
ABT
ONE OF THE MOST BEAUTIFUL SCENES IN ALL OF CLASSICAL BALLET...
...IS THE ENTRANCE OF THE *SHADES* IN *LA BAYADÈRE*.

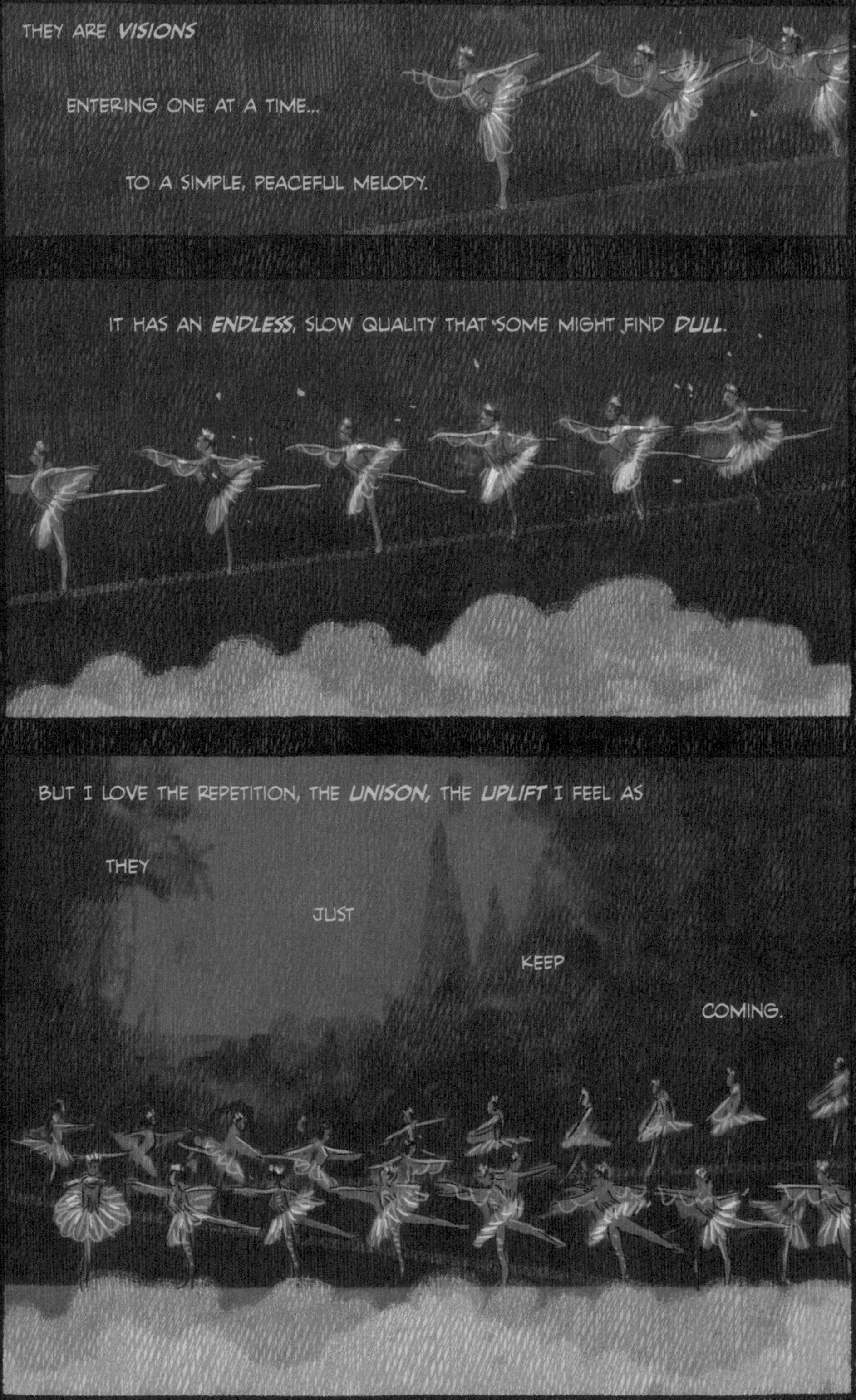
THEY ARE VISIONS
ENTERING ONE AT A TIME...
TO A SIMPLE, PEACEFUL MELODY.
IT HAS AN ENDLESS, SLOW QUALITY THAT SOME MIGHT FIND DULL.
BUT I LOVE THE REPETITION, THE UNISON, THE UPLIFT I FEEL AS
THEY
JUST
KEEP
COMING.

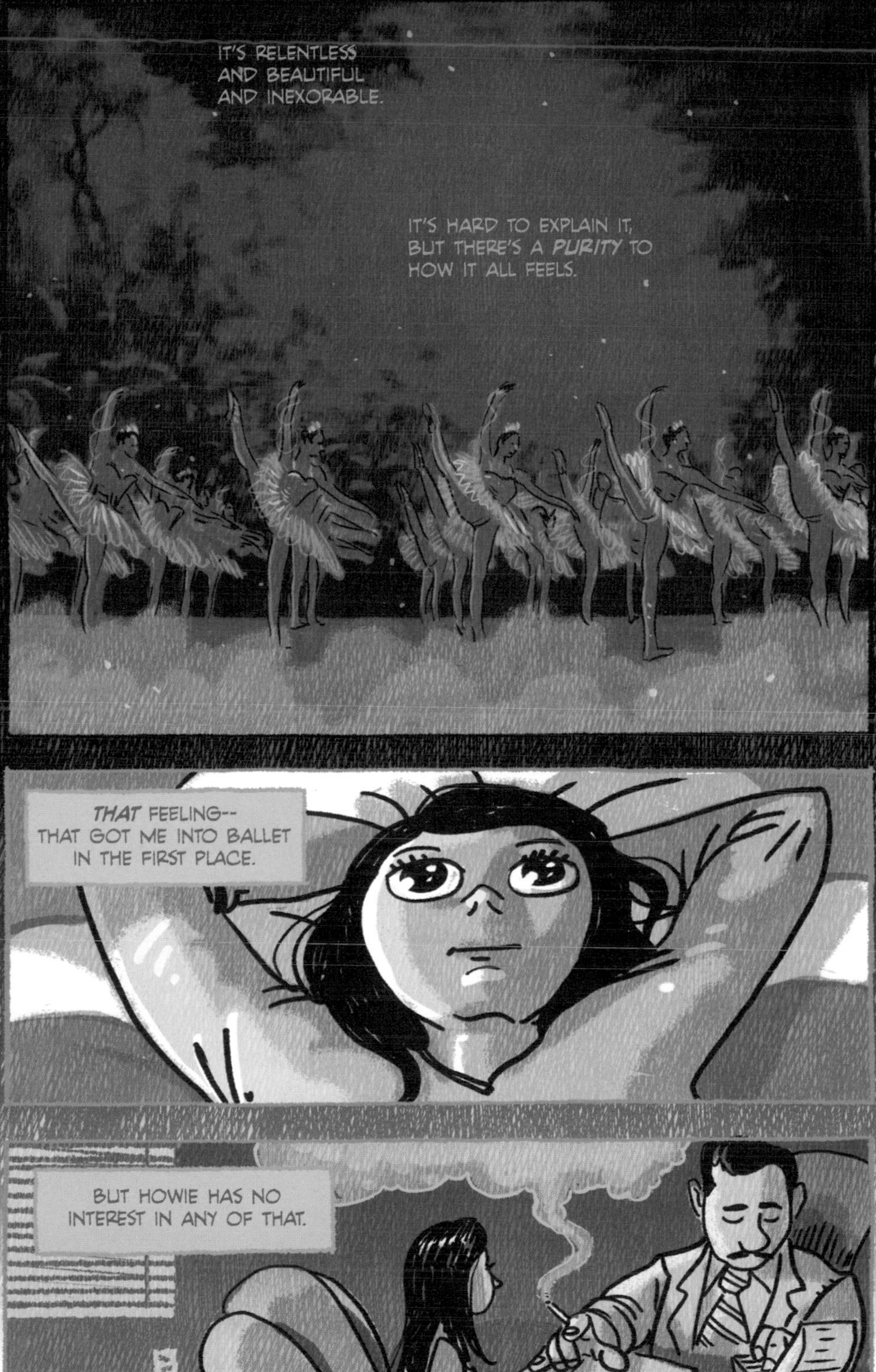
IT'S RELENTLESS AND BEAUTIFUL AND INEXORABLE.
IT'S HARD TO EXPLAIN IT, BUT THERE'S A *PURITY* TO HOW IT ALL FEELS.
THAT FEELING-- THAT GOT ME INTO BALLET IN THE FIRST PLACE.
BUT HOWIE HAS NO INTEREST IN ANY OF THAT.

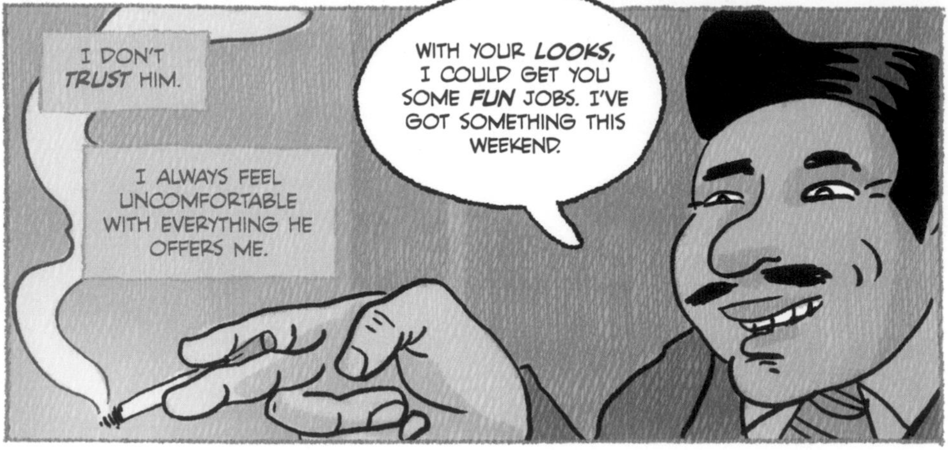
I DON'T *TRUST* HIM.
I ALWAYS FEEL UNCOMFORTABLE WITH EVERYTHING HE OFFERS ME.
WITH YOUR *LOOKS,* I COULD GET YOU SOME *FUN* JOBS. I'VE GOT SOMETHING THIS WEEKEND.

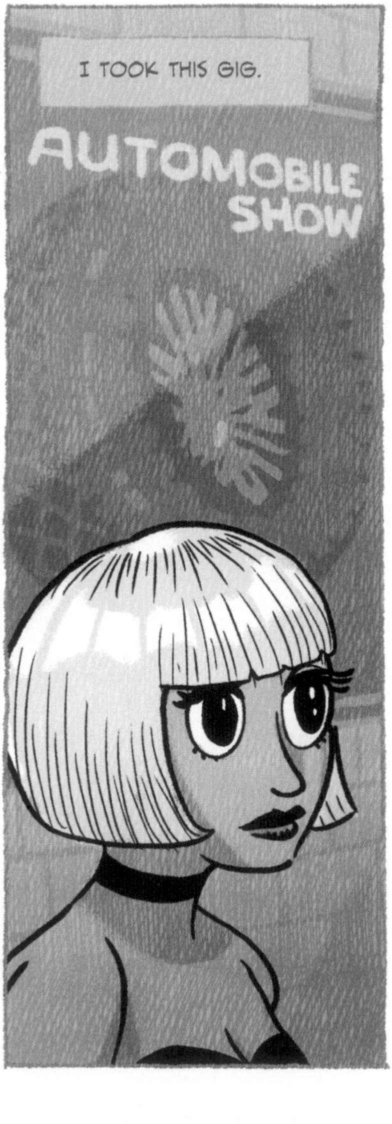
I TOOK THIS GIG.
AUTOMOBILE SHOW

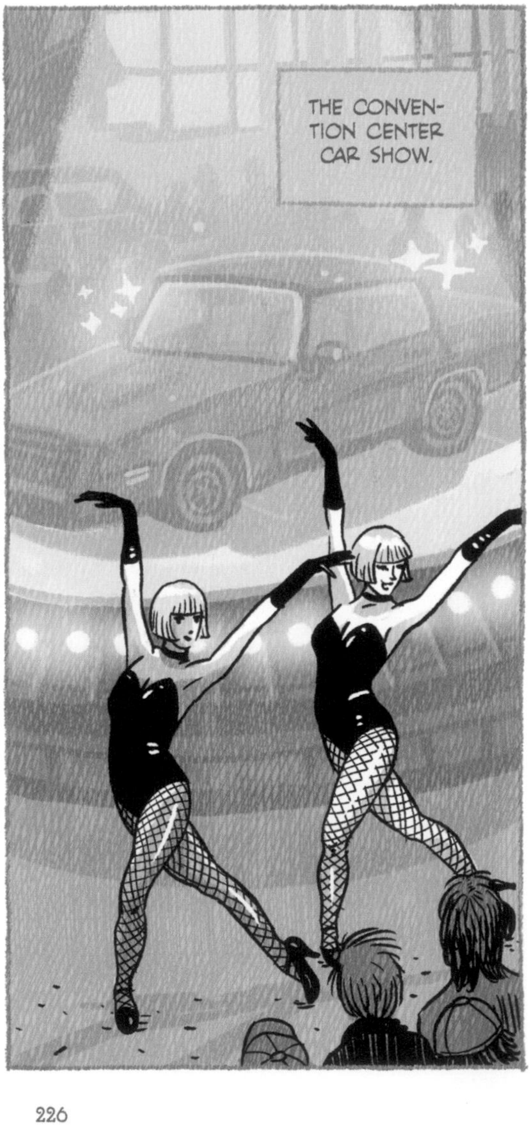
THE CONVENTION CENTER CAR SHOW.

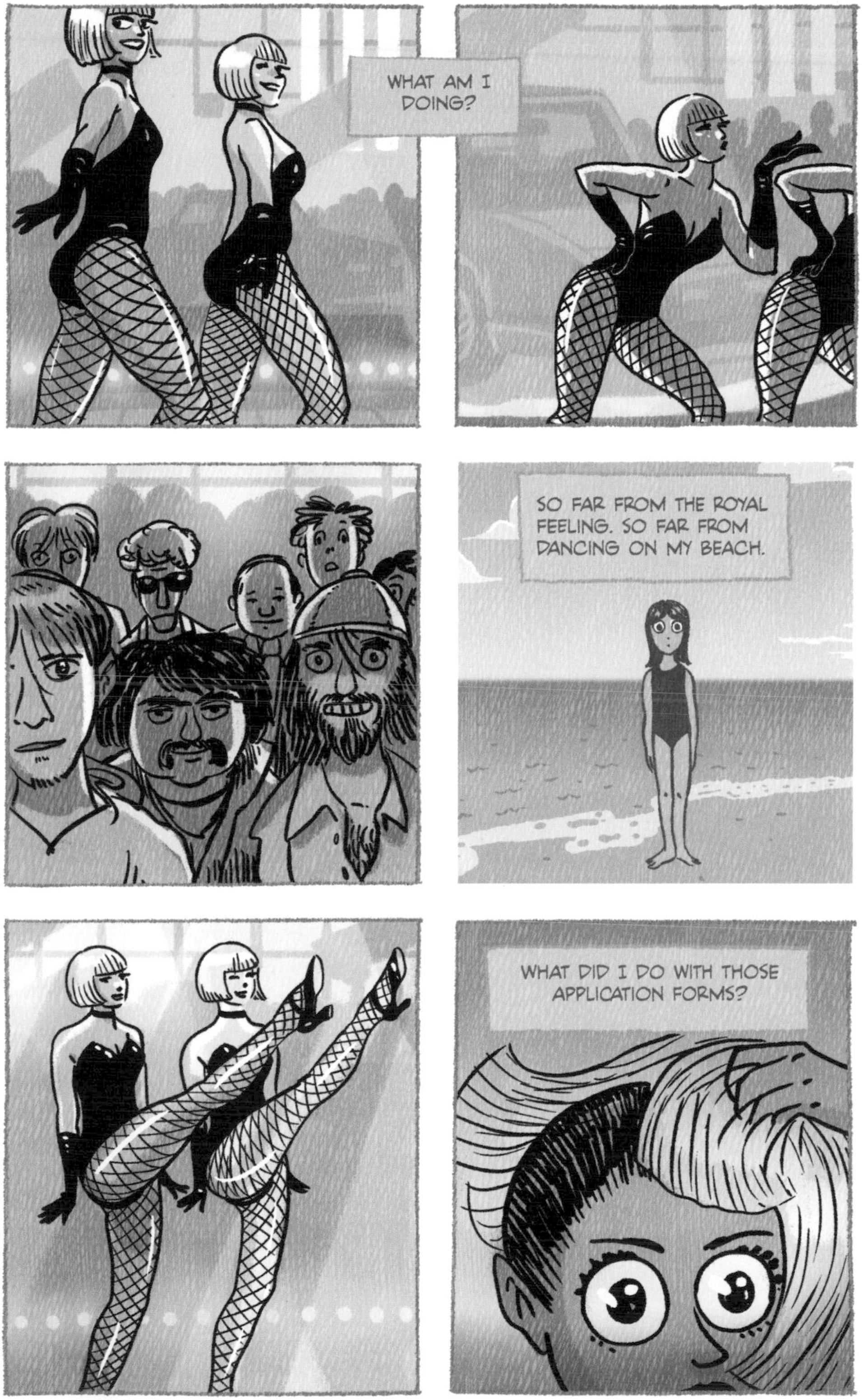
WHAT AM I DOING?
SO FAR FROM THE ROYAL FEELING. SO FAR FROM DANCING ON MY BEACH.
WHAT DID I DO WITH THOSE APPLICATION FORMS?

Part 4

Providence

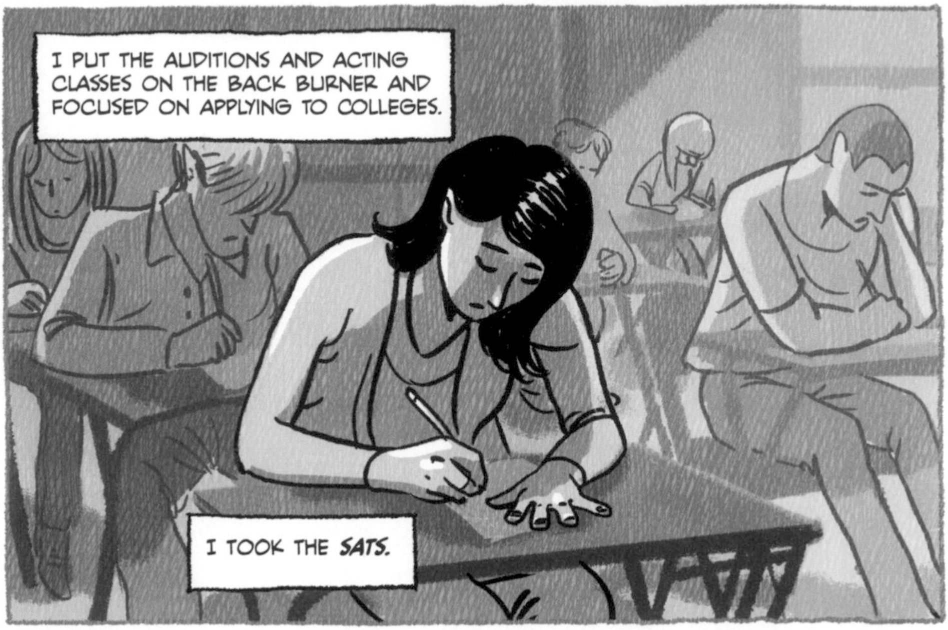
I PUT THE AUDITIONS AND ACTING CLASSES ON THE BACK BURNER AND FOCUSED ON APPLYING TO COLLEGES.
I TOOK THE ***SATS.***

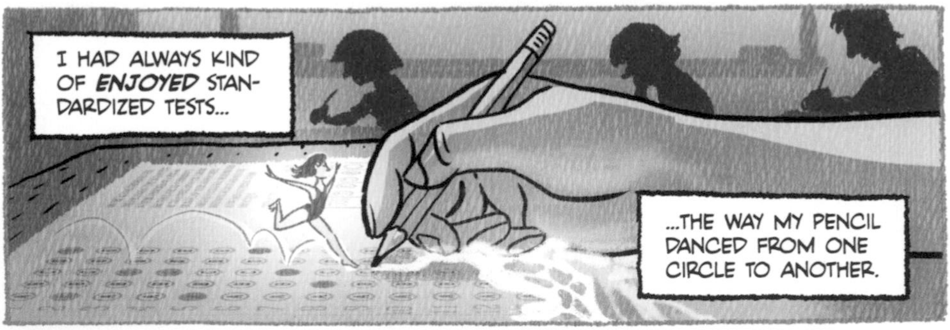
I HAD ALWAYS KIND OF ***ENJOYED*** STANDARDIZED TESTS...
...THE WAY MY PENCIL DANCED FROM ONE CIRCLE TO ANOTHER.

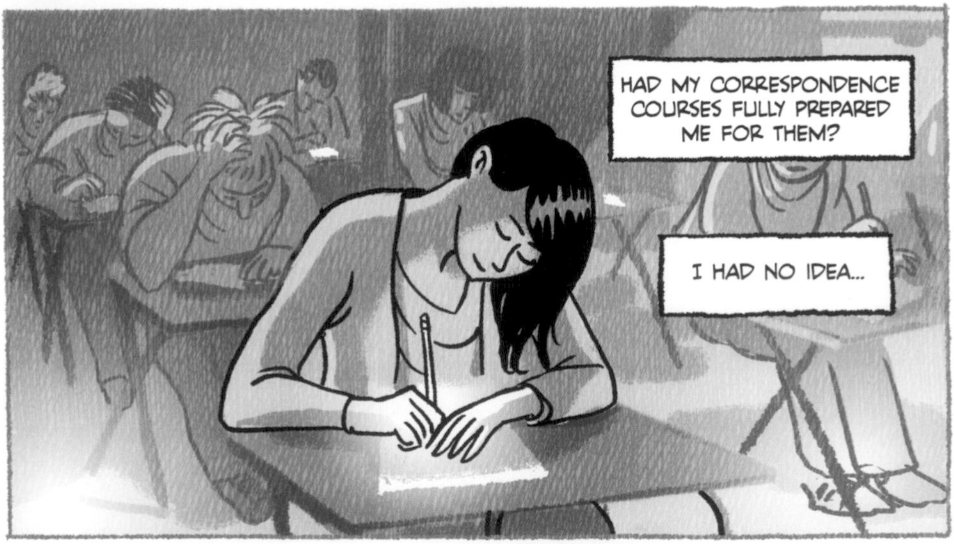
HAD MY CORRESPONDENCE COURSES FULLY PREPARED ME FOR THEM?
I HAD NO IDEA...

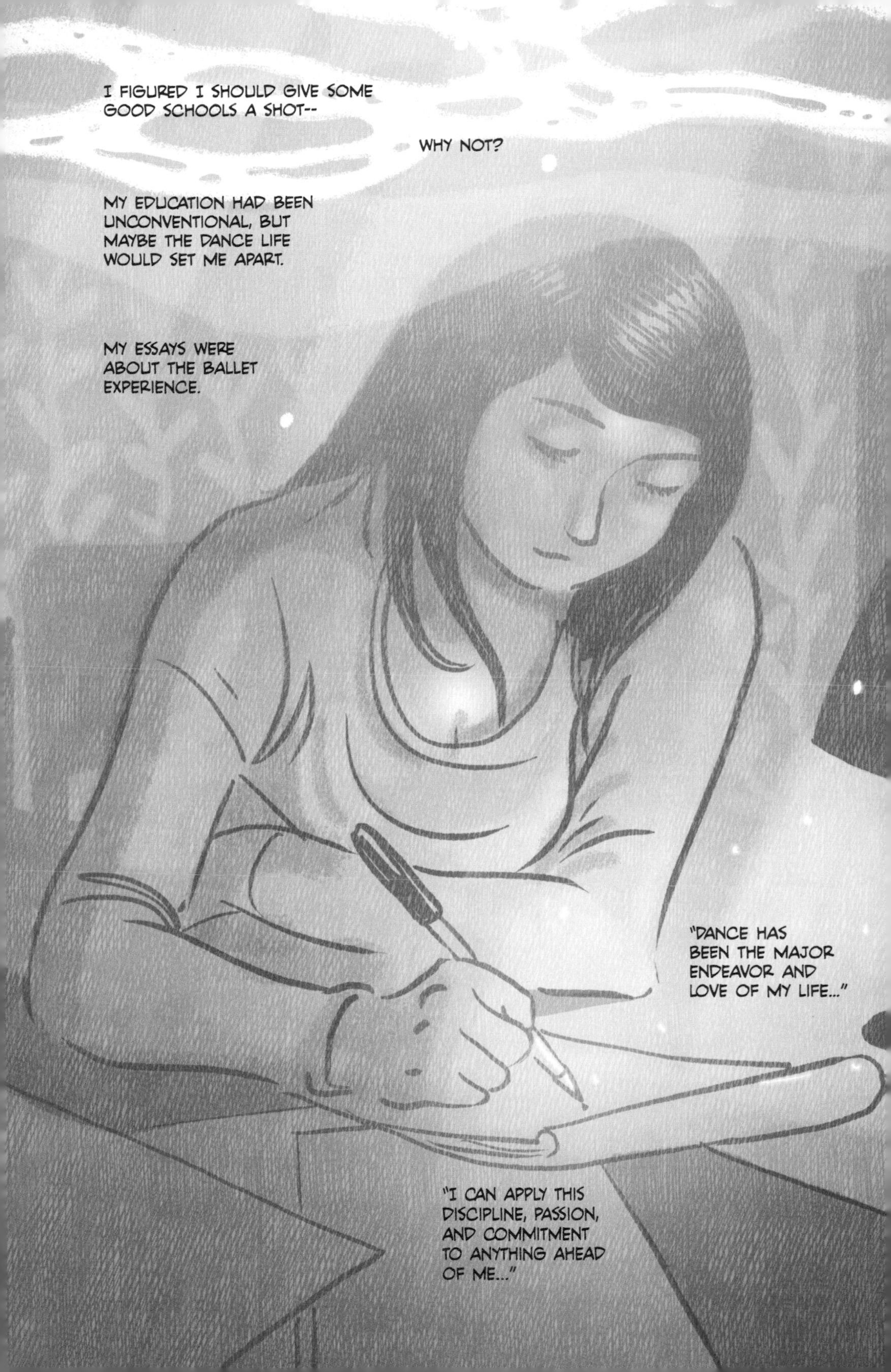
I FIGURED I SHOULD GIVE SOME GOOD SCHOOLS A SHOT--
WHY NOT?
MY EDUCATION HAD BEEN UNCONVENTIONAL, BUT MAYBE THE DANCE LIFE WOULD SET ME APART.
MY ESSAYS WERE ABOUT THE BALLET EXPERIENCE.
"DANCE HAS BEEN THE MAJOR ENDEAVOR AND LOVE OF MY LIFE..."
"I CAN APPLY THIS DISCIPLINE, PASSION, AND COMMITMENT TO ANYTHING AHEAD OF ME..."

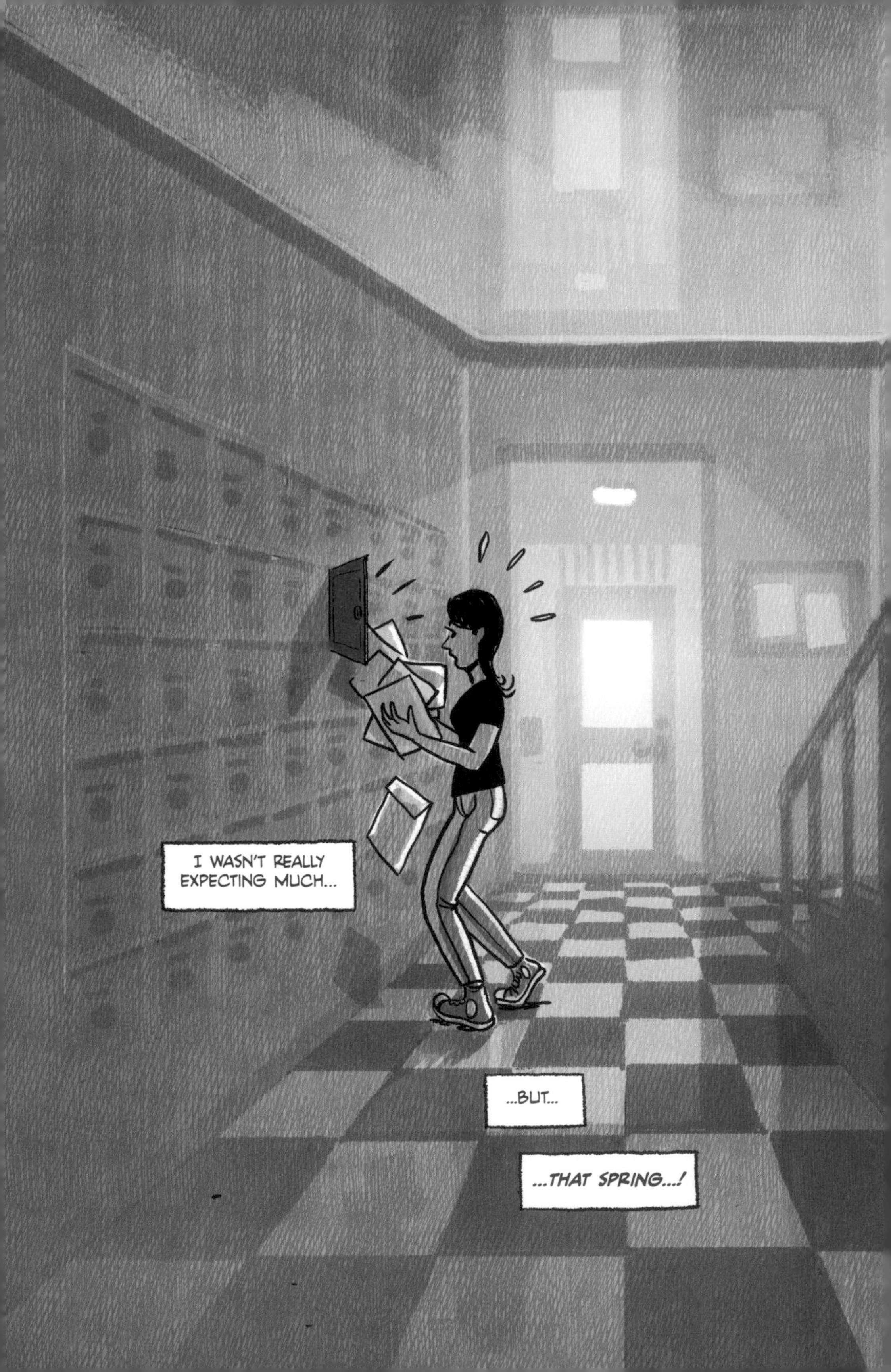
I WASN'T REALLY EXPECTING MUCH...
...BUT...
...THAT SPRING...!

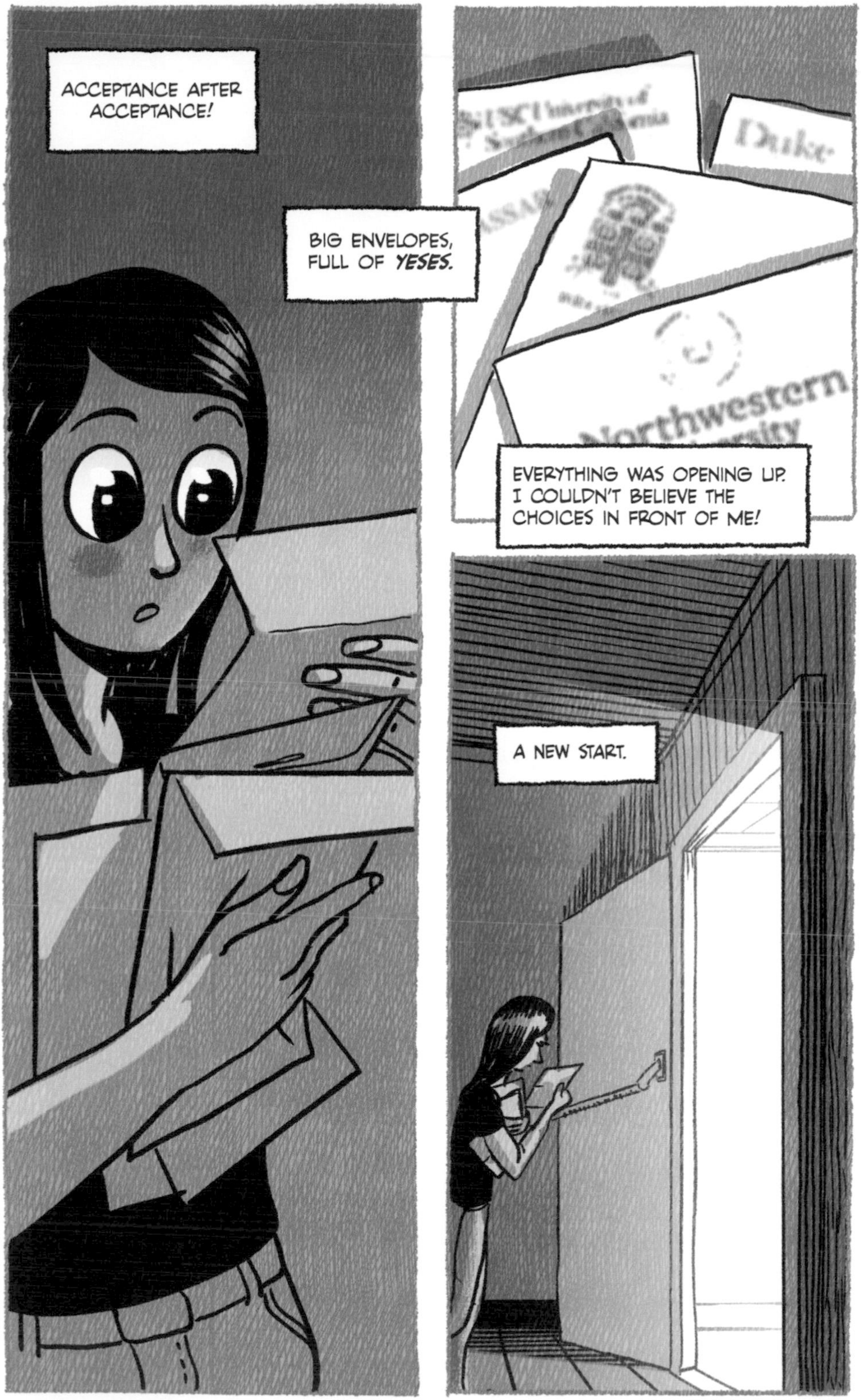
ACCEPTANCE AFTER ACCEPTANCE!
BIG ENVELOPES, FULL OF *YESES.*
Duke
Northwestern
EVERYTHING WAS OPENING UP. I COULDN'T BELIEVE THE CHOICES IN FRONT OF ME!
A NEW START.

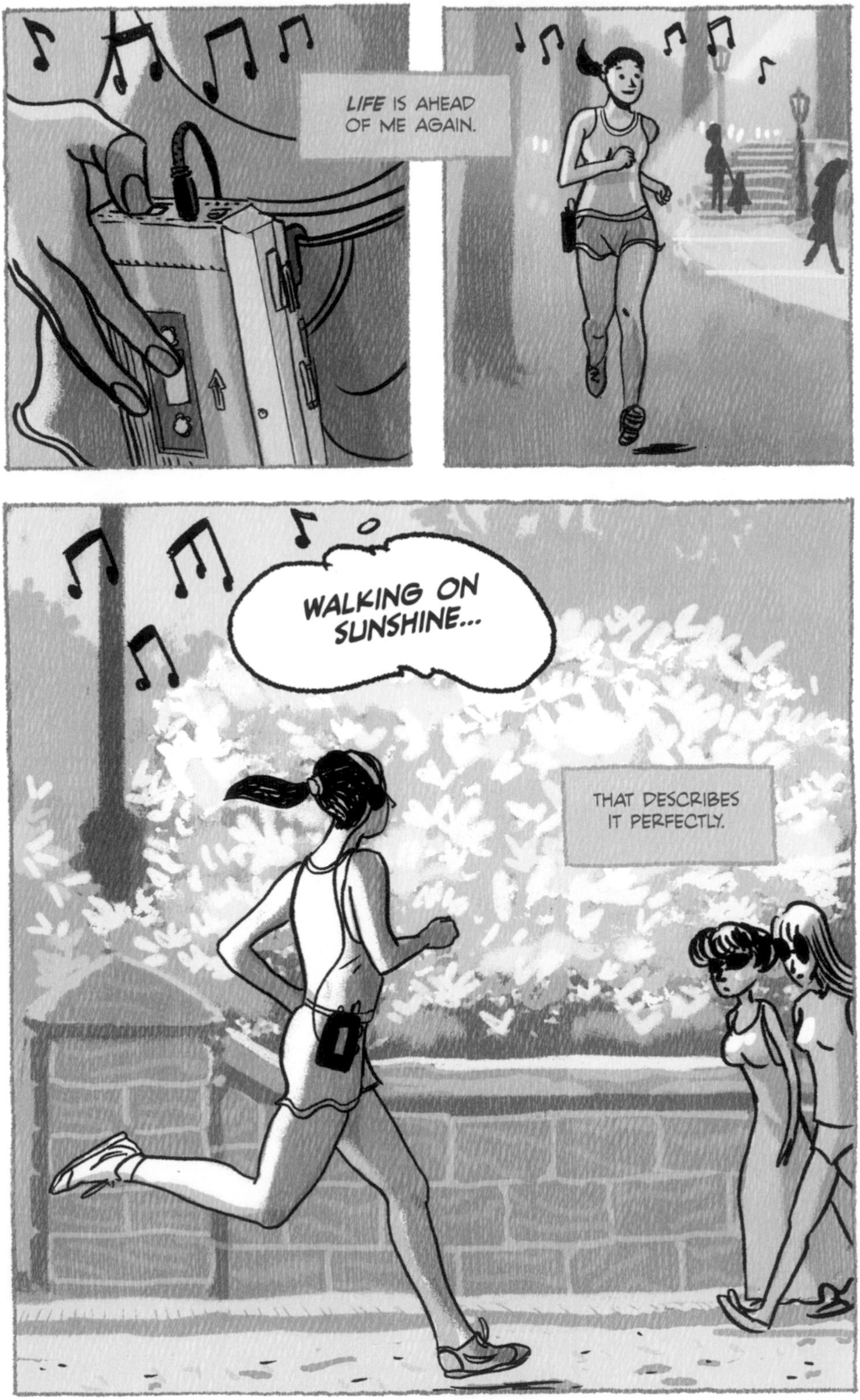

LIFE IS AHEAD OF ME AGAIN.
WALKING ON SUNSHINE...
THAT DESCRIBES IT PERFECTLY.

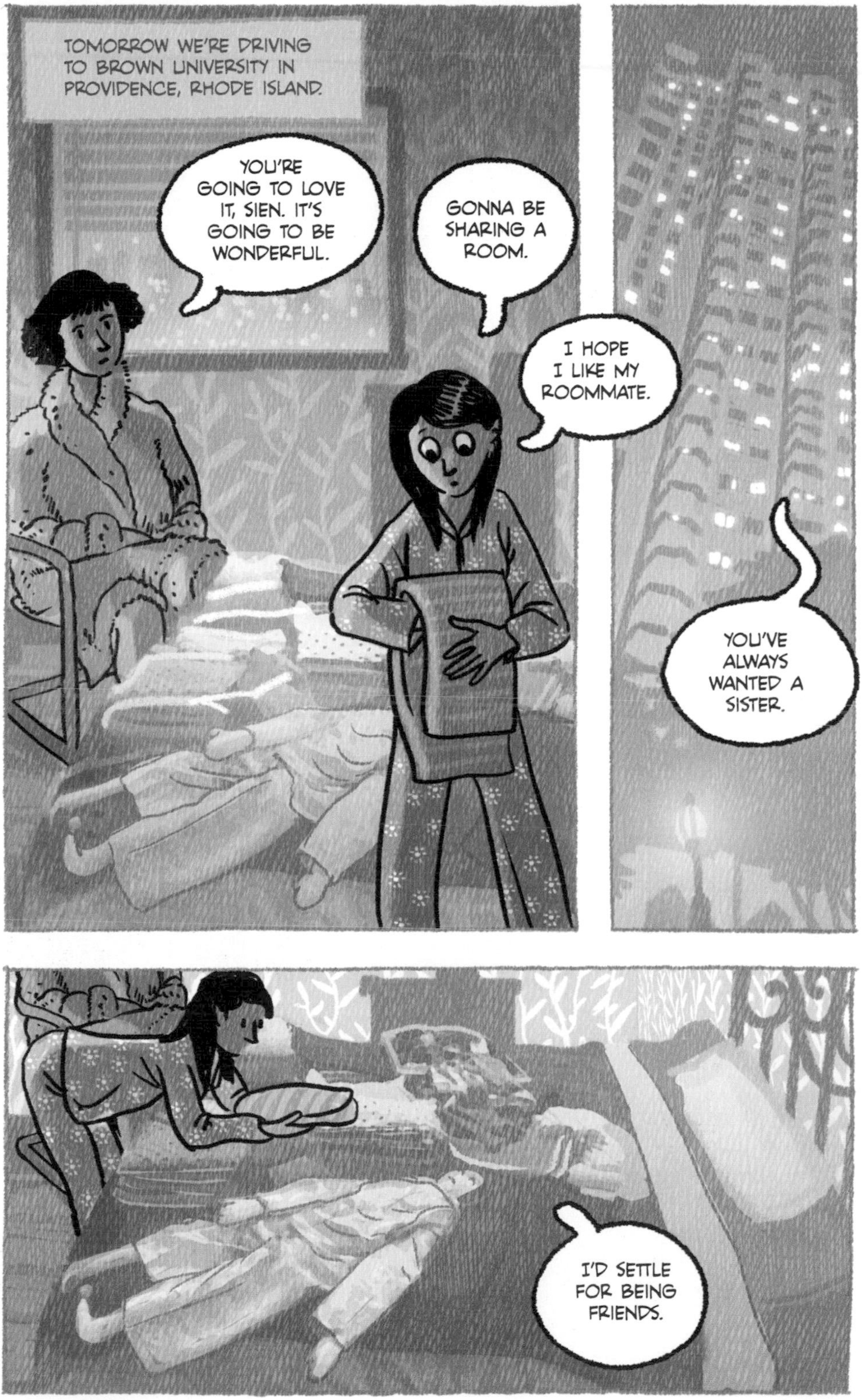
TOMORROW WE'RE DRIVING TO BROWN UNIVERSITY IN PROVIDENCE, RHODE ISLAND.
YOU'RE GOING TO LOVE IT, SIEN. IT'S GOING TO BE WONDERFUL.
GONNA BE SHARING A ROOM.
I HOPE I LIKE MY ROOMMATE.
YOU'VE ALWAYS WANTED A SISTER.
I'D SETTLE FOR BEING FRIENDS.

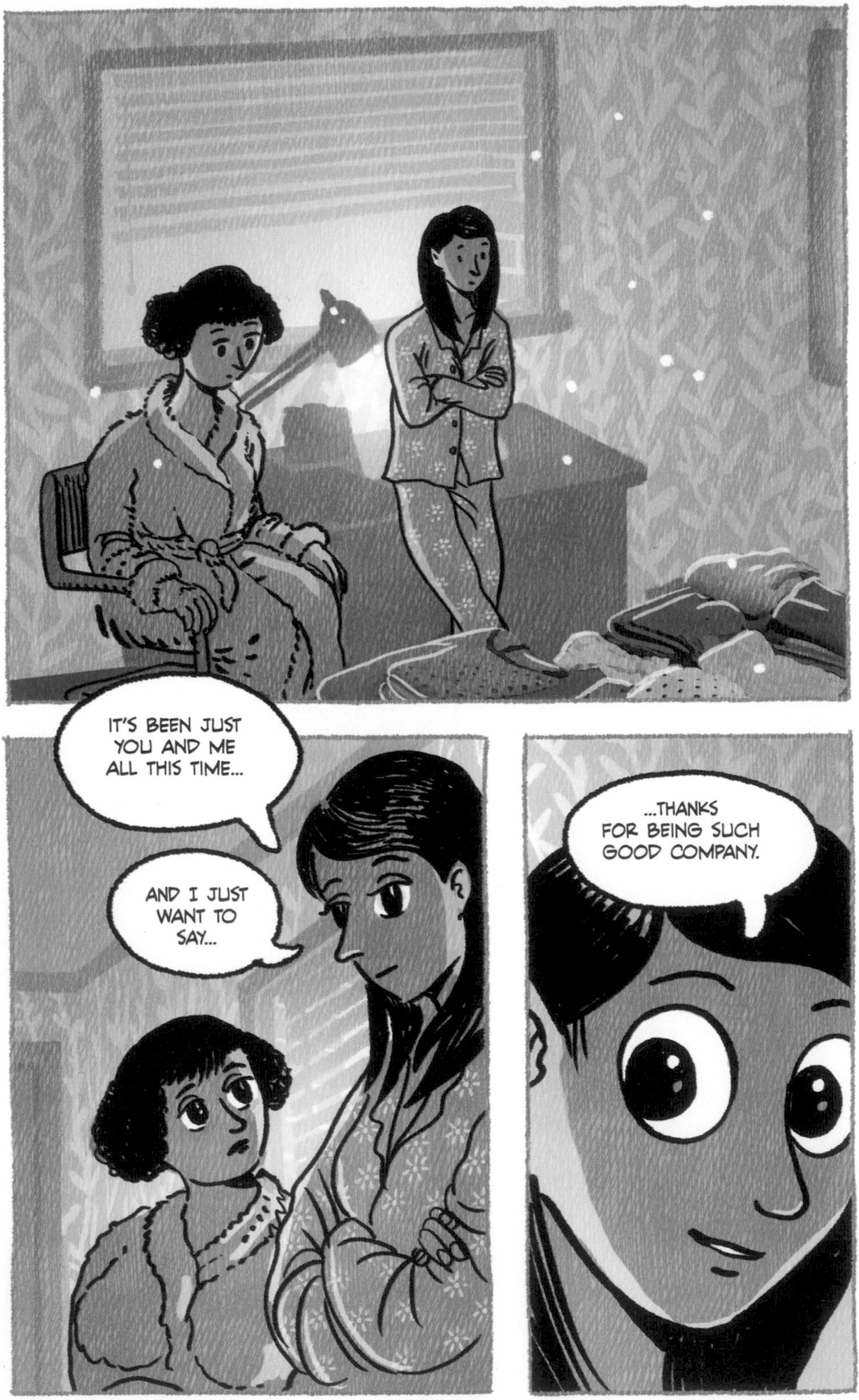
IT'S BEEN JUST YOU AND ME ALL THIS TIME...
AND I JUST WANT TO SAY...
...THANKS FOR BEING SUCH GOOD COMPANY.

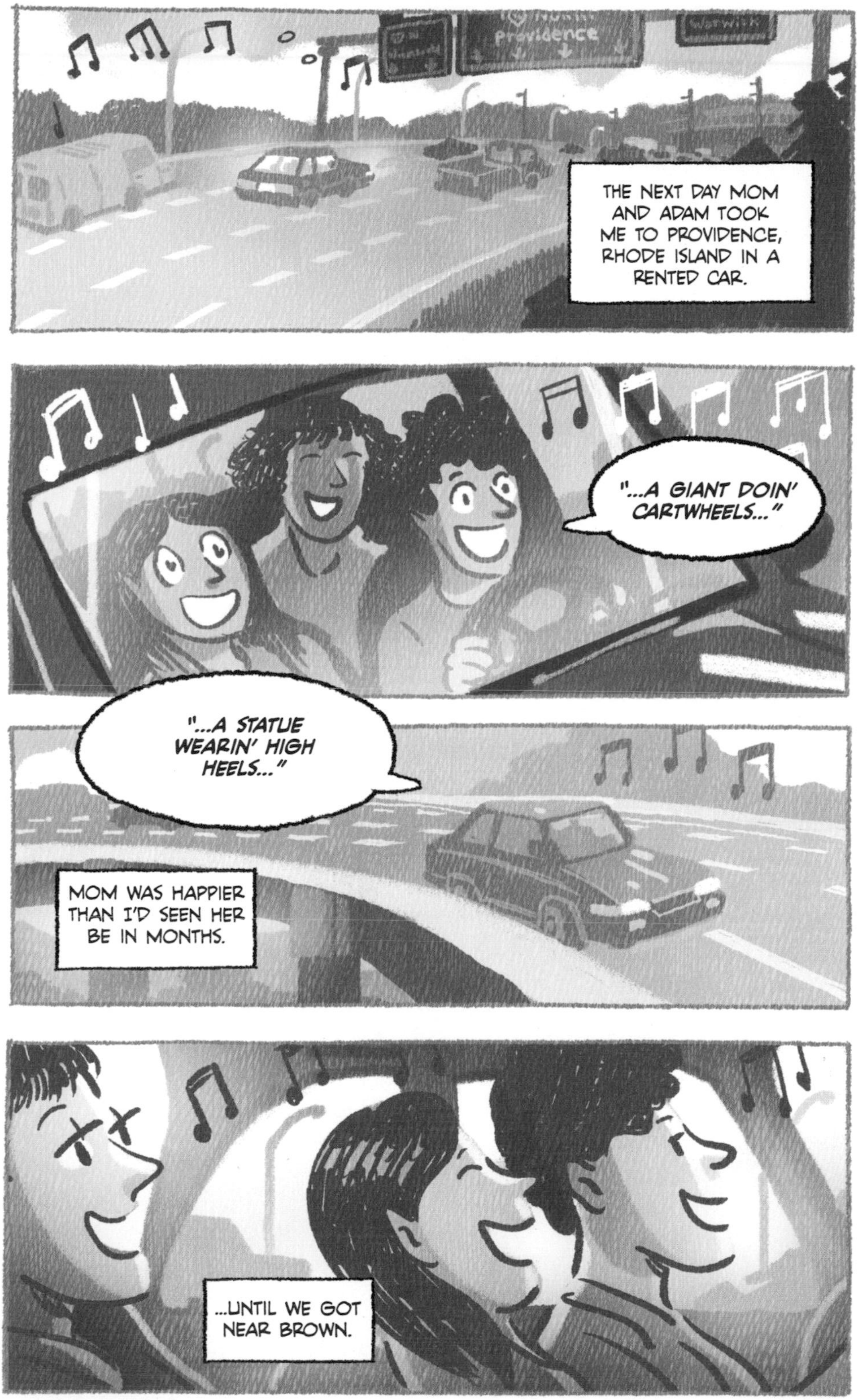
Providence
Warwick
THE NEXT DAY MOM AND ADAM TOOK ME TO PROVIDENCE, RHODE ISLAND IN A RENTED CAR.
"...A GIANT DOIN' CARTWHEELS..."
"...A STATUE WEARIN' HIGH HEELS..."
MOM WAS HAPPIER THAN I'D SEEN HER BE IN MONTHS.
...UNTIL WE GOT NEAR BROWN.

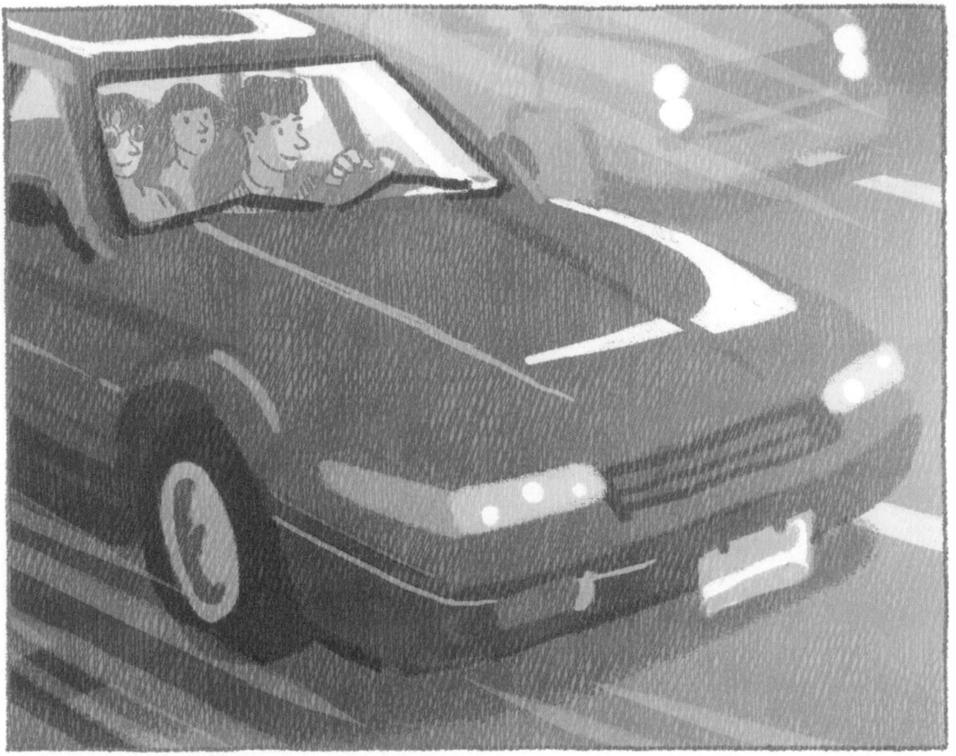

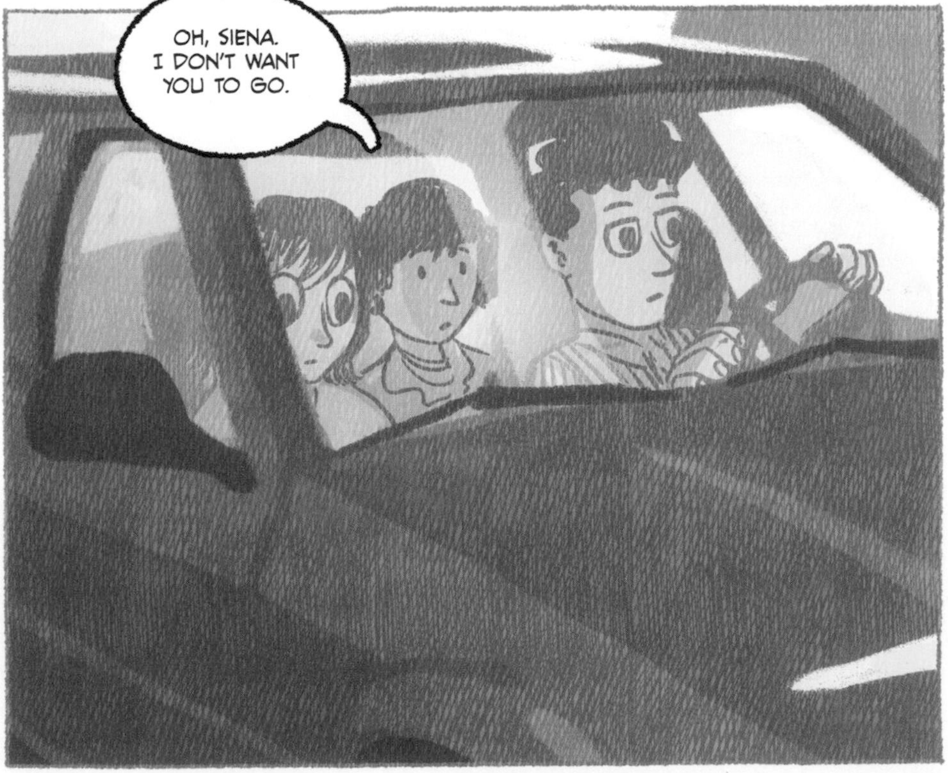
OH, SIENA. I DON'T WANT YOU TO GO.

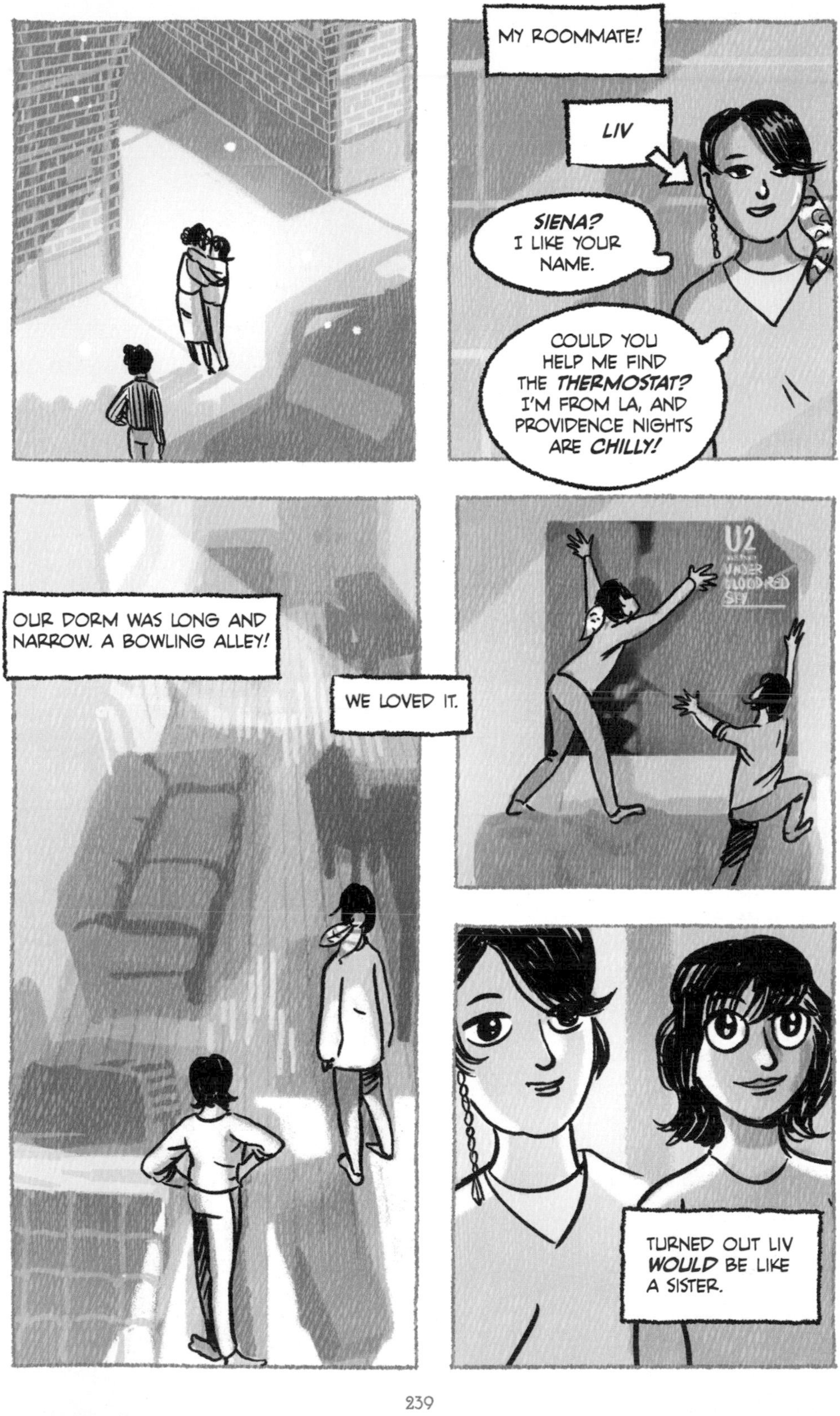
MY ROOMMATE!
LIV
SIENA? I LIKE YOUR NAME.
COULD YOU HELP ME FIND THE THERMOSTAT? I'M FROM LA, AND PROVIDENCE NIGHTS ARE CHILLY!
OUR DORM WAS LONG AND NARROW. A BOWLING ALLEY!
WE LOVED IT.
U2
TURNED OUT LIV WOULD BE LIKE A SISTER.

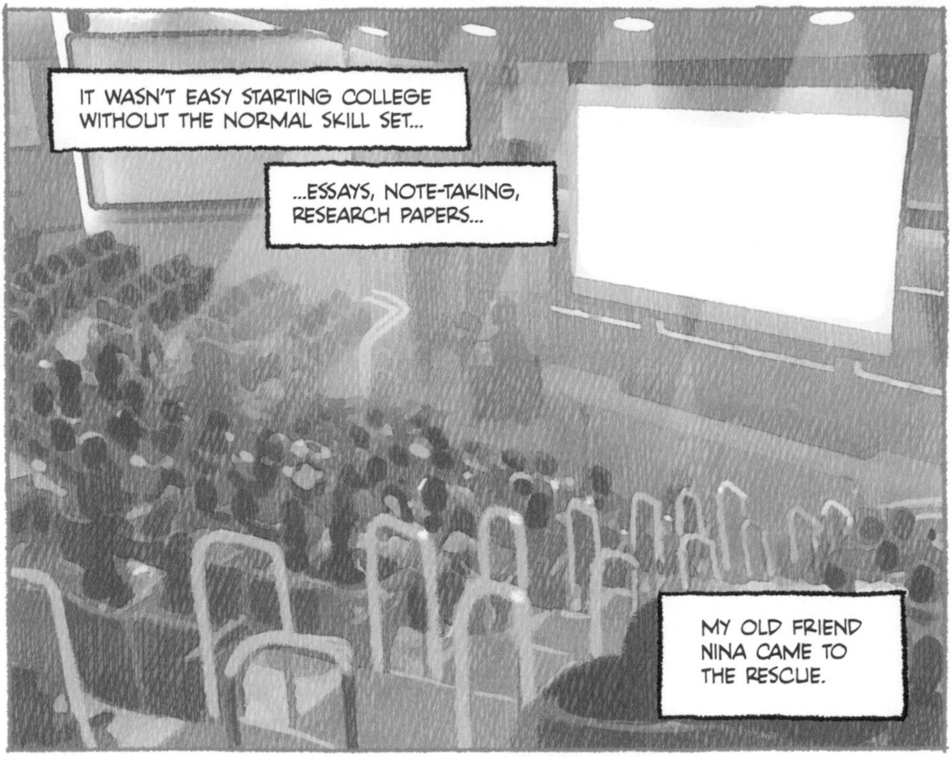
IT WASN'T EASY STARTING COLLEGE WITHOUT THE NORMAL SKILL SET...
...ESSAYS, NOTE-TAKING, RESEARCH PAPERS...
MY OLD FRIEND NINA CAME TO THE RESCUE.

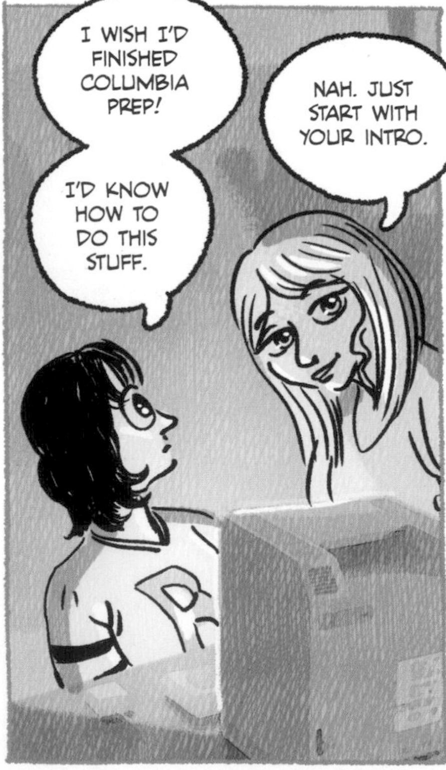
I WISH I'D FINISHED COLUMBIA PREP!
I'D KNOW HOW TO DO THIS STUFF.
NAH. JUST START WITH YOUR INTRO.

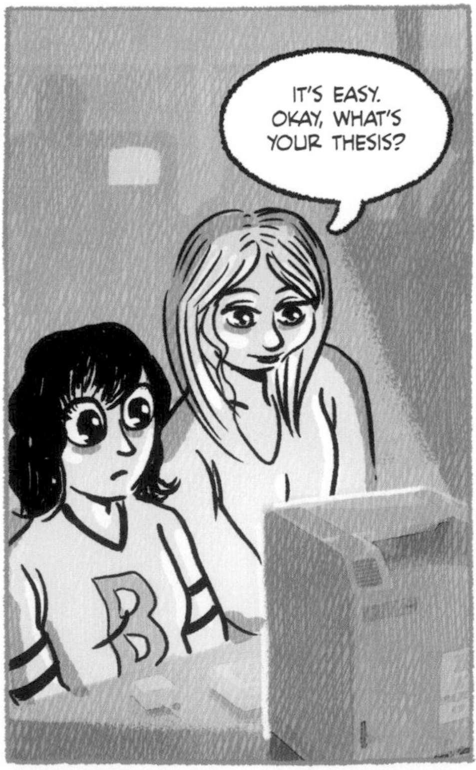
IT'S EASY. OKAY, WHAT'S YOUR THESIS?

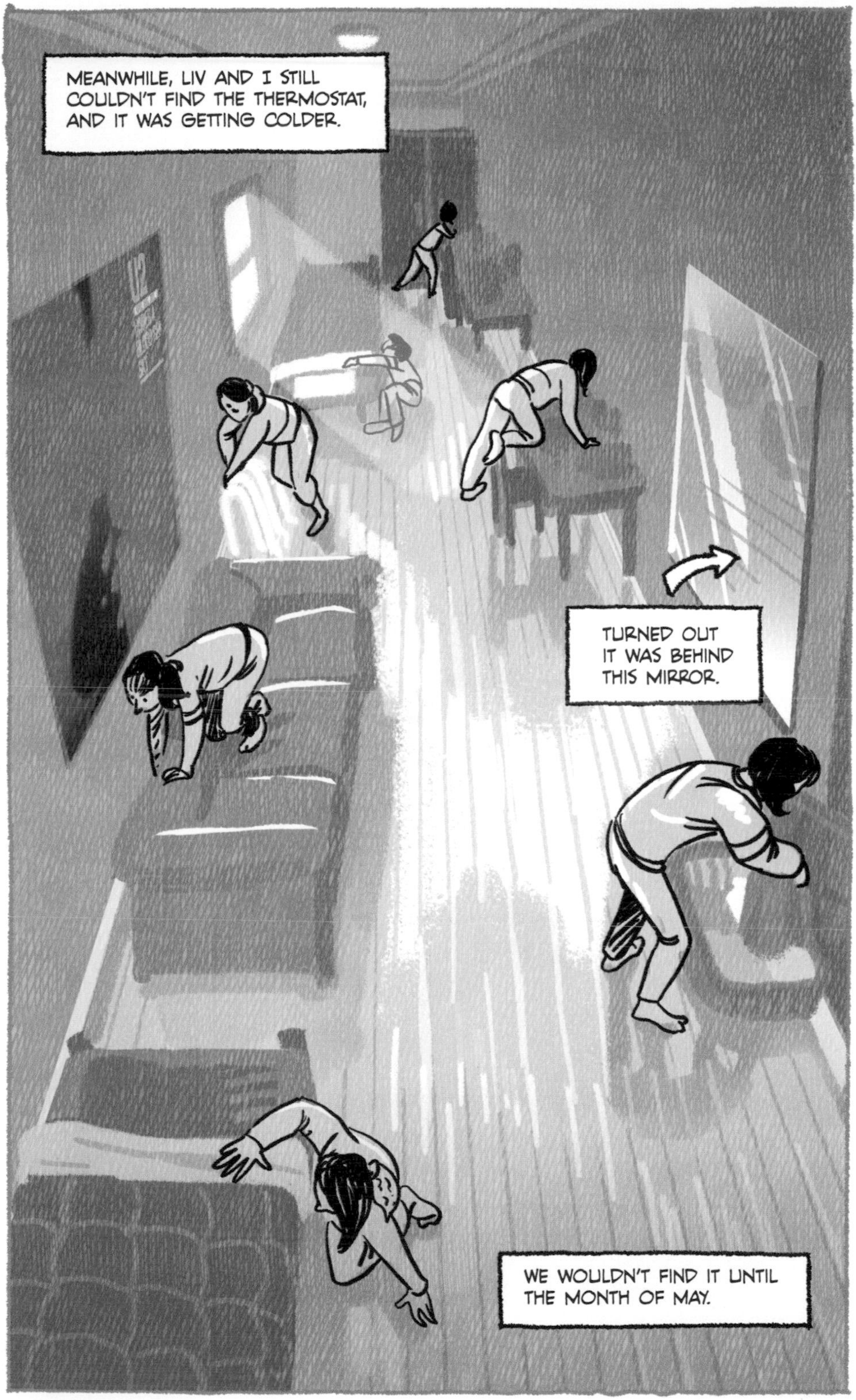
MEANWHILE, LIV AND I STILL COULDN'T FIND THE THERMOSTAT, AND IT WAS GETTING COLDER.
U2
TURNED OUT IT WAS BEHIND THIS MIRROR.
WE WOULDN'T FIND IT UNTIL THE MONTH OF MAY.

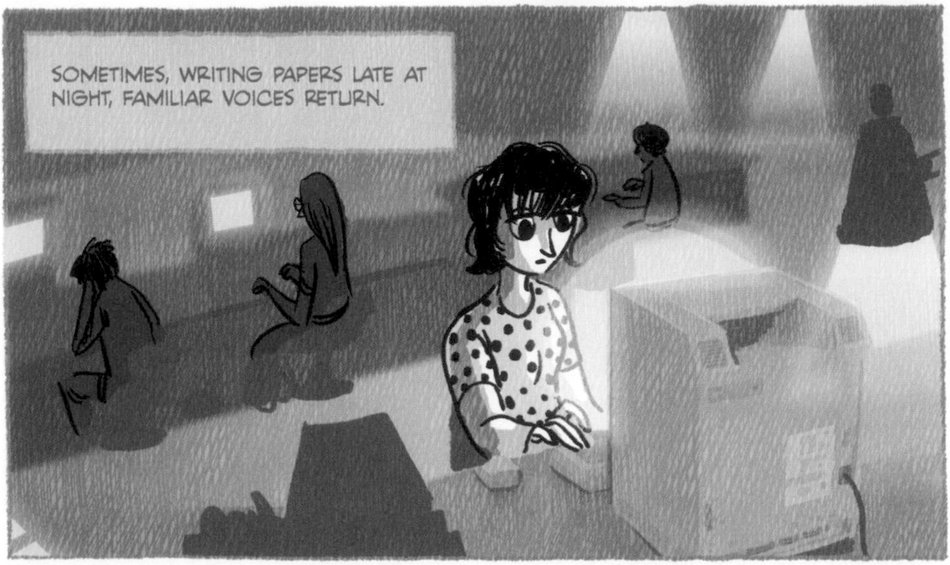
SOMETIMES, WRITING PAPERS LATE AT NIGHT, FAMILIAR VOICES RETURN.

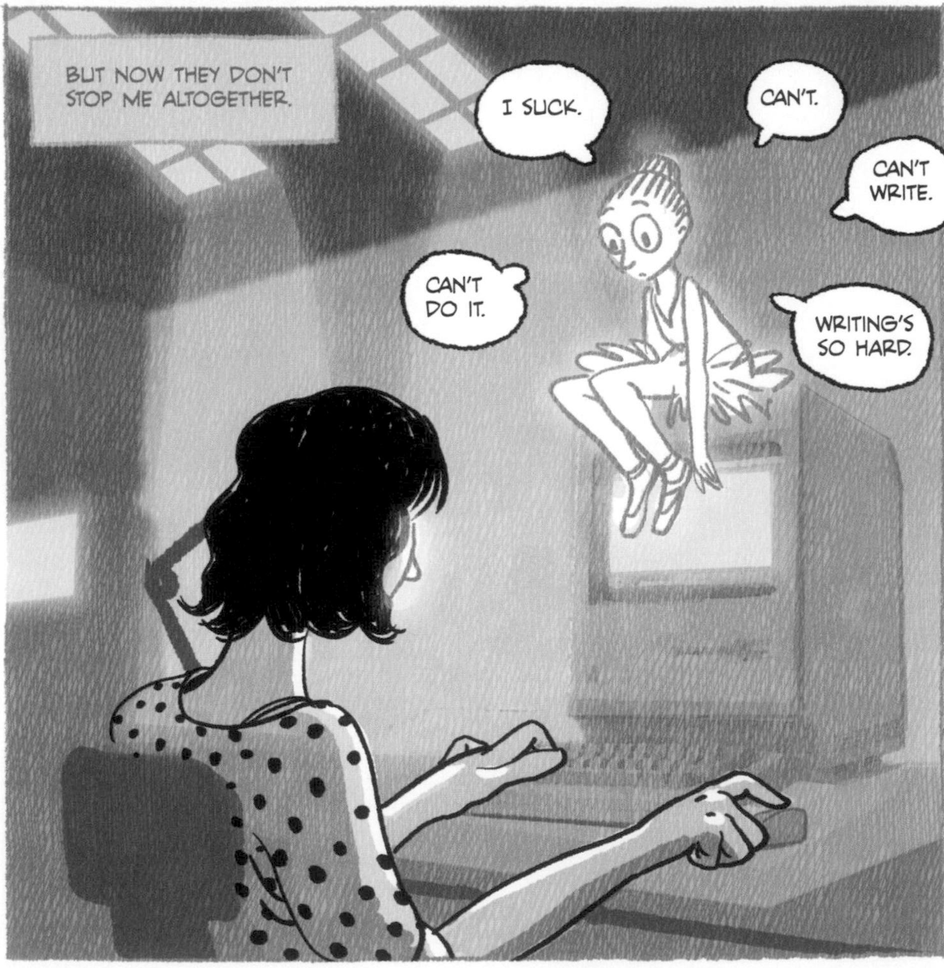
BUT NOW THEY DON'T STOP ME ALTOGETHER.
I SUCK.
CAN'T.
CAN'T WRITE.
CAN'T DO IT.
WRITING'S SO HARD.

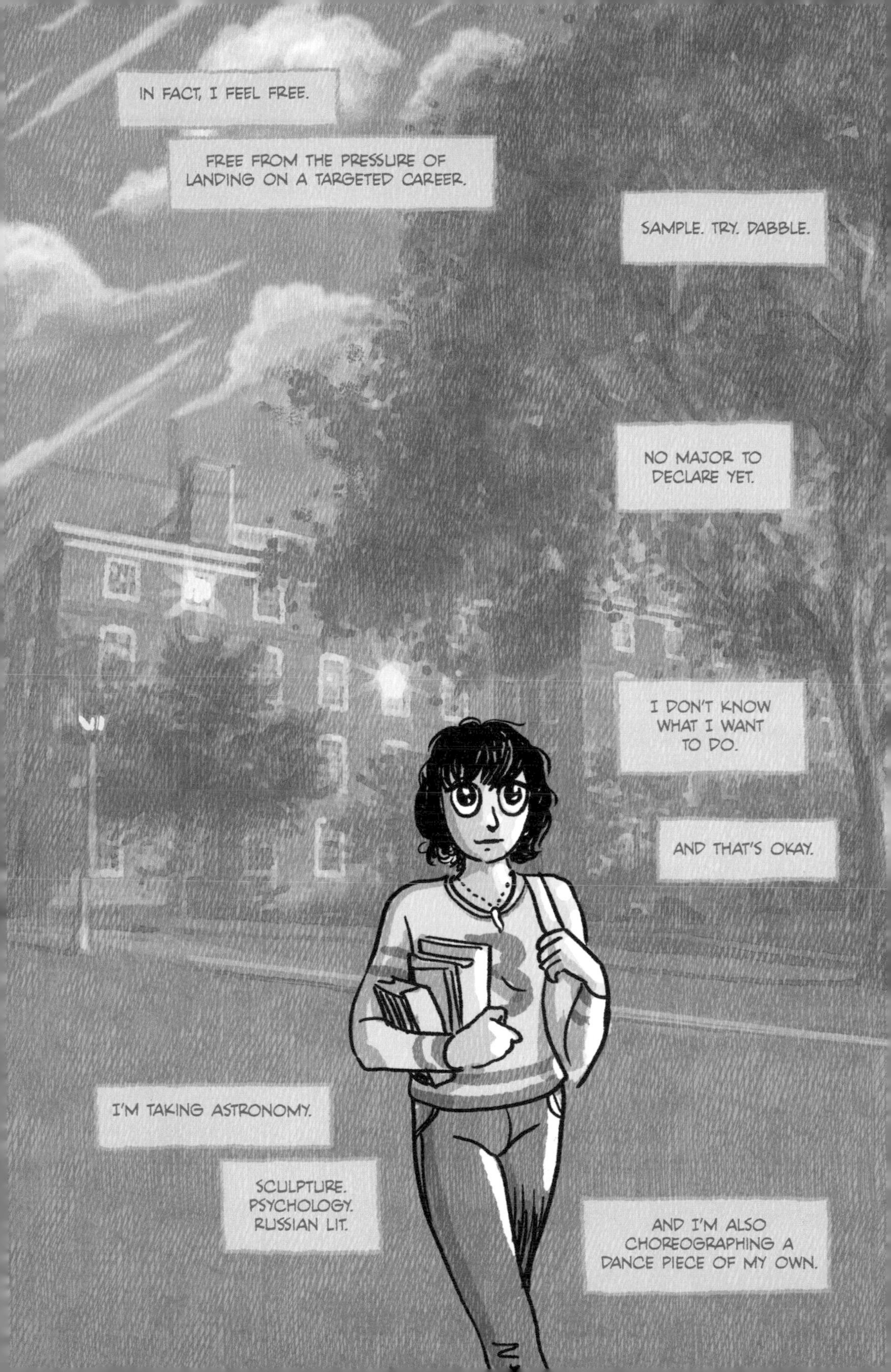
IN FACT, I FEEL FREE.
FREE FROM THE PRESSURE OF LANDING ON A TARGETED CAREER.
SAMPLE. TRY. DABBLE.
NO MAJOR TO DECLARE YET.
I DON'T KNOW WHAT I WANT TO DO.
AND THAT'S OKAY.
I'M TAKING ASTRONOMY.
SCULPTURE. PSYCHOLOGY. RUSSIAN LIT.
AND I'M ALSO CHOREOGRAPHING A DANCE PIECE OF MY OWN.

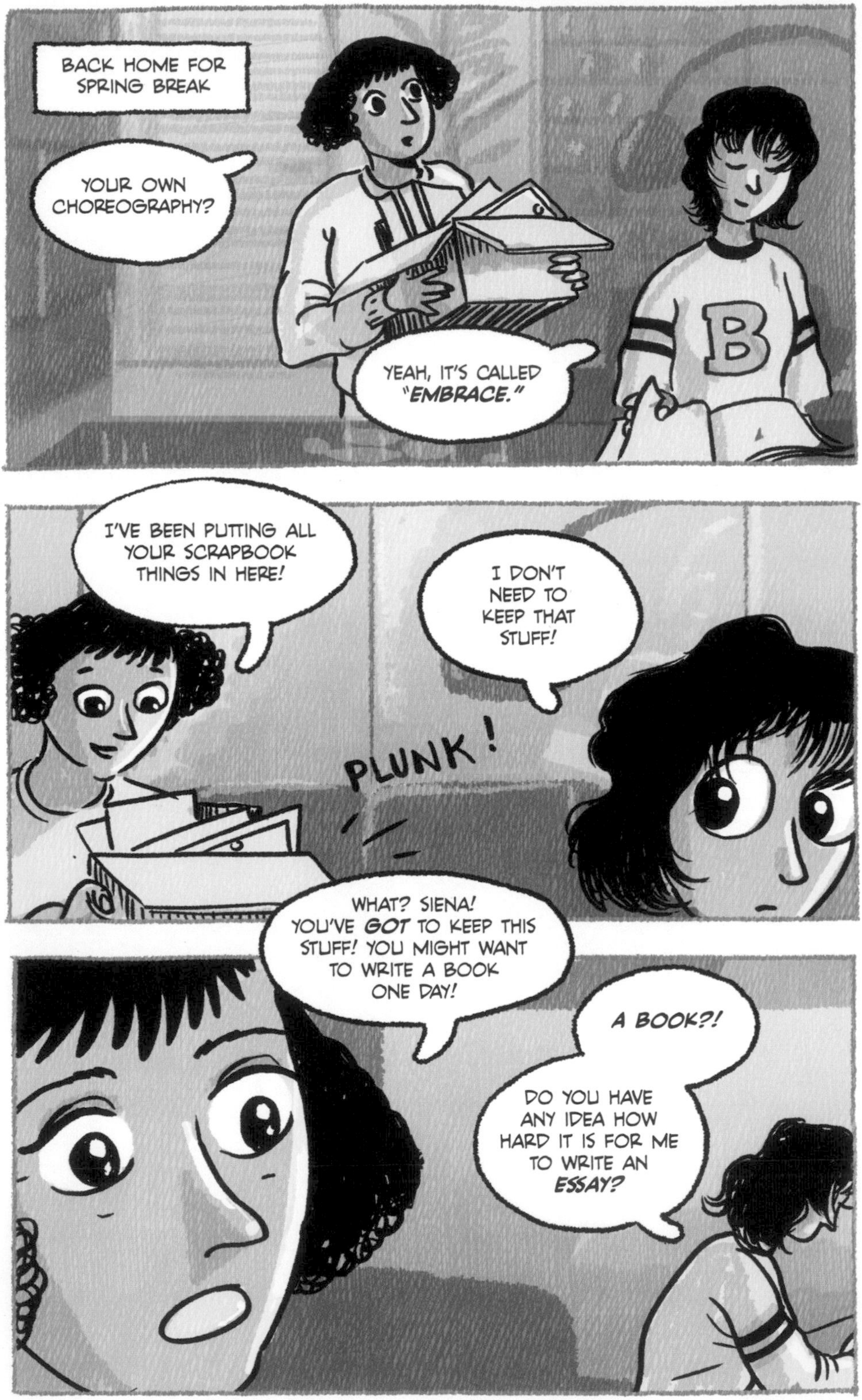
BACK HOME FOR SPRING BREAK
YOUR OWN CHOREOGRAPHY?
YEAH, IT'S CALLED "EMBRACE."
I'VE BEEN PUTTING ALL YOUR SCRAPBOOK THINGS IN HERE!
I DON'T NEED TO KEEP THAT STUFF!
PLUNK!
WHAT? SIENA! YOU'VE GOT TO KEEP THIS STUFF! YOU MIGHT WANT TO WRITE A BOOK ONE DAY!
A BOOK?!
DO YOU HAVE ANY IDEA HOW HARD IT IS FOR ME TO WRITE AN ESSAY?

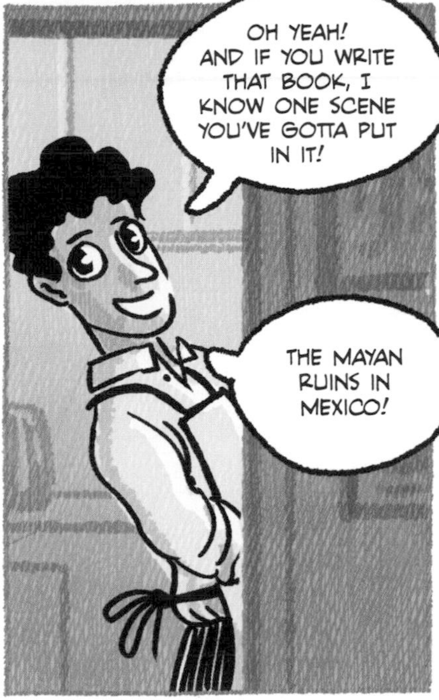
OH YEAH! AND IF YOU WRITE THAT BOOK, I KNOW ONE SCENE YOU'VE GOTTA PUT IN IT!
THE MAYAN RUINS IN MEXICO!

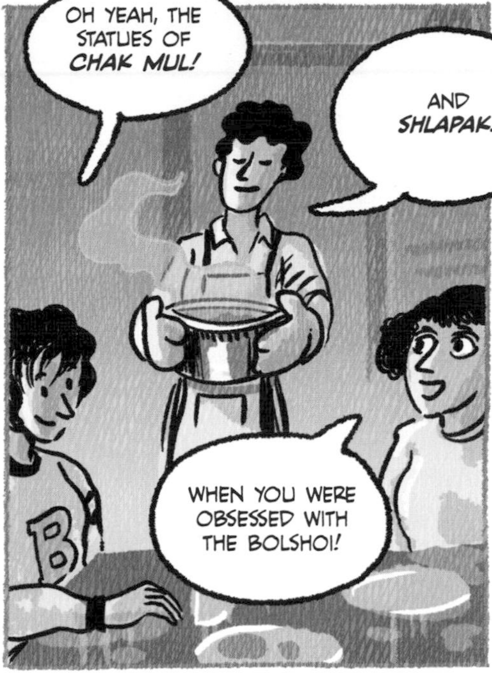
OH YEAH, THE STATUES OF *CHAK MUL!*
AND *SHLAPAK!*
WHEN YOU WERE OBSESSED WITH THE BOLSHOI!

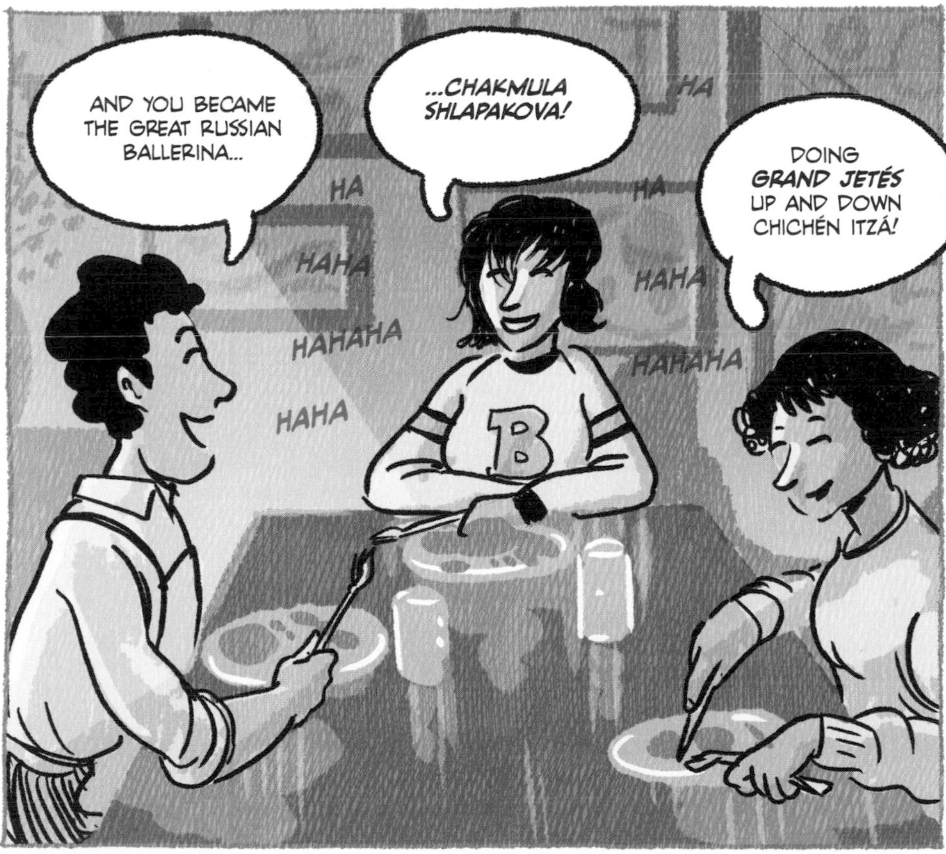
AND YOU BECAME THE GREAT RUSSIAN BALLERINA...
...CHAKMULA SHLAPAKOVA!
DOING *GRAND JETÉS* UP AND DOWN CHICHÉN ITZÁ!
HA
HA
HA
HAHA
HAHA
HAHAHA
HAHAHA
HAHA

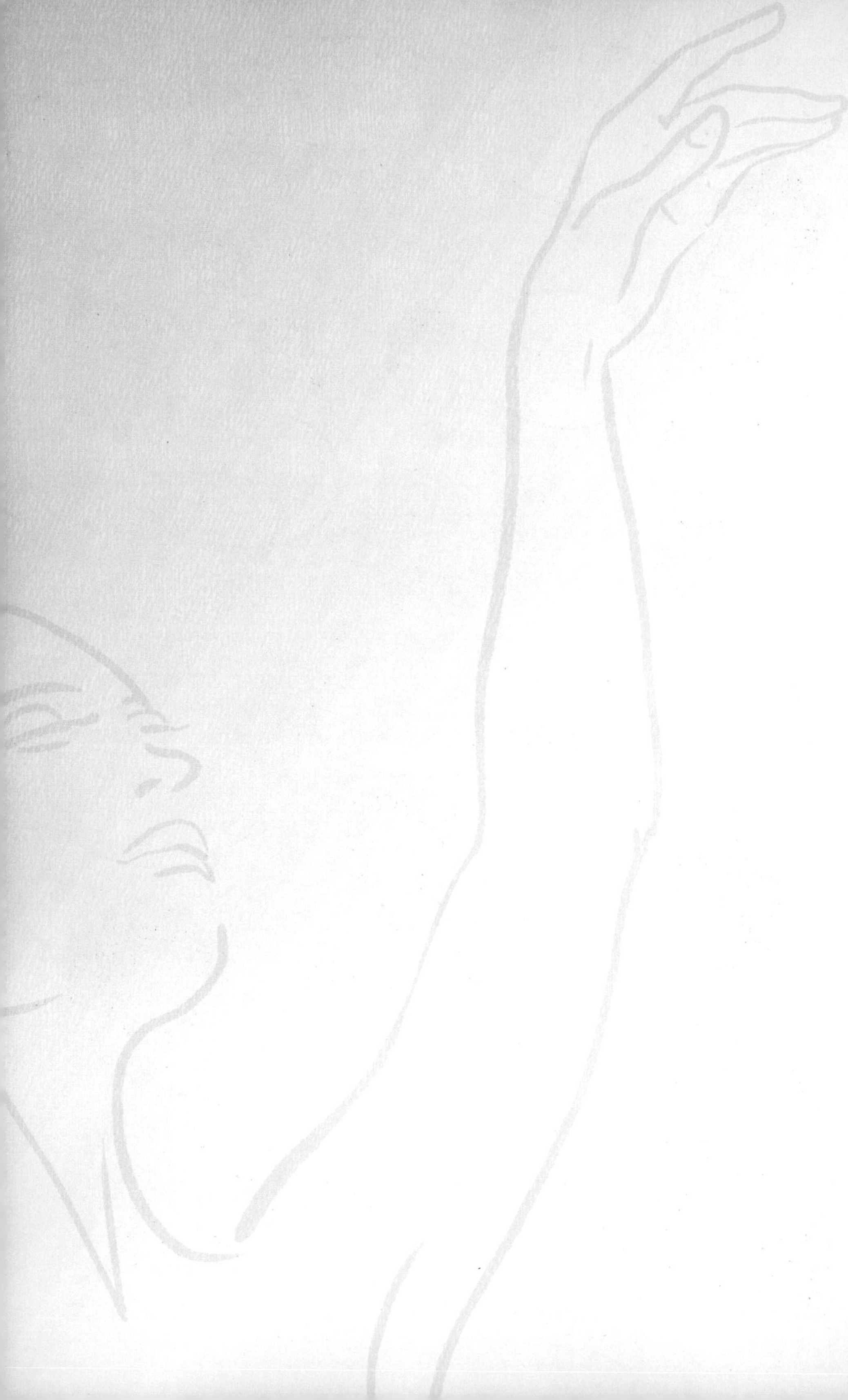

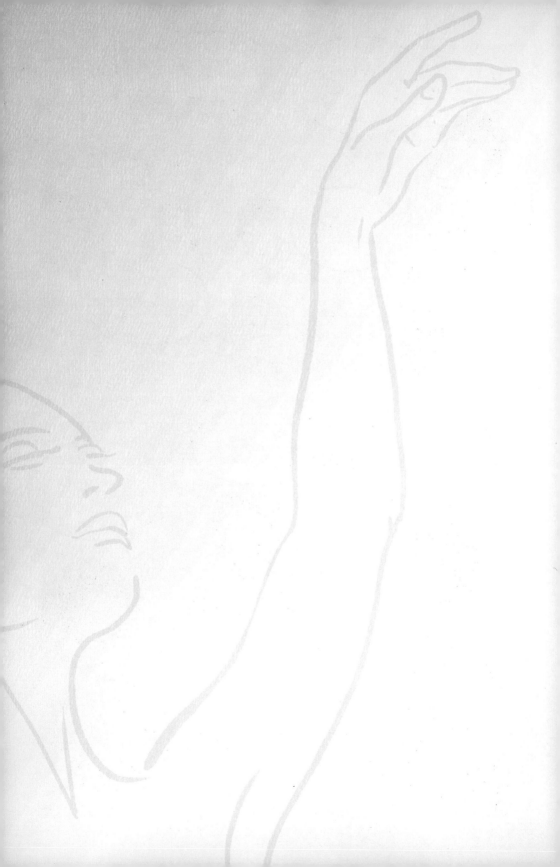

Epilogue

Tiny Dancer

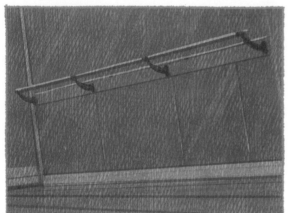

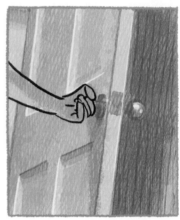

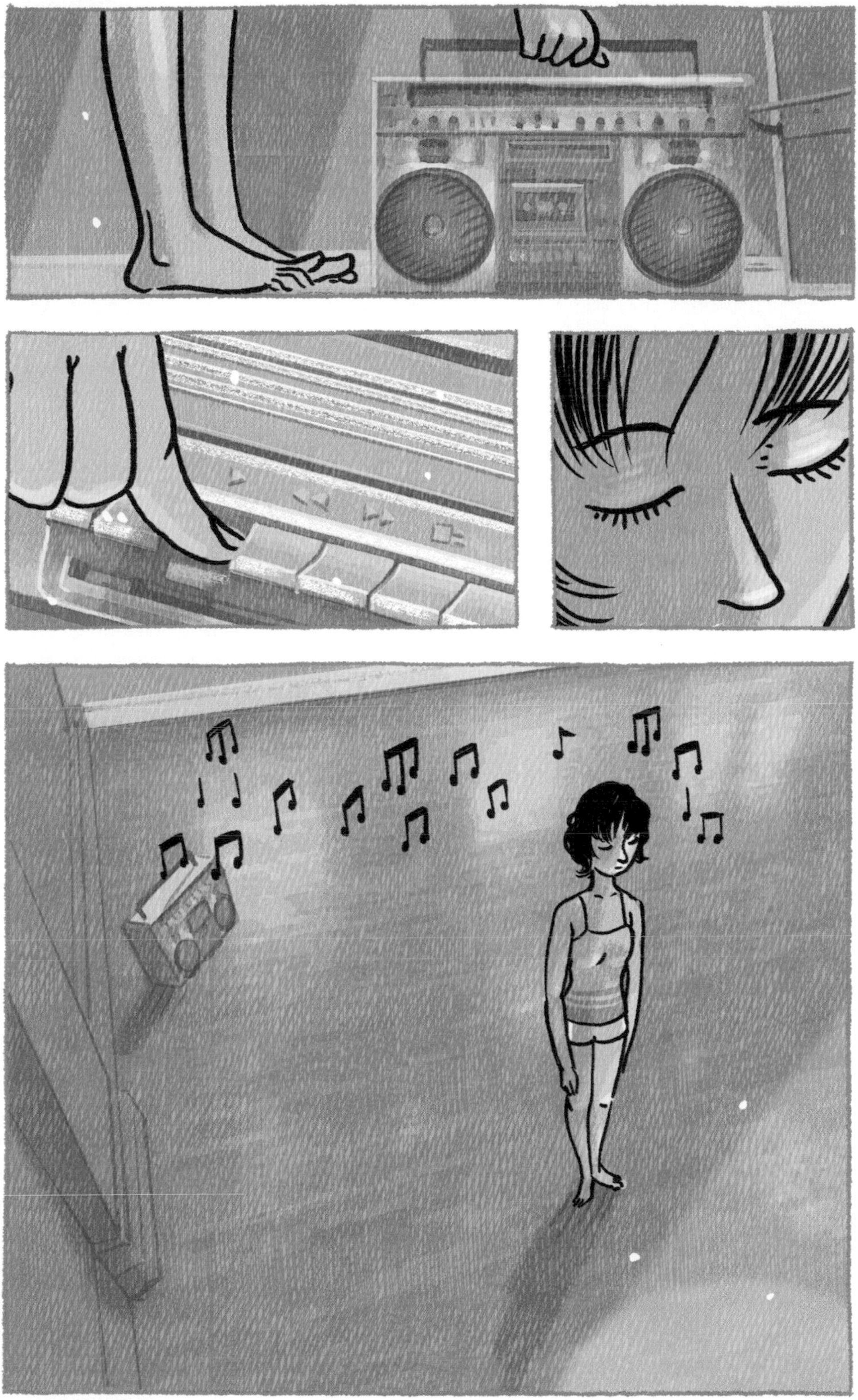

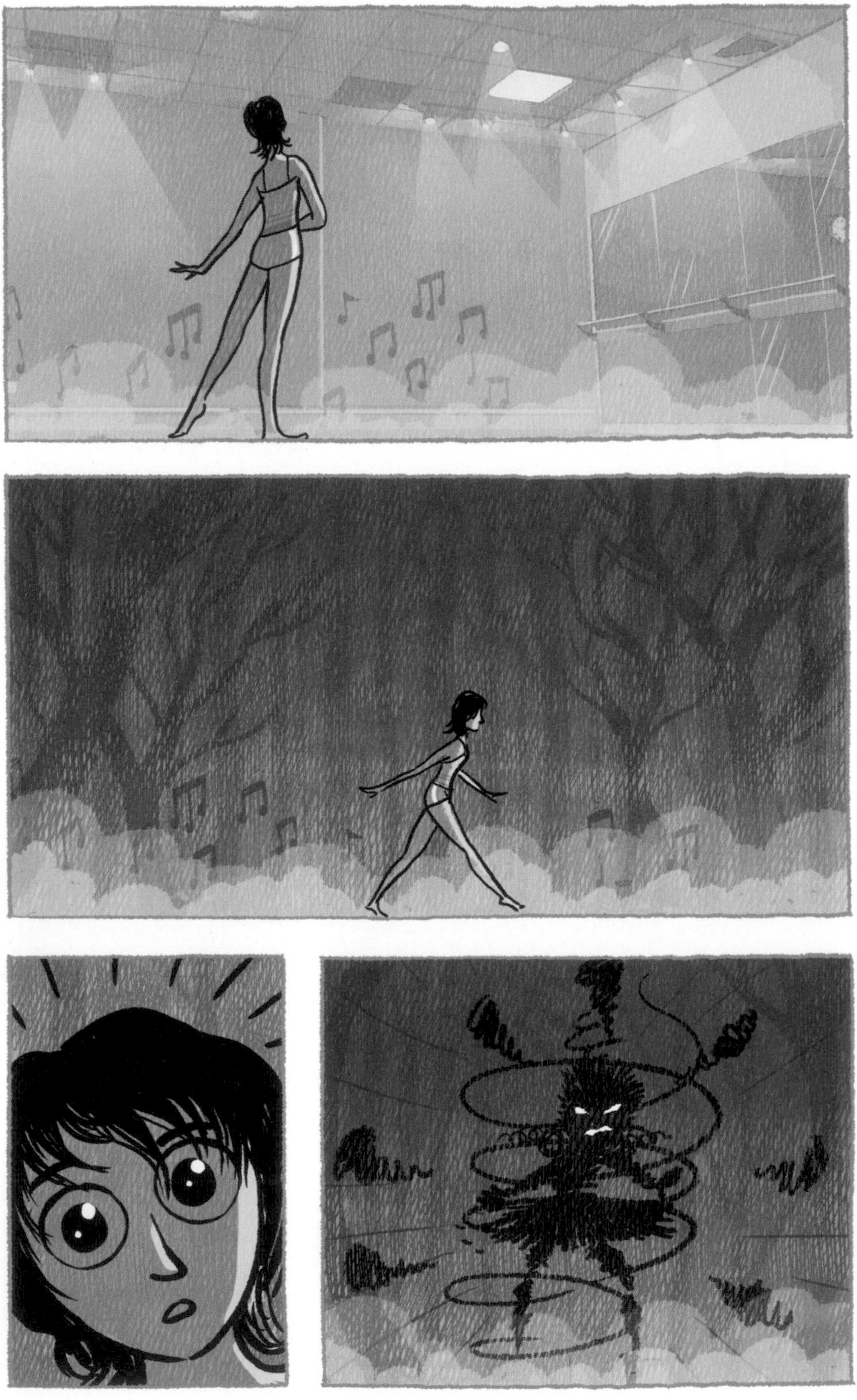

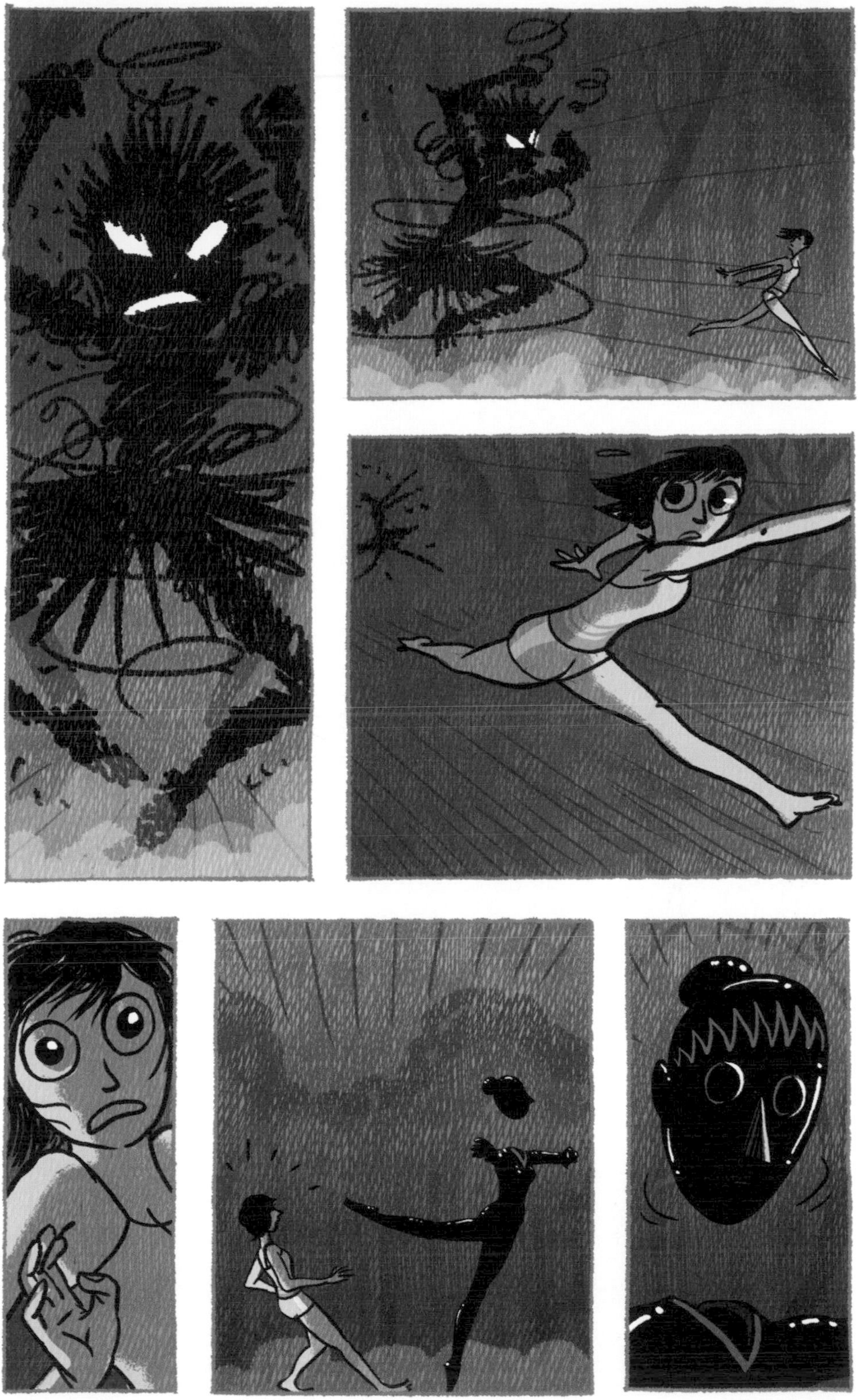

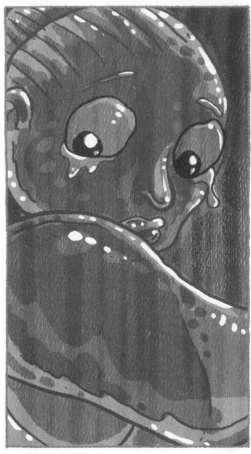

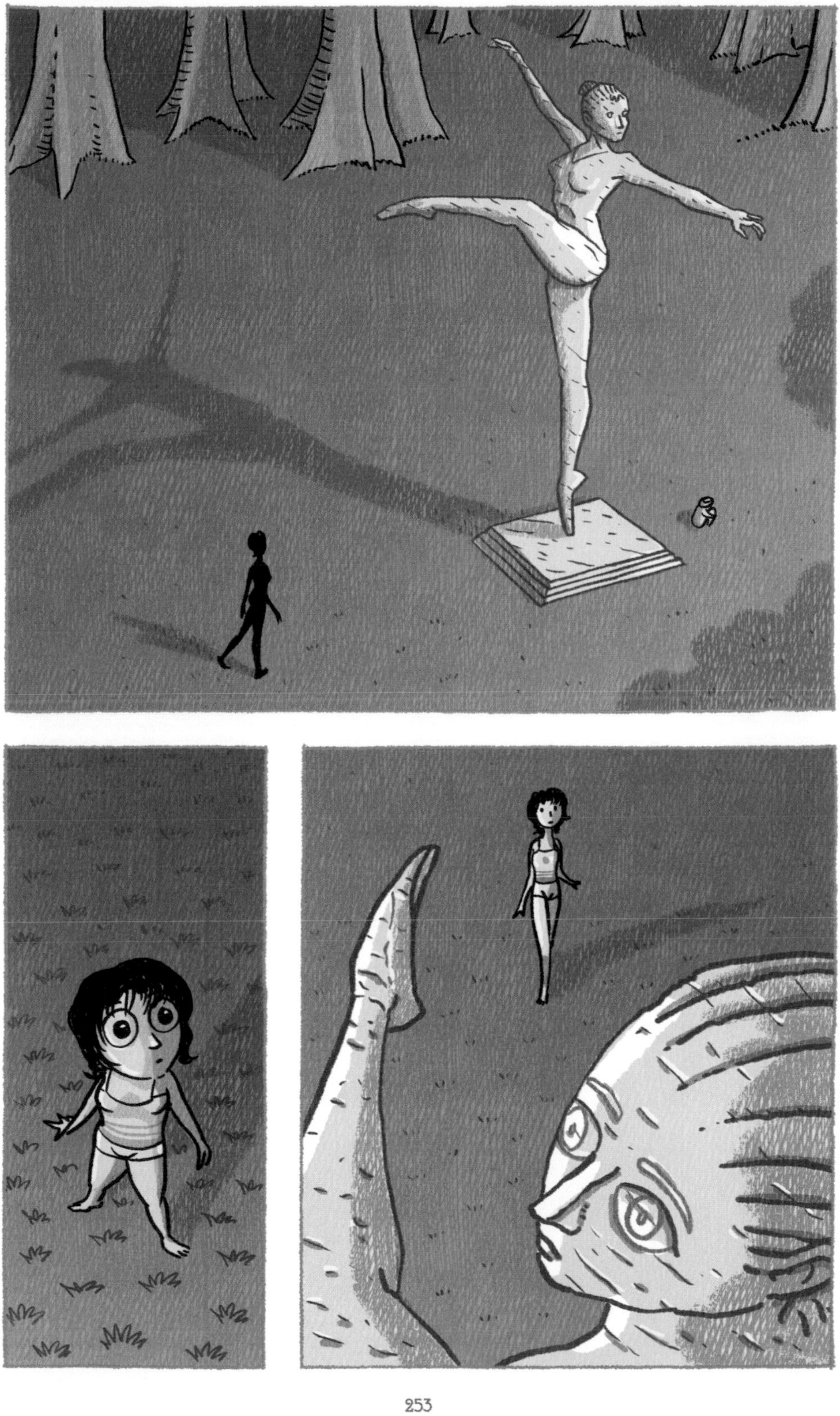

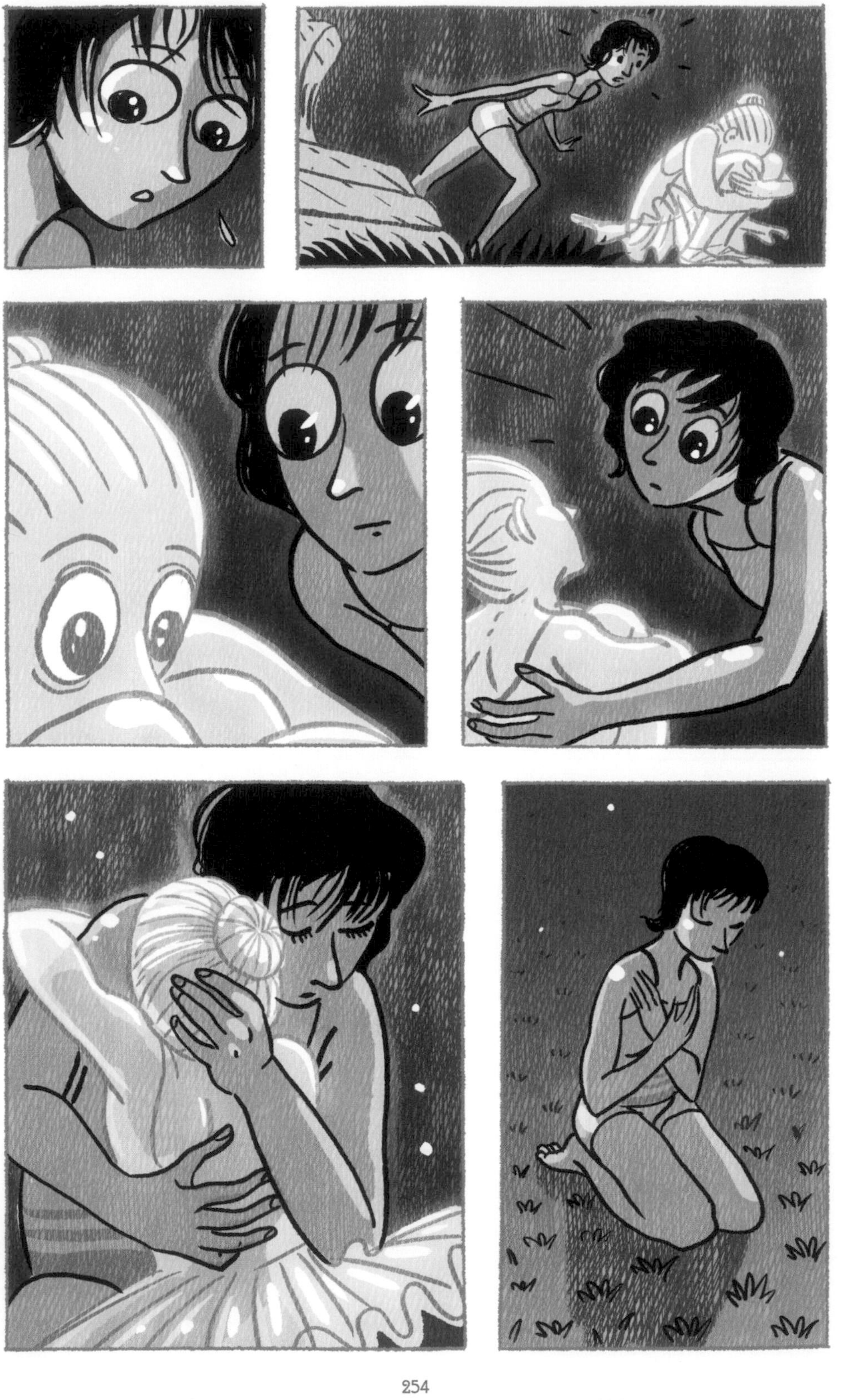

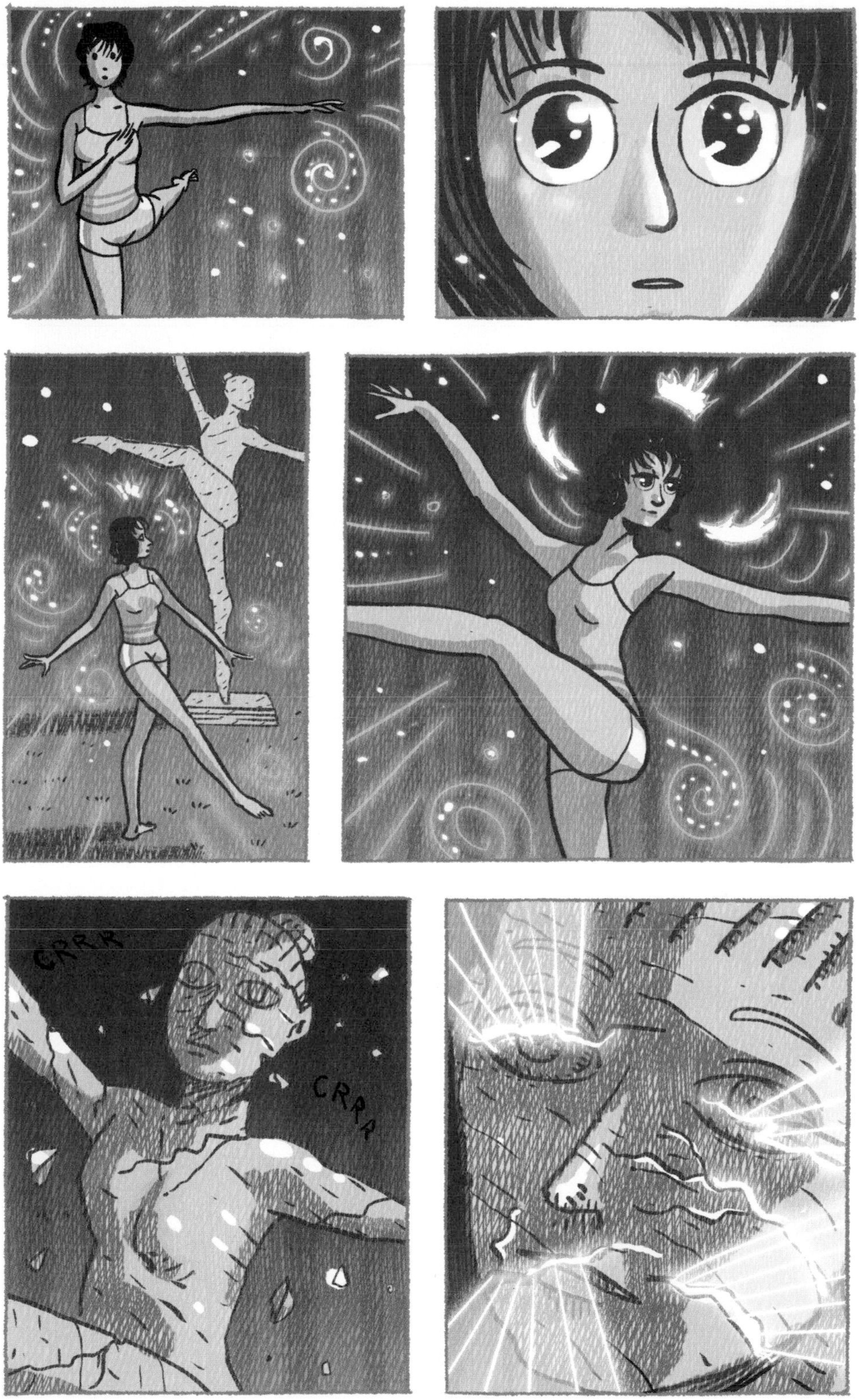
CRRR
CRRR

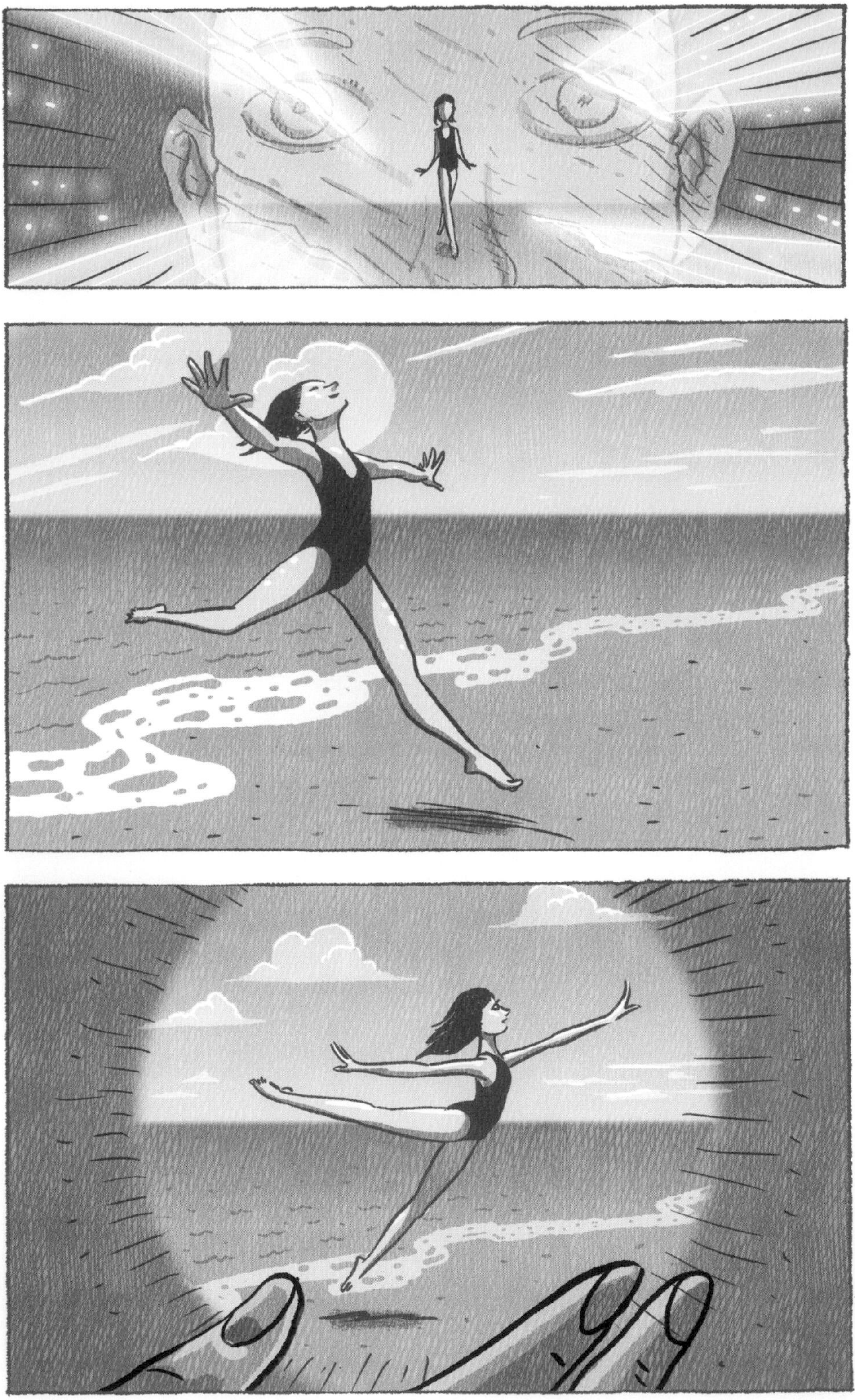

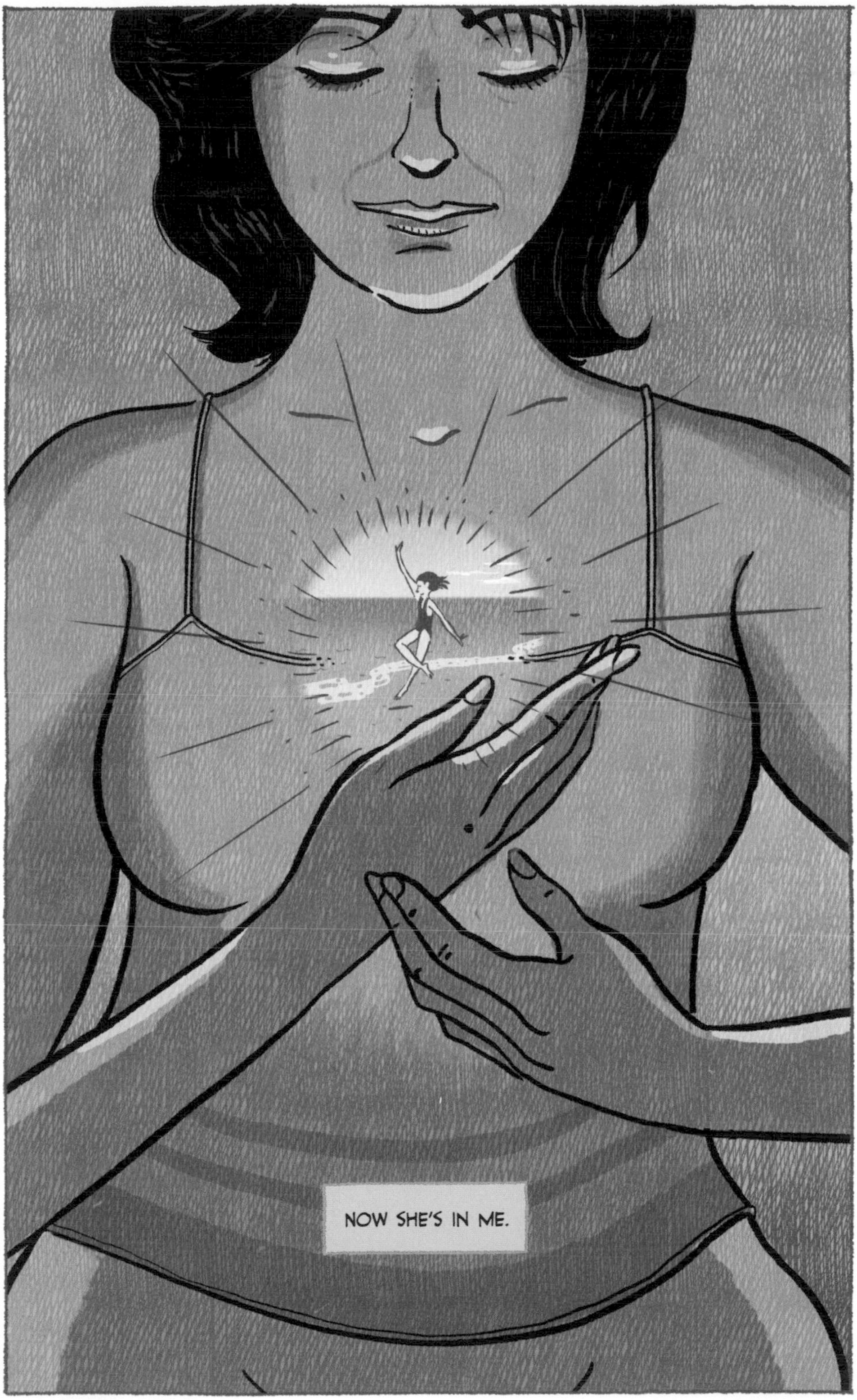
NOW SHE'S IN ME.

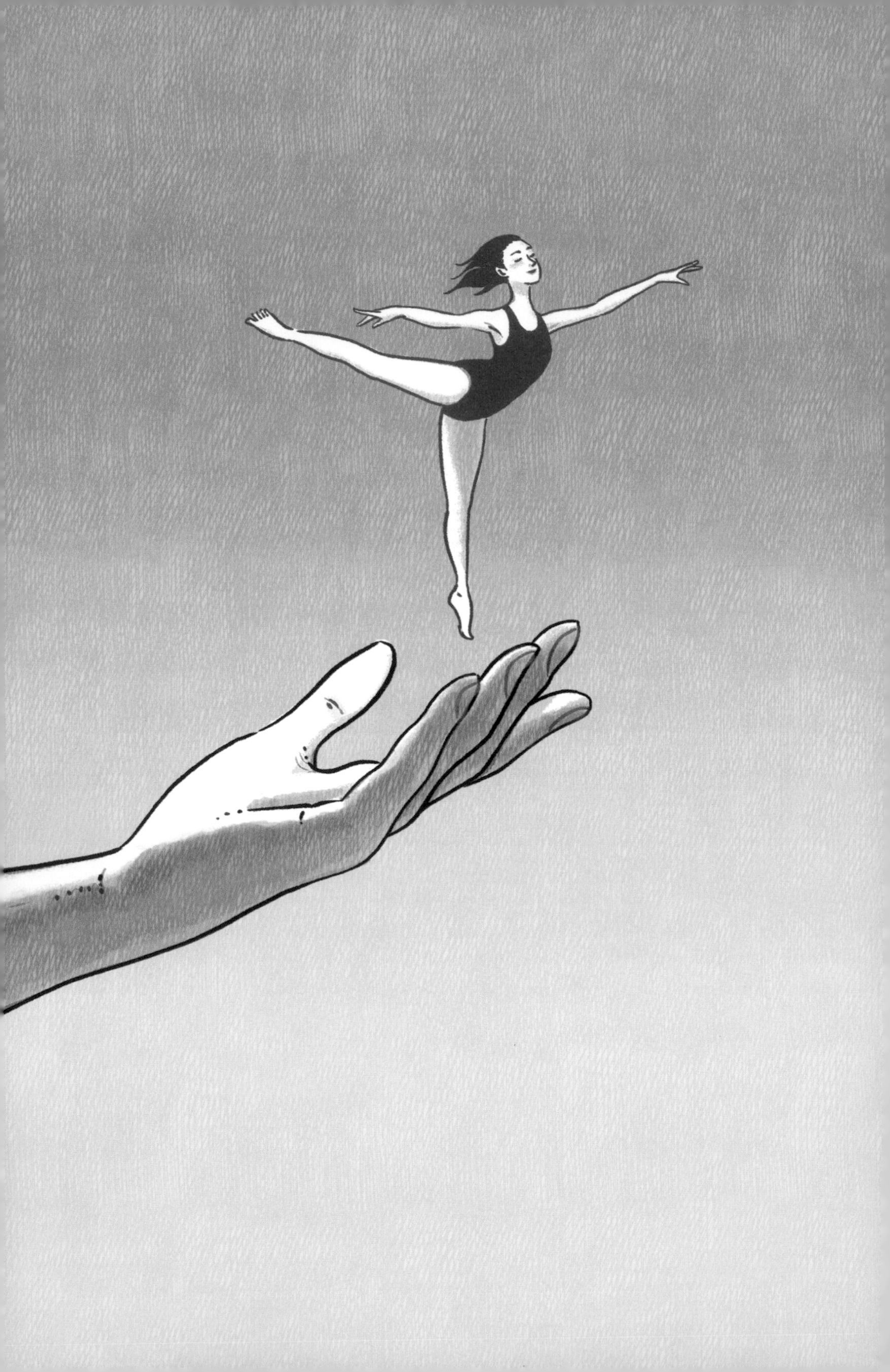

For Julien and Clio—
just the way you are

—S.C.S.

For Marie-Claire Siegel—
always with me
—M.S.

ACKNOWLEDGMENTS

Deepest thanks go to:

Adam Cherson—You're the only person on the planet with whom I share the language of my childhood.

Edward and Marie-Claire Siegel—for your unwavering enthusiasm and encouragement of our creative lives.

Tanya McKinnon—Your belief in the potential of this project, your insight, guidance, and formative questions were helpful beyond words.

Reka Simonsen—for your perceptive mind, bright instincts, and great counsel, which enhanced this dance at every step.

Greg Stadnyk, Jeannie Ng, and the Atheneum team—for your caring attention to every last detail.

Jessica Wapner—Our early conversations brought me vital clarity. And your support along the way means the world to me.

And special thanks go to:

Abe Erskine—for your lovely care and commitment.
—Siena

Thank you, Siena, for our pas de deux.
—Mark

atheneum

An imprint of Simon & Schuster Children's Publishing Division

1230 Avenue of the Americas, New York, New York 10020

For information about special discounts for bulk purchases, please contact
Simon & Schuster Special Sales at 1-866-506-1949 or business@simonandschuster.com.

The Simon & Schuster Speakers Bureau can bring authors to your live event.
For more information or to book an event, contact the Simon & Schuster Speakers Bureau
at 1-866-248-3049 or visit our website at www.simonspeakers.com.

Also available in an Atheneum paperback edition

Interior design by Mark Siegel and Greg Stadnyk

The text for this book was set in Piekos.

The illustrations for this book were rendered digitally.

Manufactured in China.

First Atheneum hardcover edition October 2021

2   4   6   8   10   9   7   5   3   1

Library of Congress Cataloging-in-Publication Data

Names: Siegel, Siena Cherson, author. | Siegel, Mark, 1967– illustrator.

Title: Tiny dancer ; with artwork by Mark Siegel.

Description: First edition. | New York : Atheneum, 2021. | Audience: Ages: 12 up | Summary: "Siena
Cherson Siegel dreamed of being a ballerina. Her love of movement and dedication to the craft earned her
a spot at the School of American Ballet. Siena has worked hard her whole life to be a professional ballet
dancer, then makes the difficult decision to quit dancing and tries to figure out what comes next. But what
do you do when you have spent your entire life working toward a goal, having that shape your identity,
and then decide it's time to move on? How do you figure out what to do with your life? And how do you
figure out who you are?" — Provided by publisher.

Identifiers: LCCN 2020035007 | ISBN 9781481486668 (hardcover) | ISBN 9781481486675 (paperback) |
ISBN 9781481486682 (eBook)

Subjects: LCSH: Siegel, Siena Cherson — Juvenile literature. | Siegel, Siena Cherson — Comic books,
strips, etc. | Ballerinas — United States — Biography — Juvenile literature. | Ballerinas — United States —
Biography — Comic books, strips, etc. | Graphic novels.

Classification: LCC GV1785.S554172 A3 2021 | DDC 792.802/8092 [B] — dc23

LC record available at https://lccn.loc.gov/2020035007

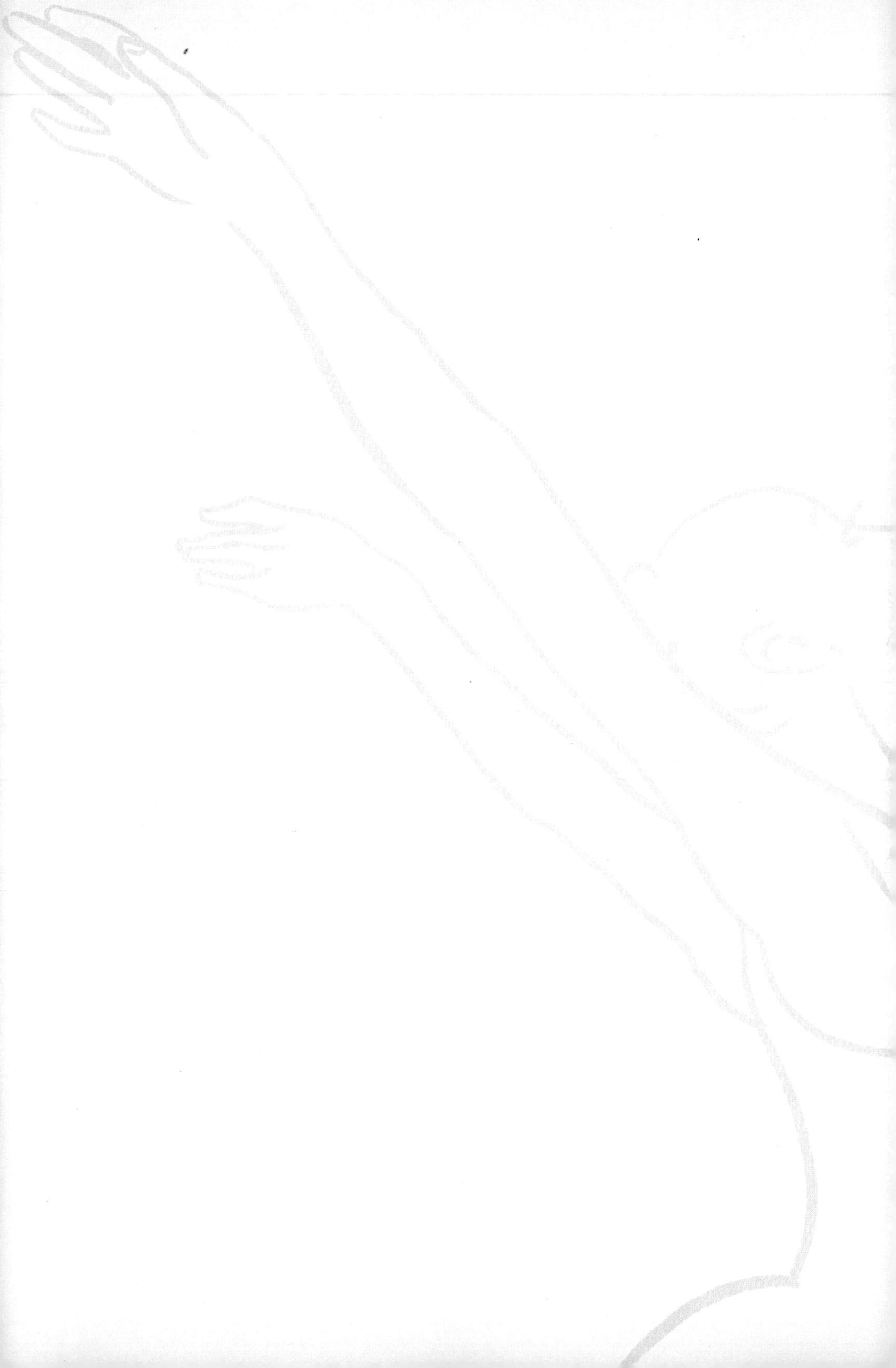